Microsoft® Windows®
Desktop Deployment Resource Kit

Jerry Honeycutt

PUBLISHED BY
Microsoft Press
A Division of Microsoft Corporation
One Microsoft Way
Redmond, Washington 98052-6399

Library of Congress Cataloging-in-Publication Data
Honeycutt, Jerry.
    Microsoft Windows Desktop Deployment Resource Kit / Jerry Honeycutt, with the
Microsoft Windows XP and Office teams.
        p. cm.
    Includes index.
    ISBN 0-7356-1898-4
    1. Microsoft Windows (Computer file)   2. Operating systems (Computers)   I. Microsoft
Corporation.   II. Title.

    QA76.76.O63H66355   2003
    005.4'4682--dc22   2003060435

Printed and bound in the United States of America.

1 2 3 4 5 6 7 8 9   QWT   9 8 7 6 5

Distributed in Canada by H.B. Fenn and Company Ltd.

A CIP catalogue record for this book is available from the British Library.

Microsoft Press books are available through booksellers and distributors worldwide. For further information about international editions, contact your local Microsoft Corporation office or contact Microsoft Press International directly at fax (425) 936-7329. Visit our Web site at www.microsoft.com/learning/. Send comments to *rkinput@microsoft.com*.

Microsoft, Active Directory, ActiveX, Authenticode, Bookshelf, DirectX, FrontPage, InfoPath, IntelliMirror, JScript, Microsoft Press, MSDN, MS-DOS, MSN, NetMeeting, the Office logo, OneNote, Outlook, PhotoDraw, PowerPoint, SharePoint, Visio, Visual Basic, Visual C++, Visual InterDev, Win32, Windows, the Windows logo, Windows Media, Windows NT, and Windows Server are either registered trademarks or trademarks of Microsoft Corporation in the United States and/or other countries. Other product and company names mentioned herein may be the trademarks of their respective owners.

The example companies, organizations, products, domain names, e-mail addresses, logos, people, places, and events depicted herein are fictitious. No association with any real company, organization, product, domain name, e-mail address, logo, person, place, or event is intended or should be inferred.

This book expresses the author's views and opinions. The information contained in this book is provided without any express, statutory, or implied warranties. Neither the authors, Microsoft Corporation, nor its resellers or distributors will be held liable for any damages caused or alleged to be caused either directly or indirectly by this book.

Acquisitions Editor: Martin DelRe
Project Editor: Denise Bankaitis
Technical Editor: Jack Beaudry
Copyeditor: Nancy Sixsmith
Indexer: Seth Maislin

Body Part No. X10-08633

Contents at a Glance

Contents

What do you think of this book?
We want to hear from you!

Microsoft is interested in hearing your feedback about this publication so we can continually improve our books and learning resources for you. To participate in a brief online survey, please visit: *www.microsoft.com/learning/booksurvey/*

23   Software Installation   665

Part V   Appendixes

Acknowledgments

I certainly wasn't able to create this book by myself, so I'd like to acknowledge the people who toughed it out with me to get it done. First, I'd like to thank Martin DelRe, my acquisitions editor at Microsoft Press, for having enough confidence in me to write this book. I'd also like to thank Alan Le Marquand for getting the ball rolling.

Maureen Zimmerman and Denise Bankaitis were this book's project editors. First there was Maureen, and then there was Denise. Both of them kept me motivated, moving forward, and helped keep track of all the balls I tossed into the air. Denise managed the second half (everyone knows things go great in the beginning but fall apart at the end), and still maintained her sanity every time I came up with another reason for being late. I can't wait to work with Denise again.

Many other folks at Microsoft Press contributed their editorial expertise to this book. Thank you, Carl Diltz, Barb Levy, Ellie Fountain, Maria Gargiulo, Jack Beaudry, Joel Panchot, Kristen Heller, Nancy Sixsmith, Seth Maislin, and Tess McMillan.

Some of the most important contributions to this book are from reviewers who examined and commented on content to help me improve it. Ralph Ramos, Chris Sherrill, Geoff Pickard, Don Freeman, and Anthony Perkins all reviewed content for this book. I'd like to specifically point out that Ralph and Anthony provided invaluable insight that comes only from experience deploying the business desktop. These two impressed me with the depth and breadth of their knowledge.

Numerous Microsoft employees also reviewed this book's contents. I thank Wes Miller, Joseph Sexton, Michael Anderson, Todd Phillips, Michael Dennis, Mark Williams, Bryan Chee, Sravan Ankaraju, Joe Giunta, Michael Brinlee, Kalpit Jain, Madhulika Narayan, Ryan Burkhardt, Alain Meeus, Ryan Cooper, Randy Holbrook, Bo Mings, Paul Spencer, David Hornbaker, Jon Markarian, John Wilson, Todd Furst, Andrew Montgomery, and Michael Murgolo for their participation.

I also thank the contributors to this book. Alex Angelopoulos wrote the WSH scripts you find on this book's CD. Alex put in long hours to produce these scripts. Tim Thomson and Glenn Fincher contributed content to chapters in this book.

I'd like to thank the folks at Studio B, my agency, for everything they've done for me. I've been with Studio B for many years, and I look forward to many more. Thank you David Rogelberg, Sherry Rogelberg, Neil Salkind, David Talbott, and Elsa Rosenberg.

Introduction

Deploying Microsoft Windows XP Professional in a corporate environment isn't a trivial task. It requires careful planning, which is often lacking in many scenarios. It also requires that you be familiar with the technologies involved, including the possibilities and limitations. This book helps you plan by asking important questions, and then describes the technologies that help you execute that plan.

Rather than just describing the deployment technologies for deploying Windows XP Professional and including Microsoft Office 2003 Editions, this book creates a framework for using them. It doesn't just describe the contents of a Windows XP Professional distribution point, for example; instead, it provides template distribution points that you can copy, customize, and use to deploy Windows XP Professional in your organization. And these templates help you do things like automatically handle long filenames, automatically distribute third-party device drivers, and automatically install applications as part of a Windows XP Professional installation.

Windows Versions

This book is targeted at current versions of Microsoft products:

- **Windows XP Professional** This book describes how to deploy Windows XP Professional, not earlier versions of Windows. Much of the content applies equally well to Microsoft Windows 2000 Professional, but Windows XP Professional provides unique features settings that Windows 2000 Professional doesn't have.

- **Office 2003 Editions** This book describes how to include Office 2003 Editions in your Windows XP Professional deployment. If you know how to deploy Microsoft Office XP, you already know much of what you need to know about Office 2003 Editions. However, Office 2003 Editions include deployment features that Office XP doesn't provide, and this book relies on them.

- **Windows 2003 Server** I vacillate a little between Microsoft Windows 2000 Server and Microsoft Windows Server 2003 because I know that many shops are still using Windows 2000 Server and will continue to do so for awhile longer. When a feature is specific to Windows 2003 Server, I point that out. Otherwise, most of this book's content applies equally well to both versions of the network operating system.

Some Terminology

Most of the terminology I use in this book is fairly standard by now, but to avoid confusion, I'll take a moment to describe how I use some of it.

Rather than give you hardcode paths, I use the standard environment variables that represent those paths instead. That way, when you read the instructions, you can apply them to your scenario even if you're using a dual-boot configuration or if user profiles exist on your computer (C:\Documents and Settings or C:\Winnt\Profiles). Additionally, on your computer, the folder that contains the Windows XP Professional system files might be in a different location—depending on whether you upgraded to the operating system, installed a clean copy of the operating system, or customized the installation path in an unattended-setup answer file. Thus, I use the following environment variables throughout this book (you can see these environment variables by typing **set** at an MS-DOS command prompt):

- **%USERPROFILE%**   This folder represents the current user profile folder. Thus, if you log on to the computer as **Jerry** and your profile folders are in C:\Documents and Settings, you'd translate %USERPROFILE% to C:\Documents and Settings\Jerry.

- **%SYSTEMDRIVE%**   This is the drive that contains the Windows XP Professional system files. That's usually drive C, but if you installed Windows XP Professional on a different drive, perhaps in a dual-boot configuration, it could be drive D, E, and so on.

- **%SYSTEMROOT%**   This is the folder containing Windows XP Professional. In a clean installation, this is usually C:\Windows, but if you upgraded from Windows NT or Windows 2000, it's probably C:\Winnt.

Aside from the environment variables, I also use abbreviations for the various root keys in the registry. *HKEY_CLASSES_ROOT* and *HKEY_LOCAL_MACHINE* are unwieldy, for example, and cause lines to wrap in funny places. To make the book more readable, I use the following instead:

HKCR	*HKEY_CLASSES_ROOT*
HKCU	*HKEY_CURRENT_USER*
HKLM	*HKEY_LOCAL_MACHINE*
HKU	*HKEY_USERS*
HKCC	*HKEY_CURRENT_CONFIG*

Companion CD

This book comes with a companion CD that includes planning aids, sample distribution points, scripts, tools, and a fully searchable electronic version (eBook) of the book. It also includes what could be the largest collection of deployment-related white papers in one place. Here is what you find in each directory of the companion CD:

- **Aids** This folder contains job aids, which are mostly planning worksheets. Simply copy each job aid to your computer and edit as appropriate.

- **Extras** This folder contains white papers and other useful documentation, mostly provided by Microsoft. There is a subfolder in Extras for each chapter, making it easier to find the documentation associated with each chapter.

- **Favorites** This folder contains shortcuts for all of the hyperlinks contained in this book. You can drag these directly to your Favorites folder to access them more quickly.

- **Samples** This folder contains sample files and distribution points. Each chapter that provides samples in this folder also provides instructions for using them. In most cases, you copy the samples to your computer and customize the files they contain by using the documentation contained in them as a guide.

- **Scripts** This folder contains a variety of scripts that are useful in deployment scenarios. Some are Windows Script Host (WSH) scripts, and others are batch scripts. In most cases, typing the name of the script without any command-line options will provide help for using them.

I continued testing the scripts after submitting this book's manuscripts, so you might find slight differences between the listings in the book and the contents of the CD. If in doubt, the contents of the CD are more current than this book's listings.

System Requirements

The systems to which you deploy Windows XP Professional will vary and must meet the Windows XP Professional minimum requirements (which you will learn about in this book's planning chapters). Most of the scripts contained on the companion CD do require at least Windows 2000 Professional, Windows 2000 Server, Windows XP Professional, or Windows Server 2003. To view the electronic version of the book, you'll need Adobe Acrobat or Adobe Reader. To obtain more information about these products or to download Adobe Reader, visit www.adobe.com.

Companion Web Site

It's my hope that this book makes your deployment job easier. Even though this book has over 800 pages, I don't for a minute believe that it is comprehensive enough to cover every scenario in every organization. Also, some topics are much bigger than the few pages I had to cover them. For example, Group Policy gets only about 60 pages in this book, but I could write another 300 useful pages about this technology.

That's why I envision this book as a *living book*. By that, I mean to support and update the book continuously via its companion Web site, which provides updated examples, chapters, and other new content. I'll also correct errors via this Web site. Most importantly, this Web site contains a bulletin board that you can use to collaborate with the rest of the deployment community. I'll answer questions on this bulletin board system, and you'll likely receive useful answers from other readers. The URL of the companion Web site is *http://www.bddreskit.com.*

Other Resources

There are three references that are absolutely necessary when deploying Windows XP Professional and Office 2003 Editions. This book refers to them frequently, in almost every chapter, and you should get to know them well:

- **Windows XP Professional Deployment Tools** These tools are on the Windows XP Professional distribution CD in the Support\Tools folder. They're in the Deploy.cab file, which you can open in Microsoft Windows Explorer to extract its contents. Aside from the tools it provides, it includes an outstanding set of documentation, "Microsoft Windows Corporate Deployment Tools User's Guide," including reference material for various deployment files such as unattended-setup answer files. This documentation is in Deploy.chm and Ref.chm. You might as well copy both of these files to your My Documents folder to keep them handy.

- **Office 2003 Editions Resource Kit** This resource kit provides documentation and tools for customizing and deploying Office 2003 Editions. This resource kit is available on Microsoft's Web site at *http://www.microsoft.com/office/ork.*

- **Microsoft Solution Accelerator for Business Desktop Deployment** The Microsoft Solution Accelerator for Business Desktop Deployment (BDD) provides guidance and tools to help you quickly deploy Windows XP Professional and Office 2003 Editions, as well as other business applications to computers across an organization. It includes technical guides that will assist you in planning and executing a rapid deployment. It also includes a variety of sample documents and templates to help you start, manage, and transition your desktop deployment project to a production environment. You can download the BDD solution accelerator from Microsoft's Web site at *http://www.microsoft.com /downloads*. If you're not a nuts-and-bolts type, the solution accelerator is a good starting point for your own deployment project. And this book is a good complement to it.

Lab Testing

This isn't your run-of-the-mill technology book. For example, I wrote an introductory book about Microsoft Windows Server 2003. Very little of that book could have serious consequences unless it was used with total abandonment of common sense.

This book is different, however. Even with the best-laid plans, using this book's contents without testing your design and implementation could have very serious consequences for your organization, its infrastructure, and your job security. To succeed, a large-scale desktop deployment requires careful planning and thorough testing. Take the ideas and techniques that I describe in this book, make them your own by extending them to suit your needs, and then test them carefully before implementing them in your organization.

Resource Kit Support Policy

Microsoft does not support the tools and scripts supplied on the *Microsoft Windows Desktop Deployment Resource Kit* companion CD. Microsoft does not guarantee the performance of the tools or scripting examples, or any bug fixes for these tools and scripts. However, Microsoft Press provides a way for customers who purchase this book to report any problems with the software and receive feedback on such issues—just send e-mail to msinput@microsoft.com. This e-mail address is only for issues related to *Microsoft Windows Desktop Deployment Resource Kit*. Microsoft Press also provides corrections for books and companion CDs through the World Wide Web at: *http://www.microsoft.com/learning/support/*. To connect directly to the Microsoft Press Knowledge Base and enter a query regarding a question or issue, go to: *http://www.microsoft.com/learning/support/search.asp*. For issues related to the Windows operating system, please refer to the support information included with your product.

Contacting Me

If you have any comments or questions, please feel free to send them my way at *jerry@honeycutt.com*. I answer my e-mail. You can also visit my Web site, *http://www.honeycutt.com* to learn more about me and the deployment services I'm able to provide.

Part I

Planning

In this part:

Chapter 1

Deployment Plan

This chapter helps you determine the best way to deploy Microsoft Windows XP Professional in your organization. Deploying the operating system requires careful planning. Before you install Windows XP Professional on your desktop computers, you must determine whether you need to upgrade your hardware and applications. Then you must decide which features to install, how much centralized control to maintain over users' computers, and which installation methods to use.

Checklist

- Have you been given a charter and do you understand it? Make sure that you have a clear charter and that you understand its objectives and constraints.

- Have you assembled an initial planning team for your deployment project? If not, invite key participants from each technical discipline (infrastructure, desktop engineering, help desk, and so on) to participate in initial planning stages.

- Do you have a clear window of time during which you can plan and deploy a new desktop? Desktop deployment projects are complicated and disruptive enough without compounding them with other ongoing projects.

Planning Overview

The first step in the deployment process is to assess your business needs so that you can define the project scope and objectives. Next, decide how best to use Windows XP Professional to meet those needs. Then, assess your current network and desktop configurations, determine whether you need to upgrade your hardware or software, and choose the tools for your deployment. Having made these decisions, you are ready to plan your deployment. An effective plan typically includes the following:

- A schedule for the deployment.

- All the details for customizing Windows XP Professional.

- An assessment of your current configuration, including information about users, organizational structure, network infrastructure, and hardware and software. Create a test environment in which you can deploy Windows XP Professional by using the features and options in your plan. Have your test environment mirror, as closely as possible, your users' network, including hardware, network architecture, and business applications.

- Test and pilot plans. When you're satisfied with the results in your test environment, roll out your deployment to a specific group of users to test the results in a controlled production environment. This is your pilot test.

- A rollout plan. Finally, roll out Windows XP Professional to your entire organization.

Creating the deployment plan is a cyclical process. As you move through each phase, modify the plan based on your experiences.

More Info   The white paper "Deploying and Supporting Windows XP" at *http://www.microsoft.com/technet/itsolutions/msit/deploy/wxpdpsp.mspx* provides a good overview of the deployment-planning process.

On the Resource Kit CD   Another excellent resource for better understanding how to plan a deployment is the white paper "Deployment Planning Blueprint for Windows XP and Office XP." You can download this white paper from Microsoft's Web site at *http://www.microsoft.com/resources/desktop /deployment.asp*. You'll also find a copy of this white paper on this book's companion CD in Extras\chap01. The file name is WinXPOfficeXP.doc.

Scheduling Templates

This book's companion CD contains a handful of planning templates for Microsoft Project 2003 that you can use to plan and document your project. They are in the folder Extras\chap01. They're also at *http://office. microsoft.com/templates* in the Meetings and Projects category:

- **Project.mpt**   A template for scheduling a deployment project
- **Offproj.mpt**   A template for scheduling a Microsoft Office 2003 Editions deployment project
- **Winproj.mpt**   A template for scheduling a Windows XP Professional deployment project
- **Lanproj.mpt**   A template for scheduling an infrastructure deployment project

Scope and Objectives

The *scope* is the baseline for creating a specification for your deployment project. The scope of your deployment project is defined largely by your answers to the following questions:

- What business needs do you want to address with Windows XP Professional?
- What are the long-term IT goals for the deployment project?
- How will your Windows XP Professional client computers interact with your IT infrastructure?

Current Environment

Document your existing computing environment, looking at your organization's structure and how it supports users. Use this assessment to determine your readiness for desktop deployment of Windows XP Professional. The three major areas of your computing environment to assess include your hardware, software, and network:

- **Hardware.**   Do your desktop and laptop computers meet the minimum hardware requirements for Windows XP Professional? In addition to meeting these requirements, all hardware must be compatible with Windows XP Professional.
- **Software.**   Are your applications compatible with Windows XP Professional? Make sure that all your applications, including custom-designed software, work with computers running Windows XP Professional. For more information about application compatibility, see Chapter 2, "Application Compatibility."

■ **Network.** Document your network architecture, including topology, size, and traffic patterns. Also, determine which users need access to various applications and data, and describe how they obtain access.

Where appropriate, create diagrams to include in your project plan. Diagrams convey more information than words alone. My favorite tool for creating these diagrams is Microsoft Office Visio 2003. See *http://www.microsoft.com/office* for information.

Testing and Piloting

Before rolling out your deployment project, you need to test it for functionality in a controlled environment. Before you begin testing your deployment project, create a test plan that describes the tests you will run, the expected results, a schedule for performing tests, and who will run each test. The test plan must specify the criteria and priority for each test. Prioritizing your tests can help you avoid slowing down your deployment because of minor failures that can be easily corrected later; it can also help you identify larger problems that might require redesigning your plan.

The testing phase is essential because a single error can be duplicated to all computers in your environment if it is not corrected before you deploy the image. Create a test lab that is not connected to your network but mirrors, as closely as possible, your organization's network and hardware configurations. Set up your hardware, software, and network services as they are in your users' environment. Perform comprehensive testing on each hardware platform, testing both application installation and operation. This can greatly increase the confidence of the project teams and the business-decision makers, resulting in a higher-quality deployment.

Microsoft recommends that you roll out the deployment to a small group of users after you test the project. Piloting the installation allows you to assess the success of the deployment project in a production environment before rolling it out to all users (crawling before walking, walking before running). To pilot the project, roll out the deployment to a small group of users. The primary purpose of pilot projects is not to test Windows XP Professional. Instead, the aim of your early pilots is to get user feedback for the project team. This feedback is used to further determine the features that you need to enable or disable in Windows XP Professional. This is particularly relevant if you upgrade from Microsoft Windows 98 or Microsoft Windows Millennium Edition (Me), which do not include features such as domain-based computer accounts, local security, and file system security. For pilots, you might choose a user population that represents a cross-section of your business in terms of job function and computer proficiency. Install pilot systems by using the same method that you plan to use for the final rollout.

The pilot process provides a small-scale test of the eventual full-scale rollout, so you can use the results of the pilot, including any problems encountered, to finalize your rollout plan. Compile the pilot results and use the data to estimate upgrade times, the number of concurrent upgrades you can sustain, and peak loads on the user support functions.

Rolling Out

After you thoroughly test your deployment plan and pilot the deployment to smaller groups of users and you're satisfied with the results, begin rolling out Windows XP Professional to the rest of your organization. To finalize the rollout plan, you need to determine the following:

- The number of computers to be included in each phase of the rollout
- The time needed to upgrade or perform a clean installation for each computer to be included
- The personnel and other resources needed to complete the rollout
- The timeframe during which you plan to roll out the installations to different groups
- Training needed for users throughout the organization

Throughout the rollout, gather feedback from users and modify the deployment plan as appropriate.

More to Think About

There are many more issues involved in planning a desktop deployment than I describe in this chapter. Examples include the following processes:

- Choosing a deployment team
- Recruiting sponsors and champions for the project
- Managing schedules and milestones
- Managing sign-off processes for milestones
- Recruiting pilot testers and training them
- Decommissioning older hardware

Aside from searching the plethora of resources for the various issues you should consider, I recommend that you sit down with the key people involved in the project and flush these issues out over the course of a few days. Assign ownership for key areas of your deployment plan to ensure that nothing slips through the cracks. Don't overcomplicate the planning process with useless steps and irrelevant documentation that just keeps the project stuck in a quagmire.

Environment Plan

As described in the section "Current Environment," your deployment plan must include an assessment of your current infrastructure as well as the steps necessary to update the environment. The answers to the following questions can help you determine what you must do to prepare the computers in your organization for Windows XP Professional:

- Are the computers and other devices in your network compatible with Windows XP Professional?

- What applications does your organization use? Are they compatible with Windows XP Professional, or do you need to upgrade to newer versions of the software before upgrading users' computers?

- Are all of your users connecting locally, or do some of them use remote access to connect to your network?

To determine whether your computers and peripheral devices are compatible with Windows XP Professional, see the Hardware Compatibility List (HCL) on Microsoft's Web site at *http://www.microsoft.com/whdc/hcl/search.mspx*. For more information about application compatibility, see the Windows Catalog at *http://www.microsoft.com/windows/catalog*. Before you can upgrade your users to Windows XP Professional, you must upgrade other software and your hardware as needed. Be sure to upgrade devices, remote access services, and your organization's applications first.

Upgrade Paths

You can't upgrade from Microsoft Windows 95 or Microsoft Windows 3.x to Windows XP Professional. If you are migrating from either of these operating systems you must do a clean installation of the operating system and then install device drivers that are compatible with Windows XP Professional. Upgrading from Microsoft Windows 98 or Microsoft Windows Me to Windows XP Professional might require some additional planning because of differences in the registry structure and the setup process.

Windows 2000 and Windows NT Workstation 4.0 provide the easiest upgrade path to Windows XP Professional because they share a common operating system structure and core features, such as support file systems, security concepts, device driver requirements, and registry structure. If you upgrade or install Windows XP Professional on a Windows NT Workstation 4.0–based computer that uses NT file system (NTFS), the installation process automatically upgrades the file system to Windows XP Professional NTFS. If you install or upgrade to Windows XP Professional and the current file system is file allocation table (FAT), you are asked if you want to upgrade to the NTFS file system. You cannot upgrade computers that run Windows NT Workstation 3.51 to Windows XP Professional. You must do a clean installation of Windows XP Professional.

Many updated drivers ship with the Windows XP Professional operating system CD. However, when critical device drivers, such as hard-drive controllers, are not compatible with Windows XP Professional or can't be found, Windows XP Setup might halt the upgrade until updated drivers are obtained. The 16-bit device drivers for Windows Me, Windows 98, Windows 95, and Windows 3.x were based on the virtual device driver (VxD) model. The VxD model is not supported in Windows XP Professional. An upgrade does not migrate drivers from Windows Me or Windows 98 to Windows XP Professional. If the driver for a particular device does not exist in Windows XP Professional, you might need to download an updated driver from the device manufacturer.

Some hardware devices that are supported by Microsoft Windows NT Workstation 4.0 also work on Windows XP Professional; however, it is best to run Windows XP Setup in Check Upgrade Only mode to check for driver compatibility issues before upgrading the operating system (see the sidebar "Using Check Upgrade Only" for more information). Windows XP Professional does not support drivers, including third-party drivers, that worked on Windows NT Workstation 4.0. You need to obtain an updated driver for Windows XP Professional from the device manufacturer. Typically, you can address issues concerning deployment or upgrade of Windows NT Workstation 4.0 during the test phase of deployment.

> **Note**   To access an NTFS volume that has been upgraded for Microsoft Windows XP Professional, you need to be running Windows NT 4.0 Service Pack (SP) 4 or later.

Client Hardware

Make sure that your hardware is compatible with Windows XP Professional, and that all the computers on which you plan to install the operating system are capable of supporting the installation. Table 1-1 shows the minimum and recommended hardware requirements for installing Windows XP Professional. For more information about hardware compatibility with Windows XP Professional, see the HCL at *http://www.microsoft.com/whdc/hcl/search.mspx*. If you're purchasing new hardware, contact the hardware vendor to confirm its compatibility with Windows XP Professional. Most hardware vendors will loan you evaluation computers so you can test your configuration on them.

Table 1-1   Hardware Requirements

Minimum Requirements	Recommended Requirements
Intel Pentium (or compatible) 233 megahertz (MHz) or higher processor	Intel Pentium II (or compatible) 300 MHz or higher processor
64 megabytes (MB) of RAM	128 MB (4 GB maximum) of RAM
2 gigabyte (GB) hard disk with 650 MB of free disk space (additional disk space required if installing over a network)	2 GB of free disk space
Video Graphics Adapter (VGA) or higher display adapter	Super VGA (SVGA) display adapter and Plug and Play monitor
Keyboard, mouse, or other pointing device	Keyboard, mouse, or other pointing device
Compact disc read-only memory (CD-ROM) or digital video disc read-only memory (DVD-ROM) drive (required for CD installations)	CD-ROM or DVD-ROM drive (12x or faster)
Network adapter (required for network installation)	Network adapter (required for network installation)

Note   Windows XP Professional supports single and dual central processing unit (CPU) systems.

Before upgrading to Windows XP Professional, check that the computer's BIOS is the latest available version and that it is compatible with Windows XP Professional. You can obtain an updated BIOS from the manufacturer. If the computer does not have Advanced Configuration and Power Interface (ACPI) functionality, you might need to update the BIOS. To get ACPI functionality after Windows XP Professional is installed, you are required to do an in-place upgrade of your current installation. Microsoft does not provide technical support for BIOS upgrades. Contact the manufacturer for BIOS upgrade instructions. For more information about BIOS issues, see the HCL at *http://www.microsoft.com/whdc/hcl/search.mspx*.

The Windows XP Professional HCL is a list of hardware devices that have successfully passed the Hardware Compatibility Tests. All hardware on the HCL works with Windows XP Professional. Hardware not included on the HCL is not guaranteed to work successfully with Windows XP Professional. Installing Windows XP Professional on a computer that has hardware that is not on the HCL might cause the installation to fail, or it might cause problems after installation. For more information about hardware compatibility, see *http://www.microsoft.com/whdc/hcl/search.mspx*. A device that is not on the HCL might function, but not be supported by Windows XP

Professional. For devices that do not function when the computer is running Windows XP Professional, contact the device manufacturer for a Windows XP Professional–compatible driver. If you have a program that uses 16-bit drivers, you need to install 32-bit Windows XP Professional–compatible drivers from the device manufacturer to ensure functionality with Windows XP Professional.

Client Software

Because there are new technologies in Windows XP Professional, you need to test your business applications for compatibility with the new operating system. Even if you currently use Windows NT Workstation 4.0, you need to test applications to make sure that they work as well on Windows XP Professional as they do in your existing environment. Also, enhancements included in Windows XP Professional, such as improved security features, might not be supported by some applications.

Identify all applications that your organization currently uses, including custom software. As you identify applications, prioritize them and note which ones are required for each business unit in your organization. Remember to include operational and administrative tools, including antivirus, compression, backup, and remote-control programs.

Applications that comply with the Windows XP Application Specification are compatible with Windows XP Professional and take advantage of the new technologies it provides. The desktop application specification applies to any software that runs on Windows XP Professional, whether it runs as a standalone program or as the client portion of a distributed application. Commercial applications that comply with the Windows XP Application Specification can be certified by an independent testing organization if they meet certain requirements, such as using Windows Installer. Applications can also comply with the specification even if they are not certified. For more information about the specification, see *http://www.microsoft.com /windowsserver2003/partners/isvs/cfw.mspx*.

More Info   For more information about overcoming compatibility issues, particularly when an upgrade for an application isn't available, see Chapter 2. This chapter describes how to use the Application Compatibility Toolkit to resolve compatibility problems with Windows XP Professional.

Using Check Upgrade Only

Windows XP Setup includes a Check Upgrade Only mode, which you can use to test the upgrade process before you do an actual upgrade. This mode produces a report that flags potential problems that might be encountered during the actual upgrade, such as hardware compatibility issues or software that might not be migrated during the upgrade. To run Windows XP Setup in this mode, select Check System Compatibility from the menu displayed when you insert the installation CD. You can also run Windows XP Setup in this mode by running Winnt32.exe from the i386 folder with the command-line parameter **/checkupgradeonly**. The Upgrade Report is a summary of potential hardware and software upgrade issues. The following entries are in the report:

- **MS-DOS configuration.** This reports entries in Autoexec.bat and Config.sys that are incompatible with Windows XP Professional. These entries might be associated with older hardware and software that are incompatible with Windows XP Professional. It also suggests that more technical information is provided in the Setupact.log file located in the %WINDIR% folder.

- **Unsupported hardware.** This reports hardware that might not be supported by Windows XP Professional without additional files.

- **Software that must be permanently removed.** This reports upgrade packs that are required for some programs because they do not support Windows XP Professional or because they can introduce problems with Windows XP Professional. Before upgrading to Windows XP Professional, gain disk space by using Add Or Remove Programs in Control Panel to remove programs not in use.

- **Software that must be temporarily removed.** This reports upgrades that are recommended for programs because they use different files and settings in Windows XP Professional. If an upgrade cannot be obtained, remove the program before upgrading by using Add Or Remove Programs in Control Panel. After upgrading to Windows XP Professional, reinstall or upgrade the program.

- **Installation requirements.** This reports how much additional disk space or memory is required to install Windows XP Professional, and whether the computer contains operating systems that cannot be upgraded to Windows XP Professional.

Some problems are *blocking issues*. If an incompatibility prevents the upgrade from continuing, a wizard appears to inform the user. You can view details about the incompatibility, if available. Unless you can fix the problem by supplying a missing file (by clicking the Have Disk button), you must quit Windows XP Setup and fix the problem before running Winnt32.exe again. Others are simply *warnings*. If the incompatibility does not prevent a successful upgrade to Windows XP Professional, you are warned that this application might not work correctly with Windows XP Professional. At this point, you can choose to quit or to continue the upgrade. The Have Disk button is also supported in this case.

The Upgrade Report also lists issues that do not prevent a successful upgrade, but might be useful for the user to know. This includes information about incompatible hardware accessories or applications that might need to be updated or are replaced by Windows XP functionality, as well as program notes. A General Information section lists information you need to be aware of before upgrading, such as files found on the computer (these might include backup files that need to be saved to a different location so they are not removed by Windows XP Setup), excluded or inaccessible drives, configurations that might be lost during the upgrade process, and other reference information.

Infrastructure

Assess your network infrastructure by identifying existing network protocols, network bandwidth, and the network hardware. Table 1-2 describes how these issues affect your deployment plan.

Table 1-2   Network Infrastructure

Attribute	Effect on Project Plan
Network Protocols	Network protocols determine how you customize several of the networking sections of answer files, such as *[NetAdapter]*, *[NetProtocols]*, and *[NetServices]*. See Chapter 6, "Answer Files," for more information about customizing answer files.
Network Bandwidth	Network bandwidth affects which method of installation to use. For example, in low-bandwidth networks or on computers that are not part of a network, you might need to use a local installation method. For high-bandwidth network connections, you might choose to install Windows XP Professional by using a network-based disk image.
Network Servers	The servers you have in your network affect the installation tools available to you. If you have an existing Microsoft Windows 2000 Server or Microsoft Windows Server 2003 infrastructure in place, you can use a wider range of tools to automate and customize client installations, including Remote Installation Services (RIS). For more information about RIS, see Chapter 16, "Remote Installation Service."

Next, collect information about both the hardware and software in your network infrastructure. This should include the logical organization of your network, name- and address-resolution methods, naming conventions, and network services in use. Documenting the location of network sites and the available bandwidth between them can help you decide which installation method to use.

Document the structure of your network, including server operating systems, file and print servers, directory services, domain and tree structures, server protocols, and file structure. You should also include information about network administration procedures, including backup and recovery strategies, antivirus measures, and data storage and access policies. If you use multiple server operating systems, note how you manage security and users' access to resources. Network security measures should also be included in your assessment of the network. Include information about how you manage client authentication, user and group access to resources, and Internet security. Document firewall and proxy configurations. Create physical and logical diagrams of your network to organize the information you gather:

- The physical network diagram can include the following information:
  - Physical communication links, including cables, and the paths of analog and digital lines.
  - Server names, Internet protocol (IP) addresses, and domain membership.
  - Location of printers, hubs, switches, routers, bridges, proxy servers, and other network devices.
  - Wide area network (WAN) communication links, their speed, and available bandwidth between sites. If you have slow or heavily used connections, it is important to note them.

- The logical network diagram can include the following information:
  - Domain architecture
  - Server roles, including primary and backup domain controllers, and WINS and DNS servers
  - Trust relationships and any policy restrictions that might affect your deployment

Configuration Plan

After you identify your business needs and decide which features of Windows XP Professional to use, determine how to implement these features to simplify the management of users and computers in your organization. An important means to simplification is standardization. Standardizing desktop configurations makes it easier to install, update, manage, support, and replace computers that run Windows XP Professional. Standardizing users' configuration settings, software, hardware, and preferences makes it easier to deploy operating system and application upgrades, and configuration changes can be guaranteed to work on all computers.

When users install their own operating system upgrades, applications, device drivers, settings, preferences, and hardware devices, a simple problem can become complex. Establishing standards for desktop configurations prevents many problems and makes it easier for you to identify and resolve problems. Having a standard configuration that you can install on any computer minimizes downtime by ensuring that user settings, applications, drivers, and preferences are the same as before the problem occurred. The following sections provide an overview of some of these features.

More Info   Chapter 3, "Windows Configuration," describes configuration planning in detail. This chapter describes how to create a preferred, standardized configuration for Windows XP Professional. It includes configuring desktop management, desktop connectivity, security, file systems, applications, settings, and more. Planning a configuration for Office 2003 Editions is also an important consideration. For help designing a preferred configuration for Office 2003 Editions, see Chapter 4, "Office Configuration."

Note   Some features are available only if you deploy Windows XP Professional in a domain that uses Active Directory. Other features are available to any computer running Windows XP Professional, using any server. After you identify your business needs, you can map desktop management, security, and networking features in Windows XP Professional to those needs.

Management

Desktop management features allow you to reduce the total cost of ownership in your organization by making it easier to install, configure, and manage clients. These features are also designed as tools to make computers easier to use. Table 1-3 describes desktop management features in Windows XP Professional that increase user productivity. See Chapter 3 for more information about them.

Table 1-3   Desktop Management Features

Feature	Description	Benefit
Group Policy Administrative Templates	Files that you can use to configure Group Policy settings to govern the behavior of services, applications, and operating system components.	Allows you to configure registry-based policy settings for domains, computers, and users.
Software Installation and Maintenance	An IntelliMirror feature that you can use to assign or publish software to users according to their job needs.	Allows you to centrally manage software installation and to repair installations by using Windows Installer.
Roaming User Profiles	A feature that ensures that the data and settings in a user's profile are copied to a network server when the user logs off and are available to the user anywhere on the network.	Provides a transparent way to back up the user's profile to a network server, protecting this information in case the user's computer fails. This is also useful for users who roam throughout the network.
Folder Redirection	An IntelliMirror feature that you can use to redirect certain folders, such as My Documents, from the user's desktop to a server.	Provides improved protection for user data by ensuring that local data is also redirected or copied to a network share, providing a central location for administrator-managed backups. Speeds up the logon process when using Roaming User Profiles by preventing large data transfers over the network.
Offline Files and Folders	A feature that you can use to make files that reside on a network share available to a local computer when it is disconnected from the server.	Allows users without constant network access, such as remote and mobile users, to continue working on their files even when they are not connected to the network. Users can also have their file synchronized with the network copy when they reconnect.
Multilingual Options	Multilanguage support in Windows XP Professional lets users edit and print documents in almost any language.	Lets administrators customize desktop computers in their organization with the language and regional support that best meets their users' needs.

Networking

You can configure computers that run Windows XP Professional to participate in a variety of network environments, including Microsoft Windows-based, Novell NetWare-based, UNIX-based, and IBM Host Systems-based networks. You can also configure Windows XP Professional to connect directly to the Internet without being part of a network environment. Windows XP Professional includes several features, such as Zero Configuration, which simplify the process of connecting to a network and allow mobile users to access network resources without physically reconnecting cables each time they move to a new location. Table 1-4 describes several features in Windows XP Professional that provide remote and local access to resources and support for communication solutions.

Table 1-4   Networking Features

Feature	Description	Benefit
TCP/IP	The standard transport protocol in Windows XP Professional.	Provides communication across networks that use diverse hardware architectures and various operating systems, including computers running Windows XP Professional, devices using other Microsoft networking products, and non-Microsoft operating systems such as UNIX.
Dynamic Host Configuration Protocol (DHCP)	A protocol that allows computers and devices on a network to be dynamically assigned IP addresses and other network configuration information.	Eliminates the need to manually configure IP addresses and other IP settings, reducing potential conflicts and administrative overhead caused by static configurations.
Telephony and Conferencing	A service that abstracts the details of the underlying telecommunications network, allowing applications and devices to use a single command set.	Allows data, voice, and video communications to travel over the same IP-based network infrastructure.
Remote Access	A connection between the local network and a remote or home office, established by dial-up modem, virtual private network (VPN), X.25, Integrated Services Digital Network (ISDN), or Point-to-Point Protocol (PPP).	Allows users to access the network from home or remote offices or in transit.
Client Service For NetWare	A feature that allows Windows XP Professional clients to transmit Network Core Protocol (NCP) packets to NetWare servers.	Allows Windows XP Professional client computers to connect to NetWare file and print servers.
Secure Home Networking	Includes Internet Connection Sharing, bridging, personal firewall, and Universal Plug and Play.	Provides easy connectivity for various devices within the home and from the home to the corporate network, along with safe access to the Internet and multiple-user accessibility over a single Internet connection.

Table 1-4   Networking Features

Feature	Description	Benefit
Wireless Connectivity	Protocols that are supported by Windows XP Professional to provide LAN and WAN connectivity, including security mechanisms that can make the wireless connection as secure as a cabled connection.	Provides ease of mobility by allowing users to access network resources and the Internet without using connection cables.
Zero Configuration	A mechanism in which a client computer goes through a list of possible network configurations and chooses the one that applies to the current situation.	Allows the administrator to set up the initial configuration options so that users do not need to know which connection configuration to use.

Security

Windows XP Professional includes features to help you secure your network and computers by controlling authentication and access to resources and by encrypting data stored on computers. Also included are preconfigured Security Templates for various security scenarios. Table 1-5 is an overview of these features.

Table 1-5   Security Features

Feature	Description	Benefit
Security templates	Four preconfigured combinations of security policy settings that represent different organizational security needs: basic, secure, highly secure, and compatible.	Allow you to implement the appropriate templates without modifications or use them as the base for customized security configurations.
Security groups	User groupings, used to administer security, which are defined by their scope, their purpose, their rights, or their role.	Allow you to control users' rights on the system. By adding or removing users or resources from the appropriate groups as your organization changes, you can change access control lists (ACLs) less frequently.
ACLs	Ordered lists of access control entries (ACEs) that collectively define the protections that apply to an object and its properties.	In combination with security groups, configuring ACLs on resources makes user permissions easier to control and audit.
Kerberos	The authentication protocol for computers running Microsoft Windows 2000 and Windows XP Professional in Active Directory domains.	Provides more efficient and secure authentication than NTLM.

Table 1-5   Security Features

Feature	Description	Benefit
NTLM	The default authentication protocol in Microsoft Windows NT 4.0 and Windows XP Professional.	Allows Windows XP Professional computers to establish connections to Windows NT–based networks.
Windows stored user names and passwords	A technology that can supply users with different credentials for different resources.	Can increase security on a per-resource basis by allowing users to store and manage credentials.
Smart card support	An integrated circuit card (ICC) that can store certificates and private keys, and perform public key cryptography operations such as authentication, digital signing, and key exchange.	Provides tamper-resistant storage for private keys and other forms of personal identification. Isolates critical security computations involving authentication, digital signatures, and key exchange. Enables credentials and other private information to be moved among computers.
Encrypting File System (EFS)	A feature of NTFS that uses symmetric key encryption and public-key technology to protect files.	Allows administrators and users to encrypt data to keep it secure. This is particularly beneficial to mobile users.

Distribution Plan

After you decide how to use Windows XP Professional in your organization and how best to manage your users and computers, you need to prepare your installations. The following questions can help you make important decisions affecting the process:

- Will you upgrade computers or perform clean installations?

- Which installation method is appropriate for you to use?

- Do you plan to install multiple operating systems on individual computers?

Your answers to the preceding questions are largely determined by your business goals and your current configuration. For example, if you plan to install Windows XP Professional to gain enhancements unavailable in current Windows 2000 Professional installations, upgrading might be the preferred strategy. However, if your desktop computers run Windows 95, you must do a clean installation of Windows XP Professional. If you have an Active Directory environment in place, you can use RIS to standardize the installations across your desktops, customize and control the installation process, and determine the media on which to distribute the installation.

The following sections describe various issues and decisions you must make. For help choosing a distribution method, see the section "Distribution Methods," later in this chapter.

Clean Installations Are Best

If you're upgrading from Windows 95, Windows 98, or Windows Me, I strongly urge you to install Windows XP Professional cleanly instead of upgrading to it from these legacy operating systems. The following list describes the many reasons why I make this recommendation:

- **System degradation over time.** Over the course of a computer's lifetime, its configuration and performance degrades significantly. If you upgrade to Windows XP Professional from a legacy operating system, you carry forward most of these issues. For example, upgrading will not resolve issues with disk fragmentation, wasted drive space, registry size and fragmentation, page file fragmentation, and so on.

- **Application migration.** Many applications don't migrate well during an upgrade to Windows XP Professional from a legacy version of Windows. The solution in most cases is to reinstall the application in Windows XP Professional.

- **Security and privacy.** Windows XP Professional is more secure than legacy versions of Windows. During an upgrade, Windows XP Setup does strengthen some settings, but it migrates many security settings from earlier versions of Windows. Therefore, Windows XP Professional is less secure after an upgrade than after a clean installation.

- **Total cost of ownership.** Upgrading a computer from an unknown state, which is true of most computers running legacy versions of Windows, to Windows XP Professional results in a big mix of issues. These issues result in more Help desk calls and more difficult management. Also, legacy versions of Windows use Windows NT–style policies and after upgrading to Windows XP Professional, those policies tattoo the registry.

- **Lost opportunity.** If you upgrade from a legacy version of Windows to Windows XP Professional, you're missing an opportunity for a clean start.

- **Deployment process.** Designing, configuring, and implementing an upgrade from legacy versions of Windows to Windows XP Professional is more difficult, time consuming, and expensive than clean installations.

In most environments, the disadvantages of upgrading far outweigh the advantages. Clean installations have far more advantages and far fewer disadvantages, making it the best choice in most cases.

Clean Installations

During an upgrade, existing user settings are retained, as well as installed applications. If you perform a clean installation, the operating system files are installed in a new folder, and you must reinstall all your applications and reset user preferences, such as desktop and application settings. You need to choose a clean installation of Windows XP Professional in the following cases:

- No operating system is installed on the computer.

- The installed operating system does not support an upgrade to Windows XP Professional. Windows XP Professional provides upgrade paths from Windows 2000 Professional, Windows NT Workstation 4.0, Windows 98, and Windows Me. If you are using Windows 95, Windows 3.x, or another operating system, you need to do clean installs.

- The computer has more than one partition and needs to support a multiple-boot configuration that uses Windows XP Professional and the current operating system.

- A clean installation is preferred. In some environments, particularly those in which desktops are currently unmanaged, a clean installation is the quickest and easiest way to gain control of the desktop configurations. Simply upgrading an unmanaged desktop to Windows XP Professional doesn't guarantee a managed configuration. However, after designing a standardized configuration and deploying it as a clean installation, your chances of success are much higher.

The most basic advantage of a clean installation is that all your systems can begin with the same configuration. All applications, files, and settings are reset. You can use a single disk image or answer file to make sure that all of the desktops in your organization are standardized. In this way, you can avoid many of the support problems that are caused by irregular configurations.

The User State Migration Tool (USMT) allows you to save and restore users' settings and files to minimize the time required to configure users' computers after installing Windows XP Professional. You can use USMT when performing clean installations, migrating from computers running Windows 95, Windows 98, Windows Me, Windows NT 4.0, Windows 2000, or Windows XP. You can run USMT from the Windows XP Professional installation CD or some other automated method, as discussed in Chapter 18, "User State Migration." By default, USMT saves the majority of user interface settings such as desktop color schemes and wallpaper, network connectivity settings such as e-mail servers and proxy servers, and some files associated with recent versions of Microsoft Office. You can customize the *.inf* files the tool uses to save only the settings you want to migrate to Windows XP Professional. You can restore these settings only on computers running Windows XP Professional or Windows XP Home Edition; you cannot use USMT to migrate to Windows XP 64-Bit Edition.

Multibooting

You can install multiple operating systems on computers so that users can choose the operating system to use each time they start the computer. You can also specify an operating system as the default that starts when the user makes no selection. Multibooting is useful in scenarios where you must support applications that aren't compatible with Windows XP Professional. A better alternative in this scenario is Microsoft Virtual PC, however. For more information, see Chapter 2 or *http://www.microsoft.com/windowsxp/virtualpc/.*

> **Warning** f you install Windows XP Professional and any other operating system on a computer, you must install Windows XP Professional on a separate partition. Installing Windows XP Professional on a separate partition ensures that it will not overwrite files used by the other operating system. Installing multiple operating systems on the same partition is not supported and can prevent one or both operating systems from working properly.

Installing multiple operating systems on a computer has some drawbacks, however. Each operating system uses disk space, and compatibility issues (especially between file systems) can be complex. Also, you cannot use dynamic disks with certain operating systems. Only Windows 2000 Professional and Windows XP Professional can access a dynamic disk. Converting a basic disk to a dynamic disk that contains multiple installations of Windows XP Professional or Windows 2000 Professional can cause startup problems.

Before setting up a computer that has more than one operating system, review the following restrictions:

- MS-DOS and Windows XP Professional:

    - Install MS-DOS first. Otherwise, important files needed to start Windows XP Professional can be overwritten.

    - Install each operating system on its own partition and then install the applications used with each operating system on the same partition. If you intend to run an application on both operating systems, install it on both partitions.

    - Format the system partition as FAT.

- Windows 95 and Windows XP Professional:

    - Install Windows 95 first. Otherwise, important files needed to start Windows XP Professional can be overwritten.

    - Install each operating system on its own partition and then install the applications used with each operating system on the same partition. If you intend to run an application on both operating systems, install it on both partitions.

    - Format the system partition as FAT. (For Windows 95 OSR2, the primary partition must be formatted as FAT or FAT32.)

    - Compressed DriveSpace or DoubleSpace volumes are not available while you run Windows XP Professional. It is not necessary to uncompress DriveSpace or DoubleSpace volumes that you access only from Windows 95.

- Windows 98 or Windows Me and Windows XP Professional:

    - Install each operating system on its own partition and then install the applications used with each operating system on the same partition. If you intend to run an application on both operating systems, install it on both partitions.

    - Format the system partition as FAT or FAT32.

    - Compressed DriveSpace or DoubleSpace volumes are not available while you run Windows XP Professional. It is not necessary to uncompress DriveSpace or DoubleSpace volumes that you access only from Windows 98.

- Windows NT Workstation 4.0 and Windows XP Professional:

    - Make sure that Windows NT 4.0 has been updated with the latest service pack.

    - Install each operating system on its own partition and then install the applications used with each operating system on the same partition. If you intend to run an application on both operating systems, install it on both partitions.

    - Using NTFS as the only file system on a computer that contains both Windows XP Professional and Windows NT is not recommended.

    - Do not install Windows XP Professional on a compressed volume unless the volume was compressed by using the NTFS compression feature.

    - If the computer is part of a domain, use a unique computer name for each installation.

- Windows 2000 Professional and Windows XP Professional; or multiple Windows XP Professional partitions:

  - Install each operating system on its own partition and then install the applications used with each operating system on the same partition. If you intend to run an application on both operating systems, install it on both partitions.

  - On a computer on which you install multiple Windows XP Professional partitions, you can install any product in the Windows XP product family. For example, you can install Windows XP Professional on one partition and Microsoft Windows XP Home Edition on another. Because Windows XP Home Edition does not support dynamic disks, you must use basic disks on computers that multiple-boot Windows XP Professional and Windows XP Home Edition.

  - If the computer participates in a domain, use a different computer name for each installation. Because a unique security identifier (SID) is used for each installation of Windows XP Professional on a domain, the computer name for each installation must be unique, even for multiple installations on the same computer.

  - If you use EFS, ensure that encrypted files are available from each of the installations.

For Windows-based computers, the available file systems are NTFS, FAT, and FAT32. For more information, see Chapter 3. The version of NTFS included in Windows 2000 and Windows XP Professional has new features that are not available for Windows NT. You might have full access to files that use new features only when the computer is started by using Windows 2000 Professional or Windows XP Professional. For example, a file that uses the new encryption feature is not readable when the computer is started with Windows NT Workstation 4.0, which was released before the encryption feature existed.

To set up a computer that has an NTFS partition to run Windows NT Workstation 4.0 and Windows XP Professional, you must use Windows NT Workstation 4.0 with the latest released service pack. Using the latest service pack maximizes compatibility between Windows NT Workstation 4.0 and the NTFS enhancements in Windows XP Professional. Specifically, SP 4 and later service packs provide this compatibility in file systems. Even the most recent service pack, however, does not provide access to files using later features in NTFS. Using NTFS as the only file system on a computer that contains both Windows XP Professional and Windows NT Workstation 4.0 is not recommended. On these computers, a FAT partition ensures that the computer has access to needed files when it is started with Windows NT Workstation 4.0. If you set up a computer with Windows NT Workstation 3.51 or earlier on a FAT partition and Windows XP Professional on an NTFS partition, the NTFS partition is not visible while you run Windows NT Workstation 3.51.

If you configure a computer so that it contains Windows 2000 Professional and Windows XP Professional or it contains multiple Windows XP Professional partitions, you must take certain steps to use EFS so that encrypted files are readable between the different installations. Use either of the following approaches:

- Ensure that all the installations are in the same domain and that the user has a roaming profile.

- Export the user's file encryption certificate and associated private key from one installation and import it into the other installations.

Dynamic Update

Dynamic Update is a feature in Windows XP Setup that works with Windows Update to download critical fixes and drivers needed for the setup process. This feature updates the required installation files to improve the process of getting started with Windows XP Professional. Dynamic Update also downloads device drivers from the Windows Update site that are not included on the Windows XP Professional operating system CD, which ensures that devices attached to the computer will work. Updates to existing drivers are not downloaded during Dynamic Update, but you can obtain them by connecting to Windows Update after setup is complete. Dynamic Update downloads the following types of files:

- **Critical fixes.**   Dynamic Update replaces files from the Windows XP Professional operating system CD that require critical fixes or updates. Files that are replaced also include *dynamic-link libraries* (DLLs) that Windows XP Setup requires. No new files are downloaded—only replacements for existing files.

- **Device drivers.**   Dynamic Update downloads new drivers for devices that are connected to the computer and are required to run Windows XP Setup. Only drivers that are not included on the operating system CD are downloaded.

For Dynamic Update to run during Windows XP Setup, the computer needs an Internet connection or access to a network share containing updates downloaded from the corporate catalog on the Windows Update Web site, and Internet Explorer 4.01 or later. If either of these requirements is not met, Dynamic Update does not connect to Windows Update or download the required files. The user is asked whether Windows XP Setup should look for updates. If the user selects Yes, Dynamic Update connects to Windows Update and searches for new drivers and critical fixes. In unattended installations, Dynamic Update is enabled by default, but can be disabled by setting the following key in the answer file: DUDisable = Yes. For more information, see Chapter 13, "Unattended Setup."

Windows XP Setup checks for required disk space, memory, and other requirements. If these requirements are not met, neither the setup process nor the Dynamic Update step proceeds. If the computer meets the setup requirements, Windows XP

Setup checks the size of the Dynamic Update download to determine whether there is enough space to download the file. The estimated size of the download is based on the size of the cabinet (*.cab*) files, and the size of the cabinet (.cab) files, and the total amount of disk space required for the downloaded files cannot be determined. Windows XP Setup checks the size of the files again after they are extracted from the downloaded .cab files.

If you plan to roll out Windows XP Professional to a large number of computers, you might not want multiple users connecting to the Windows Update Web site to download critical fixes and device drivers. Using Dynamic Update, you can download the needed files from the Windows Update Corporate site and place them on a share within your network where client computers can connect during setup. This saves bandwidth and gives you more control over what files are copied to each computer. This process also lets you choose device drivers to include during the Dynamic Update phase of setup. For more information, see Chapter 13.

Windows Product Activation

Windows Product Activation (WPA) deters piracy by requiring your Windows XP Professional installation to be activated. WPA is based on requiring each unique installation to have a unique product key.

> **Note**   WPA is not required under volume-licensing agreements.

WPA ties your product key and Product ID to your computer by creating an installation ID. The installation ID is made up of your Product Identification (PID) and a PC identifier, called a hardware ID (HWID). The installation ID is sent to a Microsoft license clearinghouse, which verifies whether Microsoft manufactured that PID and that the PID has not been used to install the operating system on more hardware than is defined by the product's End-User License Agreement (EULA). For Windows XP Professional, the EULA states that you can install on one computer. If this check fails, activation of Windows XP Professional fails. If this check passes, your computer receives a confirmation ID that activates your computer. After Windows XP Professional is activated, you never need to perform WPA again, unless you significantly overhaul the hardware in your computer. You must activate your installation within 30 days after installing Windows XP Professional. If the product key is used to install Windows XP Professional on a second computer, activation fails. Additionally, if WPA detects that the current installation of Windows XP Professional is running on a different computer than it was originally activated on, you must activate it again. In this way, WPA prevents casual copying of the operating system.

For unattended installations that are not performed using volume-licensing media, a separate answer file, including a unique product key, must be created for each computer on which Windows XP Professional is installed.

> **Tip**   Because product keys cannot be determined from within the system, it is recommended that you create a database that lists each computer and the product key that corresponds to its installation. You can then use this database with the template techniques described in Chapter 6 to use one template answer file to generate answer files for each product key, as needed.

Distribution Methods

The following questions and guidelines help you determine which of the automated installation and customization tools is most appropriate for your environment. The guidelines describe baseline requirements for each of the tools:

- **Do the client computers have compatible Hardware Abstraction Layers (HALs)?**   Before you can determine which tool to use, you have to find out whether the client computers have compatible HALs. If the client computers don't have compatible HALs, you can't use disk imaging with Sysprep or the Remote Installation Preparation tool (Riprep.exe), which is a component of RIS. For example, if the sample computer you use to build a disk image has a Standard PC HAL, the destination computer must have the same Standard PC HAL. If the sample computer has an ACPI PC HAL, the destination computer must have the same ACPI PC HAL. (Standard PC and ACPI PC are the names of HALs that are detected during the initial phase of a Windows XP Professional installation, before Sysprep.exe or Riprep.exe are run.) If the client computers have compatible HALs, you can obtain a compatible sample computer with which to build disk images.

- **Do the client computers have a fast and reliable network connection?** If the client and reference computers have compatible HALs, you have to determine whether the network connections are fast and reliable enough to enable you to use a third-party disk-imaging product or RIS. If the client computers are not connected to a network, you cannot use either. Determine whether there is a Windows 2000 Server–based or Windows Server 2003–based network infrastructure in place. Identify existing network protocols. Also, if the network connections aren't fast or reliable enough, unattended installations using answer files are not feasible.

- **Do you want to upgrade an existing installation of the operating system?**   If you are planning to perform a clean operating system installation on the client computers, you can use any of the installation tools. However, if you are planning to perform an operating system upgrade to the client computers, you cannot use RIS or disk imaging with Sysprep. Client computers running Windows 3.x and Microsoft Windows 95 cannot be upgraded to Windows XP Professional. You must perform clean installations on these client computers. Windows XP Professional supports upgrades from the following operating systems:

  - Windows NT Workstation 4.0

  - Windows 2000 Professional

  - Windows 98

  - Windows Me

- Choosing to perform a clean installation is a good course of action if you plan to standardize the desktop computers across your organization. If you decide to perform a clean installation, you can't migrate customized settings from the currently installed operating system without using a tool like "User State Migration Tool." Depending on the status of your deployment, you might have to upgrade many of your computers in addition to installing Windows XP Professional on new computers. If you plan to use currently installed applications on existing hardware, you must perform an upgrade. Table 1-6 provides an overview of support for upgrades and clean installations.

Table 1-6   Upgrades and Clean Installations

Tool	Upgrade	Clean Installation
Unattended Installation	Yes	Yes
System Preparation Tool (Sysprep.exe)	No	Yes
Remote Installation Services (RIS)	No	Yes
Systems Management Server (SMS)	Yes	No

- **Do you plan to deploy and maintain a large number of client computers?**   The number of client computers in a deployment can help you determine which installation tool to use. For example, if you have a large number of computers, RIS, SMS, or disk-imaging with Sysprep are good choices. For a small number of computers, using unattended installations with answer files is reasonable.

Table 1-7 summarizes the installation methods available for Windows XP Professional and some of the considerations for each method.

Table 1-7   Methods and Requirements

Method and Requirements	From CD-ROM	Unattended Setup	SysPrep	Remote Operating System Installation	SMS
Upgrade or clean install	Upgrade or clean install	Upgrade or clean install	Clean install only	Clean install only	Upgrade only
Required hardware	CD-ROM drive on each computer	A network boot disk if using a remote distribution share, or a CD-ROM drive and a floppy disk drive	All desktop computers need similar hardware configurations	Preboot Execution Environment (PXE)–enabled desktop computers	A fast connection to the SMS site
Server requirements	Does not require a server	Does not require a server	Does not require a server	Requires Windows 2000 Server with Active Directory	Requires a Windows server with SMS running an SMS site
Considerations for modifying project	No changes can be made	Requires updating Unattend.txt	Requires updating and reimaging the master installation	Requires modifying the answer file	

On the Resource Kit CD   This book's companion CD contains a tool to help you choose the best distribution method for your environment. Open the file plan01.xls in any recent version of Microsoft Excel. Answer the questions in the Questions worksheet and then view the recommendations on the Results worksheet.

Unattended Installation

Unattended installations use unattended-setup answer files to answer installation questions and to automate the installation process, which simplifies the installation of the operating system. Chapter 6 describes how to create answer files, and Chapter 13 describes how to use them to install Windows XP Professional. You use different versions of Windows XP Setup depending on the operating system in which you run it:

Use unattended installations to upgrade a large number of client computers that have different hardware and software configurations. The following list describes the advantages and disadvantages of using unattended installations:

- **Advantages of unattended installation.** Unattended installations save time and money because users do not have to attend to each computer and answer questions during installation. Unattended installations can also be configured to enable users to provide input during the installation process. You can perform unattended installations to upgrade many computers at once or to automate clean installations of the operating system.

- **Disadvantages of unattended installation.** You cannot use unattended installations to create reference configurations that include applications and that replicate the configurations across your client computers. Usually, unattended installation must be initiated by someone who has direct access to each client computer. Most significantly, unattended installations are slower and use more network bandwidth than most other distribution methods.

Disk Imaging with Sysprep

Disk imaging with third-party tools and Sysprep is a timesaving way to deploy Windows XP Professional. To clone a configuration, configure a sample computer with the operating system, standard desktop settings, and applications that users need; then make an image of the sample computer's hard disk. Last, transfer the image to other computers, installing the operating system, settings, and applications quickly and without the need to configure each computer.

The System Preparation tool (Sysprep.exe) prepares the reference computer for cloning. Sysprep creates a unique SID for each cloned client computer, which makes this process secure. Sysprep also detects Plug and Play devices and adjusts for systems with different devices. You can run Windows Setup Manager to select the screens you want displayed. These screens can be used to solicit user-specific information, such as user name or time zone selection. You can also provide these answers by using an answer file to deploy fully automated installations. For more information about disk imaging with Sysprep, see Chapter 15, "Disk Imaging with Sysprep."

> **Note** Sysprep performs the preparation of the system image; however, a cloning utility from a third party is required to create the image. Chapter 15 describes the tools I use most frequently and provides a list of alternatives.

Use Sysprep to deploy clean installations in large organizations where hundreds of computers need the same applications and desktop configurations. Use Sysprep if the computers in your organization have only a few standard hardware configurations, rather than many custom configurations. The following list describes the advantages and disadvantages of using disk imaging with Sysprep:

- **Advantages of disk imaging with Sysprep.** Sysprep reduces deployment time because nearly every component—including the operating system, applications, and desktop settings—can be configured without user interaction. The disk image can be copied to a CD and physically distributed to client computers, saving the time and network capacity required to load files across a network. Using Sysprep to deploy Windows XP Professional on numerous desktops in a large organization enables you to implement standardized desktops, administrative policies, and restrictions. Additionally, by default, Sysprep does not perform full hardware Plug and Play redetection, reducing this part of the installation process to just a few minutes (instead of 20 to 30 minutes for each computer). Sysprep detects any new Plug and Play hardware during the MiniSetup Wizard; however, Sysprep does not detect hardware that is not Plug and Play.

- **Disadvantages of disk imaging with Sysprep.** If you use a third-party disk-imaging utility with Sysprep to copy a reference image onto physical media, you must be able to distribute the physical media to remote client computers. The size of the reference image is limited by the capacity of the CD (approximately 650 MB). Sysprep cannot be used to upgrade earlier versions of the operating system. To preserve existing content, you must arrange to back up data and user settings prior to the installation, and then restore the data and user settings after the installation. Chapter 18, "User State Migration," describes how to do this.

Remote Installation Service

RIS enables you to perform a clean installation of Windows XP Professional on supported computers throughout your organization. You can simultaneously deploy the operating system on multiple clients from one or more remote locations. You can use RIS to create and store one or more images of a supported operating system on a RIS Server. A RIS image can then be downloaded over a network connection by a client computer that supports the PXE. You can completely automate the installation of the downloaded RIS image or you can require users to provide input by typing a computer name or an administrator password, for example.

> **Note**   To deploy Windows XP images from Windows 2000 Server–based RIS Servers, you must install the Windows 2000 Remote Installation Services update. For more information, see Chapter 16.

To use RIS, Windows 2000 Server or Windows Server 2003 must be deployed with Active Directory configured. Then, you can deploy Windows XP Professional by using PXE technology, which enables computers to boot from their network adapters. When working with a RIS server, you can make a preconfigured image of Windows XP Professional available for installation on a client computer. For computers that do not support PXE technology, RIS includes a tool called the Remote Boot Floppy Generator (Rbfg.exe) that you can use to create a remote boot disk to use with RIS. You can use the RIS remote boot disk with supported network adapters that comply with the Peripheral Component Interconnect (PCI) specification.

Use RIS on desktop computers that are newly added to a network or on which you want to perform a clean installation of the operating system. Use RIS when you want to standardize a Windows XP Professional configuration on new desktop computers or on computers with an existing operating system that you want to replace with Windows XP Professional. The following list describes advantages and disadvantages of using RIS to deploy Windows XP Professional:

- **Advantages of RIS.**   RIS offers a simple way to replace the operating system on a computer. RIS uses the Single Instance Store (SIS) method to eliminate duplicate files and to reduce the overall storage that is required on the server for system files. You can also use Riprep to install and configure a client computer to comply with specific corporate desktop standards. The following list describes some of the important advantages of using RIS:

    - You can standardize your Windows XP Professional installation.

    - You can customize and control the end-user installation. You can configure the end-user Setup Wizard with specific choices that can be controlled by using Group Policy.

    - You do not need to distribute physical media, and image size is not constrained by the capacity of distributed physical media.

■ **Disadvantages of RIS.** You can use RIS only on client computers that are connected to a network that is running Windows 2000 Server or Windows Server 2003 with Active Directory. RIS is restricted to working on computers that are equipped with PCI-compliant network adapters that are enabled for PXE technology or with the Remote Boot Floppy Generator (Rbfg.exe) that is used to create a remote boot disk that can be used with supported PCI-compliant network adapters. RIS works only with images that have been created from drive C; RIS cannot use images of other partitions on a hard disk. You cannot use RIS to upgrade an operating system; you can use RIS only for clean installations.

Systems Management Server

Microsoft SMS includes an integrated set of tools for managing Windows-based networks consisting of thousands of computers. SMS includes desktop management and software distribution tools to automate operating system upgrades. In organizations that already use SMS to manage computers from a central location, SMS provides a convenient means for administrators to upgrade computers to Windows XP Professional.

You can use SMS only for upgrades of Windows-based client computers; you cannot use SMS for clean installations. For information about how you can implement a Windows XP Professional deployment by using SMS, see Chapter 17, "Systems Management Server." The following list describes the advantages and disadvantages of using SMS to deploy Windows XP Professional:

■ **Advantages of SMS.** You can upgrade computers in a locked-down or low-rights environment. You can even upgrade computers after hours, without users being logged on. SMS enables you to set deployment policies for specific client computers. Automatic load balancing between distribution points accommodates many concurrent upgrades. As a primary advantage, SMS offers centralized control of the upgrade. For example, you can control when upgrades take place, which computers to upgrade, and how to apply network constraints.

■ **Disadvantage of SMS.** SMS is an efficient deployment tool for Windows XP Professional only if SMS is already being used within your network.

BDD Solution Accelerator

The Microsoft Solution Accelerator for Business Desktop Deployment (BDD) provides guidance and tools to help you quickly deploy Windows XP Professional and Office 2003 Editions, as well as other business applications to computers across an organization. It includes 11 technical guides that'll assist you in planning and executing a rapid deployment. They cover deployment architecture, application and infrastructure compatibility issues, security and operations, user state migration, Office 2003 Editions, disk imaging, and all phases of your deployment process.

The full BDD solution accelerator includes a variety of sample documents and templates to help you start, manage, and transition your desktop deployment project to a production environment. These documents range from project scoping and planning documents to detailed test plans and other specific project management tools. The full BDD solution accelerator also includes a comprehensive suite of scripts and configuration files to help enable you to quickly configure imaging and deployment servers to roll out your new desktop environment.

You can download the BDD solution accelerator from Microsoft's Web site at *http://www.microsoft.com/downloads*.

Best Practices

The following are best practices for planning a Windows XP Professional deployment:

- **Develop a project requirements document.** This document states the goals and objectives for a project and any constraints that may affect the project, such as budget or resource limitations. The document serves as an informal contract.

- **Document risks and assumptions.** This document should identify project risks and provide a contingency plan for mitigating serious problems.

- **Understand components of a project plan.** To manage the project efficiently and well, the project manager should understand the following six components of the project:

  - Milestones. Clearly identifiable points in the project that represent the completion of particular sets of tasks.

  - Deliverables. Clearly defined results, products, or services produced during the project or at its conclusion.

- Tasks. Particular units of work that make up the larger activities of a project.

- Durations. Estimated units of time assigned for completion of project tasks.

- Resources. The people, equipment, and material used to complete tasks in a project.

- Task Dependencies. The relationship between tasks, in which one task's beginning or end depends on the start or finish of another task.

- **Develop a project plan.**   For the project plan, the delivery date and the key infrastructure milestones must be finalized. It is important at this stage to make sure that all parties have signed off on the project requirements document and are committed to the timeline under consideration. To estimate the project duration, the project manager must research previous project plans, seek time estimates for specific tasks from experienced people, and consider how identified risks may impact the schedule.

- **Identify and resolve project issues.**   Project managers must have a clear process in place for resolving or escalating issues that occur during the life cycle of the project. First, each must identify a person to whom they can escalate unresolved issues. In the escalation process, parties must define the issue, determine the impact if an issue remains unresolved by a specific date, provide recommendations or options for resolving the issue, and communicate the information, with a required response date, to the party responsible for acting on the recommendations.

- **Identify and resolve project scope changes.**   Often, someone requests additional services or deliverables after a project is underway. It is important to maintain all change requests in a change log and to follow a documented process for managing such requests.

- **Report status.**   All concerned parties must be informed of the project status on a regular basis. When delivering a report, the project manager must state progress against the original plan, thoroughly describe project problems (once only), publicize successes, and warn of any problem areas that require decisions.

- **Complete client acceptance and handoff.**   A successful project is a project that the client accepts. Use a delivery acceptance checklist for client sign-off. The project manager owns the project delivery process.

Chapter 2

Application Compatibility

Application compatibility is often a deployment-blocking issue. It's also the issue that most deployment projects focus on the least—until things begin to fall apart. By focusing on application compatibility early, you can better ensure a successful deployment project. This chapter describes the Microsoft tools that are available for testing compatibility and distributing fixes for the problems you find.

Checklist

- Do you have standardized configurations in your environment? See Chapter 1, "Deployment Plan," for more information about the importance of standardizing your desktop configurations.

- Do you have an inventory of the applications used in your environment? If not, see the section "Compatibility Inventory," later in this chapter.

- Do you have a test lab that mimic's typical configurations in which you can test applications? If not, see the section "Building the Test Lab," later in this chapter.

- Have you contacted each application's vendor for an updated version? If not, see each application vendor's Web site for more information about upgrading the application.

Understanding Compatibility

Application compatibility is often a deployment-blocking issue. Since the arrival of Microsoft Windows as a ubiquitous application platform, independent software vendors (ISVs) and internal developers have created thousands of applications for it. Many are mission-critical applications; some of which aren't compatible with the latest version of Windows. Types of applications that might not be compatible include the following:

- Line-of-business applications such as enterprise resource-planning suites.
- Core applications that are part of standard desktop configurations.
- Administrative tools, such as antivirus, compression, and remote-control applications.
- Custom tools, such as logon scripts.

Applications designed for earlier versions of Windows have been carried forward for a number of reasons. Maybe the application is a necessary tool that is used daily to accomplish some otherwise tedious task. Maybe users have learned the application and are reticent to move to another similar application. Maybe the application has no replacement, either because the original creator is no longer in business or has left the company. All these issues make application compatibility a critical issue that you must consider when deploying a new operating system such as Microsoft Windows XP Professional. In this chapter, I'll discuss the many issues that affect application compatibility, how to discover the applications on which your users depend, and what you can do to assure that the mission-critical applications work with Windows XP Professional from the get-go.

An application is compatible with Windows XP Professional if it runs *as designed* in Windows XP Professional—that is, the application should install and remove correctly. Users should be able to create, delete, open, and save any data files that are native to the application. Common operations such as printing should work as expected. A compatible application runs on Windows XP Professional *out of the box* without any special assistance. If an application is not compatible, you might find that a newer, compatible version of the application is available or that using one of the tools that Microsoft provides to remediate the compatibility problem is all you need. You might also find that an application will require a combination of fixes to run properly. This chapter discusses all of these scenarios.

More Info   See "Windows Application Compatibility" at *www.microsoft.com /windows/appcompatibility/default.mspx* for more information about application compatibility with Windows XP Professional.

Why Applications Fail

There are a number of issues that can make applications incompatible with Windows XP Professional. Some of the more common issues are the following:

- **Applications might expect a specific operating system version.**   When an application is first developed, the developers often intend for users to run the application-specific version of Windows or a limited number of the current versions of Windows currently shipping. If a new version of Windows is released, the application might no longer run simply because the application checks for a version number that is now newer than it was designed to support. This problem is easily fixed simply by *deceiving* the application about the operating system's version.

- **Applications might use hard-coded paths for folders.**   Another common problem that Microsoft has seen is when an application uses hard-coded paths for special folders. The paths might be correct for earlier versions of Windows but no longer valid for Windows XP Professional or Microsoft Windows Server 2003. A good example is the My Documents folder. In previous versions of Windows, the default location of this folder was %SYSTEMDRIVE%. This folder is now in the user profile folder %SYSTEMDRIVE%\Documents and Settings\%USERNAME%. A program writing data into the C:\My Documents folder fails simply because Windows XP Professional creates the My Documents folder in a different location. This is easily fixed by tricking applications to use the new location via a run-time redirect function.

- **Applications might require administrator privileges in order to run.** Microsoft Windows 95, Microsoft Windows 98, and Microsoft Windows Me were all designed primarily for the home user; therefore, there was no security model in place that provided for differences in user rights or permissions. In effect, all users were administrators. In Microsoft Windows NT, Microsoft Windows 2000, Windows XP Professional, or Windows Server 2003, the security model assigns roles to certain users, allowing more rights and permissions to administrators than to a restricted user. This security model can cause compatibility issues for older applications that expect full access to the file system. It can also affect access to the registry, in which applications store their settings. Older versions of Windows allowed unlimited access to registry settings by any user, whereas Windows XP Professional does not.

- **Applications might fail to install correctly.** Installation problems can be a combination of some of the already mentioned failures. Windows version issues during installs or an inability to write data to a specific file location might be problems. Older installations may expect to be able to overwrite system files that are now protected by Windows File Protection (WFP). Or installers might be unable to correctly write to the registry as they could in the past. Even if the application does install correctly, the application doesn't remove itself cleanly but leaves traces of itself in the registry or file system when removed. Some applications might be unable to deal with newer classes of hardware, such as large hard drives. A symptom of this problem is when an application is trying to determine available disk space and fails to do so simply because it cannot deal with hard drives larger that 2GB. These issues all affect compatibility.

- **Applications might look for registry values in old locations.** Windows XP Professional stores some registry settings in different locations than earlier versions of Windows. Applications that look for those settings in old locations aren't compatible with Windows XP Professional. Many applications will choose the correct locations if you install them in Windows XP Professional directly, but they fail to adjust properly when you install them in earlier versions of Windows and then upgrade to Windows XP Professional.

- **Applications might use platform-specific drivers, such as antivirus, backup, partitioning software, low-level drivers, file-system drivers, and so on.** Applications that access hardware directly, such as antivirus software, backup software, or partitioning software, might be unable to run at all. Some of them use device drivers that are written for Windows 98 and are thus unable to run at all. Software meant to access the file system directly may not be aware of the NTFS (NT file system), file encryption, or the new dynamic disk format introduced in Windows 2000.

Windows XP Professional replaces all previous versions of Windows. Whether users are running Windows 98, Windows NT, or Windows 2000, Windows XP Professional is a valid upgrade. And although Microsoft designed Windows XP Professional to replace these legacy versions of Windows, it was also designed to *favor stability over compatibility*. Windows 2000 and Windows XP Professional both introduce changes that could impact overall application compatibility. Some of these changes include the following:

- **Windows File Protection.** Critical system files are protected from being changed or overwritten. In Windows XP Professional, Windows File Protection prevents applications from overwriting system components such as *.dll*, *.exe*, and *.ocx* files. An application written to an earlier version of Windows may attempt to overwrite one of these system files with an older version. WFP will allow the operation to appear to succeed. The problem may come later when the application attempts to run and expects a certain version of the file to be present. This may cause application problems because the application may be depending on an obsolete function in the older file.

■ **Windows XP Professional Shared Environment.**   In workgroup networks, multiple users may be logged on simultaneously. Windows XP Professional presents particular problems for applications that are unaware of the shared environment presented by Fast User Switching.

■ **Remote Desktop And Remote Assistance.**   Based on Terminal Services technology, applications need to run without problems in a remote fashion. The remote access technologies such as Remote Desktop and Remote Assistance. All these features are provided by the underlying technology of Terminal Services. Applications must be able to run remotely as well as resume normal operations when a user switches to a currently running session.

■ **Advanced Configuration Power Interface (ACPI) Support.**   Applications need to be able to handle standby and hibernate modes correctly. ACPI support on Windows XP Professional allows users to enter standby or hibernate modes. Upon powerup, the system resumes where it left off. Applications should deal gracefully with these states as well so that the user can continue without application interruption.

Windows Logo Requirements

Applications receive the *Designed for Microsoft Windows XP* logo after they have passed stringent compliance testing and completed a license agreement with Microsoft. The baseline requirements for receiving the logo stress stability and reliability, and can be summarized under three key areas:

■ **Windows Fundamentals.**   The application will run on Windows XP Professional and perform its primary functionality while maintaining stability. If an application installs kernel mode drivers, the drivers must pass independent driver verification. Applications must support Fast User Switching and Remote Desktop as well as supporting the visual styles of Windows XP Professional.

■ **Install And Remove.**   An application will install without degrading the system or other applications. Applications will not attempt to replace files protected by Windows File Protection. Applications will correctly support Add/Remove programs. Also, an application that receives the logo will support migration from an earlier version of Windows.

■ **Data And Settings Management.**   An application designed for Windows XP Professional will support multiple users as well as running under limited user permissions. Applications that produce data will store both user data and application settings data in the appropriate locations in the file system and the registry.

Adherence to these standards ensures that the system will remain stable through the life of the system. Because primary goals for Windows XP Professional were reliability and stability, an application shouldn't compromise these features. The Designed for Microsoft Windows XP logo assures that the end user can get the most out of the Windows experience, whether using built-in features or applications provided by a third-party vendor. Making the Designed for Microsoft Windows XP logo a requirement for all new applications that are purchased for the system should be a key requirement of any deployment plan.

More Info   See "Designed for Windows Logo Program" at *www.microsoft.com /winlogo/default.mspx* for information about the Windows logo program.

Compatibility Technologies

This section describes the compatibility technologies that are available for planning and mitigating application compatibility.

Migration Technologies

One of the key areas in which compatibility comes in to play is in an upgrade scenario. Users are running some version of Windows 98, Windows NT, or Windows 2000; and have multiple applications installed. In an upgrade, if Windows XP–Setup knows about the installed application and what needs to be done to allow the application to continue to run after the upgrade, Windows XP Setup can correctly handle the upgrade. The end result is an application that continues to run correctly after the upgrade.

During the development of Windows 2000, Microsoft developed the concept of a *migration dynamic-link library (DLL)*: a shared library that Windows XP Setup could use to correct anything that needed changing in an upgrade scenario. The ISV was responsible for creating migration DLLs for their applications and providing them to the end user either as part of the Windows 2000 CD media or via standard support channels from the vendor's Web site. When provided online or via CD, these were known as *upgrade packs*—whose purpose was to allow the user to continue to run their application after the upgrade. The main problem with migration DLLs was that not many application vendors wanted to dedicate the developer resources to create them when it might be better to concentrate on a new version of the product (maybe even one that would require an upgrade to support the new operating system). Some vendors felt that Windows XP Professional was such a significant upgrade that they concentrated their efforts on an entirely new version of the product.

In either case, Windows XP Professional ships with a large amount of information about installed applications and how to make those applications run during an upgrade scenario. Whether via migration information or the software compatibility database, more applications written for previous versions of Windows will continue to run after an upgrade than ever before possible in a similar scenario.

Some applications will still require new versions that are specifically designed for Windows XP Professional, however, simply because of the type of application that they are. For example, antivirus applications require low-level access to the file system to be able to adequately protect data from viruses. Because the NTFS file system changed on Windows XP Professional, a new version that understands the changes must be purchased.

Other categories of application that require new versions are partitioning software, backup software, or third-party quota management tools. All these applications usually require administrative permission to install because they install kernel mode components. Applications that interact with devices—such as Web cams, wireless network adapters, or digitizer tablets—may require Windows XP-specific software.

Compatibility Modes

The compatibility modes that Microsoft built into Windows 2000 were expanded significantly in Windows XP Professional. Primarily because Windows XP Professional was designed to finally replace Windows 98, as well as NT and Windows 2000, Windows XP Professional supports literally hundreds of applications out of the box. The compatibility database that is periodically updated covers hundreds of business and home use applications, provides a stable working environment for those applications, and ensures compatibility from day one. In the chance that an application doesn't run when you first attempt to use it on Windows XP Professional, there are several things that you can attempt. Two tools that come to mind are part of the built-in compatibility mode features of Windows XP Professional. The two tools this chapter describes are:

- Program Compatibility Wizard
- Compatibility Shell Extensions

The Program Compatibility Wizard is a simple wizard used when you have a single application that will not run on Windows XP Professional. It may be an application that a small portion of your users need or even an application that a single person has come to depend on. In either case, using the Program Compatibility Wizard is simple and to the point. The wizard is accessed from Windows XP Professional's Help subsystem and can be accessed from either Help or the Start menu: Click Start, All Programs, Accessories, Program Compatibility Wizard. Using the wizard is very straightforward:

1. Open the wizard using either Help or the Start menu as described previously.

2. Click Next to advance to the first options page, which asks about the location of the program you want to run with compatibility settings. The options on this page are as follows:

    ■ I Want To Choose From A List Of Programs
    This option allows you to choose a program that is listed in Add/Remove Programs or located in the Program Files folder.

    ■ I Want To Use The Program In The CD-ROM Drive
    This option is usually used when attempting to install a new program and the install fails for some reason. Sometimes, simply getting the application to install is the only hurdle to compatibility.

    ■ I Want To Locate The Program Manually
    This allows you to browse to the application in question if you know the location and select compatibility options from the resulting dialog box.

3. If you choose to locate the program manually, you are presented with a page that enables you to browse to the application to select it.

4. After you choose the way in which you want to locate the application, click Next to advance to the next page.

5. The compatibility mode page shown in Figure 2-1 allows you to choose one of the standard sets of compatibility modes for the application to run under.

    ■ The choices include Windows 95, Windows 98/Windows Me, Windows NT 4.0, and Windows 2000. You are also allowed to choose Do Not Apply A Compatibility Mode. Based on your choices from this page, a set of compatibility fixes will be applied to the application so it runs as if it is running under that older operating system instead of Windows XP Professional.

Figure 2-1 Use the compatibility mode page to choose present compatibility modes.

6. The next page provides a few simple choices that often cause older applications to fail under Windows XP Professional:

- 256 Colors
  Forces the application to use only 256-color depth.

- 640 x 480 Screen Resolution.
  Forces the application to use a 640 X 480 screen resolution.

- Disable Visual Themes
  Forces the application to use Windows classic look and feel.

After making your choices to allow the application to run correctly, you select Next to advance to the test page that enables you to run the application using the compatibility fixes that you have chosen.

If the application runs without failures, you are asked whether the application ran correctly and gives you options to set the program to always use these settings, try other settings, or simply abandon any other attempts at compatibility mode correction of the application. If you choose to save the settings, the application will always run using those settings.

Similar to the Program Compatibility Wizard are the shell extensions that provide a Compatibility tab in an application's Properties dialog box, shown in Figure 2-2. The options that are available are the same as those offered by the Program Compatibility Wizard, and are all conveniently arranged in one dialog box. Simply make your choices and click OK; the next time the application is run, it will run with those compatibility fixes in place.

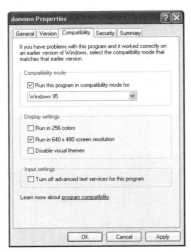

Figure 2-2   The Compatibility Mode tab is similar to the Program Compatibility Wizard.

Though both of these features are built in to the operating system and available to any user, they are not the primary tools that are typically used in an enterprise deployment. Any compatibility settings made through either of these two tools will be stored on a per-user basis and thus will affect only the user who made the settings.

Application Help

A key piece of the overall approach to application compatibility in Windows XP Professional is what to do when an application is shown to simply not work at all. An application may have been determined to not work at all under Windows XP Professional, and rather than attempting remediation of the application, a help message may be displayed, stating that the application is not designed to run under Windows XP Professional. This is a message that is displayed when a user installs or runs an incompatible application and an application compatibility fix or mode is not available or viable. An Application Help message can warn a user about an incompatibility, but still let the user install or run the incompatible application, or it can block the user from installing or running the application. This Help dialog box may have been provided to Microsoft from the application vendor, but it can also be created using one of the tools in the Application Compatibility Toolkit that I'll discuss later in this chapter.

Compatibility Fixes

The real key to legacy applications running under Windows XP Professional are the many compatibility fixes that Microsoft's Application Experience team have developed. These fixes—which range from simple version lies to fixes that redirect older application programming interfaces (APIs) to the newer equivalent API—provide the real core to making older applications behave properly under Windows XP Professional.

> **More Info** The full list of compatibility fixes is documented in the SYMPTOMS.XLS spreadsheet and the "Common Application Compatibility Issues" white paper that are installed with the Application Compatibility Toolkit. Some of the fixes are applied when you select one of the compatibility modes such as the Windows 95 mode. When this mode is selected, approximately 50 common fixes are applied to allow the application to run on Windows XP Professional or Windows Server 2003.

Compatibility Databases

Windows XP Professional and Windows Server 2003 solve application compatibility issues by dynamically matching problems with known solutions. The matching mechanism runs each time an application is installed or during run time. The solutions are packaged in a set of compatibility databases that ship with the product or are periodically updated. These databases contain a list of known applications and a set of fixes that are known to remediate the application. In addition, a mechanism exists to allow you to create custom databases for specific applications. The database files are located in the %SYSTEMROOT%\AppPatch folder on Windows XP Professional and Windows Server 2003. The Application Compatibility Databases that ship with Windows XP Professional and Windows Server 2003 are listed in Table 2-1.

Table 2-1   Application Compatibility Databases

File	Description
MigDB.inf	Migration database that contains a list of Windows 95, Windows 98, and Windows Me Edition applications that are incompatible with Windows XP Professional.
NTCompat.inf	Migration database that contains a list of Windows NT Server 4.0 and Windows 2000 applications that are incompatible with Windows XP Professional.
Apphelp.sdb	Prepackaged database that contains a list of third-party applications and associated Application Help messages. You can add third-party applications and custom Application Help messages to this database, but you cannot change or delete the existing list of names and Application Help messages.
Sysmain.sdb	Prepackaged database that contains a list of third-party applications and their associated application compatibility fixes and modes. You cannot change or delete the information in this database, but you can use the application compatibility fixes and modes that it contains to create custom databases.

Table 2-1   Application Compatibility Databases

File	Description
Drvmain.sdb	Prepackaged database that contains a list of device drivers and their associated Application Help messages.
Msimain.sdb	Prepackaged database that contains a list of *.msi* files and their associated Application Help messages.

There are three types of databases: migration databases, prepackaged databases, and custom databases. Table 2-1 lists the migration databases and prepackaged databases that ship with the product. Custom databases are created with the Compatibility Administrator tool that I'll detail later.

Application Compatibility Toolkit

The principal set of tools available to deal with application compatibility issues is the Application Compatibility Toolkit. This toolkit (currently at version 3.0) contains documentation, usage guides, and several tools that support the deployment of third-party applications in Windows XP Professional and Windows Server 2003. An earlier version of the Application Compatibility Toolkit shipped on the Windows XP Professional product CD, but the latest version has greatly improved tools as well as new functionality, so you should use this newer version. The URL is *http://www.microsoft.com/windows/appcompatibility/toolkit.mspx*. You can also order a CD that contains the latest version.

The Application Compatibility Toolkit contains the tools and documentation needed to design, deploy, and support applications on these platforms: Windows 2000 SP3, Windows XP Professional, and Windows Server 2003. Included in the toolkit are the following:

- Latest versions of the Microsoft Windows Application Compatibility Analyzer, Windows Application Verifier, and Compatibility Administrator

- Training videos of each tool in action

- Documentation on deployment, certification, and application compatibility

Microsoft provides a range of tools including, but not limited to, the Application Compatibility Toolkit to assist in your application compatibility issues. These tools and features can be divided into four groups, one for each of the four major phases in the overall application compatibility testing process: planning, testing, resolving, and deploying. Figure 2-3 is an overview of the compatibility testing process. It represents each major step in the process and directs you to sections in this chapter that contain more detailed information.

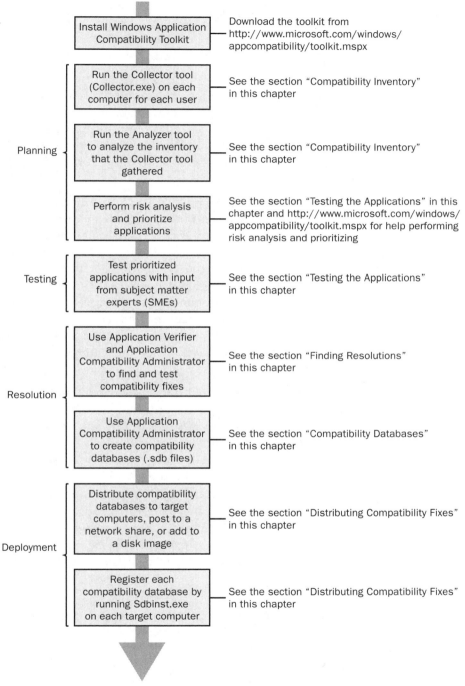

Figure 2-3   The application compatibility testing process includes planning, testing, resolution, and deployment. This diagram provides an overview of each step.

- **Planning Tools.**   These tools include the Application Compatibility Analyzer, Systems Management Server (SMS), Windows Catalog, and Windows Upgrade Advisor. Use these tools to collect information about the applications in your organization and to identify applications that are known to have compatibility problems.

- **Testing Tools.**   These tools include the Application Verifier and debugging tools. Use these tools to create a test environment for identifying hard-to-find application compatibility, stability, and security problems. Testing tools also include Windows Upgrade Advisor and the Windows Catalog, which identify applications that have already been tested and certified for Windows XP Professional and Windows Server 2003.

- **Resolution Tools.**   These tools include the Compatibility Administrator, the Program Compatibility Wizard, and the Compatibility property sheet. You use the Compatibility Administrator to apply compatibility modes to custom *.sdb* files, which you can distribute throughout your organization. You use the Program Compatibility Wizard and the Compatibility property sheet to resolve compatibility problems on a standalone computer. The Program Compatibility Wizard and the Compatibility property sheet are rarely used to address application compatibility issues in a large enterprise. Any compatibility settings made through either of these two methods will be stored on a per-user basis and thus will affect only the user who made the settings.

- **Deployment Tools.**   These tools include System Preparation Tool (Sysprep) and Remote Installation Services (RIS) for deployment and Group Policy Software Installation and logon scripts for distribution. You can use these tools to deploy applications, patches, and *.sdb* files during an operating system rollout; or to distribute applications, patches, and *.sdb* files to computers that already have an operating system installed. These tools also include the Application Compatibility Database Installer (Sdbinst.exe) and the Windows Installer program (Msiexec.exe), both of which you use in conjunction with the deployment and distribution tools to install applications, patches, and custom database (*.sdb*) files. In addition, they include the Windows Installer Software Development Kit, which you use to package applications, application updates, and *.sdb* files into Windows Installer packages (*.msi* files).

More Info   See "Windows Application Compatibility Toolkit" at *http://www.microsoft.com/windows/appcompatibility/toolkit.mspx* to download the Windows Compatibility Toolkit.

Compatibility Inventory

An important first step in a deployment process is completing an accurate inventory of exactly what applications you currently have deployed. Many organizations already feel that they have a good handle on this until they use an inventory program for the first time and discover that users have installed many more applications than expected. Especially in environments running Windows 98, users have had the ability to install just about anything they might want to install because the environment simply allows it. Using a tool such as SMS or a similar third party tool used to be the only answer other than a simple paper survey. Imagine the daunting task of inventorying each and every desktop by hand. Such an inventory is actually the way some organizations have gone about the task. A technician would be sent to each machine in turn and record manually the applications listed in Add/Remove Programs and under the Program Files folder. This method only slightly beats the best-guess approach—simply getting users to tell you what it is that they run on a day-to-day basis.

If you have an automated tool to gather inventories, by all means use that tool. SMS, for example, not only gathers software inventories, but hardware inventories as well (which are also needed if you are planning a Windows XP Professional deployment). Other third-party tools may have similar features as well. But because an accurate software inventory is a key step in planning a deployment, Microsoft included a new tool in the Application Compatibility Toolkit 3.0: the Application Compatibility Analyzer. This tool consists of two parts:

- The Collector tool that actually gathers the information.

- The Analyzer that allows you to analyze the information in a number of ways. The Analyzer also can look up compatibility information online as part of its analysis.

The Application Compatibility Analyzer is the first tool in the toolkit that this chapter describes.

Risk analysis is one of the more important aspects of application compatibility. This includes identifying the priority of applications for testing (business critical, high priority, daily use, nice-to-have, and so on), which ensures that the most important applications work properly after deployment. It's essential to use this information to plan which applications you must test. For more information about risk analysis, see the Application Compatibility Toolkit at *http://www.microsoft.com /windows/appcompatibility/toolkit.mspx.*

Taking the Inventory

To take an inventory of a machine or a whole group of machines, you simply need to run the collector.exe application on each machine. Because this executable does not need administrative permission to run, you can add a line to run the Collector to a logon script or create a dedicated script or batch file to run the tool. If multiple users use a specific computer, you may need to run the Collector several times to make sure that the information is complete. When the Collector runs, it does not display an application window; instead, an icon is seen in the status area for the duration of its operation, which usually only takes one to two minutes. The Collector supports a number of command-line switches to allow the administrator to customize the process to suit the needs of the organization. The command-line options for collector.exe are listed in Table 2-2, and the following describes the command's syntax:

```
collector.exe [/o filename][/f path] [/e department] [/n] [/d days] [/a] [/p profile]
```

Table 2-2   Collector.exe Command-Line Options

Option	Description
/cw	Causes the Collector to wait five minutes before running, reducing CPU usage during startup.
/o filename	Directs the Collector to produce output on the specified *filename*. By default, the Collector places the output file onto the user's desktop.
/f path	Provides the source *path* for the Collector to gather information from; it can be either file or directory. If file or directory is not specified, directs the Collector to gather information from all drives on the machine.
/e department	Provides *department* information for use in processing Collector logs. This data helps separate collected information into useful categories after the logs are merged later in the process.
/n	Directs the Collector not to collect information from mapped (network) drives. By default, network drives are included.
/d days	Directs the Collector to collect information only if the Collector had not run within the number of *days* specified by the parameter. If the number of days is not specified, Collector will not run if it had already been executed on the machine once.
/a	Combines collecting information from shell/installed programs with the collection from specified drives/paths.
/p profile	Directs the Collector to use a specified *profile* (initialization file) instead of the default collector.ini file.

A sample run of the Collector might be similar to the following: *server-name**sharename*\collector.exe /D 20 /O /CW *servername**logshare*\pilot. This command line would run the collector.exe application from the *servername**sharename* folder as long as it has been 20 days since the last time it was run, and the output logs will be created in the *servername**logshare*\pilot folder on the network. The resulting log data that the Collector creates is compressed and saved as a CAB file. The /CW switch causes the Collector to wait five minutes before running to reduce the CPU load at startup.

The Collector can be run to inventory applications on the following:

- Windows 95, Windows 98, Windows 98 Second Edition, Windows Me
- Windows NT 4.0
- Windows 2000 Professional
- Windows 2000 Server
- Windows XP Professional
- Windows Server 2003

Note Instead of using the command line, you can include all options in an *.ini* file called collector.ini. This file is fully documented in the help file for the Application Compatibility Analyzer.

After an inventory has been run, you use the Analyzer tool shown in Figure 2-4 to load the results and analyze. The Analyzer can be run on the following:

- Microsoft Internet Explorer 5.5 or higher
- Windows 2000 Professional
- Windows 2000 Server
- Windows XP Professional
- Windows Server 2003

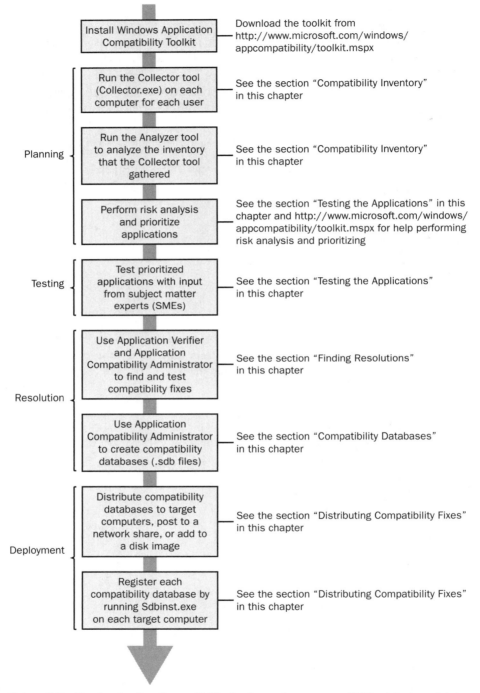

Figure 2-4 The Application Compatibility Analyzer stores compatibility data in a database.

The Analyzer stores its data in either an Access or SQL Server database. Subsequent runs of the Collector from other machines may be easily added to the database using the Analyzer console. The resulting data may be evaluated, and reports may be generated from the data. Additionally, you can download compatibility information from Microsoft to compare with the inventoried applications in your own enterprise. When you request compatibility information for an application from the application compatibility database, one of four levels of compatibility is returned:

- **Compatible.**   The application is compatible with Windows XP Professional.

- **Compatible With Issues.**   The application typically is compatible, but might have problems when run in certain contexts.

- **Incompatible.**   The application is incompatible with Windows XP Professional.

- **Unknown.**   Either the application or its compatibility with Windows XP Professional is unknown to Microsoft.

The compatibility levels returned by the application compatibility database are combined with the information in your inventory to create a local application compatibility database for your organization.

> **More Info**   See "Microsoft Application Compatibility Analyzer" at *http: //www.microsoft.com/windows/appcompatibility/analyzer.mspx* to download the Application Compatibility Analyzer.

Scripting the Inventory

The script applist.wsf is a simple tool that lists the applications installed on a computer. This script is on the book's companion CD in the Scripts folder. It's simpler than the Compatibility Analyzer because it records only the Windows Installer-based applications and legacy programs listed in the Add/Remove Programs dialog box to a log file. You can run this script for each computer, storing each computer's log file in a separate file on a network share. Although this script doesn't tell you whether a program is compatible with Windows XP Professional or not, it helps you discover which applications are installed on the network clients. Table 2-3 lists the command-line options that this script supports, and the following describes the script's syntax:

```
applist.wsf [/?] /L:logfile [/COMPUTER:computername] [/APPEND]
[/DELIMITER: character] [/USER] [/MSI[+|-]] [/LEGACY[+|-]]
```

Table 2-3   Applist.wsf Command-Line Options

Option	Description
/?	Displays a help message.
/L:logfile	Outputs the application list to the log file *logfile*. If omitted when using Cscript.exe to run the script, it outputs to StdOut.
/COMPUTER:computername	Logs the applications installed on the computer *computername*. If not specified, logs the applications installed locally.
/APPEND	Appends the application list to an existing log file.
/DELIMITER:character	Uses *character* as the log file delimiter.
/USER	If specified, logs the applications that the user has run using the Run dialog box. This list is extracted from the registry (HKCU\Software\Microsoft\Windows\CurrentVersion\Explorer\RunMRU).
/MSI[+ |-]	Skips logging Windows Installer-based programs if **/MSI-** is specified; otherwise, logs all installed Windows Installer-based programs.
/LEGACY[+ |-]	Skips logging legacy programs if **/LEGACY-** is specified; otherwise, logs all installed legacy programs.

The following command, which you can learn more about in Appendix E, "Batch Script Syntax," executes the script applist.wsf for each computer contained in the text file Computers.txt, which must exist in the current folder: `for /f %i in (Computers.txt) do applist.wsf /SERVER:%i /LOG:%i.txt`. It outputs the results to a log file *Computer*.txt, where *Computer* is the name of each computer listed in the file Computers.txt. The quickest way to build Computers.txt is to type **net view >Computers.txt** and then edit the text file to remove extra lines and the \\ characters before each name.

On the Resource Kit CD   The script applist.wsf is available on this book's companion CD in the Scripts folder.

Building the Test Lab

You probably will not be building a test lab just for application testing; instead, you will establish a lab for your overall deployment effort. Collecting and analyzing current installed software will be done as already detailed, of course, but testing of each application that will be included in your final deployed image must be done in a lab environment. A well-maintained lab environment that closely mimics your real production environment can be a real lifesaver to an operating system deployment. Remember that you should establish a lab that is physically separate from the production corporate network.

You should configure the deployment test lab with at least the following items readily available. And to the extent that it is possible, you should configure the lab to fully represent the production environment. Your deployment lab should include the necessary hardware to host the following environment:

- A Windows domain for the machines to join and to host user accounts. This could be a Windows NT 4.0, Windows 2000, or Windows 2003 domain. If a Windows NT 4.0 domain is used, the domain controllers must be running at least Service Pack 3 to allow Windows XP Professional machines to properly communicate with the domain.

- Dynamic Host Configuration Protocol (DHCP) services, for providing Transmission Control Protocol/Internet Protocol (TCP/IP) addresses to client machines.

- *Domain Name Server* (DNS) services, for providing TCP/IP host name resolution to client and server machines.

- Windows Internet Naming Service (WINS), for providing NetBIOS name resolution to client and server machines.

- A build server, at least a Windows NT 4.0 or newer Windows machine, in the domain to host the build files and images. This can be a workstation or server class machine as long as it has sufficient amount of disk space to host the data for the deployment.

- Remote Installation Services (RIS), optionally a server hosting RIS to allow for the uploading and downloading of RIS images. RIS servers require a Windows 2000 or newer domain.

- Network switches and cabling; 100 megabytes/sec (MBPS) is recommended to accommodate the potential high volumes of data.

- Client workstations. Any unique type of workstation configuration that will be found in production should be duplicated in the lab. This duplication allows for testing each separate hardware configuration.

- KVM switches. It can be helpful to have the client workstations connected to a keyboard\video\mouse switch to minimize the floor space needed to host the workstations.

- CD burner. A system should be available in the lab for creating CD-ROMs.

- Internet access. The lab (or a portion of the lab) should have access to the Internet for downloading software updates and application compatibility information.

- Original Windows XP Professional media and license keys, available on the volume license media (select CDs).

- Original Windows XP Professional Tablet Edition media (two CDs) and license keys, available on the volume license media (select CDs).

- Windows XP Service Pack 1 or Service Pack 2 media, available on the volume license media (select CDs).

- Microsoft Office 2003 Editions media and license keys, available on the volume license media (select CDs).

- Windows PreInstall Environment media, available on volume license media (select CDs).

- Business desktop deployment media.

- Any additional application media to be included in the images.

- Any hardware-specific software, such as drivers, CD-ROM burner software, and DVD viewing software.

Testing the Applications

Whether you use the Application Compatibility Analyzer tool, SMS, or a third-party tool to generate your application inventory, review the inventory to see if you can consolidate your organization's application base. Limiting the applications used in your organization to those provided by the vendors that you plan to support in the future and to the specific version numbers that you plan to support can minimize your testing effort, decrease configuration variability during deployment, and increase the likelihood of a successful deployment. Look for the following in your inventory:

- **Several versions of the same application.**   Consider updating older applications to newer versions or moving all users to a full-featured version of a particular application. For example, if some of your users use Microsoft Office XP and others use Microsoft Office 2003 Editions, you might decide to support only Office 2003 Editions in the future.

- **Redundant applications.**   If there are groups in your organization who are using different applications to accomplish the same tasks, consider moving everyone to the same application.

- **Obsolete applications.**   Review your inventory for applications that are rarely or never used in your organization, and consider retiring them.

Most medium-to-large organizations use so many applications that it is not possible to test them all thoroughly. Consequently, most organizations prioritize the applications they plan to test. After you have consolidated your application base so that only the applications you plan to support with the new operating system are listed, you can prioritize your list based on factors such as whether applications are compatible with Windows XP Professional and Windows Server 2003, how critical they are to your business operations, and the number of users who depend on them. The ultimate goal of prioritizing inventoried applications is to identify the core group of applications that must function properly before you begin to roll out the new version of the Windows operating system.

You can prioritize your testing by using several different guidelines or a combination of guidelines. Categorizing applications by whether they are compatible with Windows XP Professional is one approach as is frequency of use. Another approach is based on the somewhat subjective measurement of how critical the application is to your business needs. An application that is considered mission-critical has a high priority, whereas an application that is more of a personal preference application can be relegated to a lower priority. The documentation that ships with the Application Compatibility Toolkit has more details of how best to prioritize your application testing. Remember that one method may not be sufficient; it may take a combination of methods to best categorize your testing.

When you test your applications, you need to use Subject Matter Experts (SMEs) who are familiar with the details of the application you are testing. Use the SME to assist in generating a reasonable test scenario for the application that you want to test. Pay careful attention to common uses such as opening and saving data, printing, and other similar operations.

On the Resource Kit CD   See "Windows Fundamentals Testing Checklist" in the file plan03.doc on this book's companion CD in the Aids folder. Use this worksheet to document test results for each application that you test for Windows XP Professional compatibility.

Finding Resolutions

When your testing discovers incompatible applications, you need to find resolutions to the problems. There are two tools that are included in the Application Compatibility Toolkit that are designed to resolve these problems. One tool is for developers who have access to the source code for an application, such as an in-house line of business application or a third-party software vendor. The other tool is used to remediate applications in which you do not have access to the original source code.

Shown in Figure 2-5, Application Verifier is the tool used by developers to test an application for the most common application problems, including incorrect version checking, bad registry usage, and hard-coded file paths. This tool also can be used to assist in testing applications in preparation for the Designed for Windows Logo Program. Using the tool is very simple.

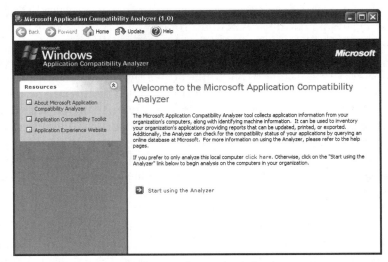

Figure 2-5   Use Application Verifier to check for the most common compatibility problems.

To use the Application Verifier tool, simply load the application that you want to test by using the Add button and browsing to the application executable. Then select any of the tests in the right pane of the Application Verifier. After you have chosen the tests that you want to run, you simply double-click the application listed in the application pane or click the Run button. As you exercise the application, the chosen test will be performed. Note that some of the tests require running under the services of a debugger; thus the design of this tool is to be run by developers. The Options dialog box also has some additional tests that can be configured, such as common folder handling and the capability of the application to handle permissions correctly. Application Verifier records its results in a log file that can be viewed after the application has been executed and tested, as shown in Figure 2-6.

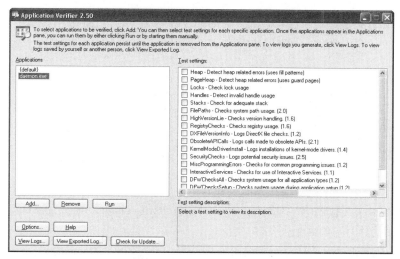

Figure 2-6   The Application Verifier log file displays problems and possible resolutions.

This log shows errors and gives possible resolutions, sometimes requiring a rewrite of the application to use a current API call instead of an obsolete call. If the application source code is no longer available, it may still be possible to remediate the application using the Application Compatibility Administrator tool, which allows you to test applications and if necessary add specific compatibility fixes to a custom database that will serve to remediate the application every time it is run. Application Compatibility Administrator (shown in Figure 2-6) ships with a small demo application that can be used to acquaint yourself with using the tool. This demoapp.exe file allows you to test for both installation and runtime issues to familiarize yourself with running the application.

To assist in understanding how best to utilize the tools and test your applications, the toolkit ships a number of documents that will be of great assistance. One of these documents, Application Compatibility Testing Checklist, is a straightforward approach to application testing that covers the basic Windows fundamentals of an application running on Windows XP Professional. Another document, Common Application Compatibility Issues, discusses the most common issues with legacy applications to assist in understanding the real issues you are likely to encounter when you test your applications.

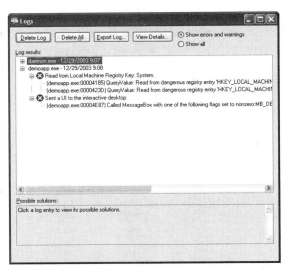

Figure 2-7   Use Application Compatibility Administrator to search for compatibility fixes already used on the system.

When you first open the Application Compatibility Administrator tool, you can use the Search menu to search for any compatibility fixes that are already in use on the system. You can also list the individual fixes by selecting the compatibility fixes node in the left pane of the tool. But for most IT professionals, the individual fixes aren't that informative. Testing still requires SMEs and application testing experts to identify and remediate the fixes. Some of the troubleshooting techniques learned by using an application over time are most useful during application testing. Also, a test matrix or plan developed with the input of SMEs will be useful for recording each individual test that is performed and whether it passed or failed. A good working knowledge of the built-in fixes that are part of the system fix database will assist in discovering what fixes may be needed for an individual application to run correctly under Windows XP Professional or Windows Server 2003.

On the Resource Kit CD   See "Compatibility Solutions Spreadsheet" in the file plan02.xls on this book's companion CD in the Aids folder. Use this worksheet as a tool to match compatibility fixes to symptoms that applications exhibit when running Windows XP Professional.

Compatibility Databases

When you discover that one or more of your applications will not run correctly under Windows XP Professional, the easiest way to remediate the application is to create a custom compatibility database. In Compatibility Administrator, the steps to create a fix for an application are as follows:

1. Under Custom Databases, select New Database, right-click to select New, and then select whether you are creating an Application Fix, AppHelp message, or Compatibility Mode.

2. To create an Application Fix, select that option and browse to locate the application that you want to fix.

3. If the application was originally designed to run under a previous version of Windows, you can choose to simply select that version using one of the listed compatibility modes, as shown in Figure 2-8.

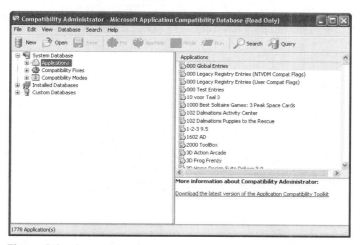

Figure 2-8   Choose one of the compatibility modes if the application was designed to run in an earlier version of Windows.

4. If you have determined by your research that only one or a couple of fixes are needed, you can individually select them from the list of available fixes on the next page, as shown in Figure 2-9.

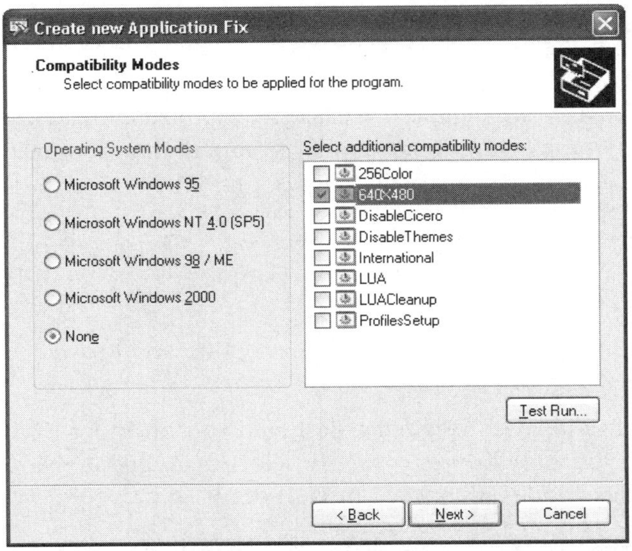

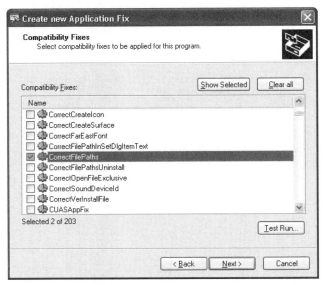

Figure 2-9   Use compatibility fixes to fix specific individual problems.

5. After you have selected the fixes that you need, you can run the application and exercise it through your test matrix to see whether the fix was sufficient to allow it to run.

6. When you are sure that the fixes you chose have taken care of the problem that you were seeing during testing, you can advance to the final page that selects the matching methods that will be used to tie the fixes that you have created to the application, as shown in Figure 2-10.

Figure 2-10   You can match fixes to applications with a variety of criteria.

7. The final step in creating a custom database is saving the database so that you can include it in your deployed image.

   ■ Click File, Save As to save the currently selected database under any file-name you choose. It is a good practice to simply name the file the same name as the application you are fixing, unless you have created fixes for multiple applications in one database.

8. After you have created one or more custom database files, you need to install them on your master system so that the fixes will be available when the application is installed and run on your business desktops.

Distributing Compatibility Fixes

Distribution of the custom databases can be facilitated using a variety of methods such as logon scripts, Group Policy, or simple file copy operations. After the file is on the target system, the actual installation of the custom databases is done using a tool that ships with the operating system, called SDBINST.EXE. After the file exists on the target computer, the custom database file must be installed (registered) before the operating system will identify the fixes present when launching the affected applications. (An example command line could be like `sdbinst c:\Windows \AppPatch\myapp.sdb`.) After the database file is registered on a computer, the compatibility information will be used any time the application is launched. Table 2-4 describes the command-line options for sdbinst.exe, and the following shows the command's syntax:

sdbinst [-?] [-q] filename.sdb [-u] [-g {guid}] [-n name]

Table 2-4 Sdbinst.exe Command-Line Options

Option	Description
-?	Displays help text.
-q	Runs quietly with no message boxes.
filename.sdb	Specifies the file name of the database to install.
-u	Uninstalls the database.
-g {guid}	Specifies the GUID of the database to uninstall.
-n name	Specifies the name of the database to uninstall

The SDBINST.EXE command can be written into a logon script to automatically install the custom database from a shared network location when the users log on to their computers. This process could even be accomplished as part of a custom job to be pushed out to the desktops via SMS or another third-party management application. One of the best methods of distribution of these custom databases is to include them in your master Windows XP Professional image. Installing them as part of the original image before adding the application that needs the fixes assures that the application will run from the first time the user needs it. You can deliver the fixes as part of the master image, but still use Group Policy application installation to deploy the application.

Maintaining Compatibility

Periodically, new information becomes available from Microsoft regarding application compatibility. Microsoft then gathers the resulting information into new compatibility updates, which become available on the Windows Update servers for download. There are three methods of keeping your compatibility information current.

The first method is manually going to Windows Update to see if new updates are available. This process, of course, is fine for a standalone machine, but it isn't useful for an enterprise. The other two methods involve automating the collection of the new updates when they become available. One method, which occurs only when Windows XP Professional is installed, is known as Dynamic Update; the other method is Windows Update with the addition of Software Update Services. First let's look at Dynamic Update.

Dynamic Update

Dynamic Update is a feature of Windows XP Setup that allows it to contact the Windows Update servers during the installation of Windows XP Professional to download newly released information pertinent for installation. The information that can be downloaded includes enhancements and fixes to the actual installation engine, new application compatibility information, and new driver files. Because this is an automated process that occurs when Windows XP Professional is being installed, there is nothing that needs to be done to ensure that the latest files are made available during installation. The only problem is that Dynamic Update runs only during an interactive or unattended installation of Windows XP Professional. Imaged installations or RIS installations cannot directly benefit from the automated retrieval of the files needed for Dynamic Update. If there is no current connection to the Internet during installation, or if you are using one of the other mentioned methods of deployment, you can download the files that contain the update ahead of time from the Windows Update site. The download packages contain some or all of the following files:

- Updates.cab: replacement files
- Upginfs.cab: updated INF files for upgrades from Microsoft Windows 98 or Microsoft Windows 95
- Winnt32.cab: fixes to the Winnt32.exe file
- Duasms.cab: assembly fixes

■ Drvx.cab: updated drivers

Several knowledge base articles address Dynamic Update and how to prepare to download and use the updates as part of your deployment. These articles will be your best source of information on the current status of Dynamic Update availability as well as the best methods of deployment. Please see the following articles for more information on Dynamic Update:

■ "Description of the Dynamic Update Feature in Windows XP Setup" at
   http://support.microsoft.com/default.aspx?scid=kb;EN-US;311220

■ "How to Deploy the Windows XP Dynamic Update Package" at
   http://support.microsoft.com/default.aspx?scid=kb;EN-US;312110

Windows Update

Most users of Windows, whatever the version, have become familiar with Windows Update. From its original inception with Windows 95 some eight years ago, Windows Update has been the principal method to keep Windows systems up to date. From driver fixes to security fixes to replacement applications such as the Windows Media Player, Windows Update is the primary vehicle to be used to keep Windows XP Professional up to date. But, one drawback that has hampered enterprise deployments of Windows is that there used to be no automated method or corporate method of downloading just the fixes that were known to work within an in enterprise under the control of a system administrator.

Approximately two years ago (at the time of this writing in 2003), Microsoft released the Corporate Windows Update site, which allowed an administrator to independently select the Windows platforms that were in place in their own organization and download all the available fixes for that platform. After the files were downloaded, they could be individually tested for compatibility on sample systems before being distributed to the individual workstations. The Corporate Windows Update site has since been replaced with the Software Update Services (SUS), a new feature of Windows 2000 and Windows Server 2003 systems that enables an enterprise to download fixes as they become available on a regularly scheduled basis, approve the fixes that are needed, and then automatically propagate them out to desktops. Windows XP SP1 includes an updated update mechanism, so it can be configured to automatically take these fixes as they become available from the SUS server.

More Info   For detailed information on setting up Software Update Services in your enterprise, see the information online at *http://www.microsoft.com /windows2000/windowsupdate/sus/default.asp*

Another method of deploying fixes to your desktop is used when you create master images for deployment. It is actually an extension of Windows Update and simply involves downloading the most recent fixes at the time of creation of the master image. Going to Windows Update from one of the Windows XP Professional machines in your build lab and choosing Windows Catalog allows you to download all the fixes that are available for the system. After you have downloaded all these fixes, you can then deploy them as part of your base image to have a fully patched Windows XP Professional master image for duplication.

Virtual PC as Safety Net

Microsoft Virtual PC 2004 is software that lets users run two or more operating systems on their computers—at the same time. It prevents complicated configurations in environments where people must use multiple operating systems (whether because of incompatible legacy applications or as a safeguard during migration). Users install multiple guest operating systems in virtual machines. These virtual machines look like any other applications people use on their physical computers. For example, users bring virtual machines to the foreground simply by clicking its title bar. Virtual machines' similarity to applications stops at look-and-feel, however. Virtual PC mimics physical computers so exactly that the applications users install in them don't distinguish the virtual machine from a physical computer. Instead of installing operating systems on multiple, costly computers or creating unwieldy multi-boot installations, you can install the operating systems in multiple, inexpensive virtual machines. And changes that users make in virtual machines don't affect their physical computers.

Virtual PC enables companies to take advantage of new operating systems while continuing to support legacy applications that aren't compatible with them. Some of the applications on which companies rely might not run on Windows XP Professional. If you're migrating to Windows XP Professional and have a legacy application that doesn't work in it, then you might have believed you had two choices. You could scratch your deployment until the developers update the legacy applications, or you could allow people who use those applications to have two computers until the developers update them. Now you can install Virtual PC on those users' computers, which allows them to run the operating system version with which those legacy applications are compatible. If your accounting department uses bookkeeping software that works only in Windows 98, you can delay the migration until the vendor updates the software. Better yet, you can install Virtual PC, install Windows 98 as a guest operating system, and then install the bookkeeping software in that virtual machine. Those users can reap all of the benefits that Windows XP Professional offers but continue using their bookkeeping software in their virtual machines.

> **More Info**   For more information about Virtual PC, including how to deploy virtual machines on a large-scale deployment, see *http://www.microsoft.com /virtualpc*.

Best Practices

The following are best practices for Windows XP Professional application compatibility:

- **Inventory your environment.**   Know what applications that you currently have in place and are in regular use, and how many copies you are running and actually need.

- **Prioritize your applications.**   You must determine which of your installed applications are crucial to the success of your business and your overall deployment.

- **Use your Subject Matter Experts.**   Recruit SMEs to assist in designing adequate tests to fully exercise the applications you have in place. Good SMEs can make or break an application compatibility test plan.

- **Create and use a test plan.**   Following a test plan (remember that the Application Compatibility Toolkit includes great documentation on how to design a test plan) for each and every application is essential.

- **Fix compatibility issues using Application Compatibility Administrator.** Use the Application Compatibility Administrator tool to fix any essential line of business application that you cannot find a compatible replacement for from the original vendor or another software company.

Chapter 3

Windows Configuration

Standardizing desktop configurations makes it easier to install, update, manage, support, and replace computers that run Microsoft Windows XP Professional. Standardizing users' configuration settings, software, hardware, and preferences makes it easier to deploy operating system and application upgrades, and configuration changes can be guaranteed to work on all computers. This chapter describes planning considerations for building preferred Windows XP Professional configurations.

Checklist

- Have you defined the scope and objectives of your deployment? See Chapter 1, "Deployment Plan," for more information.

- Have you created an environment plan that describes how to migrate the current environment to the planned environment? See Chapter 1 for more information.

- Have you built a test lab in which you can test your preferred configuration? See Chapter 1 for more information.

Management

By running Windows XP Professional in a Windows Server 2003 domain, you can specify the level of control exercised over users. Table 3-1 describes how you can use the desktop management features to manage computer and user settings. For example, by using Active Directory and Group Policy, you can manage desktops as follows:

■ Prevent users from installing applications that are not required for their jobs.

■ Make new or updated software available to users without visiting their workstations.

■ Customize desktop features or prevent users from making changes to their desktop settings.

■ Refresh policy settings from the server without requiring the user to log off or restart the computer.

Table 3-1   Desktop Management Tasks and Features

Task	Feature
Configure registry-based policy settings for computers and users	Group Policy Administrative Templates
Manage local, domain, and network security	Security Settings
Manage, install, upgrade, repair, or remove software	Software Installation And Maintenance
Manage Internet Explorer configuration settings	Internet Explorer Maintenance, Microsoft Management Console (MMC), Group Policy settings, Internet Explorer Administration Kit
Apply scripts during user logon/logoff and computer startup/shutdown	Group Policy–based scripts
Manage users' folders and files on the network	Folder Redirection
Manage user profiles	Roaming User Profiles
Make shared files and folders available offline	Offline Files And Folders (in conjunction with Folder Redirection)

If you deploy Windows XP Professional desktops in a domain that does not include Active Directory, you can still take advantage of some management features. For example, you can manage Windows XP Professional desktops by implementing the following IntelliMirror features:

■ Roaming User Profiles

■ Logon Scripts

■ Folder Redirection

■ Internet Explorer Maintenance

■ Administrative Templates (registry-based policy)

Desktop

For desktop computers that are used for specific functions, such as running certain line-of-business applications, you can use a management structure that prevents users from installing any application or device or from modifying the desktop or changing settings. To improve security and manage data storage, you can use Folder Redirection to save all data to a server location instead of on the local computer. You can also use Group Policy settings to manage configurations, restrict user access to certain features, and limit the customizations that users can make to their configurations. To configure a computer for a single application and no other tasks, you can remove desktop features such as the Start menu and set that application to start when the user logs on.

If users need to exercise a great deal of control over their desktops, and if tightly managing them is not acceptable, you can use desktop management strategies to reduce support costs and user downtime. You can allow users to install approved applications and to change many settings that affect them while preventing them from making harmful system changes. For example, you might allow users to install or update printer drivers but not to install unapproved hardware devices. To ensure that the user's profile and data are saved to a secure location in which it can be backed up regularly and restored in the event of a computer failure, use Roaming User Profiles and Folder Redirection.

> **More Info**   For more information about implementing the preceding desktop management strategies, see Chapter 21, "Desktop Management." For more information about implementing Group Policy to manage desktop computers, see Chapter 20, "Policy Management."

Laptop

If your mobile users travel frequently, or work from remote sites and use slow or intermittent network connectivity, you might want to give them more control over their computers than you allow users who use their computers primarily onsite (where administrators can provide full support). For example, you might allow traveling users to install or update device drivers and applications but restrict them from performing tasks that can damage or disable their computers.

Mobile users who work mostly offsite, whether or not they are connected to your network, have less access to support personnel. Therefore, when you install applications for users who are seldom connected to the network or who do not have a reliable fast connection to it, make sure that all necessary components are also installed. You can use scripts to make sure that all files associated with the installed applications are installed locally. To allow mobile computer users to install software, make them members of the Power Users security group. For more information about security groups, see "Security," later in this chapter on page 77.

Users who connect to your network remotely might need to configure virtual private network (VPN) connections. To allow them to make necessary configuration changes, enable the following settings:

- Delete remote access connections belonging to the user.

- Rename connections belonging to the current user.

- Display and enable the New Connection Wizard.

- Display the Dial-up Preferences item on the Advanced menu.

- Allow status statistics for an active connection.

- Allow access to the following:

  - Current user's remote access connection properties.

  - Properties of the components of a local area network (LAN) connection.

  - Properties of the components of a remote access connection.

If mobile users rarely connect to your network, you might not want to use features such as Roaming User Profiles and Folder Redirection. However, these features help maintain a seamless work environment from any computer for users who frequently connect to the network or roam between portable and desktop computers.

More Info   For more information about supporting mobile users, see Appendix A, "Mobile Scenarios."

Connectivity

Determining how to connect clients to your network depends largely on where they are located and the type of network you are running. Those located within the corporate infrastructure can use a variety of network media, such as Asynchronous Transfer Mode (ATM), Ethernet, or Token Ring; those outside of the corporate infrastructure need to use Routing and Remote Access or virtual private networking.

Windows XP Professional uses Transmission Control Protocol/Internet Protocol (TCP/IP) as its standard network protocol. For a Windows XP Professional–

based computer to connect to a NetWare or Macintosh server, you must use a protocol that is compatible with the server. NWLink is the Microsoft implementation of the Novell Internetwork Packet Exchange/Sequenced Packet Exchange (IPX/SPX) protocol, which allows you to connect to NetWare file and print servers. However, the IPX/SPX protocol is not available on Windows XP 64-Bit Edition.

In the Properties dialog box for your network adapter, you can specify which protocols to install and enable. Windows XP Professional attempts to connect to remote servers by using the network protocols in the order specified in this dialog box. You can configure these protocols in your unattended-setup answer file, as described in Chapter 6, "Answer Files."

> **Note** Install only the necessary protocols. For example, installing and enabling Internetwork Packet Exchange (IPX) when you need only TCP/IP generates unnecessary IPX and Service Advertising Protocol (SAP) network traffic.

TCP/IP Networks

Client computers running on TCP/IP networks can be assigned an Internet Protocol (IP) address statically by the network administrator or dynamically by a Dynamic Host Configuration Protocol (DHCP) server. Windows XP Professional uses *Domain Name Server* (*DNS*) as the namespace provider, whether you use static IP addresses or DHCP. Networks that include Microsoft Windows NT Server 4 or earlier or client computers running versions of Windows earlier than Windows 2000 Professional might require a combination of DHCP and Windows Internet Name Server (WINS). DNS is required for integration with Active Directory, and it provides the following advantages:

- Interoperability with other DNS servers, including Novell NDS and UNIX Bind.

- Integration with networking services by using WINS and DHCP.

- Dynamic registration of DNS names and IP addresses.

- Incremental zone transfers and load balancing between servers.

- Support for resource record types such as Services Locator (SRV) and Asynchronous Transfer Mode Addresses (ATMA) records.

DHCP allows Windows XP Professional-based computers to receive IP addresses automatically. This helps to prevent configuration errors and address conflicts that can occur when previously assigned IP addresses are reused to configure new computers on the network. As computers and devices are removed from the network, their addresses are returned to the address pool and can be reallocated to other clients. The DHCP lease-renewal process ensures that needed changes are made automatically when client configurations must be updated. The advantages of using DHCP follow:

- Conflicts caused by assigning duplicate IP addresses are eliminated.

- DNS or WINS settings do not need to be manually configured if the DHCP server is configured to those settings.

- Clients are assigned IP addresses regardless of the subnet to which they connect, so IP settings need not be manually changed for roaming users.

If you assign IP addresses statically, you need to have the following information for each client:

- The IP address and subnet mask for each network adapter installed on each client computer.

- The IP address for the default gateway.

- Whether the client is using DNS or WINS.

- The name of the client computer's DNS domain and the IP addresses for the DNS or WINS servers.

- The IP address for the proxy server.

> **Note**   It is recommended that you assign static IP addresses to servers and dynamic ones to client computers. However, there are exceptions that might require you to assign static addresses to computers running Windows XP Professional. For example, a computer that runs an application that has the IP addresses hard-coded into it requires a static address.

IPX Protocol

IPX is the network protocol used by NetWare networks to control addressing and routing of packets within and among LANs. Windows XP Professional computers can connect to NetWare servers using Client Service for Netware. Windows XP Professional includes NWLink and Client Service for NetWare to transmit NetWare Core Protocol (NCP) packets to and from NetWare servers.

> **Note**   Although TCP/IP is used on some Novell NetWare–based networks, Client Service for NetWare does not support it.

NWLink and Client Service for NetWare provide access to file and print resources on NetWare networks and servers that are running either Novell Directory Services (NDS) or bindery security. Client Service supports some NetWare tools applications. It does not support IP, including NetWare/IP. You can install Client Service or the current network client by using Novell Client. However, you cannot use Novell Client to connect a computer running Windows XP Professional to a Windows 2000 Server–based computer.

> **Caution**   Do not install both Client Service and Novell Client for Windows NT/2000 on the same computer running Windows XP Professional. Doing so can cause errors on the system.

When upgrading to Windows XP Professional from Windows Me, Windows 98, or Windows NT 4 Workstation, Windows XP Professional upgrades Novell Client version 4.7 or earlier to the latest version of Novell Client, allowing for a seamless upgrade. All other versions of Novell Client should be removed before upgrading the operating system; then reinstall and reconfigure Novell Client.

Security

The Windows XP Professional security model is based on the concepts of authentication and authorization. Authentication verifies a user's identity, and authorization verifies that the user has permission to access resources on the computer or the network. Windows XP Professional also includes encryption technologies, such as Encrypting File System (EFS) and public key technology, to protect confidential data on disk and across networks.

Authentication

When the user logs on to a computer, a user name and password are required before the user can access resources on the local computer or the network. Windows XP Professional authentication enables single sign-on to all network resources, so that a user can log on to a client computer by using a single password or smart card and gain access to other computers in the domain without re-entering credential information. The Windows XP Professional authentication model protects your network against malicious attacks, such as the following:

- **Masquerade attacks**   Because a user must prove identity, it is difficult to pose as another user.

- **Replay attacks**   It is difficult to reuse stolen authentication information because Windows XP Professional authentication protocols use timestamps.

■   **Identity interception**   Intercepted identities cannot be used to access the network because all exchanges are encrypted.

Kerberos V5 is the primary security protocol within Windows 2000 Server–based and Windows Server 2003–based domains. Windows XP Professional–based clients use NTLM to authenticate to servers running Windows NT Server 4 and to access resources within a Windows NT Server 4–based domain. Computers running Windows XP Professional that are not joined to a domain also use NTLM for authentication.

If you use Windows XP Professional on a network that includes Active Directory, you can use Group Policy settings to manage logon security, such as restricting access to computers and logging users off after a specified time.

Authorization

Authorization controls user access to resources. Using access control lists (ACLs), security groups, and NT file system (NTFS) file permissions, you can make sure that users have access only to needed resources such as files, drives, network shares, printers, and applications. Security groups, user rights, and permissions can be used to manage security for numerous resources while maintaining fine-grained control of files and folders and user rights. The four main types of security groups are the following:

■   Domain local groups

■   Global groups

■   Universal groups

■   Computer local groups

Using security groups can streamline the process of managing access to resources. You can assign users to security groups and then grant permissions to those groups. You can add and remove users in security groups according to their need for access to new resources. To create local users and place them within local security groups, use the Computer Management snap-in of MMC or the User Accounts option in Control Panel. To automate the process, you can use a WMI (Windows Management Instrumentation) script. Within the domain local and computer local security groups, there are preconfigured groups to which you can assign users:

■   **Administrators**   Members of this group have total control of the local computer and have permissions to complete all tasks. A built-in account called Administrator is created and assigned to this group when Windows XP Professional is installed. When a computer is joined to a domain, the Domain Administrators group is added to the local Administrators group by default. Assigning users to the Administrators group is not a best practice because doing so makes it difficult to restrict what users can do.

- **Power Users** Members of this group have read and write permissions to other parts of the system in addition to their own profile folders, can install applications, and can perform many administrative tasks. Members of this group have the same level of permissions as Users and Power Users in Windows NT Workstation 4. Assign mobile users to the Power Users group to give them enough control to be self-sufficient because they are away from IT support.

- **Users** Members of this group are authenticated users with read-only permissions for most parts of the system. They have read and write access only within their own profile folders. Users cannot read other users' data (unless it is in a shared folder), install applications that require modifying system directories or the registry, or perform administrative tasks. User permissions under Windows XP Professional are more limited than under Windows NT Workstation 4. Assigning users to this group is a best practice because it allows you to better restrict what users can do in restricted environments. This brings up the issue of installing applications, however, which Chapter 23, "Software Installation," addresses.

- **Guests** Members of this group can log on using the built-in Guest account to perform limited tasks, including shutting down the computer. Users who do not have an account on the computer or whose account has been disabled (but not deleted) can log on using the Guest account. You can set rights and permissions for this account, which is a member of the built-in Guests group by default. The Guest account is enabled by default. You can use the utility Cusrmgr.exe from the Microsoft Windows 2000 Server Resource Kit to automatically disable this account during installation. Alternatively, you can write a WMI script to disable this account during installation.

You can configure access control lists (ACLs) for resource groups or security groups, and add or remove users or resources from these groups as needed. The ability to edit the membership of groups that you assign to resources makes user permissions easier to control and audit. It also reduces the need to change ACLs. You can grant users permissions to access files and folders, and specify what tasks users can perform on them. You can also allow permissions to be inherited, so that permissions for a folder apply to all its subfolders and the files in them. You can use Group Policy settings to assign permissions to resources and grant rights to users as follows:

- **To restrict which types of users can run certain applications** This reduces the risk of exposing the computer to unwanted applications, such as viruses.

- **To configure many rights and permissions for client computers** You can also configure rights and permissions on an individual computer to be used as the base image for desktop installations, to ensure standardized security management even if you do not use Active Directory.

You can use preconfigured security templates that meet the security require-ments for a given workstation or network. Security templates are files with preset security settings that can be applied to a local computer or to client computers in a domain by using Active Directory. Security templates can be used without modifica-tion or customized for specific needs. For more information about security tem-plates, see Chapter 20.

Encryption

You can use EFS to encrypt data on your hard disk. For example, because portable computers are high-risk items for theft, you can use EFS to enhance security by encrypting data on the hard disks of your company's portable computers. This pre-caution protects data and authentication information against unauthorized access. Before implementing EFS, it is important to understand the proper backup structure for EFS keys and to know how to restore them.

Disk Partitions

Disk partitioning is a way of dividing hard disks into sections that function as sepa-rate units. Partitions can be set up to organize data or to install additional operating systems for multiple-boot configurations. Partitioning involves dividing a disk into one or more areas, each formatted for use by a particular file system. Depending on your existing hard disk configuration, you have the following options during Windows XP Setup:

- If the hard disk is unpartitioned, you can create and size the Windows XP Pro-fessional partition.

- If an existing partition is large enough, you can install Windows XP Profes-sional on that partition.

- If the existing partition is too small but you have adequate unpartitioned space, you can create a new Windows XP Professional partition in that space.

- If the hard disk has an existing partition, you can delete it to create more unpartitioned disk space for the Windows XP Professional partition. Keep in mind that deleting an existing partition also erases any data on that partition.

Caution   Before you change file systems on a partition or delete a parti-tion, back up the information on that partition because reformatting or deleting a partition deletes all existing data on that partition.

If you install Windows XP Professional as part of a multiple-boot configuration, it is important to install Windows XP Professional on its own partition. Installing Windows XP Professional on the same partition as another operating system might overwrite files installed by the other operating system and overwrites the system directory unless you specify a different directory in which to install Windows XP Professional. If you install Windows XP Professional as part of a multiple-boot configuration, make sure that you install it after you install all other operating systems. If you install another operating system after Windows XP Professional, you might not be able to start Windows XP Professional.

It is recommended that you install Windows XP Professional on a 2-GB or larger partition. Although Windows XP Professional requires a minimum of 650 MB of free disk space for installation, using a larger installation partition provides flexibility for adding future updates, operating system tools, and other files. During installation, you only need to create and size the partition on which you plan to install Windows XP Professional. After Windows XP Professional is installed, you can use the Disk Management snap-in to make changes or create new partitions.

More Info   Partitioning disks manually is not efficient in a large-scale deployment. Chapter 13, "Unattended Setup," and Chapter 14, "Preinstallation Environment," describe how to use Diskpart.exe with a script to partition disks automatically prior to installing Windows XP Professional. Third-party tools are also available for partitioning disks as part of a scripted installation.

File Systems

Windows XP Professional supports the FAT16, FAT32, and NTFS file systems. Table 3-2 describes the sizes and limitations of each file system. Because NTFS has all the basic capabilities of FAT16 and FAT32, with the added advantage of advanced storage features such as compression, improved security, and larger partitions and file sizes, it is the recommended file system for Windows XP Professional. Some features that are available when you choose NTFS include the following:

- File encryption allows you to protect files and folders from unauthorized access.

- Permissions can be set on individual files, as well as on folders.

- Disk quotas allow you to monitor and control the amount of disk space used by individual users.

- Better scalability allows you to use large volumes. The maximum volume size for NTFS is much greater than it is for the file allocation table (FAT). Additionally, NTFS performance does not degrade as volume size increases as it does in FAT systems.

- Recovery logging of disk activities helps restore information quickly in the event of power failure or other system problems.

When you perform a clean installation of Windows XP Professional, it is recommended that you use NTFS. If you upgrade computers that use NTFS as the only file system, continue to use NTFS with Windows XP Professional.

Table 3-2   Comparison of NTFS and FAT File Systems

Subject of Comparison	NTFS	FAT16	FAT32
Operating system compatibility	A computer running Windows 2000 Professional or Windows XP Professional can access files on an NTFS partition. A computer running Windows NT Workstation 4 with Service Pack 4 or later can access files on the partition, but some NTFS features, such as Disk Quotas, are not available. Other operating systems allow no access.	File access is available to computers running MS-DOS, all versions of Windows, Windows NT Workstation, Windows XP Professional, and OS/2.	File access is available only to computers running Windows 95 OSR2, Windows 98, Windows Me, Windows 2000 Professional, and Windows XP Professional.
Volume size	<ul><li>Recommended minimum volume size is approximately 10 MB.</li><li>Recommended practical maximum for volumes is 2 TB. Much larger sizes are possible.</li><li>Cannot be used on floppy disks.</li></ul>	<ul><li>Volumes up to 4 GB.</li><li>Cannot be used on floppy disks.</li></ul>	<ul><li>Volumes from 512 MB to 2 TB.</li><li>In Windows XP Professional, you can format a FAT32 volume only up to 32 GB.</li><li>Cannot be used on floppy disks.</li></ul>
File size	Maximum file size is 16 TB minus 64 KB (2^{44} minus 64 KB).	Maximum file size is 4 GB.	Maximum file size is 4 GB.
Files per volume	4,294,967,295 (2^{32} minus 1 files).	65,536 (2^{16} files).	Approximately 4,177,920.

Converting versus Formatting

Before you run Windows XP Setup, you must decide whether to keep, convert, or reformat an existing partition. The default option for an existing partition is to keep the existing file system intact, thus preserving all files on that partition.

Windows XP Professional provides support for Windows 95, Windows 98, or Windows Me file systems, including FAT16 and FAT32 file systems. If you upgrade computers that use FAT or FAT32 as their file system, consider converting the partitions to NTFS. You cannot upgrade compressed Windows 98 volumes; you must uncompress them before you upgrade them to Windows XP Professional. Use the conversion option if you want to take advantage of NTFS features such as security or disk compression and you are not dual-booting with another operating system that needs access to the existing partition. You cannot convert an NTFS volume to FAT or FAT32. You must reformat the NTFS volume as FAT. However, when you convert a volume from FAT to NTFS, you cannot use the uninstall feature to roll back to a previous operating system installation.

> **Note**   Once you convert to NTFS, you cannot revert to FAT or FAT32.

You can reformat a partition during a clean installation only. If you decide to convert or reformat, select an appropriate file system (NTFS, FAT16, or FAT32). You can reformat a partition as either FAT or NTFS; however, reformatting a partition erases all files on that partition. Make sure to back up all files on the partition before you reformat it.

File System Compatibility

NTFS is the recommended file system for Windows XP Professional. However, you might need a different file system to multi-boot Windows XP Professional with an operating system that cannot access NTFS volumes. If you use NTFS to format a partition, only Windows XP Professional, Windows 2000 Professional, and Windows NT Workstation 4 with Service Pack 4 can access the volume.

If you plan to install Windows XP Professional and another operating system on the same computer, you must use a file system that all operating systems installed on the computer can access. For example, if the computer has Windows 95 and Windows XP Professional, you must use FAT on any partition that Windows 95 must access. However, if the computer has Windows NT Workstation 4 and Windows XP Professional, you can use FAT or NTFS because both operating systems can access all those file systems. However, certain features in the version of NTFS included with Windows XP Professional are not available when the computer runs Windows NT Workstation 4.

Note You can access NTFS volumes only when running Windows NT Workstation 4, Windows 2000 Professional, or Windows XP Professional.

Hardware Devices

Windows XP Professional includes support for a range of hardware devices, including USB- and IEEE 1394–compliant devices. Device drivers for most devices are included with the operating system. Drivers can be configured to be dynamically updated by connecting to the Windows Update Web site and downloading the most recent versions. If you can connect to the Internet, Dynamic Update can connect to Windows Update during Windows XP Setup to install device drivers that were not included on the Windows XP Professional operating system CD. You can add devices, such as mass storage and Plug and Play devices, to your installation. For more information about adding hardware devices to your installation, see Chapter 7, "Distribution Points."

Multilingual

Windows XP Professional supports companies that need to equip their users to work with various languages or in multiple locale settings. This includes organizations in any of the following scenarios:

- Operate internationally and must support various regional and language options, such as time zones, currencies, or date formats
- Have employees or customers who speak different languages, or require language-dependent keyboards or input devices
- Develop an internal line of business applications to run internationally or in more than one language

If you have roaming users who need to log on anywhere and edit a document in several languages, you need the appropriate language files installed or installable on demand, on a server or workstation. You can also use Terminal Services to allow users to initiate individual Terminal Services sessions in different languages. See Appendix B, "Multilingual Scenarios," for more information.

Accessibility

Windows XP Professional includes multiple features and options that improve accessibility for people with disabilities. You can use the Accessibility Wizard or individual Control Panel properties to set options to meet the needs of users with vision, mobility, hearing, and learning disabilities.

For users with vision impairments or learning disabilities, you can set size and color options for the display of text and screen elements such as icons and windows. You can also adjust the size, color, speed, and motion of the mouse cursor to aid visibility on the screen. Options such as StickyKeys, BounceKeys, ToggleKeys, and MouseKeys benefit some users with mobility impairments. SoundSentry and ShowSounds can assist users with hearing impairments.

Accessibility tools such as Magnifier, Narrator, and On-Screen Keyboard allow users with disabilities to configure and use computers without additional hardware or software. These tools also allow some users with disabilities to roam multiple computers in their organization.

> **Note** Accessibility features such as Narrator, Magnifier, and On-Screen Keyboard provide a minimum level of functionality for users with special needs. Most people with disabilities require tools with higher functionality.

You can use Group Policy and set user profiles to make sure that accessibility features are available to users wherever they log on in your network. You can also enable some accessibility features when you run Windows XP Setup by specifying them in your answer file.

Applications

During installation, you can choose to install standard productivity applications such as Microsoft Office 2003 Editions, as well as custom applications. If certain core applications need to be available to users at all times, you can install them along with the operating system. If you are automating installations by using Remote Installation Services or disk imaging with Sysprep, you can install the applications on the disk image that you create; if you are doing unattended installations by using answer files, you can include applications and make them available from your distribution folder. For more information about distributing applications with Windows XP Professional, see Chapter 11, "Chaining Installations," and Chapter 23.

If you use Active Directory, you can use the Software Installation And Maintenance feature of IntelliMirror to make applications available to users. You can assign critical applications to users and publish applications users might need to access:

- **Publishing an application**   When you publish applications, users can install the application by using Add Or Remove Programs in Control Panel. For more information about using Software Installation And Maintenance to make applications available to your users, see Chapter 23.

- **Assigning an application to a user**   When you assign an application to a user, it appears to the user that the application is already installed, and a shortcut appears in the user's Start menu. When the user clicks the shortcut, the application is installed from a server share.

- **Automating deployment and upgrades**   You can also use Microsoft Systems Management Server (SMS) to automate the deployment and upgrade applications during and after installing the operating system. SMS is a good option for large-scale software-deployment projects because SMS can be set to run when it will cause minimal interruption to your business, such as at night or on weekends. For more information about SMS, see the documentation included with SMS.

Settings

Creating a preferred configuration for Windows XP Professional includes planning user and computer settings. Document the settings that you plan to configure for users and computers. The following are suggestions for settings to configure:

- **Internet Explorer**   Document the Internet Explorer settings for the preferred configuration, including the home page, proxy server addresses, certificates, and so on. Chapter 10, "Internet Explorer Settings," describes methods for deploying these settings. A more complete list of settings is in the Internet Explorer Administration Kit at *http://www.microsoft.com/windows/ ieak/techinfo/deploy/60/en*. In the left pane, click Deployment Guide, Custom Package Checklist.

- **Windows Explorer**   Document settings for Windows Explorer. For example, your preferred configuration might show file extensions rather than hiding them. Chapter 8, "Windows Settings," describes methods for deploying these settings.

- **System Restore** Document how System Restore will work in your preferred configuration. Some organizations will want to disable System Restore because it potentially rolls configurations past virus and security updates. If you choose to enable System Restore in your preferred configuration, I recommend that you configure it for scheduled updates by using policies. Chapter 20 contains more information about Group Policy.

- **Remote Desktop** By default, Windows XP Professional disables Remote Desktop. Consider enabling this feature and using it as a remote administration and troubleshooting tool, however. Doing so can prevent many trips to users' desks. You can automatically enable Remote Desktop for domain Administrators by including a *.reg* file in your distribution point, as described in Chapter 11, or by configuring it in your answer file, as described in Chapter 6.

- **Automatic Updates** Chapter 19, "Software Update Services," describes the corporate version of Automatic Update. Although configuring Automatic Update to update from Microsoft's Windows Update Web site isn't appropriate in most enterprise environments (although it's a good idea in small-business scenarios), you can deploy Software Update Services on your network and then configure Automatic Updates to retrieve critical updates and security fixes from it. I recommend that you configure it to automatically install updates on a schedule to avoid user interaction with it.

On the Resource Kit CD Plan the methods that you intend to use for deploying these settings. In addition to policies, Chapter 8 describes various methods you can use for configuring these settings. Create a spreadsheet that lists the settings you'll configure and how you intend to deploy them. This spreadsheet becomes part of your deployment plan. This book's companion CD contains a sample spreadsheet in the Aids folder. The file is Settings.xls.

Best Practices

The following are best practices for planning preferred Windows XP Professional configurations:

- **Review the Windows XP Professional deployment white papers** Microsoft publishes two Windows XP Professional deployment white papers that are essential reading before you start planning your project. To review them, see *http://www.microsoft.com/technet/prodtechnol/winxppro/deploy/default.mspx.* The first white paper is "Deploying Windows XP Part I: Planning"; the second is "Deploying Windows XP Part II: Implementing."

- **Separate managed settings from unmanaged settings** For each setting in your preferred configuration, decide whether it's a managed setting or not. Use policies to enforce managed settings.

- **Plan to put users in the appropriate local security groups** For desktop computers, put users in the local Users group, which is restricted. For mobile computers, put users in the local Power Users group, which is less restricted. You can mitigate application-installation issues by using security templates, as described in Chapter 20.

- **Use the NTFS file system** The best file system to use with Windows XP Professional is NTFS. It provides security, encryption, compression, and so on. Use the FAT and FAT32 file systems only in multiboot scenarios in which the other operating systems cannot read the NTFS file system.

- **Document settings and assign to a method** Document each and every setting in your preferred configuration, and assign each to a deployment method. A variety of methods are available for deploying settings (default user profiles, inclusion on the disk image, installation chaining, and so on). For each setting, indicate at which point in the process you will configure that setting.

Chapter 4

Office Configuration

Configuring Microsoft Office 2003 Editions provides options similar to those for configuring Microsoft Office XP. These options give you the flexibility to customize Office 2003 Editions to suit your enterprise's environment. This chapter describes the choices you must make when planning an Office 2003 Editions deployment.

Checklist

- Have you defined the scope and objectives of your deployment? See Chapter 1, "Deployment Plan," for more information.

- Have you created an environment plan that describes how to migrate the current environment to the planned environment? See Chapter 1 for more information.

- Have you built a test lab in which you can test your preferred configuration? See Chapter 1 for more information.

- Have you downloaded the Office 2003 Editions Resource Kit from Microsoft's Web site? Download it from *http://www.microsoft.com /office/ork.*

- Are you familiar with essential Office 2003 Editions concepts, such as the types of files that customize an installation? It's essential that you understand the steps Office 2003 Setup takes to install the product. For more information, see "Setup Sequence of Events" at *http://www.microsoft.com/office/ork/2003/two/ch3/DepA03.htm*.

Packages

Office 2003 Editions is available in a variety of editions and standalone products. Rarely does a single edition meet all of your requirements, though. For example, you might deploy Microsoft Office Standard Edition 2003 to most users in the enterprise but deploy Microsoft Office Professional Edition 2003 to those users who need Office Access 2003 or Office InfoPath 2003.

Table 4-1 describes the Office 2003 Editions that are available through Microsoft Volume Licensing programs. For more information about other editions, including original equipment manufacturer (OEM) and retail editions, see *http://www.microsoft.com/office*. You can purchase standalone products through the Microsoft Volume Licensing program, too. For more information on these products please visit *http://www.microsoft.com/office/howtobuy/default.mspx*.

The product CD for each edition contains a Microsoft Windows Installer database that installs the product. For example, the Office Professional Edition 2003 CD contains the package file Pro11.msi. Document not only the name of the editions that you must deploy, but also document the name of the package files that you must deploy.

Table 4-1   Volume-License Editions

Microsoft Office Professional Enterprise Edition 2003	Microsoft Office Standard Edition 2003	Microsoft Office Small Business Edition 2003
<ul><li>Access 2003</li><li>Excel 2003</li><li>InfoPath 2003</li><li>Outlook 2003</li><li>Outlook 2003 with Business Contact Manager</li><li>PowerPoint 2003</li><li>Publisher 2003</li><li>Word 2003</li></ul>This edition includes additional support for Extensible Markup Language (XML) and information rights management (IRM) content creation and authoring.	<ul><li>Excel 2003</li><li>Outlook 2003</li><li>PowerPoint 2003</li><li>Word 2003</li></ul>	<ul><li>Excel 2003</li><li>Outlook 2003</li><li>Outlook 2003 with Business Contact Manager</li><li>PowerPoint 2003</li><li>Publisher 2003</li><li>Word 2003</li></ul>

Office 2003 Editions Resource Kit

The Microsoft Office 2003 Editions Resource Kit is the primary tool you use to customize and deploy Office 2003 Editions. It's designed for administrators, IT professionals, and support technicians who deploy and maintain Office 2003 Editions in their organizations. It features a collection of tools designed specifically to support the Office 2003 Editions, as well as comprehensive documentation on such areas as deployment, security, messaging, and worldwide support.

The Microsoft Office 2003 Editions Resource Kit is available both on the Web and as a book published by Microsoft Press. The Web site includes all the information provided with the book, plus new information about software updates, emerging technologies, and software management issues. The printed book is available through your local bookseller, online bookstores, or directly from Microsoft Press. Included with the book is a CD that contains Office Resource Kit tools, reference information, and supplementary documents. You can download the Office Resource Kit tools from *http://www.microsoft.com/office/ork*. You need to download and install these tools to follow this book's Office 2003 Editions content.

Environment

After choosing the combination of editions and standalone products you're deploying and selecting their corresponding package files, assess your environment to ensure that it meets the requirements. The following sections describe the specific considerations that affect your deployment project.

Network Capacity

Plan the following network-capacity issues:

- **Do your installation servers have sufficient disk space for the Office 2003 Editions administrative installation point?** The disk space required for Office 2003 distribution points varies. Compressed CD images require a minimum of 400 MB, and you need additional space for customizations. Administrative installations require substantially more disk space.

- **Will network-bandwidth limitations affect how and when you distribute Office 2003 Editions to users?** Low-bandwidth scenarios, particularly mobile computers, alter your distribution plan for Office 2003 Editions. If you have low network bandwidth, you'll want to consider disabling features installation states such as Run From Network, and you'll want to plan for a distribution method that is an alternate to an administrative installation.

■ **Do you have plans to upgrade your operating system, messaging servers, or other server applications soon?** The minimum operating system requirement for Office 2003 Editions is Windows 2000 with Service Pack 3 or Windows XP Professional. If you're planning to upgrade from an earlier version of Windows, you can plan to deploy Office 2003 Editions as part of or after that project. As well, if you're planning an Exchange migration project, you might want to consider holding Office Outlook 2003 back until that project. In this staged scenario, you'd deploy all of Office 2003 Editions except for Office Outlook 2003 now, and then deploy Outlook 2003 as part of your migration.

Client Computers

Plan the following client-computer issues:

■ **What operating systems and service packs are installed on client computers?** The minimum requirement for Office 2003 Editions is Windows 2000 with Service Pack 3 or Windows XP Professional. Deploying Office 2003 Editions to either operating system is much simpler than deploying Office XP to earlier versions.

■ **Do users' computers meet the minimum requirements?** Table 4-2 describes the minimum requirements for installing and running Office 2003 Editions. Some advanced features, such as Office Outlook 2003 with Business Contact Manager have additional requirements.

■ **How many laptop users do you have?** You might choose to deploy a compressed CD image instead of an administrative installation to mobile computers in order to ensure continuous access to the source files when mobile users aren't connected to the network or are using slow connections.

Because you can easily stage your deployment of Office 2003 Editions to selected groups of users or computers, a mix of hardware configurations and operating systems within your organization does not prevent you from starting your rollout. You can roll it through your organization as part of a hardware and operating system refresh, for example, or you can deploy Office 2003 Editions by attrition.

Table 4-2 Office 2003 Editions System Requirements

Component	Requirement
Computer and processor	Personal computer with an Intel Pentium III or equivalent processor recommended; 233-megahertz (MHz) required. Intel Pentium 4 or equivalent processor will provide optimal performance for Microsoft Office Professional Edition 2003 and Microsoft Office Professional Enterprise Edition 2003.
Memory	128 megabytes (MB) of RAM or above recommended.

Table 4-2   Office 2003 Editions System Requirements

Component	Requirement
Hard disk	Hard disk usage will vary depending on configuration; custom installation choices may require more or less hard disk space. Listed following are the hard disk requirements for individual Office 2003 Editions. Microsoft Office Standard Edition 2003: ■ 260 MB of available hard disk space ■ Optional installation files cache (recommended) requires an additional 250 MB of available hard disk space Microsoft Office Professional Edition 2003: ■ 400 MB of available hard disk space; 190 MB of hard disk space for Microsoft Office Outlook 2003 with Business Contact Manager ■ Optional installation files cache (recommended) requires an additional 290 MB of available hard disk space Microsoft Office Small Business Edition 2003: ■ 380 MB of available hard disk space; 190 MB of additional hard disk space to use optional installation of Outlook 2003 with Business Contact Manager ■ Optional installation files cache (recommended) requires an additional 280 MB of available hard disk space Microsoft Office Student and Teacher Edition 2003: ■ 260 MB of available hard disk space ■ Optional installation files cache (recommended) requires an additional 250 MB of available hard disk space
Operating system	Microsoft Windows 2000 with Service Pack 3 (SP3) or later; or Windows XP Professional or later.
Display	Super VGA (800 × 600) or a higher-resolution monitor.

Preparation

You can deploy Office 2003 Editions from an administrative installation, similar to Office 2000 and Office XP. You can also deploy it from a customized compressed CD image, which is a new capability for Office 2003 Editions. By deploying Office 2003 Editions from an administrative installation, you can do the following:

■ Manage one set of Office 2003 Editions files from a central location.

■ Create a standard Office 2003 Editions configuration for a group of users.

■ Take advantage of flexible installation options.

■ Manage updates of Office 2003 Editions by patching one administrative image.

> **Note**   Only Office 2003 Editions acquired through a Volume License agreement or other non-retail channel allow you to create an administrative installation point. You can't run Setup.exe in administrative mode (**/a**) with a retail edition of Office 2003 Editions.

Need help choosing between administrative installations and compressed CD images? I strongly prefer the compressed CD image because it provides better support for mobile computers by caching the source files locally. It also makes patching Office 2003 Editions easier in the future because the link between the client installation and the administrative installation on the server doesn't exist (you can install client patch files). The only good reason I've come up with for creating Office 2003 Editions administrative installations is if you want to decompress the source files so you can use the Run From Network feature installation state. If in doubt, deploy a compressed CD image. Regardless of which method you choose, document your choice and the reason for your choice in your deployment plan.

> **More Info**   For more information about compressed CD images and local installation sources, see *http://www.microsoft.com/office/ork/2003/two /ch3/DepC06.htm*.

Administrative Installation

Administrative installations are decompressed copies of the Office 2003 Editions CD that include the product key and organization name. Chapter 7, "Distribution Points," shows you how to create administration installations. Before creating administrative installation points for Office 2003 Editions, consider the following issues:

- **How many installation servers do you need?**   Windows Installer continues to reference the installation source after Office 2003 Editions is deployed. To make them more resilient, you can copy the original administrative image to any number of servers. You specify additional sources in a transform (*.mst* files). For more information, see Chapter 9, "Office Settings."

- **How reliable are users' network connections?**   To use administrative installations, users must have reliable access to the network share, not only for installing Office 2003 Editions initially, but also for installing features on demand and repairing or removing Office applications.

- **What additional software do you want to include on the administrative image?** You can add packages from the Office 2003 Editions product CD or add packages that you plan to chain to the Office 2003 Editions installation. For your own convenience, you can also store tools from the Office 2003 Editions Resource Kit on the same network share. For more information about chaining packages, see Chapter 11, "Chaining Installations."

- **Are you deploying to international users?** Each Office 2003 Editions Multilingual User Interface (MUI) Pack corresponds to one language and is installed in its own package. You can install any number of MUI Packs on the Office 2003 Editions administrative installation and then chain them to the Office 2003 Editions installation or deploy them separately later on. For more information about installing MUI Packs, see Appendix B, "Multilingual Scenarios."

- **Will laptop users in the field use the Office CD as a source?** The compressed cabinet (*.cab*) files on the CD are extracted when you run **setup /a** to create an administrative installation point. Users who install Office 2003 Editions from the network cannot use the compressed Office 2003 Editions CD as an interchangeable source. For more information, see the following section.

Compressed CD Image

When users install Office 2003 Editions from the CD or from a compressed CD image on the network, Office 2003 Setup uses a system service named Office Source Engine (Ose.exe) to copy required installation files to a hidden folder on the local computer. Windows Installer uses this local installation source to install Office 2003 Editions, and the local source remains available for repairing, reinstalling, or updating Office 2003 Editions later. Users can install features on demand or run Office 2003 Setup in maintenance mode to add new features.

Office 2003 Setup creates a local installation source by default, but only when you install Office 2003 Editions from the CD or a compressed CD image. If sufficient hard disk space exists on the local computer, Office 2003 Setup caches the entire installation source by default. Maintaining this local installation source after Office 2003 Editions is installed offers a number of benefits to users in large organizations:

- Traveling users, or users with slow or intermittent network connections, can install features on demand or run Office 2003 Setup in maintenance mode to add new features without requiring a source on the network.

- When Office 2003 Editions is updated, administrators can distribute smaller client patches, and users can apply them even when they do not have access to the original source.

- Because Office 2003 Setup caches the compressed cabinet (*.cab*) files, the local installation source requires considerably less hard disk space than a copy of the entire uncompressed administrative image.

When you run Office 2003 Setup with the **/a** option to create an administrative installation point, it extracts the compressed *.cab* files on the network share, and Office 2003 Setup can no longer create the local installation source. However, installing Office 2003 Editions from a compressed CD image offers almost all of the same deployment options as an administrative installation point:

- You can create a transform and modify Setup.ini to customize Office 2003 Editions, and you can create multiple configurations from the same compressed CD image.

- You can set features to be installed on demand (Install On First Use); however, you cannot run Office 2003 Editions applications over the network (Run From Network).

- You can chain additional packages to the Office 2003 Editions installation, including standalone products such as Microsoft Office FrontPage 2003 and Microsoft Office OneNote 2003. Chained packages that support creation of a local installation source inherit the local installation source settings specified for the core Office 2003 Editions package.

- You can use deployment tools such as Microsoft Systems Management Server to install Office 2003 Editions on users' computers.

- You can deploy compressed CD images by using Group Policy and Active Directory; however, Windows Installer will not create a local installation source because you're bypassing Setup.exe.

Note   The creation and maintenance of the local installation source is managed entirely by Office 2003 Setup and the Office Source Engine (Ose.exe), not by Windows Installer.

Customization

After you create an administrative installation point for Office 2003 Editions, you can make extensive customizations before installing Office 2003 Editions on users' computers. You can also customize many aspects of the installation process itself. Begin by evaluating who your users are and how they use Office 2003 Editions. Some users may work exclusively in English, for example, whereas others routinely view or edit documents in multiple languages. Consider the following when planning your Office 2003 Editions customizations:

■ **Do you want a uniform configuration throughout your organization?**
If multiple users share one computer, or if users roam from one computer to
another, establish a standard Office 2003 Editions configuration.

■ **How many different configurations of Office 2003 do you need and for
which groups of users?**   You can distribute different configurations of
Office 2003 Editions from a single administrative installation point.

■ **Which applications are essential and must be installed locally? Which
applications can be advertised (installed on demand)?**   When users have
fast and reliable access to the network, advertising can speed the initial deployment by installing only the features users actually need on the local hard disk.
However, avoid the Install-On-Demand setting for laptop users (who may have
intermittent or slow access to the network) and install all features locally.

■ **Are you staging your deployment of Office 2003 Editions
applications?**   Many organizations stagger their deployment of Office 2003
Editions applications. With the Custom Installation Wizard, you can specify settings for applications that will be installed later. You use the Custom Maintenance Wizard to add standalone Office 2003 Editions applications to an
existing configuration. For example, you can schedule an Office Outlook 2003
installation to coincide with a mail server upgrade instead of the Office 2003
Editions installation.

■ **What other products do you want to include in the Office 2003 Editions
installation?**   You can specify additional Windows Installer packages to
install with Office 2003 Editions, such as MUI Packs. Office 2003 Setup coordinates these installations after the Office 2003 Editions installation is complete.

■ **Do you want to install Office 2003 Editions quietly, or will users be able
to select options during the installation?**   For automated distributions of
Office 2003 Editions, such as when deploying it by using Systems Management
Server (SMS), you'll want to display no user interface at all.

■ **Do you want users to be able to change the default settings and customize Office 2003 Editions for themselves, or do you want to enforce your
settings?**   Settings that you distribute in a transform or Office 2003 Editions
profile settings file (*.ops* file) appear as the default settings when users install
Office 2003 Editions, but users can modify them. To enforce your settings, use
policies.

■ **Do some users need to keep previous versions of Office 2003 Editions
on their computers?**   By default, when you run Office 2003 Setup in quiet
mode, all previous versions of the Office applications being installed are
removed. However, you can specify previous versions to keep.

■ **What is the best way to customize Office Outlook 2003 to work in your messaging environment?**   In the Custom Installation Wizard, you can create or modify Office Outlook 2003 profiles, set up new e-mail accounts, or configure Office Outlook 2003 to work with an Exchange server.

■ **Do you plan to use Microsoft Office Application Error Reporting (Dw.exe) to report installation failures to Microsoft?**   This feature is turned off by default when you create an administrative installation point. To turn it back on, set the SETUPDW property to True before users install Office 2003 Editions.

When you're planning your customizations, one of the best tools to use is the Custom Installation Wizard. This is your primary customization tool, so it's an obvious place to start. Think of it as taking a dry run through the wizard. Here's how I use it to take an initial stab at a configuration: I step through each and every screen, filling in the blanks and taking screen shots that I can later print. You can even include the screen shots in your planning document. Although the initial settings will likely change, it jump starts the configuration by showing you the possibilities. Spend the majority of your time looking at the settings on the Change Office User Settings screen to get an idea of what you can customize. Also, spend some time looking at the Specify Security Settings screen and the Office Outlook 2003 profile screens.

Each transform (*.mst* file) you create by using the Custom Installation Wizard roughly corresponds to a configuration for one group of users. Document in your deployment plan each unique configuration and its corresponding transform file. For example, if you're deploying two Office 2003 Editions configurations, one for the majority of the organization and one for users who require Office Access 2003, document the transform files for each configuration. If you're also creating a configuration that includes language support for multilingual users, document the name and contents of that transform file.

Removal

When you upgrade to Office 2003 Editions, the Removal Wizard (Offcln.exe) removes unnecessary or obsolete components from previously installed versions of Office and related applications. The wizard components run behind the scenes during Setup, but you can also run the Removal Wizard on its own. You can use the default behavior, which is to remove all previous versions of Office and their components, or you can customize it to remove specific components while leaving others. When planning your deployment, decide which of the following you want to leave on users' computers when you upgrade:

■ Microsoft Word

   ▪ Microsoft Word 2002

   ▪ Microsoft Word 2000

- Microsoft Word 97
- Microsoft Word 95

■ Microsoft Excel

- Microsoft Excel 2002
- Microsoft Excel 2000
- Microsoft Excel 97
- Microsoft Excel 95

■ Microsoft PowerPoint

- Microsoft PowerPoint 2002
- Microsoft PowerPoint 2000
- Microsoft PowerPoint 97
- Microsoft PowerPoint 95

■ Microsoft Outlook

- Microsoft Outlook 2002
- Microsoft Outlook 2000
- Microsoft Outlook 97
- Microsoft Outlook 98

■ Microsoft Access

- Microsoft Access 2002
- Microsoft Access 2000
- Microsoft Access 97
- Microsoft Access 95

■ Microsoft Publisher

- Microsoft Publisher 2002
- Microsoft Publisher 2000
- Microsoft Publisher 97
- Microsoft Publisher 95
- Microsoft Publisher 3

■ Microsoft Multilingual User Interface Packs
■ Obsolete Microsoft Office Files

Features

When you install Office 2003 Editions from an administrative installation point or compressed CD image, you can determine which applications and features are installed on users' computers, including how and when features are installed. When running Office 2003 Setup interactively, users can choose which applications and features are installed by selecting options from the feature tree that Office 2003 Setup displays. Features can be installed in any of the following states:

- **Run From My Computer**   Office 2003 Setup copies files and writes registry entries and shortcuts associated with the feature to the user's hard disk, and the application or feature runs locally.

- **Run All From My Computer**   Same as Run From My Computer, except that all child features belonging to the feature are also set to this state.

- **Run From Network**   Office 2003 Setup leaves components for the feature on the administrative installation point, and the feature is run from there. The Run From Network option is available only when users install from an uncompressed administrative image.

- **Run All From Network**   Same as Run From Network, except that all child features belonging to the feature are also set to this state. Note that some child features do not support Run From Network; these child features are installed on the local computer.

- **Installed On First Use**   Office 2003 Setup leaves components for the feature and all its child features on the administrative installation point until the user first attempts to use the feature, at which time the components are automatically copied to the local hard disk. If the user installed from a compressed CD image with the local installation source enabled, the components are installed from the local source. Note that some child features do not support Installed On First Use; these features are set to Not Available.

- **Not Available**   The components for the feature and all of the child features belonging to the feature are not installed on the computer. Users can change this installation state during Setup or later in maintenance mode.

- **Not Available, Hidden, Locked**   The components for the feature are not installed, and the feature does not appear in the feature tree during Office 2003 Setup—nor can users install it by changing the state of the parent feature or by calling Windows Installer directly from the command line.

In addition to setting the installation state, you can hide the feature from the user. Office 2003 Setup does not display hidden features in the feature tree when users run Office 2003 Setup interactively; instead, the feature is installed behind the scenes according to the installation state that you have specified. When you hide a feature, all the child features belonging to the feature are also hidden. The best use of hiding features is to simplify the feature tree for users. For example, you might hide the Office Tools branch of the feature tree so that users do not have to decide which tools they need. Only the tools that you select are installed.

Installing features on demand or running features over the network is not always efficient. Both of these installation states require a fast connection and reliable access to the administrative installation point on the network—which laptop users in the field might not always have. The Custom Installation Wizard includes two options on the Set Feature Installation States page that disable these installation states and help ensure that users do not reset features to these states during Setup or in maintenance mode (you can apply these settings to entire branches of the feature tree):

- **Disable Run From Network**   When you select a feature in the feature tree and then select this check box, users are prevented from setting the feature to run from the network. The installation state does not appear in the list of options during initial Office 2003 Setup or in maintenance mode.

- **Disable Installed On First Use**   When you select a feature in the feature tree and then select this check box, users are prevented from setting the feature to be installed on first use. The installation state does not appear in the list of options during initial Setup or in maintenance mode.

To make an Office 2003 Editions installation more efficient, Office 2003 Setup automatically migrates feature installation states. When you upgrade to Office 2003 Editions, Office 2003 Setup detects and matches feature installation states from the previous version. Also, when you install MUI Packs from the Office 2003 Multilingual User Interface Pack, Setup matches the feature installation states specified for the core version of Office. Last, when you install Office 2003 Editions under Microsoft Windows Terminal Services, Setup applies the most efficient installation state for each feature. You can override this behavior by preventing feature state migration for any feature or entire branches of the feature tree.

By using the Custom Installation Wizard, you can make these choices for users ahead of time. When users run Office 2003 Setup interactively, the installation states that you specify in the transform (*.mst* file) appear as the default selections. When you run Office 2003 Setup quietly, your choices determine how the features are installed. The best way to plan feature installation states, assuming that you're not going to accept the default states, is to view the feature installation states in the Custom Installation Wizard. I recommend that you make as few changes as possible to the default feature installation states. I tend to configure feature installation states at the higher levels of the tree, such as to prevent the installation of an entire program, and then configure just a few lower-level feature installation states in order to meet specific deployment requirements.

Settings

Office 2003 Editions applications are highly customizable. Users can change how Office 2003 Editions functions by setting options or adding custom templates or tools. For example, a sales department can create a custom template for invoices or a custom dictionary with industry-specific terms. Users can change everything from toolbar layouts to the default file format for saving documents. Most of these user-defined settings are recorded as values in the registry.

As an administrator, you can customize user-defined settings and distribute a standard Microsoft Office 2003 configuration to all the users in your organization by using the Profile Wizard to capture settings in a profile settings file (*.ops* file). When you add the *.ops* file to a transform (*.mst* file), your customized settings are included when Office 2003 Editions is installed on client computers. The Custom Installation Wizard also allows you to customize user-defined settings directly in the transform by using the Change Office User Settings screen. You can set user options and add or modify registry entries. You can even add the *.ops* to a transform and run it separately to distribute new default settings. When Office 2003 Editions is installed, your customizations modify values in the registry, and your settings appear as the defaults on users' computers. Last, you can configure specific registry settings by using the Add/Remove Registry Entries screen. You must know the key, value name, value type, and data for each setting.

Of the three methods for customizing settings available (Change Office User Settings, *.ops* files, and Add/Remove Registry Entries), I prefer using the Change Office User Settings screen most. Making changes to these settings is very easy because I can open the transform, edit them, and then save the new transform. My next preference is the Add/Remove Registry Entries screen. You can easily edit these values by using Custom Installation Wizard. Using *.ops* files is my least-preferred method because you can't edit these files, and they contain more settings than the small handful that you might want to deploy. For example, if you use an *.ops* file to configure the location of workgroup templates for Office 2003 Editions, you're also deploying hundreds of other settings because *.ops* files are essentially a snapshot of the Office 2003 Editions user profile (registry settings and files). That includes window positions, and so on. This method is too imprecise for my liking. When you're choosing the methods you'll use to customize settings, consider these points (Table 4-3 compares the different methods):

- **How extensively you want to configure Office 2003**   You can create a custom configuration for all of Office 2003 Editions or you can preset just a few key options.

- **How complex your deployment scenarios are**   You can distribute the same custom settings to all the users in your organization or you can configure Office 2003 Editions applications differently to meet the needs of different groups of users.

- **How and when you deploy Office 2003 applications** If you are staging your Office 2003 Editions deployment, you can customize only the applications that you are installing at a given time. Or, if you have already deployed Office 2003 Editions, you can distribute a standard configuration to all users.

- **Whether you want to enforce your custom settings** Settings that you distribute through a transform (*.mst* file) or Office 2003 Editions profile settings file (*.ops* file) appear to users as the default settings—but users can choose different options for themselves. By contrast, using Office 2003 Editions policies ensures that your settings are always applied.

Table 4-3 Customization Methods

Scenario	Method	Tool
Distribute a standard default Office 2003 configuration.	Add an *.ops* file to a transform.	Profile Wizard and Custom Installation Wizard (Customize Default Application Settings page)
Set just a few options or adjust your Office 2003 configuration without recreating the *.ops* file.	Add user settings to a transform.	Custom Installation Wizard (Change Office User Settings page)
Set default security levels.	Specify security settings in a transform.	Custom Installation Wizard (Specify Office Security Settings page)
Distribute a default Microsoft Office Outlook 2003 profile.	Specify Outlook settings in a transform.	Custom Installation Wizard (Outlook: Customize Default Profile page)
Specify settings that are not captured in an *.ops* file.	Add registry values to a transform.	Custom Installation Wizard (Add/Remove Registry Entries page)
Distribute a default Office 2003 configuration, but store one or more *.ops* files separately from the *.mst* file.	Run the Profile Wizard during Setup.	Profile Wizard and Custom Installation Wizard (Add Installations And Run Programs page)
Preserve users' custom settings from a previous version instead of specifying new default settings.	Allow Setup to migrate settings from a previous version of Office.	Default Setup behavior
Set unique options for Microsoft Office 2003 Multilingual User Interface Packs or other chained packages.	Specify settings in the transform applied to the chained package.	Custom Installation Wizard and Setup settings file (Setup.ini)

Table 4-3   Customization Methods

Scenario	Method	Tool
Distribute a default Office 2003 configuration that overrides individual users' settings.	Run the Profile Wizard as a standalone tool after Office is installed.	Profile Wizard
Modify user settings after Office is installed.	Distribute a configuration maintenance file (.*cmw* file) after Office is installed.	Custom Maintenance Wizard
Prevent users from modifying the options you set.	Set Office policies.	Group Policy snap-in
Customize Microsoft Office Visio 2003 application settings and user-defined options.	Set policies or run the Profile Wizard as a standalone tool after Office is installed.	Group Policy snap-in or Profile Wizard

Files

Office 2003 Setup allows you to add your own files to the installation. You can deploy corporate templates, images, custom dictionaries, custom applications, or other files along with Office 2003 Editions. In your deployment plan, list the files that you want to include in your Office 2003 Editions configuration and indicate where they go. You might also provide reviewers with copies of those files.

Shortcuts

Shortcuts for Office 2003 Editions applications are stored in a new subfolder: Microsoft Office. Shortcuts to Office tools are stored in a subfolder in the same location: Microsoft Office\Microsoft Office Tools. If you upgrade to Office 2003 Editions but retain some applications from a previous version, the shortcuts for the applications you have chosen to keep, and those for any shared components, remain in their original location. Shortcuts to the new versions of the applications and tools appear in the new location.

By using the Custom Installation Wizard, you can customize the shortcuts that Office 2003 Setup creates for Office 2003 Editions applications and files. You can control which shortcuts are installed, and you can also specify which folder a shortcut is stored in and which command-line options to use with a shortcut. While planning, decide whether you want to change the name or location of any shortcut. Also decide whether you want to remove any shortcuts. Table 4-4 describes the default shortcuts and their locations. I like to leave the shortcuts in their default location, but I remove the 2003 from each shortcut name so that they fit better when users pin them to the Start menu.

Table 4-4   Office 2003 Editions Shortcuts

Shortcut	Location	Default
Digital Certificate for VBA Projects	\<StartMenu\Programs\>\Microsoft Office\Microsoft Office Tools	Installed
Microsoft Clip Organizer	\<StartMenu\Programs\>\Microsoft Office\Microsoft Office Tools	Installed
Microsoft Office 2003 Language Settings	\<StartMenu\Programs\>\Microsoft Office\Microsoft Office Tools	Installed
Microsoft Office 2003 Save My Settings Wizard	\<StartMenu\Programs\>\Microsoft Office\Microsoft Office Tools	Installed
Microsoft Office Access Snapshot Viewer	\<StartMenu\Programs\>\Microsoft Office\Microsoft Office Tools	Installed
Microsoft Office Application Recovery	\<StartMenu\Programs\>\Microsoft Office\Microsoft Office Tools	Installed
Microsoft Office Document Imaging	\<StartMenu\Programs\>\Microsoft Office\Microsoft Office Tools	Installed
Microsoft Office Document Scanning	\<StartMenu\Programs\>\Microsoft Office\Microsoft Office Tools	Installed
Microsoft Office Picture Manager	\<StartMenu\Programs\>\Microsoft Office\Microsoft Office Tools	Installed
Microsoft Office Access 2003	\<StartMenu\Programs\>\Microsoft Office	Installed
Microsoft Office Excel 2003	\<StartMenu\Programs\>\Microsoft Office	Installed
Microsoft Office InfoPath 2003	\<StartMenu\Programs\>\Microsoft Office	Installed
Microsoft Office Outlook 2003	\<StartMenu\Programs\>\Microsoft Office	Installed
Microsoft Office PowerPoint 2003	\<StartMenu\Programs\>\Microsoft Office	Installed
Microsoft Office Publisher 2003	\<StartMenu\Programs\>\Microsoft Office	Installed
Microsoft Office Word 2003	\<StartMenu\Programs\>\Microsoft Office	Installed
New Office Document	\<StartMenu\>	Not Installed
Open Office Document	\<StartMenu\>	Not Installed

Distribution

You can always run Office 2003 Setup interactively to install Office 2003 Editions or allow users to run Office 2003 Setup interactively. However, by using command-line options or setting values for Office 2003 Setup properties in the Setup.ini settings file or in a transform (*.mst* file), you can customize the way Office 2003 Setup installs Office 2003 Editions throughout your organization. Make and document the following decisions in your deployment plan:

- When you distribute Office 2003 Editions, you can determine how much of the Office 2003 Setup user interface is displayed to users. You can allow users to interact fully with Office 2003 Setup and make choices that differ from the defaults you specify, or you can run Office 2003 Setup silently so that your configuration of Office 2003 Setup is installed with no opportunities to make changes. You can even set different display settings for different portions of the installation process. The following are your choices:

  - **None**   No user interface is displayed; Office 2003 Editions is installed silently.

  - **Basic**   Only simple progress indicators, error messages, and a completion message are displayed.

  - **Reduced**   Full progress indicators and error messages are displayed, but Office 2003 Setup collects no information from the user.

  - **Full**   All dialog boxes and messages are displayed to the user, and the user can enter information during the Setup process.

- Both Office 2003 Setup and Windows Installer generate log files during the installation process. You can't set options for the Office 2003 Setup log file; however, Windows Installer allows you to set a number of logging options that apply to each package that it installs during Office 2003 Setup. Any logging options you set apply to all log files created by Windows Installer during the Office 2003 Editions installation; you cannot specify unique logging options for a chained package.

- When Office 2003 Editions is installed from the product CD or a compressed CD image, Office 2003 Setup automatically copies required installation files to a hidden folder on the local computer. Windows Installer uses this local installation source to install Office 2003 Editions, and the local source remains available for repairing, reinstalling, or updating Office 2003 Editions later on. Users can install features on demand or run Office 2003 Setup in maintenance mode to add new features, even when they do not have access to the original source. You can customize the installation source as follows:

  - Specify a different drive for the local installation source.

  - Enable or disable local caching.

  - Give users the option to delete the local installation source at the end of Setup.

In addition to customizing how Office 2003 Setup runs, you must plan to run Office 2003 Setup with elevated privileges. Users in the Users and Power Users groups can't install Office 2003 Editions. Only members of the Administrators group can install the product. Chapter 23, "Software Installation," describes some strategies for dealing with this issue. And some distribution methods, such as disk imaging, Group Policy, and SMS, don't have this issue.

Best Practices

The following are best practices for planning an Office 2003 Editions configuration:

- **Separate managed settings from unmanaged settings**   Configure managed Office 2003 Editions by using policies. Settings that you configure by using the Profile Wizard or Custom Installation Wizard are only defaults.

- **Document settings and assign to a method**   Document each and every setting in your Office 2003 Editions configuration and assign each to a deployment method (Profile Wizard, Custom Installation Wizard, and so on). For each setting, indicate at which point in the process you will configure that setting. You can use the file Settings.xls to document these settings. Settings.xls is on this book's companion CD in the Aids folder.

Chapter 5

Office Migration

Migration planning is the least understood and often the most complex part of deploying Microsoft Office 2003. This chapter describes the issues, technologies, and techniques for migrating from earlier versions of Office, particularly Microsoft Office 97 and earlier. It also includes scripts that you can use to discover your migration issues.

Checklist

- Do you know which versions of Office users are running? See Chapter 1, "Deployment Plan," for help inventorying your environment. Also see the section "Network Inventory," later in this chapter.

- Do you know which groups of users share documents with which other groups of users? Do they share documents one way or two ways? See the section "Phased Rollouts" for more information.

- Do users store their Office 2003 documents in a central network location, such as a redirected My Documents folder or home folder? See Chapter 3, "Windows Configuration," for more information about folder redirection.

- Do you have an inventory of the third-party and internally built Office-based programs and customizations? See Chapter 1 for more information about inventorying your environment.

- Have you tested each third-party and internally built Office-based solution for compatibility with Office 2003 Editions? See the section "Solution Migration," later in this chapter, for more information.

Migration Issues

Deploying Office 2003 Editions would be straightforward if it weren't for migration. You'd simply install Office 2003 Editions and move on to the next computer; however, users have documents, databases, and macros that might not work in the newer version of Office. This is primarily true if you're migrating from Office 97 or earlier. Migrating large numbers of existing documents—including corporate templates, user templates, and user-created documents—from earlier versions of Office is complex. Your organization might have tens of thousands of existing documents that it must maintain across versions of Office.

Also, organizations must migrate their Visual Basic for Applications (VBA) or Component Object Model (COM)–based LOB (Line of Business) applications and customizations. LOB applications and customized add-ins, whether created internally or purchased from a third party, often delay or entirely prevent Office 2003 Editions migrations due to their mission-critical importance to the business. In other words, it's not uncommon for an entire migration to derail because a third-party add-in doesn't work with the latest version of Office. Risks (whether real or perceived) related to add-ins failing in a new version of Office require extensive testing before migration.

Other issues affecting your migration plans include the following:

- Global IT logistics, which is how you will manage and maintain a worldwide Office 2003 Editions deployment.

- Industry and organizational requirements. Organizations such as the Food and Drug Administration (FDA), the legal community, and other organizations enforce strict document specifications. You must determine how the latest version of Office affects these requirements.

- Compatibility between the different versions of Office. The file formats changed after Microsoft Office 95. Office 97, Office 2000, Office XP, and Office 2003 Editions have more compatible file formats, though—with the exception that the file format changed between Microsoft Access 97 and Access 2000.

- Object model changes between different versions of Office. These changes can break existing LOB applications and customizations. Changes to the way features work might require end-user training and could also break customizations.

You can address compatibility challenges after you understand the differences between the version of Office you're using now and Office 2003 Editions.

> **More Info**   The following section, "Versions Compatibility," contains more detailed information about this topic.

■ Negative experiences from earlier Office migrations. Prior negative experiences affect users, IT professionals, and decision makers and can include concerns about risks associated with users losing productivity and costs in migrating to a newer version of Office. Such experiences affect decision-making, adoption, and even attitudes moving forward. Although prior experience provides valuable input into the process, it doesn't dictate future success or failure.

> **More Info**   See "Microsoft Office 2003 Editions Resource Kit" at *http://www.microsoft.com/office/ork* for more information about planning your migration to Office 2003 Editions. Also, see the white paper called "Microsoft Office XP Migration Blueprint" at *http://www.microsoft.com/technet/prodtechnol/office/officexp/deploy/migratbp.mspx* for more information about migration planning for Office 2003 Editions. Although this white paper talks specifically about Office XP, it applies equally well to Office 2003 Editions.

Versions Compatibility

Most of the compatibility issues between Office 97 and Office XP or Office 2003 Editions are associated with changes to the object model, virus scanner interoperability bugs, automation failures, and legitimate bugs. The following four sections describe all four topics in more detail.

Microsoft provides the "Microsoft Office 97 to Office 2003 Migration Issues" white paper (also known as the 97-03delta white paper), which is part of the Microsoft Office 2003 Editions Resource Kit. This document shows the differences between Office 97 and Office 2003 Editions at a very detailed level. It describes what users might see differently in the user interface (UI) and what they might experience as a possible bug, depending on their usage of the various Office 2003 Editions programs. The white paper does reference numerous Knowledge Base articles that provide confirmation that the more serious bugs are being dealt with and were corrected in various service packs. Also, it provides a summary of the most likely migration issues that an IT professional might encounter during and after a migration of Office 97 to Office 2003 Editions.

> **More Info**   Microsoft publishes the "Microsoft Office 97 to Microsoft Office 2003 Migration Issues" white paper on its Web site at *http://www.microsoft.com/office/ork/2003/journ/97-03DeltaWPIntro.htm*. This white paper is the ultimate reference for uncovering any problems you're likely to encounter when migrating from Microsoft Office 97 to Office 2003 Editions. It includes 78 pages of known issues, their descriptions, and links to Knowledge Base articles that contain more information. Although reading this chapter is a start, it does not replace the migration issues white paper. For your convenience, I included this white paper on this book's companion CD in the Extras\chap05 folder. The file name is 97-03Delta.doc.

Object Model Changes

The differences between the Office 97 and Office 2003 Editions object models are significant and require research for developers to properly update legacy programs for Office 2003 Editions. Developers can help reduce potential migration issues in businesses with large-scale customizations by understanding these issues.

Over time, improvements to Office applications caused the necessary upgrading of code modules and coding techniques. These updates, in some cases, force changes as to how legacy custom macros (any custom code created under an earlier version of Office and intended to be used in a newer version) interact with the newer object models of the Office applications they reference. Generally speaking, custom applications from older versions of Office work well with newer versions of the object model, but in some cases they do require updating. Most problems occur for new custom solutions created under a new version of the object model and the attempted use of these solutions on older versions of Office applications in which the object model interfaces did not exist. Therefore, new solutions, intended to be used on older versions of Office, can be problematic. The basic solution is to develop these custom solutions by using the oldest version of Office that the solution is intended to be used on (making sure only the object model library for that version of Office is installed on the development computer).

For custom applications developed on newer versions of Office, when the need to have backward compatibility is necessary, a change in binding techniques to problematic objects is necessary. (Some changes have required significant reworking of custom applications.) There are three basic methods of binding to objects within Office 2003 Editions programs: early binding, DISPID, and late binding.

With new coding paradigms, it is now recommended to use late binding with some objects. Doing so helps you avoid issues that might arise from design changes within some objects that no longer resolve the older interfaces to the newer interfaces of these objects. In some cases, early binding may actually slow a custom application down due to problems resolving the v-table and, therefore, is worth the effort to modify existing legacy applications to a late-binding paradigm for some objects.

Unfortunately, the specific change to some of the object models in Office 2003 Editions forced a significant change to how some custom macro solutions that are developed with a newer object model must interact with older Office objects. Late binding avoids the majority of these issues. Several Knowledge Base articles address this issue and are described in the 97-03delta white paper to help with any problems programmers might be experiencing. Some legacy custom solutions that are running extremely slowly, fail, spawn errors, or appear unreliable may actually require a change with regard to how objects are bound.

These issues are relevant only when attempting to run custom solutions against object models older than the object model the solutions were created from. For instance, a solution created for Office Word 2003 might not run properly with requests to objects that use early binding on Word 97 because of the changes in the interfaces of the objects. However, it is very likely that the custom solution will work just fine if it was created under Word 97 and used with Office Word 2003. The reason is that the legacy interfaces (which might be hidden in the newer version of the object) will probably be found, provided that the custom solution is not recompiled under the Office Word 2003 library if it was created from the Word 97 library.

Virus Scanner Problems

Some virus-checking software can cause Office 2003 Editions applications to slow unexpectedly. In most cases, the vendor supplying the virus-checking software can provide updated versions of their software, and you can typically obtain and install these updates by visiting their Web site. However, in some cases, you might need to request a CD. Usually, upgrading to the appropriate version of the virus-checking program eliminates or reduces the effects of slowed applications.

This issue is an important consideration and in some cases can make some custom macro programs almost useless if not corrected. Contact the virus-checking software manufacturer if you have noticed considerable slowing in your applications or custom macros. In most cases, a new version of the program eliminates this slowing. It is also advised to examine the settings of the computer to determine whether the system was optimized.

A Knowledge Base article about system optimization for Word is provided in the Knowledge Base; article 239431 is good for all applications running on a Windows operating system and is an advised read for all administrators.

Automation Failures

Some object model changes have led to automation failure of custom applications, so a thorough review of the object binding techniques used in these applications is recommended. See the Knowledge Base article 247579 for more information about using DISPID binding. When you are automating an Office 2003 Editions application from Visual Basic or Visual C++ and you expect to communicate with more than one version of the application, Microsoft recommends the use of late binding with cached DISPIDs (DISPID binding), or late binding in general, to remain compatible across current and future versions.

Legitimate Bugs

There are legitimate bugs in all software. However, with the advent of new testing methods devised exclusively for Office XP and Office 2003 Editions, fewer serious bugs shipped with either version than with any previous version of Office. In addition, service releases addressed many known issues raised to Microsoft through the Office 2003 Editions error-reporting features. This feature is a defining tool in the way Office XP and Office 2003 Editions programs are developed and how they are updated for service releases. The major benefit is the elimination of almost all memory leaks and a reduced turnaround time from recognition of a bug to a fix available in a service release.

Microsoft provides the Office 2003 Editions Administrative Updates Web site at *http://www.microsoft.com/office/ork/updates/2003/default.htm*. Check this Web site frequently for updates, which include fixes for known problems.

Network Inventory

This book's companion CD contains the script offdocs.wsf, which helps automate the process of locating documents created by earlier versions of Office in your environment. To use this script, you must also install Dsofile.exe, which is also on CD, on each client. Both are in the Scripts folder. The following shows the syntax of this script, which you must run on each client computer, and Table 5-1 describes each option:

```
offdocs.wsf [/?] path [/L value] [/A] [/Q]
```

Table 5-1   Offdocs.wsf Command-Line Options

Option	Description
/?	Displays help and usage information.
path	Specifies the path to search for documents created by Office 95 and databases created in Access 97. This can be a UNC path. If no path is specified, the script scans all of the computer's local drives.

Table 5-1   Offdocs.wsf Command-Line Options

Option	Description
/L:value	Logs the results to the log file specified by **value**.
/A	Appends output to the log file specified by **value**.
/Q	Suppresses all output.

The following are notes about using the script offdocs.wsf:

- You must use the /l command-line option with the script offdocs.wsf or use Cscript.exe as the host.

- This script tests Excel and Word documents using the custom DSOFile.dll's *DSOleFile.PropertyReader* class and looking at the string returned from the *Version* property; an Access database is checked by opening an ADO connection to it and checking its *DBMS Version* property.

- If a Word or Excel document explicitly has a version of 97/2000 (which also applies to Office XP and Office 2003 Editions documents), it is recognized as a post–Office 95 document; if it has an explicit 6/95 or 5.0/95 string, it is recognized as a known Office 95 document.

- If the version string and application name returned by DSOfile.dll are both blank and if there are no macros found, this is very clearly not an Office document in a sense that matters: it is either a very clean Word document or some other file that happens to have an Office-like extension.

- An Access database is verified by looking at the DBMS version. If it is any number under 4.00, it is known to be an older database format.

- The script offdocs.wsf cannot test Access databases to determine whether or not they contain embedded macros; thus, this property will always show a ? in the log file.

Accessing the properties on some files can cause errors. The script doesn't anticipate all of them, but it logs them:

- **2.**   Returned by some documents that are actually simple text files.

- **57.**   Indicates a document that is seriously damaged; it may have been recovered from a damaged file system. Such documents should be viewed with suspicion.

- **88.**   Permissions problems accessing a file. This implies restrictions on the account accessing the indicated file path and is sometimes due to documents with an orphaned SID as the owner in NTFS.

- **432.**   Occurs for some files saved from 16-bit versions of Word.
- **Permission Errors.**   These will typically occur only for Access databases that are password-protected.

On the Resource Kit CD   The script offdocs.wsf is on this book's companion CD in the Scripts folder. To use this script, you must also install Dsofile.exe, which is also on the CD in the Scripts folder.

Document Conversion

This section describes the resources available for converting documents from earlier versions of Office to Office 2003 Editions. It also includes information about converting WordPerfect documents to Office 2003 Editions. Key points to take away from these sections include the following:

- Word, Excel, and PowerPoint in Office 97, Office 2000, Office XP, and Office 2003 Editions share the same file format and thus don't require conversion to use earlier versions of those documents with Office XP or Office 2003 Editions.

- Office XP and Office 2003 Editions can open individual files created with earlier versions of Office, and they include the Batch Conversion Wizard for converting multiple documents at a time.

- You can deploy the Office Converter Pack to convert files in formats that Office 2003 Editions doesn't natively support.

More Info   Download Office Converter Pack from *http://www.microsoft.com /office/ork/2003/tools/BoxA07.htm*.

More Info   Powerlan OfficeConverter is a product that comes highly recommend by my customers. OfficeConverter can convert legacy Office documents to Office 2003 Editions file formats. It can upgrade your Access databases. OfficeConverter also provides technology for automating the conversion of documents in bulk. For more information about OfficeConverter, see *http://www.officeconverter.com*.

Office

A key resource for converting documents from earlier versions of Office to Office 2003 Editions is the "Microsoft Office XP and File Sharing in a Heterogeneous Office Environment" white paper. It describes the different file formats; examines file migration and coexistence strategies; defines the information-sharing options that are available; and suggests additional resources. The paper further describes the different file formats for each program in each version of Office and outlines how to prepare for the migration process when you have different combinations of versions. Last, it describes strategies for allowing users of different versions to share documents.

Key Knowledge Base articles that aid in the process of converting documents to Office 2003 Editions include the following:

- **Word.** "WD2002: What's New in Word 2002?" (Q288725)
- **Excel.** "XL2002: List of Supported File Formats in Microsoft Excel 2002." (Q291051)
- **PowerPoint.** "PPT2002: Converting Corel 9 Presentations to PowerPoint Format." (Q291873)

Office 2003 Editions provides filters for file formats from earlier versions of Office. Thus, to convert documents created with earlier versions of Office, simply open the document in the appropriate program and then save it using the newer file format. Office 2003 Editions provides the Batch Conversion Wizard to convert multiple documents at one time. To start the wizard, choose New on the File menu; and in the New Document task pane, click On My Computer. Next, click the Other Documents tab and double-click Batch Conversion Wizard. If you need support for file formats that Office 2003 Editions doesn't support natively, deploy and use the Office Converter Pack.

More Info   See "Office XP and File Sharing in a Heterogeneous Office Environment" at *http://www.microsoft.com/technet/prodtechnol/office /officexp/maintain/fileshar.mspx* for more information about sharing Office 2003 Editions files in a mixed environment. Although this white paper specifically addresses Office XP, it applies equally well to Office 2003 Editions.

WordPerfect

Office Word 2003 doesn't convert files directly from WordPerfect 7.0 or 8.0. Both versions of WordPerfect support alternative file formats that Word can open, however. The default file format for WordPerfect 7.0 is WordPerfect 6.0, for example, and Office Word 2003 can convert files saved in that format. The default file format for WordPerfect 8.0 is WordPerfect 6/7/8, so Office Word 2003 can convert files saved in that format. The Knowledge Base article Q212379 ("WD2000: How to Convert Word-Perfect 6.x Data Files and Address Books") describes how to convert WordPerfect files to Word.

Here's how to convert multiple WordPerfect files to Word:

1. Place the documents you want to convert in a single folder.

2. On the File menu, click New.

3. In the New Document task pane, under Templates, click On My Computer.

4. Click the Other Documents tab and double-click the Batch Conversion Wizard.

5. Select either WordPerfect 5.x or 6.x from Convert From Another Format To Word.

The following Knowledge Base articles describe issues you might encounter with converting WordPerfect documents to Word:

- **291312 ("WD2002: Limitations of Converting WordPerfect 5.x Documents").** This article contains a table that lists features that are not completely converted, that are not supported on one product or the other, or that require some comment. For best results converting to and from Office Word 2003, use the WordPerfect 5.<x> converter shipped with Office Word 2003.

- **291451 ("WD2002: WordPerfect File Contains Garbled Text When Opened in Word").** When you attempt to open a WordPerfect file in Office Word 2003, and the file has an extension other than *.doc* or *.wpd*, Word might unexpectedly open the file in text-only format.

- **210396 ("OFF2000: Descriptions and Limitations of Graphics Filters Included with Microsoft Office").** This article includes WordPerfect graphics import and export filters topics and the WordPerfect graphics import filter limitations.

There is no WordPerfect macro conversion, but most macros were used to format text. You can insert them into a WordPerfect file and then convert the file and make AutoText entries from the formatted text to provide replacement functionality for those macros with little time and work involved.

Database Conversion

Potentially the most technical and complex part of the migration process is converting Access databases from older versions to Office Access 2003. A key resource for converting Access databases is the "Microsoft Access 2002 Conversion" white paper, which contains essential information for converting Access 2.0, Access 95, and Access 97 to Office Access 2003. Another essential resource is the Office 2003 Editions Resource Kit.

Key points to keep in mind when converting databases to Office Access 2003 include the following:

- As soon as you convert a database to Office Access 2003, you cannot open that database by using earlier versions of Access. However, Office Access 2003 does allow you to convert a database back to Access 97 or an Access 2000 format.

- Although you can enable a database from an earlier version of Access without converting it to Office Access 2003, you cannot use Office Access 2003 to change the design of any objects in that database. You can't modify any of the objects in an Access 97 or earlier database version, nor can you add objects. But you can modify the data that is stored in the tables.

- When you open a database in Office Access 2003 that was created in Access 2000, you can make some design changes without converting the database because both Access 2000 and Office Access 2003 use the Microsoft Jet database engine version 4.0 for Jet database formats.

Here's how to enable a database created with an earlier version of Access:

1. On the File menu, choose Open.

2. Choose the database you want to enable, and then click Open.

3. In the Convert/Open Database dialog box, click Open Database.

Office Access 2003 enables the database without making any permanent changes to it. An enabled database can still be opened with the original version of Access that was used to create it.

Coexistence

You should convert databases to the Office Access 2003 file format only if all users have upgraded to Access 2000, Access 2002, or Access 2003 and if you have been successfully using the file in the Access 2000 file format. If all users have upgraded to Office Access 2003, you can develop an application in the Office Access 2003 file format without having to make sure that any object, method, property, or function you use is also available in Access 2000. After all users have upgraded to Office Access 2003, you can change the default file format by using the following methods:

- Using the user interface (choose Options on the Tools menu, click the Advanced tab, and then select Access 2002–2003 in the Default File Format list box).

- Setting the registry value for the default file format: HKEY_CURRENT_USER \Software\Microsoft\Office\11.0\Access\Settings\Default File Format. The following are valid values:

  - 9. Access 2000 file format

  - 10. Access 2002 file format

    Until all users have upgraded to Office Access 2003, you must provide a way to allow users to access shared databases. If your Access database is a multiuser (shared) database, and all users cannot upgrade to Access 2000 or later at the same time, you can split the database so that it is a front-end/back-end application. You can then have different versions of the front end connected to the back end, which remains unaltered. Users of Access 2000 or later can use a converted version of the front end and thereby take advantage of new features.

> **More Info**   For more information about splitting Access databases into front-end/back-end applications, see the topic "About Using an Access File with Multiple Versions of Access" in Office Access 2003 Help.

Also, you can prevent users from accidentally converting older databases to the Office Access 2003 file format by using policies. Use Group Policy or System Policy. See "Managing Users' Configuration by Policy" in the Office 2003 Editions Resource Kit. Enable the policy *Do Not Prompt To Convert Older Databases* policy, which prevents Office Access 2003 from prompting users to convert earlier databases to the new file format.

Conversion

Unless you enabled the *Do Not Prompt To Convert Older Databases* policy, Office Access 2003 prompts users to convert individual database files. You can programmatically convert multiple databases to Office Access 2003, though, and use the *ConvertAccessProject* method to convert databases to the format that you specify. A second method uses the *Shell* function to run Msaccess.exe with the **/convert** switch. See the Knowledge Base article 304318 ("ACC2002: How to Programmatically Convert Multiple Access Databases") for more information.

Common Issues

The following list contains important points to keep in mind while migrating database files to Office Access 2003:

- **Size of an enabled Access database.** Your Access database might increase in size when you enable it because the Visual Basic for Applications project must store information in the format of each version. In other words, if you multienable a database, the Visual Basic for Applications project is stored multiple times, which causes the database to increase in size.

- **Compilation errors in an enabled Access database.** If you enable your Access 97 or earlier database on a computer that has never had the earlier version installed, you may receive errors when you try to compile Data Access Objects (DAO) because Office Access 2003 doesn't install the Jet 2.5/3.5 compatibility library and might not be able to compile code that uses syntax that is specific to the earlier versions of the DAO library.

- **New style of toolbars and menu bars.** Access 97 and later versions support a new style of toolbars and menu bars. When you enable a database, custom toolbars are converted to the new style, but the converted toolbars and menus are not saved. Custom menu bars are interpreted as the new style menu bar, but the menu bar macros are not converted and continue to be supported.

- **Converting databases with many code or class modules (or both).** When you convert an Access database that has many forms, reports, and modules, the conversion process fails with a "Can't Create Any More Class Modules" or an "Out Of Memory" error. Office Access 2003 has a limit of 1000 Visual Basic for Application modules; Microsoft Access 97 has a limit of 1024. If you use lightweight forms and reports (with the *HasModule* property set to *No*) in Office Access 2003, you greatly reduce the impact of this limitation.

Best Practices

The following are best practices for migrating databases to Office Access 2003:

- Always work with a local copy of the file when you convert a database. You can reduce the chance of corrupting your file during the conversion process because of a network communication problem if you work on your local drive.

- Before you convert a database, it is also a good idea to compact the database in the earlier version to remove outdated information from the system tables.

- Earlier versions of Access allowed you to use reserved words in or as object names. Office Access 2003 no longer allows you to use reserved words in or as an object name.

Security Migration

Security is a migration issue because earlier versions of Office did not implement code signing, and many businesses did not even use code signing in Office 2000. Due to the obvious increase in threats, such as macro viruses, leveraging the Office 2003 Editions security features is paramount. Doing so means that you must plan for deploying trusted sources along with Office 2003 Editions, enforcing high security through policies, and preventing users from adding to the list of trusted sources. The ultimate resource for securing Office 2003 Editions is the "Security" chapter in the Office 2003 Editions Resource Kit. The URL is *http://www.microsoft.com/technet /prodtechnol/office/officexp/maintain/fileshar.mspx.*

Security Policy

Configuring policies to set the security level for each program to high is straightforward. You install the Office 2003 Editions Resource Kit on the server and then create a policy by using the Office 2003 Editions policy templates that set the security level for each program. Likewise, locking the list of trusted sources is straightforward. You use the Resource Kit's Custom Installation Wizard to lock the list. Also, deploying a list of trusted sources is more straightforward in Office 2003 Editions than in Office XP. That's because the Custom Installation Wizard now provides a user interface for deploying trusted sources, so you don't have to rely on registry hacks. See the Office 2003 Editions Resource Kit for step-by-step instructions about all of these tasks.

Office 2000 introduced code signing for VBA macros, and Office 2003 Editions leverages that technology and adds an additional object-model enhancement: *Application.AutomationSecurity.* This property allows macros to choose to open a document and to trigger the appropriate security warning, which is the same as if an end user is manually opening the document. This new property does not affect the behavior when the end user uses the user interface to open files. In this case, this property does not change the settings in the Security dialog box (on the Tools menu, choose Macro and then click Security to open the Security dialog box). The following are the *MsoAutomationSecurity* constants that you can choose from:

- ■ *msoAutomationSecurityLow.*   Current default, macros are enabled.

- ■ *msoAutomationSecurityForceDisable.*   Disable macros by default.

- ■ *msoAutomationSecurityByUI.*   Use the security value that is currently set in the security UI for each of the applications.

Solution Migration

The following sections describe migrating VBA and COM add-ins.

VBA Add-Ins

The default location for VBA add-ins changed in Office 2000, Office XP, and Office 2003 Editions. Placing add-ins in these locations will result in per-user availability of the add-ins. The locations listed below contain VBA add-ins:

- %USERPROFILE%\Application Data\Microsoft\Word\Startup
- %USERPROFILE%\Application Data\Microsoft\Excel\XLStart

The original add-in paths are still available, and note that it is not necessary to explicitly set the File Location Startup options for add-ins to load from those paths. The following are per-computer locations:

- C:\Program Files\Microsoft Office\Office11\Startup
- C:\Program Files\Microsoft Office\Office11\XLStart

COM Add-Ins

A COM add-in is a DLL that is specially registered for loading by the Microsoft Office 2003 applications. You can build COM add-ins with any of the Office 2003 Editions programs in Office 2003 Developer Edition. In addition, you can create COM add-ins with Microsoft Visual Basic or Microsoft Visual C++.

> **More Info**   For more information about these tools, see the Microsoft Developer Network (MSDN).

A COM add-in also can be a Microsoft ActiveX *.exe* file for Visual Basic. However, DLLs generally provide better performance. COM add-ins use the Component Object Model that makes it possible for you to create a single add-in that is available to one or many of the Office 2003 Editions programs (Word, Excel, Access, PowerPoint, Outlook, FrontPage, or even the Visual Basic Editor). By developing COM add-ins, you can extend the functionality of your Office 2003 Editions–based applications without adding complexity for users.

Phased Rollouts

During an Office 2003 Editions rollout, a variety of solutions are available to enable users to share documents from version to version of Office. If you're migrating from Office 95 to Office 2003 Editions, for example, these solutions ensure that the users you haven't yet migrated can still exchange information with the users you have migrated.

> **More Info**   The white paper "Microsoft Office XP and File Sharing in a Heterogeneous Office Environment" provides a full treatment of these solutions. This white paper is at *http://www.microsoft.com/technet/prodtechnol /office/officexp/maintain/fileshar.mspx*.

The solutions you choose to use depend on whether users share documents with other groups or not. They'll also depend on whether they share documents one way or two ways; and on whether or not they need to change the documents they're sharing. Groups of users who don't share documents with other departments can be migrated to Office 2003 Editions at any time without adversely affecting their productivity.

If a group of users shares documents with other groups, you must decide whether the recipients need read-only access to those documents or whether they need to be able to edit and return those documents. If they need read-only access to those documents, a larger variety of solutions is available, including file viewers, saving documents as Web pages, and so on. If they need to edit and return documents to the sending group, you should consider restricting both groups to a common file format until both groups are fully migrated to Office 2003 Editions. Also, in order to ensure continuity, you could plan to migrate dependent groups within the same time frame.

Best Practices

The following are best practices for planning an Office 2003 Editions migration:

- Prevent Office Access 2003 from converting databases in older formats by setting the policy *Do Not Prompt To Convert Older Databases*.

- Identify groups of users that share documents two ways (reviewing and editing documents) and then deploy Office 2003 Editions to all users in those related groups together.

- Identify groups of users that share documents one way (reviewing only) and then deploy interim solutions to those groups until you deploy Office 2003 Editions to them.

Part II

Configuring

Chapter 6

Answer Files

Answer files are scripts that you can use to automate the installation of Microsoft Windows XP Professional. They provide automatic responses to the Windows XP Setup prompts so users don't have to interact with the process. This chapter describes how to create answer files and includes sample settings you can use in your own.

Checklist

- Have you identified and planned the settings you need for installing Windows XP Professional? If not, see Chapter 3, "Windows Configuration," and the file dist01.doc on this book's companion CD in the Aids folder.

- Do you need a fully automated setup process, or is technician or user interaction with Windows XP Setup allowed? For issues regarding a fully automated process, see the section "Running Setup Fully Unattended" later in this chapter on page 143.

- Have you planned and created a restricted domain account that can join computers to the domain? For more information, see the section "Join Domain," later in this chapter on page 149.

- Do you need to include additional files, such as device drivers, with the Windows XP Professional source files? If so, see Chapter 7, "Distribution Points," for more information about including them in your distribution point.

- Do you need to run any commands after Setup installs Windows XP Professional? If so, see the section "Run Once" later in this chapter on page 151 and Chapter 11, "Chaining Installations."

Getting Started

Answer files are text files that look like Configuration Settings (*.ini*) files. Answer files have many sections, and each section contains settings. They provide responses for Windows XP Setup, rather than Setup prompting users for the settings. Not only do answer files automate the setup process, they also enable you to configure Windows XP Professional in ways that aren't possible through the user interface. For example, you can change the location of user profiles from C:\Documents and Settings to another location, including a different volume. Importantly, you must use an answer file to automate preinstallation and post-installation tasks.

Unattend.txt is the traditional name for answer files, but I prefer to give names to my answer files that make deciphering their purpose easier. Just make sure you use 8.3 filenames so you can read their names when installing Windows XP Professional using MS-DOS. Also, I don't like to use the *.txt* extension for answer files. I prefer to use the *.sif* file extension, which is the file extension for Setup Information Files, so I can easily differentiate a text file from an answer file. For example, I might have an answer file to install Windows XP Professional on a lab computer called Labprep.sif. You might create different answer files for different departments called Sales.sif, Legal.sif, and so on. Regardless, use descriptive names that help you discern the differences between answer files because you'll grow a collection.

Where do you create and store answer files? In Chapter 7, you learn how to build a Windows XP Professional distribution point that includes custom files, third-party device drivers, and so on. You'll typically store the answer files you create in the distribution points. In fact, I recommend that you store answer files in the parent folder of the OEM folder, which you'll also learn about in Chapter 7. You don't have to have distribution points to use an answer file, though; they can be independent of distribution points. The primary example is that you can use an answer file to install Windows XP Professional from a CD without requiring user interaction. When using answer files independently of distribution points, you can store them anywhere that's convenient. But if you want to use an answer file to automate the installation of Windows XP Professional from an uncustomized product CD, you must put the answer file on a floppy disk and name it Winnt.sif.

You use an answer file to install Windows XP Professional by using the Winnt.exe command-line option */u* or Winnt32.exe command-line option */unattend*. You must also use the */s* or */source* command-line option to specify the location of the Windows XP Professional source files if they are in a different location.

> **More Info**   This chapter doesn't describe how to run Windows XP Setup. But Chapter 13, "Unattended Setup," describes how to run Setup in detail, including how to use answer files to fully automate installation.

Sample Answer File

Listing 6-1 shows a sample answer file (most tend not to be this complicated and so well-documented with comments). This sample is in the file sample.sif on this book's companion CD in the Samples\chap06 folder. You learn more about the settings in this answer file throughout this chapter (see also Appendix D, "Answer File Syntax"). For now, take a note of how I formatted this file. For example, sections begin and end with brackets (*[Unattended]*), and each section contains settings that have the syntax *name=value*. Comments begin with a semicolon (*;*), and Windows XP Setup ignores anything after the semicolon on each line.

> **More Info**   Some of these settings might not make complete sense to you until you read Chapter 7 and Chapter 11.

A description of some of the settings in Listing 6-1 will help you better understand how answer files automate the installation process. The setting `OemSkipEula=Yes` accepts the End User License Agreement on behalf of the organization, skipping it during the installation so users don't have to accept it. And the setting `UnattendMode=ReadOnly` causes Windows XP Setup to prevent users from changing settings that you specify in the answer file. If Setup displays a page that contains settings requiring user input as well as a setting that you specified in the answer file, Setup disables the setting you specified in the answer file while allowing the user to edit the setting that requires user input; otherwise, if you specify all the settings for a page in the answer file, Setup skips the page entirely. Incidentally, both settings, *OemSkipEula* and *UnattendMode*, are in the section *[Unattended]*.

> **More Info**   The section "Specializing Answer Files" later in this chapter on page 145 describes different settings in more detail.

Use this sample as a template for the answer files you create. Although you can use Windows Setup Manager to create answer files (see the section "Setup Manager" later in this chapter on page 139), starting with a template is often easier, particularly after you create a library of specialized answer files from which you can assemble bits and pieces to build new answer files in just a few minutes.

> **More Info**   Appendix D, "Answer File Syntax," is a reference that describes the most common settings for answer files. Appendix D describes the majority of settings that I use throughout this book. For information about answer file settings you don't find in Appendix D, see "Microsoft Windows Preinstallation Reference," which is the file Ref.chm in Deploy.cab, and "Microsoft Windows Corporate Deployment Tools User's Guide," which is the file Deploy.chm in Deploy.cab, for more information about building Windows XP Professional answer files. Deploy.cab is on the Windows product CD in Support\Tools.

Listing 6-1   Sample.sif

```
[Unattended]
    DriverSigningPolicy=Ignore
    FileSystem=ConvertNTFS

; Replace OemFilesPath with path to the $OEM$ folder:

    OemFilesPath=\\Server\Share\win2002.pro\OEM1\$OEM$

; Replace OemPnPDriversPath with the path of the third-party
; device drivers (separate folders with a semicolon):

    OemPnPDriversPath=\WINDOWS\DRIVERS

    OemPreinstall=Yes
    OemSkipEula=Yes
    Repartition=No
    TargetPath=\WINDOWS
    UnattendMode=ReadOnly
    UnattendSwitch=Yes
```

```
[GuiRunOnce]

; Add commands in this section that you want Windows XP
; to run the first time a user logs on to it (enclose each
; command in quotation marks). See AdminPassword, AutoLogon,
; and AutoLogonCount in the [GuiUnattended] section.

[GuiUnattended]

; Uncomment the following three lines to have the setup
; program automatically log on to Windows XP after installation:

;     AdminPassword=*
;     AutoLogon=Yes
;     AutoLogonCount=1

    OemSkipRegional=1
    OemSkipWelcome=1

; Replace TimeZone with the correct time zone for the computer.
; See Ref.chm or Appendix D, "Answer File Syntax," for values:

    TimeZone=020

[UserData]

; Replace ComputerName, FullName, and OrgName with appropriate
; values. If any of these values is missing, the setup program
; will prompt the installer for the value:

    ComputerName="Sample"
    FullName="User Name"
    OrgName="Company Name"

; Replace ProductID with your product ID. If you don't provide
; a product key here, the setup program will prompt the installer:

    ProductKey=XXXXX-XXXXX-XXXXX-XXXXX-XXXXX

[TapiLocation]

; Replace AreaCode and CountryCode with appropriate values. See
; Ref.chm or Appendix D, "Answer File Syntax," for values:

    AreaCode=972
    CountryCode=1
    Dialing=Tone

[Identification]

; Replace DomainAdmin and DomainAdminPassword with the credentials
; of an account that can join the computer to the domain. The setup
; program will prompt the installer for these values if missing:
```

```
            DomainAdmin=Administrator
            DomainAdminPassword=Password

    ; Replace JoinDomain with the name of the domain to join:

            JoinDomain=DOMAIN

    ; Optionally, uncomment and replace MachineObjectOU with the LDAP
    ; path of the OU in which to create the computer account, if the
    ; account doesn't already exist:

    ;    MachineObjectOU="OU=Accounts,DC=honeycutt,DC=corp"

[Networking]

    ; This empty section is necessary if the answer file will include
    ; additional network settings described in Ref.chm. It's not necessary
    ; to use InstallDefaultComponents=Yes in this section. This answer
    ; file configures the computer with default networking components,
    ; including Client for Microsoft Networks, File and Printer Sharing
    ; for Microsoft Networks, QoS Packet Scheduler, and Internet Protocol
    ; (TCP/IP) configured to use DHCP.

[Components]

    ; Uncomment and set each of the following components to On to install
    ; it or Off to not install it (see Ref.chm or Appendix D, "Answer File
    ; Syntax," for more information about each component). These settings
    ; don't necessarily correspond to the operating system defaults:

    ;    accessopt=On
    ;    calc=On
    ;    certsrv=Off
    ;    certsrv_client=Off
    ;    certsrv_server=Off
    ;    charmap=On
    ;    chat=Off
    ;    deskpaper=On
    ;    dialer=On
    ;    fax=Off
    ;    fp_extensions=Off
    ;    fp_vdir_deploy=Off
    ;    freecell=On
    ;    hearts=On
    ;    hypertrm=On
    ;    IEAccess=On
    ;    iis_common=Off
    ;    iis_ftp=Off
    ;    iis_htmla=Off
    ;    iis_inetmgr=Off
    ;    iis_nntp=Off
    ;    iis_nntp_docs=Off
    ;    iis_pwmgr=Off
```

```
;    iis_smtp=Off
;    iis_smtp_docs=Off
;    iis_www=Off
;    iis_www_vdir_printers=Off
;    iis_www_vdir_terminalservices=Off
;    iisdbg=Off
;    indexsrv_system=Off
;    media_clips=On
;    media_utopia=Off
;    minesweeper=On
;    mousepoint=On
;    mplay=On
;    msmq_ADIntegrated=Off
;    msmq_Core=Off
;    msmq_HTTPSupport=Off
;    msmq_LocalStorage=Off
;    msmq_MQDSService=Off
;    msmq_RoutingSupport=Off
;    msmq_TriggersService=Off
;    msmsgs=On
;    msnexplr=On
;    mswordpad=On
;    netcis=Off
;    netoc=On
;    objectpkg=On
;    OEAccess=On
;    paint=On
;    pinball=On
;    rec=On
;    reminst=Off
;    rstorage=Off
;    solitaire=On
;    spider=On
;    templates=On
;    TerminalServer=Off
;    TSClients=Off
;    TSWebClient=Off
;    vol=On
;    wms=On
;    wms_admin_asp=On
;    wms_admin_mmc=On
;    wms_server=On
;    zonegames=On

;end
```

Settings Categories

Table 6-1 categorizes the different types of answer-file settings. For each category, it describes the types of settings in that category and which answer-file sections you use to configure those settings.

See Appendix D for information about these settings. You learn more about many of them in the section "Specializing Answer Files" later in this chapter on page 145.

> **On the Resource Kit CD**   See the "Answer File Settings Worksheet" in the file dist01.doc on this book's companion CD in the Aids folder. This worksheet helps you plan and document the settings for your unattended-setup answer file.

Table 6-1   Automating Tasks

Category	Description
Hardware Installation And Configuration	This category includes installing and configuring mass storage controllers that are required at startup, such as SCSI hard disks and Plug and Play devices that are not included on the operating system CD. The answer-file sections you use to configure hardware settings include the following: ■ [MassStorageDrivers] ■ [OEMBootFiles] ■ *[Unattended]*
Setup Configuration	This category includes partitioning and formatting hard disks prior to Setup, and configuring Setup options that are usually configured by end users during the GUI mode and text mode stage of Setup. This also includes configuring upgrade options, uninstall options, and other settings that affect the way Setup runs. The answer-file sections you use to configure Setup include the following: ■ [Data] ■ [GuiUnattended] ■ [Unattended] ■ *[Win9xUpg]*

Table 6-1   Automating Tasks

Category	Description
Operating System Configuration	This category includes configuring power management, telephony, display settings, and regional options. This also includes configuring error reporting, Windows file protection, remote assistance, system restore, licensing, and shell settings. The answer-file sections you use to configure operating system settings include the following: ■ [Display] ■ [LicenseFilePrintData] ■ [PCHealth] ■ [RegionalSettings] ■ [Shell] ■ [SystemFileProtection] ■ [SystemRestore] ■ [TapiLocation] ■ *[UserData]*
Internet Explorer Configuration	This category includes configuring Internet Explorer options such as favorites, proxy server settings, branding, and default Home and Search pages. This also includes configuring Internet Explorer Enhanced Security Configuration settings, which apply only to Windows Server 2003. The answer-file sections you use to configure Internet Explorer settings include the following: ■ [Branding] ■ [FavoritesEx] ■ [Proxy] ■ [URL] ■ [Components] ■ *[IEHardening]*

Table 6-1 Automating Tasks

Category	Description
Networking Configuration	This category includes configuring Internet Connection Sharing (ICS), Internet Connection Firewall (ICF), and domain membership settings. It also includes the installation and configuration of protocols, network adapters, and networking services and components. The answer-file sections you use to configure networking settings include the following:

- *[Homenet]*
- [Identification]
- [MS_AppleTalk parameters]
- [MS_ATMArps parameters]
- [MS_ATMLANE parameters]
- [MS_ATMUni parameters]
- [MS_L2TP parameters]
- [MS_MSClient parameters]
- [MS_NetMon parameters]
- [MS_NWClient parameters]
- [MS_NWIPX parameters]
- [MS_NwSapAgent parameters]
- [MS_PPTP parameters]
- [MS_Psched parameters]
- [MS_RAS parameters]
- [MS_RasSrv parameters]
- [MS_Server parameters]
- [MS_TCPIP parameters]
- [MS_WLBS parameters]
- [NetAdapters]
- [NetBindings]
- [NetClients]
- [NetOptionalComponents]
- [NetProtocols]
- [NetServices]
- *[Networking]*

Table 6-1   Automating Tasks

Category	Description
Services Configuration	This category includes configuring Internet Information Services (IIS), Certificate Services, Remote Installation Services, Terminal Server, fax service, and Simple Network Management Protocol (SNMP) service. It also includes installing and configuring a domain controller by using Active Directory. Most of these settings apply to Microsoft Windows Server 2003, not Windows XP Professional. The answer-file sections you use to configure services include the following: ■ *[DCInstall]* ■ [Fax] ■ [InternetServer] ■ [OsChooser] ■ [RemoteInstall] ■ [SNMP] ■ [TerminalServices] ■ [CertSrv_Client] ■ *[CertSrv_Server]*
Windows XP Professional Components And Services Installation	This category includes all Windows XP Professional components listed in Add or Remove Programs in Control Panel, such as accessories, games, media services, and Indexing Service. The answer-file section you use to configure optional components includes the following: ■ *[Components]*
Software Application Installation And Configuration	This category includes Windows Installer (*.msi*) packages and staged software. Software installation must run in quiet mode, which means that the installation must be fully automated and cannot rely on user interaction. Usually, when you run an installation program in quiet mode, you must provide an answer file or use command-line options. The answer-file sections you use to install software include the following: ■ *[GuiRunOnce]* ■ *[SetupParams]*
Running Programs, Scripts, And Batch Files	Programs, scripts (JS, VBS, and so on), and batch files must be fully automated and cannot rely on user interaction, which means you must provide an answer file for any programs, scripts, or batch files you are running; and you must be able to run the programs, scripts, or batch files in quiet mode. The answer-file sections you use to run programs include the following: ■ *[GuiRunOnce]* ■ *[SetupParams]*

Avoiding Answer Files

Think you can avoid answer files? Wrong.

Answer files are the centerpiece of every distribution method you'll use for deploying Windows XP Professional. You'll use an answer file to build disk images automatically and another answer file to automate the installation process when you distribute the disk image. Remote Installation Service uses answer files. Scripted installations use answer files, even if you deploy a Windows XP Professional upgrade using Microsoft Systems Management Server. There's just no getting around answer files.

Because answer files are the centerpiece of every distribution method, master them. Create a library of answer files from which you can draw to build new answer files. Fortunately, building answer files is fairly easy, and 90% of the settings are straightforward enough to require very little explanation.

Editing Answer Files

There are two ways to create answer files for Windows XP Setup. You can use Windows Setup Manager, which walks you step-by-step through creating an answer file and distribution point, or you can use a text editor. This section describes both.

At first glance, using Windows Setup Manager might seem like the easiest option. It's really not. First, Windows Setup Manager doesn't support all the settings that you're likely going to configure in an answer file. Second, it's many times quicker to start with a template answer file and customize it than to create an answer file by stepping through the wizard. Last, when you do use a template answer file that you've previously tested and confirmed to work properly, you can benefit from regression testing, whereas you must assume that you have to test everything in an answer file that you create with Windows Setup Manager. In any case, turnaround time is almost always faster when using templates.

Tip   An exception to that templates-are-better-than-the-wizard rule is when you want to create an answer file based on a computer's current configuration. For example, you can configure a network connection on a computer and then use Windows Setup Manager to capture that configuration in an answer file. In this case, using Windows Setup Manager can save hours of work over creating an answer file from a template. Another exception is that using Windows Setup Manager is the only way to generate encrypted passwords for use in answer files.

Setup Manager

You can use Windows Setup Manager to create answer files for unattended Windows XP Professional installations, automated installations using Sysprep, or automated installations using Remote Installation Service. Windows Setup Manager is on the Windows XP Professional CD in the Deploy.cab file of the Support\Tools folder (use the version that comes with Service Pack 1, as the original version is now outdated).

Windows Setup Manager is a wizard that helps you create and modify answer files by prompting for the information required to create answer files. Windows Setup Manager can create new answer files, import existing answer files, and create new answer files based on a computer's current configuration. The last option is useful when you want to configure network settings in an answer file and you don't understand all the settings available, or when you don't want to risk errors—which are likely, considering how complex these sections are sometimes.

To install and run Windows Setup Manager, double-click Deploy.cab in the Windows XP Professional CD's Support\Tools folder. Then, copy the cabinet file's contents to a folder on your disk and double-click Setupmgr.exe to run Setup Manager, as shown in Figure 6-1. The result of the wizard is an answer file. Table 6-2 describes Windows Setup Manager's different pages, in the order you see them.

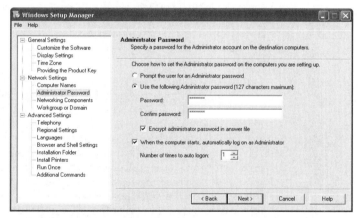

Figure 6-1 Windows Setup Manager is greatly improved over Windows 2000's version. Most of the changes are in its user interface, but encrypting the local administrator password is a new feature.

Table 6-2 Windows Setup Manager Pages

Page	Description
Set User Interaction	Use this page to set the level of user interaction during Setup. Select Provide Defaults to display the configurable values supplied in the answer file or select Fully Automated to create a setup process that requires no user interaction.
Customize The Software	Use this page to specify an organization and user name.
Display Settings	Use this page to configure the display color depth, screen resolution, and refresh frequency display settings. I prefer to allow Windows XP Professional to automatically adjust these settings to the best available, and you should generally avoid setting a refresh frequency if you're not 100 percent sure that all the monitors in use by your organization can support that frequency. Generally, 70 is a safe bet and LCD monitors perform best with 60.
Time Zone	Use this page to set the time zone.
Providing The Product Key	Use this page to specify a product key, which is required for a fully automated installation.
Computer Names	Use this page to tell Windows Setup Manager to generate a Uniqueness Database File (UDF) that the setup program uses to give each computer a unique name. If you import names from a text file, Windows Setup Manager converts them into a UDF. You can also set an option to generate unique computer names.
Administrator Password	Use this page to tell Windows Setup Manager to encrypt the local administrator password in the answer file so that users can't gain unauthorized access to the local administrator account. You can also configure the answer file to prompt users for the local administrator password during installation. If the Administrator Password box is blank, you can use the AutoLogon feature to automatically log on to the client computer as an administrator. For more information about using the AutoLogon feature, see "AutoLogon" later in this chapter on page 151.
Networking Components	Use this page to configure any network setting in Windows Setup Manager that you can configure on the desktop. The interface for setting network settings in Windows Setup Manager is the same as you see in Windows XP Professional.
Workgroup Or Domain	Join computers to a domain or workgroup You can also automatically create computer accounts in the domain.
Telephony	Use this page to set telephony properties, such as area codes and dialing rules.

Table 6-2 Windows Setup Manager Pages

Page	Description
Regional Settings	Use this page to set regional options, such as date, time, and currency formats.
Languages	Use this page to add support for other language groups.
Browser And Shell Settings	Use this page to configure Internet connections, including proxy server settings. If you need to customize the browser, you can use Windows Setup Manager to access the Internet Explorer Administration Kit (IEAK), available from *http://www.microsoft.com/windows/ieak*.
Installation Folder	Use this page to specify the default Windows folder, generate a unique folder during setup, or install Windows XP Professional in a custom folder. For example, if you plan to keep Microsoft Windows 2000 in parts of your company or are upgrading to Windows XP Professional from Windows 2000, you can move Windows XP Professional from the Windows folder to the Winnt folder so that you have a consistent folder structure throughout the organization. Microsoft strongly recommends that you move away from naming this folder Winnt, however.
Install Printers	Use this page to install printers as part of the installation process.
Run Once	Use this page to add commands that run automatically the first time a user logs on to the computer. Windows Setup Manager adds these commands to the answer file's *[GuiRunOnce]* section. For example, you can fire off Microsoft Office 2003 Editions's setup program from here. For more information about using this feature to deploy user settings, see "Run Once" later in this chapter on page 151.
Additional Commands	Use this page to add commands that run at the end of the setup process and before users log on to the system, such as when starting a setup program or adding user settings. These commands should run silently in order to ensure an unattended installation. For more information, see Chapter 11.

Text Editors

Even with all of Windows Setup Manager's features, I prefer to create answer files manually. Now, before you think I'm silly and just making work for myself, let me add that I have a library of answer-file templates that I call on when required. After you create your first answer file and you have it just right, you can reuse it over and over again because there are few changes from job to job. You can use a text editor, Notepad for example, to create answer files. A typical answer file for a computer that you're joining to a Microsoft-based network is only about 20 lines long, so editing it with a text editor isn't difficult. If you add errors to an answer file, the setup program reports the line number containing the syntax error.

My absolute favorite text editor is TextPad from Helios Software Solutions. You can learn more about it and download it at *http://www.textpad.com*. It does everything from text sorting to syntax highlighting and it has a powerful macro-recording feature. It's the perfect text editor for Windows Script Host scripts, *.reg* files, batch scripts, and answer files. UltraEdit is another popular text editor, which I've never used, but you can learn more about it at *http://www.ultraedit.com*.

The syntax highlighting feature in TextPad makes editing answer files particularly easy. If you type a keyword correctly, TextPad highlights the keyword. If you mistype the keyword, the editor doesn't highlight it. That way, you're more likely to create error-free files. In order to use this feature for editing answer files, you'll need a syntax file, though, and I've included one in the Samples\textpad folder on this book's companion CD (see Figure 6-2). The file is sif.syn. Using my syntax file, keywords are blue, comments are green, and settings are black. Here's how to use it with TextPad:

1. Install TextPad.

2. Copy sif.syn from the Samples\textpad folder on this book's companion CD to %USERPROFILE%\Application Data\TextPad.

3. Import sif.reg from the Samples\textpad folder on this book's companion CD into the registry.

This file configures the syntax file sif.syn in TextPad.

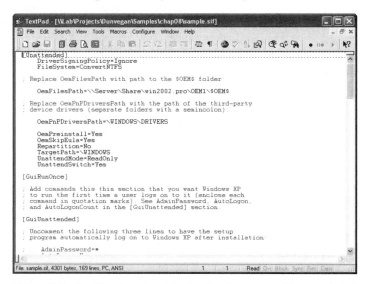

Figure 6-2 TextPad is a great text editor for answer files, and syntax highlighting helps you prevent errors that would otherwise go unnoticed.

Word: Answer File Editor

I sometimes use Microsoft Word 2003 to edit answer files. Here's why:

- Word includes built-in version control, enabling me to manage the different versions of an answer file over time. I can refer to an earlier version of an answer file to see what I changed.

- Word includes revision tracking, which enables me to see the changes I made to the current version of my answer file. This is a great feature for documenting answer files as well as sending answer files out for review.

- Word enables reviewers to comment on answer files without actually changing them. This is another great feature for sending answer files out for review.

- Word enables me to build custom dictionaries. I build custom dictionaries that include answer file section and value names, which ensures that I don't add errors to answer files with something as silly as a typo. I included a custom dictionary in the Samples\chap06 folder on this book's companion CD. The filename is custom.dic.

I'm willing to bet that these four features are enough to convince you to start using Word to edit answer files. Doing so will make you many times more productive as an IT professional. The process requires one bit of explanation, though. I edit and review answer files as document files (*.doc* files). Only when I'm ready to build a distribution share do I export the answer file from Word to a text file. Enjoy!

Running Setup Fully Unattended

Most of the answer-file settings you learn about in this book are optional; however, to fully automate Windows XP Setup, you must configure the following sections and settings in your answer file. Listing 6-2 shows what this minimal answer file looks like. This file is in the Samples\chap06 folder on this book's companion CD.

The settings you must configure to fully automate installation include the following:

- ■ *[Unattended].*   You must specify values for *OemSkipEULA*, *UnattendMode*, and *TargetPath*.

- ■ *[GuiUnattended].*   You must specify values for *AdminPassword*, *OemSkip-Regional*, *OemSkipWelcome*, and *TimeZone*. The value for *AdminPassword* cannot begin with an asterisk (*). Using a password that begins with an asterisk can cause the password to be set to a null value.

- ■ *[UserData].*   You must specify values for *FullName*, *ComputerName*, *OrgName*, and *ProductKey*.

- ■ *[Identification].*   You must specify values for *JoinDomain*, *DomainAdmin*, and *DomainAdminPassword* if you want to join the domain.

- ■ *[Networking].*   If your destination computer requires network connectivity, you must specify values for various network protocol entries.

Listing 6-2   Minimal.sif

```
[Unattended]
    OemSkipEula=Yes
    TargetPath=\WINDOWS
    UnattendMode=ReadOnly

[GuiUnattended]
    AdminPassword=Password
    OemSkipRegional=1
    OemSkipWelcome=1

; Replace TimeZone with the correct time zone for the computer.
; See Ref.chm or Appendix D, "Answer File Syntax," for values:

    TimeZone=020

[UserData]

; Replace ComputerName, FullName, and OrgName with appropriate
; values. If any of these values is missing, the setup program
; will prompt the installer for the value:

    ComputerName="Sample"
    FullName="User Name"
    OrgName="Company Name"

; Replace ProductID with your product ID. If you don't provide
; a product key here, the setup program will prompt the installer:

    ProductKey=XXXXX-XXXXX-XXXXX-XXXXX-XXXXX
```

```
[Identification]

; Replace DomainAdmin and DomainAdminPassword with the credentials
; of an account that can join the computer to the domain. The setup
; program will prompt the installer for these values if missing:

    DomainAdmin=Administrator
    DomainAdminPassword=Password

; Replace JoinDomain with the name of the domain to join:

    JoinDomain=DOMAIN

;end
```

Specializing Answer Files

The following sections are templates for specialized settings you can add to your own answer files. All of these settings are from the file sample.sif in the Samples\chap06 folder on this book's companion CD. I split them out in this section to better explain the purposes of different settings. The sections are the following:

- **Custom Files.**   Copy custom files to each target computer.
- **User Settings.**   Configure users' names, organizations, and so on.
- **Device Drivers.**   Include third-party device drivers with Windows XP Professional.
- **Local Password.**   Configure the local Administrator password.
- **Join Domain.**   Join each target computer to the domain.
- **AutoLogon.**   Automatically log on to the target computer.
- **Run Once.**   Run programs the first time a user logs on to the computer.
- **Components.**   Configure Windows XP Professional optional components.
- **Remote Desktop.**   Automatically enable Remote Desktop.

More Info   The settings you learn about in this section are documented in Appendix D. A more portable reference for these settings is Ref.chm, however, which is in Deploy.cab on the Windows XP Professional product CD in the Support\Tools folder.

Custom Files

Listing 6-3 shows the settings necessary to copy custom files to each target computer with the Windows XP Professional source files. Chapter 7 describes this topic in great detail. In order to copy files to the target computer, you must create an OEM folder and then set *OemFilesPath* to the path of that folder. Organize the OEM folder as described in Chapter 7. Last, you must set `OemPreinstall=Yes` in order for Windows XP Setup to copy the files to each target computer.

Here are a couple of examples. First, you can copy third-party device drivers to each target computer, as described in the section "Device Drivers" later in this chapter on page 148. You can also copy additional help files, system files, and program files to the target computer. Last, you might want to copy settings files (*.reg, .inf,* and so on) to each target computer so you can apply settings during the installation process. For all of this to work, however, you must organize the OEM folder correctly, as shown in Chapter 7.

Listing 6-3

```
[Unattended]
; Replace OemFilesPath with path to the $OEM$ folder:

    OemFilesPath=\\Server\Share\win2002.pro\OEM1\$OEM$
    OemPreinstall=Yes
```

User Settings

Listing 6-4 shows the settings necessary to personalize Windows XP Professional for the user. Set *ComputerName* to the name of the computer. Set *FullName* to the user's full name. Set *OrgName* to the company name. Set *ProductKey* to your Windows XP Professional product key. Other than *OrgName*, which is straightforward, the other three values are often problematic:

- The first is *ComputerName*. The problem is that you don't want to put a specific computer name in the answer file because each computer must have a unique name. If you set `ComputerName=*`, Windows XP Setup creates a unique name for the computer based on the organization name and the computer's MAC address. If this doesn't meet the naming requirements for your enterprise, you have three choices: allow Setup to prompt the user or technician for the computer name; rename the computer after installation; or build custom answer files from templates after looking up the computer name from a database based on the computer's MAC address. If technicians will visit each desktop during deployment, the first option isn't so bad. Renaming the computer after installation isn't a suitable option in most cases. Building custom answer files based on templates is such a keen solution, however, that I describe it in the section "Templating Answer Files" later in this chapter on page 154.

■ The second problem is *FullName*. Most organizations simply set the name to something like *Valued Company Employee*. This avoids the issue altogether. Because most users can get their name correct without error, this isn't necessarily a bad setting for which to prompt users, except that it interrupts a fully unattended Setup. If you will template answer files (as I describe in the section "Templating Answer Files" later in this chapter on page 154), you might as well add the user's name along with the computer name, however.

■ The last problematic setting is *ProductKey*, which generally won't change from computer to computer. The problem is that it's in the answer file as plain text, and you don't want to see your enterprise product key plastered all over the Internet. The solution is to encrypt the product key, which is only possible with Windows XP Professional Service Pack 1, Windows Server 2003, or later. With Service Pack 1 integrated into your Windows XP Professional source files, run the following command to encrypt the product key in your answer file:

winnt32.exe /encrypt:"*productkey*:*y*"/unattend:*filename*

productkey is the enterprise product key. *y* is the number of days from 5 to 60 for which you want the encrypted product key to be valid. *filename* is the path and filename of the answer file in which you want Winnt32.exe to store the encrypted product key. Although this solution doesn't prevent users from copying encrypted product keys, it does ensure that they have limited life spans when they do.

More Info   See Chapter 7 for more information about including custom files in a Windows XP Professional distribution point.

Listing 6-4

```
[UserData]

; Replace ComputerName, FullName, and OrgName with appropriate
; values. If any of these values is missing, the setup program
; will prompt the installer for the value:

    ComputerName="Sample"
    FullName="User Name"
    OrgName="Company Name"

; Replace ProductID with your product ID. If you don't provide
; a product key here, the setup program will prompt the installer:

    ProductKey=XXXXX-XXXXX-XXXXX-XXXXX-XXXXX
```

Device Drivers

Listing 6-5 shows the settings necessary to copy third-party device drivers to each target computer with the Windows XP Professional source files. Chapter 7 describes this topic in great detail. In order to copy files to the target computer, you must configure the answer file, as I described in the section "Custom Files" earlier in this chapter on page 146.

Then, set the value `DriverSigningPolicy=Ignore` so Windows XP Setup will install unsigned device drivers during installation without requiring user feedback. While I recommend against installing unsigned device drivers, it's often necessary to do so after careful testing. This setting doesn't affect policy after installation, and you presumably are testing unsigned device drivers before including them in your source files. So preventing user interaction with Setup is a good idea.

The last setting you must configure is *OemPnPDriversPath*, which you must set to the path of the device drivers relative to the target computer's file system. You can include multiple folders in this path, each separated by a semicolon. For Windows XP Professional, the maximum length for this setting is 4,096 characters, which is an improvement over earlier versions of Windows. You can't use environment variables in this setting.

> **More Info**   See Chapter 7 for more information about adding third-party device drivers to a Windows XP Professional distribution point.

Listing 6-5

```
[Unattended]
    DriverSigningPolicy=Ignore

; Replace OemFilesPath with path to the $OEM$ folder:

    OemFilesPath=\\Server\Share\win2002.pro\OEM1\$OEM$

; Replace OemPnPDriversPath with the path of the third-party
; device drivers (separate folders with a semicolon):

    OemPnPDriversPath=\WINDOWS\DRIVERS
    OemPreinstall=Yes
```

Local Password

Listing 6-6 shows the settings necessary to configure the local Administrator password. You can set *AdminPassword* to a specific password, or you can set it to *, which configures the local Administrator account with no password (null password).

Configuring *AdminPassword* with a plain text or null password isn't a good idea, however, because it gives users easy access to the local Administrator account. However, Windows XP Professional and Windows Server 2003 prevent user accounts with a blank password from connecting over the network. Windows XP Setup does remove *AdminPassword* from any local copies of the answer file that it creates, but it doesn't guarantee that resourceful users won't find the file in your distribution points. Instead, encrypt the password. The only way I know to do that is to use Windows Setup Manager, which you learned about in the section "Setup Manager" earlier in this chapter on page 139.

Run Windows Setup Manager and skip to the Administrator Password page shown earlier in Figure 6-1. Then, click the Use The Following Administrator Password option, type a password in the spaces provided, and click to select the Encrypt Administrator Password In Answer File check box. Last, save your answer file. The result is shown in Listing 6-7. Copy the values *AdminPassword* and *Encrypted-AdminPassword* to your answer file. The result is a local Administrator password that users won't see.

Listing 6-6

```
[GuiUnattended]
    AdminPassword=Password
```

Listing 6-7

```
[GuiUnattended]
    AdminPassword=5358ba2ad0d8fb22aad3b435b51404eec8a1a77b0ed80df6ddb93e00de1ef4e7
    EncryptedAdminPassword=Yes
```

Join Domain

Listing 6-8 shows the three settings necessary to join the target computer to a domain. The first is *DomainAdmin*, which is the name of the account you want to use to join the domain. The second is *DomainAdminPassword*, which is the account's password. The last is *JoinDomain*, which is the name of the domain to join.

The problem is obvious: To automatically join the computer to the domain, you must set *DomainAdminPassword*. If you use the domain Administrator account, however, you're publishing the account's password for everyone to see. Bad idea. And to make matters worse, Windows XP Setup doesn't support encryption for the value *DomainAdminPassword*. There are three strong solutions to this problem, though, so all is not lost:

- **Prestaging computer objects.** In Active Directory, prestage computer objects, delegating ownership to the user responsible for joining the computer to the domain. Then, leave *DomainAdmin* and *DomainAdminPassword* out of the answer file so that Setup prompts users for their credentials. For that matter, create an Installers group in Active Directory and assign each prestaged computer object to the Installers group as you create it.

> **More Info**   For more information about prestaging computer objects in Active Directory, see Windows Server 2003 Help and Support Center. The Microsoft Knowledge Base article 238793 provides step-by-step procedures for this technique.

- **Creating a restricted account.** In Active Directory, create a severely restricted account that has the rights and permissions necessary to join computers to the domain. Then, use that account and its password in *DomainAdmin* and *DomainAdminPassword*. Because the domain account you created is restricted to joining computers to the domain, publishing the account's password has minimal risk. See Windows Server 2003 Help and Support Center for more information about adding accounts to Active Directory and configuring their privileges. This is the best practice for joining computers to a domain.

- **Scripting domain joins.**   Use a script to join the computer to the domain after installation. The Microsoft Knowledge Base article 315273 describes this technique and provides a sample script. You can also use the utility Netdom.exe to join a computer to the domain after installation (See Appendix E, "Batch Script Syntax," for a description of the Netdom.exe command-line options). In either case, you don't have to run the script or Netdom.exe locally on the computer you're joining to the domain. See "Scripting Domain Adds" later in this chapter on page 157 for more information.

Listing 6-8

```
[Identification]

; Replace DomainAdmin and DomainAdminPassword with the credentials
; of an account that can join the computer to the domain. The setup
; program will prompt the installer for these values if missing:

    DomainAdmin=Administrator
    DomainAdminPassword=Password

; Replace JoinDomain with the name of the domain to join:

    JoinDomain=DOMAIN
```

AutoLogon

Listing 6-9 shows the settings necessary to automatically log on to the computer after finishing installation. Set `AutoLogon=Yes`. This sets the value AutoAdminLogon in the key HKLM\Software\Microsoft\Windows NT\CurrentVersion\WinLogon. You must also set *AutoLogonCount*. This setting specifies the number of times that you want to automatically log on to Windows XP Professional. This sets the value *AutoLogonCount* in HKLM\Software\Microsoft\Windows\CurrentVersion\WinLogon. Normally, you'd log on to Windows XP Professional only one time by setting `AutoLogonCount=1`. The value of *AutoLogonCount* is decremented by one following each reboot. When the value of *AutoLogonCount* reaches *0*, the value *DefaultPassword* is deleted from the registry. You can log on to the operating system as many times as is necessary, such as when a setup program restarts the computer in the middle of the installation process.

This setting logs the local Administrator on to the computer. When you set a password using the *AdminPassword* setting, Windows XP Professional uses that password to log the local Administrator on to it. However, if you encrypt the password and set `EncryptedAdminPassword=Yes`, Windows XP Professional disables this feature. If the password is blank by setting `AdminPassword=*`, Windows XP Setup restricts *AutoLogonCount* to a maximum value of *1*. It's a trade-off between security and deployment convenience. Don't panic, though, because after Windows XP Professional finishes installing, it removes the password from any local copies of the answer file, such as %SYSTEMROOT%\System32\$winnt$.sif.

Listing 6-9

```
[GuiUnattended]
    AdminPassword=*
    AutoLogon=Yes
    AutoLogonCount=1
```

Run Once

Listing 6-10 shows the setting necessary to run commands the first time a user logs on to Windows XP Professional. The *[GuiRunOnce]* section contains a list of commands that run the first time a user logs on to the computer after Windows XP Setup finishes. Enclose each command in quotes. The commands in the *[GuiRunOnce]* section run in the context of the console user, so you must ensure that the user has the privileges necessary to run each command. In most cases, you'll use *[GuiRunOnce]* in conjunction with the *AutoLogon* setting described in the previous section.

You must provide any programs and data files that you want to use, and you do that by deploying them through the OEM distribution folders that you learn about in Chapter 7. Also, you want to make sure that a program you run from *[GuiRunOnce]* has a command-line option to run quietly; you don't want to display a user interface while installing registry settings, for example. Setup will not finish until each of the commands you launch in this section finishes, so a program that you run from *[GuiRunOnce]* that requires user interaction could hang the installation.

Here are three things you should consider when using *[GuiRunOnce]*:

- From *[GuiRunOnce]*, you can't run programs that force Windows XP Professional to restart. That's because Windows XP Professional looses any entries remaining in *[GuiRunOnce]* when it restarts, and those commands will not run. If you can't prevent the program from restarting the computer, try repackaging it as a Windows Installer package file or add it as the last command in *[GuiRunOnce]*.

- Any program that relies on Windows Explorer will not work properly because Windows Explorer is not running when the commands in the *[GuiRunOnce]* section are. Again, you can consider repackaging these applications.

- If you're trying to install Windows Installer package files from *[GuiRunOnce]*, you must use the */wait* command-line option to ensure that two packages don't try to install at the same time. Otherwise, both packages fail. This is only an issue when installing Windows Installer packages using Setup.exe, however, because Setup.exe launches Windows Installer and then returns, allowing the next package to begin installing immediately. If you install Windows Installer packages using Msiexec (the Windows Installer command-line interface) instead, this problem isn't an issue.

More Info See Chapter 11 for more information about adding packages to a distribution point and running commands during installation.

Listing 6-10

```
[GuiRunOnce]
   "%SYSTEMROOT%\APPS\setup.exe /q"
   "%regedit /s SYSTEMROOT%\SETTINGS\setup.exe /q"
```

Components

Listing 6-11 shows the settings necessary to install or remove optional Windows XP Professional components. Setting a component to *On* installs it. Setting it to *Off* doesn't. For a complete list of components, see Appendix D. Some components have dependencies on other components, which Appendix D describes.

Listing 6-11

```
[Components]

; Uncomment and set each of the following components to On to install
; it or Off to not install it (see Ref.chm or Appendix D, "Answer File
; Syntax," for more information about each component):

    accessopt=On
    calc=On
    certsrv=Off
    certsrv_client=Off
    certsrv_server=Off
    charmap=On
    chat=Off
    deskpaper=On
    dialer=On
    fax=Off
    fp_extensions=Off
    fp_vdir_deploy=Off
    freecell=On
    hearts=On
    hypertrm=On
    IEAccess=On
    iis_common=Off
    iis_ftp=Off
    iis_htmla=Off
    iis_inetmgr=Off
    iis_nntp=Off
    iis_nntp_docs=Off
    iis_pwmgr=Off
    iis_smtp=Off
    iis_smtp_docs=Off
    iis_www=Off
    iis_www_vdir_printers=Off
    iis_www_vdir_terminalservices=Off
    iisdbg=Off
    indexsrv_system=Off
    media_clips=On
    media_utopia=Off
    minesweeper=On
    mousepoint=On
    mplay=On
    msmq_ADIntegrated=Off
    msmq_Core=Off
    msmq_HTTPSupport=Off
    msmq_LocalStorage=Off
    msmq_MQDSService=Off
    msmq_RoutingSupport=Off
    msmq_TriggersService=Off
    msmsgs=On
    msnexplr=On
    mswordpad=On
    netcis=Off
    netoc=On
```

Continued

```
objectpkg=On
OEAccess=On
paint=On
pinball=On
rec=On
reminst=Off
rstorage=Off
solitaire=On
spider=On
templates=On
TerminalServer=Off
TSClients=Off
TSWebClient=Off
vol=On
wms=On
wms_admin_asp=On
wms_admin_mmc=On
wms_server=On
zonegames=On
```

Remote Desktop

Listing 6-12 shows how to enable Remote Desktop in Windows XP Professional. Remote Desktop is a fabulous tool for remote administration, but it's disabled by default. In order to use it without having to remotely edit the registry or visit the desktop, you must enable it during installation. Add the settings shown in Listing 6-12 to do that. By default, only members of the local Administrators group can access the computer using Remote Desktop. Once enabled, only user accounts with a nonblank password can connect via Remote Desktop.

Listing 6-12

```
[TerminalServices]
AllowConnections=1
```

Templating Answer Files

You've created the perfect answer file. You've verified all of the settings in the lab. Now you're ready to start thinking about building distribution points with it and installing Windows XP Professional on a few thousand computers. Will your answer file work for the different users and computers in the organization without requiring user input? It probably won't work well unless you find a way to customize the answer file for different computers and users.

The problem settings tend to be *FullName* and *ComputerName*. The setting *ComputerName* must be unique from computer to computer. You might have additional settings that must be unique per computer, too. For example, you might want to set *OrgName* to the user's department name. You might want to join different groups of computers to different domains or create their computer accounts in different organizational units. Another example is customizing telephony, time zone, and regional settings in a geographically dispersed deployment without requiring unique answer files for each permutation.

The solution is the template processor that you find in the script siftemp.wsf, which is a variable process for answer files. It substitutes text for variables that begin and end with percent signs (%), similar to environment variables. For example, if you run the script with FULLNAME="Jerry Honeycutt", the script will substitute *Jerry Honeycutt* for each occurrence of *%FULLNAME%* in the answer file. The script siftemp.wsf is on this book's companion CD in the Scripts folder. This script is also in each sample distribution folder's Scripts folder, which are in the Samples folder. Table 6-3 shows the command-line options for siftemp.wsf, and the following shows its syntax (see the following sections for examples of using this script):

```
siftemp.wsf [/I:value] [/O:value] [/CS] [name=value, …] [/L:value] [/?]
```

Table 6-3   Siftemp.wsf Command-Line Options

Option	Description
/I:value	Specifies the path and filename of the template answer file that contains variables for this script to expand. The filename *value* can be a local, mapped network drive or UNC path.
/O:value	Specifies the path and filename of the answer file to create using the template answer file specified with the */I* command-line option and the command-line variables. The filename *value* can be a local, mapped network drive or UNC path. If you're creating the answer file in a network share, make sure the user has write permission.
/CS	Specifies that variable names are case-sensitive. If this command-line option isn't specified, variable names are not case-sensitive.
name=value	Specifies the variable *name* and the text *value* to substitute for that variable in the template answer file. COMPUTERNAME=TEST will substitute each occurrence of the variable *%COMPUTERNAME%* in the template answer file with the text *TEST.* Specify as many variables on the command line as necessary.
/L:value	Logs the results to the log file specified by *value.*
/?	Displays help and usage information.

On the Resource Kit CD   The script siftemp.wsf is on this book's companion CD in the Scripts folder. This script requires the file windeploy.wsc, which is in the same folder. Sample distribution folders that include siftemp.wsf are on this book's companion CD in the Samples folder. Simply copy these sample distribution folders to your hard disk and customize them as described in Chapter 7.

Creating Templates

Listing 6-13 shows a template answer file that's designed for use with siftemp.vbs. The variables in this answer file are *TIMEZONE*, *COMPUTERNAME*, and *USERNAME*. You can define any variable you want simply by including it in the answer file delimited by percent signs (%) on either side of the name. You define the text to substitute for each variable on the script's command line.

Listing 6-13   Template.sif

```
[Unattended]
    OemSkipEula=Yes
    TargetPath=\WINDOWS
    UnattendMode=ReadOnly

[GuiUnattended]
    AdminPassword=*
    OemSkipRegional=1
    OemSkipWelcome=1
    TimeZone=%TIMEZONE%

[UserData]
    ComputerName=%COMPUTERNAME%
    FullName="%USERNAME%"
    OrgName="My Company"
    ProductKey=XXXXX-XXXXX-XXXXX-XXXXX-XXXXX

[Identification]
    DomainAdmin=Installer
    DomainAdminPassword=Password
    JoinDomain=DOMAIN

;end
```

Scripting Templates

To expand the variables in the answer file, run the following command: **siftemp.wsf /I:template.sif /O:winnt.sif TIMEZONE=020 USERNAME="Jerry Honeycutt" COMPUTERNAME=JERRY1**. The script opens the template file template.sif, replaces each occurrence of *%TIMEZONE%* with *020*, *%USERNAME%* with *Jerry Honeycutt*, and *%COMPUTERNAME%* with *JERRY1*.

If you had to run this command manually for each installation, it wouldn't be much better than customizing the answer file each time. The first option is to run the batch script template.cmd, shown in Listing 6-14. This file is in the Samples\chap06 folder on this book's companion CD. In order to run template.cmd, the script siftemp.wsf must be in the same folder or in the path. So you can run the script directly from the CD, I've copied siftemp.wsf and windeploy.wsc to Samples\chap06. The batch script siftemp.wsf prompts the user for the user name, computer name, and time zone. Then it runs siftemp.wsf to expand those values in the file template.sif.

Of course, the next step would be to run Windows XP Setup, which you learn more about in Chapter 11.

Listing 6-14   Template.cmd

```
@echo off
@rem template.cmd: sample template processor

setlocal enableextensions

  set /p SIF.USERNAME="Full name: "
  set /p SIF.COMPUTERNAME="Computer name: "
  set /p SIF.TIMEZONE="Time zone: "

  siftemp /i:template.sif /o:winnt.sif USERNAME="%SIF.USERNAME%" "
COMPUTERNAME="%SIF.COMPUTERNAME%" TIMEZONE="%SIF.TIMEZONE%"
:end
```

The batch script template.cmd is very rudimentary. It simply moves all user interaction from the middle of the installation process to the very beginning. A better solution than using a batch script is to build an HTA application that collects settings from the user or technician and then runs siftemp.wsf to process the template answer file. With an HTA application, you have a cleaner user interface and a better opportunity to validate users' input.

What if you want to use template answer files without requiring any user input whatsoever? This solution is more complicated but elegant. You can create a script that looks up the computer's MAC address in a database and then extracts the remaining data from the database. For example, the database can include columns for each computer's MAC address, computer name, user name, time zone, area code, and so on. The script could look up the MAC address, retrieve each column, and then run siftemp.wsf to replace each variable with the values from the database. This book's companion CD contains a working example of this type of script in the folder Samples\chap14. For more information about using this script to fully automate the installation of Windows XP Professional based on a computer's MAC address, see the section "Automating Installations" in Chapter 14, "Preinstallation Environment."

Scripting Domain Adds

As you learned in the section "Join Domain" earlier in this chapter on page 149, joining computers to the domain can be a potential security risk if you include the domain Administrator password in your answer files. One solution is to create restricted accounts for adding computers to the domain; then including their passwords in answer files isn't much of a problem. The Microsoft Knowledge Base article 315273 provides additional solutions for this problem.

Another solution is to script joining the domain after Windows XP Setup finishes. You can use Netdom.exe, as described in Appendix E, to join the computer to the domain. You can run Netdom.exe locally or remotely, making it a versatile utility for joining computers to domains after installing Windows XP Professional. You can also use the script joindom.wsf, which is in the Scripts folder on this book's companion CD. The benefit of the script is that you can specify a list of computers on the command line. In either case, there is no way for Windows XP Setup to communicate to you its need to join the computer to the domain, so you must be aware of which computers are waiting to join the domain and then use Netdom.exe or joindom.wsf to join them.

Tip You can use Sysinternals' Psexec to run Netdom.exe on remote computers. To download Psexec, see *http://www.sysinternals.com*. Also, this book's companion CD contains batch scripts that you can use to automate this command for a list of computers.

More Info For more information about these batch scripts, see Appendix E. In particular, use the batch script forlist.cmd to run Psexec for a list of computers contained in a text file or forcmd.cmd to run Psexec for a list of computers generated by the command *net view*.

Table 6-4 describes the command-line options for joindom.wsf, and the following describes the script's syntax:

```
joindom.wsf [/ME] [/U:value] /D:value [/P:value] [computer, . . .] [/?]
```

Table 6-4   Joindom.wsf Command-Line Options

Option	Description
computer	Specifies the computer to join to the domain. If not specified, this script joins the local computer to the domain.
/D:value	Specifies the domain to join.
/ME	Specifies to run this script using the console user's credentials. If you use the */ME* command-line option, this script ignores the */U* command-line option.
/U:value	Specifies the account's user name to use for joining *computer* to the domain. This script ignores the */U* command-line option if you use the */ME* option.
/P:value	Specifies the account's password to use for joining *computer* to the domain. If not specified, this script prompts for the password.
/?	Displays help and usage information.

On the Resource Kit CD   The script joindom.wsf is on this book's companion CD in the Scripts folder. This script requires the file windeploy.wsc, which is in the same folder. Sample distribution folders that include joindom.wsf are on this book's companion CD in the Samples folder. Simply copy these sample distribution folders to your hard disk and customize it as described in Chapter 7.

Best Practices

The following are best practices for creating Windows XP Setup answer files:

- **Build a library of template answer files.**   Build and test answer files in a lab. Once you've verified them, you can confidently reuse them in your projects, and testing them is easier since you only have to regression test your changes.

- **Use Windows Setup Manager to get a quick start on complex answer files.**   Windows Setup Manager isn't ideal if you already have a library of answer files. But it's a great tool for capturing a computer's current configuration in an answer file. Windows Setup Manager is also a necessity when configuring specialized network settings, since these sections are error prone and Windows Setup Manager can capture a computer's network settings in an answer file; then, you can copy those sections to your answer files.

- **Use an editor that helps reduce errors.**   Notepad is out. Editors like TextPad and Word help reduce errors in answer files by using syntax highlighting or custom dictionaries. Both features call your attention to typos without requiring you to go through a two-hour test cycle to discover a bug in the first place.

- **Build answer files appropriate for the audience.**   If you already know that technicians are attending each installation, then you can allow some interaction, such as naming the computer or joining the domain. Otherwise, limit the input required by Windows XP Setup. Fully unattended is best for users.

- **Create a restricted account for joining computers to the domain.**   In Active Directory, create a restricted account with just enough rights and permissions to join computers to a domain. Then, use that account's name and password for the *DomainAdmin* and *DomainAdminPassword*

- **Use answer file templates to make them more generic.**   By using answer file templates with the script siftemp.wsf, you can support more configurations with fewer answer files.

Chapter 7

Distribution Points

Microsoft Windows XP Professional and Microsoft Office 2003 Editions distribution points are the portals from which your deployment project leaves your capable hands and installs on client computers. They are also containers for all of your customizations, including answer files, scripts, and so on. This chapter describes how to build distribution points for both Windows XP Professional and Office 2003 Editions as the first step in the technical deployment process.

Checklist

- Have you created an answer file for Windows XP Professional? If not, see Chapter 6, "Answer Files."

- Have you obtained your product key for Windows XP Professional? Contact Microsoft if you haven't yet obtained a Windows XP Professional product key.

- Have you identified the files that you want to add to the installation? If not, see Chapter 1, "Deployment Plan," for more information.

- Have you identified the third-party device drivers you must add to the installation? If so, have you received those device drivers from the hardware vendor? Otherwise, see the section "Adding Third-Party Drivers," later in this chapter.

- Do you have Windows XP Professional and Office 2003 Editions media sets for the versions that you're deploying? If so, do you have the latest service pack for Windows or service release for Office 2003 Editions available for integration into your existing source files? See Chapter 3, "Windows Configuration," and Chapter 4, "Office Configuration."

- Have you identified the hot fixes that you want to add to the Windows installation? If so, have you received these files from Microsoft? Otherwise, see Chapter 3 for more information.

- Have you identified the distribution servers from which you're deploying Windows? If not, see Chapter 1 for more information.

- Have you identified the distribution servers from which you're deploying Office 2003 Editions? If not, see Chapter 1 for more information.

Getting Started

A Windows distribution point contains the source files that install the product. These source files include the I386 folder from the Windows product CD, third-party device drivers, and any other files you require to customize the installation. A Windows distribution point boils down to a specific folder hierarchy and related files that Setup expects to find. Some of the folders and files in this hierarchy have special meaning, based on their locations and names, and some of them require you to add additional values to your unattended-setup answer file (Unattend.txt).

You can use Windows Setup Manager, shown in Figure 7-1, to create a Windows distribution point for unattended installations, disk images, or Remote Installation Services (RIS). You can even use it to add third-party device drivers to distribution points. Windows Setup Manager is in Deploy.cab on the Windows product CD in the Support\Tools folder. Although Windows Setup Manager is an easy tool to use, it seldom covers the depth and breadth of your requirements; so this chapter focuses on building distribution points by hand. Nonetheless, if you don't want to use the templates on this book's companion CD, you can use Windows Setup Manager to start your distribution point quickly and then further customize it using the information contained in this chapter.

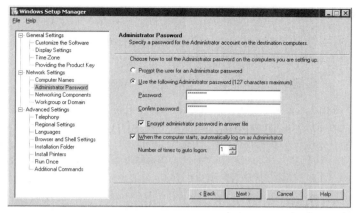

Figure 7-1 Windows Setup Manager is useful for a quick start building a distribution point, but copying an existing distribution point is quicker still.

On the Resource Kit CD   See "Distribution Share Worksheet" in the file dist02.doc on this book's companion CD in the Aids folder. This worksheet helps you plan the contents of your distribution points.

After you build a distribution point, you can copy it to one or more deployment servers for deployment. And you can use distributed file system (DFS) to replicate the distribution point across sites.

More Info   For more information about securing your distribution points, see "Sharing Distribution Points," later in this chapter on page 189.

For more information about using multiple servers to load-balance the installation process, see "Balancing Installation," later in this chapter on page 190.

For more information about using Distributed File System, see Help and Support Center in Microsoft Windows Server 2003.

See "Microsoft Windows Preinstallation Reference," which is the file Ref.chm in Deploy.cab, and "Microsoft Windows Corporate Deployment Tools User's Guide," which is the file Deploy.chm in Deploy.cab, for more information about building Windows XP Professional distribution points. Deploy.cab is on the Windows product CD in Support\Tools.

Building a Development Server

You can initially create your distribution point anywhere—even on your desktop. As odd as it sounds, however, I recommend that you use a high-powered laptop computer with ample disk space to create and test your initial distribution points. When building and testing a distribution, you seldom want to be tied to a physical location. You might want to demonstrate the distribution point in a meeting. You might want to take it with you to a training class so you can get feedback from the instructor. And building an initial distribution point on a laptop makes it easier to test the configuration on computers that aren't connected to the corporate network. On more than one occasion, I've regretted not using a laptop for development.

Hardware Recommendations

The following list is a recommendation for the hardware configuration of a development server:

- **1 GB of memory.**   The obscene amount of memory I recommend is to allow you to use tools such as Microsoft Virtual PC to create virtual computers that you can use for quick and dirty testing. Rather than finding a computer on which to test your configuration, you can simply create a virtual computer and then deploy your configuration to it. See Chapter 2, "Application Compatibility," for more information about Virtual PC.

- **60 GB of disk space.**   If you're building disk images, you'll need ample disk space. Even if you're not building disk images, you'll need space for source files, application packages, device drivers, utilities, and so on. You'll also need a lot of extra space to store ISO images of your product CDs, which makes copying source files less time-consuming. I do recommend that you split the disk into two partitions, however, or even install a second hard disk in the computer. Use the first partition for Windows Server 2003 system files, and the second partition for your developmental distribution point. A second partition is required if you intend to use RIS, which I explain later in this section.

- **Floppy disk drive.**   You'd think that this is obvious, but more and more computers come without a floppy disk drive. It's a must for building bootable floppy disks or creating a floppy disk for use with Microsoft Windows Preinstallation Environment (Windows PE). If your development server doesn't have a built-in floppy disk drive, you can use an inexpensive universal serial bus (USB) device.

- **CD/RW drive.**   If you're using a laptop as a development server, make sure it comes with a CD burner. It's useful for copying disk images and necessary for building Windows PE CDs.

- **USB Flash Disk (UFD).** Not as obvious as a floppy disk drive, a USB flash disk is often incredibly useful for copying device drivers to the development server, lifting files from a computer when you can't connect the server to the network, and so on. This $50 device will save you a lot of time.

- **Ethernet switch or crossover cables.** In order to test your configurations on real computers, you must be able to connect them to the development server. I keep a 5-port Netgear switch (*http://www.netgear.com*) handy for this purpose. I also have a short crossover cable handy, just in case.

Software Recommendations

In addition to hardware configurations, I recommend the following invaluable software for use in building distribution points:

- **Disk-imaging software.** If you're building disk images, as described in Chapter 15, "Disk Imaging with Sysprep," install the disk-imaging software on the development server. Chapter 15 describes a workflow you can use for building disk images on your server.

- **CD-burning software.** The CD-burning software that comes with Windows Server 2003 isn't adequate for building distribution points. You need software that can write ISO images to a CD. My preference is Ahead Nero Burning ROM, which you can purchase from *http://www.nero.com*. Also, the Microsoft Windows Server 2003 Resource Kit includes utilities for burning CDs and DVDs. The CD burning utility is called CDBurn, and the DVD burning utility is called, oddly enough, DVDBurn.

> **More Info** A product that my associates recommend highly is ISO Recorder, which is a free product from Alex Feinman. You can learn more about ISO Recorder at *http://isorecorder.alexfeinman.com/isorecorder.htm*.

- **Disk-capture software.** Disk-capture software creates a binary file that contains an image of a floppy disk or CD. You can add the floppy disk image to RIS or use virtual CD software to mount the CD image without requiring you to fumble around with the actual CDs. This software is also useful for building libraries of bootable floppy disks. My choice for disk-capture software is WinImage from Gilles Vollant (*http://www.winimage.com*).

- **Virtual CD software.** Product CDs are much easier to handle if you create ISO images of them and then store them on your development server. You can use Microsoft Virtual CD, which is available to Microsoft beta testers to mount ISO images as virtual drives. You can also use Daemon Tools—downloadable from your favorite shareware Web site. My preference is Daemon tools because it works better through Remote Desktop than does Virtual CD. For more information, see *http://www.daemon-tools.cc*.

- **SysInternals PsTools.** SysInternals (*http://www.sysinternals.com*) provides numerous free tools that are extremely useful when building distribution points. Make sure you download PsTools: They provide a variety of other free tools, and the company also sells some high-powered administrator tools under the brand Winternals (*http://www.winternals.com*). For example, its ERD Commander 2003 is essentially Windows PE on a huge dose of steroids. Its products are a bit pricey, however, so be prepared to justify your need before handing your manager a purchase order.

- **SysInternals Regmon and Filemon.** These two tools are essential for customizing a distribution point. You use them to monitor the computer in real-time so that you can see which processes are changing which settings and files. These tools are the most efficient way to customize settings and files.

- **Scriptomatic tool.** This simple utility helps you write Windows Management Instrumentation (WMI) scripts without requiring significant scripting expertise on your part, as shown in Figure 7-2. WMI scripts are necessary for many Windows XP Professional customizations. Download this free tool from *http://www.microsoft.com/technet/scriptcenter/tools/wmimatic.asp*.

- **Microsoft Windows XP Professional Support Tools.** The support tools contain a number of useful utilities, many of which you'll want to install in your configurations for use by administrators and help desk technicians down the line. These support tools are on the Windows XP Professional CD in the Support\Tools folder.

- **WinDiff.** WinDiff is actually part of Windows Support Tools, but I list it separately because of its immense usefulness. WinDiff compares text files and shows you the differences. That's it. But you can use it to compare *.reg* files to locate settings in the registry. You can use it to compare versions of unattended-setup answer files to locate changes. It's a sanity saver.

- **Support\Tools folder from the Windows XP Professional product CD.** This folder contains the Windows XP Professional deployment tools, including Windows Setup Manager, Sysprep, and the documentation. You should copy these tools to your Windows XP Professional distribution points for easy access, as I recommend later in this chapter.

- **Helios TextPad.** Helios TextPad is my favorite text editor for most tasks, including editing answer files, administrative templates, Windows Script Host scripts, and so on. I even provide you with TextPad syntax files on this book's companion CD in the folder Samples\textpad. For more information, see *http://www.textpad.com*.

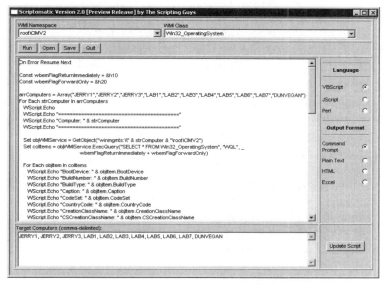

Figure 7-2 The Scriptomatic tool helps you write WMI scripts without requiring expertise.

Whether you're building distribution points on a desktop computer or laptop, install Windows Server 2003 on it. And configure the computer to match the configuration of the servers that will be supporting your configurations. Doing so makes testing your configurations easier. For example, if your company uses Active Directory, configure Active Directory on the development server complete with a matching domain name so that you can test that your answer files correctly join the computer to the domain. If you're going to configure the development server with Dynamic Host Configuration Protocol (DHCP), though, make sure you don't connect it to the corporate network. Even if you don't load DHCP, don't put a Domain Controller on the network with the same domain name as the production document. Keep your testing environment isolated. I also like to install and configure RIS on the development server, as described in Chapter 16, "Remote Installation Service." I don't do this to install Windows XP Professional. I do it to start Windows PE quickly and to use Argon RISme for providing quick access to boot-floppy disk images. See Chapter 14, "Preinstallation Environment," for more information about Windows PE. See Chapter 18 or *http://www.argontechnology.com* for more information about RISme.

Creating the Distribution Point

There is no one right way to build a distribution point for Windows XP Professional. The folder structure that I use is based on trial and error over time and it reflects my own quirks. Feel free to customize my suggestions to suit your requirements.

Figure 7-3 tells you more about how I organize distribution points than I can describe with text alone. The top folder is the shared distribution point. The root folder contains three files. The first is diskpart.txt, which is the script file for automating Diskpart.exe (see the section "diskpart.txt"), the utility that comes with Windows XP Professional and Windows PE for partitioning the hard disk. The second file is setup32.cmd (see the section "setup32.cmd"), which is a batch script that installs one of the configurations, OEM1, OEM2, and so on. The third file is setup.bat, which is an MS-DOS version of the batch script setup32.cmd. Right under the distribution point, you see the following folders:

- **I386.**   This is a copy of the Windows XP Professional product CD's I386 folder.

- **OEM1.**   This folder contains a configuration, which is the combination of an answer file called winnt.sif that automates the installation (see the section "winnt.sif"), a batch script called winnt32.cmd that starts Setup with the appropriate command-line options (see the section "winnt32.cmd"), and the OEM folder that contains customizations.

- **OEM2.**   This folder contains another configuration similar to OEM1. You can create as many configures as required—OEM1, OEM2, through OEM*N*—and install the appropriate configuration by passing it as a command-line option to the batch scripts Setup32.cmd or Setup.bat.

- **Scripts.**   This folder contains scripts that are useful for building and customizing Windows XP Professional. This is where I copy the scripts that you see in this chapter.

- **Tools.**   This folder contains the deployment tools from the Support\Tools folder of the Windows XP Professional product CD. It includes Windows Setup Manager, Sysprep, and the deployment documentation.

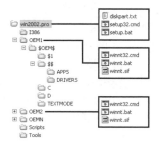

Figure 7-3   This organization allows you to have multiple configurations with a single copy of the Windows XP Professional source files in the I386 folder.

On the Resource Kit CD   The folder structure and files that you see in Figure 7-3 are on this book's companion CD in Samples\chap07\win2002.pro. For a quick start, simply copy the template folder from the CD to your development server and then copy the I386 folder from your Windows XP Professional product CD to the root of the distribution point. See the section "Customizing the Sample Folder" for step-by-step instructions on customizing the sample distribution folder for this chapter.

The section "Sharing Distribution Points," later in this chapter describes how to properly secure your distribution points. While testing, I give the Everyone group only read permission on the share to prevent accidental changes while testing it. You can create another folder on your development server called Incoming and give the group Everyone full control of it for copying files back to the server from client computers, though. Don't forget that you can access the client computer's hard disk from the server using the administrator shares *Computer*\C$, and so on.

diskpart.txt

Listing 7-1 shows the contents of diskpart.txt from Figure 7-3. This file selects the first disk installed on the computer, removes its current partitions, creates a new primary partition using all of the available space, assigns the drive letter C, and then marks the partition as active so that it'll boot. The command to use diskpart.txt in Windows PE is *diskpart /s diskpart.txt*. The batch script setup32.cmd, which you learn about in the next section, automatically runs this Diskpart.exe with this script, though. You can't use Diskpart.exe with MS-DOS.

Diskpart.exe does not format the disk, so you must format the disk after partitioning it. The command *format c: /q /fs:ntfs /v:"" /y* quickly formats the newly partitioned disk with the NT file system (NTFS) and without a volume label. The command-line option */y* runs Format without prompting for input. You can run both commands within a batch script to automatically partition and format a disk, which is what you see happening in setup32.cmd in the next section.

Diskpart.exe doesn't work in MS-DOS, but it does work in Windows PE. That's one reason I prefer to use Windows PE for installing Windows XP Professional. If you don't have Windows PE or aren't ready to give up your MS-DOS boot disks, you don't need Diskpart.txt. Instead, you can use a tool such as Gdisk, which comes with Symantec Ghost (*http://www.symantec.com*) to partition and format the disk. The Gdisk command to erase a disk is *gdisk /del /all*. The Gdisk command to partition and format a disk with the FAT32 file system is *gdisk /cre /pri /for /q /y*. The downfall of using MS-DOS and Gdisk to prepare a disk for installation is that you have to restart the computer after formatting the disk. That's another reason I prefer using Windows PE to prepare the computer for installing Windows XP Professional.

> **More Info**   For more information about using Diskpart.exe in Windows PE, see Chapter 14.

Listing 7-1   diskpart.txt

```
select disk=0
clean
create partition primary
assign letter=c
active
```

setup32.cmd

Listing 7-2 shows the file setup32.cmd from Figure 7-3. This batch script expects a single command-line option, which is the name of the folder with the configuration you want to install. Referring to Figure 7-3, to install the configuration OEM1, you run the command *setup32 OEM1*. After checking that the folder exists and contains an OEM folder, it runs Diskpart.exe with the script in the previous section to partition the hard disk and then it formats the disk with the NTFS file system.

After preparing the disk, the batch script switches to the directory containing the configuration you want to install and calls the batch script winnt32.cmd, which just contains the command for starting Setup with the proper command-line options. The purpose of splitting the process into two batch files, setup32.cmd and winnt32.cmd, is that each configuration might require a different command. This is particularly true if you're installing Microsoft Windows XP Tablet PC Edition, which requires the extra */2* or */copysource* command-line options. You can install any of the configurations using the single batch script setup32.cmd, but maintain the flexibility of using different setup commands with each configuration.

Because I designed setup32.cmd for using with Windows PE, the batch script winnt32.cmd uses the Setup command-line option */syspart* to copy the installation files to the target computer without restarting the computer to continue the installation process. Therefore, setup32.cmd uses the *exit* command to reboot the computer after the batch script winnt32.cmd returns. If you have just repartitioned the drive and you don't use the */syspart* command-line option to install Windows XP Professional when using Windows PE, Setup will fail to find a partition for installation.

If you're using MS-DOS boot disks instead of Windows PE, the batch script setup32.cmd will not work. First, the MS-DOS batch-script language doesn't support all of the features that the Windows PE command processor supports. Second, this batch script uses Diskpart.exe to prepare the hard disk, formats the hard disk, and then starts Setup without restarting the computer. Listing 7-3 shows the batch script setup.bat, which you'd use for MS-DOS installations instead. This batch script assumes that the hard disk is already prepared, whether using Fdisk and Format or using a utility such as Gdisk. Incidentally, there is no harm in keeping both setup32.cmd and setup.bat in a distribution point; doing so gives you the flexibility to use both MS-DOS boot disks and Windows PE to install the distribution point.

Listing 7-2   setup32.cmd

```
@echo off
@rem setup32.cmd: install Windows XP

setlocal enableextensions

if '%1'=='' goto help
if not exist %1 goto help
if not exist %1\$OEM$ goto help

  diskpart /s diskpart.txt
  format c: /q /fs:ntfs /v:"" /y

  cd %1
  call winnt32.cmd
  exit

:help

  echo.
  echo Usage: setup.cmd FOLDER
  echo.
  echo FOLDER can be one of the following:
  echo.
  for /d %%i in (*) do (
    if exist %%i\$OEM$ echo %%i
  )
  goto end

:end
```

Listing 7-3   setup.bat

```
@echo off
@rem setup.bat: install Windows XP

if '%1'=='' goto help
if not exist %1\winnt.bat goto help

  cd %1
  call winnt.bat
  goto end

:help
```

```
echo.
echo Usage: setup.bat FOLDER
echo.
echo FOLDER can be one of the following:
dir /ad
echo.
goto end

:end
```

winnt32.cmd

Listing 7-4 shows the batch script winnt32.cmd, which setup32.cmd calls in order to start Setup. You learned that each configuration has its own winnt32.cmd so that you have a single batch script with which to launch the setup process while keeping the flexibility of using different setup commands for different configurations. The command in winnt32.cmd simply calls the setup program winnt32.exe, which works only in a 32-bit Windows environment like Windows PE, using the */unattended* command-line option to specify the unattended-setup answer file and the */syspart* command-line option to instruct Setup to copy the installation source files to the target computer without rebooting the computer to continue the installation process. Chapter 13, "Unattended Setup," describes the command-line options for winnt.exe.

If you're using an MS-DOS boot disk to install Windows XP Professional, the batch script winnt32.cmd shown in Listing 7-4 won't work; it uses the 32-bit setup program winnt32.exe and the */syspart* command-line option. Instead, the batch script *setup.bat* you learned about in the previous section calls winnt.bat, shown in Listing 7-5. This batch script calls the 16-bit setup program to install Windows XP Professional, and it assumes that you've already partitioned the disk, formatted it, and restarted the PC. Chapter 13 describes the command-line options for winnt.exe.

Listing 7-4   winnt32.cmd

```
@..\i386\winnt32 /unattended:winnt.sif /syspart:c:
```

Listing 7-5   winnt.bat

```
@..\i386\winnt /s:..\i386 /u:winnt.sif
```

winnt.sif

Listing 7-6 shows the answer file winnt.sif that you saw in Figure 7-3. Chapter 6, "Answer Files," described how to create answer files. This answer file is only a sample. The important bit here is that I set OemFilesPath to the UNC path of the OEM folder in the configuration I'm installing. That means that this setting will be different for each configuration in the distribution point. This is necessary because I'm not putting the OEM folder beneath the I386 folder, which is where Setup expects to find it.

Listing 7-6   winnt.sif

```
[Unattended]
    DriverSigningPolicy=Ignore
    FileSystem=ConvertNTFS

; Replace OemFilesPath with path to the $OEM$ folder:

    OemFilesPath=\\Server\Share\win2002.pro\OEM1\$OEM$

; Replace OemPnPDriversPath with the path of the third-party
; device drivers (separate folders with a semicolon):

    OemPnPDriversPath=\WINDOWS\DRIVERS

    OemPreinstall=Yes
    OemSkipEula=Yes
    Repartition=No
    TargetPath=\WINDOWS
    UnattendMode=ReadOnly
    UnattendSwitch=Yes

[GuiRunOnce]

; Add commands in this section that you want Windows XP
; to run the first time a user logs on to it (enclose each
; command in quotation marks). See AdminPassword, AutoLogon,
; and AutoLogonCount in the [GuiUnattended] section.

[GuiUnattended]

; Uncomment the following three lines to have the setup
; program automatically log on to Windows XP after installation:

;     AdminPassword=*
;     AutoLogon=Yes
;     AutoLogonCount=1

    OemSkipRegional=1
    OemSkipWelcome=1

; Replace TimeZone with the correct time zone for the computer.
; See Ref.chm or Appendix D, "Answer File Syntax," for values:

    TimeZone=020

[UserData]

; Replace ComputerName, FullName, and OrgName with appropriate
; values. If any of these values is missing, the setup program
; will prompt the installer for the value:

    ComputerName="Sample"
    FullName="User Name"
    OrgName="Company Name"
```

```
; Replace ProductID with your product ID. If you don't provide
; a product key here, the setup program will prompt the installer:

    ProductKey=XXXXX-XXXXX-XXXXX-XXXXX-XXXXX

[TapiLocation]

; Replace AreaCode and CountryCode with appropriate values. See
; Ref.chm or Appendix D, "Answer File Syntax," for values:

    AreaCode=972
    CountryCode=1
    Dialing=Tone

[Identification]

; Replace DomainAdmin and DomainAdminPassword with the credentials
; of an account that can join the computer to the domain. The setup
; program will prompt the installer for these values if missing:

    DomainAdmin=Administrator
    DomainAdminPassword=Password

; Replace JoinDomain with the name of the domain to join:

    JoinDomain=DOMAIN

; Optionally, uncomment and replace MachineObjectOU with the LDAP
; path of the OU in which to create the computer account, if the
; account doesn't already exist:

;    MachineObjectOU="OU=Accounts,DC=honeycutt,DC=corp"

[Networking]

; This empty section is necessary if the answer file will include
; additional network settings described in Ref.chm. It's not necessary
; to use InstallDefaultComponents=Yes in this section. This answer
; file configures the computer with default networking components,
; including Client for Microsoft Networks, File and Printer Sharing
; for Microsoft Networks, QoS Packet Scheduler, and Internet Protocol
; (TCP/IP) configured to use DHCP.

[Components]

; Uncomment and set each of the following components to On to install
; it or Off to not install it (see Ref.chm or Appendix D, "Answer File
; Syntax," for more information about each component). These settings
; don't necessarily correspond to the operating system defaults:

;    accessopt=On
;    calc=On
;    certsrv=Off
;    certsrv_client=Off
;    certsrv_server=Off
```

```
;    charmap=On
;    chat=Off
;    deskpaper=On
;    dialer=On
;    fax=Off
;    fp_extensions=Off
;    fp_vdir_deploy=Off
;    freecell=On
;    hearts=On
;    hypertrm=On
;    IEAccess=On
;    iis_common=Off
;    iis_ftp=Off
;    iis_htmla=Off
;    iis_inetmgr=Off
;    iis_nntp=Off
;    iis_nntp_docs=Off
;    iis_pwmgr=Off
;    iis_smtp=Off
;    iis_smtp_docs=Off
;    iis_www=Off
;    iis_www_vdir_printers=Off
;    iis_www_vdir_terminalservices=Off
;    iisdbg=Off
;    indexsrv_system=Off
;    media_clips=On
;    media_utopia=Off
;    minesweeper=On
;    mousepoint=On
;    mplay=On
;    msmq_ADIntegrated=Off
;    msmq_Core=Off
;    msmq_HTTPSupport=Off
;    msmq_LocalStorage=Off
;    msmq_MQDSService=Off
;    msmq_RoutingSupport=Off
;    msmq_TriggersService=Off
;    msmsgs=On
;    msnexplr=On
;    mswordpad=On
;    netcis=Off
;    netoc=On
;    objectpkg=On
;    OEAccess=On
;    paint=On
;    pinball=On
;    rec=On
;    reminst=Off
;    rstorage=Off
;    solitaire=On
;    spider=On
;    templates=On
;    TerminalServer=Off
;    TSClients=Off
```

```
;    TSWebClient=Off
;    vol=On
;    wms=On
;    wms_admin_asp=On
;    wms_admin_mmc=On
;    wms_server=On
;    zonegames=On

;end
```

Copying the Source Files

You already learned that you must copy the I386 folder of the Windows XP Professional product CD to your distribution point. Put this folder at the root of the distribution point so that you can create multiple configurations without requiring separate I386 folders.

If you're deploying Windows XP Tablet PC Edition, you must copy a second folder to the distribution point. The media set for Windows XP Tablet PC Edition contains two CDs. After copying the I386 folder from the first CD to the distribution point, copy the CMPNENTS folder from the second CD. Both the I386 and CMP-NENTS folders should be at the same level within the distribution point. When you've finished creating a distribution point for Windows XP Tablet PC Edition, the distribution point should look similar to Figure 7-4.

Figure 7-4   For Windows XP Tablet PC Edition, copy the CMPNENTS folder to the root of the distribution folder, side by side with the I386 folder.

Creating the OEM Folder

Each OEM*N* folder you saw in Figure 7-3 contains an OEM folder. The OEM folder contains your customizations. These are the files that you add to the Windows XP Professional source files, such as third-party device drivers. You must add the line OemPreinstall=Yes to the *[Unattended]* section of your answer file, as shown in Listing 7-6, in order for Setup to add this folder to the target computer. If you don't set OemPreinstall in your answer file, Setup does not copy the OEM folder to the target computer.

The OEM folder can contain the file cmdlines.txt, which contains commands you want Setup to execute before the installation process finishes. This file is useful for running commands that configure Windows XP Professional or chain installations to the installation. Chapter 11, "Chaining Installations," describes the format of this file and how to use it to install additional programs with Windows XP Professional. If you're already familiar with this file and intend to use it without reading Chapter 11, keep in mind that environment variables are not available when the commands in this file run, so you can't use %SYSTEMROOT%, %SYSTEMDRIVE%, and so on in the paths of the commands that you run from this file. Additionally, file associations don't work at this point, so you must launch scripts using Wscript.exe:

```
wscript.exe //e:vbscript script.vbs options
```

Refer to Figure 7-3, which showed the assorted folders that you can create under the OEM folder. The following list describes each folder that you see:

- **TEXTMODE.**   This folder contains hardware-specific files that Setup and text-mode setup install on the target computer during the text-mode phase of the installation process. These files might include original equipment manufacturer (OEM) hardware abstraction layers (HALs), mass-storage device drivers, and the txtsetup.oem file. The txtsetup.oem file describes how to load and install these files. You must list these files in the [OemBootFiles] section of the unattended-setup answer file. This folder and the txtsetup.oem file aren't typically used during desktop deployments, however, because you don't often find specialized mass-storage devices on these computers; and Windows 2000 and Windows XP Professional support most of the common mass-storage devices on the market today. It's more common to use this section during a server deployment. Ref.chm in Deploy.cab on the Windows product CD in Support\Tools contains more information about adding text-mode device drivers to this folder.

- **$$.**   Setup copies the contents of this folder to %SYSTEMROOT% on each target computer. It replicates all the folders, subfolders, and files that this folder contains in the %SYSTEMROOT% folder of each target computer. If you want Setup to copy a file to %SYSTEMROOT%\System32 on each target computer, for example, put the file in OEM\$$\System32. I tend to create two folders within $$:

  - The first is DRIVERS. You can store third-party device drivers in this folder so that Setup copies them to each target computer; then, those device drivers are available later in this process (see "Adding Third-Party Drivers"). Ensure that you set the value OemPnPDriversPath in the [Unattended] section of your answer file to the path of the third-party device drivers on the target computer.

■ The second is APPS. You can store installations in this folder that you want to chain to the Windows installation. These can include packages that contain settings or install programs. They all tend to be self-contained package files that install silently, though. Note that this folder will persist on users' computers after installation, but you can remove the folder after installation is complete by adding the command to remove the folder to the Cmdlines.txt file.

> **More Info**   See Chapter 11 for more information.

■ **$1.**   Setup copies the contents of this folder to %SYSTEMDRIVE% on each target computer. It replicates all the folders, subfolders, and files that this folder contains in the %SYSTEMDRIVE% folder on each target computer. This is typically drive C on most computers. I tend to create a single folder in $1 when using disk-imaging techniques to deploy Windows. That is Sysprep. This is the Sysprep folder that you must create on the sample computer when you're building a disk image. By creating the Sysprep folder in $1, you can automate the disk-imaging process, as described in Chapter 15.

■ **Drive.**   *Drive* is a drive letter: C, D, E, and so on. Setup copies the contents of this folder to the root of the corresponding drive on each target computer. It replicates all the folders, subfolders, and files that this folder contains in the corresponding drive during the text-mode phase of the setup process. For example, Setup copies any files that you put in OEM\D to the root of drive D on each target computer. I recommend that you don't use these folders. They rely on a very specific disk configuration on the target computer. Use $1 to represent %SYSTEMDRIVE% instead.

> **Caution**   In most installations, OEM\$1 and OEM\C write to the same location: the root of drive C. If you add files to either of these folders, make sure that you don't have duplicate filenames; otherwise, if a file with the same name exists in both OEM\$1 and OEM\C, the copy in OEM\C overwrites OEM\$1 on the target computer during the installation process.

Adding Third-Party Drivers

The most common reason for customizing an OEM folder is adding third-party device drivers to the Windows XP Professional source files. If you're using recently released hardware, chances are good that Windows XP Professional doesn't ship with all of the device drivers needed to properly configure the computer. Don't deploy a configuration that doesn't work on the hardware configurations in your enterprise. First, in locked-down environments, users won't be able to install device drivers. Second, configurations that don't work properly *out-of-the-box* have a severely detrimental effect on users' satisfaction. Adding third-party device drivers is too easy to let it slip.

First, you must identify the device drivers that you need to add to the configuration. The best way I've found to do that is to install an un-customized version of Windows XP Professional on each type of computer that I'm supporting with the configuration. Then, I take a look in Device Manager to see which devices have bangs (icons next to a device's name that indicates an error). If all the devices are working properly, I move on to the next computer; otherwise, I make a note of the devices that aren't working. To make finding drivers easier, I sometimes look in the registry to find each device's Plug and Play ID. Armed with that information, I set out to find the device drivers:

- **Vendor Web sites.** I usually end up downloading device drivers from vendor Web sites. Most hardware vendors are very good about posting the latest device drivers. If you're given the choice between signed and unsigned device drivers, make sure that you download the signed drivers, regardless of which is newer. You can often find device drivers in two places. First is the component OEM's Web site. For example, you can download a video adapter's device driver from the adapter OEM's Web site. You can also download device drivers from the computer OEM's Web site. For example, you can download device drivers for most of IBM's computers from its Web site. Given the choice between downloading a device driver from the component OEM's or computer OEM's Web sites, I'd download it from the computer OEM's. They often provide device drivers that are further customized for their specific configurations.

- **Factory Image.** If the hardware to which you will be deploying the image ships from the factory with Windows XP Professional installed, the OEM might include the drivers on the factory disk image. However, vendors typically delete these drivers following the first boot of the factory image. Capture a disk image of the factory image by using a tool such as Symantec Ghost before starting the operating system; then gather the driver files from the disk image.

■ **Windows Update.**   You can download signed device drivers from Windows
Update. Instead of using Windows Update to install device driver updates, you
can use the Windows Update catalog to search for device drivers and then
download the driver packages to your hard disk. Open Windows Update by
clicking Tools, Windows Update in Internet Explorer; then, in the left pane,
click Personalize Windows Update. In the right pane, select the Display The
Link To The Windows Update Catalog Under See Also check box, and click
Save Settings. After personalizing Windows Update, you can search the catalog
by clicking Windows Update Catalog in the left pane and then download drivers to your hard disk. When you download device drivers from the catalog,
you'll find each in the subfolder Driver*Language**Type**Platform**ID**File*.cab.
You can extract the driver files from the .cab file using Windows Explorer or
WinZip from WinZip Computing (*http://www.winzip.com*).

> **Tip**   The device drivers that you download from Windows Update are
> already in a form suitable for addition to a Windows XP Professional distri-
> bution folder. They're already split into their .inf, .cat, .sys, and other files,
> so you don't have to decompress a self-extracting installation program and
> find the files yourself. Simply copy all of the files from the .cab file to your
> OEM folder, as described in the next section.

> **On the Resource Kit CD**   See "Unattended Installation Worksheet" in the
> file dist04.doc on this book's companion CD in the Aids folder. Use this
> worksheet to document the device drivers you must include in your distribu-
> tion point.

Manual Process

As shown in Figure 7-3, I store device drivers in OEM\\$$\\DRIVERS. You copy the
device driver files to this folder. You can create subfolders under the DRIVERS
folder, but add each path to OemPnPDriversPath. For example, if you store device driv-
ers for network adapters in OEM\\$$\\DRIVERS\\LAN and device drivers for video
adapters in OEM\\$$\\DRIVERS\\VIDEO, add the following line to the *[Unattended]*
section of the answer file:

```
OEMPnpDriversPath=\WINDOWS\DRIVERS\LAN;\WINDOWS\DRIVERS\VIDEO
```

You don't want all the files that a device driver contains. If you copy every file from every device driver that you downloaded, you're likely to get a lot of useless and duplicate files. Instead, copy only the essential files for each device driver. How do you know which files are essential? Easy. Listing 7-7 is an excerpt from the .inf file for the Intel PRO/100 VE network adapter. You need to copy the .inf file for the device driver to the OEM\$$\DRIVERS folder (Plug and Play uses the .inf file to match the IDs of the devices installed on the computer to their device drivers). You also need the .cat file that contains the device driver's signature. To find the name of the .cat file, look in the .inf file's *[Version]* section for the *CatalogFile* setting. This setting indicates the name of the .cat file, which is e100b325.cat in Listing 7-7. Last, you need to copy to the OEM\$$\DRIVERS folder each file listed in the *[SourceDisks-Files]* section. In this case, that includes e100b325.bin, e100b325.sys, Prounstl.exe, IntelNic.dll, and e100bmsg.dll.

A very few device drivers indicate that a file listed in the *[SourceDisksFiles]* section is in a subfolder. You must duplicate this folder structure exactly in your OEM\$$\DRIVERS folder in order for Setup to find all of the device driver's files. For example, if you see a line in the *[SourceDisksFiles]* section that looks like `Example.sys=1,FOLDER`, you must copy the file Example.sys to OEM\$$ \DRIVERS\FOLDER for Setup to find it; otherwise, Setup will prompt the user for the file's location.

Listing 7-7   e100b325.inf

```
[Version]
CatalogFile      = e100b325.cat

[SourceDisksFiles]
e100b325.din = 1,,
e100b325.sys = 1,,
Prounstl.exe = 1,,
IntelNic.dll = 1,,
e100bmsg.dll = 1,,
```

Scripted Process

This book's companion CD contains the script infcopy.wsf, which automates the process of copying a device driver's files to the OEM\$$\DRIVERS or any other folder. It simply automates the process described in the previous section. The following shows the syntax of this script, and Table 7-1 describes each option:

`infcopy.wsf filename folder [/Y] [/L:value] [/Q] [/?]`

Table 7-1   Infcopy.wsf Command-Line Options

Option	Description
filename	Specifies the path and filename of the device driver's .inf file.
Folder	Specifies the path of the folder in which to copy the device driver's file.
/Y	Overwrites existing device driver files.
/L:value	Logs the results to the log file specified by *value*.
/Q	Suppresses all output.
/?	Displays help and usage information.

Running this script manually is not the most efficient way to use it. For example, to copy the required files from the device driver that the .inf file D:\Device\Driver.inf describes to the target folder D:\Target, overwriting existing files, run the command infcopy.wsf d:\device\driver.inf d:\target /y. You'd have to repeat this for each device driver that you wanted to add to your distribution folder. Instead, you can put a list of device driver .inf files in a text file such as drivers.txt and then use the command *for /f %i in ("drivers.txt") do infcopy.wsf %i d:\target*. This command runs infcopy.wsf for each .inf file in the text file drivers.txt, copying them to the folder D:\Target.

The sample distribution folder in Samples\chap07\win2002.pro on this book's companion CD takes this one step further. It includes the batch script drivers.cmd, shown in Listing 7-8, which assumes that the script infcopy.wsf is in the Scripts subfolder and processes the list of device driver .inf files contained in each OEM*N* folder's drivers.txt file. It uses the *for /d* statement to examine each of the distribution folder's subfolders. Then, it runs infcopy.wsf for any subfolder that contains an OEM folder. The *for /f* statement parses the drivers.txt file's contents. It expects each line in this file to follow the syntax `Subfolder=Inffile`, where `Subfolder` is a subfolder you want to create beneath the OEM\$$\DRIVERS folder and `Inffile` is the path and filename of the device driver's *.inf* file. If you want to put the device driver's files in the OEM\$$\DRIVERS folder and not in a subfolder, use `Inffile.=`. The period (.) represents the DRIVERS folder. This batch script also calls rename.wsf, a script that you learn about in the next section, to make sure that any long filenames that device drivers contain are handled in $$Rename.txt.

Listing 7-9 is an example drivers.txt file. It stores the files for the Intel 815 Audio and IDE device drivers in the OEM\$$\DRIVERS folder. It stores the files for the Intel 815 LAN device driver in the OEM\$$\DRIVERS\LAN folder. It stores the files for the Intel Extreme and S3 Graphics Twister display adapters in the OEM\$$\DRIVERS\VIDEO folder.

Listing 7-8   drivers.cmd

```
@echo off
@rem drivers.cmd: make $OEM$ drivers folders

setlocal enableextensions

if not '%1'=='' cd /d %1

  echo.

  for /d %%i in (*) do (

    rem Find each subfolder that contains an $OEM$ folder

    if exist %%i\$OEM$ (

      rem Run incopy.wsf for each subfolder=inffile listed in drivers.txt
      rem Also run rename.wsf to create $$rename.txt for FAT32 targets

      for /f "usebackq tokens=1-2 delims==" %%j in ("%%i\drivers.txt") do (
        echo Copying %%~nxk to %%i\$OEM$\$$\DRIVERS\%%j
        .\scripts\infcopy.wsf "%%k" "%%i\$OEM$\$$\DRIVERS\%%j"
        .\scripts\rename.wsf "%%i\$OEM$"
      )
    )
  )

  echo.

  goto end

:end
```

Listing 7-9   drivers.txt

```
.=D:\Drivers\Intel 815 Audio Driver 5.12\SMAXWDM\W2K\smwdm.inf
.=D:\Drivers\Intel 815 IDE Drivers 603\Win2000\IntelATA.inf
LAN=D:\Drivers\Intel 815 LAN Driver 383\Net82557.inf
VIDEO= D:\Drivers\Intel Extreme Graphics Controller 6.13\ialmnt5.inf
VIDEO= D:\Drivers\S3 Graphics Twister Video Driver 6.13\tw5333.inf
```

On the Resource Kit CD   Infcopy.wsf is on this book's companion CD in the Scripts folder. This script requires the file windeploy.wsc, which is in the same folder. A sample distribution folder that includes drivers.cmd and drivers.txt is on this book's companion CD in the folder Samples\chap07\win2002.pro. Simply copy this folder to your hard disk and customize it as described in the section "Customizing the Sample Folder."

Fixing Long Filenames

Windows XP Professional stores two versions of every filename. The long filename is what you normally see, such as This Is A Long File Name.txt. It also stores a short filename, which is the first six alphanumeric characters of the long filename with a ~*N*, where *N* is a number beginning with 1. So, the short filename version of This Is A Long File Name.txt is THISIS~1.txt.

If you're installing Windows XP Professional from Windows PE, you don't have to worry about the length of filenames. Windows PE can read and write long file-names, and you're starting off with the NTFS file system. If you're installing Windows XP Professional using an MS-DOS boot disk, you have a problem. MS-DOS can't see long filenames, and you're starting off with the FAT32 file system, so Setup copies files from the distribution point to the target computer using the short filename (8.3). Setup already handles long filenames in the original Windows XP Professional source files, but you'll sometimes add third-party device drivers to your distribution points that contain long filenames. After Setup copies these files to the target computer, changing their names to short filenames, Setup can't find the files it needs to configure device drivers, and applications' setup programs fail because they can't find their files.

> **On the Resource Kit CD**   See "Renamed Files and Folders Worksheet" on this book's companion CD in the Aids folder for help planning renamed files and folders. The filename is dist03.doc. You need this worksheet only if you're creating $$Rename.txt files manually.

Manual Process

You can use $$Rename.txt files to restore long filenames after Setup converts the file system to NTFS. An example of this file is in Listing 7-10, which you'd create in the OEM\$$ folder. Each section name is the path of the files contained in the section, and the paths are relative to the folder that contains the $$Rename.txt file. Each entry has the format short.exe="long file name.exe".

Forget everything you've read in the documentation ($$Rename.txt isn't limited to the OEM\$1 folder), which is confusing at best, and put a $$Rename.txt file only in the OEM folders $$, $1, C, D, and so on. Don't put them in subfolders and don't rely on a single $$Rename.txt at the root of %SYSTEMDRIVE%, either of which is too confusing.

> **Caution** Don't create an empty $$Rename.txt file or a $$Rename.txt file that contains an empty section. Doing so prevents Setup from properly renaming Windows XP Professional source files. The most obvious symptom of this problem is that Windows XP Professional starts with the classic theme because Setup wasn't able to rename the *.theme* files to their long filenames. If you don't have a short filename that you need to restore to a long filename, don't create $$Rename.txt.

Listing 7-10 $$Rename.txt

```
[DRIVERS]
THISIS~1.TXT = "This is a test.txt"
THISIS~2.TXT = "This is another test.txt"

[DRIVERS\LAN]
THISIS~1.TXT = "This is a test.txt"
THISIS~2.TXT = "This is another test.txt"

[DRIVERS\VIDEO]
THISIS~1.TXT = "This is a test.txt"
THISIS~2.TXT = "This is another test.txt"
```

Scripted Process

Now that I've described why and how to create the $$Rename.txt file, forget about it. Instead, run the script rename.wsf, which is on this book's companion CD. This script automatically checks your distribution point for long filenames and automatically creates the appropriate $$Rename.txt files. The following shows the syntax of this script, and Table 7-2 describes each option:

```
rename.wsf folder [/L] [/Y] [/V] [/Q] [/?]
```

Table 7-2   Rename.wsf Command-Line Options

Option	Description
folder	Specifies the path of the OEM folder to scan for long filenames.
/L	Lists long filenames without creating $$Rename.txt files.
/Y	Overwrites existing $$Rename.txt files.
/V	Creates verbose output.
/Q	Suppresses all output.
/?	Displays help and usage information.

To scan the folder D:\win2002.pro\OEM1\$OEM$ for long filenames, use the command rename.wsf d:\win2002.pro\oem1\$OEM$. If the subfolders $$ and C both contain long filenames, rename.wsf creates $$Rename.txt files in both folders. You don't have to run this script manually, however, as the batch script drivers.cmd, which you learned about in the section "Adding Third-Party Drivers," automatically runs rename.wsf after copying third-party device drivers to OEM\$$\DRIVERS.

On the Resource Kit CD   This book's companion CD contains rename.wsf in the Scripts folder. This script requires the file windeploy.wsf, which is in the same folder. It also contains a fully customized distribution point with the batch script drivers.cmd that calls rename.wsf to account for long names in device driver files. The sample distribution point is in the folder Samples\chap07\win2002.pro. Simply copy this folder to your hard disk and customize it as described in the section "Customizing the Sample Folder."

Customizing the Sample Folder

The Samples\chap07\win2002.pro folder on this book's companion CD contains the sample distribution folder for this chapter. It's fully customized using the scripts that this chapter describes. Here's how to use that sample to jumpstart your own distribution (Figure 7-5 shows what this fully customized distribution point looks like):

1. Copy Samples\chap07\win2002.pro from this book's companion CD to your development server, and do one of the following:

   - If you're creating a distribution point for Windows XP Professional, rename the folder to win2002.pro (I use the naming convention *version.edition* for distribution folders).

   - If you're creating a distribution point for Windows XP Table PC Edition, name the folder win2002.tab.

2. Do one of the following:

   - If you're creating a distribution point for Windows XP Professional, copy the I386 folder from your Windows XP Professional media to win2002.pro.

■ If you're creating a distribution point for Windows XP Tablet PC Edition, copy the I386 folder from your Windows XP media to win2002.tab; then copy the CMPNENTS folder from the second CD to win2002.tab.

3. Create a folder in win2002.pro or win2002.tab to store original device drivers, such as win2002.pro\Drivers. Within that folder, create a subfolder for each device driver that you download form OEMs and expand.

4. Determine how many configurations you want to create (the sample folder includes OEM1, OEM2, and OEMN). Create addition OEM*N* folders if necessary or remove unused OEM*N* folders. For example, if you need only two configurations, delete the folder win2002.pro\OEMN. If you need four configurations, copy win2002.pro\OEMN to OEM3 and OEM4.

5. In each OEM*N* folder under win2002.pro or win2002.tab, update drivers.txt to point to each device driver's .inf file that you want to include. If you examine the drivers.txt file, you'll find an example of the file's syntax.

6. In each OEM*N* folder under win2002.pro or win2002.tab, update winnt.sif, which is the unattended-setup answer file. In particular, you must update the following settings (see the sample winnt.sif file for more settings that you must replace when customizing a distribution point):

   ■ OemFilesPath. Set this property to the UNC path of the OEM folder. For example, if you're editing winnt.sif in win2002.pro\OEM2 and the UNC path of the distribution point will be \\Server\Windows, add OemFiles-Path=\\Server\Windows\win2002.pro\OEM2\OEM to the *[Unattended]* section of winnt.sif.

   ■ OemPnPDriversPath. Update this property with the path of each folder that contains third-party device drivers. This path is relative to the folders on the target computer. So, if you have files in OEM\DRIVERS, OEM\DRIVERS\LAN, and OEM\DRIVERS\VIDEO, add OemPnPDriversPath=\WINDOWS\DRIVERS;\WINDOWS\DRIVERS\LAN;\WINDOWS\DRIVERS\VIDEO to the *[Unattended]* section.

7. In win2002.pro or win2002.tab, run drivers.cmd, which will copy the device driver files described by the .inf files in drivers.txt to the distribution point. It will also run rename.wsf to create $$Rename.txt files for long filenames.

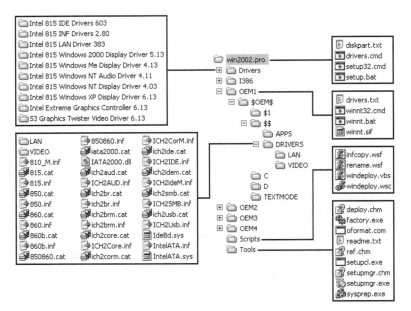

Figure 7-5   After customizing the sample distribution point in
Samples\chap07\win2002.pro on the companion CD, this is the result.

More Info   To learn how to customize your distribution point to run commands during the installation, see Chapter 11. For more information about customizing unattended-setup answer files, see Chapter 7. And for more information about installing Windows XP Professional after customizing your distribution point, see Chapter 13.

Integrating Service Packs

Most of you will have received from Microsoft a Windows XP Professional product CD with the latest service pack already integrated into it. If so, you're set to go. If your deployment requirements specify that you're deploying a service pack level that you don't already have, you can download the latest Windows XP Professional service pack and integrate it into the source files that you already have. This process applies the service pack files directly to the Windows XP Professional source files, preventing you from having to install the service pack after installing Windows XP Professional on the client computer. And doing so requires very little additional disk space in the distribution point because service packs tend to replace existing files and add very few.

Chapter 22, "Patch Management," describes how to slipstream service packs into existing Windows XP Professional source files. In short, after you've downloaded the service pack from Microsoft's Web site or received the service pack CD from Microsoft, use the following steps to integrate a service pack:

1. Type *spfile* **–x** in the Run dialog box or at the command prompt to extract the service pack files to your hard disk. *spfile* is the cabinet file that contains the service pack. The wizard will prompt you for the folder into which you want it to extract the files.

2. Type **folder\i386\Update\Update.exe –s:share**, where **folder** is the folder into which you extracted the service pack and **share** is the distribution point, in the Run dialog box or at the command prompt. The wizard slipstreams the service pack files into the distribution point.

Don't slipstream a service pack into a distribution point after you've deployed the distribution point. Windows XP Professional occasionally restores files from the distribution point to the client computer, and if you integrate a service pack into the distribution point, the operating system might restore an incorrect file version. You should integrate service packs into distribution points prior to deploying the operating system, and then deploy the service pack to individual client computers after deployment.

> **More Info**   See Chapter 22 for more information about deploying service packs to individual client computers.

Sharing Distribution Points

After you customize your distribution point, you'll post it to the intranet deployment server and share it. Secure your distribution point as follows:

- **NTFS security.**   Configure NTFS security for the distribution point to give administrators full control and users read and execute permission.

- **Share security.**   Configure the share security for the distribution point to give all users read-only access to it. Even though giving administrators full control is tempting, there is seldom any good reason to change a distribution point remotely, and doing so can only lead to errors.

Balancing Installation

You can create distribution points on multiple servers to load-balance installations. This applies to unattended installations only. Creating distribution points on multiple servers also improves the performance of the file-copy phase of the setup process. You can run the 32-bit setup program with up to eight distribution points, and it'll copy source files from each of them.

More Info   See Chapter 13 for more information about installing Windows from multiple distribution points.

Office Distribution Points

Creating distribution points for Microsoft Office 2003 Editions is more straightforward than creating Windows XP Professional distribution points. Office 2003 Editions distribution points are even simpler than creating Office XP distribution points because you can now create distribution points simply by copying the contents of the product CD to the distribution point. This new capability is called *compressed CD images*. You can still create administrative installations of Office 2003 Editions, however. You can only create administrative installations of Office 2003 Editions using product CDs that you receive through a Volume License Agreement.

My recommendation in most cases is that you create Office 2003 Editions distribution points from compressed CD images. As you'll learn in the section "Compressed CD Images," these distribution points provide numerous advantages over administrative installations without any significant disadvantages. For example, when you install Office 2003 Editions from a compressed CD image, Office 2003 Setup creates a local installation source on the target computer that allows users to add features and repair the installation without a network connection. If you support any number of mobile users, this capability alone makes using compressed CD images an easy decision to make.

More Info   The following sections, "Administrative Installations" and "Compressed CD Images," describe both techniques. Although these sections provide a starting point for creating Office 2003 Editions distribution points, the ultimate resource for information about configuring Office 2003 Editions distribution points is the Office 2003 Editions Resource Kit at *http://www.microsoft.com/office/ork*. On the left side of the Web page, click Deployment.

Administrative Installations

Most administrators are familiar with creating Office 2003 Editions administrative installations because this has been the only way to build distribution points for Microsoft Office 2000 and Office XP. The process involves decompressing the contents of the product CD and embedding the organization name, product key, and acceptance of the End User License Agreement into the distribution point.

First, create a distribution folder for Office 2003 Editions. You can initially create this folder on your development server and then replicate it to distribution servers. If you intend to configure features to run from the network (Run from Network or Run All from Network), you must create the administrative installation in a subfolder of the distribution point. For example, *server**share**admin*, where *server* is the distribution server, *share* is the distribution point, and *admin* is a subfolder.

After you've created the distribution folder, run the setup program in administrative-installation mode. From the Office 2003 Editions CD, run the command *setup /a*, and then follow the instructions you see on the screen. It prompts you for the organization name, product key, distribution point location, and end user license agreement. Because you provide the product key when you create the administrative installation, Office 2003 Editions doesn't prompt users for the key when they run it the first time. It then decompresses the contents of the CD to the distribution point and prepares it for distribution to client computers.

After you create a distribution point, you can customize it, as you learn in Chapter 9, "Office Settings." You use the Office 2003 Editions Resource Kit tools, including the Custom Installation Wizard, to configure Office 2003 Editions for deployment. Afterward, you deploy Office 2003 Editions using any of the methods that you learn about in Chapter 23, "Software Installation," such as Active Directory.

More Info See "Office 2003 Editions Resource Kit" at *http://www.microsoft.com/office/ork* for more information about creating administrative installations of Office 2003 Editions. Specifically, point to Deployment, and then click Preparing to Deploy Office 2003.

Compressed CD Images

When users install Office 2003 Editions from a compressed CD image on the network, Office 2003 Setup uses a system service named Office Source Engine (Ose.exe) to copy required installation files to a hidden folder on the local computer. Windows Installer uses this local installation source to install Office 2003

Editions, and the local source remains available for repairing, reinstalling, or updating Office 2003 Editions later. Users can install features on demand or run Office 2003 Setup in maintenance mode to add new features.

Office 2003 Setup creates a local installation source by default, but only when users install Office 2003 Editions from a compressed CD image. If sufficient hard disk space exists on the local computer, Office 2003 Setup caches the entire installation source by default. Maintaining this local installation source after Office 2003 is installed offers a number of benefits to users in large organizations. The most important benefit is to mobile users. Local installation sources allow them to add or repair features without requiring access to the network source files. This solves a particularly nasty problem that has plagued administrators since Office 2000. There is only one significant disadvantage of creating distribution points with compressed CD images: users can't run features from the network by using the Run From Network installation state. In most enterprises, however, this isn't necessarily a disadvantage because you don't typically want users wasting network bandwidth by running features from the network.

Office 2003 Editions source files are compressed in cabinet (CAB) files to fit on the Office 2003 Editions product CD. To create a distribution point as a compressed CD image, you simply copy the compressed CAB files to a network share before customizing the CD image. You don't run Office 2003 Setup to create an administrative installation point; instead, you just copy the compressed files directly to the network share. Unlike the process of running Office 2003 Setup with the /a option, which expands the compressed files on the administrative installation point, the files in the CD image remain compressed. Here's how to create a distribution point from a compressed CD image:

1. In Windows Explorer, display hidden files so that you see the entire contents of the Office 2003 Editions CD. To do so, choose Tools, Folder Options; then, on the View tab, click Show Hidden Files And Folders.

2. Select all the folders on the CD, and copy the CD contents to a network share. The complete CD image for Office 2003 Professional Edition requires approximately 250MB of space.

Copying the CD to a distribution point doesn't embed the product key or accept the End-User License Agreement (EULA) automatically on behalf of all users who install Office 2003 Editions from this network share. You must configure the product key, organization name, and acceptance of the EULA when you customize Office 2003 Editions using the Custom Installation Wizard (CIW). For more information about using CIW to customize these settings, see Chapter 9.

> **More Info**   I recommend that you distribute Office 2003 Editions from compressed CD images. As you've read, you create these distribution points by simply copying the CD to a network folder. You customize a compressed CD image by using the CIW. This includes controlling how Office 2003 Setup creates local installation sources, specifying the product key, and accepting the EULA. For more information about using CIW to customize your compressed CD image, see Chapter 9.

> **More Info**   A new version of the Office 2003 Setup program is available in the Office 2003 Editions Resource Kit Toolbox. Version 11.0.6176.0 helps ensure that every desktop in the organization gets and keeps a complete local installation source. The new Office 2003 Setup also allows administrators to deploy the local installation source first, and then launch the installation of Office 2003 Editions. I strongly recommend that you update the version of Office 2003 Setup in your current distribution points with the latest version.

Integrating Service Releases

Office 2003 Editions service releases are interim upgrades that address performance, reliability, and security issues. You're likely to have received an Office 2003 Editions product CD that contains Office 2003 Editions with the current service release already integrated. Otherwise, if your deployment plans require, you might need to integrate the latest service release with your existing Office 2003 Editions source files.

Microsoft issues two versions of each service release. You can download either from *http://www.microsoft.com/office/ork*. One is for updating administrative installations, and the other is for updating client computers (also called binary updates). Both are patch files with the .msp extension. The administrative update is a full-file replacement that contains all the service release's changes. The client update updates existing files instead of replacing them. You must use the administrative update to integrate the service release into your Office 2003 Editions distribution point, if you created it as an administrative installation, and the client update to update client computers, if you created the distribution point as a compressed CD image.

Chapter 22 describes how to integrate a service release into your Office 2003 Editions source files. You should update your Office 2003 Editions distribution points prior to deploying them, however. Here is the shorthand version of the process to integrate a service release into your administrative installation. Type **msiexec /p** *mspfile* **/a** *msifile* **SHORTFILENAMES=TRUE /qb /L*** *logfile*—where *mspfile* is the path and filename of the patch file; *msifile* is the path and filename of the administrative installation's package file; and *logfile* is the path and filename of the log file in which you want to record the results—in the Run dialog box or the command prompt. Some service releases contain multiple patch files, and you need to run the previous command once for each patch file.

Distribution Point Contents

Table 7-3 describes key files in an Office 2003 Editions distribution point.

Table 7-3 Distribution Point Contents

File	Location	Description
Setup.exe	Root of distribution folder	You use Setup.exe to install Office 2003 Editions on computers that don't already contain the correct version of Windows Installer. This typically includes versions of Windows earlier than Windows 2000. Setup.exe installs Windows Installer, manages reboots, and handles package chaining.
Setup.ini	FILES\SETUP	This configuration settings file controls how Setup.exe runs. This file contains information for package chaining, too.
Office 2003 Editions Package	Root of distribution folder	The Office 2003 Editions package file has the .msi extension. This package file contains the instructions necessary to install Office 2003 Editions on the client computer.
Source files	FILES\PFILES	The Office 2003 Editions package file doesn't actually contain the program files. The package file installs the program files from this folder.

Sharing Distribution Points

After you've customized your Office 2003 Editions distribution point, post it to your intranet distribution server. You can replicate the distribution point to multiple servers in order to improve resiliency. If you do so, make sure you add each distribution point to the Office 2003 Editions source list, as described in Chapter 9. When you replicate Office 2003 Editions distribution points that you created as administrative installations, each new administrative installation has the same organization name and product key as the original distribution point that you replicated.

On each Office 2003 Editions distribution point that you share, configure security as follows:

■ **NTFS security.** Configure NTFS security for the distribution point to give administrators full control and users read and execute permission.

- **Share security.** Configure the share security for the distribution point to give all users read-only access to it. Even though giving administrators full control is tempting, there is seldom any good reason to change a distribution point remotely, and doing so can only lead to errors.

Best Practices

The following are best practices for building Windows XP Professional and Office 2003 Editions distribution points:

- **Automate the development process.** To prevent human error, automate as much of the development process as possible. Use batch scripts and Windows Script Host scripts to automate repetitive processes that are prone to error, as shown throughout this chapter.

- **Use the templates provided on the companion CD.** To quickly create a distribution folder, use the template distribution folder on this book's companion CD or use Windows Setup Manager to build it. Then customize the distribution point to suit your requirements. The companion CD contains sample distribution folders in the Samples folder.

- **Conserve space and maintain flexibility.** To conserve space, distribute different Windows XP Professional configurations using a single I386 folder with multiple OEM folders and configure the OemFilesPath value in the *[Unattended]* section of the answer file for each configuration.

- **Use multiple distribution servers.** In large-scale deployments, install Windows XP Professional from multiple distribution servers to load-balance the deployment.

- **Improve the performance of the file-copy phase.** To improve the performance of the installation's file-copy phase, specify multiple distribution servers on the Setup command line, as described in Chapter 13.

- **Distribute Office 2003 Editions from compressed CD images.** Unless you have a specific reason for using administrative installations, deploy Office 2003 Editions from compressed CD images. Doing so allows Office 2003 Setup to create local installation sources on target computers so that users can add and repair features without a network connection.

- **Create Office 2003 Editions administration installations in subfolders of the network share.** If you do deploy Office 2003 Editions from an administrative installation, create administrative installations in subfolders of their distribution points to ensure that the installation state Run from Network works properly.

Chapter 8

Windows Settings

Configuring settings for Microsoft Windows XP Professional is seldom overlooked by administrators, but they don't always do it the most efficient way possible. This chapter describes automated approaches to deploying Windows XP Professional settings as part of a Windows XP Professional configuration that makes the task easier and more rigorous.

Checklist

- Have you documented in your deployment plan the Windows XP Professional settings you must deploy? See Chapter 3, "Windows Configuration," for more information.

- Have you examined which settings you can configure by using answer files? See Chapter 6, "Answer Files," for more information.

- Have you built a Windows XP Professional distribution from which you can deploy settings? See Chapter 7, "Distribution Points," for more information.

- Do you already have a method in place for deploying settings? If not, see Chapter 11, "Chaining Installations," to learn how to deploy them from distribution points.

- Have you documented in your deployment plan which settings are policy rather than default settings? If so, see Chapter 20, "Policy Management," to learn more about deploying policies.

Settings Overview

Choose the settings-deployment method that's most appropriate for the type of setting that you're deploying. And choose one that's automated, requiring no manual work beyond packaging the setting, and robust enough to withstand rigorous testing. The following list describes various methods that are available for deploying settings:

- **Required settings via Group Policy**   Group Policy is at the top of this list because it's the primary way to deploy settings that are policies. Although this chapter describes how to deploy default settings for computers, Chapter 20 describes how to configure policy settings, which users can't change.

- **Default settings via manual configuration on a disk image**   Using this technique, you click through the Windows XP Professional user interface while you're building a disk image. The problem with this technique is that it's manual, so testing and repeating the configuration after fixing bugs is difficult. For this reason, I don't recommend that you manually configure any setting. With that said, realistically there will be times when a setting is so difficult to configure automatically that you must configure it manually. Use your best judgment when building disk images.

> **More Info**   For more information about disk imaging, see Chapter 15, "Disk Imaging with Sysprep," and Chapter 16, "Remote Installation Service."

Default settings via automated techniques during distribution   This technique involves using a combination of Registration Entries (*.reg*) files, Setup Information (*.inf*) files, Windows Script Host (WSH) scripts, and Windows Installer databases (*.msi* package files) to deploy settings as part of your Windows XP Professional distribution. And methods for deploying the settings range from inclusion in the distribution point to configuration through a logon script. This chapter focuses on these techniques for configuring Windows XP Professional default settings during distribution.

When you think about and document the settings you're deploying, you tend to picture the Windows XP Professional user interface. But the majority of the default settings you want to configure during a distribution are actually registry settings or files. I use scripts to configure these settings. As you're planning these settings, also plan which methods you intend to use to distribute each. You can divide most settings into two categories: managed and unmanaged. Obviously, you'll prefer to deploy managed settings by using Group Policy. Chapter 20, "Policy Management," provides more information about policies. The techniques that this chapter describes are more appropriate for unmanaged settings.

Scripting is a more efficient way to deploy and change default settings for Windows XP Professional. Notice that I didn't use the word *manage*, which better applies to policies than scripting. (If you need to manage settings, see Chapter 20.) Scripting is useful on many levels. You can write a script that changes some group of settings and then test it in the lab before deploying. And if you need to update the script, you can easily regression-test it to see how your changes affect the results. Simply put, I like scripting registry changes because scripts are repeatable without the potential for human error each time I use them to change settings. You can also deploy scripts without visiting desktops. You can use your software management infrastructure (Microsoft Systems Management Server, Active Directory, and so on) or some dodgier methodology if you don't have an infrastructure to deploy scripts without having to interrupt users' work.

AutoProf Profile Maker

In environments where I have a choice, I use a product from AutoProf called Profile Maker to configure unmanaged settings (I still use Group Policy to configure managed settings, except in heterogenous environments).

Profile Maker makes short work of configuring any setting, including registry values, files, and so on. Profile Maker even provides a user interface for configuring common settings, such as Microsoft Office 2003 Editions settings, Microsoft Office Outlook 2003 mail profiles, printer connections, network drive mappings, and so on.

Most important, Profile Maker provides an easy-to-use, centralized console that you can use to configure settings for the entire enterprise. It allows you to filter settings based on a huge variety of criteria (certain settings can apply only to laptop computers or computers in a certain organizational unit, for example), and Profile Maker allows you to configure computer settings in a locked-down environment by configuring them with elevated permissions.

Profile Maker can significantly reduce the cost, time, and effort required to deploy settings in any organization. For more information about Profile Maker, see *http://www.autoprof.com* and read Chapter 12, "User Profiles."

This chapter describes five of my favorite scripting methods. The first is using *.inf* files. I like the simplicity of *.inf* files and the fact that there's no registry setting they can't edit, so I describe them first. The second is *.reg* files, which are easy to make by exporting settings from Registry Editor (Regedit). I also describe how to use Console Registry Tool for Windows (Reg.exe) to edit the registry from the MS-DOS command prompt, which is a terrific tool for changing settings from batch files. Also, I describe how to write scripts that change settings. Windows XP Professional comes with WSH, and this chapter shows you how to write scripts using the JScript and VBScript languages. Finally, I describe how to build a Windows Installer package file to deploy settings. This technique is great because you can sometimes deploy those settings through Active Directory and Group Policy.

Finding Settings

The most difficult part when creating a script to configure Windows XP Professional is actually finding the setting. The following two sections describe techniques and tools to do just that.

Comparing *.reg* Files

Comparing two *.reg* files is often the easiest way to discover where in the registry Windows XP Professional stores a setting. Create these *.reg* files before and after changing a setting that is in the user interface and that you know is somewhere in the registry. First, I exported HKCU to a *.reg* file. I changed a setting in Tweak UI and exported the same branch to a second *.reg* file. Then I compared the two files to figure out which value changed when I changed the setting in Tweak UI. You can use this method to trace just about any setting that has a user interface to its location in the registry.

The only disadvantage of comparing two registry files is that the process requires a file-comparison tool. Windows XP Professional comes with such a tool, which I'll tell you about later in this section. The advantages of this method are many. First, it's quick and easy. Second, its results are dead-on accurate. If you don't let a lot of time pass between each snapshot, the differences between the two should include only those settings you changed. Also, *.reg* files are easy to read, so you won't have any problems deciphering the results.

Now for some details. Recall that Registry Editor (Regedit) can export all or part of the registry to text files that have the *.reg* extension (*.reg* files). A *.reg* file looks similar to an INI file. It contains one or more sections; the name of each section is the path of a registry key, and each section contains the key's values. The format of each value is `name=value`. If the value is a string containing spaces, `value` must be quoted. Each key's default value looks like `@=value`. The section "Setting Values with *.reg* Files" describes *.reg* files in all their glory, including how to interpret the different types of values in them. To export the registry to a *.reg* file, click the key that you want to export. Then on the File menu, click Export. In the Export Registry File dialog box, click Win9x/NT4 Registration Files (*.reg) to export to a version 4 ANSI *.reg* file. Regedit supports *.reg* files in two different file formats: American National Standards Institute (ANSI) and Unicode. Many file-comparison tools work only with the first, thus you must create version 4 ANSI *.reg* files for them. The tools I talk about in this chapter support both ANSI and Unicode text files, though.

The sections following this one describe tools you can use to compare two *.reg* files. My personal favorite is WinDiff, which comes with the Windows Support Tools on your Windows XP Professional product CD. I like this tool so much because of its simple user interface, and more importantly, the speed at which it compares very large text files. Another choice is probably already installed on your computer: Microsoft Office Word 2003. It's slower than WinDiff, but you're probably already familiar with how to use this word processor. In any case, the overall process is the same:

1. Export the registry to a *.reg* file and name the file something like Before.reg. If you have a general idea where the setting is in the registry, export that branch; otherwise, export the entire registry, including HKU and HKLM.

2. Change a setting in the user interface or perform some other action that you're trying to trace to the registry. For example, if you want to see where a program stores its settings during installation, install the program.

3. Export the registry to a second .reg file and name it After.reg. Make sure you export the same branch using the same file format as you did in step 1. If you don't duplicate the process exactly, the files won't match and finding the difference will be difficult.

4. Compare Before.reg and After.reg by using your favorite file-comparison utility. The differences between the two files are your changes. The file-comparison tool points out only the values that changed because only the values under each section heading change, but if you look a little higher in the file, you'll see the key that contains the values.

There are a few ways to make this process more efficient. Comparing two large *.reg* files can take a while—even using WinDiff. If you're pretty certain you know the general vicinity of a setting in the registry, export just that branch. For example, if you know that a setting is a per-user setting, export just HKCU. If you suspect it's somewhere in HKLM\SOFTWARE\Microsoft, search just that branch. You can always resort to exporting the entire registry if your hunch isn't right. Another way to streamline the process is to ignore differences that are irrelevant. Some settings change, whether or not you do anything. For example, Plug and Play values change frequently, as does the configuration of some services. The easiest way to eliminate the confusion that these inherent changes cause is to exclude HKLM\SYSTEM in your *.reg* files. Also, the less time that elapses between snapshots, the less noise you'll have in your comparison results.

All-in-One Solutions

LastBit Software produces a program called RegSnap that performs the process I described in this section. You don't have to create any *.reg* files or compare two *.reg* files with a file-comparison tool. RegSnap does the whole bit for you, making it a cool program to have around if you do this sort of thing on a regular basis. You can download the shareware version of RegSnap from *http://www.webdon.com*. Give it a try; if you like it, it's very inexpensive. It comes in a standard edition and a professional edition. The professional edition enables you to work with remote registries; otherwise, the standard edition is sufficient to locate a setting in the registry. The only problem I have with RegSnap is that its user interface is very clunky.

That leads me to RegView from Vincent Chiu. This program is available at *http://www.regview.com*. I like this program because it has a cleaner user interface. It also serves as an admirable replacement for Regedit because you can use it to edit and search the registry and to compare different versions of it. RegView doesn't have a setup program, but it really doesn't need one. Figure 8-1 shows the result in RegView of comparing a snapshot to the current registry. RegView's output is a little easier to read than RegSnap's output, but RegView is quite a bit slower at producing it.

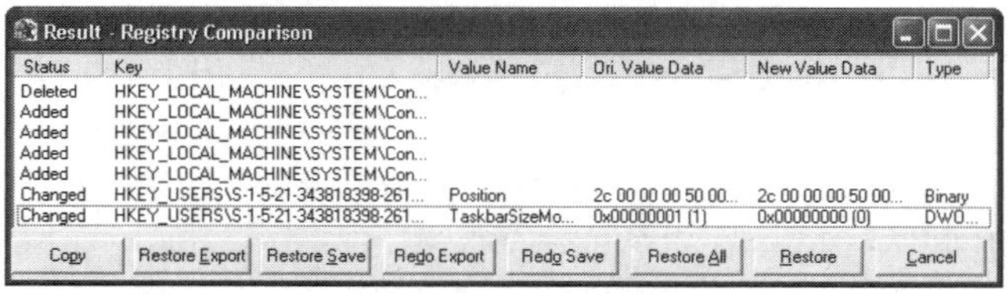

Figure 8-1   RegView is an enhanced registry editor.

If turnaround time is important to you, use RegSnap. If you're after an enhanced registry editor that can do a search-and-replace as well as compare snapshots of the registry, you should consider RegView. Both shareware programs are inexpensive, but if you don't want to shell out the money, stick with the methods you learn in this chapter.

WinDiff is the ultimate tool for comparing two versions of a text file. Its roots are as a developer tool for comparing different versions of source files to see changes before checking them into version control. It was also useful as a debugging tool to figure out which changes in a source file might have introduced a problem. WinDiff was originally available in the Windows Software Development Kit (SDK). Microsoft included it in the last several Windows resource kits. It comes with Windows XP Professional as part of the Windows Support Tools. Install the tools from \Support\Tools on your Windows XP Professional product CD. Type **windiff** in the Run dialog box to start it.

After starting WinDiff, here's how to compare two *.reg* files with it:

1.   On the File menu, click Compare Files.

2.   Type the path and name of the first file, and click Open.

3.   Type the path and name of the second file, and click Open.

4.   On the View menu, click Expand or double-click the files in the list.

After comparing the two files, you see results similar to Figure 8-2. WinDiff combines both files and highlights the differences in red and yellow. Differences are relative to the second file, which is why I had you open the second file after the first one. Deleted lines, present in the first file but not in the second, are red. Inserted lines, absent in the first file but present in the second, are yellow. White lines are the same in both files. You also see arrows that indicate whether a line is deleted or inserted. A left arrow (<!) indicates a line deleted from the second file, and a right arrow (!>) indicates a line inserted into the second file. WinDiff represents changed lines as deletions followed by insertions, as shown in Figure 8-2. Because WinDiff compares files line by line instead of character by character, you have to judge for yourself whether a deleted line followed by an inserted line represents a changed line of text. Press F8 to move to the next block of differences that WinDiff found; press F7 to move to the previous block of differences.

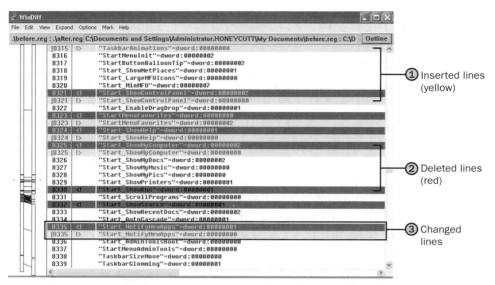

Figure 8-2   The two columns you see on the left side of the window represent the two files that you're comparing. These columns are a roadmap of the files' differences.

Monitoring a Sample

Monitoring the registry for changes is different from comparing snapshots in that you're watching registry access as it happens. Thus, you can change a setting in the user interface and then look at the monitor to see what value Windows XP Professional wrote to the registry. I tend to monitor the registry instead of compare snapshots when I'm looking for a large number of settings. When doing this, it's helpful to keep the noise down to a minimum.

My favorite monitoring tool is Regmon from Winternals. You can download a freeware version of this tool from *http://www.sysinternals.com*. Regmon Enterprise Edition, which is inexpensive, is available at *http://www.winternals.com*. The difference between the two is that the Enterprise Edition enables you to monitor a remote registry, which makes the process a little easier if you can work on one computer and see the results on a different computer. Although the freeware version of Regmon contains all the enterprise edition's other features, I purchased and use Regmon Enterprise Edition for the convenience of remote monitoring.

Download either version of Regmon. The freeware version doesn't have a setup program, so you just run it from the directory in which you unzip it. Regmon Enterprise Edition comes with a setup program that adds a shortcut for Regmon to the Start menu.

> **More Info** For more information about Regmon, including downloading freeware versions, see the Sysinternals Web site at *http://www.sysinternals.com*.

Choosing a Technique

Table 8-1 lays out the substantial differences—as I see them—between the scripting methods covered in this chapter. Each column represents one of the five scripting methods that I describe in this chapter. For example, the Batch column describes using Reg.exe in a batch file. The MSI (Windows Installer setup databases) column describes Windows Installer package files that include registry settings. First, the similarities: all five methods enable you to change values as well as add keys or values. Also, Windows XP Professional supports all five methods without installing third-party tools or any resource kits.

Now I'll describe the differences. As the table shows, using *.reg* files is the easiest method, scripts and Windows Installer package files are the most difficult, and the rest fall somewhere in between. No matter which method you choose, they all become rather easy after you learn how to use them. Access to the operating system is important only if you're trying to do more than just edit the registry. For example, if you want to read values from the registry and then dump them to a text file, you'll need access to the operating system. The most important difference is that only *.inf* files and scripts provide high support for the many different types of values you can store in the registry. The remaining methods support the basic value types, though, and that's often all you need. If you need to edit more esoteric types, however, you're better off writing an *.inf* file or a script. Likewise, *.inf* files and scripts are the only two methods you can use to set and clear bits in values. For example, the bits in the value UserPreferencesMask indicate different user interface settings, and you enable or disable them by setting or clearing the corresponding bit. If this is your requirement, you're left with *.inf* files or scripts as your method of choice.

Nine times out of ten, my preference is to write an *.inf* file. You'll notice that most of the scripts in this book are *.inf* files. I chose this method because I'm familiar with *.inf* files, they're easy to create, and they're easy to read. I use scripts only when I have to query values from the registry. *.inf* files' strong suit is that they offer the flexibility to do anything I want in the registry without requiring me to put on a programmer hat for the weekend. Choose whatever methods best suit you, but give more weight to *.inf* files and scripts. You won't end up using just one of these techniques, though. In fact, you'll find that you'll use a combination of these methods, depending on the *scenario*. After you start using the script methods I describe in this chapter, you'll master them in no time.

Table 8-1   Comparison of Scripting Methods

Features	.inf	.reg	Batch	Script	MSI
Difficulty	Medium	Low	Medium	High	Medium
OS access	Basic	None	Full	Full	Basic
Built-in support	Yes	Yes	Yes	Yes	Yes
Change values	Yes	Yes	Yes	Yes	Yes
Add keys/values	Yes	Yes	Yes	Yes	Yes
Delete keys/values	Yes	Yes	Yes	Yes	Yes
Querying values	No	No	Yes	Yes	No
Support for value types	High	Medium	Medium	Low	Medium
Bitwise support	Yes	No	No	Yes	No

Installing *.inf* Files

Setup Information files have the *.inf* extension; I call them *.inf* files. The Windows XP Professional setup API (application programming interface) uses *.inf* files to script installations. Most people associate *.inf* files with device-driver installation, but applications often use them, too. Most actions that you associate with installing device drivers and applications are available through *.inf* files. You can copy, remove, and rename files. You can add, change, and delete registry values. You can install and start services. You can install most anything using *.inf* files. For example, you can use them to customize registry settings—obviously. You can also create *.inf* files that users can uninstall using Add Or Remove Programs.

.inf files look similar to INI and *.reg* files. They're text files that contain sections that look like *[Section]*. Each section contains items, sometimes called *properties*, that look like `Name=Value`. Windows XP Professional happens to come with the perfect *.inf* file editor: Notepad. When you create a new *.inf* file using Notepad, make sure that you enclose the filename in quotes or choose All Files in the Save As Type list in the Save As dialog box. That way, your file will have the *.inf* extension instead of the *.txt* extension. Installing an .inf file is straightforward: Right-click the *.inf* file and then click Install. To deploy an *.inf* file and prevent users from having to install it manually, use the following command, replacing *Filename* with the name of your *.inf* file. (This is the command line that Windows XP Professional associates with the *.inf* file extension in the registry.)

```
rundll32.exe setupapi,InstallHinfSection DefaultInstall 132 Filename.inf
```

Listing 8-1 shows a simple *.inf* file, which is the file simple1.inf in the Samples\chap08 folder of this book's companion CD. The first section, *[Version]*, is required. The name of the second section is arbitrary, but is usually *[DefaultInstall]* so that users can right-click the file to install it. The linkage to this section is through the command line you saw just before this paragraph. The command is *rundll32.exe*, which executes the API in Setupapi.dll called *InstallHinfSection*. The next item on the command line, *DefaultInstall*, is the name of the section to install. The *132* you see before the filename tells the setup API to prompt the user before rebooting the computer, if necessary. The last item on the command line is the name of the *.inf* file to install. Because this is the command that Windows XP Professional associates with the *.inf* file extension, you should name this installation section *[DefaultInstall]*. Within this section, you see two directives: *AddReg* and *DelReg*. The directive AddReg=Add.Settings adds the settings contained in the section *[Add.Settings]*, which changes the default action for *.reg* files to Edit. The directive DelReg=Del.Settings deletes the settings listed in the section *[Del.Settings]*, which removes the last key opened in Registry Editor and removes saved view settings. The names of these sections are arbitrary; you should adopt names that make sense to you and stick with them so you don't confuse yourself down the road. For example, I often use the section name *[Reg.Settings]* in my *.inf* files.

On the Resource Kit CD This chapter's sample files are on this book's companion CD in the folder Samples\chap08.

Listing 8-1 Sample1.inf

```
[Version]
Signature=$CHICAGO$

[DefaultInstall]
AddReg=Add.Settings
DelReg=Del.Settings

[Add.Settings]
HKCR,regfile\shell,,0,"edit"

[Del.Settings]
HKCU,Software\Microsoft\Windows\CurrentVersion\Applets\Regedit
```

Now you've had my two-dollar tour of an *.inf* file. The sections that follow describe how to write the different parts of an *.inf* file. I'm focusing on using *.inf* files to edit the registry, but you can do much more with them. The ultimate resource for writing *.inf* files is *http://msdn.microsoft.com/library/en-us /install/bh/install/inf-format_7soi.asp* on Microsoft's Web site. This is the ".*INF* Files and Directives" section of the Windows Driver Development Kit (DDK). Don't let the fact that this information is in the DDK scare you; it's really straightforward and useful for much more than installing device drivers.

Customizing Default Settings

Windows XP Professional doesn't invent its settings out of thin air. It uses *.inf* files in the i386 distribution folder to initially create the registry's hive files when you install the operating system. These *.inf* files use the same syntax I described in this chapter, so you should be able to customize them easily. Here are the *.inf* files:

- **Hivecls.inf**   This *.inf* file creates the settings in HKLM\SOFTWARE (HKCR).

- **Hivedef.inf**   This *.inf* file creates the settings in HKU\.DEFAULT. It also creates the settings for the default user profile.

- **Hivesft.inf**   This *.inf* file creates the settings in HKLM\SOFTWARE.

- **Hivesys.inf**   This *.inf* file creates the settings in HKLM\SYSTEM.

You can change any of the Windows XP Professional default settings by changing the setting in the hive files listed. This is in lieu of creating a default user profile for Windows XP Professional. If you want to change file associations for every computer in the organization, change them in the file Hivecls.inf.

Starting with a Template

I never start *.inf* files from scratch. I can't be bothered to remember the format of the sections and directives, so I use a template. I'm lazy enough (or efficient enough) that I add the template you see in Listing 8-2 to the Templates folder in my user profile so that I can right-click in a folder and then click New, Setup Information File. The easiest way is to first create the file Setup Information File.inf with the contents of Listing 8-2 or copy it from the Samples\chap08 folder on this book's companion CD. The file name is template.inf. Then use Microsoft Tweak UI to add the template. It's a real timesaver.

> **More Info**   Tweak UI is a killer utility that Microsoft provides for free. You use it to customize a large variety of settings in Windows XP Professional. You can download Tweak UI from *http://www.microsoft.com/downloads*.

The reason why this template makes creating *.inf* files so easy is because I've added comments to it. Comments begin with the semicolon (;) and add descriptive information to the file. In this case, I described the format of the different directives for each section. In the *[Reg.Settings]* section, for example, you see the syntax for adding values to the registry. In the *[Bits.Set]* section, you see the format for setting individual bits in a number. I often write *.inf* files that users can uninstall using Add Or Remove Programs; the template in Listing 8-2 shows you how to do that. If you don't want users to uninstall the file and its settings, remove the *[DefaultUninstall]*, *[Reg.Uninstall]*, *[Inf.Copy]*, *[DestinationDirs]*, *[SourceDisksNames]*, and *[SourceDisks-Files]* sections and any linkages to those sections. In this template, all-capitalized words are placeholders that I replace when I create an *.inf* file. For example, I replace *FILENAME* with the *.inf* file's actual name.

Listing 8-2   Template.inf

```
[Version]
Signature=$CHICAGO$

[DefaultInstall]
BitReg=Bits.Set
AddReg=Reg.Settings
AddReg=Reg.Uninstall
CopyFiles=Inf.Copy

[DefaultUninstall]
BitReg=Bits.Clear
DelReg=Reg.Settings
DelReg=Reg.Uninstall
DelFiles=Inf.Copy

[Reg.Settings]

; ROOT,SUBKEY[,NAME[,FLAG[,DATA]]]
;
; FLAG:
;
;  0x00000 - REG_SZ
;  0x00001 - REG_BINARY
;  0x10000 - REG_MULTI_SZ
;  0x20000 - REG_EXPAND_SZ
;  0x10001 - REG_DWORD
;  0x20001 - REG_NONE

[Bits.Set]

; ROOT,SUBKEY,NAME,FLAG,MASK,BYTE
;
; FLAG:
;
```

```
;   0x00000 - Clear bits in mask
;   0x00001 - Set bits in mask

[Bits.Clear]

; ROOT,SUBKEY,NAME,FLAG,MASK,BYTE
;
; FLAG:
;
;   0x00000 - Clear bits in mask
;   0x00001 - Set bits in mask

[Reg.Uninstall]
HKCU,Software\Microsoft\Windows\CurrentVersion\Uninstall\%NAME%
HKCU,Software\Microsoft\Windows\CurrentVersion\Uninstall\%NAME%,
DisplayName,,"%NAME%"
HKCU,Software\Microsoft\Windows\CurrentVersion\Uninstall\%NAME%,
UninstallString,,"Rundll32.exe setupapi.dll,InstallHinfSection
DefaultUninstall 132 %53%\Application Data\Custom\FILENAME"

; ROOT:
;
;   HKCU
;   HKLM

[Inf.Copy]
FILENAME

[DestinationDirs]
Inf.Copy=53,Application Data\Custom

; DIRID:
;
;   10 - %SystemRoot%
;   11 - %SystemRoot%\System32
;   17 - %SystemRoot%\Inf
;   53 - %UserProfile%
;   54 - %SystemDrive%
;   -1 - Absolute path

[SourceDisksNames]
55=%DISKNAME%

[SourceDisksFiles]
FILENAME=55

[Strings]
NAME     = "Jerry's NAME"
DISKNAME = "Setup Files"
```

The first two lines in Listing 8-2 are the only ones required. The *[Version]* section and the *Signature* property identify the file as a valid *.inf* file. You must include these two lines at the top of all your *.inf* files. Incidentally, *Chicago* was Microsoft's code name for Microsoft Windows 95, and so version=$CHICAGO$ identifies the file as a Windows 95 *.inf* file. These days, *$CHICAGO$* indicates an *.inf* file that's compatible with all versions of Windows. Use *$Windows 95$* if you want to indicate that your *.inf* file is compatible with 16-bit versions of Windows only. Use *$Windows NT$* to indicate that your *.inf* file is compatible with 32-bit versions of Windows only. Generally, I leave *Signature* set to *$CHICAGO$*.

Linking Sections Together

After the *[Version]* section is usually the *[DefaultInstall]* section. As I said earlier, the name of this section is arbitrary, but you should use *[DefaultInstall]* if you want users to be able to install your *.inf* file by right-clicking it. The command associated with the *.inf* file extension references this section by name. This is the section that links together your *.inf* file. You fill it with directives that tell the Setup API which sections in the *.inf* file to process and what to do with them.

You saw this section in Listing 8-2. Each line in this section is a directive. The Setup API supports a number of different directives, but the ones we care about in this book are *AddReg*, *DelReg*, and *BitReg*. In the listing, you see a line that says AddReg=Reg.Settings. This adds the settings listed in the *[Reg.Settings]* section. The line BitReg=Bits.Set sets the bit masks listed in the section *[Bits.Set]*. As well, you can list more than one section for each directive. You can duplicate a directive on multiple lines, for example, or you can assign multiple sections to it: AddReg= Section1,Section2,SectionN. For an example, see Listing 8-3, which is the file sample2.inf in the Samples\chap08 folder on this book's companion CD.

Listing 8-3   sample2.inf

```
[Version]
Signature=$CHICAGO$

[DefaultInstall]
AddReg=Reg.Settings1,Reg.Settings2,Reg.Settings3
AddReg=Reg.Settings4
AddReg=Reg.Settings5
DelReg=Reg.Settings6

[Reg.Settings1]
; Registry settings to add or change

[Reg.Settings2]
; Registry settings to add or change
```

```
[Reg.Settings3]
; Registry settings to add or change

[Reg.Settings4]
; Registry settings to add or change

[Reg.Settings5]
; Registry settings to add or change

[Reg.Settings6]
; Registry keys and values to remove
```

> **Note**   The order of the *AddReg* and *DelReg* directives doesn't matter. The Setup API processes all *DelReg* directives first, followed by the *AddReg* sections.

Adding Keys and Values

As you just saw, the *AddReg* directive in *[DefaultInstall]* indicates the names of sections that contain settings you want to add to the registry. These are *[add-registry-section]* sections. You can add new keys, set default values, create new values, or modify existing values using an *[add-registry-section]* section. And each section can contain multiple entries. Each *[add-registry-section]* name must be unique in the *.inf* file.

Syntax

```
[add-registry-section]
rootkey, [subkey], [value], [flags], [data]
```

rootkey	This is the root key containing the key or value you're modifying. Use the abbreviations: HKCR, HKCU, HKLM, or HKU.
subkey	This is the subkey to create or the subkey in which to add or change a value. This is optional. If missing, all operations are on the root key.
value	This is the name of the value to create or modify if it exists. This value is optional. If value is omitted and the flags and data parameters are given, operations are on the key's default value. If value, flags, and data are omitted, you're adding a subkey.

flags
- 0x00000000. Value is REG_SZ. This is the default if you omit flags.
- 0x00000001. Value is REG_BINARY.
- 0x00010000. Value is REG_MULTI_SZ.
- 0x00020000. Value is REG_EXPAND_SZ.
- 0x00010001. Value is REG_DWORD.
- 0x00020001. Value is REG_NONE.
- 0x00000002. Don't overwrite existing keys and values. Combine this flag with others by ORing them together.
- 0x00000004. Delete subkey from the registry, or delete value from subkey. Combine this flag with others by ORing them together.
- 0x00000008. Append data to value. This flag is valid only if value is REG_MULTI_SZ. The string data is not appended if it already exists. Combine this flag with 0x00010000 by ORing them together.
- 0x00000010. Create subkey, but ignore value and data if specified. Combine this flag with others by ORing them together.
- 0x00000020. Set value only if it already exists. Combine this flag with others by ORing them together.
- 0x00001000. Make the specified change in the 64-bit registry. If not specified, the change is made to the native registry. Combine this flag with others by ORing them together.
- 0x00004000. Make the specified change in the 32-bit registry. If not specified, the change is made to the native registry. Combine this flag with others by ORing them together.

data
This is the data to write to value. If the value doesn't exist, the Setup API creates it; if the value exists, the API overwrites it; if the value is REG_MULTI_SZ and you set the 0x00010008 flag, the API adds the value to the existing string list. If you omit data, the Setup API creates the value without setting it. See the following example to learn how to format each type of value.

Example

```
[Version]
Signature=$CHICAGO$

[DefaultInstall]
AddReg=Reg.Settings

[Reg.Settings]
; Sets the default value of HKCU\Software\Sample
HKCU,Software\Sample,,,"Default"

; Creates a REG_SZ value called Sample
HKCU,Software\Sample,String,0x00000,"String"

; Creates a REG_BINARY value called Binary
HKCU,Software\Sample,Binary,0x00001,00,01,30,05

; Creates a REG_MULTI_SZ value called Multisz
```

```
HKCU,Software\Sample,Multisz,0x10000,"String list"

; Creates a REG_DWORD value called Dword
HKCU,Software\Sample,Dword,0x10001,0x01010102

; Creates a REG_SZ value called Hello
HKLM,SOFTWARE\Sample,Hello,,"World"

; Creates a REG_DWORD value and sets it to 0x0000
HKLM,SOFTWARE\Sample,Nothing,0x10001
```

Deleting Keys and Values

The *[DefaultInstall]* section's *DelReg* directive specifies sections containing registry keys and values to delete. These are *[del-registry-section]* sections. They are much simpler than the *[add-registry-section]* sections, but have similar rules: Each section can contain multiple entries, and the name of each section must be unique.

Syntax

```
[del-registry-section]
rootkey, [subkey], [value], [flags], [data]
```

rootkey	This is the root key containing the key or value you're deleting. Use the abbreviations: HKCR, HKCU, HKLM, or HKU.
subkey	This is the subkey to delete or subkey from which to delete a value. This is optional. If missing, all operations are on the root key.
value	This is the name of the value to delete. This value is optional. If value is omitted, you're deleting subkey.
flags	■ 0x00002000. Deletes the entire subkey. ■ 0x00004000. Make the specified change in the 32-bit registry. If not specified, the change is made to the native registry. Combine this flag with others by ORing them together. ■ 0x00018002. If value is REG_MULTI_SZ, remove all strings matching the string indicated by data.
data	This is used only when flags is 0x00018002. This specifies the string to remove from a REG_MULTI_SZ value.

Example

```
[Version]
Signature=$CHICAGO$

[DefaultInstall]
DelReg=Reg.Settings

[Reg.Settings]
; Removes the key HKCU\Software\Sample
HKCU,Software\Sample
```

```
; Removes the value Hello from HKCU\Software\Sample
HKCU,Software\Sample,Hello

; Removes the string "World" from the REG_MULTI_SZ value Hello
HKCU,Software\Sample,Hello,0x00018002,"World"
```

Setting and Clearing Bits

The *BitReg* directive is similar to the *AddReg* directive. You add it to the *[DefaultInstall]* section to indicate the names of sections that contain bits you want to set and clear. These are *[bit-registry-section]* sections. Use the *BitReg* directive when you want to work with bit masks in the registry. For example, if you want to enable certain user-interface features in the value *UserPreferencesMask*, use this directive. Like the other directives you learned about, each section can contain multiple entries, and the name of each section must be unique.

In the following description of the syntax, notice the differences between the *[bit-registry-section]* and *[add-registry-section]* sections. The parameter *value* is not optional. Also, the parameters *mask* and *byte* replace the value *data*. The parameter *mask* is 8-bits long and indicates which bit you want to enable or disable. The parameter *byte* indicates which byte in the binary value you want to modify. This indicates bytes left to right, starting from 0. This is straightforward when working with REG_BINARY values, but less so when working with REG_DWORD values. Windows XP Professional stores REG_DWORD values in the registry in reverse-byte order (little-endian architecture). To be sure, test your *.inf* files carefully to make sure that you're masking the bits you think you're masking. Figure 8-3 shows the relationship between *value, mask*, and *byte*. The value to which I'm applying the mask is a REG_DWORD value stored in the registry in reverse-byte notation: 0x0180C000. Set the mask in byte 0, and the result is 0x0180C080. Clear the mask in byte 1, and the result is 0x0140C080.

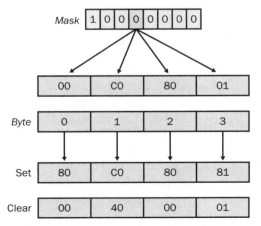

Figure 8-3 The parameter *byte* indicates to which of a number's bytes you want to apply *mask*.

Syntax

```
[bit-registry-section]
rootkey, [subkey], value, [flags], mask, byte
```

rootkey	This is the root key containing the value you're modifying. Use the abbreviations: HKCR, HKCU, HKLM, or HKU.
subkey	This is the subkey in which to change a value. This is optional. If missing, all operations are on the root key.
value	This is the name of the value to modify. This value is not optional and should be a REG_DWORD or REG_BINARY value.
flags	■ 0x00000000. Clear the bits specified by mask. ■ 0x00000001. Set the bits specified by mask. ■ 0x00040000. Make the specified change in the 32-bit registry. If not specified, the change is made to the native registry. Combine this flag with others by ORing them together.
mask	This is the byte-sized mask specifying the bits to set or clear in the specified byte of value. Specify this value in hexadecimal notation. Bits that are 1 will be set or cleared, depending on flags, and bits that are 0 will be ignored.
byte	This specifies the byte in value to which you want to apply mask. The leftmost byte is 0, the next is 1, and so on. Keep in mind that Windows XP Professional stores REG_DWORD values in reverse-byte order when specifying which byte on which to apply mask. Thus, in REG_DWORD values, the rightmost byte is stored first in memory.

Example

```
[Version]
Signature=$CHICAGO$

[DefaultInstall]
BitReg=Bit.Settings

[Bit.Settings]
; Changes 50,00,10,00 to 31,00,10,00
HKCU,Software\Sample,Mask,0x0001,0x01,0

; Changes 50,00,F0,00 to 30,00,70,00
HKU,Software\Sample,Mask,0x0000,0x80,2
```

Using Strings in *.inf* Files

You can make your *.inf* files far easier to read if you use the *[Strings]* section. Each line in this section is a string in the format name="string". Then you can use that string elsewhere in the *.inf* file by referencing it as *%name%*. This makes *.inf* files easier to read in numerous ways (see Listing 8-4, which is also a good example of using the *BitReg* directive and is on this book's companion CD in the Samples\chap08 folder):

- The *[Strings]* section collects strings at the bottom of your *.inf* file so that you can see them in one place.

- The *[Strings]* section enables you to type a string one time and then use that string in numerous places. The string is consistent throughout your *.inf* file.

- The *[Strings]* section makes translating .inf files easier because localizable strings are at the bottom of the file.

Listing 8-4   Sample3.inf

```
[Version]
Signature=$CHICAGO$

[DefaultInstall]
BitReg=Bits.Set
AddReg=Add.Settings
DelReg=Del.Settings

[Add.Settings]
HKCU,%HK_DESKTOP%,ActiveWndTrkTimeout,0x10001,1000
HKLM,%HK_SETUP%,RegisteredOwner,,%OWNER%

[Del.Settings]
HKCU,%HK_EXPLORER%\MenuOrder
HKCU,%HK_EXPLORER%\RunMRU
HKCU,%HK_EXPLORER%\RecentDocs
HKCU,%HK_EXPLORER%\ComDlg32\LastVisitedMRU
HKCU,%HK_SEARCH%\ACMru
HKCU,%HK_INTERNET%\TypedURLs

[Bits.Set]
HKCU,%HK_DESKTOP%,UserPreferencesMask,1,0x01,0
HKCU,%HK_DESKTOP%,UserPreferencesMask,1,0x40,0

[Strings]
HK_DESKTOP="Control Panel\Desktop"
HK_EXPLORER="Software\Microsoft\Windows\CurrentVersion\Explorer"
HK_SEARCH="Software\Microsoft\Search Assistant"
HK_INTERNET="Software\Microsoft\Internet Explorer"
HK_SETUP="SOFTWARE\Microsoft\Windows NT\CurrentVersion"
OWNER="Fuzzy Wuzzy Was a Bear"
```

> **Note**   Here's the truth-in-advertising bit: I seldom use strings because I don't often localize *.inf* files. I use strings only when doing so really does make the *.inf* file easier to read. In particular, when a line becomes so long that it wraps, I use a string to shorten it. Alternatively, you can use the line-continuation character, a backslash (\), to split lines. I also use strings for values that change frequently, particularly in template *.inf* files. Strings make using templates easier.

Setting Values with *.reg* Files

Registry Entries (*.reg*) files are the classic method for adding and changing values in the registry, but as I said in the section "Choosing a Technique," they're not as powerful as the other methods you learn about in this chapter. Their big weakness is that you can't remove values using a *.reg* file; you can only add or modify values, or remove keys.

After you've created a *.reg* file, which has the *.reg* file extension, you import it into the registry by double-clicking the file. This is great if you want users to import the file themselves, but you need the following command if you want to import a *.reg* file using your software management infrastructure or some method such as providing a link to it on the intranet: **regedit /s *filename*.reg**. Replace ***filename*.reg** with the path and name of your *.reg* file. The */s* command-line option imports the file into the registry without prompting the user, which is what you want to do most of the time. To edit a *.reg* file, right-click it and then click Edit. Don't accidentally double-click a *.reg* file thinking that you will open it in Notepad because double-clicking a *.reg* file imports it into the registry, after a confirmation message.

Remember that Regedit supports two different file formats for *.reg* files. Version 4 *.reg* files are ANSI. ANSI character encoding uses one byte to represent each character. Also, Regedit writes REG_EXPAND_SZ and REG_MULTI_SZ strings to *.reg* files using ANSI character encoding, so each character is a single byte. Unicode character encoding uses two bytes for each character, and when you create a Unicode *.reg* file, Regedit writes REG_EXPAND_SZ and REG_MULTI_SZ strings to the file using the two-byte Unicode encoding scheme. What you need to know is that choosing to create a version 4 *.reg* file means that the file and the values in the file use ANSI; likewise, creating a version 5 *.reg* file means that the file and the values in the file use Unicode. I tend to use version 4, ANSI *.reg* files except when I know that the registry data contains localized text that requires Unicode to represent it. If in doubt, always create version 5 Unicode files.

Listing 8-5 shows a sample *.reg* file, which is the file sample4.reg on this book's companion CD in the Samples\chap08 folder. The first line in this file is the header, which identifies the file's version. The header *Windows Registry Editor Version 5.00* indicates a version 5 Unicode *.reg* file. The header *REG_EDIT4* indicates a version 4, ANSI *.reg* file. A blank line usually follows the header, but the file works okay without it. Notice how similar the remainder of this file looks to *.inf* and INI files. Each section contains the fully qualified name of a key. They use the full names of root keys, not the abbreviations. Listing 8-5 imports settings into three keys:

HKCU\Control Panel\Desktop, HKCU\Control Panel\Desktop\WindowMetrics, and HKCU\Control Panel\Mouse. The lines below each section are values that Regedit will add to that key when Regedit imports the file into the registry. The format is `"name"=value`. The value named @ represents the key's default value. Some of the values in Listing 8-5 contain *dword* and *hex*, whereas others are enclosed in quotes. Values enclosed in quotes are strings. Values in the form *dword:value* are REG_DWORD values. Values in the form *hex:values* are REG_BINARY values. This gets more complicated when you add subtypes, such as *hex(type):value*, and I'll talk about those a bit later.

Text Editor

To edit *.reg*, *.inf*, and similar files, I use xxxTextPad from Helios Software Solutions. You can learn more about it and download it at *http://www.textpad.com*. I've mentioned this text editor several times in this book, so you have to assume it's my favorite. UltraEdit is another popular text editor, which I've never used, but you can learn more about it at *http://www.ultraedit.com*.

The syntax highlighting feature in TextPad makes editing *.reg*, *.inf*, and similar files easy. If you type a keyword correctly, TextPad highlights the keyword. If you mistype the keyword, the editor doesn't highlight it. That way, you're more likely to create error-free files. In order to use this feature for editing *.reg* and *.inf* files, you'll need a syntax file, though, and I've included samples for *.adm*, *.inf*, *.reg*, *.sif*, and *.vbs* files in the Samples\textpad folder on this book's companion CD. Here's how to use it with TextPad:

- Install TextPad.

- Copy ext.syn from the Samples\textpad folder on this book's companion CD to %USERPROFILE%\Application Data\TextPad.

- Import ext.reg from the Samples\textpad folder on this book's companion CD into the registry.

This file configures the syntax file ext.syn in TextPad. To configure the remaining syntax files, copy the appropriate *.syn* file as described in step 2, and then import the corresponding *.reg* file as described in step 3.

Listing 8-5   Sample4.reg

```
Windows Registry Editor Version 5.00

[HKEY_CURRENT_USER\Control Panel\Desktop]
"ActiveWndTrkTimeout"=dword:00000000
"ForegroundFlashCount"=dword:00000003
"ForegroundLockTimeout"=dword:00030d40
"MenuShowDelay"="400"
"PaintDesktopVersion"=dword:00000000
"UserPreferencesMask"=hex:9e,3e,07,80

[HKEY_CURRENT_USER\Control Panel\Desktop\WindowMetrics]
"Shell Icon BPP"="16"
"Shell Icon Size"="32"
"MinAnimate"="1"

[HKEY_CURRENT_USER\Control Panel\Mouse]
@="Rodent"
"ActiveWindowTracking"=dword:00000000
"DoubleClickHeight"="4"
"DoubleClickSpeed"="500"
"DoubleClickWidth"="4"
"MouseSensitivity"="10"
"MouseSpeed"="1"
"MouseThreshold1"="6"
"MouseThreshold2"="10"
"SnapToDefaultButton"="0"
"SwapMouseButtons"="0"
```

> **On the Resource Kit CD**   This chapter's sample files are on this book's companion CD in the folder Samples\chap08.

Exporting Settings to *.reg* Files

The easiest way to create a *.reg* file is by using Regedit to export keys to *.reg* files. Follow these steps to export branches of the registry to files:

1. Click the key at the top of the branch you want to export.

2. On the File menu, click Export. The Export Registry File dialog box appears, shown in Figure 8-4.

3. In the File Name box, enter a name for the file you're creating.

4. Select the option for the export range you want:

   ■ To back up the entire registry, select the All option.

   ■ To back up the selected branch, select the Selected Branch option.

5. In the Save As Type list, click the type of file you want to create: Registration (*.reg) or Win9x/NT4 Registration (*.reg).

6. Click Save.

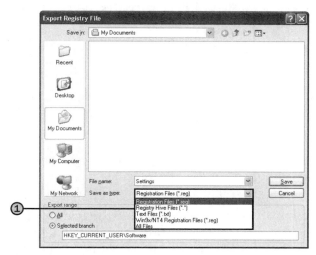

Figure 8-4 The only two types of files that create *.reg* files are Registration Files (*.reg) and Win9x/NT4 Registration Files (*.reg).

The *.reg* file you create contains all the subkeys and values under the key you exported. The likelihood that you want all the key's subkeys and values isn't very high, so you should open the file in Notepad by right-clicking it, click Edit, and then remove any keys and values that you don't want to keep in the file. You can also change any of the values in the *.reg* file. For example, you can export a key from your own computer, just to get you started, and then edit it to suit your requirements—removing keys, changing values, and so on.

Caution IIf you're creating a *.reg* file for versions of Windows that don't support version 5 Unicode *.reg* files, use version 4 ANSI *.reg* files. Microsoft Windows 95, Windows 98, and Windows Me do not support Unicode *.reg* files, and any attempt to import Unicode *.reg* files into their registries could yield results that you don't like. Windows 2000 and Windows XP Professional support UNICODE *.reg* files.

Creating .reg Files Manually

Creating *.reg* files by hand is an error-prone process that I don't recommend. Nonetheless, many of you are likely to do it anyway, so I will show you how. First, decide whether you will create an ANSI or Unicode *.reg* file, and then follow these instructions to create it:

- Create a new file in Notepad.

- At the top of the file, add one of the following, followed by a blank line:

    - Add *REG_EDIT4* at the top of the file to create a version 4 *.reg* file.

    - Add *Windows Registry Editor Version 5.00* at the top of the file to create a version 5 *.reg* file.

- For each key into which you want to import values, add a section to the file in the format *[key]*, where *key* is the fully qualified name of the key. Don't use the root key abbreviations; use their full names: HKEY_CURRENT_USER.

- For each value that you want to import into the registry, add the value in the format `"name"=value` to the key's section. Use @ for a key's default value. See Table 8-2 for information about how to format the different types of values in a *.reg* file. You can continue an entry from one line to the next using the line-continuation character, a backslash (\).

- Click File, Save As, type the name of the file in File Name, including the extension *.reg* (enclose the filename in quotes so that Notepad doesn't use the *.txt* extension), do one of the following, and then click Save:

    - In the Encoding list, choose ANSI to create a version 4 *.reg* file.

    - In the Encoding list, choose Unicode to create a version 5 *.reg* file.

Table 8-2   Value Formats in .reg files

Type	Version 4	Version 5
REG_SZ	*"String"*	*"String"*
REG_DWORD	*dword:00007734*	*dword:00007734*
REG_BINARY	*hex:00,00,01,03*	*hex:00,00,01,03*
REG_EXPAND_SZ	*hex(2):25,53,59,53,54, 45,4d,52,4f,4f,54,25,00*	*hex(2):25,00,53,00,59,00,53,00,54,00,45,0 0,4d,00,52,00,4f,00,4f,00,54,00,25,00, 00,00*
REG_MULTI_SZ	*hex(7):48,65,6c,6c,6f,20, 57,6f,72,6c,64,00,4a,65, 72,72,79,20,77,61,73,20, 68,65,72,65,00,00*	*hex(7):48,00,65,00,6c,00,6c,00,6f,00,20, 00,57,00,6f,00,72,00,6c,00,64,00,00,00, 4a,00,65,00,72,00,72,00,79,00,20,00,77, 00,61,00,73,00,20,00,68,00,65,00,72,00, 65,00,00,00,00,00*

Encoding Special Characters

Within .*reg* files, certain characters have special meaning. Quotation marks begin and end strings. The backslash character is a line-continuation character. So how do you include these characters in your values? You use escaping, which is an ages-old method for prefixing special characters with a backslash. For example, the string \n represents a newline character and the string \" represents a quotation mark. Table 8-3 describes the special characters you can use and shows you examples.

Table 8-3   Special Characters in .*reg* Files

Escape	Expanded	Example
\\	\	*C:\\Documents and Settings\\Jerry*
\"	"	*A \"quoted\" string*
\n	newline	*This is on \n two lines*
\r	return	*This is on \r two lines*

Deleting Keys or Values Using a .*reg* File

You can use a .*reg* file to remove entire keys or individual values. This is an undocumented feature of .*reg* files: To delete a key, just prefix a key's name with a minus-sign (-): *[-key]*. Here's a brief example that removes the key HKCU\Software\Honeycutt when you import the .*reg* file into the registry:

```
Windows Registry Editor Version 5.00

[-HKEY_CURRENT_USER\Software\Honeycutt]
```

To remove a value, place a minus sign (-) after the equals sign (=), like this: *value*=-. The following example removes a value from the key HKCU\Software" \Honeycutt when you import the .*reg* file into the registry:

```
Windows Registry Editor Version 5.00

[-HKEY_CURRENT_USER\Software\Honeycutt]
RemoveThis=-
```

Rather than manually create a .*reg* file to remove keys and values, I prefer to export a key to a .*reg* file and then edit it. After exporting the key to a .*reg* file, remove all the values and keys that you don't want to delete. Then, add the minus sign to the names of the keys and values that you do want to delete. Then, you can remove those keys quickly and easily by double-clicking the .*reg* file or using the command **regedit /s *filename*.reg**.

Editing from the Command Prompt

Windows XP Professional comes with the Console Registry Tool for Windows (Reg.exe), which is nothing short of marvelous. You use it to edit the registry from the MS-DOS command prompt. You can do with Reg.exe just about anything you can do with Regedit, and more. The best part of Reg.exe is that you can use it to write simple scripts in the form of batch files that change the registry. And unlike in earlier versions of Windows, you don't have to install Reg.exe. It's installed by default and combines the numerous registry tools that came with the resource kits for earlier versions of Windows.

This tool is cool enough for me to start with an example. Listing 8-6 is a simple batch file that installs Microsoft Office 2003 Editions the first time the batch file runs (think login script). It's the file sample5.cmd in the Samples\chap08 folder on this book's companion CD. After installing Office 2003 Editions, the batch file calls Reg.exe to add the REG_DWORD value Flag to HKCU\Software\Example. The batch file checks for this value's presence each time the file runs and skips the installation if it exists. Thus, the batch file installs the application only one time. This is a method you can use to deploy software through users' logon scripts. Instead of checking for a value that you add, as Listing 8-6 does, you can check for a value that the application stores in the registry. For example, the second line in the batch file could just as easily be **Reg QUERY HKCU\Software\Microsoft\Office\11.0 >nul**, which checks to see whether Office 2003 Editions is installed for the user.

Listing 8-6   Sample5.cmd

```
@Echo Off

Reg QUERY HKCU\Software\Example /v Flag >nul

goto %ERRORLEVEL%

:1

    Echo Installing software the first time this runs
    \\Camelot\Office\Setup.exe /settings setup.ini

    Reg ADD HKCU\Software\Example /v Flag /t REG_DWORD /d "1"
    goto CONTINUE

:0

    Echo Software is already installed, skipping this section

:CONTINUE

Set HKMS=HKCU\Software\Microsoft
Set HKCV=HKCU\Software\Microsoft\Windows\CurrentVersion

REM Clear the history lists
```

```
Reg DELETE %HKCV%\Explorer\MenuOrder /f
Reg DELETE %HKCV%\Explorer\RunMRU /f
Reg DELETE %HKCV%\Explorer\RecentDocs /f
Reg DELETE %HKCV%\Explorer\ComDlg32\LastVisitedMRU /f
Reg DELETE "%HKMS%\Search Assistant\ACMru" /f
Reg DELETE "%HKMS%\Internet Explorer\TypedURLs" /f
```

The syntax of the Reg.exe command line is straightforward: **reg *command options*. *Command*** is one of the many commands that Reg.exe supports, including **ADD**, **QUERY**, and **DELETE**. ***Options*** is the options that the command requires. Options usually include the name of a key and sometimes a value's name and data. If any key or value name contains spaces, you must enclose the name in quotes. It gets more complicated for each of the different commands you can use with it, however, and I cover each of those in the sections following this one. If you're without this book and need a quick refresh, just type **reg /?** at the MS-DOS command prompt to see a list of commands that Reg.exe supports.

Filling the Environment

Have you ever written a batch or logon script and ran in to roadblocks because a setting you need doesn't exist in the environment? I have. You can use WMI to fill the environment with a variety of settings, however. For example, you can fill the environment with information about the Windows XP Professional page file. You can fill the environment with information about the operating system, such as the installation date, owner, and version.

The command is *for /f %i in ('wmic PATH Class GET /VALUE') do set Prefix.%i.*, where *Class* is the name of the WMI class you want to use to fill the environment and *Prefix* is the prefix you want to put in front of the environment variable. The prefix simply keeps settings for different WMI classes from overwriting each other and makes it easier to see at a glance where a value comes from when you view it in the environment. For example, to query the WMI class Win32_OperatingSystem and store its values in the environment by prefixing the value names with *OS.*, use the command *for /f %i in ('wmic PATH Win32_OperatingSystem GET /VALUE') do set OS.%i*. After dumping the WMI class in to the environment, you can use the values in your batch scripts like you'd use any other environment variable.

To see which WMI classes are available, see the WMI Reference at *http://msdn.microsoft.com/library/default.asp?url=/library/en-us/wmisdk /wmi/wmi_start_page.asp*. Look under Windows Management Instrumentation, WMI Reference, WMI Classes, Win32 Classes.

On the Resource Kit CD   This chapter's sample files are on this book's companion CD in the folder Samples\chap08.

Adding Keys and Values

Use the ADD command to add keys and values to the registry.

Syntax

```
Reg.exe ADD [\\computer\]key [/v value | /ve] [/t type] [/s separator]
[/d data] [/f]
```

\\computer	If omitted, Reg.exe connects to the local computer; otherwise, Reg.exe connects to the remote computer.
key	This is the key's path, beginning with the root key. Use the root key abbreviations HKCR, HKCU, HKLM, and HKU. Only HKLM and HKU are available when connecting to remote computers.
/v value	This adds or changes value.
/ve	This changes the key's default value.
/t type	This is the value's type: REG_BINARY, REG_DWORD, REG_DWORD_LITTLE_ENDIAN, REG_DWORD_BIG_ENDIAN, REG_EXPAND_SZ, REG_MULTI_SZ, or REG_SZ. The default is REG_SZ.
/s separator	This specifies the character used to separate strings when creating REG_MULTI_SZ values. The default is \0, or null.
/d data	This is the data to assign to new or existing values.
/f	This forces Reg.exe to overwrite existing values with prompting.

Example

```
Reg.exe ADD \\JERRY1\HKLM\Software\Honeycutt
Reg.exe ADD HKLM\Software\Honeycutt /v Data /t REG_BINARY /d CCFEF0BC
Reg.exe ADD HKLM\Software\Honeycutt /v List /t REG_MULTI_SZ /d Hello\0World
Reg.exe ADD HKLM\Software\Honeycutt /v Path /t REG_EXPAND_SZ /d
%%SYSTEMROOT%%
```

> **Note** The percent sign (%) has a special purpose on the MS-DOS command prompt and within batch files. You enclose environment variables in percent signs to expand them in place. Thus, to use them on the Reg.exe command line, and elsewhere for that matter, you must use double percent signs (%%). In the previous example, if you had used single percent signs, the command prompt would have expanded the environment variable before running the command. Using double percent signs prevents the command prompt from expanding the environment variable.

Querying Values

The QUERY command works three ways. First, it can display the data in a specific value. Second, it can display all of a key's subkeys. Third, it can list all the subkeys and values in a key by adding the /s command-line option. How it works depends on the options you use.

Syntax

```
Reg.exe QUERY [\\computer\]key [/v value | /ve] [/s]
```

computer	If omitted, Reg.exe connects to the local computer; otherwise, Reg.exe connects to the remote computer.
key	This is the key's path, beginning with the root key. Use the root key abbreviations HKCR, HKCU, HKLM, and HKU. Only HKLM and HKU are available when connecting to remote computers.
/v value	This queries a value in the key. If you omit /v, Reg.exe queries all values in the key if you use the /s option.
/ve	This queries the key's default value.
/s	This queries all the key's subkeys and values.

Example

```
Reg.exe QUERY HKLM\SOFTWARE\Microsoft\Windows\CurrentVersion /s
Reg.exe QUERY HKLM\SOFTWARE\Microsoft\Windows NT\CurrentVersion
/v CurrentVersion
```

Note   Reg.exe sets ERRORLEVEL to 0 if the command succeeds and 1 if it doesn't. Thus, you can test ERRORLEVEL in a batch file to determine whether a value exists or not. You saw an example of this in Listing 8-6. Although you can use the *If* statement to test ERRORLEVEL, I prefer creating labels in my batch file, one for each level, as shown in Listing 8-6. Then I can just write statements that look like *Goto %ERRORLEVEL%* or *Goto QUERY%ERRORLEVEL%*, which branches to the label *QUERY1* if *ERRORLEVEL* is 1.

Deleting Keys and Values

Use the DELETE command to remove keys and values from the registry.

Syntax

```
Reg.exe DELETE [\\computer\]key [/v value | /ve | /va] [/f]
```

computer	If omitted, Reg.exe connects to the local computer; otherwise, Reg.exe connects to the remote computer.
key	This is the key's path, beginning with the root key. Use the root key abbreviations HKCR, HKCU, HKLM, and HKU. Only HKLM and HKU are available when connecting to remote computers.
/v value	This deletes value from the key.
/ve	This deletes the key's default value.
/va	This deletes all values from the key.
/f	This forces Reg.exe to delete values with prompting.

Example

```
Reg.exe DELETE \\JERRY1\HKLM\Software\Honeycutt
Reg.exe DELETE HKLM\Software\Honeycutt /v Data /f
Reg.exe DELETE HKLM\Software\Honeycutt /va
```

Comparing Keys and Values

Use the COMPARE command to compare two registry keys. Those keys can be on the same computer or different computers, making this command a useful troubleshooting tool.

The /on command-line option seems odd at first. Why would you compare keys or values and not show the differences? Reg.exe sets ERRORLEVEL depending on the comparison's result, and you can use it in your batch files to execute different code depending on whether the two are the same or different—without displaying any results. Here's the meaning of ERRORLEVEL:

- **0**   The command was successful and the keys or values are identical.

- **1**   The command failed.

- **2**   The command was successful and the keys or values are different.

```
Reg.exe COMPARE [\\computer1\]key1 [\\computer2\]key2 [/v value | /ve]
[/oa|/od|/os|/on] [/s]
```

computer1	If omitted, Reg.exe connects to the local computer; otherwise, Reg.exe connects to the remote computer.
computer2	If omitted, Reg.exe connects to the local computer; otherwise, Reg.exe connects to the remote computer.
key1	This is the key's path, beginning with the root key. Use the root key abbreviations HKCR, HKCU, HKLM, and HKU. Only HKLM and HKU are available when connecting to remote computers.
key2	This is the key's path, beginning with the root key. Use the root key abbreviations HKCR, HKCU, HKLM, and HKU. Only HKLM and HKU are available when connecting to remote computers.
/v value	This compares value.
/ve	This compares the key's default value.
/oa	This shows all differences and matches.
/od	This shows only differences.
/os	This shows only matches.
/on	This shows nothing.
/s	This compares all the key's subkeys and values.

Example

```
Reg.exe COMPARE HKCR\txtfile HKCR\docfile /ve
Reg.exe COMPARE \\JERRY1\HKCR \\JERRY2\HKCR /od /s
Reg.exe COMPARE HKLM\Software \\JERRY2\HKLM\Software /s
```

Copying Keys and Values

The COPY command copies a subkey to another key. This command is useful to back up subkeys.

```
Reg.exe COPY [\\computer1\]key1 [\\computer2\]key2 [/s] [/f]
```

computer1	If omitted, Reg.exe connects to the local computer; otherwise, Reg.exe connects to the remote computer.
computer2	If omitted, Reg.exe connects to the local computer; otherwise, Reg.exe connects to the remote computer.
key1	This is the key's path, beginning with the root key. Use the root key abbreviations HKCR, HKCU, HKLM, and HKU. Only HKLM and HKU are available when connecting to remote computers.
key2	The key's path, beginning with the root key. Use the root key abbreviations HKCR, HKCU, HKLM, and HKU. Only HKLM and HKU are available when connecting to remote computers.
/s	This copies all the key's subkeys and values.
/f	This forces Reg.exe to copy with prompting.

Example

```
Reg.exe COPY HKCU\Software\Microsoft\Office HKCU\Backup\Office /s
Reg.exe COPY HKCR\regfile HKCU\Backup\regfile /s /f
```

Exporting Keys to *.reg* Files

Use the EXPORT command to export all or part of the registry to *.reg* files. This command has a few limitations, though. First, it works only with the local computer. You can't create a *.reg* file from a remote computer's registry. Second, it creates only version 5 Unicode *.reg* files. There's no option available to create ANSI *.reg* files. The EXPORT command is the same as clicking File, Export in Regedit.

```
Reg.exe EXPORT key filename
```

key	This is the key's path, beginning with the root key. Use the root key abbreviations HKCR, HKCU, HKLM, and HKU. This is the key you want to export to a *.reg* file.
filename	This is the path and name of the *.reg* file to create.

Example

```
Reg.exe EXPORT "HKCU\Control Panel" Preferences.reg
```

Importing *.reg* Files

Use the IMPORT command to import a *.reg* file into the registry. This command does the same thing as running *regedit /s filename*. It imports a *.reg* file silently. This command can handle both version 4 and version 5 *.reg* files, but it works only on the local computer.

```
Reg.exe IMPORT filename
```

filename   This is the path and name of the *.reg* file to import.

Example

```
Reg.exe IMPORT Settings.reg
```

Saving Keys to Hive Files

The SAVE command saves a key as a hive file. This command is similar to clicking File, Export in Regedit and then changing the file type to Registry Hive Files (*.*). Hive files are binary files that contain registry settings, and they're the native format that Windows XP Professional uses to store the registry. It's a convenient method for backing up the registry before making substantial changes. This command works only on the local computer.

```
Reg.exe SAVE key filename
```

key   This is the key's path, beginning with the root key. Use the root key abbreviations HKCR, HKCU, HKLM, and HKU. This is the key you want to save as a hive file.

filename   This is the path and name of the hive file to create.

Example

```
Reg.exe SAVE HKCU Backup.dat
```

Restoring Hive Files to Keys

The RESTORE command overwrites a key and all its contents with the contents of a hive file. This is similar to importing a hive file in Regedit. The difference between this command and loading a hive file is that this command overwrites any existing key, whereas loading a hive file creates a new temporary key to contain the hive file's contents. Use this command to restore a backup hive file. This command works only on the local computer.

```
Reg.exe RESTORE key filename
```

key   This is the key's path, beginning with the root key. Use the root key abbreviations HKCR, HKCU, HKLM, and HKU. This is the key you want to overwrite with the contents of the hive file.

filename   This is the path and name of the hive file to restore.

Example

```
Reg.exe RESTORE HKCU Backup.dat
```

Loading Hive Files

The LOAD command loads a hive file into a temporary key. You reference the hive file's keys and values through the temporary key you specify on the command line. This command is similar to loading hive files in Regedit. This command works only on the local computer.

```
Reg.exe LOAD key filename
```

key	This is the key's path, beginning with the root key. Use the root key abbreviations HKCR, HKCU, HKLM, and HKU. This is the new temporary key into which you want to load the hive file.
filename	This is the path and name of the hive file to load.

Example

```
Reg.exe LOAD HKU\Temporary Settings.dat
```

Unloading Hive Files

The UNLOAD command removes a hive file that you've loaded using the LOAD command. It simply unhooks the hive file from the registry. You must remember to unload a hive file that you've loaded before trying to copy or do anything else with the hive file because Windows XP Professional locks the file while it is in use.

```
Reg.exe UNLOAD key
```

key	This is the key's path, beginning with the root key. Use the root key abbreviations HKCR, HKCU, HKLM, and HKU. This is the name of the key containing the hive file you want to unload.

Example

```
Reg.exe UNLOAD HKU\Temporary
```

Scripting Using Windows Script Host

Scripts give IT professionals the ultimate ability to control and automate Windows XP Professional. These aren't batch files; they're full-fledged administrative programs that are surprisingly easy to create, considering the wealth of power they enable. You can write a script that inventories a computer and writes the result to a file on the network, for example. You can automate an application to perform redundant steps automatically. The sky is the limit, really, but I'm here to tell you how to use scripts to edit the registry, so I'm confining myself a bit.

The scripting technology in Windows XP Professional is WSH. The current version is technologically leaps and bounds over what Microsoft Windows 2000 provided. WSH is called a *host* because it's not aware of a script's language. Microsoft calls this language-*agnostic*. WSH uses different scripting engines to parse the different languages in which you might write a script. Windows XP Professional provides two scripting engines: VBScript and JScript. If you've ever used the C or C++ languages, you'll be more comfortable writing scripts using JScript. If you've ever used Visual Basic in any of its incarnations, you'll be more comfortable using VBScript to write scripts.

The problem with focusing this chapter on how to use scripts to edit the registry is that doing so assumes that you're already familiar with WSH. If that's not true, I suggest that you find a good book about scripts. If you don't want a book, see *http://msdn.microsoft.com/library/default.asp?url=/nhp/default.asp?contentid= 28001169*. This is Microsoft's Scripting Web site and it contains everything you need to know about writing scripts for Windows XP Professional, including accessing Windows Management Instrumentation (WMI) via scripts. After you've mastered the languages, which aren't difficult, you'll appreciate this Web site's reference content. The content describes the object model and how to use it—the hardest part of writing scripts for Windows XP Professional.

Creating Script Files

Script files can have two file extensions, and the script's file extension indicates which language the file contains. Use the *.js* extension for files that contain JScript. Use the *.vbs* extension for files that contain VBScript. Regardless, script files are nothing more than text files that contain the language's keywords, so you can use your favorite text editor, Notepad, to create them. When you save a script file, make sure you enclose the file's name in quotation marks or choose All Files from the Save As Type list, so Notepad doesn't add the *.txt* extension to the file.

Without going into detail about the object model, you access the registry through the *Shell* object. This object contains the methods you call to add, remove, and update values in the registry. You'll add one of the following statements to every script in which you want to access the registry. The first line shows you how to create the *Shell* object using VBScript, and the second shows you how to do it using JScript. Just to show you how easy it is to create a script, open Notepad, and type Listing 8-7. The JScript language is case-sensitive, so type Listing 8-7 carefully. VBScript has the benefit of not being case-sensitive. Save the file using the *.js* extension and then double-click the file to run it. You'll see a message from me. Because double-clicking the script file runs it, you must right-click the file and then click Edit to edit the file.

```
set WshShell = WScript.CreateObject( "WScript.Shell")
var WshShell = WScript.CreateObject( "WScript.Shell");
```

Listing 8-7   Sample6.js

```
var WshShell = WScript.CreateObject( "WScript.Shell");

WshShell.Popup( "Hello from Jerry Honeycutt" );
```

Why Write Scripts When *.inf* Files Are Easier?

I usually write *.inf* files to edit the registry. If I'm not using *.inf* files, I write batch files and use Reg.exe. I like the simplicity of these methods. There are times when writing a script is the only suitable method, however.

Writing a script is necessary in a number of cases. The first is when you must have a user interface. If you want to display settings to or collect settings from users, scripting is the best choice. Also, scripting is the only method that provides rather full access to Windows XP Professional. For example, you can use a script to inventory the computer and dump the information to a text file on the network. You can use a script to configure users' computers using logic, if-this-then-that, which isn't possible with the other methods. So if you're doing anything more complicated than just adding, changing, or removing values, you'll end up writing scripts. I've seen some fairly complicated scripts. For example, one fellow I worked with wrote a script that searched the registry for services that Sysprep disabled and then permanently removed them from the registry. This is a great example of scripting.

Combined with WMI, scripting is nothing short of amazing. The following script shows you how to use VBScript and WMI to inventory a computer's configuration. It displays the amount of physical memory installed on the computer, the name of the computer, the basic input/output system (BIOS) version, the type of processor, and more. This script and many more like it are available on Microsoft's Script Center, which is a large library of scripts that you can download, modify, and use. All these scripts are at *http://www.microsoft.com/technet/scriptcenter.*

```
strComputer = "."
Set objWMIService = GetObject("winmgmts:" _
    & "{impersonationLevel=impersonate}!\\" & strComputer &
"\root\cimv2")
Set colSettings = objWMIService.ExecQuery _
    ("Select * from Win32_OperatingSystem")
For Each objOperatingSystem in colSettings
    Wscript.Echo "OS Name: " & objOperatingSystem.Name
    Wscript.Echo "Version: " & objOperatingSystem.Version
    Wscript.Echo "Service Pack: " & _
        objOperatingSystem.ServicePackMajorVersion _
            & "." & objOperatingSystem.ServicePackMinorVersion
    Wscript.Echo "OS Manufacturer: " & objOperatingSystem.Manufacturer
    Wscript.Echo "Windows Directory: " & _
        objOperatingSystem.WindowsDirectory
    Wscript.Echo "Locale: " & objOperatingSystem.Locale
```

```
        Wscript.Echo "Available Physical Memory: " & _
            objOperatingSystem.FreePhysicalMemory
        Wscript.Echo "Total Virtual Memory: " & _
            objOperatingSystem.TotalVirtualMemorySize
        Wscript.Echo "Available Virtual Memory: " & _
            objOperatingSystem.FreeVirtualMemory
        Wscript.Echo "OS Name: " & objOperatingSystem.SizeStoredInPagingFiles
    Next
    Set colSettings = objWMIService.ExecQuery _
        ("Select * from Win32_ComputerSystem")
    For Each objComputer in colSettings
        Wscript.Echo "System Name: " & objComputer.Name
        Wscript.Echo "System Manufacturer: " & objComputer.Manufacturer
        Wscript.Echo "System Model: " & objComputer.Model
        Wscript.Echo "Time Zone: " & objComputer.CurrentTimeZone
        Wscript.Echo "Total Physical Memory: " & _
            objComputer.TotalPhysicalMemory
    Next
    Set colSettings = objWMIService.ExecQuery _
        ("Select * from Win32_Processor")
    For Each objProcessor in colSettings
        Wscript.Echo "System Type: " & objProcessor.Architecture
        Wscript.Echo "Processor: " & objProcessor.Description
    Next
    Set colSettings = objWMIService.ExecQuery _
        ("Select * from Win32_BIOS")
    For Each objBIOS in colSettings
        Wscript.Echo "BIOS Version: " & objBIOS.Version
    Next
```

Running Script Files

Windows XP Professional provides two scripting hosts. The Windows-based version runs scripts when you double-click a script file. The script engine is Wscript.exe. You can also use the command-line version, which is handy when the script outputs data similar to the way most command-line programs do. The example in the sidebar "Why Write Scripts When *.inf* Files Are Easier?" is one script that's better from the command line. The command-line scripting engine is Cscript.exe:

```
cscript script [//B|//I] [//D] [//E:engine] [//H:cscript|//H:wscript]
[//Job:name] [//Logo|//Nologo] [//S] [//T:time] [//X] [//?]
```

//B	This specifies batch mode, which does not display alerts, scripting errors, or input prompts.
//I	This specifies interactive mode, which displays alerts, scripting errors, and input prompts. This is the default and the opposite of //B.
//D	This turns on the debugger.

//E:engine	Specifies the scripting language that is used to run the script.
//H:cscript | //H:wscript	This registers either Cscript.exe or Wscript.exe as the default script host for running scripts. If neither is specified, the default is Wscript.exe.
//Job:name	This runs the job identified by name in a .wsf script file.
//Logo	This specifies that the WSH banner is displayed in the console window before the script runs. This is the default and the opposite of //Nologo.
//Nologo	This specifies that the WSH banner is not displayed before the script runs.
//S	This saves the current command-line options for the current user.
//T:time	This specifies the maximum time the script can run (in seconds). You can specify up to 32,767 seconds. The default is no time limit.
//X	This starts the script in the debugger.
//?	This displays available command parameters and provides help for using them. (This is the same as typing Cscript.exe with no parameters and no script.)

You can specify some of the same options when using the Windows-based scripting host. Right-click the script file and then click Properties. You'll see the dialog box shown in Figure 8-5. You can set the amount of time that the script is allowed to run and whether or not the host displays a log or not. The result is a file with the *.wsh* extension that contains these settings. It looks like your average INI file. You then execute the script by double-clicking the WSH file.

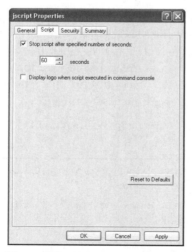

Figure 8-5   You create a WSH file, which contains a script file's settings, by right-clicking the script, clicking Properties, and then clicking the Script tab.

Formatting Key and Value Names

Before I show you how to edit the registry with a script, there's one more detail: how to format the names of keys and values in a script. Unlike other scripting methods I've described in this chapter, the WSH object model doesn't have separate parameters for the key and value name. Thus, you distinguish between key names and value names by the way you format them. The rule is simple: If a string ends with a backslash, it's a key name; if a string doesn't end with a backslash, it's a value name. Also, the JScript language reserves the backslash character (\) as the escape character: *n* is a newline character and *t* is a tab, for example. That means that you must escape the backslashes in your keys. Thus, any time you have a backslash in a key, you must use two backslashes (\\). To keep these clear, see Table 8-4.

Table 8-4 Key and Value Formatting

Object	VBScript	JScript
Value	*"HKLM\Subkey\Value"*	*"HKLM\\Subkey\\Value"*
Key	*"HKLM\Subkey\"*	*"HKLM\\Subkey\\"*

Adding and Updating Values

The *Shell* object's *RegWrite* method adds keys and values or changes existing values. If you want to change a key's default value, set **strName** to the name of the key, including the trailing backslash, and then assign a value to it.

> **Tip** One of the *RegWrite* method's biggest weaknesses is that it only writes 4 bytes of REG_BINARY values. It can't handle larger binary values. If you want to change longer binary values or change the types of values that this method doesn't support, use the *Shell* object's *Run* method to import a *.reg* file. For example, you can put your settings in a *.reg* file called Settings.reg. Then import that *.reg* file using the statement `WshShell.Run("Settings.reg")`. Your script could even create a settings.reg file in a temporary location, import that file using the Run method, and then delete the temporary file.

```
object.RegWrite( strName, anyValue [,strType] )
```

object	This is the Shell object.
strName	This is the string indicating the name of the key or value. You can add keys. You can add or change values. strName must be a fully qualified path to a key or value and begin with one of the root keys: HKCR, HKCU, HKLM, or HKU.
anyValue	This is the data to assign to new or existing values. Use the format appropriate for the value's type.
strType	This is the type of value to create: REG_SZ, REG_EXPAND_SZ, REG_DWORD, or REG_BINARY. The *RegWrite* method doesn't support the REG_MULTI_SZ value type. Also, this method writes only 4-byte REG_BINARY values.

Example (VBScript)

```
Set WshShell = WScript.CreateObject( "WScript.Shell" )

WshShell.RegWrite "HKCU\Software\Sample\", 1, "REG_BINARY"
WshShell.RegWrite "HKCU\Software\Sample\Howdy", "World!", "REG_SZ"
```

Example (JScript)

```
var WshShell = WScript.CreateObject( "WScript.Shell" );

WshShell.RegWrite( "HKCU\\Software\\Sample\\", 1, "REG_BINARY" );
WshShell.RegWrite( "HKCU\\Software\\Sample\\Howdy", "World!", "REG_SZ");
```

Removing Keys and Values

The *Shell* object's *RegDelete* method removes keys and values from the registry. Be careful, however, because removing an entire branch is easy; there's no confirmation. To remove a key, end *strName* with a backslash; otherwise, you're removing a value.

```
object.RegDelete( strName )
```

object	This is the shell object.
strName	This is the string indicating the name of the key or value to delete. strName must be a fully qualified path to a key or value and begin with one of the root keys: HKCR, HKCU, HKLM, or HKU.

Example (VBScript)

```
Set WshShell = WScript.CreateObject( "WScript.Shell" )

WshShell.RegDelete "HKCU\Software\Honeycutt\Howdy"
WshShell.RegDelete "HKCU\Software\Honeycutt\"
```

Example (JScript)

```
var WshShell = WScript.CreateObject( "WScript.Shell" );

WshShell.RegDelete ( "HKCU\\Software\\Honeycutt\\Howdy" );
WshShell.RegDelete ( "HKCU\\Software\\Honeycutt\\" );
```

Querying Registry Values

The *Shell* object's *RegRead* method returns a value's data. To read a key's default value, end *strName* with a backslash; otherwise, you're reading a value.

```
object.RegRead( strName )
```

object	This is the shell object.
strName	This is the string indicating the name of the value to read. strName must be a fully qualified path to a key or value and begin with one of the root keys: HKCR, HKCU, HKLM, or HKU.

Example (VBScript)

```
Dim WshShell, dwFlag, strValue
Set WshShell = WScript.CreateObject( "WScript.Shell" )

dwFlag = WshShell.RegRead( "HKCU\Software\Honeycutt\" )
strValue = WshShell.RegRead( "HKCU\Software\Honeycutt\Howdy" )
```

Example (JScript)

```
var WshShell = WScript.CreateObject( "WScript.Shell" );

var dwFlag = WshShell.RegRead( "HKCU\\Software\\Honeycutt\\" );
var strValue = WshShell.RegRead( "HKCU\\Software\\Honeycutt\\Howdy" );
```

Creating Windows Installer Packages

The last method of deploying registry settings I discuss in this chapter is creating Windows Installer package files. You've undoubtedly encountered package files by now. Office 2003 Editions ships as a package file, which is a database of files and settings that Windows Installer installs on the computer. Creating a package file for a large application is an intense process, but creating package files that contain registry settings is straightforward.

To create a package file, you need an editor. One of the most popular package editors is VERITAS WinINSTALL, and you can learn more about this enterprise-class tool at *http://www.veritas.com*. If you don't want to fork over the cash necessary to purchase a full version of WinINSTALL, how'd you like a free version? If you still have your Microsoft Windows 2000 Professional CD laying around, look in the Valueadd\3rdparty\Mgmt\Winstle folder, which is an older limited edition version of WinINSTALL. It's clunky and short on features when compared to recent versions of WinINSTALL, but it's suitable for creating package files to deploy registry settings. Install the program by double-clicking Swiadmle.msi. This installs WinINSTALL on the Start menu: Click Start, All Programs, VERITAS Software, VERITAS Software Console to run it. OnDemand Software now publishes WinINSTALL, and you can download an evaluation copy at *http://www.ondemandsoftware.com*.

Package files contain features, and features contain components. To deploy registry settings in a package file, you must create all the above. Follow these steps to create a new package file and add registry settings to it:

1. In the left pane, right-click Windows Installer Package Editor, New. In the File-name box, type the path and name of the package file and click OK.

2. In the left pane, right-click the package file you created and then click Add Feature. In the right pane's Name box, type a new name for the feature.

    This is likely to be the only feature that you add to the package file because all you're doing is deploying registry settings. You can create multiple features, though, with each feature containing different registry settings; then, users can install or not install individual features.

3. In the left pane, right-click the feature you created in step 2 and then click Add Component.

    The package editor automatically gives the component a globally unique identifier (GUID), which is a globally unique number that identifies the package. Components typically contain all the files and settings required to implement a program unit, so applications often have multiple components. When using a package file to deploy settings, creating multiple components doesn't make a lot of sense.

4. In the left pane, select the component you added and click Registry.

5. In the right pane, right-click the root key that you want to edit and click New Key. Continue creating subkeys by right-clicking a key and clicking New Key until you've created the full path of the key that you want to edit.

6. In the right pane, click the key in which you want to add or change a value and then click New Value. In the Value Name box, type the name of the value. In the Data Type list, select the type of value's type; click OK. In the *Type* Editor dialog box, type the value's data and then click OK.

7. Click File, Save to save your package file.

After you've created a package file, you can deploy it as any other package file. For example, users can simply double-click the package file to install it. If the package file contains settings that users don't have permission to change, you can deploy it through Active Directory and Group Policy, which installs package files with elevated privileges. You can also execute the command that installs a package file, which is **msiexec.exe" /i** *filename***.msi**.

> **Tip**   If you're trying to customize the settings of an application that's already packaged as a Windows Installer setup database (.msi file), there is an easy way to do it: edit the package with a package editor. Chapter 23, "Software Installation," describes some of the package editors available. The package editor with which I'm the most familiar is Wise for Windows Installer (*http://www.wise.com*). You can add, change, and remove registry settings and files in any existing package file. For example, I edited the package file for Helio TextPad (*http://www.textpad.com*) to include syntax highlighting files that I use frequently.

Configuring Specific Settings

One of the more common questions I receive, and one of the biggest requests from reviewers who read this chapter, is recommendations about specific settings to configure in Windows XP Professional. There are thousands of settings in Windows XP Professional, many of which an enterprise might want to configure in different combinations. Documenting them all isn't possible.

I've attempted the next best thing, however. This book's companion CD contains sample *.inf*, *.reg*, *.vbs*, and *.cmd* files for numerous settings that are useful to configure during a desktop deployment. They're in the Samples\chap08\settings folder. Instead of trying to anticipate what every reader might want to configure, I looked at the last few desktop deployments I did and borrowed their settings. The Samples\chap08 folder contains the spreadsheet Settings.xls, which describes each of the *.inf*, *.reg*, *.vbs*, and *.cmd* files in the Samples\chap08\settings folder.

Best Practices

The following are best practices for distributing settings with Windows XP Professional:

- **Use Group Policy to deploy required settings.**   The techniques that this chapter describes are for default settings. If you don't want users to change a particular setting, deploy that setting as a policy.

- **Use the formalized techniques before resorting to the techniques in this chapter.**   Some settings have formalized methods for distributing them. For example, you can configure numerous settings using an unattended-setup answer file. Thus, use the answer file for those settings before resorting to scripting.

- **Choose a distribution method with which you are most comfortable.** By relying on scripting techniques with which you're already familiar, you reduce the chances of errors that come from inexperience.

Chapter 9

Office Settings

After creating an installation source on the network, as described in Chapter 7, "Distribution Points," you can customize Microsoft Office 2003 Editions before distributing it to users' computers. You can configure which Office features are available and specify default settings for most options, for example. This chapter describes how to customize Office 2003 Editions for distribution.

Checklist

- Have you documented the feature installation states and settings you want to configure? See Chapter 4, "Office Configuration," for more information.

- Have you gathered the files and registry settings you must deploy with Office 2003 Editions? See Chapter 4 for more information.

- Have you planned your Office 2003 Editions security configuration? See Chapter 4 to learn best practices for Office 2003 Editions security.

- Have you identified the need for a staged Office 2003 Editions deployment? See Chapter 1, "Deployment Plan," for more information.

- Have you created an Office 2003 Editions distribution point? See Chapter 7 to learn how to create one.

Customization Methods

After you create an administrative installation point or compressed CD image for Office 2003 Editions, you can customize it before distributing it to users' computers:

- Specify default settings for Office 2003 Editions applications.

- Add files or shortcuts to an Office 2003 Editions installation.

- Determine which Office 2003 Editions applications and features are installed.

- Determine which previous versions of Office are removed.

- Distribute a default Microsoft Office Outlook 2003 profile.

You can accomplish many of the customizations you make to an Office 2003 Editions installation by one of several methods. Table 9-1 describes these methods and recommends when to use each:

- Specifying options on the command line.

- Customizing the Setup.ini file.

- Creating a transform (.*mst* file) with the Custom Installation Wizard.

- Creating an Office 2003 Editions profile settings file (.*ops* file) with the Profile Wizard.

- Running the Removal Wizard during or after the Office 2003 Editions installation.

Table 9-1   Customizing Packages

Customization	MSI File	Command Line	INI File	MST File	OPS File	Removal Wizard
Setup process (display, logging, installation location, organization name, and so on)	Pro11.msi	Yes	Yes	Yes		
Local installation source (compressed CD image only)	Pro11.msi	Yes	Yes			
Office features, added files, and shortcuts	Pro11.msi			Yes		

Table 9-1 Customizing Packages

Customization	MSI File	Command Line	INI File	MST File	OPS File	Removal Wizard
Security settings	Pro11.msi			Yes	Yes	
Outlook settings	Pro11.msi			Yes	Yes	
Other user settings	Pro11.msi			Yes	Yes	
Removal options	Pro11.msi			Yes		Yes

More Info The Office 2003 Editions Resource Kit at *http://www.microsoft.com /office/ork* is your primary resource for customizing Office 2003 Editions. The Office 2003 Editions Resource Kit toolbox includes the Custom Installation Wizard, Profile Wizard, and Removal Wizard. The resource kit Setup program installs these tools by default. For more information, see the Toolbox at *http://www.microsoft.com/office/ork/2003/tools/default.htm*. Download the tools from *http://www.microsoft.com/office/ork/2003/tools/ddl /default.htm*.

Options

When you run Setup, you can use command-line options to change how Setup installs Office 2003 Editions. By using command-line options, you can identify the package file and transform to use, specify a custom settings file, configure display options, set logging options, and change Setup properties. For example, the command `setup.exe /qb+ /l* %temp%\office11.txt COMPANYNAME="Jerry Honeycutt"` does the following:

- Setup does not prompt the user for information, but displays progress indicators and a completion message when it installs Office 2003 Editions (**/qb+**).

- Windows Installer logs all information and any error messages (**/l***) for Setup to the file C:\Documents and Settings*Username*\Local Settings\Temp\Office11.txt on the user's computer, where *username* is the logged-on user's name.

- Setup sets the default organization name to Jerry Honeycutt.

- Because no custom .ini or *.mst* file is specified, Setup installs the same Office 2003 Editions features that it would if the user clicked Typical Install during installation.

The Setup command line is most useful when you have few customizations to make or when you want to create several different installations quickly. You can use one custom .ini file or apply the same *.mst* file to install a basic Office 2003 Editions configuration to everyone but define different command lines for targeted groups of users. For example, you can have your Engineering and Accounting departments install the same set of Office 2003 Editions features and settings but specify unique organization names. On the installation image, you create two shortcuts that have the following command lines:

- `setup.exe /q /settings Custom.ini COMPANYNAME="Engineering"`
- `setup.exe /q /settings Custom.ini COMPANYNAME="Accounting"`

Command-line options are also useful if you use Microsoft Systems Management Server or another systems management tool to create multiple deployment packages, each of which requires a different command line.

Tip Any settings that you can specify on the command line can also be added to Setup.ini—including the command line itself. For extensive or complex command-line customizations, use Setup.ini to make the installation process easier to track and troubleshoot.

When users double-click Setup.exe on the installation image, Setup runs with no command-line options. To apply your custom command-line options, users must use the Run dialog box or a command prompt. To simplify this process, you can create a batch script that runs Setup.exe with your command-line options. Or, you can create a shortcut and add your custom options to the command-line box. Users double-click the batch script or shortcut to run the Setup command line that you have defined. You can store the batch file or shortcut in the root folder of the installation image. If you run Setup from a network logon script or through a systems management tool such as Systems Management Server (SMS), you can add your custom options to the Setup command line in the script or deployment package.

Setup properties are different from command-line options, but you can use them on the command line. They control many aspects of the installation process, including display settings, logging options, Setup user interface, feature installation states, and so on. The difference between setup properties and command-line options is that setup properties are defined in the Windows Installer package (*.msi* file) whereas Setup interprets command-line options. You can specify new values for properties on the command line, in Setup.ini, or on the Modify Setup Properties page of the Custom Installation Wizard. During the installation, Setup passes all Setup property values to Windows Installer.

> **More Info**   For more information about customizing how Office 2003 Setup runs, see Chapter 13, "Unattended Setup." This chapter describes how to configure the Setup user interface, logging options, and so on.

Settings Files

Before applying the values specified on the command line, Setup reads the properties specified in the Setup settings file (Setup.ini), in which you can set all the properties that you can on the command line. For example, you can do the following:

- Specify the *.msi* and *.mst* files to use in the *[MSI]* and *[MST]* sections.

- Direct Setup to run in quiet mode in the *[Display]* section.

- Set logging options for Windows Installer and Office 2003 Setup in the *[Logging]* section.

- Change the default values of Setup properties in the *[Options]* section.

- Customize the way Setup creates a local installation source on users' computers when you install Office 2003 Editions from a compressed CD image.

Because the Setup settings file organizes options in an easy-to-read format, it is more convenient to use than long or complex command lines. If you use Setup.ini to set most Setup properties, you can reserve the command line for specific and targeted modifications or changes that you need to make late in the deployment process. Another scenario in which the Setup settings file is the preferred customization method to use when you want users to run Setup.exe directly from the installation image, instead of creating a batch file or shortcut to install a customized version of the Office 2003 Editions client. You also use a settings file when you want to chain installations, as described in Chapter 11, "Chaining Installations."

In most sections of Setup.ini, including the *[Options]* section, you use the syntax *property=value* to specify custom property values.

If you are installing Office 2003 Editions from a compressed CD image and you want to customize the way Setup creates the local installation source on users' computers, you set properties in the *[Cache]* section of Setup.ini. Because Setup creates the local installation source before a transform is applied, you cannot set most local installation source options in a transform.

When you edit the default Setup settings file (Setup.ini), users can run Setup without using command-line options to install Office with your customizations. To create multiple custom installations that use different Setup options, however, you can create several custom .ini files that have different names and store them in the root folder of the installation image. Users specify the name of a settings file by using the /**settings** command-line option. You can simplify this process by creating a batch file or shortcut that contains the appropriate /**settings** command-line option. If your custom .ini file is stored in any location other than the folder that contains Setup.exe, you must include the relative or absolute path with the /**settings** option: **setup.exe /settings ***server******share***\files\setup\off11eng.ini**.

> **More Info**   For more information about customizing how Office 2003 Setup runs, see Chapter 13, which describes how to configure the Setup user interface, logging options, and so on.

Transforms

When you install Office 2003 Editions from an administrative installation point or compressed CD image, you can customize the configuration that is installed on users' computers by applying a Windows Installer transform (.*mst* file). Many of the customizations that you make in Setup.ini or on the command line can also be made in a transform, but some tasks are better handled in a transform. For example, a transform is typically used to set default installation states for Office 2003 Editions features or to specify default application settings.

You create a Windows Installer transform by using the Custom Installation Wizard. The transform contains the changes that you want to make to the Windows Installer package (.*msi* file). When you apply the transform during the installation, your modifications become the default settings for anyone who runs Setup from your installation image. If you run Setup in quiet mode (with no user interaction), your selections define precisely how Office 2003 Editions is installed on users' computers.

> **More Info**   The Office 2003 Editions Resource Kit toolbox includes the Custom Installation Wizard, Profile Wizard, and Removal Wizard. The resource kit Setup program installs these tools by default. For more information, see the Toolbox at http://*www.microsoft.com/office/ork/2003 /tools/default.htm*. Download the tools from http://*www.microsoft.com /office/ork /2003/tools/ddl/default.htm*.

A Windows Installer transform is most useful when you want to make extensive customizations, particularly customizations that you can't readily make by using the Setup command line or Setup settings file. By creating multiple transforms, you can also install different Office 2003 Editions configurations to different groups of users from the same installation image. When you create a transform, the Custom Installation Wizard allows you to do the following:

- Define the path where Office 2003 Editions is installed on users' computers.

- Accept the End-User License Agreement (EULA) and enter a product key on behalf of users who are installing from a compressed CD image.

- Define the default installation state for Office 2003 Editions applications and features. For example, you can install Microsoft Office Word 2003 on the local computer, but set Microsoft Office PowerPoint 2003 to be installed on demand or run from the network. You can also hide and lock features so that users cannot make changes after Office 2003 Editions is installed.

- Add your own files and registry entries to Setup so that they are installed with Office 2003 Editions.

- Modify Office 2003 Editions application shortcuts, specifying where they are installed and customizing their properties.

- Define a list of servers for Office 2003 Editions to use if the primary installation source is unavailable.

- Specify other products to install or programs to run on users' computers after Setup is completed.

- Configure Outlook. For example, you can specify a default user profile.

- Specify which previous versions of Office 2003 Editions are removed.

For users to install Office 2003 Editions with your customizations, you must specify the name and path to the transform by setting the **TRANSFORMS** property on the command line or by adding an entry to the *[MST]* section of the Setup settings file. For example, to direct Setup to use the transform Custom.mst (stored in the same folder as Setup.exe), you use the command **setup.exe TRANSFORMS =custom.mst**. This command-line option is equivalent to adding the following entry to the [MST] section of Setup.ini:

```
MST1=Custom.mst
```

> **Warning**   If you misspell the **TRANSFORMS** option on the command line as **TRANSFORM** (singular), Setup returns an error and your transform is not applied. Watch out! This is a common error.

If you create unique transforms for different groups of users, you must specify—on the command line or in Setup.ini—which transform to use. For example, users in your Accounting department might need all the add-ins included with Microsoft Office Excel 2003, and users in the Engineering department might need a custom set of Microsoft Office Access 2003 features. In this scenario, you can create different transforms that specify different installation states for Excel and Access features and then create two shortcuts on the installation image by using the following command lines:

- `setup.exe TRANSFORMS=off11eng.mst`

- `setup.exe TRANSFORMS=off11act.mst`

> **More Info**   You can apply a transform only when Office 2003 Editions is initially installed. To make changes to an Office 2003 Editions configuration after it's installed, you must use the Custom Maintenance Wizard. For more information, see Chapter 21, "Desktop Management."

Precedence

Office 2003 Editions offers many ways to customize an installation, and using a combination of methods can result in conflicting settings. If you specify different values for the same options on the Setup command line, in the Setup settings file, and in a transform, Setup uses the following rules to determine which value to use:

- If you set an option in the Custom Installation Wizard that corresponds to a Setup property, the wizard automatically sets the corresponding property in the *.mst* file. For example, when you customize removal behavior on the Remove Previous Versions page, the Custom Installation Wizard sets the *SKIPREMOVEPREVIOUSDIALOG* property to *True*.

- If you modify a Setup property on the Modify Setup Properties page of the Custom Installation Wizard, this setting overrides any corresponding options that you set on previous pages of the wizard. Your modified Setup property is written to the *.mst* file.

- If you set options (including Setup properties) in the Setup settings file that conflict with options in the transform, the values in the .ini file take precedence over the transform.

- If you set options on the command line, those settings take precedence over any conflicting values in either the .ini file or the transform.

Note   The *COMPANYNAME* property is an exception to the normal precedence of settings. If you supply an organization name when you create an administrative installation point and then specify a new default organization name on the Specify Default Path And Organization page of the Custom Installation Wizard, that setting takes precedence over any other *COMPANYNAME* setting you specify later in the wizard, in Setup.ini, or on the command line.

More Info   For more information about each page of the Custom Installation Wizard, see "Custom Installation Wizard" in the Office 2003 Editions Resource Kit Reference at http://*www.microsoft.com/office/ork/2003/ref /default.htm*.

Customizing Features

When you install Office 2003 Editions from an administrative installation point or compressed CD image, you can determine which applications and features are installed on users' computers, including how and when features are installed. You can also customize the way that Setup creates shortcuts for Office 2003 Editions applications and even add your own custom files to the Office installation.

When running Office 2003 Setup interactively, users can choose which applications and features to install by selecting options from the feature tree that Setup displays. Office features can be installed in any of the following states:

- Installed to the local hard disk.

- Run from the network server (administrative installation point only).

- Installed on first use, which means that Setup does not install the feature until the first time it is used.

- Not installed but accessible to users through Add/Remove Programs or the command line.

- Not installed, not displayed during Setup, and not accessible to users after Office 2003 Editions is installed.

By using the Custom Installation Wizard, you can make these choices for users ahead of time. When users run Setup interactively, the installation states that you specify in the transform (*.mst* file) appear as the default selections. When you run Setup quietly, your choices determine how the features are installed.

Installation States

The Set Feature Installation States page of the Custom Installation Wizard displays the same feature tree that users see when they select the Customize option during Setup. The feature tree is a hierarchy. Parent features contain child features, and child features can contain subordinate child features. For example, the Microsoft Word for Windows feature includes the child feature Help, and the Help feature includes the child feature Help for WordPerfect Users.

When you click a feature in the feature tree, you can select one of the following installation states:

- **Run From My Computer**   Setup copies files and writes registry entries and shortcuts associated with the feature to the user's hard disk, and the application or feature runs locally.

- **Run All From My Computer**   Same as Run From My Computer, except that all child features belonging to the feature are also set to this state.

- **Run From Network**   Setup leaves components for the feature on the administrative installation point, and the feature is run from there. The Run From Network option is available only when users install from an uncompressed administrative image. It's not available from a compressed CD image.

- **Run All From Network**   Same as Run From Network, except that all child features belonging to the feature are also set to this state. Note that some child features do not support Run From Network; these child features are installed on the local computer.

- **Installed On First Use**   Setup leaves components for the feature and all its child features on the administrative installation point until the user first attempts to use the feature, at which time the components are automatically copied to the local hard disk. If the user installed from a compressed CD image with the local installation source enabled, the components are installed from the local source. Some child features do not support Installed On First Use; these features are set to Not Available.

- **Not Available**   The components for the feature and all the child features belonging to the feature are not installed on the computer. Users can change this installation state during Setup or later in maintenance mode. Also, you can make features unavailable and then change them at a later date by using the Custom Maintenance Wizard, which is a good way to stage deployments.

- **Not Available, Hidden, Locked**   The components for the feature are not installed and the feature does not appear in the feature tree during Setup—nor can users install it by changing the state of the parent feature or by calling Windows Installer directly from the command line. Once deployed with this state, you can't change it.

Not all installation states are available for every feature. For example, if a feature contains a component that cannot be run over the network, Run From Network is not included in the list of available installation states.

When you change the installation state of a feature, Windows Installer may automatically change the installation state of a parent or child feature to match. If you set the Help feature to Installed On First Use, for example, but set the child feature Help For WordPerfect Users to Run From My Computer, Setup installs the entire Help feature on the local hard disk. You can work around this behavior by not configuring the parent feature and then configuring child feature individually.

> **Tip**   If you run the Custom Installation Wizard (Custwiz.exe) with the **/x** command-line option, the wizard displays the feature tree fully expanded on the Set Feature Installation States page.

Hiding and Locking Features

In addition to setting the installation state, you can right-click any feature on the Set Feature Installation States page and click Hide to hide the feature from the user. Setup does not display hidden features in the feature tree when users run Setup interactively; instead, the feature is installed behind the scenes according to the installation state that you have specified. When you hide a feature, all the child features belonging to the feature are also hidden. When you edit the transform in the Custom Installation Wizard, you can reverse the Hide setting by right-clicking the feature and clicking Unhide. However, you cannot use the Custom Maintenance Wizard to expose a hidden feature after Office is installed.

The best use of the Hide setting is to simplify the feature tree for users. For example, you might hide the Office Tools branch of the feature tree so that users do not have to decide which tools they need. Only the tools that you select are installed.

Even if you set a feature to Not Available and hide it in the feature tree, users can still change the setting and install the feature by installing the parent feature or by running Office 2003 Setup in maintenance mode. For example, if you set the Help For WordPerfect Users feature to Not Available and hide it, users can still install it by setting the parent Help feature to Run All From My Computer. If you want to help prevent users from installing hidden features, choose the Not Available, Hidden, Locked installation state. In this case, the feature or application is not installed and is not available in maintenance mode. Users cannot install it by changing the state of the parent feature or by calling Windows Installer directly from the command line. The only way to reverse the Not Available, Hidden, Locked installation state after Office 2003 Editions is installed is to use the Custom Maintenance Wizard.

> **More Info**   See Chapter 21 for more information about the Custom Maintenance Wizard.

When users install Office 2003 Editions, Setup does not display the feature tree by default. Clicking the Custom Install option displays a top-level list of applications. Users can select the check box next to an application to install a typical set of features. When you set an application to Not Available, Hidden, Locked, the check box on this page remains visible but appears grayed-out—users cannot select the application. To hide this page during Setup altogether, set the *SKIPCHECKBOXDIALOG* property to **1**.

Preventing Network Features

Installing features on demand or running features over the network is not always efficient. Both of these installation states require a fast connection and reliable access to the administrative installation point on the network—which laptop users in the field might not always have. The Custom Installation Wizard includes two options on the Set Feature Installation States page that disable these installation states and help ensure that users do not reset features to these states during Setup or in maintenance mode:

- **Disable Run From Network**   When you select a feature in the feature tree and then select this check box, users are prevented from setting the feature to run from the network. The installation state does not appear in the list of options during initial Setup or in maintenance mode.

- **Disable Installed On First Use**   When you select a feature in the feature tree and then select this check box, users are prevented from setting the feature to be installed on first use. The installation state does not appear in the list of options during initial Setup or in maintenance mode.

Child features do not inherit these settings from parent features automatically. You must select each feature in the tree and set Disable Run From Network or Disable Installed On First Use for only that feature. You can also select a feature and click Apply To Branch to apply either of these settings to a feature and all its subordinate features.

> **Note** The Disable Run From Network and Disable Installed On First Use settings remain in effect for as long as Office 2003 Editions is installed on the user's computer. You cannot reverse these settings by using the Custom Maintenance Wizard.

Configuring Feature State Migration

To make an Office 2003 Editions installation more efficient, Setup automatically sets default feature installation states in the following circumstances:

- When you upgrade to Office 2003 Editions, Setup detects and matches feature installation states from the previous version. For example, if Microsoft Word 2002 is installed to run from the network, Setup installs Microsoft Office Word 2003 to run from the network. If Microsoft PowerPoint 2002 is set to Not Available, Setup does not install Office PowerPoint 2003.

- When you install Multilingual User Interface (MUI) Packs from the MUI Pack, Setup matches the feature installation states specified for the core version of Office 2003 Editions. For example, if the core English version of Microsoft Office Access 2003 is set to be installed on demand, Setup automatically sets international versions of Office Access 2003 features to Installed On First Use. When you install Office under Microsoft Windows Terminal Services, Setup applies the most efficient installation state for each feature. For example, because the speech recognition feature does not run efficiently over most networks and might not be supported by all clients, Windows Terminal Services automatically changes the feature installation state from Installed On First Use to Not Available.

This intelligent Setup behavior works to your advantage in most situations. However, you can override Setup and specify your own default feature installation states in a transform by using one of the following two settings:

- *NOFEATURESTATEMIGRATION* **property**   Setting this property to **1** for the Office 2003 Editions package overrides intelligent Setup behavior for the entire package. Note that this property has no effect on Windows Terminal Services logic; you must override optional Windows Terminal Services installation states on a per-feature basis.

- **Do Not Migrate Previous Installation State Check Box On The Set Feature Installation States Page Of The Custom Installation Wizard**   Selecting an Office 2003 Editions feature in the feature tree and then selecting this check box overrides intelligent Setup behavior and enforces the installation state you set in the transform. If you have already set the *NOFEATURESTATEMIGRATION* property for the entire package, selecting this check box for a given feature has no effect. This check box has no effect on default feature installation state matching for MUI Pack features.

Table 9-2 summarizes the results of setting the *NOFEATURESTATEMIGRATION* property for an Office 2003 Editions package or selecting the Do Not Migrate Previous Installation State check box for a feature.

Table 9-2   NOFEATURESTATEMIGRATION Property

Package	Property Set To True	Check Box Selected
Office	Default feature installation state migration is disabled for all of Office.	Does not apply the installation state from a previous version to the selected feature.
MUI Pack	Default feature installation state matching is disabled for the entire package.	Has no effect on default feature installation state matching.
Proofing Tools	Default feature installation state matching is disabled for the entire package.	Has no effect on default feature installation state matching.

Although the *NOFEATURESTATEMIGRATION* property has no effect on Windows Terminal Services logic, you can override default Windows Terminal Services settings for some features by selecting the Do Not Migrate Previous Installation State check box. For example, if your network and clients support the speech recognition feature, you can set that feature to Run From My Computer and select the Do Not Migrate Previous Installation State check box to enforce your setting. However, you cannot override all the installation states set by default under Windows Terminal Services. For example, Windows Terminal Services does not allow any feature to be set to Installed On First Use.

Microsoft Access 2000 and Office 2003

When you upgrade from Microsoft Office 2000 to Office 2003 Editions, you might choose to keep Access 2000 installed on users' computers. In this scenario, if you set Office Access 2003 to Not Available and install Office quietly, Windows Installer removes the .mdb file extension registration, and Access 2000 no longer recognizes the databases. Selecting the Do Not Migrate Previous Installation State check box for Microsoft Access does not prevent this problem.

To help ensure that Access 2000 users can continue to use their .mdb files after the upgrade, you can take one of two steps:

- Set Microsoft Office Access 2003 to Not Available, Hidden, And Locked in the transform.

- Set the *NOFEATURESTATEMIGRATION* property to **True** for the entire Office 2003 Editions package.

Customizing Office Shortcuts

By using the Custom Installation Wizard, you can customize the shortcuts that Setup creates for Office 2003 Editions applications and files. You can control what shortcuts are installed, and you can also specify which folder a shortcut is stored in and what command-line options to use with a shortcut. On the Add, Modify, Or Remove Shortcuts page, the Custom Installation Wizard displays shortcuts for all the features that you selected on the Set Feature Installation States page.

An additional tab displays shortcuts for Office 2003 Editions features that you did not set to be installed. Use the Not Installed tab to customize shortcuts for applications that you plan to install later. For example, if you omitted Office Access 2003 from your initial installation, you can use the Custom Maintenance Wizard to install Access later. Because the Custom Maintenance Wizard does not allow you to customize the way shortcuts are installed, you must customize Access shortcuts ahead of time in the transform.

For more information about the Custom Maintenance Wizard, see Chapter 21.

> **Note** Shortcuts for Office 2003 Editions applications are stored in a new subfolder: Start\Programs\Microsoft Office. Shortcuts to Office 2003 Editions tools are stored in a subfolder in the same location: Start\Programs \Microsoft Office\Microsoft Office Tools. If you upgrade to Office 2003 Editions but retain some applications from a previous version, the shortcuts for the applications you have chosen to keep and those for any shared components remain in their original location: Start\Programs and Start\Programs \Microsoft Office Tools. Shortcuts to the new versions of the applications and tools appear in the new location.

Modifying Shortcuts

On the Add, Modify, Or Remove Shortcuts page, you modify any existing shortcut by selecting the shortcut and clicking Modify. In the Add/Modify Shortcut Entry dialog box, you can make the following changes:

- Change the target application associated with a shortcut.
- Change the location in which the shortcut (*.lnk* file) is created.
- Rename a shortcut.
- Change the starting folder for the application—that is, the folder in which the application starts when the user clicks the shortcut.
- Specify a keyboard shortcut for a shortcut.
- Change the icon associated with a shortcut.

> **Note** Windows Installer shortcuts support automatic repair of Office 2003 Editions features and allow you to advertise applications. Advertised applications are installed the first time a user clicks the shortcut or opens a file associated with the application. In some circumstances, you might not want Setup to create Windows Installer shortcuts. For example, if you are deploying to roaming users who sometimes log on to computers that do not support Windows Installer shortcuts, you can circumvent the default behavior by clearing the Create Windows Installer Shortcuts If Supported check box on the Add, Modify, Or Remove Shortcuts page.

You can click Add to add a new shortcut for any file being installed by Setup. This step allows you to create duplicate shortcuts for the most frequently used Office 2003 Editions applications on the user's computer. It also allows you to create shortcuts for custom files or applications that you add to the installation. To remove a shortcut from the list, select the shortcut and click Remove.

Migrating Existing Shortcuts

Office users can create shortcuts with custom names or command-line options. For example, a custom shortcut might open a particular document whenever Office Word 2003 is started. In versions of Office prior to Office XP, these shortcuts were left behind and broken when users upgraded to a new version of Office. When you upgrade to Office 2003 Editions, however, Setup automatically migrates custom shortcuts to point to the corresponding Office 2003 Editions application. For example, if a user has created a shortcut to Word 2002 on the desktop, Setup replaces it with a shortcut to Office Word 2003. If you associated a custom command line with the shortcut, Setup preserves that as well.

> **Note**   Custom shortcuts for previous versions of Access are not updated to point to Office Access 2003 when you upgrade.

Setup handles shortcut migration for each application separately. If you upgrade most of your applications to Office 2003 Editions but retain Microsoft Excel 2002, for example, all your shortcuts point to the correct versions: Office 2003 Editions applications and Excel 2002. This is an improvement over earlier versions of Office.

But if you install more than one version of the same application on your computer—for example, both Excel 2002 and Microsoft Office Excel 2003—Setup updates all custom shortcuts to point to the Office 2003 Editions application. In this multiple-version scenario, you might later uninstall Office 2003 Editions; however, your custom shortcuts are not migrated back to the previous version. If you are installing Office 2003 Editions in a multiple-version environment, and you do not want to update custom shortcuts to point to the new version, you can prevent Setup from upgrading existing custom shortcuts. Set the *DISABLESCMIGRATION* property to **True** in a transform or on the command line.

Setup handles migration of custom shortcuts when Office 2003 Editions is first installed, when an advertised application is installed, and when an installation state of an installed application is changed to Not Available. Setup searches the following locations for custom shortcuts:

- Desktop
- Start menu, including the Programs and Microsoft Office Tools submenus
- Quick Launch toolbar

You can specify additional custom shortcuts in other locations by editing the Oclncust.opc file. For more information about this file, see the section "Customizing Removal Behavior," later in this chapter on page 273.

Removing Custom Shortcuts

Office 2003 Editions removes custom shortcuts to Office 2003 Editions applications more efficiently than versions prior to Office XP. For example, if a user copies a shortcut to Office Excel 2003 onto the desktop and then removes Office Excel 2003 from the computer, Setup automatically removes that shortcut.

In addition to the default locations that Setup checks for custom shortcuts to remove, you can direct Setup to search additional folders for outdated custom shortcuts by setting the *CIWEXTRASHORTCUTDIRS* property in a transform or on the command line. You specify additional locations by using a list delimited by semicolons. For example, to direct Setup to clean up custom shortcuts in the Startup and Favorites\My Office folders, add the following to the Setup command line: **CIWEXTRASHORTCUTDIRS=<StartMenu\Programs\Startup>;<Favorites> \My Office**. When you specify additional folders, you can use any of the following folder keywords, appending other path information to them:

- <Desktop>
- <StartMenu>
- <StartMenu\Programs>
- <StartMenu\Programs\Startup>
- <ProgramFiles\Microsoft Office>
- <ApplicationData>

- <Favorites>

- <NetHood>

You can also specify additional locations by using a full path, such as C:\Office\My Office. Wildcards—both asterisks (*) and question marks (?)—are supported. For example, the following setting causes Setup to search the Start Menu\Programs folder for all folders that include Office in the name: **CIWEXTRASHORTCUTDIRS=<StartMenu\Programs*Office*>**.

Adding Files to Office 2003

In addition to selecting which Office 2003 Editions files are installed, Setup allows you to add your own files to the installation. You can deploy corporate templates, clip art, custom applications, or other files along with Office 2003 Editions. On the Add/Remove Files page of the Office Custom Installation Wizard, click Add to add a new file to the installation.

After you select one or more files to add, enter the destination path for the file or files in the File Destination Path dialog box. You can enter an absolute path on the user's computer or you can select a path from the list. If you select a path, you can add a subfolder to it by appending a backslash (\) followed by the subfolder name. When you click OK, the wizard adds the file to the transform. Setup installs the file on the user's computer, in the folder you specified, when the user installs Office.

> **Note** Files that you add to the installation on this page are not removed if the user subsequently modifies the file or removes, repairs, or reinstalls Office 2003 Editions.

After you add the file, you can add a shortcut for the file on the Add, Modify, Or Remove Shortcuts page of the wizard. On that page, click Add; the file you added appears in the Target box. Because the file is copied into the transform, you must update the transform if the file changes later on:

1. On the Open The MST File page, enter the name of the Windows Installer transform (*.mst* file).

2. On the Select The MST File To Save page, enter the name of the *.mst* file again.

3. On the Add/Remove Files page, select the file that has changed and then click Remove.

4. Click Add and then enter the information for your modified file.

The Custom Installation Wizard also allows you to specify files to remove from users' computers when Office 2003 Editions is installed. For example, you can have Setup delete custom templates designed for Word 2002 or Word 2000 when you upgrade to Office Word 2003. Click the Remove Files tab to list files to remove.

Customizing User Settings

Office 2003 Editions applications are highly customizable. Users can change the way Office 2003 Editions functions by setting options or adding custom templates or tools. For example, a sales department can create a custom template for invoices or a custom dictionary with industry-specific terms. Users can change everything from the screen resolution to the default file format for saving documents. Most of these user-defined settings are recorded as values in the registry.

As an administrator, you can customize user-defined settings and distribute a standard Office 2003 Editions configuration to all the users in your organization by using the Profile Wizard to capture settings an Office 2003 Editions profile settings file (.*ops* file). When you add the .*ops* file to a transform (.*mst* file), your customized settings are included when Office 2003 Editions is installed on client computers.

The Custom Installation Wizard also allows you to customize user-defined settings directly in the transform. You can set user options and add or modify registry values. You can even add the Profile Wizard to a transform and run it separately to distribute new default settings. When Office 2003 Editions is installed, your customizations modify values in the registry, and your settings appear as the defaults on users' computers.

Table 9-3 lists typical scenarios for customizing user settings and the recommended methods and tools to use in each case. The method you choose to customize user-defined settings depends on the following:

- **How extensively you want to configure Office 2003 Editions**   You can create a custom configuration for all of Office 2003 Editions or preset just a few key options.

- **How complex your deployment scenarios are**   You can distribute the same custom settings to all the users in your organization or you can configure Office 2003 Editions applications differently to meet the needs of different groups of users.

- **How and when you deploy Office 2003 Editions applications**   If you are staging your Office 2003 Editions deployment, you can customize only the applications that you are installing at a given time. Or, if you have already deployed Office 2003 Editions, you can distribute a standard configuration to all Office 2003 Editions users.

- **Whether you want to enforce your custom settings** Settings that you distribute through a transform (*.mst* file) or Office 2003 Editions profile settings file (*.ops* file) appear to users as the default settings—but users can choose different options for themselves. By contrast, using Office 2003 Editions policies ensures that your settings are always applied.

Table 9-3 Customizing User Settings

Scenario	Method	Tool
Distribute a standard default Office 2003 Editions configuration.	Add an OPS file to a transform.	Profile Wizard and Custom Installation Wizard (Customize Default Application Settings page)
Set just a few options or adjust your Office 2003 Editions configuration without re-creating the OPS file.	Add user settings to a transform.	Custom Installation Wizard (Change Office User Settings page)
Set default security levels.	Specify security settings in a transform.	Custom Installation Wizard (Specify Office Security Settings page)
Distribute a default Microsoft Office Outlook 2003 profile.	Specify Outlook settings in a transform.	Custom Installation Wizard (Outlook: Customize Default Profile page)
Specify settings that are not captured in an OPS file.	Add registry values to a transform.	Custom Installation Wizard (Add/Remove Registry Entries page)
Distribute a default Office 2003 Editions configuration, but store one or more OPS files separately from the MST file.	Run the Profile Wizard during Setup.	Profile Wizard and Custom Installation Wizard (Add Installations And Run Programs page)
Preserve users' custom settings from a previous version instead of specifying new default settings.	Allow Setup to migrate settings from a previous version of Office.	Default Setup behavior
Set unique options for Microsoft Office 2003 Editions MUI Packs or other chained packages.	Specify settings in the transform applied to the chained package.	Custom Installation Wizard and Setup settings file (Setup.ini)
Distribute a default Office 2003 Editions configuration that overrides individual users' settings.	Run the Profile Wizard as a standalone tool after Office is installed.	Profile Wizard

Table 9-3   Customizing User Settings

Scenario	Method	Tool
Modify user settings after Office is installed.	Distribute a configuration maintenance file (CMW file) after Office is installed.	Custom Maintenance Wizard
Prevent users from modifying the options you set.	Set Office policies.	Group Policy snap-in
Customize Microsoft Office Visio 2003 application settings and user-defined options.	Set policies or run the Profile Wizard as a standalone tool after Office is installed.	Group Policy snap-in or Profile Wizard

Most customized user options correspond to entries in the registry. If you define conflicting values for the same setting, Windows Installer must determine which value to use. In most cases, a setting applied later in the installation process overwrites any settings applied earlier. Settings for user options are applied in the following order:

1. Settings in an *.ops* file included in a transform.

2. Settings specified in a transform.
   These settings can be entered on the Change Office User Settings, Specify Office Security Settings, or Outlook: Customize Default Settings pages of the Custom Installation Wizard.

3. Registry settings specified in a transform.

4. Settings applied by running the Profile Wizard during Setup.

5. Settings that migrate from a previous version of Office.

6. Settings applied by using the Profile Wizard or Custom Maintenance Wizard after Office 2003 Editions is installed. This precedence assumes that users have already started each Office 2003 Editions application and any migrated settings have already been applied.

7. Settings managed through policies.

Using the Profile Wizard

The Profile Wizard saves and restores user-defined settings in Office 2003 Editions applications. Most user-defined settings can be stored in an Office 2003 Editions user profile. When you run the Profile Wizard to save a user profile, you create an Office 2003 Editions profile settings file (*.ops* file). Setup uses the *.ops* file to apply default settings when Office 2003 Editions is installed.

For Office 2003 Editions, the Profile Wizard allows you to save settings for only a selected application or group of applications. This feature is particularly useful when you are staging your Office 2003 Editions deployment; you can limit the settings saved in the *.ops* file to only the applications that you are deploying at a given time.

By design, the Profile Wizard excludes some settings, including user-specific information such as the username and the Most Recently Used file list (File menu). Nor does the Profile Wizard capture all Office Outlook 2003 settings. See "Office Profile Wizard" in the Office 2003 Editions Resource Kit Reference at *http://www.microsoft.com/office/ork/2003/ref/default.htm* for a list of the settings not captured by the Profile Wizard.

Creating an OPS File

Before you create an *.ops* file, you must start each Office 2003 Editions application on a lab computer and set all the options you want to customize. You can set most options by using the Options command on the Tools menu. To customize toolbars and menus, use the Customize command on the Tools menu. After you have customized the Office 2003 Editions applications, run the Profile Wizard to save the settings to an *.ops* file. Here's how to save settings to an *.ops* file:

1. Start the Profile Wizard.

2. On the Save Or Restore Settings page, select Save The Settings From This Machine, and enter the name and path for the *.ops* file.

3. Select the check boxes next to the Office 2003 Editions applications you want to include in your *.ops* file and then click Finish. The Profile Wizard saves the Office 2003 Editions application settings on your computer to the *.ops* file.

> **Note**   If an OPS file contains settings for an application that is not installed on a user's computer, those settings are still written to the registry.

Adding to a Transform

Adding an *.ops* file to a transform is a convenient way to deploy a collection of custom settings throughout your organization. Settings contained in the *.ops* file are implemented when users install Office 2003 Editions, and those settings apply to every user who logs on using that computer. However, any other method of customizing user options—including specifying user settings elsewhere in the transform or choosing to migrate settings from a previous version of Office—overwrites default settings in the *.ops* file.

To customize default options for users by using an *.ops* file, use these steps:

1. Use the Profile Wizard to create an *.ops* file that contains your default settings for Office 2003 Editions application options.

2. Use the Custom Installation Wizard to create a transform (MST file) that contains the *.ops* file.

3. Install Office 2003 Editions on users' computers with your transform.

You use the Custom Installation Wizard to create a transform that includes the OPS file. Start the Custom Installation Wizard. On the Customize Default Application Settings page, select Get Values From An Existing Settings Profile, and enter the filename and path of the *.ops* file you created. The Custom Installation Wizard creates a transform that contains your *.ops* file and any other customizations you have made.

Migrating Existing Settings

By default, if a previous version of Office 2003 Editions is installed on a user's computer, Windows Installer copies the previous application settings for that version to Office 2003 Editions. Migrated settings are applied the first time each user starts an Office 2003 Editions application, and the user's migrated settings overwrite any duplicate settings contained in an *.ops* file or added to the transform.

You can modify this behavior on the Customize Default Application Settings page of the Custom Installation Wizard. If you are not including an *.ops* file in the installation, the wizard selects the Migrate User Settings check box by default. When users install Office 2003 Editions with your transform, Setup migrates relevant settings from a previous version. If you add an *.ops* file to the transform, the wizard clears the Migrate User Settings check box and uses the values in your *.ops* file instead. If you add an *.ops* file to the transform and also select the Migrate User Settings check box, the settings from your *.ops* file are applied during the initial installation. However, the first time a user starts an Office 2003 Editions application, Windows Installer migrates settings from a previous version of Office and overwrites any corresponding settings previously applied.

Running During Setup

Adding an *.ops* file to the *.mst* file increases the size of the transform and also requires that you re-create the transform whenever you modify the *.ops* file. Alternatively, you can store the *.ops* file on a network share and direct Setup to run the Profile Wizard with that *.ops* file during the Office 2003 Editions installation.

Running the Profile Wizard during Setup applies a standard default Office 2003 Editions configuration to users' computers. However, because the *.ops* file is stored separately, you can modify the configuration without changing the transform. You can also create different *.ops* files for different groups of users. When you run the

Profile Wizard separately, you can choose whether to apply the settings in the *.ops* file once per user (the recommended option) or once per computer. You can also specify whether user-defined options are returned to their original default settings before your customized settings are applied; this step ensures that all users begin with exactly the same Office 2003 Editions configuration. Here's how to run Profile Wizard during Setup:

- Copy the Profile Wizard executable file (Proflwiz.exe) and your customized *.ops* file to the Office 2003 Editions administrative installation point. You can place the files in the same folder as Office 2003 Setup, or you can create a sub-folder.

- Start the Custom Installation Wizard.

- On the Add Installations And Run Programs page, click Add.

- In the Target box, type the filename and path to Proflwiz.exe or click Browse to select the file. Make sure you specify a Universal Naming Convention (UNC) path in the Target box; otherwise, the command won't work on client comput-ers.

- In the Arguments box, add command-line options directing the Profile Wizard to apply the *.ops* file to the user's computer and then click OK. Make sure you specify a UNC path in the Arguments box.

- Do one of the following:

  - Choose Run This Program Once Per Machine To Apply Your Default Settings The First Time A User Logs On.

  - Choose Run This Program Once Per User To Apply Your Default Settings To Every User Of The Computer. This option requires a connection to the network every time a new user logs on.

For example, to run the Profile Wizard from the Profile folder in the Office 2003 Editions administrative installation point, type **server\share\admin\profile\proflwiz.exe** in the Target box. Then type **profile\newprofile.ops /r /q** in the Arguments box. These arguments run the Profile Wizard quietly (/**q**), reset all options to their original default settings (/**r**), and apply settings from the file Newprofile.ops.

More Info   For more information about running the Profile Wizard, see "Office Profile Wizard" in the Office 2003 Editions Resource Kit Reference at *http://www.microsoft.com/office/ork/2003/ref/default.htm*.

When you add the Profile Wizard (Proflwiz.exe) to a transform, it runs after Office 2003 Editions is installed, so settings from this *.ops* file overwrite any duplicate settings specified in the transform, including the following:

- Settings specified in an *.ops* file added to a transform

- Settings specified on the Change Office User Settings page

- Microsoft Outlook e-mail options specified on the Outlook: Customize Default Settings page

- Security levels specified on the Specify Office Security Settings page

- Registry entries added on the Add/Remove Registry Entries page

> **Note** When you run the Custom Installation Wizard with the Visio 2003 package, the Customize Default Application Settings page is not displayed, and you can't add an *.ops* file to the transform. However, on the Add Installations And Run Programs page, you can specify that the Profile Wizard run at the end of the installation and apply an *.ops* file stored in another location.

Running After Installation

You can run the Profile Wizard as a standalone tool after you deploy Office 2003 Editions. This method allows you to distribute a standard user profile that overwrites any other settings distributed through a transform, migrated during Setup, or set by users. Running the Profile Wizard separately also allows you to customize the process more precisely and include only the particular applications settings you want to manage.

To customize the performance of the Profile Wizard, you edit the .ini file (Opw11adm.ini). Open the file in Notepad or another text editor, and then add or delete references to settings that you want to include or exclude. You can include or exclude registry settings, Application Data folders, template files, and so on. You can also run the Profile Wizard from the command line with no loss in functionality. Every option available in the wizard has a corresponding command-line switch. You do not need to edit the Profile Wizard .ini file to include or exclude individual Office 2003 Editions applications. On the Save Or Restore Settings page of the wizard, select the check boxes next to the applications for which you want to save settings.

More Info   For more information about customizing the Profile Wizard, editing its .ini file, or specifying its command-line options, see "Office Profile Wizard" in the Office 2003 Editions Resource Kit Reference at *http://www.microsoft.com/office/ork/2003/ref/default.htm*.

Using a Transform

If you do not want to distribute an entire Office 2003 Editions configuration, as does the Profile Wizard, you can customize selected user-defined options in a transform. Most of the options captured by the Profile Wizard can also be set on the Change Office User Settings page of the Custom Installation Wizard. This method is useful for presetting just a few key options or for modifying a standard configuration without re-creating the *.ops* file.

When users install Office with your transform, the settings you specify are applied to every user of the computer. However, only settings that differ from existing default settings are applied. Options that you set on this page of the wizard overwrite corresponding settings in an *.ops* file added to the transform.

When you run the Custom Installation Wizard with Visio 2003, the Change Office User Settings page is not displayed. To deploy Visio with custom settings, use the Profile Wizard to capture and then distribute settings to users. Alternatively, you can manage Visio settings by using Group Policy and the Visio 2003 policy template (Visio11.adm).

More Info   For more information about Group Policy, see Chapter 20, "Policy Management."

Registry Values

Because most Office 2003 Editions options are registry values, you can customize those options by adding or modifying registry values in a transform. Setup applies your new default options when users install Office 2003 Editions. Depending on which branch of the registry you customize, your settings are applied once per user (HKCU) or once per computer (HKLM). In addition, you can add registry settings to customize some options that can't be set with the Office 2003 Editions user interface and are not captured by the Profile Wizard in an *.ops* file. For example, you can include custom applications in Office 2003 Setup that require custom registry settings. After Setup finishes, Windows Installer copies the registry entries that you added to the transform to users' computers. Options that you set by adding or modifying registry values override duplicate values that you set on other pages of the Custom Installation Wizard, including the following:

- Settings specified in an *.ops* file added to a transform
- Settings specified on the Change Office User Settings page
- Options on the Outlook: Customize Default Settings page
- Settings configured on the Specify Office Security Settings page

You add or modify registry values on the Add Registry Entries page of the Custom Installation Wizard. You need to know the complete path for each registry entry, as well as the value name and the data type for that entry. Use the following steps to add registry values to a transform:

1. Start the Custom Installation Wizard.
2. On the Add Registry Entries page, click Add.
3. In the Root box, select the portion of the registry you want to modify.
4. In the Data Type box, enter a data type for the new entry.
5. In the remaining boxes, enter the full path for the registry value you want to add, enter the value name and data, and click OK.

To add multiple registry values to a transform, you can create a registration entry (*.reg*) file and then use the Add Registry Entries page of the Custom Installation Wizard to import the registry file. This is the most efficient and least-error-prone method of adding registry values to a transform. If your computer already has the registry values you want to copy to users' computers, use the following steps to import those settings in to a transform:

1. In Registry Editor (Regedit.exe), export the branch containing the settings you want to add to the transform to a registration entries file.
2. Start the Custom Installation Wizard.
3. On the Add Registry Entries page, click Import.
4. Select the registration entries file you created and click Open.

    The wizard adds the registry entries from the registry file to the list on the Add Registry Entries page. If the wizard encounters an entry in the registration entries file that is a duplicate of an entry already in the list, and the two entries contain different value data, the wizard prompts you to select the entry you want to keep.

> **More Info** When you install Office 2003 Editions, you can modify registry values by using Office 2003 Editions Group Policy settings. Policy settings take effect when the user logs on to the network, and they override any duplicate values set during installation. Unlike default application settings set by means of an *.ops* file, policies are not optional. In most cases, users can't change settings that you define as policies. For more information about Office 2003 Editions policies, see Chapter 20.

Office Security

You can customize Office 2003 Editions security settings in a transform or *.ops* file, but some security settings are implemented differently from other user-defined settings. Security levels—High, Medium, or Low—apply to each Office 2003 Editions application. However, the default security level can be set in one of two areas of the registry:

- **HKCU\Software\Microsoft\Office\11.0*Application*\Security** The Level value in this subkey is the security setting captured by the Profile Wizard when you create an *.ops* file or when you customize the setting on the Specify Office Security Settings page of the Custom Installation Wizard. It is applied once for each user of the computer.

- **HKLM\Software\Microsoft\Office\11.0*Application*\Security** The Level value in this subkey is the security setting that applies to the local computer. This setting takes precedence over the per-user setting, regardless of how the per-user setting is customized. You can customize this setting on the Change Office User Settings page or the Add/Remove Registry Entries page of the Custom Installation Wizard.

For example, on the Specify Office Security Settings page, you can set the default security level for Office Word 2003 to Medium. This step sets the Level value in the Security subkeys in HKCU to 2. However, on the Change Office User Settings page, you can also set the Level value in the Security subkey in HKLM to 3. In this scenario, Office Word 2003 is installed on the computer with the default security level set to High for all users. You can also set security levels by using policies—a policy that applies to the security level in the HKCU or another policy that applies to the HKLM. In this case, the security level set by policy for the local computer takes precedence over the policy set for the current user.

On the Specify Office Security Settings page of the Custom Installation Wizard, you can manage the list that identifies trusted sources for digitally signed macros, add-ins, ActiveX controls, and other executable code used by Office 2003 Editions applications. You can add Microsoft digital certificates (*.cer* files) to help ensure that all add-ins and templates are installed with Office 2003 Editions. On the same page of the wizard, you can determine whether unsigned, and therefore potentially unsafe, ActiveX controls can initialize using persisted data.

> **More Info**   For more information about configuring security settings for Office 2003 Editions, see "Security Overview" at *http://www.microsoft.com/office/ork/2003/seven/default.htm*.

Outlook Settings

Many Office Outlook 2003 options appear on the Change Office User Settings page, and you customize them the same way you customize options for any other Office 2003 Editions application. However, several important Office Outlook 2003 settings appear on their own pages of the Custom Installation Wizard.

You can't define an Outlook profile by running the Profile Wizard, adding registry entries, or setting Office 2003 Editions policies. Instead, you must create or modify an Office Outlook 2003 profile on the Outlook: Customize Default Profile page of the Custom Installation Wizard. These settings are not overwritten by any other method of customizing user options. An alternative method for creating Office Outlook 2003 profiles is to use a product such as AutoProf Profile Maker (*http://www.autoprof.com*) to create them in a variety of scenarios.

When you add or modify an Office Outlook 2003 profile, you can also configure e-mail account information. For example, on the Outlook: Specify Exchange Settings page, you can configure an Exchange connection and specify whether users work with a local copy of their Exchange mailbox (Cached Exchange Mode feature). On the Outlook: Add Accounts page, you can include more e-mail accounts in the user's Office Outlook 2003 profile.

Last, you specify default settings for the following options or items on the Outlook: Customize Default Settings page of the wizard:

- Whether to convert the personal address book (PAB) file to an Outlook Address Book

- Default e-mail editor

- Default e-mail format

> **More Info**   For more information about configuring Office Outlook 2003, see "Messaging Overview" at *http://www.microsoft.com/office/ork/2003/three/default.htm*.

Customizing Removal Behavior

When you upgrade to Office 2003 Editions, the Removal Wizard (Offcln.exe) removes unnecessary or obsolete components from previously installed versions of Office and related applications. The wizard components run behind the scenes during Setup, but you can also run the Removal Wizard on its own.

Both the wizard and Office 2003 Setup use the same logic and the same text file (.opc file) to detect and remove unneeded or obsolete files and settings from users' computers. You can determine which previous versions of Office applications are removed by setting options in a transform (*.mst* file). You can also customize the .opc file so that only the files and components that you specify are removed.

> **More Info**   The Office 2003 Editions Resource Kit includes the same standalone Removal Wizard (Offcln.exe) that is included with Office 2003 Editions. The Removal Wizard is installed by default when you run the Office Resource Kit Setup program. For more information, see the Toolbox at *http://www.microsoft.com/office/ork/2003/tools/default.htm*. Download the tools from *http://www.microsoft.com/office/ork/2003/tools/ddl/default.htm*.

Removal Wizard components (which are used by both the wizard and Setup) include the following files:

- **Offcln.exe**   Provides the user interface that lets you run the wizard as a standalone utility. It's located in the \Files\Pfiles\MSOffice\Office11 folder on the installation image. The wizard is also available in the Office 2003 Editions Resource Kit.

- **Oclean.dll**   Used by the standalone Removal Wizard and Setup to carry out instructions in the .opc files and clean up the user's hard disk.

- **Oclncore.opc**   Global *.opc* file for Office 2003 Editions, located in the \Files\Pfiles\MSOffice\Office11 folder on the installation image. This file specifies files, registry entries, .ini file settings, and shortcuts associated with all components in the core English version of Office 2003 Editions.

- **Oclnintl.opc**   Satellite *.opc* file for each language version of Office 2003 Editions, located in the *LCID* subfolders. Specifies language-specific components including files, registry entries, .ini file settings, and shortcuts.

- **Oclncust.opc**   Template file for adding content to be deleted by the Removal Wizard, including all content that was commented out in previous versions of the wizard; located in the \Files\Pfiles\MSOffice\Office11 folder on the installation image. Modify this file if you want to delete additional files or registry keys.

> **Note**   Microsoft Visio 2003 does not use the .opc file to customize removal behavior. By default, Visio 2003 removes previous versions of Visio installed on the user's computer. If you want to keep a previous version, set the *REMOVEALLPREVIOUS* property to keep on the command line, in Setup.ini, or in a transform. This property sets the corresponding option in the Setup user interface. If you do not want users to change the setting during the installation, run Setup in quiet mode.

Removing Previous Versions

When users install Office 2003 Editions, Setup detects files, settings, and shortcuts from previously installed versions of Office and removes them. When you run Setup in quiet mode (**/q**), default Setup behavior removes all previous versions of Office applications that are also included in the version of Office 2003 Editions that you are installing. For example, if you are installing the standalone version of Office Word 2003 over Microsoft Office XP Professional, only Word 2002 is removed by default during the update process. If you run Setup with a full user interface, users can choose which previous-version applications to remove.

> **Note**   The Setup user interface allows users to keep or remove all previous versions of a particular application. However, you can use the Custom Installation Wizard or standalone Removal Wizard to select particular versions to keep or remove. For example, you can keep Word 2000 but remove Word 97.

Because Setup recognizes components at the application level, the removal process detects and removes standalone versions of applications such as Word and Microsoft Excel. If all the core applications are removed, Setup also removes shared components such as Office Binder and Equation Editor. Setup can detect and remove the following versions of Office and Office-related products (Setup does not remove documents or other user files from the user's hard disk):

- Microsoft Office 95, Office 97, Office 2000, Office XP (including standalone applications)

- Microsoft Outlook 97, Outlook 98, Outlook 2000, Outlook 2002 (does not include Outlook Express)

- Microsoft FrontPage 1.1, FrontPage 97, FrontPage 98, FrontPage 2000, FrontPage 2002

- Microsoft Publisher 95, Publisher 97, Publisher 98, Publisher 2000, Publisher 2002

- Microsoft Office 2000 and Office XP MUI Packs

- Obsolete files, including orphaned files, registry settings, Start menu shortcuts, and .ini file settings used by any previously installed edition of Office applications

- MUI Packs, which are removed by default only if all other Office 2000 or Office XP applications are also being removed. If you are installing MUI Packs or Proofing Tool Kits separately, Offcln.exe does not run.

In addition, Setup detects the following products to avoid deleting shared files that overlap with Office 2003 Editions:

- Microsoft Project 95, Project 98, Project 2000, Project 2002

- Microsoft PhotoDraw 1, PhotoDraw 2

- Hagaki 1, Hagaki 2, Hagaki 3, Hagaki 4, Hagaki 5

- Team Manager 97

- Microsoft Bookshelf 1 (Office 97)

Setup also detects the following as candidates for removal:

- Incompletely installed or uninstalled components that leave unusable files on the hard disk

- Files that begin with a tilde (~)

- Files in temporary folders

Setup removes files according to instructions contained in the global .opc file (Oclncore.opc) plus any language-specific .opc files (Oclnintl.opc) that you add to the *LCID* subfolders on your installation image. For example, a user might have a French version of Word and an English version of Excel. The global .opc file cleans up all components included in the core English version of Office. If you add the Oclnintl.opc file to the 1036 subfolder, Setup also removes components unique to the French version of Office.

> **Note** By default, Setup removes previous versions of Visio when you install Visio 2003. However, if you use Group Policy to assign or publish Visio 2003 to users, and a user has a per-computer installation of Visio 2000, Visio 2000 is not removed. And instead of coexisting with Visio 2003, the Visio 2000 application is broken. The user must reinstall Visio 2000 with administrative privileges. To avoid this scenario, uninstall Visio 2000 before upgrading to Visio 2003.

Removing Small Business Tools

Office 2003 Editions does not include the Microsoft Small Business Tools programs (Small Business Customer Manager, Business Planner, Direct Mail Manager, and Financial Manager) that were part of Microsoft Office 2000 Premium Edition. If you are upgrading from Office 2000, Small Business Tools components are not removed by default. If you want Office 2003 Setup to remove Small Business Tools during the installation, set the following properties on the command line, in Setup.ini, or in a transform:

- **OPCREMOVESBT2000**   Setting this property to 1 allows Office 2003 Setup to remove Small Business Tools from users' computers.

- **OPCREMOVESBTTEXT**   Setting this property to a string value—for example, "&Small Business Tools"—adds a check box to the Remove Previous Versions page of Setup so that users can choose to remove Small Business Tools the same way they remove any other previous-version Office application.

Customizing the Removal Process

There are several ways that you can specify how Office 2003 Setup or Removal Wizard cleans up users' computers:

- In the Custom Installation Wizard, specify which Office components to remove on the Remove Previous Versions page.

- Customize the .opc file used by Setup to include or exclude additional files or registry entries during the removal process. When users run Setup, your custom removal routine runs automatically.

- Create your own .opc file and run the Removal Wizard with a command-line option that specifies your custom .opc file.

You can use the Custom Installation Wizard to customize removal behavior during Office 2003 Setup. On the Remove Previous Versions page of the wizard, you specify exactly which previous versions of each application are removed from users' computers. In this case, Setup does not display the Remove Previous Versions page to users during the installation—the instructions in the transform are carried out regardless of the display setting.

Setup follows the instructions in the global .opc file and any language-specific .opc files to determine which components to remove. The .opc files identify files, registry entries, .ini file entries, and Start menu items that were installed or modified by previously installed versions of Office and Office-related products. The .opc file also contains rules that describe which of these files or entries to remove, where they are located, and under what conditions they can be deleted.

By editing the default .opc file or by creating a custom .opc file, you can specify which components to remove from the users' computers. You can also use the .opc file to remove non-Office components, such as custom applications. To add components to the removal list, customize the Oclncust.opc file. To exclude components from removal, you must edit the default Oclncore.opc file.

More Info   For more information about customizing the .opc files, see "OPC File Syntax" in the Office 2003 Editions Resource Kit Reference at *http://www.microsoft.com/office/ork/2003/ref/default.htm*.

Running the Removal Wizard Standalone

After Setup removes files and settings from previously installed versions of Office or Office components, other unneeded files might remain on users' computers. For example, font files and dynamic-link libraries (.dll files) might not be removed. You can run the Removal Wizard as a standalone utility to remove all Office-related files from users' computers. Situations in which it makes sense to run the Removal Wizard as a standalone utility include the following:

- Before you upgrade to Office 2003 Editions to clean up existing Office-related files.

- When you stage your upgrade to Office 2003 Editions applications. For example, if you upgrade to Office Word 2003 before upgrading to the rest of Office 2003 Editions, you can remove previously installed versions of only Word.

- When upgrading to Office 2003 Editions replaces the need for a custom application on users' computers. You can use the wizard to remove the custom application.

> **Note**   You must have administrator rights to run the Removal Wizard. If a user does not have administrator rights, you must log on as an administrator and run the wizard with the proper permissions.

You can run the Removal Wizard in one of three modes, depending on the degree to which you want to clean up users' hard disks:

- **Aggressive mode**   Removes all Office-related components, including components shared by more than one Office application. Before installing Office 2003 Editions, you might run the wizard in aggressive mode for users who are upgrading from a variety of Office versions. In aggressive mode, the wizard marks all items listed in the .ocp file for removal.

- **Safe mode**   Removes only components that are no longer needed. Components deleted in safe mode are not being used by any application. In safe mode, the wizard marks items listed in the .opc file for removal only if it does not detect a corresponding application.

- **Safe mode with user discretion**   Runs in safe mode, but allows users to select which detected applications to keep and which to delete.

> **Caution**   Never run the Removal Wizard in aggressive mode after you install Office 2003 Editions. The wizard might remove shared components that are needed by other applications installed on the computer.

The final page of the Removal Wizard lists all files scheduled for removal. This list is accurate for all Office applications from Microsoft Office 97 or earlier. Because the Removal Wizard relies on Windows Installer to manage removal of files associated with a particular application, however, the list might be incomplete for Office 2000 and Office XP. This behavior results in a cleaner and safer removal of Office files, even though the list in the Removal Wizard might be incomplete.

Creating a custom .ocp file and running the Removal Wizard with command-line options gives you the greatest amount of flexibility. To run the Removal Wizard with command-line options, click Run on the Start menu and then type **Offcln.exe** followed by the command-line options you want. Table 9-4 describes each command-line option, and the following shows the command's syntax:

offcln.exe [/a | /s [/q[/r]] [/l][!][logfile]] [directory]

Table 9-4   Offcln.exe Command-Line Options

Option	Description
/a	Indicates aggressive mode. The Removal Wizard removes files associated with all previously installed versions of Office and Office-related applications. When you use this command-line option, the wizard does not allow you to select which files to keep.
/s	Indicates safe mode. The Removal Wizard removes only those files for which it does not detect an associated application. When you use this command-line option, the wizard does not allow you to select which files to keep.
/q	Indicates quiet mode. The Removal Wizard runs without prompting the user for information or displaying progress indicators. The wizard does not restart the user's computer; therefore, changes might not be completed until the user restarts the computer.
/r	Used with the /q option to restart the computer automatically if necessary. The user has no opportunity to save files before the computer restarts.
/llogfile	Generates a log with the filename *logfile*. If no log filename is specified, the Removal Wizard creates a default log file, Offcln11.log, in the current folder of the wizard.
/l!logfile	Generates a log file in the same manner as /l, but the Removal Wizard does not perform the removal process. This option is useful to test the Removal Wizard before running it to remove files.
directory	Specifies the folder that contains the files used by the Removal Wizard: Oclncore.opc, Oclncust.opc, and *LCID*\Oclnintl.opc files. By default, the Removal Wizard searches the same folder that contains Offcln.exe.

Tip   The Removal Wizard returns a value to indicate whether the wizard ran with any errors. If you create a batch file to run the wizard, you can include code that captures this value. The wizard returns 0 to indicate that no errors occurred; any other value indicates errors.

Using a Custom OPC File

When you run the Removal Wizard separately, you can create a custom .opc file that controls the removal process. For example, suppose that you want to remove an internal company tool that is being replaced by Office 2003 Editions functionality. The internal tool, Chart.exe, resides on users' computers in the folder C:\Program Files\Internal\Chart. In addition, the folder contains support files: Chartsub.dll, Chartprt.dat, and Readme.txt. The following procedure shows you how to modify the .opc file to accomplish all these aims. Here's how to modify the Oclncust.opc for a custom removal routine:

1. Create a backup copy of the default Oclncust.opc file.

2. Open Oclncust.opc in a text editor.

3. Add the following lines, which direct the wizard to always delete files in the *[SAFE]* section and specify the name and location of the files to delete.

   ```
   [SAFE] "Internal charting tool"
   C:\program files\internal\chart\chart.exe
   C:\program files\internal\chart\chartsub.dll
   C:\program files\internal\chart\chartprt.dat
   C:\program files\internal\chart\readme.txt
   ```

4. Save and close Oclncust.opc.

> **Tip** Test your customized OPC file on a computer by using the */l!logfile* command-line option. This step generates a log of the files that will be deleted by your customized .opc file without actually removing any files.

Customizing Installation

In Chapter 7, you learned the difference between an Office 2003 Editions administrative installation and compressed CD image. Only by deploying Office 2003 via compressed CD images can you take advantage of local installation sources, which ensures that users always have access to the Office 2003 Editions source files because Office 2003 Setup copies them to the local computer.

Compressed CD Images

After you copy the contents of the Office 2003 Editions CD to a network share, the process of customizing a CD image is similar to the process of customizing an administrative installation point. You can edit the Setup.ini file and use the Custom

Installation Wizard to create a transform (*.mst* file) as long as you point to the transform file on the compressed image. You can also customize files that reside outside the Office 2003 Editions CAB files, such as the .opc file used by Office 2003 Setup or the Removal Wizard to remove previous versions.

Unlike deploying from administrative installation point, however, you must accept the EULA and enter a valid Volume License Key before users can install Office 2003 Editions from the compressed CD image. New functionality has been added to the Custom Installation Wizard to handle these settings and to hide those pages from users during interactive installation. Here's how to customize the CD image with the product key and to accept the EULA:

- Start the Custom Installation Wizard and open the *.msi* file on the CD image.

- On the Configure Local Installation Source page, select the option Configure local installation source.

- In the Product Key box, enter a valid 25-character Volume License Key.

- Select the I Accept The Terms In The License Agreement check box.

- Make any additional customizations you want and save the transform.

- Do one of the following:

  - Run Office 2003 Setup from the network share with your transform.

  - Copy the entire compressed image onto a CD and distribute copies to users. The volume label of the CDs you create must match the volume label of the Office 2003 Editions CD for Office 2003 Setup to run properly from the custom CDs. The CDs that you create can be used in the same way as the original Office CD, except that Office 2003 Setup runs with your modifications.

> **Note** You must obtain the proper user licenses before copying, modifying, or distributing a customized version of the Office 2003 CD. For more information about volume licensing programs, contact your software reseller or see the Microsoft Licensing Web site.

Users do not need administrator rights to install new features from the local installation source. However, installing features on demand directly from the Office 2003 Editions CD requires administrator rights each time a feature is installed. This scenario is the only exception to persistent administrator rights after an initial installation with elevated privileges. For this reason, users who rely on an Office 2003 Editions CD as an alternate source must be administrators of their computers.

Local Installation Sources

Because Office 2003 Setup creates the local installation source by default when you deploy from a compressed CD image, you do not need to set any additional options. Office 2003 Setup creates the local installation source in *Drive*:\Msocache, where *Drive* is the drive with the most free space. This folder is a hidden folder on users' computers.

Office 2003 Setup caches the entire source by default; if the user's computer has insufficient disk space, Office 2003 Setup caches installation files for only the selected features. It retains the local installation source after the installation is complete. You can modify how Office 2003 Setup handles the local installation source by setting the following properties in the *[Cache]* section of Setup.ini:

■ **LOCALCACHEDRIVE**   Specify a different fixed drive for the local installation source. By default, Office 2003 Setup searches for the drive with the most space or uses an existing MsoCache folder, if one exists.

■ **DELETEABLECACHE**   Give users the option to delete the local installation source at the end of installation.

■ **CDCACHE**   Enable or disable creation of a local installation source. You can set this property to cache the entire source, to cache installation files for only selected features, or to run the installation directly from the source and bypass creation of a local installation source entirely.

When you force creation of a local installation source, the installation fails if the local computer lacks sufficient disk space. The default setting (CDCACHE=auto) allows Office 2003 Setup to fall back on options to cache installation files for only selected features or to install from the network source when the user's computer has insufficient disk space; however, this scenario might result in inconsistent local installation source configurations across an organization.

Note   Because Office 2003 Setup creates the local installation source before applying a transform (*.mst* file), you should set local installation source properties in the Setup.ini settings file, not on the Modify Setup Properties page of the Custom Installation Wizard.

More Info   For more information about the *[CACHE]* section of Setup.ini, see "Setup Settings File" in the Office 2003 Editions Resource Kit Reference. The URL is *http://www.microsoft.com/office/ork/2003/ref /default.htm.*

Best Practices

The following are best practices for customizing Office 2003 Editions:

- **Hide and lock feature installation states that you don't want users to change.**   The Custom Installation Wizard allows you to lock down feature installation states to prevent users from changing them. For more information, see the section "Hiding and Locking Features" in this chapter on page 253.

- **Configure volatile settings late in the process.**   Configure settings that aren't likely to change from installation to installation using the Custom Installation Wizard. Configure settings that are more likely to change using command-line options, a settings file, or an *.ops* file that you run after setup. Doing so makes updating these settings easier.

- **Customize workgroup paths instead of adding files.**   Rather than copying corporate templates and clip art to each user's computer, copy those files to a shared network location and then configure paths to them using the Custom Installation Wizard or Profile Wizard. Doing so makes it easier to update templates and artwork after deployment.

- **Use the Change Office User Settings page of the Custom Installation Wizard.**   The Change Office User Settings page's user interface is similar to using the System Policy Editor. It's less error-prone than changing registry settings directly and more flexible than deploying *.ops* files.

- **Configure Office 2003 Editions security settings using policy.**   Don't rely solely on the security settings you configure in the Custom Installation Wizard. Back them up by defining security policies, as described in Chapter 20.

Chapter 10

Internet Explorer Settings

Microsoft Internet Explorer 6 is an integral part of Microsoft Windows XP Professional. It's also users' portal to the Internet and your intranet. By configuring Internet Explorer as part of a Windows XP Professional deployment, you control security, prepare it for use with your intranet, and prevent users from configuration snafus. This chapter describes how to configure Internet Explorer as part of Windows XP Professional.

Checklist

- Have you determined which Internet Explorer settings you want to customize? See Chapter 3, "Windows Configuration," for more information.

- Have you prepared any custom graphics and files you need for Internet Explorer? See Chapter 3 for more information.

- Have you planned how you're going to distribute your customizations? See the section "Overview" in this chapter on page 286.

Overview

A variety of methods is available for you to configure Internet Explorer settings. Each method is appropriate for different phases of deployment, though. For example, using an unattended-setup answer file, as described in the following list, is only appropriate for configuring Internet Explorer when installing the operating system:

- **Internet Explorer Customization Wizard**   The Internet Explorer Administration Kit (IEAK) contains the Internet Explorer Customization Wizard. This is a tool for customizing and distributing Internet Explorer. You can build and distribute a customized Internet Explorer 6 package to computers that don't already have the Web browser installed, for example. Using the wizard is more complicated than the other methods this chapter describes, and it's more suitable for distributing and updating Internet Explorer than it is for primarily configuring Internet Explorer settings. For more information about Internet Explorer Customization Wizard, see the section "Administration Kit," later on this page.

- **IEAK Profile Manager**   You use IEAK Profile Manager to configure Internet Explorer settings after the browser is already installed. IEAK Profile Manager produces two files: an Internet settings file and a cabinet file. Internet settings files (*.ins* files) are similar to unattended-setup answer files. They contain specific sections and settings that are unique to Internet Explorer, though. The cabinet file contains .inf files that customize the registry for Internet Explorer settings. See the section "Internet Settings Files" on page 287 for more information.

- **Unattended-Setup Answer Files**   You learned how to create answer files in Chapter 6, "Answer Files." Answer files contain three sections for customizing Internet Explorer: *[FavoritesEx]*, *[Proxy]*, and *[URL]*. These sections support only basic customizations, though. If a setting you want to configure isn't available in these sections, use IEAK Profile Manager. For more information about using these settings, see the section "Unattended-Setup Answer Files" on page 294.

- **Group Policy Settings**   After you deploy Windows XP Professional with Internet Explorer, you can use Group Policy to manage Internet Explorer settings. See the section "Group Policy Settings" on page 297 for more information.

Administration Kit

IEAK makes Internet Explorer easier to deploy and support by helping you build distribution packages that include customizations as well as the Internet Explorer program files. IEAK is a toolkit that you'd primarily use to distribute the latest version of Internet Explorer to existing client computers. If you've ever used IEAK, you'll like that it's now easier to download, install, and use. It includes an integrated license agreement that eliminates the need to use customization codes, for example.

You can do the following with IEAK:

- Control versions throughout your organization.

- Centrally distribute and manage browser settings.

- Configure automatic connection profiles for users.

- Customize virtually every aspect of Internet Explorer, including features, security, communications settings, and so on.

IEAK includes three components. The Internet Explorer Customization Wizard provides five stages of step-by-step screens that help you build and customize Internet Explorer distribution packages. It's not the best tool for customizing Internet Explorer settings when deploying Windows XP Professional, though. IEAK Profile Manager enables you to change users' settings and apply restrictions automatically—after Internet Explorer is already installed. The IEAK Toolkit has useful tools, programs, and sample files, which are in the Toolkit folder in the IEAK installation.

Windows XP Professional includes Internet Explorer, so you won't use Internet Explorer Customization Wizard to distribute Internet Explorer initially. Service packs for Windows XP Professional include updates for Internet Explorer, too. In the event that Microsoft releases a new version of Internet Explorer after you've deployed Windows XP Professional, however, you'll want to evaluate using the Internet Explorer Customization Wizard for packaging and distributing Internet Explorer. See *http://www.microsoft.com/windows/ieak/techinfo/deploy/60/en* for detailed information about using IEAK.

> **More Info**   The most recent version of IEAK is available from Microsoft at *http://www.microsoft.com/windows/ieak/downloads/ieak6/ieak6sp1.asp*. Run the installation file and follow the instructions you see on the screen to install IEAK. Check this Web site frequently for updates to IEAK. It also contains links to technical documentation about using IEAK.

Internet Settings Files

Internet settings files (*.ins* files) are similar to Windows XP Professional unattended-setup answer files. You use them to configure Internet Explorer during a Windows XP Professional installation. The first step is creating an *.ins* file. The easiest way to create an *.ins* file is by using IEAK Profile Manager. You can create an *.ins* using any text editor, but all except the most basic *.ins* files are difficult to create manually. The section "Creating the Settings File" on page 288 describes how to create the *.ins* file using IEAK Profile Manager.

The next step is deploying the *.ins* file. How you deploy the file depends on how you create it and which method you want to use. For example, you can include the file in an Internet Explorer distribution package, deploy it from a Web server, or add it to your Windows XP Professional distribution point. For this book's purposes, I will show you how to add it to your Windows XP Professional distribution point and link it to your unattended-setup answer file. The section "Distributing the Settings File" on page 290 describes how to add the *.ins* file to your answer file.

More Info For detailed information about the settings you can configure by using Internet settings files, see "Microsoft Windows Preinstallation Reference," which is the file Ref.chm in Deploy.cab; and "Microsoft Windows Corporate Deployment Tools User's Guide," which is the file Deploy.chm in Deploy.cab. In particular, see the "Internet Settings (*.ins*) Files." Deploy.cab is on the Windows product CD in Support\Tools.

Creating the Settings File

To run IEAK Profile Manager after installing IEAK, click Start, All Programs, Microsoft IEAK 6, IEAK Profile Manager. Click File, New to create a new *.ins* file, as shown in Figure 10-1.

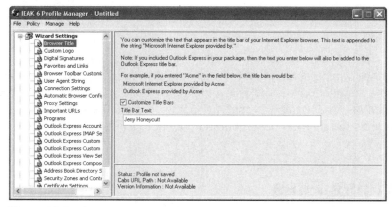

Figure 10-1 Click a settings category in the left pane and configure settings in the right pane.

IEAK Profile Manager creates two files when you save an *.ins* file. The first is the actual *.ins* file that contains many of your settings, including text for the title bar, important URLs, favorite URLs, and so on. The second file is a cabinet file that contains registry settings that customize specific Internet Explorer settings, such as Security Zones. The *.ins* file contains a reference to the cabinet file. You must store the cabinet file on a Web server, so you must know the URL of the cabinet file in advance. For example, you can store the *.ins* and cabinet file on your Web server at *http://sample/settings*. After configuring the settings you want to customize, click File, Save As to save your *.ins* file. In the Save *.ins* and .CAB Files dialog box, type the path and name of the *.ins* file and the URL where you intend to store the cabinet file.

If you enable automatic configuration, Internet Explorer will automatically update its settings when you change the *.ins* file. The default behavior is to update its settings each time users start the browser. You can configure Internet Explorer to update its settings periodically, though. First, store both your *.ins* file and cabinet file on the intranet. In IEAK Profile Manager, click Automatic Browser Configuration in the left pane; then click to select the Enable Automatic Configuration check box and type the URL of the *.ins* and cabinet files in Auto-Config URL. If you want Internet Explorer to update periodically, type the number of minutes between updates in Automatically Configure Every *N* Minutes.

Listing 10-1 shows a sample *.ins* file: Sample.ins. I created this file using IEAK Profile Manager. IEAK Profile Manager also created a matching cabinet file, Sample.cab, which I stored on my Web server. Notice also that I enabled automatic configuration and have set *AutoConfigURL* to the URL containing my *.ins* file and cabinet file.

Listing 10-1   Sample.ins

```
[Branding]
Language Locale=en
Language ID=1033
Window_Title_CN=Jerry Honeycutt
Window_Title=Microsoft Internet Explorer provided by Jerry Honeycutt
FavoritesOnTop=0
NoLinks=1
Platform=2
CabsURLPath=http://camelot/settings
InsVersion=2003.12.03.00
ProfMgrVersion=6.00.2800.1106
Type=2
[URL]
AutoConfig=1
AutoDetect=1
AutoConfigURL=http://camelot/settings/sample.ins
Home_Page=http://camelot
Search_Page=http://camelot/search
Help_Page=http://camelot/support
[Internet_Mail]
Window_Title=Outlook Express provided by Jerry Honeycutt
Use_IMAP=No
POP_Server=
SMTP_Server=
Logon_Using_SPA=No
SMTP_Logon_Using_SPA=No
SMTP_Logon_Required=0
[FavoritesEx]
```

```
Title1=Outlook Web Access.url
URL1=http://camelot/exchange
Title2=Intranet Home Page.url
URL2=http://camelot
[Favorites]
Outlook Web Access.url=http://camelot/exchange
Intranet Home Page.url=http://camelot
[Proxy]
HTTP_Proxy_Server=
FTP_Proxy_Server=
Gopher_Proxy_Server=
Secure_Proxy_Server=
Socks_Proxy_Server=
Use_Same_Proxy=1
Proxy_Enable=0
Proxy_Override=<local>
[Internet_News]
NNTP_Server=
Logon_Using_SPA=No
Logon_Required=0
[Outlook_Express_Global]
Read_Only=0
Disable_Account_Access=0
[Security Imports]
ImportSecZones=1
[ExtRegInf]
SecZones=*,seczones.inf,DefaultInstall
[ExtRegInf.Hklm]
SecZones=seczones.inf,IeakInstall.Hklm
[ExtRegInf.Hkcu]
SecZones=seczones.inf,IeakInstall.Hkcu
[Custom Branding]
Branding=http://camelot/settings/sample.cab,2003.12.03.00,-1,
```

Distributing the Settings File

To add your *.ins* file to the Windows XP Professional installation, you link the unattended-setup answer file to it. The *[Branding]* section contains settings for specifying the name of your *.ins* file.

Table 10-1 describes the two settings you must configure for Windows XP Setup to process the *.ins* file. Listing 10-2 shows a sample that uses those settings. The first setting, *BrandIEUsingUnattended*, indicates whether to configure Internet Explorer using the answer file or an *.ins* file. The second, *IEBrandingFile*, specifies the name of the *.ins* file to use if you set *BrandIEUsingUnattended=No*. You must store the *.ins* file in the root of the distribution point's OEM folder.

When Windows XP Setup installs Windows XP Professional, it'll apply the settings specified in the *.ins* file, including those in the cabinet file that it finds at the specified URL. Because the *.ins* file in Listing 10-1 enables automatic configuration, Internet Explorer will also check for updates at the same URL every time the user opens the Web browser, making it easy to update settings after deployment.

Table 10-1 [Branding] Section Entries

Entry	Description
BrandIEUsingUnattended	Specifies whether to use the answer file or an *.ins* file to configure Internet Explorer during Windows XP Setup:
	■ **Yes** Configures browser settings by using the entries specified in the answer file's [FavoritesEx], [Proxy], and [URL] sections.
	■ **No** Uses the *.ins* file specified in *IEBrandingFile*.
IEBrandingFile	■ Specifies the name of the *.ins* file to use for configuring Internet Explorer. You do not have to specify the full path of the *.ins* file, but you must place the file in the root of the distribution point's OEM folder.

Listing 10-2 Sample.sif

```
[Unattended]
    DriverSigningPolicy=Ignore
    FileSystem=ConvertNTFS

; Replace OemFilesPath with path to the $OEM$ folder:

    OemFilesPath=\\Server\Share\win2002.pro\OEM1\$OEM$

; Replace OemPnPDriversPath with the path of the third-party
; device drivers (separate folders with a semicolon):

    OemPnPDriversPath=\WINDOWS\DRIVERS

    OemPreinstall=Yes
    OemSkipEula=Yes
    Repartition=No
    TargetPath=\WINDOWS
    UnattendMode=ReadOnly
    UnattendSwitch=Yes

[GuiRunOnce]

; Add commands to this section that you want Windows XP
; to run the first time a user logs on to it (enclose each
; command in quotation marks). See AdminPassword, AutoLogon,
; and AutoLogonCount in the [GuiUnattended] section.

[GuiUnattended]

; Uncomment the following three lines to have the setup
; program automatically log on to Windows XP after installation:

;    AdminPassword=*
;    AutoLogon=Yes
;    AutoLogonCount=1
```

```
    OemSkipRegional=1
    OemSkipWelcome=1

; Replace TimeZone with the correct time zone for the computer.
; See Ref.chm or Appendix D, "Answer File Syntax," for values:

    TimeZone=020

[UserData]

; Replace ComputerName, FullName, and OrgName with appropriate
; values. If any of these values is missing, the setup program
; will prompt the installer for the value:

    ComputerName="Sample"
    FullName="User Name"
    OrgName="Company Name"

; Replace ProductID with your product ID. If you don't provide
; a product key here, the setup program will prompt the installer:

    ProductKey=XXXXX-XXXXX-XXXXX-XXXXX-XXXXX

[Branding]
BrandIEUsingUnattended=No
IEBrandingFile=Sample.ins

[TapiLocation]

; Replace AreaCode and CountryCode with appropriate values. See
; Ref.chm or Appendix D, "Answer File Syntax," for values:

    AreaCode=972
    CountryCode=1
    Dialing=Tone

[Identification]

; Replace DomainAdmin and DomainAdminPassword with the credentials
; of an account that can join the computer to the domain. The setup
; program will prompt the installer for these values if missing:

    DomainAdmin=Administrator
    DomainAdminPassword=Password

; Replace JoinDomain with the name of the domain to join:

    JoinDomain=DOMAIN

; Optionally, uncomment and replace MachineObjectOU with the LDAP
; path of the OU in which to create the computer account, if the
; account doesn't already exist:

;    MachineObjectOU="OU=Accounts,DC=honeycutt,DC=corp"

[Networking]
```

```
; This empty section is necessary if the answer file will include
; additional network settings described in Ref.chm. This answer
; file configures the computer with default networking components,
; including Client for Microsoft Networks, File and Printer Sharing
; for Microsoft Networks, QoS Packet Scheduler, and Internet Protocol
; (TCP/IP) configured to use DHCP.

[Components]

; Uncomment and set each of the following components to On to install
; it or Off to not install it (see Ref.chm or Appendix D, "Answer File
; Syntax," for more information about each component):

;    accessopt=On
;    calc=On
;    certsrv=Off
;    certsrv_client=Off
;    certsrv_server=Off
;    charmap=On
;    chat=Off
;    deskpaper=On
;    dialer=On
;    fax=Off
;    fp_extensions=Off
;    fp_vdir_deploy=Off
;    freecell=On
;    hearts=On
;    hypertrm=On
;    IEAccess=On
;    iis_common=Off
;    iis_ftp=Off
;    iis_htmla=Off
;    iis_inetmgr=Off
;    iis_nntp=Off
;    iis_nntp_docs=Off
;    iis_pwmgr=Off
;    iis_smtp=Off
;    iis_smtp_docs=Off
;    iis_www=Off
;    iis_www_vdir_printers=Off
;    iis_www_vdir_terminalservices=Off
;    iisdbg=Off
;    indexsrv_system=Off
;    media_clips=On
;    media_utopia=Off
;    minesweeper=On
;    mousepoint=On
;    mplay=On
;    msmq_ADIntegrated=Off
;    msmq_Core=Off
;    msmq_HTTPSupport=Off
;    msmq_LocalStorage=Off
;    msmq_MQDSService=Off
;    msmq_RoutingSupport=Off
;    msmq_TriggersService=Off
```

```
;    msmsgs=On
;    msnexplr=On
;    mswordpad=On
;    netcis=Off
;    netoc=On
;    objectpkg=On
;    paint=On
;    pinball=On
;    rec=On
;    reminst=Off
;    rstorage=Off
;    solitaire=On
;    spider=On
;    templates=On
;    TerminalServer=Off
;    TSClients=Off
;    TSWebClient=Off
;    vol=On
;    wms=On
;    wms_admin_asp=On
;    wms_admin_mmc=On
;    wms_server=On
;    zonegames=On

;end
```

Unattended-Setup Answer Files

Unattended-setup answer files for Windows XP Professional support three types of basic Internet Explorer customizations. First, you can add shortcuts to the Web browser's Favorites menu. Second, you can configure the Web browser's proxy settings. Last, you can configure important URLs, such as the user's home page. The following sections describe the sections and settings for customization. For Windows XP Setup to use these settings, set **BrandIEUsingUnattended=Yes** in your answer file, as shown in Listing 10-3.

Listing 10-3

```
[Branding]
BrandIEUsingUnattended=Yes
```

Favorites

The *[FavoritesEx]* section contains the default Favorites settings for Internet Explorer. Listing 10-4 shows an example of using this section:

Listing 10-4

```
[FavoritesEx]
Title1="Outlook Web Access.url"
URL1="http://camelot/exchange"
Title2="Intranet Home Page.url"
URL2="http://camelot"
```

Proxy Settings

The *[Proxy]* section contains entries for specifying proxy server settings for Internet Explorer. If these settings are not present, Windows XP Setup uses default settings. Listing 10-5 shows an excerpt of an answer file that configures proxy settings for Internet Explorer. Table 10-2 describes each possible setting in this section.

Table 10-2   [Proxy] Section Entries

Entry	Description
FTP_Proxy_Server	Specifies the IP address or URL of the FTP proxy server on the network: `FTP_Proxy_Server = http://proxyserver:80`.
Gopher_Proxy_Server	Specifies the IP address or URL of the Gopher proxy server on the network: `Gopher_Proxy_Server = http://proxyserver:80`.
HTTP_Proxy_Server	Specifies the IP address or URL of the HTTP proxy server on the network: `HTTP_Proxy_Server = http://proxyserver:80`. This setting is required if you enable Use_Same_Proxy.
Proxy_Enable	Specifies whether to use a proxy server to connect to the Internet: ■ **0** Don't use a proxy server. ■ **1** Do use a proxy server.
Proxy_Override	Specifies a semicolon-delimited list of IP addresses to bypass the proxy server. You must enclose the list in quotation marks if it includes more than one address. Use the string *<local>* to override local addresses.
Secure_Proxy_Server	Specifies the IP address or URL of the Secure proxy on the network: `Secure_Proxy_Server = http://proxyserver:80`.
Socks_Proxy_Server	Specifies the IP address or URL of the Socks proxy on the network: `Socks_Proxy_Server = http://proxyserver:80`.
Use_Same_Proxy	Specifies whether to use the same proxy server for all protocols: ■ **0** Don't use the same proxy server. ■ **1** Do use the same proxy server. If you enable this setting, all protocols use the HTTP proxy server.

Listing 10-5

```
[Proxy]
FTP_Proxy_Server = http://proxyserver:80
Gopher_Proxy_Server = http://proxyserver:80
HTTP_Proxy_Server = http://proxyserver:80
Proxy_Enable = 1
Proxy_Override = <local>
Secure_Proxy_Server = http://proxyserver:80
Socks_Proxy_Server = http://proxyserver:80
Use_Same_Proxy = 1
```

> **Note** In the *[Unattended]* section, if `AutoActivate = Yes` and `ActivateProxy = Proxy`, Windows Product Activation (WPA) attempts to activate this installation of Windows XP Professional by using the proxy settings specified in this section. If *ActivateProxy* is a value other than *Proxy*, WPA uses the proxy settings specified in *[section_name]* of the answer file. The entries in *[section_name]* must match the syntax specified for the *[Proxy]* section.

Important URLs

The *[URL]* section contains entries for specifying default URLs for Internet Explorer. Table 10-3 describes the settings available in this section. Listing 10-6 is an example of using the *[URL]* section.

Table 10-3 *[URL]* Section Entries

Entry	Description
AutoConfig	Specifies whether to configure the browser automatically from a server: ■ **0** Doesn't configure Internet Explorer with an *.ins* file located on a server. ■ **1** Configures Internet Explorer with an *.ins* file located on a server.
AutoConfigJSURL	Specifies the URL of a Jscript file that automatically configures the proxy-server settings for Internet Explorer: `AutoConfigJSURL = http://configserver/autoconfig.js`.
AutoConfigURL	■ Specifies the URL of an *.ins* file that automatically configures the proxy-server settings for the browser: `AutoConfigURL = http://configserver/autoconfig.ins`.
Help_Page	Specifies the URL for HTML-based help: `Help_Page = http://configserver/help`.
Home_Page	Specifies the URL for the default home page: `Home_Page = http://defaulthome`.
Quicklink	Specifies shortcuts in the link folder of the [FavoritesEx] section. See Listing 10-6 for an example of using QuickLink.

Listing 10-6

```
[URL]
AutoConfig = 1
AutoConfigJSURL = http://configserver/autoconfig.js
AutoConfigURL = http://configserver/autoconfig.ins
Help_Page = http://configserver
Home_Page = http://www.msn.com/
Quick_Link_1_Name = "MS HomePage"
Quick_Link_1 = http://www.microsoft.com/
Quick_Link_2_Name = "MS Japan HomePage"
Quick_Link_2 = http://www.microsoft.com/Japan
```

Group Policy Settings

In homogeneous organizations that use Active Directory and Group Policy, I recommend that you rely on Group Policy to manage Internet Explorer while using the other techniques this chapter describes to configure default settings. First, review the settings that are available in Group Policy to conclude whether they cover the breadth and depth of your requirements. If so, you can easily manage Internet Explorer settings by using Group Policy. Otherwise, you can configure Internet Explorer to automatically configure itself from an *.ins* file.

Chapter 20, "Policy Management," describes using Group Policy to manage Windows XP Professional. To help you decide whether you want to use Group Policy to manage Internet Explorer settings, the following list describes many of the settings available in Group Policy for managing the Web browser's settings:

- Browser User Interface
    - Browser Title
    - Custom Logo
    - Browser Toolbar Customizations
- Connection
    - Connection Settings
    - Automatic Browser Configuration
    - Proxy Settings
    - User Agent String
- URLs
    - Favorites and Links
    - Important URLs

- Security

    - Security Zones and Content Ratings

    - Authenticode Settings

- Programs

In addition to the settings in the previous list, Group Policy provides administrative templates for restricting the Internet Explorer user interface. You can disable virtually any portion of the Web browser's user interface, preventing users from changing those settings.

Best Practices

The following are best practices for configuring Internet Explorer for deployment:

- In a homogeneous Windows XP Professional network with Active Directory, use Group Policy to manage Internet Explorer settings.

- In heterogeneous networks with different versions of Windows and Internet Explorer, use IEAK Profile Manager to create *.ins* files, load those *.ins* files on a Web server, and then configure automatic configuration in Internet Explorer.

Chapter 11

Chaining Installations

You must usually install extra programs as part of the Microsoft Windows XP Professional desktop-deployment process. For instance, you might need to install support tools, networking clients, or file-system utilities when you deploy the desktop operating system. This chapter describes how to chain installations to Windows XP Professional and Office 2003 Editions installations; and it provides a sample distribution folder for getting started.

Checklist

- Have you identified in your deployment plan the applications that you want to deploy with Windows XP Professional? See Chapter 1, "Deployment Plan," if not.

- Have you chosen which applications you want to chain to your Windows XP Professional installation or add to your disk image? See Chapter 1.

- Have you verified that each program you want to chain to your Windows XP Professional installation has a silent-installation option and is in a self-contained package? See Chapter 23, "Software Installation," to learn more about repackaging.

- Have you recorded the command-line options required to install each package silently? If not, see the section "Unattended Packages," later in this chapter on page 316.

- Have you identified at which phase of the Windows XP Professional installation process you want to install each chained application? If not, see the section "Package Installation," later in this chapter on page 304.

- Have you already created an unattended-setup answer file for Windows XP Professional? If not, see Chapter 6, "Answer Files."

- Have you already built a Windows XP Professional distribution share on your development server that includes third-party device drivers and additional customizations? If not, see Chapter 7, "Distribution Points."

Chaining Overview

Chaining installations is the process of installing extra programs during the installation of Windows XP Professional. You can install Adobe Acrobat Reader while installing the operating system, for example. Chaining has at least two useful scenarios:

- **Unattended installations**   While installing Windows XP Professional using an unattended-setup answer file, you can install additional applications without requiring user interaction. For example, you can install Tablet PC button applications during the installation of Microsoft Windows XP Tablet PC Edition so the computer works properly the first time the user logs on to it.

- **Disk-image deployment**   A common practice is to include additional programs with Windows XP Professional in a disk image. Doing so has numerous benefits: Users don't have to install programs so they get to work faster; applications are easier to deploy on a disk image than by most other methods; and including applications on a disk image uses less time and less network bandwidth. Just as in the previous example, you can start these installations from your unattended-setup answer file so that Windows XP Setup automatically installs the applications on the image.

The last sentence of the previous bullet needs more explanation. As you're undoubtedly beginning to notice, I prefer completely automated processes for installing Windows XP Professional, building disk images, and so on. In a typical deployment project, you might build and test a disk image repeatedly—dozens of times. To prevent human error from creeping in to your installations like a ghoulish game of Whack-a-Mole and enable you to regression test your installations between revisions, you must completely automate the build process. Chapter 15, "Disk Imaging with Sysprep," describes an automated build process for building disk images. This chapter describes an automated build process for unattended installations.

Figure 11-1 shows the two key opportunities you have for chaining installations to Windows XP Professional. The first opportunity is before Windows XP Setup finishes installing the operating system but before the first user logs on to it. You configure installations at this point using the Cmdlines.txt file, which is in the distribution folder's OEM folder. The second opportunity is after Windows XP Setup finishes and the first user logs on to Windows XP Professional. You configure installations at this point using the *[GuiRunOnce]* section of the unattended-setup answer file. To automatically log on to the computer as local Administrator and run the commands in the *[GuiRunOnce]* section, you also configure the *AutoLogon, AutoLogonCount,* and *AdminPassword* settings in the *[GuiUnattended]* section of the answer file.

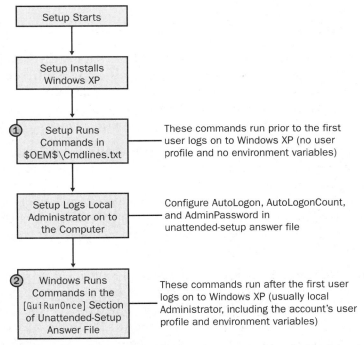

Figure 11-1 This diagram shows key opportunities for chaining installations during the setup process: prior to Windows XP Setup finishing the installation of Windows XP Professional and after the first user logs on to it.

Note In most cases, for applications to work the way you expect, their packages must install for all users. In essence, that means the application must install its shortcuts in the All Users profile folder and it must create default settings for each user that runs the program. Windows Installer databases have the capability to install for all users by adding the **ALLUSERS=2** property to the command line, transform, or database. Other types of packages might install for all users by default or provide a command-line option to install for all users. Otherwise, packages that you chain to your Windows XP Professional installation might not work for all users who share the PC.

More Info   See "Microsoft Windows Preinstallation Reference," which is the file Ref.chm in Deploy.cab, and "Microsoft Windows Corporate Deployment Tools User's Guide," which is the file Deploy.chm in Deploy.cab, for more information about running programs from an unattended-setup answer file. Deploy.cab is on the Windows XP Professional product CD in Support\Tools.

Package Distribution

Chapter 7 described how to build Windows XP Professional distribution points, including the OEM folder. Windows XP Setup copies the OEM folder to the target computer during installation (OEM\\$1 to %SYSTEMDRIVE% and OEM\\$$ to %SYSTEMROOT%), so this is the perfect location for distributing packages. Success is greatly enhanced by minding the following considerations:

- **Single file**   Chained installations are easier to manage if they are in self-contained, compressed package files. If you try adding an installation to a distribution point that contains numerous files, keeping track of them is tedious. Additionally, requiring a self-contained package file makes automating the installation process much easier, as you'll see in "Package Installation." With that said, the section "Package Installation" shows you how to neatly distribute an installation that you can't package in to a single file.

- **Silent installation**   To install Windows XP Professional and chained programs fully unattended, each chained program must support silent installation. Many programs support the **/q** or **/s** command-line options for silent installations. If a program that you're chaining to Windows XP Professional doesn't support silent installation, consider repackaging the program as a Windows Installer database, which does support silent installation. The repackaging program that I use most often is Wise for Windows Installer (*http://www.wise.com*). Chapter 23, "Software Installation," describes how to repackage applications as Windows Installer databases.

After a program is in a self-contained package file that you can install silently, store it in your distribution point's OEM directory so that Windows XP Setup will copy it to the target computer during installation. I prefer to copy package files to a subfolder of %SYSTEMROOT% so they're not immediately visible to users, who don't need additional distractions. Also, as you learned in "Chaining Overview," you can install programs at different points in the process: before Windows XP Setup finishes installing Windows XP Professional and after the first user logs on to it. The easiest way to automate the installations, which you learn how to do in the next section, is to store package files in different subfolders, depending on the phase during which you want to install them: CMDLINES and RUNONCE, as shown in Figure 11-2.

> **Note**   Some Windows Installer databases don't include the program files. This is typically true for large applications, such as Office. They contain registry settings, shortcuts, and other installation instructions, but not program files. You can use most Windows Installer packaging tools, including Wise for Windows Installer, to recompile the package files so they contain compressed program files, and you have a single package file to copy to the Windows XP Professional distribution point. If you have an application that you don't want to recompile into a self-contained package file, probably because the resulting file would be too large, install the application from an administrative installation on the network instead of copying it to the Windows XP Professional distribution point. This is my recommendation for Office 2003 Editions, for example.

- **Prior to Windows XP Setup finishing the installation (Cmdlines.txt)**
  These are packages that you want to install before Windows XP Setup finishes installing Windows XP Professional but before the Log on to Windows dialog box displays. Place these packages in your distribution point in the folder OEM\$$\APPS\CMDLINES. You can't install Windows Installer databases from Cmdlines.txt.

- **After the first user logs on to Windows XP Professional (*[GuiRunOnce]*)**
  These are packages that you want to install after Windows XP Setup is finished installing Windows XP Professional and the first user logs on to it. You'll typically use the *AutoLogon* and *AutoLogonCount* settings in the unattended-setup answer file to automatically log on to the computer as the local Administrator and install these packages. This is the phase during which you'll install most chained packages because you can't install Windows Installer databases using Cmdlines.txt. Put these packages in your distribution point in the folder OEM\$$\APPS\RUNONCE.

Figure 11-2   Put packages to install before Windows XP Setup finishes in APPS\CMDLINES and packages you want to install after the first user logs on to Windows XP Professional in APPS\RUNONCE.

On the Resource Kit CD   The folder structure and files that you see in Figure 11-2 are on this book's companion CD in Samples\chap11\win2002.pro. This sample folder is a superset of the sample from Chapter 7, "Distribution Points." For a quick start, simply copy the template folder from the CD to your development server and then copy the I386 folder from your Windows XP Professional product CD to the root of the distribution point. See the section "Sample Distribution Folder" for step-by-step instructions on customizing the sample distribution folder for this chapter.

Package Installation

Listing 11-1 shows the script runinst.vbs, which I use to install the packages in the subfolders of OEM\$$\APPS. The script runinst.vbs is on this book's companion CD in the Scripts folder (because the lines in Listing 11-1 wrap, making it difficult to retype, I recommend that you copy the script from the CD). It accepts a single command-line option: the folder containing the packages you want to install. This script launches all of the packages that the folder contains, and it can launch different types of package files, including files with the extensions *.exe*, *.msi*, *.bat*, *.js*, *.vbs*, *.reg*, and *.inf*. It waits to launch a Windows Installer setup database if Windows Installer is already running because you can install only one setup database at a time. These files run the gamut from setup programs and Windows Installer databases to scripts to registry settings deployed via files with the *.reg* extension.

The point of this script is to prevent you from having to edit Cmdlines.txt or the *[GuiRunOnce]* section of your unattended-setup answer file just to add a setting to the target computer's registry or install a Windows Installer database. Run this script from both locations, and you'll never again have to change either just to run a batch script or install a program. Instead, you'll just drop the file in the appropriate folder, OEM\$$\APPS\CMDLINES or OEM\$$\APPS\RUNONCE, and the script will automatically run it at the appropriate point in the installation process. For example, I can drop the files settings.reg and joindom.vbs in the RUNONCE folder; and without changing any other files, runinst.vbs automatically loads settings.reg into the registry and runs joindom.vbs using Windows Script Host. You can configure most of the per-computer settings that you learned about in Chapter 8, "Windows Settings," by using this method. In fact, some of those settings apply properly only if you configure them before Windows XP Setup finishes installing Windows XP Professional, so you add those to the CMDLINES folder as *.reg* files to automatically configure them.

I put this script in OEM\$$\APPS so that it's easy to access from unattended-setup answer files. %SYSTEMROOT%\APPS\runinst.vbs is the path on the target computer. The addition of this script is possibly over the top, so Figure 11-3 illustrates the locations of the script, installation packages, and answer files. The sections following this one, "Cmdlines.txt" and "*[GuiRunOnce]*," give you more information about running this script from Cmdlines.txt and the *[GuiRunOnce]* section of your answer files. The following list shows the location from which to execute each command:

- **Cmdlines.txt in the OEM directory** Add the following line to Cmdlines.txt, which installs the package files contained in OEM\$$\APPS \CMDLINES:

```
[Commands]
"wscript.exe //e:vbscript \WINDOWS\APPS\runinst.vbs \WINDOWS\APPS\CMDLINES"
```

- **_[GuiRunOnce]_ in the unattended-setup answer file** Add the following line to the *[GuiRunOnce]* section of your unattended-setup answer file, which installs the package files contained in OEM\$$\APPS\RUNONCE:

```
[GuiRunOnce]
"%SYSTEMROOT%\APPS\runinst.vbs %SYSTEMROOT%\APPS\RUNONCE"
```

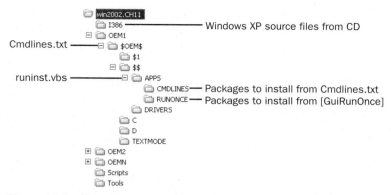

Figure 11-3   This diagram shows a sample distribution point that's fully customized to chain installations at different phases of the process.

On the Resource Kit CD   This book's companion CD contains the script runinst.vbs in the Scripts folder. You can copy this script to the OEM\$$\APPS folder of your distribution point and then add it manually to the Cmdlines.txt file and the *[GuiRunOnce]* section of the unattended-setup answer file. Alternatively, you can use the sample distribution folder in the Samples\chap11\win2002.pro folder on the companion CD. Just copy this folder to your development server, as described in the section "Sample Distribution Folder," later in this chapter on page 313.

Listing 11-1   runinst.vbs

```
' runinst.vbs: run commands in the given folder
' runinst.vbs: run commands in the given folder
'
' USAGE
'
'   runinst.vbs FOLDER
'
'   FOLDER  Path of folder containing installations to run
'
' NOTES
'
'   This script supports files with the extensions EXE,
'   MSI, BAT, CMD, JS, VBS, REG, and INF.
'
'   If the folder doesn't exist, this script displays an error
'   message that times out in 10 seconds, since it's for use during
'   the Windows setup process and the folder doesn't always exist.
'

Option Explicit

Main()
```

```vbscript
Sub Main()

  ' Check the command-line argument (which must be the path of
  ' a folder that contains installations to run); then, call
  ' LaunchInstallations to silently run each installation contained
  ' in the folder.
  '
  Dim intRC
  Dim objArguments
  Dim objFileSystem
  Dim objShell

  Set objArguments = WScript.Arguments
  Set objFilesystem = CreateObject( "Scripting.FileSystemObject" )
  Set objShell = CreateObject( "WScript.Shell" )

  If objArguments.Count > 0 Then
    If objFileSystem.FolderExists( objArguments(0) ) Then
      LaunchInstallations( objArguments(0) )
    Else

      ' The folder doesn't exist

      intRC = objShell.Popup( "The folder " & objArguments(0) & _
                " doesn't exist.", 10, "Folder Missing", 0 )

    End If

  Else

    ' No folder was given on the command line

    WScript.Echo "Usage: runinst.vbs FOLDER"

  End If

End Sub

Sub LaunchInstallations( strPath )

  ' Execute each installation file contained in strPath silently:
  '
  '    strPath Path of the folder containing installations
  '

  Dim objFileSystem
  Dim objShell

  Set objFilesystem = CreateObject( "Scripting.FileSystemObject" )
  Set objShell = CreateObject( "WScript.Shell" )

  ' Build a list of files in the given subfolder

  Dim intRC
  Dim objFolder
  Dim colFiles
  Dim objFile
```

```
      Set objFolder = objFileSystem.GetFolder( strPath )
      Set colFiles = objFolder.Files

      ' Launch each file in the list using the appropriate command

      For Each objFile in colFiles
        Select Case UCase( objFileSystem.GetExtensionName( objFile ))

          Case "EXE"
            intRC = objShell.Run( objFile, 1, True )

          case "MSI"

            Dim objWMIService
            Dim strProcessName

          ' Wait for any current MSI processes to finish

            strProcessName = "msiexec.exe"
            Set objWMIService = GetObject("winmgmts:\\.\root\cimv2")

            Do While objWMIService.ExecQuery( "Select Name from " & _
              "Win32_Process where Name='" & strProcessName & "'""").Count > 1
              WScript.Sleep 5000
            Loop

            intRC = objShell.Run( "msiexec.exe /qb /i " & _
                                 objFile & " ALLUSERS=2", 1, True )
          Case "BAT"
            intRC = objShell.Run( "cmd.exe /c " & objFile, 1, True )

          Case "CMD"
            intRC = objShell.Run( "cmd.exe /c " & objFile, 1, True )

          Case "JS"
            intRC = objShell.Run( "wscript.exe //e:jscript " & _
                        objFile, 1, True )

          Case "VBS"
            intRC = objShell.Run( "wscript.exe //e:vbscript " & objFile, 1, True )

          Case "REG"
            intRC = objShell.Run( "regedit.exe /s " & objFile, 1, True )

          Case "INF"
            intRC = objShell.Run( _
            "rundll32.exe setupapi,InstallHinfSection DefaultInstall 132 " _
            & objFile, 1, True )

        End Select
      Next

  End Sub
```

Cmdlines.txt

The file Cmdlines.txt contains commands that the GUI-mode phase of Windows XP Setup runs when installing optional components, including applications that Windows XP Setup must install immediately after installing Windows XP Professional, but before the first user logs on to it. The commands in Cmdlines.txt run as a system service, so they run with elevated privileges. You put the Cmdlines.txt file in the OEM subfolder of the Windows XP Professional distribution folder. You use the OEM folder to copy chained installations to the target computer, as described in the section "Package Distribution," previously in this chapter on page 302.

The format of Cmdlines.txt is simple. It has a single section called *[Commands]*, followed by zero or more commands. Enclosing each command in quotes is a good idea if the command contains spaces. Here's a sample that executes the script runinst.vbs, which you learned about earlier in this chapter (environment variables aren't available to commands executed from Cmdlines.txt):

```
[Commands]
"wscript.exe //e:vbscript \WINDOWS\APPS\runinst.vbs \WINDOWS\APPS\CMDLINES"
```

On the Resource Kit CD   The companion CD contains a fully customized distribution point that you can copy and use for your own Windows XP Professional distribution points. This sample is in the Samples\chap11 \win2002.pro folder, and it contains a Cmdlines.txt file that executes the script runinst.vbs as shown in this example.

Using Cmdlines.txt is different from the *[GuiRunOnce]* section in some important aspects:

- You must create the OEM distribution folders, and you must set OEMPreinstall =Yes in your answer file.

More Info   See Chapter 9, "Office Settings," for more information about this setting.

- Windows XP Setup runs the commands in Cmdlines.txt under the Local System security account, giving the commands elevated privileges.
- When Windows XP Setup runs the commands in Cmdlines.txt, no user is logged on to Windows XP Professional, and for that matter, no network connection is guaranteed. As a result, Windows XP Professional stores settings in the default user hive file, so all users receive the same settings.

- You can't install Windows Installer databases using Cmdlines.txt. Be wary because some self-contained, self-extracting setup programs actually decompress in to Windows Installer databases during installation.

- You can't use Cmdlines.txt if you are using an operating system CD and a Winnt.sif file to perform an unattended installation. You can use Cmdlines.txt only if you are installing from a distribution share.

For these reasons, installing applications using Cmdlines.txt is not common. The more common task for the Cmdlines.txt file is to configure computer settings, install hotfixes, and so on. For example, you can install a number of *.reg* files to configure operating system settings. You can apply hotfixes to the computer (see Chapter 22, "Patch Management," for more information). For installing applications, the better choice is using the *[GuiRunOnce]* section of the unattended-setup answer files, as described in the next section.

Adding Loose Files

I recommend that you put only self-contained package files in the CMDLINES and RUNONCE subfolders of OEM*N*\$OEM$\$$\APPS. If doing so is possible, it makes managing the packages much easier. This is not an issue for batch scripts, *.reg* files, Windows Script Host scripts, and so on. They are naturally discrete files. Large applications that are difficult to repackage into self-contained package files are a bit troublesome, though.

For those large applications that you can't or don't want to repackage, there is a solution for keeping them manageable. Under OEM*N*\$OEM$\$$ \APPS\CMDLINES or OEM*N*\$OEM$\$$\APPS\RUNONCE, create a subfolder for the application's installation files. For example, you can copy the Office 2003 Editions installation files to the folder OEM*N*\$OEM$\$$\APPS \RUNONCE\OFFICE. Then, create a batch script called office.cmd in OEM*N*\$OEM$\$$\APPS\RUNONCE to launch the setup program in the OFFICE subfolder. The batch script would contain a simple command, such as %SYSTEMROOT%\APPS\RUNONCE\OFFICE\setup.exe /qn, to run the installation silently (environment variables are available to commands run from the *[GuiRunOnce]* section). The name of the batch script file doesn't matter.

[GuiRunOnce]

The *[GuiRunOnce]* section contains a list of commands that run the first time a user logs on to the computer after Windows XP Setup finishes. You must enclose each command in quotes. The commands in the *[GuiRunOnce]* section run in the context of the console user, so you must ensure that the user has the privileges necessary to run each command. The following example uses the script runinst.vbs to install the installation packages, as described earlier in this chapter (environment variables are available to commands that you execute in the *[GuiRunOnce]* section):

```
[GuiRunOnce]
"%SYSTEMROOT%\APPS\runinst.vbs %SYSTEMROOT%\APPS\RUNONCE"
```

On the Resource Kit CD   The companion CD contains a fully customized distribution point that you can copy and use for your own Windows XP Professional distribution points. This sample is in the Samples\chap11 \win2002.pro folder, and it contains a Cmdlines.txt file that executes the script runinst.vbs, as shown in this example.

Here are two things you should consider when using the *[GuiRunOnce]* section of your unattended-setup answer file:

■ From the *[GuiRunOnce]* section, you can't run programs that force Windows XP Professional to restart because Windows XP Professional loses any entries remaining in the *[GuiRunOnce]* section when it restarts, and those commands do not run. If you can't prevent the program from restarting the computer, try repackaging it as a Windows Installer database or add it as the last command in the *[GuiRunOnce]* section of the answer file.

■ Any program that relies on Windows Explorer does not work properly because Windows Explorer is not running when the commands in the *[GuiRunOnce]* section are running. Again, you can consider repackaging these applications.

Tip   The commands in the *[GuiRunOnce]* section run asynchronously, which means that they could potentially all run at the same time. If you'd rather run commands synchronously—one at a time—create a batch script that runs the program using the Start command's **/wait** command-line option. The syntax is **Start /wait** program, where program is the path and name of the program file. The **/wait** command-line option prevents the Start program from returning control to the batch script until program finishes. Then, run this batch file from *[GuiRunOnce]*. The script you learned about earlier in this chapter, runinst.vbs, already handles this situation. If you're using the script runinst.vbs, put your batch scripts in the OEM\$$\APPS \RUNONCE folder instead of calling them directly from the *[GuiRunOnce]* section, and allow the script to run them automatically.

If you're using the *[GuiRunOnce]* section to chain installations, you'll want to automatically log on to the operating system immediately after installation is finished. On top of that, you'll likely want to log on as local Administrator to install applications that require elevated privileges or change settings in *HKLM* that restricted users can't change. Use the *AutoLogon* setting in the *[GuiUnattended]* section of your answer file. Set AutoLogon=Yes. This sets the value *AutoAdminLogon* in the registry key HKLM\Software\Microsoft\Windows NT\CurrentVersion\WinLogon. You must also set *AutoLogonCount* in the *[GuiUnattended]* section. This setting specifies the number of times that you want to automatically log on to Windows XP Professional as local Administrator. This sets the value *AutoLogonCount* in the registry key HKLM\Software\Microsoft\Windows NT\CurrentVersion\WinLogon. Normally, you'd only log on to Windows XP Professional one time by setting AutoLogonCount=1. However, you can log on to the operating system as many times as is necessary, such as when a setup program restarts the computer in the middle of the installation process. The following lines show you the settings necessary to use this feature:

```
[GuiUnattended]
AdminPassword=*
AutoLogon=Yes
AutoLogonCount=1


[GuiRunOnce]
"%SYSTEMROOT%\APPS\runinst.vbs %SYSTEMROOT%\APPS\RUNONCE"
```

The previous lines set the local Administrator password to a blank, which isn't recommended unless you're using Sysprep (see Chapter 15, "Disk Imaging with Sysprep"); instead, you should specify a password for the local Administrator account. When you set a password using the *AdminPassword* setting in the *[GuiUnattended]* section, Windows XP Professional uses that password to log the local Administrator on to it. However, if you encrypt the password, which is available only in Windows XP Professional and Microsoft Windows Server 2003, Windows XP Setup disables this feature. It's a trade-off between security and deployment convenience. Don't panic, though, because when Windows XP Professional finishes installing, it removes the password from any local copies of the answer file, such as %SYSTEMROOT%\System32\$winnt$.sif.

On the Resource Kit CD   You'll usually want to restart the computer after automatically logging on to it and installing applications. The companion CD contains the script reboot.vbs, which you can use for this purpose. It's in the Scripts folder. Copy this script to a subfolder of your distribution point's OEM\$$ or OEM\$1 folders, and then run the script from your unattended-setup answer file's *[GuiRunOnce]* section. Make sure that it's the last line in the section.

Sample Distribution Folder

The following two sections show you how to configure your distribution share to use the runinst.vbs script that you've learned about in this chapter:

- See the section "Modifying a Folder" if you already have an existing distribution folder, such as the one you created in Chapter 7.

- See the section "Creating a New Folder" to create a new distribution folder.

Modifying a Folder

Chapter 7 showed you how to create a distribution folder for Windows XP Professional. The sample distribution folder on this book's companion CD was in Samples\chap07\win2002.pro, and it included scripts for automatically adding third-party device drivers and automatically building $$Rename.txt files. The following steps describe how to add the runinst.vbs script to this folder:

1. Copy the script file runinst.vbs from the Scripts folder of this book's companion CD to the OEM*N*\$OEM$\$$\APPS in your distribution point.

2. Create the following subfolders under OEM*N*\$OEM$\$$\APPS:

   - CMDLINES

   - RUNONCE

3. Add the following line to Cmdlines.txt in OEM*N*\$OEM$, which installs the package files contained in OEM*N*\$OEM$\$$\APPS\CMDLINES:

   ```
   [Commands]
   "wscript.exe //e:vbscript \WINDOWS\APPS\runinst.vbs \WINDOWS\APPS\CMDLINES"
   ```

4. Add the following line to the *[GuiRunOnce]* section of your unattended-setup answer file in OEM*N*, which installs the package files contained in OEM*N*\$OEM$\$$\APPS\RUNONCE:

   ```
   [GuiRunOnce]
   "%SYSTEMROOT%\APPS\runinst.vbs %SYSTEMROOT%\APPS\RUNONCE"
   ```

5. Do the following:

   - Add packages that you want to install after Windows XP Setup finishes but before the user logs on to Windows XP Professional to the OEM*N*\$OEM$\$$\APPS\CMDLINES folder. These are typically hotfixes, settings, and so on.

   - Add packages that you want to install after the first user logs on to Windows XP Professional (typically local Administrator) to the folder OEM*N*\$OEM$\$$\APPS\RUNONCE. These are typically applications.

6. Optionally, add the following lines to your unattended-setup answer file (specify a local Administrator password, as described earlier in this chapter):

```
[GuiUnattended]
AdminPassword=*
AutoLogon=Yes
AutoLogonCount=1
```

Creating a New Folder

The folder Samples\chap11\win2002.pro on this book's companion CD contains the sample distribution folder for this chapter. It's fully customized, using the scripts that Chapter 7 and this chapter describe. Here's how to use that sample to jumpstart your own distribution:

1. Copy Samples\chap11\win2002.pro from this book's companion CD to your development server, and do one of the following:

   - If you're creating a distribution point for Windows XP Professional, rename the folder to win2002.pro (I use the naming convention *version.edition* for distribution folders).

   - If you're creating a distribution point for Windows XP Table PC Edition, name the folder win2002.tab.

2. Do one of the following:

   - If you're creating a distribution point for Windows XP Professional, copy the I386 folder from your Windows XP Professional media to win2002.pro.

   - If you're creating a distribution point for Windows XP Tablet PC Edition, copy the I386 folder from your Windows XP media to win2002.tab; then, copy the CMPNENTS folder form the second CD to win2002.tab.

3. Create a folder in win2002.pro or win2002.tab to store original device drivers, such as win2002.pro\Drivers. Within that folder, create a subfolder for each device driver that you download from OEMs and expand.

4. Determine how many configurations you want to create (the sample folder includes OEM1, OEM2, and OEMN). Create additional OEM*N* folders, if necessary, or remove unused OEM*N* folders. For example, if you need only two configurations, delete the folder win2002.pro\OEMN. If you need four configurations, copy win2002.pro\OEMN to OEM3 and OEM4.

5. In each OEM*N* folder, under the win2002.pro or win2002.tab, update drivers.txt to point to each device driver's *.inf* file that you want to include. If you examine the drivers.txt file, you'll find an example of the file's syntax.

6. In each OEM*N* folder, under the win2002.pro or win2002.tab, update winnt.sif, which is the unattended-setup answer file. In particular, you must update the following settings (see the sample winnt.sif file for more settings that you must replace when customizing a distribution point):

■ ***OemFilesPath***   Set this property to the UNC path of the OEM folder. For example, if you're editing winnt.sif in win2002.pro\OEM2, and the UNC path of the distribution point will be \\Server\Windows, add `Oem-FilesPath= \\Server\Windows\win2002.pro\OEM2\$OEM$` to the *[Unattended]* section of winnt.sif.

■ ***OemPnPDriversPath***   Update this property with the path of each folder that contains third-party device drivers. This path is relative to the folders on the target computer. So, if you have files in OEM\DRIVERS, OEM\DRIVERS\LAN, and OEM\DRIVERS \VIDEO, add `OemPnPDriversPath=\WINDOWS\DRIVERS;\WINDOWS\DRIVERS\LAN;\WINDOWS\DRIVERS\VIDEO` to the *[Unattended]* section.

7. In win2002.pro or win2002.tab, run drivers.cmd, which copies the device driver files described by the *.inf* files in drivers.txt to the distribution point. It will also run rename.wsf to create $$Rename.txt files for long file names.

8. Do the following:

■ Add packages that you want to install after Windows XP Setup finishes but before the user logs on to Windows XP Professional to the OEM*N*\$OEM$\$$\APPS\CMDLINES folder. These are typically hotfixes, settings, and so on.

■ Add packages that you want to install after the first user logs on to Windows XP Professional (typically local Administrator), to the folder OEM*N*\$OEM$\$$\APPS\RUNONCE. These are typically applications.

9. Optionally, add the following lines to your unattended-setup answer file:

```
[GuiUnattended]
AdminPassword=*
AutoLogon=Yes
AutoLogonCount=1
```

More Info   For more information about customizing unattended-setup answer files, see Chapter 6. For more information about adding third-party device drivers to your distribution point and creating $$Rename.txt files, see Chapter 7. And for more information about installing Windows XP Professional after customizing your distribution point, see Chapter 13, "Unattended Setup."

Unattended Packages

To achieve a fully unattended and automated installation, the packages you chain to your Windows XP Professional installation must support unattended installation. Many setup programs support a **/s** or **/q** command-line option for such a thing. Others don't.

Often, you can find out whether the package supports unattended installation by typing **setup /?** at the command prompt, where **setup** is the file name of the setup program. If the setup program doesn't provide clues, you need to know which vendor's product was used to create the package. You can usually tell by running the setup program and looking for logos, for example. You can also examine the setup program's Properties dialog box. Armed with that information, the following sections describe how to install packages created by different packaging software unattended. Table 11-1 summarizes the necessary commands.

Table 11-1   Unattended Package Installation

Package Type	Unattended Installation
Windows Installer	**msiexec.exe /i** *package.msi* **/qn ALLUSERS=2**
InstallShield	**setup.exe /s /sms**
	To create the Setup.iss file necessary to run setup silently, type **setup.exe /r** to create a Setup.iss from your responses to the setup program's dialog boxes and then copy Setup.iss from %SYSTEMROOT% to the folder containing the package.
InstallShield PackagefortheWeb	**setup.exe /a /s /sms**
	To create the Setup.iss file necessary to run setup silently, type **setup.exe /a /r** to create the Setup.iss based on your responses and then copy Setup.iss from %SYSTEMROOT% to the folder containing the package.
Wise Installation System	**setup.exe /s**

More Info   Two Web-based resources are essential for scripting the installation of packages. The first is SourceForge at *http://unattended.sourceforge.net*. This Web site shows how to run various setup programs silently. The second, AppDeploy.com at *http://www.appdeploy.com*, contains detailed information about deploying applications, including how to run setup programs silently and repackage them as Windows Installer databases.

Windows Installer

The number of applications packaged as Windows Installer databases is multiplying rapidly. And what often looks like a self-contained, self-extracting setup program, with a file name such as Setup.exe, is often a file that decompresses to a Windows Installer database. You can usually extract the database by using a tool such as WinZip (from WinZip Computing at *http://www.winzip.com*), by running the setup program and looking in the %USERPROFILE%\Local Settings\Temp for the package file or by running the setup program with the **/x** command-line option. Windows Installer databases have the *.msi* file extension.

To install Windows Installer databases unattended using Msiexec.exe, use the **/qb** command-line option for a basic user interface or the **/qn** command-line option for no user interface. Also, to ensure that the package installs for user by all users, add the **ALLUSERS=2** property. For example, the command msiexec.exe /i program.msi /qn ALLUSERS=2 installs the package file program.msi with no user interaction and for use by all users who share the computer.

InstallShield

Packages created by InstallShield (*http://www.installshield.com*) usually have the file name Setup.exe. To create an unattended installation for an InstallShield package, you need to create an InstallShield script, which has the .iss file extension. Many applications come with such a file, but they're easy to create otherwise:

1. Run the setup program using the **/r** command-line option. This creates a Setup.iss file based on how you configure the installation as you step through the setup program. The result is the file Setup.iss in %SYSTEMROOT%.

2. Copy Setup.iss from %SYSTEMROOT% to the folder containing the package. If you're using the distribution folder described in this chapter, you'll want to create a subfolder in OEM*N*\$OEM$\$$\APPS\RUNONCE for the package and then start the setup program from a batch file that you put in OEM*N*\$OEM$ \$$\APPS\RUNONCE. This avoids duplicate file names.

3. Run the setup program using the **/s** command-line option. The setup program runs silently using the responses provided by the Setup.iss file.

Tip   Packages created by InstallShield spawn a separate process and then return immediately to the calling program. This means the setup program runs asynchronously, even if you start the setup program using **setup /wait**. You can add the **/sms** command-line option to force the setup program to pause until installation is finished, however, making the process synchronous.

PackagefortheWeb

PackagefortheWeb is an InstallShield-packaged application contained in a self-contained, self-extracting file. Creating a Setup.iss file and using it is almost the same as described in the previous section. The difference is that you must use the **/a** command-line option to pass the command-line options to the setup program after the file extracts its contents. For example, a file that you downloaded called Prog.exe will expand its contents in to the temporary folder and then run Setup.exe when finished. To pass command-line options to Setup.exe, you must use the **/a** command-line option. Here's how this extra option changes the steps:

1. Run the setup program using the **/a /r** command-line options: **setup.exe /a /r**. This creates a Setup.iss file based on how you configure the installation as you step through the setup program. The Setup.iss file is in %SYSTEMROOT%.

2. Copy Setup.iss from %SYSTEMROOT% to the folder containing the package. If you're using the distribution folder described in this chapter, you'll want to create a subfolder in OEM*N*\$OEM$\$$\APPS\RUNONCE for the package and then start the setup program from a batch file that you put in OEM*N*\$OEM$ \$$\APPS\RUNONCE. This avoids duplicate file names.

3. Run the setup program using the **/a /s** command-line options: **setup.exe /a /s**. The setup program runs silently using the responses in the Setup.iss file.

Wise Installation System

Packages created using Wise Installation System (*http://www.wise.com*) recognize the **/s** command-line option for unattended installation. There isn't a tool available to script the installation, however.

Office Chaining

After Office 2003 Setup program installs the core Microsoft Office 2003 Editions package, it calls Windows Installer to install any number of chained packages in the order that you specify them in the setup settings file (Setup.ini). You customize chained packages by setting properties in Setup.ini or by creating a transform that includes the Add Installations and Run Programs screen.

The setup program reads the Setup.ini file at the start of the installation process and writes a set of tasks to the registry that installs each package listed in the *ChainedInstall_1* through *ChainedInstall_n* sections. By default, the setup program passes to Windows Installer the command-line options and properties defined for Office 2003 Editions; however, you can set unique properties for a chained package in Setup.ini. You can include Office 2003 Editions Multilingual User Interface Packs (MUI Packs) in your installation by adding the appropriate Lpk.msi files to Setup.ini, as shown in this example:

```
[ChainedInstall_1]
PATH=\\server\share\admin\1036\Lpk.msi
DISPLAY=None
MST=French.mst
CMDLINE="SOURCELIST=\\server\share\admin\1036"
```

These lines add the French Language Pack to the Office 2003 Editions installation. The French Language Pack is installed silently (regardless of the display setting specified for the Office 2003 Editions installation), the customizations in the transform French.mst are applied, and an alternate source is identified for when the primary administrative installation point is unavailable.

More Info   See "Deploying Office and Other Products Together" in the Microsoft Office 2003 Editions Resource Kit for more information about chaining packages to Office 2003 Editions. The resource kit is at *http://www.microsoft.com/office/ork*. Point to Deployment, and then click Installing Office 2003.

Package Customization

In most sections of Setup.ini, including the *Options* and *SystemPackOptions* sections, you use the syntax `property=value` to specify custom property values. In the *ChainedInstall*_n sections, you can set the *DISPLAY* and *MST* property values with this syntax, along with several additional settings that customize the installation process. However, you must use the *CMDLINE* property to add other options to the command line that the setup program passes to Windows Installer for the package.

You can set the following properties for chained packages in Setup.ini:

- **TASKNAME=task_name**   Assigns a friendly name to the installation. Office 2003 Setup program uses this name in the setup log file.

- **TASKTYPE=task_type**   Identifies whether the chained installation is an MSI file or EXE file. If you edit Setup.ini directly, you must specify *TaskType=exe* to chain an executable file; the value *exe* is case-sensitive and must be all lowercase. The Setup INI Customization Wizard enters the correct value automatically when you add an .exe file to the Office 2003 Editions installation.

- **PATH=path_to_msi_or_exe**   Specifies the relative or full path to the *.msi* file or .exe file.

- **DISPLAY=user interface display level**   Specifies a display setting for the chained installation. Use *Basic* to display only progress indicators; use *None* for a completely silent installation.

- **_MST=transform.mst_**   Specifies the path and file name of a transform (.mst file) to apply to the chained package.

- **_CMDLINE=command_line_options_**   Specifies other property=value pairs or command-line options that the Office 2003 Setup program passes to Windows Installer during the call to install the chained package.

- **_IGNORERETURNVALUE=[0|1]_**   To continue installing successive chained packages even if this installation fails, set this property to _1_.

- **_REBOOT=[0|1]_**   To restart the computer after the installation completes, set this property to _1_.

> **More Info**   Chaining by using the *ChainedInstall*_n sections is a good method for deploying Office 2003 Editions product updates. This is particularly necessary if you created your Office 2003 Editions distribution points as compressed CD images to take advantage of local installation sources. For more information, see Chapter 22.

Requirements and Limitations

Office 2003 Setup is designed to support chaining of other Windows Installer packages and simple executable programs (.exe files). This chaining functionality makes it more efficient to deploy MUI Packs from the Multilingual User Interface Pack at the same time you deploy Office 2003 Editions. However, chaining is not the best method to use in all circumstances:

- **Adding programs through the Custom Installation Wizard**   Custom Installation Wizard allows you to add installations and run programs during the Office 2003 Editions installation. However, you cannot use the Add Installations and Run Programs page of Custom Installation Wizard to chain additional Windows Installer packages. If Windows Installer tries to start installation of a second package before it has completed installation of the first package, the entire installation process fails.

- **Deploying software using Active Directory**   Active Directory software installation, a feature of IntelliMirror, installs Windows Installer databases directly, bypassing Office 2003 Setup program and Setup.ini file. For this reason, you cannot use Setup.exe to chain Office 2003 Editions installations when you assign or publish packages. Instead, Active Directory deploys the Office 2003 Editions, Multilingual User Interface Pack, and other Office 2003 Editions–related packages separately and in random order.

- **Restarting the computer after a chained installation**   Office 2003 Setup program does not support forced reboots for chained packages. In other words, you cannot chain a package that must restart the computer to complete its installation because restarting interrupts the Setup.exe thread and stops the installation process. To avoid this problem, Office 2003 Setup program sets the *REBOOT* property to *REALLYSUPPRESS* by default for all but the last chained package. You can direct Office 2003 Setup to restart the computer, and then resume to complete a chained installation by setting the *REBOOT* property. For example, if you chain a Japanese Language Pack that includes an Input Method Editor (IME), you can set the *REBOOT* property to *1* in the *ChainedInstall*_n section of Setup.ini. This setting adds a task to the registry that directs Office 2003 Setup to restart the computer and then resume the installation.

- **Elevating installation of a chained package**   If you chain a package that requires elevated privileges to install, you must take the same steps to elevate the installation that you do for Office 2003 Editions. Setup.exe does not automatically install a chained package with administrator privileges when the Office 2003 Editions installation is elevated. However, several of the methods that you use to elevate the Office 2003 Editions installation also elevate any chained installations (See Chapter 23, "Software Installation," for more ideas about handling elevated privileges):

- Use the */jm* option to advertise Office 2003 Editions; then every installation listed in Setup.ini is also advertised and therefore elevated.

- Use a tool such as Systems Management Server to install Office 2003 Editions. For more information, see Chapter 17, "Systems Management Server."

- Log on as an administrator when you begin the Office 2003 Editions installation and do not log off or restart before it completes; then chained installations run with elevated privileges.

Best Practices

The following are best practices for chaining packages to a Windows installation:

- **Chain appropriate installations to Windows XP Professional**   For example, Adobe Acrobat Reader and a small networking client are appropriate for chaining to the Windows XP Professional installation because they are small and easy to package for silent installation. These are natural choices for inclusion on disk images, too. Bigger applications such as Office 2003 Editions should be installed from a network administrative installation.

- **Run chained installations silently**   By running chained installations silently, you can completely automate the installation process so that it requires no interaction. A completely automated process is easier to repeat and regression test. For example, after you start Windows XP Setup to install Windows XP Professional, you should be able to walk away from the computer and expect to find a completed installation when you return.

- **Package chained installations in self-contained files**   Packaging chained installations in self-contained files makes managing them easier in the long run. It also makes possible automating the installation process.

- **Install Windows Installer databases using the *[GuiRunOnce]* section**   You can't install Windows Installer databases using Cmdlines.txt.

- **Chain Office 2003 Editions–related packages using the Office 2003 Editions Setup.ini file**   Limit the packages that you chain to your Office 2003 Editions installation using Setup.ini to Office 2003 Editions–related packages, such as MUI Packs.

Chapter 12

User Profiles

A user profile stores a user's settings separately from other users' settings. Even in locked-down environments, users can still change most settings in their own user profiles. But seldom are the default settings that come with Microsoft Windows XP Professional ideal for every environment. Thus, you will likely want to customize default user profiles to start users with the most appropriate settings. This chapter describes how to create and deploy user profiles in your organization.

Checklist

- Have you planned and specified the default user settings that you must change? See Chapter 3, "Windows Configuration," for more information.

- Do you intend to deploy default user profiles from the network or from a disk image? See Chapter 3 for more information. And see Chapter 15, "Disk Imaging with Sysprep," for more information about including default user profiles on a disk image.

- Have you planned on deploying settings for Windows Installer–based applications by using default user profiles? If so, see Chapter 3 to learn why you shouldn't use default user profiles for these settings.

- Have you planned to migrate users' existing settings? See Chapter 18, "User State Migration," for more information.

- Have you planned to deploy managed settings in default user profiles? If so, see Chapter 20, "Policy Management," to learn how to use Group Policy to deploy these settings instead of default user profiles.

User Profiles Overview

Windows XP Professional stores user settings separate from computer settings. The computer's settings affect every user who logs on to Windows XP Professional. Computer settings include hardware configuration, network configuration, and so on. Typically, only the administrators group can change computer settings, but some settings are within reach of the Power Users group. On the other hand, a user profile contains settings for a specific user. Users customize the operating system to their liking, and their settings don't affect other users. Users have full control of their own profiles, which contain more than just settings. They also contain files and folders specific to each user.

Deploying and managing user profiles are two of the most significant issues facing IT professionals. Properly deploying and managing user profiles can save companies money. That's because most of the behaviors that users experience in Windows XP Professional have settings in user profiles, and IT professionals can deploy user profiles that contain defaults for these settings, starting users off on the right foot. For example, they can populate the Favorites folder with links to the intranet so users don't have to find those links for themselves. They can add printer connections to a default user profile so users can print right away without having to figure out how to add a printer. Importantly, most of the useful policies that manage operating system and application settings are in user profiles. IT professionals manage the settings in user profiles by applying policies to them.

In this chapter, you learn about the contents of a user profile. Then you learn how to use roaming user profiles on a business network. The most compelling part of this chapter shows you how to build and deploy default user profiles. In that part, I show you two techniques for building default user profiles. The first is traditional but rather dirty. I prefer the second method, which is a more surgical (and tidier) method of building default user profiles. I wrap up this chapter with alternatives to using default user profiles, including an interesting combination of a default user profile and batch script that makes default settings much easier to update and maintain in the long run.

Exploring User Profiles

Windows XP Professional loads users' profiles when they log on to the computer and unloads their profiles when they log off. A user profile contains a registry hive that contains per-user settings, and folders that contain documents and data files. The following section, "Profile Hives," describes the registry hive that the operating system loads. The section "Profile Folders" describes the folders in a user profile.

Before delving into the contents of user profiles, knowing their location on the file system is useful. The default location is different from what it was in Microsoft Windows NT 4.0 or other operating systems of that era. Remember that Windows NT 4.0 stored user profiles in %SYSTEMROOT%\Profiles, but this location made it difficult to secure the operating system files while allowing access to users' data. Microsoft Windows 2000 and Windows XP Professional store user profiles in a different location, which enables you to pull user data out from under an operating system folder: %SYSTEMDRIVE%\Documents and Settings, C:\Documents and Settings on most computers. This is the case only with a clean installation of Windows XP Professional, however.

If you upgrade from a version of Windows earlier than Windows 2000, the profiles remain where they were in the previous operating system. For example, if you upgrade from Windows NT 4.0 to Windows XP Professional, the profiles remain in %SYSTEMROOT%\Profiles. The location of user profiles after upgrading from Windows 2000 to Windows XP Professional depends on whether you installed Windows 2000 cleanly or upgraded from an earlier version of Windows. In other words, Windows XP Setup never moves user profiles during an upgrade. Table 12-1 summarizes where you'll find profile folders, scenario by scenario.

Table 12-1   Location of User Profiles

Scenario	Location
Clean installation	%SYSTEMDRIVE%\Documents and Settings
Upgrade from Windows 2000	%SYSTEMDRIVE%\Documents and Settings
Upgrade from Windows NT 4.0	%SYSTEMROOT%\Profiles
Upgrade from Windows 98	%SYSTEMDRIVE%\Documents and Settings

Windows XP Professional creates and stores a list of user profiles. The key HKLM\SOFTWARE\Microsoft\Windows NT\CurrentVersion\ProfileList corresponds to the list you see in the User Profiles dialog box. To open the User Profiles dialog box, click Start, Control Panel, Performance And Maintenance, and System. In the System Properties dialog box, on the Advanced tab, click Settings in the User Profiles area. Each subkey is a user profile, and the subkey's name is the security identifier (SID) of the account that owns the profile. Each profile in ProfileList contains the REG_SZ value ProfileImagePath that points to a user profile folder in %SYSTEMDRIVE%\Documents and Settings. Figure 12-1 illustrates the relationship between the ProfileList key and the user profile folders. This relationship is the reason you shouldn't just remove a user profile from the file system. Instead, use the User Profiles dialog box to remove user profiles, which cleans the user profile out of the ProfileList key as well as off the file system.

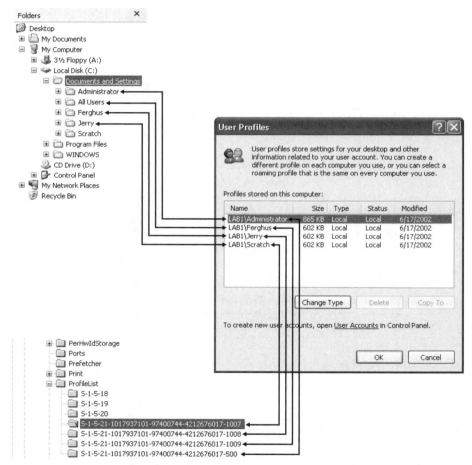

Figure 12-1 The subkeys of ProfileList contain a wealth of information about the user profiles that Windows XP Professional has created, including their paths on the file system.

Note   In enterprises that use Windows NT 4.0, IT professionals sometimes move profiles to %SYSTEMROOT%\Profiles when deploying Windows XP Professional because managing the profiles is often easier if they are in the same location, regardless of the platform. Windows XP Professional answer files offer a setting that enables you to do that. The setting is *ProfilesDir* and it's in the *[GuiUnattended]* section. Set *ProfilesDir* to the path of the folder in which you want to store profiles. You should begin the path with either %SYSTEMROOT% or %SYSTEMDRIVE%; otherwise, Windows XP Setup ignores it.

Advantages of User Profiles

The primary goal of user profiles is to keep each user's settings and data distinct from those of other users as well as from the computer's settings. This has several advantages for enterprise environments and makes Windows XP Professional more convenient to use at home, too. User profiles enable *stateless* computing. A company can configure Windows XP Professional to store key user settings and data separately from the computer. This makes backing up and replacing computers much easier because users' data is tucked safely away on the network and maintained separately from the computer's configuration. The first time users log on to a replacement computer, the operating system copies their settings from the network. They get back to work more quickly.

User profiles also allow users' settings to follow them from computer to computer. They don't have to reconfigure settings at each computer. When they log on to a network that supports roaming user profiles, the operating system downloads their settings from the network. When they log off the computer, the operating system copies users' settings back to the network. Roaming user profiles makes sharing computers more feasible because each user has his or her personalized configuration. Roaming user profiles are a must-have in environments such as call centers, in which users aren't guaranteed to sit down at the same computer twice. You learn about roaming user profiles in the section "Using Roaming User Profiles," later in this chapter.

Profile Hives

The first half of a user profile is the profile hive: Ntuser.dat. You learn about the second half in "Profile Folders." This file is in the root of users' profile folders. You find all the per-user settings for Windows Explorer and persistent network connections in profile hives. Profile hives also contain per-user taskbar, printer, and Control Panel settings. Accessories that come with Windows XP Professional store per-user settings in the profile hive.

When Windows XP Professional loads a user profile, the operating system loads the hive file Ntuser.dat into the subkey HKU\SID, where SID is the user's SID. Then Windows XP Professional links the root key HKCU to HKU\SID. Figure 12-2 shows this relationship. Windows XP Professional and most applications reference users' settings through HKCU, not HKU\SID, because HKCU resolves which subkey of HKU contains the console user's settings. HKU contains a second hive file, HKU\SID_Classes, which contains per-user file associations and class registrations.

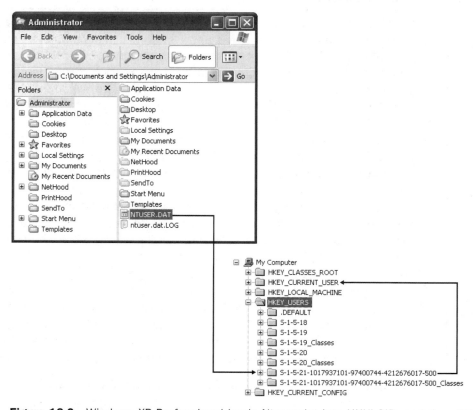

Figure 12-2   Windows XP Professional loads Ntuser.dat into HKU\SID, and then links HKCU to it.

The list of profile hives is in the key ProfileList, which you learned about in the previous section. It contains one subkey for each user profile. The subkey's name is the name of the hive in HKU or the account's SID. The REG_SZ value ProfileImage-Path is the path of the profile hive file Ntuser.dat for that user profile. ProfileList does not contain a value for the SID_Classes hives, however. HKLM\SYSTEM\Current-ControlSet\Control\hivelist contains one REG_SZ value for each hive in HKLM and HKU that the operating system is currently using. The difference between the values ProfileList and hivelist is that ProfileList contains a list of all user profiles that Windows XP Professional knows about, loaded or not, and hivelist contains a list of all currently loaded hive files.

Tip   You can load and edit profile hives in Registry Editor (Regedit) without logging on to the computer using the account that owns that user profile. This is one of the techniques you use later in this chapter to build default user profiles.

Profile Folders

The folders in a user profile contain per-user application files. For example, Microsoft Office 2003 Editions installs templates and custom dictionaries in the user profile. Internet Explorer stores its cookies and favorites in the user profile. The most interesting folder in a user profile is the Application Data folder. Figure 12-3 shows a user profile in Windows Explorer. Some of the folders are hidden; show the hidden files in Windows Explorer if you want to see all the following folders for yourself:

- **Application Data**   This folder contains application files, such as a mail files, shortcuts, templates, and so on. Each application's vendor chooses what files to store here. You can redirect this folder to a network location using Group Policy.

- **Cookies**   This folder contains Internet Explorer cookies.

- **Desktop**   This folder contains files, folders, and shortcuts on the desktop. Users see the contents of this folder on the Windows XP Professional desktop. You can redirect this folder to a network location using Group Policy.

- **Favorites**   This folder contains Internet Explorer favorite shortcuts. Users see the contents of this folder on Internet Explorer's Favorites menu. Group Policy doesn't support redirecting this folder, but you can redirect it manually with some care. Microsoft does not support redirecting Favorites folders, however.

- **Local Settings** This folder contains application files that do not roam with the profile. The files you find in this folder are either per-computer or too large to copy to the network. This folder contains four interesting subfolders:

    - **Application Data** This subfolder contains computer-specific application data.

    - **History** This subfolder contains Internet Explorer history.

    - **Temp** This subfolder contains per-user temporary files.

    - **Temporary Internet Files** This subfolder contains Internet Explorer offline files.

- **My Documents** This folder contains the default location for users' documents. Applications should save users' documents to this folder by default, and this is the location to which the common dialog boxes open by default. This folder also contains the My Pictures folder, which is the default location for users' pictures, and optionally the My Music folder, which is the default location for users' music files. You can redirect this folder to a network location using Group Policy.

- **NetHood** This folder contains shortcuts to objects on the network. Users can browse the folders to which these shortcuts are linked in the My Network Places folder.

- **PrintHood** This folder contains shortcuts to objects' printer objects. Users see the contents of this folder in the Printers folder.

- **Recent** This folder contains shortcuts to the most recently used documents. Users see these shortcuts on the My Recent Documents menu, which is on the Start menu.

- **SendTo** This folder contains shortcuts to drives, folders, and applications that are copy targets. Users see the contents of this folder when they right-click an object and then click Send To.

Figure 12-3 The user profile folders you see in this figure are the default folders in a clean installation of Windows XP Professional.

- **Start Menu**   This folder contains shortcuts to program items. Users see the contents of this folder on the Start menu and on the Start menu's All Programs menu. IT professionals can redirect this folder to a network location using Group Policy.

- **Templates**   This folder contains template files. Users see the contents of this folder when they right-click in a folder and then click New.

HKCU\Software\Microsoft\Windows\CurrentVersion\Explorer\User Shell Folders is the key where Windows XP Professional stores the location of each folder that's part of a user profile. Each value in this key represents a folder, as shown in Table 12-2. These are REG_EXPAND_SZ values, so you can use environment variables in them. Use %USERPROFILE% to direct the folder somewhere inside users' profile folders and %USERNAME% to include users' names, particularly when you want to redirect a profile folder to a network location. Redirect users' Favorites folders to the network by setting Favorites to \\Server\Share\%USERNAME%\Favorites, where \\Server\Share is the server and share containing the folders, for example. Windows XP Professional does not use the similar key Shell Folder.

Table 12-2   User Profile Folders

Name	Default path
AppData	%USERPROFILE%\Application Data
Cache	%USERPROFILE%\Local Settings\Temporary Internet Files
Cookies	%USERPROFILE%\Cookies
Desktop	%USERPROFILE%\Desktop
Favorites	%USERPROFILE%\Favorites
History	%USERPROFILE%\Local Settings\History
Local AppData	%USERPROFILE%\Local Settings\Application Data
Local Settings	%USERPROFILE%\Local Settings
My Pictures	%USERPROFILE%\My Documents\My Pictures
NetHood	%USERPROFILE%\NetHood
Personal	%USERPROFILE%\My Documents
PrintHood	%USERPROFILE%\PrintHood
Programs	%USERPROFILE%\Start Menu\Programs
Recent	%USERPROFILE%\Recent
SendTo	%USERPROFILE%\SendTo
Start Menu	%USERPROFILE%\Start Menu
Startup	%USERPROFILE%\Start Menu\Programs\Startup
Templates	%USERPROFILE%\Templates

Special Profiles

The profile folders you saw in Figure 12-1 contain more than the standard user profiles that Windows XP Professional creates when users log on to the operating system. The figure shows four special user profiles about which any IT professional should learn:

- **All Users**   This profile folder contains settings that apply to all users who log on to the computer. This profile folder contains a profile hive, Ntuser.dat, which the operating system doesn't load. Also, this profile folder contains the shared documents and music folders; shared Start menu shortcuts, and so on. The key User Shell Folders in HKLM\SOFTWARE\Microsoft\Windows \CurrentVersion\Explorer contains the linkages to the subfolders in the All Users profile folder.

- **Default User**   This profile folder contains the default user profile that Windows XP Professional copies when it creates new user profiles. It contains most of the files and folders that you learned about in the previous section. Customizing this folder is a good way to start each user who logs on to the computer with the same settings. Windows XP Professional first checks for a Default User folder on the NETLOGON share of the server and uses the local Default User folder only if the network copy isn't available. Customizing this folder is a good way to deploy settings that you don't want to manage. You learn how to customize it in the section, "Deploying Default User Profiles" later in this chapter.

- **LocalService**   This profile folder is for the built-in LocalService account, which the Service Control Manager uses to host services that don't need to run in the LocalSystem account. This is a normal user profile with limited data. You don't see it in the User Profiles dialog box, and the LocalService folder is super-hidden.

- **NetworkService**   This profile folder is for the built-in NetworkService account, which the Service Control Manager uses to host network services that don't need to run in the LocalSystem account. This is a normal user profile. You don't see it in the User Profiles dialog box, and the NetworkService folder is super-hidden.

In the previous list, the first two profile folders are far more interesting than the last two. IT professionals often customize the All Users profile folder on disk images. The customization, such as a shortcut on the Start menu, affects all users who log on to the computer. IT professionals more frequently customize the \Default User folder, though. Doing so is a great way to create custom settings that you don't want to manage. In other words, it's one method for deploying common user preferences while still allowing users to change those preferences if necessary. As you'll learn throughout this chapter, customizing the Default User folder on a disk image isn't necessarily the most efficient means to deploy default user settings. Instead, create a customized Default User folder on the server's NETLOGON share. See the section "Deploying Default User Profiles," later in this chapter.

Improvements to User Profiles

In Windows 2000, poorly written applications and services that keep registry keys open during logoff prevent Windows 2000 from unloading the user's registry hive. When this occurs, changes that a user made to his or her profile are not saved to the server, if you're using roaming user profiles. Locked user profiles have three symptoms:

■ The roaming user experience is affected because changes are not saved when users log on to another computer.

■ Because *locked* profiles never get unloaded, they end up using a lot of memory on a terminal server that has many users logging on to it.

■ If a profile is marked for deletion at logoff (to clean up the machine or for temporary profiles), profiles do not get deleted.

The three problems are solved as follows:

■ In Windows XP Professional, when a user logs off and the profile is locked, the operating system polls the profile for 60 seconds before giving up. Windows XP Professional then saves the user's profile hive and roams the profile correctly.

■ When the application or service closes the registry key and unlocks the profile, Windows XP Professional unloads the user's profile hive, freeing memory used by the profile.

■ If a profile is marked for deletion, when the reference count drops to zero, Windows XP Professional unloads and deletes it. In the event that the application never releases the registry key, Windows XP Professional deletes all profiles marked for deletion at the next machine boot.

> **Tip**   Many programs install themselves per-user, which means they install for use by a single user, when you really want all users who share the computer to use it. You can tell that a program installed per-user because its shortcut is in the profile folder belonging to the account you used to install it. If the program re-creates missing settings as it starts, then you can change the program from per-user to per-computer by simply moving its shortcut from the user profile folder in which it installed the shortcut to the All Users profile folder. This works the other way, too. You can move a shortcut from the All Users profile folder to a specific user's profile folder so that only a single user sees the shortcut.

Getting User Profiles

How users get their profiles depends on the type of profile you've configured their accounts to use:

- **Local user profile**   This profile is created the first time users log on to their computers. Local user profiles are stored on the local hard disk. Changes that users make to their profiles don't follow them from computer to computer.

- **Roaming user profile**   These profiles are available to users from any computer on the network, and changes that users make to their profiles follow them from computer to computer.

- **Mandatory user profile**   This profile is similar to roaming user profiles. Administrators assign mandatory user profiles to users, and Windows XP Professional throws away users' changes when they log off the operating system. In other words, users start with the same settings every time they log on to the operating system. Microsoft provides mandatory user profiles to provide compatibility with Windows NT 4.0, but you should consider using Group Policy instead.

The following sections describe how Windows XP Professional creates a profile when users log on to the operating system. The section "Using Roaming User Profiles" describes how to create and manage roaming user profiles. Also, the section "Managing Roaming User Profiles" shows you how to prevent Windows XP Professional from merging the local copy of a profile with the server copy using Group Policy.

Local Profiles

Here's an overview of how Windows XP Professional creates and uses a local user profile for users the first time they log on to their computers:

1. The user logs on to Windows XP Professional.

2. Windows XP Professional checks the list of user profiles in the key ProfileList to determine whether a local profile exists for the user. If an entry exists, the operating system uses it; otherwise, the operating system does one of the following:

   ■ If the computer is a domain member, Windows XP Professional checks the NETLOGON share on the domain controller that authenticated the user's account for a default user profile in a subfolder called Default User. If it exists, the operating system copies NETLOGON\Default User to %SYSTEMDRIVE%\Documents and Settings\Username, where Username is the name of the user's account.

   ■ If the computer is not a domain member or if Windows XP Professional doesn't find a default user profile on the NETLOGON share, it uses the local default user profile. It copies %SYSTEMDRIVE%\Documents and Settings\Default User to %SYSTEMDRIVE%\Documents and Settings \Username.

3. Windows XP Professional loads the profile hive Ntuser.dat into HKU*SID* and links the root key HKCU to it.

When the user logs off of Windows XP Professional, the operating system saves any changes to the profile in the user profile folder. It doesn't copy the profile folder to the network. It also unloads the profile hive from the registry.

Roaming Profiles

Here's an overview of how Windows XP Professional creates and uses a roaming user profile for users the first time they log on to their computers:

1. The user logs on to Windows XP Professional.

2. Windows XP Professional checks the list of user profiles in the key ProfileList to determine whether a local profile exists for the user. If an entry exists, the operating system merges the network copy of the profile into the local profile folder; otherwise, the operating system does one of the following:

   ■ Windows XP Professional checks the NETLOGON share on the domain controller for the Default User folder. If it exists, the operating system copies the Default User folder to %SYSTEMDRIVE%\Documents and Settings\Username, where Username is the name of the user's account.

- If Windows XP Professional doesn't find a default user profile on the NETLOGON share, it copies %SYSTEMDRIVE\Documents and Settings \Default User to %SYSTEMDRIVE%\Documents and Settings\Username.

3. Windows XP Professional loads the profile hive Ntuser.dat into HKU*SID* and links the root key HKCU to it.

When users log off Windows XP Professional, the operating system saves their changes to the local profile folders and then unloads the profile hives from HKU. Afterward, the operating system copies their profile folders to the network location specified by the administrator. If the profile folder already exists on the network, the operating system merges the local copy into the network copy. For more information, see "Understanding the New Merge," later in this chapter.

> **Note**   There are two differences between roaming and mandatory user profiles. First, you create the mandatory profile and copy it to the user's profile folder instead of allowing Windows XP Professional to create it when the user logs on to the computer. Second, rename the Ntuser.dat to **Ntuser.man**. Windows XP Professional uses the *.man* file extension to make the profile mandatory. Windows XP Professional doesn't merge mandatory user profiles to the network when the user logs off of the computer.

Using Roaming User Profiles

You configure roaming user profiles on the server, so the user must be a member of and log on to the domain to use a roaming user profile. Both Microsoft Windows NT Server 4.0 and Microsoft Windows 2000 Server support roaming user profiles, as does Microsoft Windows Server 2003. The following instructions show you how to configure roaming user profiles in Active Directory on Windows 2000 Server:

1. Create a folder on the server where you want to store user profiles. This is the top-level folder that will contain individual user profile folders.

2. Share the folder, giving all users full control. (I sometimes reduce users' permissions to read and execute in this folder, and then give them full control of their individual profile folders.)

3. In Active Directory Users And Computers, double-click the account that you want to configure to use a roaming user profile.

4. On the Profile tab of the name Properties dialog box, shown in Figure 12-4, type the path in which you want to store the user's profile in the Profile Path box. The path is *Server**Share**Username*, where *Server* is the name of the

server, *Share* is the share you created in step 1, and *Username* is the name of the account. Optionally, use %USERNAME% for *Username*, and Active Directory substitutes the current account's name for it.

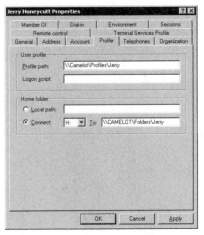

Figure 12-4   Typing a path in the Profile Path box is all it takes to enable roaming user profiles.

If you want to configure a lot of accounts to use roaming user profiles, doing the job by hand is a monumental task. Instead, use a third-party tool or write an Active Directory Scripting Interface (ADSI) script to do the job. You access ADSI through Windows Script Host (WSH) using VBScript or JScript. This subject is beyond the scope of this book, but you can find more information about it on Microsoft's Web site: *http://www.microsoft.com.*

Folder Redirection is a great complement to user profiles, particularly the roaming variety. It enables an IT professional to redirect the location of some profile folders to the network. There's nothing magical about Folder Redirection. Group Policy simply changes the folder's location in the User Shell Folders key so that applications automatically look for the folder on the network. It also manages the folder's permissions. From users' perspectives, redirected folders are similar to roaming user profiles because their documents follow them from computer to computer. Unlike roaming user profiles, however, redirected folders always remain in the same place. You can use redirected folders with or without roaming user profiles. If you use them with roaming user profiles, you can reduce the amount of data that Windows XP Professional transfers when users log on to and off of the operating system. Furthermore, redirected folders are often useful even when you don't intend to use roaming user profiles; you can allow users' documents to follow them without the complexity and sometimes difficulty of using roaming user profiles. You learn about roaming user profiles in the section "Getting User Profiles." Table 12-3 describes which folders can roam and which can redirect.

Table 12-3   Roaming and Redirecting Folders

Folder	Can Roam?	Can Redirect?
Application Data	Yes	Yes
Cookies	Yes	No
Desktop	Yes	Yes
Favorites	Yes	No
Local Settings	No	No
My Documents	Yes	Yes
My Recent Documents	Yes	No
NetHood	Yes	No
PrintHood	Yes	No
SendTo	Yes	No
Start Menu	Yes	Yes
Templates	Yes	No

Best Practices for Roaming User Profiles

The following are best practices for roaming user profiles:

- **Redirect the My Documents folder outside of roaming user profiles.** Doing so decreases logon time. Folder Redirection is the best way to do this, but you can redirect the My Documents folder manually.

- **Don't use Encrypting File System (EFS) on files in a roaming user profile.** EFS is not compatible with roaming user profiles. Encrypting a roaming user profile prevents the user profile from roaming.

- **Don't make disk quotas for roaming user profiles too restrictive.** If they're too low, roaming user profile synchronization might fail. The server debits the user's quota for temporary files that Windows XP Professional creates during the synchronization process, so ensure that enough disk space is available on the server. Also, make sure that enough disk space is available on the workstation to create temporary duplicate copies of the profile.

- **Don't make folders in roaming user profiles available offline.** If you use Offline Folders with roaming user profile folders, synchronization problems occur because both Offline Folders and roaming user profiles try to synchronize at the same time. However, you can use Offline Folders with folders you redirect, such as My Documents.

- **Use Group Policy loopback policy processing in moderation if you're also using roaming user profiles.**   Loopback processing enables you to apply different per-user Group Policy settings to users based on the computers they're using.

- **Match the home folder to the redirected My Documents folder.** When redirecting the My Documents folder outside of a roaming user profile, set the home folder to the redirected My Documents folder for compatibility with applications that aren't compatible with folder redirection.

- **Disable fast network logon using Group Policy if you're using roaming user profiles.**   This prevents conflicts that occur when user profiles change from local to roaming. For more information, see "Understanding Fast Network Logon," later in this chapter.

Managing Roaming User Profiles

Group Policy provides a number of policies that you can use to manage how Windows XP Professional handles user profiles. You can configure these policies in a local Group Policy Object (GPO) or in a network GPO. Chapter 20 describes this topic in more detail. For now, here's a description of policies for user profiles:

- **Connect Home Directory To Root Of The Share**   This policy restores the definitions of the %HOMESHARE% and %HOMEPATH% environment variables to those used in Windows NT 4.0 and earlier.

- **Limit Profile Size**   This policy sets the maximum size of each roaming user profile and determines the system's response when a roaming user profile reaches the maximum size. If user profiles become excessively large, consider redirecting the My Documents folder to a location outside of the profile.

- **Exclude Directories In A Roaming Profile**   This policy enables you to add to the list of folders excluded from the user's roaming profile.

- **Delete Cached Copies Of Roaming Profiles**   This policy determines whether the system saves a copy of a user's roaming profile on the local computer's hard drive when the user logs off.

- **Do Not Detect Slow Network Connections**   This policy disables the slow link detection feature.

- **Slow Network Connection Timeout For User Profiles**   This policy defines a slow connection for roaming user profiles.

- **Wait For Remote User Profile**   This policy directs the system to wait for the remote copy of the roaming user profile to load, even when loading is slow. Also, the system waits for the remote copy when the user is notified about a slow connection, but does not respond in the time allowed.

- **Prompt User When Slow Link Is Detected**   This policy notifies users when their roaming profile is slow to load. Users can then decide whether to use a local copy or to wait for the roaming user profile.

- **Timeout For Dialog Boxes**   This policy determines how long the system waits for a user response before it uses a default value.

- **Log Users Off When Roaming Profile Fails**   This policy logs a user off automatically when the system cannot load the user's roaming user profile.

- **Maximum Retries To Unload And Update User Profile**   This policy determines how many times the system will try to unload and update the profile hive. When the number of trials specified by this setting is exhausted, the system stops trying. As a result, the user profile might not be current, and local and roaming user profiles might not match.

- **Add The Administrators Security Group To Roaming User Profiles**   This policy adds the Administrators security group to the roaming user profile share. The default behavior prevents administrators from managing individual profile folders without taking ownership of them.

- **Prevent Roaming Profile Changes From Propagating To The Server**   This policy determines whether the changes a user makes to his or her roaming profile are merged with the server copy of their profile. This is a policy-based method for implementing mandatory user profiles.

- **Only Allow Local User Profiles**   This policy determines whether roaming user profiles are available on a particular computer. By default, when roaming-profile users log on to a computer, their roaming profile is copied to the local computer. If they have already logged on to this computer in the past, the roaming profile is merged with the local profile. Similarly, when the user logs off this computer, the local copy of the profile, including any changes made, is merged with the server copy of the profile.

The first three policies in this list are per-user, and the remaining are per-computer policies; Figure 12-5 shows them in the Group Policy editor. All of them are administrative policies in System\User Profiles under User Configuration and Computer Configuration.

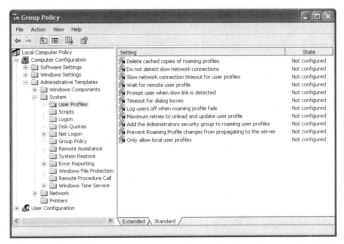

Figure 12-5   These policies give you management control of how Windows XP Professional uses profiles.

> **More Info**   Windows XP Professional Service Pack 1 introduced a change to roaming user profiles. Beginning with Service Pack 1, the operating system checks the target roaming profile folder's permissions, if it already exists. It doesn't permit roaming if the permissions aren't correct. For more information about how Windows XP Professional Service Pack 1 verifies roaming user profile folders and the impact on your deployment, see Knowledge Base article 327462 at *http://support.microsoft.com*.

Understanding Fast Network Logon

Windows XP Professional doesn't wait for the network to start before displaying the Logon To Windows dialog box. This substantially improves start time over Windows 2000. Users who have previously logged on to the computer get to their desktops faster because the operating system uses cached credentials and loads Group Policy in the background after the network becomes available. Although fast network logon improves perceived performance, it has effects you should understand. The most important thing to take away from this section is that Windows XP Professional doesn't use fast network logon if you use roaming user profiles.

Because background refresh is the default behavior, users might have to log on to Windows XP Professional up to three times for Group Policy extensions such as Software Installation and Folder Redirection to take effect. Windows XP Professional must process these types of extensions in the background without any users logged on to it. Also, because advanced Folder Redirection is based on group membership, users must log on to Windows XP Professional three times: once to update the cached user object and group membership, a second time to detect the change in group membership and require a foreground policy application, and a third time to apply folder redirection policy in the foreground. The operating system might require users to log on two times to update the properties of other Group Policy objects.

Another thing to keep in mind is the effect that fast network logon has on Windows XP Professional when users' profiles change from local to roaming. When the operating system uses fast network logon, it always uses the locally cached copy of the profile. By the time the operating system detects that the user has a roaming user profile, it has already loaded the local profile hive and changed its timestamp. The result is that if users log on to multiple computers, the operating system can replace newer profile hives with older ones. To handle this scenario, Windows XP Professional treats the change from local to roaming as a special case. First, the operating system checks the following conditions:

- Is the user changing from a local to a roaming profile?
- Is there a copy of the user profile on the server?

If both these conditions are true, Windows XP Professional merges the contents of the local user profile with the server copy, without the profile hive Ntuser.dat. Then, the operating system copies the server copy of the profile to the local copy, regardless of the profile hives' timestamps. After the user's profile becomes a roaming profile, Windows XP Professional always waits for the network so it can download the user profile. In other words, fast network logon and roaming user profiles don't work together.

> **Note** Considering the changes that Windows XP Professional makes to roaming user profiles, if you remove the roaming profile path from a user in Active Directory, you should remove the profile folder from the server. If you reconfigure the user to use roaming user profiles and you use the same path, the user will receive the older server copy of the user profile.

Understanding the New Merge

Many IT professionals are shy about using roaming user profiles because they have experience with the merge algorithm that Windows NT 4.0 uses. That algorithm assumes that there is a single master copy of the user profile. When the user logs on to the computer, the operating system assumes that the master profile is on the local computer; when the user logs off of the computer, it assumes that the master profile is on the server. It mirrors the entire profile from the local computer to the server and vice versa, completely replacing the profile at the target location. This works perfectly well when people use a single computer, but it creates havoc when they use multiple computers.

The merge algorithm in Windows XP Professional is more advanced; it merges user profiles at the file level. In other words, it's a real merge, not a wipe-and-load. The merged profile then becomes a superset of the files in the local and server copies of the user profile, and when a file exists in both copies, the operating system uses the most recent version of the file. New files don't turn up missing, and updated files are not replaced—both of which are symptoms that occur with the merge algorithm in Windows NT 4.0. In the case of the Windows NT 4.0 merge, if a profile changes on two computers, only the last one copied to the network persists.

Behind the new and improved merge algorithm is the timestamp that Windows XP Professional saves in the ProfileList key. When a user logs on to the computer, the operating system saves the current time in ProfileList. When the user logs off of the computer, the operating system uses the timestamp to determine which files have been added or removed from the server's copy of the user profile. For example, if a file called Example.doc is in the server copy of the user profile but not in the local copy, the timestamp helps Windows XP Professional determine whether the file was added to the server copy or removed from the local copy. If the timestamp of the file is later than the timestamp of the local user profile, then the file was added to the server copy. The result is that Windows XP Professional doesn't touch the file when it merges the local profile into the server copy. If the timestamp of the file is earlier than the timestamp of the local user profile, the file was removed from the local user profile. The result is that Windows XP Professional removes the file from the server copy of the profile when the operating system merges the local copy into it. With Windows XP Professional, if a profile changes on two computers, both of them are merged file by file into the server copy.

Note   There is another issue that keeps many IT professionals from using roaming user profiles. Roaming user profiles are terrific when configurations are similar from desktop to desktop. When users log on to different computers with different sets of applications, screen sizes, power management requirements, and so on, roaming user profiles are cumbersome and users' experiences aren't very good. Roaming user profiles are great in scenarios such as call centers and other environments in which configurations are standardized, but they are not very useful when configurations are not standardized in the organization.

Deploying Default User Profiles

Deploying default user profiles is one of the easiest ways to deploy settings to new users. You can't use default user profiles to deploy settings to existing users, though, because they already have user profiles. These aren't settings that you want to manage. They're defaults that you want to establish for users while allowing users to change them when necessary. Essentially, deploying default user profiles is like modifying the default settings in Windows XP Professional. If you want to define a setting that users *can't* change, use policies. Chapter 20 contains more information about managing settings.

To deploy a default user profile, follow these steps:

1. Create a template account.

   You can use a local or a domain account, but the user profile is generally cleaner if you use a local account on a computer that's not joined to a domain. (Because I include network shortcuts in my profiles, I usually use a domain account to create default user profiles.) Also, use a name for the template account that you're sure is unique in the registry and is shorter than eight characters. You'll learn why using a unique name is important a bit later.

2. Log on to the computer using the template account and customize its settings. The section "Customizing User Settings," later in this chapter, describes settings that I frequent.

3. Clean up the user profile to remove artifacts that you don't want to deploy. The section "Cleaning User Profiles," later in this chapter, describes how to clean the profile.

4. Copy the template account's user profile folder to a new location and name it Default User.

   Don't replace %SYSTEMDRIVE%\Documents and Settings\Default User, however, because you might need to repeat the process a few times to get it right and you'll want the original default user profile handy. In the section "Creating Default User Folders," later in this chapter, I describe an alternative method for building the Default User folder, which I think is more precise and yields a cleaner default user profile.

5. Deploy the default user profile.

   You can put the Default User folder in %SYSTEMDRIVE%\Documents and Settings on disk images and then deploy them, or you can put the Default User folder on the NETLOGON share of the server. I prefer the second method because it separates settings from the disk images, which allows me to update settings much more easily.

Customizing User Settings

Log on to the template account you created in step 1 of the previous section and customize the account's settings. When customizing settings for a default use profile, less is more. Preferably, you'll work from a list of settings that you have vetted with other members of the deployment planning team. The following list gives you an idea of the settings I frequently target with default user profiles:

- Taskbar
- Quick Launch toolbar
- Start menu
- Windows Explorer
- Internet Explorer
- My Network Places
- Search Assistants
- Tweak UI
- Control Panel, in particular:
    - Display
    - Folder Options
    - Mouse
    - Power Options
    - Printers And Faxes
    - Sounds And Audio Devices
    - Taskbar And Start Menu

You want to customize per-user settings because they are the only settings in the user profile. How do you know that a setting is per-user when you're customizing a user profile? You don't, necessarily, which is why you must test the settings in your list ahead of time. Sitting down to construct a default user profile isn't the time to begin wondering whether a particular setting is per-user or per-computer. The easiest way to figure this out is to log on to a new account and customize the settings in your list. Then copy that user profile to a clean installation of Windows XP Professional and see which settings made it. The settings that didn't make it are per-computer settings, and you'll want to scratch them off your list. There are a small number of settings that are per-user but still don't work well in default user profiles, and there is generally little you can do about it except hack the profile to make them work. The most prominent example is desktop wallpaper. Including wallpaper in a default user profile requires you to include the wallpaper graphic file inside the profile folder and then hack the profile hive to point to the new location.

You might also want to include settings for applications you're deploying, whether you include them on your disk images or deploy them by using other methods.

> **Caution**   First, a caveat: don't include settings for Windows Installer–based applications in a default user profile. Windows Installer provides superior methods for deploying settings. That means you shouldn't deploy settings for Office 2003 Editions using default user profiles. Instead, use tools such as the Custom Installation Wizard and the Office Profile Wizard. Both tools come with the *Microsoft Office 2003 Editions Resource Kit*, and Chapter 20 describes how to use them. Install other types of applications and customize their settings to your requirements just as you would customize Windows XP Professional settings.

This last part is optional, but I recommend it: Remove artifacts from the user profile that you don't want to deploy. Artifacts include history lists and the like. I have a preset route that I use to clean up a user profile. First, I clear the Start menu and Internet Explorer's history lists by doing the following:

- Click Start, Control Panel, Appearance And Themes, and Taskbar And Start Menu. On the Start Menu tab, click Customize. On the Customize Start Menu dialog box's Advanced tab, click the Clear List button.

- Click Start, Control Panel, Network and Internet Connections, and Internet Options. In the Internet Options dialog box, click Clear History to remove Internet Explorer's history lists.

You don't need to worry about removing temporary Internet files because they are in the profile's Local Settings folder, and Windows XP Professional doesn't copy them with the profile. If you opened Internet Explorer to customize it, however, you might clear out the cookies and AutoComplete lists. In the Internet Options dialog box, on the General tab, click Delete Cookies; on the Content tab, click AutoComplete followed by Clear Forms and Clear Passwords.

After you're finished customizing and cleaning the account's settings, log off Windows XP Professional. My last word of advice is to tread lightly; don't open dialog boxes and programs you don't intend to customize. Doing so keeps their settings out of the default user profile. For example, if you don't intend to customize Windows Media Player, don't open the program.

> **Tip**   In some cases, customizing default user profiles is more straightforward than this chapter describes (for example, when you have just one or two settings to customize, and they're all in the registry). In those cases, you simply load the hive file Ntuser.dat from the Default User folder, change the settings, and then unload the hive file. This process avoids the unpleasantness of the methods discussed in this chapter.

Cleaning User Profiles

You cleaned the user profile a wee bit in the previous section, but only to remove some artifacts from the profile hive. The next major step is to open the profile hive in Regedit and scour it for settings that you don't want to deploy or that you must change before deploying.

The most significant example is paths. User profiles contain references to the profile folder: %SYSTEMDRIVE%\Documents and Settings\Name. If you deploy the user profile to countless users, they'll all have different profile folders. When they try accessing the profile folder Name, Windows XP Professional and programs will fail because the user doesn't have access to that folder.

A more concrete example makes this clear. Assume that you created a user profile using a template account called DefUser and deployed that profile to a user named Jerry. The user Jerry has access to %SYSTEMDRIVE%\Documents and Settings\Jerry, but the folder %SYSTEMDRIVE%\Documents and Settings\DefUser doesn't even exist. When the user Jerry runs a program that uses a setting containing the path to the DefUser user profile folder, the program causes an error. To correct this situation, follow these steps:

1. Log on to the computer containing the template user profile as Administrator.

2. In Regedit, load the Ntuser.dat hive file from the template user profile folder.

3. Search the hive file for references to the template user profile folder. If the name of the folder is longer than eight characters, search for the long and short versions of the folder's name.

4. Remove values that contain the path of the template user profile folder.

5. Unload the hive file and restart the computer.

     Restarting the computer is often necessary because Windows XP Professional locks the file and you can't copy it. Restarting the computer is the quickest way to force it to let go of the file.

When you remove values that contain the path of the template user profile folder in step 4, you're assuming that Windows XP Professional and other programs re-create missing settings. This isn't always true. Some of my favorite applications fail to re-create missing settings. You'll learn which do and which don't through trial and error. You can handle the problem easily, though. Rather than removing the value permanently, replace a REG_SZ value with a REG_EXPAND_SZ value of the same name. Then set the value to the original path, substituting %USERPROFILE% for the portion that is the user profile folder. For example, if you see a REG_SZ value called Templates that contains C:\Documents and Settings\Jerry\Templates, remove the value; then add the value Templates back as a REG_EXPAND_SZ value and set it to %USERPROFILE%\Templates. Test these changes in your lab to make sure that they work properly.

In the previous section, you cleared some of the history lists using the Windows XP Professional user interface. Take this opportunity to further cover your tracks by removing the keys listed in Table 12-4. These keys correspond to most of the history lists that Windows XP Professional keeps, including the Search Assistant and command dialog boxes.

Table 12-4   History Lists to Remove

History List	Key
Internet Explorer's address bar	HKCU\Software\Microsoft\Internet Explorer\TypedURLs
Run dialog box	HKCU\Software\Microsoft\Windows\CurrentVersion\Explorer\RunMRU
Documents menu	HKCU\Software\Microsoft\Windows\CurrentVersion\Explorer\RecentDocs
Common dialog boxes	HKCU\Software\Microsoft\Windows\CurrentVersion\Explorer\ComDlg32\LastVisitedMRU
Search Assistant	HKCU\Software\Microsoft\Search Assistant\ACMru

Creating Default User Folders

The template user profile is ready to go. All you have to do now is copy it. To open the User Profiles dialog box, click Start, Control Panel, Performance And Maintenance, and then System. On the Advanced tab, click Settings in the User Profiles area. In the User Profiles dialog box, click the template user profile and then click Copy To. In the Copy Profile To box shown in Figure 12-6, type the path to which you want to copy the profile. To keep things simple, I usually copy the profile folder to C:\Default User. Just make sure that the folder doesn't already exist. Also, give the Everyone group permission to use the profile, which is appropriate for a default user profile: Click Change, type **Everyone**, and then click OK. The default user profile is ready to deploy, and you learn how to do that in the next section.

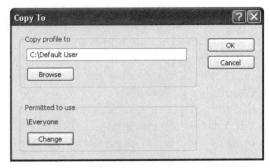

Figure 12-6   Copy the template user profile using this dialog box; don't copy the folder using Windows Explorer because doing so copies artifacts that you don't want in the profile.

The method I just described is common for creating a default user profile from a template user profile. I don't like it because user profiles expand greatly in size and complexity after Windows XP Professional loads and uses them. A default user profile created using the method I just described contains more files and folders than are necessary. To use the more surgical method that I prefer, follow these steps:

1. Copy %SYSTEMDRIVE%\Documents and Settings\Default User to another location, such as C:\Default User.

    You want to keep the original Default User folder around, just in case you have to start over again.

2. Copy the Ntuser.dat hive file from the template user profile to your copy of the Default User folder C:\Default User.

3. Copy other files from the template user profile folder to your copy of the Default User folder, C:\Default User. I tend to copy files from the following folders, assuming that they contain files I want to deploy:

    ■ \Application Data\Microsoft\Internet Explorer\Quick Launch

    ■ \Desktop

    ■ \Favorites

    ■ \NetHood

    ■ \PrintHood

    ■ \SendTo

    ■ \Templates

Deploying Default User Folders

After completing the steps in the last section, you have a default user profile that's ready to deploy. You have two choices. If you're deploying Windows XP Professional using disk-imaging techniques, you can include the default user profile on the disk image. Replace %SYSTEMDRIVE%\Documents and Settings\Default User with your own Default User folder. After replacing the Default User folder with your own, clone and deploy the disk image. When new users log on to the computer, they'll receive your default user profile and thus your settings.

I don't like customizing the local Default User folder as my sole means of deploying default settings, though. I prefer to separate settings from configurations. What if I need to update a setting down the line? I don't want to update the Default User folder on each computer in the organization.

The alternative is to copy the customized Default User folder to the NETLOGON share of the server. As you learned earlier in the chapter, Windows XP Professional looks first for the network version of the Default User folder and then the local version. The first time users log on to a computer, Windows XP Professional gets my default user profile from the network. Of course, the benefit is that I can always update it later. The primary problem with this method is that if users log on to their computers locally, they still get the local default user profile. That's the reason that I prefer doing both at the same time. I replace the Default User folder on disk images and also copy the same folder to the NETLOGON share of the server.

Note   An alternative to copying a default user profile to the NETLOGON share is keeping a user profile handy on the network and then copying it to users' network profile folders when you create new accounts. For example, stash away a default user profile somewhere on your server. Assuming that you're using roaming user profiles, copy the default user profile into new accounts' profile folders. The first time those users log on to Windows XP Professional, the operating system downloads their roaming user profile, which you've already preconfigured. This is useful in one-off scenarios in which you want users to have a profile other than the default. It's also useful in a heterogeneous environment, which often requires different user profiles for different versions of Windows.

Coexisting with Earlier Versions of Windows

Coexistence is an issue that affects roaming user profiles only. If you're not using roaming user profiles on your network, coexistence isn't an issue because you won't be deploying user profiles to different versions of Windows. In general, though, roaming user profiles are compatible between Windows 2000 and Windows XP Professional. Here are a few precautions you can take to minimize problems:

- Try to make sure that users with roaming user profiles are logging into the same version of Windows on each computer. You should choose your rollout units so that you're picking up all the computers that users in a unit use.

- At the very least, make sure that the same application versions are on each computer and that you've installed applications to the same path on each computer.

- If you're using roaming user profiles with Windows 2000 and Windows XP Professional, make sure that your %SYSTEMDRIVE% and %SYSTEMROOT% are the same. Also, make sure that profiles are stored in the same path. If you're using roaming user profiles with Windows NT 4.0 and Windows XP Professional, you should move the location of user profiles that Windows XP Professional uses by setting the *ProfilesDir* property in the *[GuiUnattended]* section of your answer file.

There's nothing in the documentation that says user profiles don't roam between Windows NT and Windows XP Professional. However, I suspect that this scenario isn't workable. First, Windows XP Professional converts Windows NT-based profiles. Second, having knowledge of both versions of the registry, I suspect that subtle differences between the two are likely to cause configuration problems in the long run. If anybody suggests that you can use roaming user profiles with any combination other than Windows 2000 and Windows XP Professional, I'd ask for more information and test these scenarios carefully in a lab.

Migrating User Settings to Windows XP

Default user profiles give settings to new users, but what do you do about users who already have user profiles? You can let Windows XP Professional migrate the user profile. Throw disk imaging into the mix and you have a whole different bag of problems. One of the drawbacks of using disk imaging to deploy the operating system is that users lose their documents and settings. This doesn't have to be a barrier to deployment, though. A variety of third-party utilities are available to migrate users' settings. Also, Microsoft provides two tools, one for the user and one for the IT professional.

All these tools work roughly the same way. First, you siphon users' documents and settings off their computers and store them on the network. You install a new disk image to their computers and then you reapply their settings. Users get to keep their documents and settings. Here are the tools that Microsoft provides:

- **Files And Settings Transfer Wizard**   This tool is designed for the user. This wizard is also useful in enterprise environments when employees want to migrate their own documents and settings without the IT department's help.

- **User State Migration Tool (USMT)**   This tool is designed for IT professionals performing large-scale deployments of Windows XP Professional in an enterprise. USMT provides the same functionality as Files And Settings Transfer Wizard, but on a larger scale. USMT gives IT professionals precise control over the documents and settings that it migrates.

Files And Settings Transfer Wizard

The Files And Settings Transfer Wizard is a fast and easy way for you to copy all your documents and settings from your previous configuration to Windows XP Professional. To start it, click Start, All Programs, Accessories, System Tools, Files And Settings Transfer Wizard. It migrates settings in four major groups:

- **Action**   This group includes settings such as the key repeat rate, whether double-clicking a folder opens it in a new window or the same window, and whether you need to double-click or single-click an object to open it.

- **Internet**   This group includes settings that enable you to connect to the Internet and control how Internet Explorer works. These settings include your home page URL, favorites, Internet shortcuts, cookies, security settings, dial-up connections, and so on.

- **Mail**   This group includes settings for connecting to your mail server, your signature file, views, mail rules, local mail, and contacts. The wizard supports only Microsoft Outlook and Outlook Express.

- **Application**   This group includes application settings such as Office 2003 Editions. The wizard migrates only application settings, not the applications. You must reinstall each setting after upgrading to Windows XP Professional.

Files And Settings Transfer Wizard also migrates your documents. It does so by type (*.doc), folder (C:\Documents and Settings\Administrator\My Documents), or name (C:\Documents and Settings\Administrator\My Documents\Jerry.doc). The wizard is preconfigured to copy the most common types of files and the most useful folders. It also gives you the option to change the folders, file types, and file lists.

User State Migration Tool

The User State Migration Tool (USMT) is similar to the Files And Settings Transfer Wizard, but it adds the ability for you to fully customize exactly what it migrates. The USMT is designed for IT professionals only; individual users do not need to use USMT. The tool is designed for large-scale migrations and it requires a domain controller on which to store settings during migration.

The USMT consists of two programs: ScanState.exe and LoadState.exe; and has four migration rule information files: Migapp.inf, Migsys.inf, Miguser.inf, and Sysfiles.inf. ScanState.exe collects users' documents and settings based on the information contained in Migapp.inf, Migsys.inf, Miguser.inf, and Sysfiles.inf. LoadState.exe deposits this user state data on a computer running a clean installation of Windows XP Professional. Both of these tools are on the Windows XP Professional CD in the \Valueadd\Msft\Usmt folder. The shared set of INF files drives the USMT. IT professionals can modify these files to customize the documents and settings that the tool migrates. In fact, during any real deployment project, you'll most likely have to modify the INF files to handle your unique requirements.

Note   The white paper *Step-by-Step Guide to Migrating Files and Settings* is a good guide for learning how to use the USMT. This white paper is on the Web at *http://www.microsoft.com/windowsxp/pro/techinfo/deployment/filesettings /default.asp*.

Scripting as an Alternative

An alternative to customizing a bunch of settings in default user profiles is scripting. Create a script that configures Windows XP Professional user settings per your company's requirements. This assumes that you have a specification (or at the very least, a list of settings that you want to customize for users). Then, run this script each time a new user logs on to the computer. The sections following this one describe this technique as well as using logon scripts to customize user settings.

One problem common to all scripting methods for customizing user profiles is the order of operations. If you run a customization script as soon as the user logs on and the desktop becomes available, then Windows XP Professional might not have created all of the user's settings and files. For example, the operating system creates some shortcuts several seconds after the user gets to the desktop for the first time. The solution to this problem is to wait for Windows XP Professional to completely finish building the user's profile folder before you begin customizing it. You can use the script waitprof.vbs for this. Just run this script in your batch scripts. The script waitprof.vbs returns control only after Windows XP Professional has finished building the user profile. Be careful of where you call this script, by the way. If you call it from a synchronous logon script, your logon script might never finish running because logon scripts are run from the process that waitprof.vbs is waiting to finish. In other words, the logon script won't finish until the logon script finishes (this won't happen). Thus, use waitprof.vbs only with asynchronous logon scripts.

On the Resource Kit CD   The script waitprof.vbs is in the Scripts folder on this book's companion CD.

> **On the Resource Kit CD** Chapter 8, "Windows Settings," provides numerous *.reg*, *.vbs*, and *.cmd* files for settings I frequently configure. Many of these files apply to user profiles (as opposed to per-computer settings in HKLM). These files are on this book's companion CD in the Samples\chap08\settings folder. The file settings.xls, which is in Samples\chap08, describes each of the settings.

Logon Scripts

You can customize user settings by using logon scripts; this assumes that you know the exact registry settings and files that you want to customize. From the logon script, for example, you can import *.reg* files using the command **regedit /s *filename***. This command silently imports the settings contained in the file *filename* into the registry. Alternatively, you can configure registry settings by using Reg.exe, which comes with Windows XP Professional. You can also use the logon script to manipulate files in the user's profile. For example, you can remove shortcuts from the Start menu, copy shortcuts to the Favorites menu, and so on.

The problem is that you want to configure default settings only once. From then on, you want to allow users to change default settings. If this is not true, then you should be managing the setting as a policy. For more information about policies, see Chapter 20. Listing 12-1 is a batch script that shows an example of how to deal with this scenario. First, you use the script guid.wsf to generate a globally unique identifier (GUID). This script just outputs a GUID to the console that you can copy to the clipboard and paste into the batch script. Then, use the script runonce.wsf to run that portion of the script one time for the GUID. The script runonce.wsf just checks for the presence of the GUID in the registry. If it finds the GUID, it sets the environment variable GUIDEXISTS to 1; otherwise, the script sets GUIDEXISTS to 0. You configure settings only if the GUID doesn't exist or if GUIDEXISTS is 0.

Listing 12-1 Logon.cmd

```
@echo off
@rem logon.cmd: configure settings one time only

setlocal enableextensions

  ' Check the GUID
  cscript runonce.wsf /USER {CCC59E6F-20C9-4D5A-A375-7C982106FE4A}

  if GUIDEXISTS==0 (

    cscript waitprof.vbs
```

```
    ' Configure user settings here

   )
   goto end

:end
```

On the Resource Kit CD   The scripts guid.wsf and runonce.wsf are on this book's companion CD in the Scripts folder. To generate a GUID, simply run **guid.wsf** at the command prompt. For more information about guid.wsf, type **guid /?** at the command prompt. For more information about runonce.wsf, type **runonce /?** at the command prompt.

RunOnce Key

An alternative to using logon scripts is to configure a default user profile that calls a batch file to configure settings the first time a user logs on to the computer. Edit the Ntuser.dat hive file in the disk image's Default User folder, adding the command that executes the script to the key HKCU\Software\Microsoft\Windows\CurrentVersion \RunOnce. The Ntuser.dat hive file in the Default User folder doesn't contain the RunOnce key by default, so you must add it. Then add a REG_SZ value to this key—the name is arbitrary—and put the command line you want to execute in it. Each time Windows XP Professional creates a new user profile, it executes the script to customize the user's settings.

Also, you can add a script that customizes the current user profile to HKLM\Software\Microsoft\Windows\CurrentVersion\Run. Windows XP Professional runs this script every time a user logs on to the computer. If you want to configure settings only the first time the user logs on to the computer, use the example shown in Listing 12-1 to check for a GUID in the user's hive file. It configures users' settings only the first time they log on to the computer.

Combination of Both

My favorite solution for environments that don't use logon scripts is a combination of both methods. Here's how it works:

1. Customize the default user profile to run a batch script *Server*\NETLOGON \Settings.cmd. To do so, add a REG_SZ value to HKCU\Software\Microsoft \Windows\CurrentVersion\RunOnce in the default user profile.

2. Create Settings.cmd in *Server*\NETLOGON. This batch script should configure the user profile's settings, files, and so on.

The advantage that this method has is that you're not making any changes to the default user profile that you might have to update in the future. If the batch script doesn't exist, Windows XP Professional just skips it. If the batch script does exist, the operating system executes it. This gives you the flexibility to change your customizations in the future without having to update your default user profiles.

Controlling Just-in-Time Setup

Every IT professional I've spoken with, particularly desktop-deployment types, have the same problem: They want to know how to prevent Windows XP Professional from creating icons for Outlook Express in the Quick Launch toolbar and Start menu when users log on to the computer the first time. More specifically, Windows XP Professional creates these icons when it creates user profiles for new users. These icons aren't in the default user profile, so you can't just remove them from it to avoid creating them.

At this point, you might be asking why you can't just remove those components from Windows XP Professional. Well, you can't remove them, but you can hide their visible entry points by customizing the *[Components]* section of your unattended-setup answer file. For example, you can hide the entry points to Outlook Express by adding *OEAccess=Off* to the *[Components]* section. You can hide the visible entry points to Internet Explorer by adding *IEAccess=Off* and to Windows Media Player by adding *WMAccess=Off*. The reason you can't remove them is that some components are required for the operating system or applications to work properly. For example, Windows XP Professional requires Internet Explorer. If you're deploying Microsoft Office Outlook 2003, you must install Outlook Express because Office Outlook 2003 depends on many of the components in Outlook Express. The best you can do is not advertise these programs so users don't get sidetracked while using their computers.

Windows XP Professional actually creates these icons as part of its *just-in-time* setup process for user profiles. The operating system creates a user profile for a new user and then runs this just-in-time setup process to finish configuring it. Another way to think of the process is that Windows XP Setup defers configuring per-user settings until Windows XP Professional creates user profiles, when decisions about those settings are better made. Controlling the just-in-time setup process is no longer necessary to prevent advertising Outlook Express and Windows Media Player, but I'm including this content for other scenarios you might encounter.

The key HKLM\SOFTWARE\Microsoft\Active Setup\Installed Components drives the just-in-time setup process. Each subkey is a component. For example, the subkey {2179C5D3-EBFF-11CF-B6FD-00AA00B4E220} is for NetShow. Within each subkey, you might see the REG_EXPAND_SZ value StubPath. If this value exists, Windows XP Professional executes the command it contains when the operating system creates a new user profile. If you don't see this value or if the value is empty, it does nothing. So to keep Windows XP Professional from running a component's just-in-time setup process, remove the value StubPath from that component's subkey in Installed Components. The next several sections describe how to use this hack to control different components. You should include changes to Installed Components on disk images. Chapter 15 describes how to deploy settings on your disk images.

> **Note** Why care if Outlook Express has an icon on the Quick Launch tool-bar? It's distracting and keeps users from their work. Specifically, your enterprise isn't likely to use Outlook Express as its mail client; you probably deployed a full-featured client such as Office Outlook 2003 or similar. If you advertise Outlook Express on the desktop, users will have two mail clients. If that doesn't confuse them and cause problems, it'll certainly tease them into playing with Outlook Express. This goes for many of the other programs that come with Windows XP Professional, including Windows Media Player, NetMeeting, and so on.

Outlook Express

When Windows XP Professional creates a new user profile, it executes the command in the REG_EXPAND_SZ value HKLM\SOFTWARE\Microsoft\Active Setup\Installed Components\{44BBA840-CC51-11CF-AAFA-00AA00B6015C}\StubPath, which (among other things) creates the Outlook Express icon in the Start menu and on the Quick Launch toolbar. This command is **"%ProgramFiles% \Outlook Express \setup50.exe" /APP:OE/CALLER:WINNT /user /install**. To prevent this command from running, remove the StubPath value or change its name to **HideStubPath**, as shown in Figure 12-7.

Name	Type	Data
(Default)	REG_SZ	Microsoft Outlook Express 6
CloneUser	REG_DWORD	0x00000001 (1)
ComponentID	REG_SZ	MailNews
HideStubPath	REG_EXPAND_SZ	"%ProgramFiles%\Outlook Express\setup50.exe" /APP:OE /C...
IsInstalled	REG_DWORD	0x00000001 (1)
Locale	REG_SZ	EN
Version	REG_SZ	6,0,2600,0000

Figure 12-7 Prevent Windows XP Professional from creating Outlook Express shortcuts by hiding StubPath.

This customization is common on disk images, so I'm providing you with a script to do it. Save the script shown in Listing 12-2 to a text file with the *.inf* extension. Right-click it and then click Install. Keep this script handy as a disk-image customization tool.

Listing 12-2

```
[Version]
Signature=$CHICAGO$

[DefaultInstall]
DelReg=Reg.Settings

[Reg.Settings]
HKLM,SOFTWARE\Microsoft\Active Setup\Installed Components\{44BBA840-
CC51-11CF-AAFA-00AA00B6015C},StubPath
```

> **Tip**   An alternative to hiding the Outlook Express icon is making Outlook
> Express a newsreader client only. Add the option **/outnews** to the target of
> each icon (put this command-line option outside of the quotation marks).
> When users choose the shortcut, Outlook Express opens with all its news-
> client features working but its mail-client features don't work. This is useful
> in scenarios in which you must provide access to newsgroups to users,
> such as developers, who usually require access to Microsoft and developer
> newsgroups. To easily deploy this customized Outlook Express shortcut,
> add it to the default user profile. Alternatively, because this hack usually
> accompanies an Office Outlook 2003 deployment, you can add this short-
> cut to your Office 2003 Editions transform.

Windows Media Player

Windows Media Player has two subkeys in HKLM\SOFTWARE\Microsoft\Active
Setup\Installed Components:

- {22d6f312-b0f6-11d0-94ab-0080c74c7e95} is for version 6.4 and the value
  StubPath is **rundll32.exe advpack.dll,LaunchINFSection C:\WINDOWS
  \INF\mplayer2.inf,PerUserStub.NT**.

- {6BF52A52-394A-11d3-B153-00C04F79FAA6} is for version 8 and the value
  StubPath is **rundll32.exe advpack.dll,LaunchINFSection C:\WINDOWS
  \INF\wmp.inf,PerUserStub**.

These values are responsible for the numerous Windows Media Player shortcuts. Remove both StubPath values to prevent Windows XP Professional from adding the Windows Media Player shortcut to the Quick Launch toolbar. Also, if you
want to keep the Windows Media Player shortcut off the top of the Start menu,
remove it from the default user profile. You also find Windows Media Player shortcuts

in the All Users profile folder in %SYSTEMDRIVE%\Documents and Settings\All Users\Start Menu\Programs\Accessories\Entertainment. Ideally, remove the shortcut from your network-based Default User profile and then remove the shortcut from the All Users profile folder on your disk images.

Desktop Themes

Preventing Windows XP Professional from configuring desktop themes when it creates a user profile is an easy way to revert to the classic user interface (see Figure 12-8). Remove or hide the REG_EXPAND_SZ value StubPath from the key HKLM\SOFTWARE \Microsoft\Active Setup\Installed Components\{2C7339CF-2B09-4501-B3F3-F3508C9228ED}. The command that this value contains is **%SystemRoot% \system32\regsvr32.exe /s /n /i:/UserInstall %SystemRoot% \system32 \themeui.dll**.

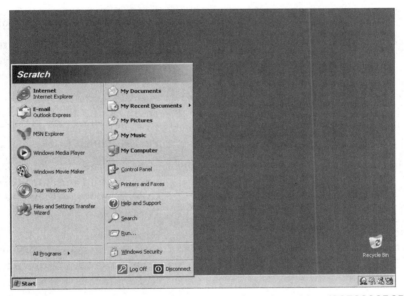

Figure 12-8 Removing the value StubPath from the subkey {2C7339CF-2B09-4501-B3F3-F3508C9228ED} prevents Windows XP Professional from configuring the new user interface.

Other Shortcuts

The key HKLM\SOFTWARE\Microsoft\Active Setup\Installed Components contains other components with StubPath values that I haven't mentioned yet. You can prevent Windows XP Professional from configuring any of the components when the operating system creates a user profile by removing or hiding the StubPath value in the corresponding subkey. Table 12-5 lists all the components I've already described plus the ones I haven't.

Keep in mind that even if you prevent Windows XP Professional from configuring every component I show in the table, you might still have unwanted icons. These icons come from the Default User and All User profile folders. Remove the shortcuts that you don't want from any default user profile you've deployed. Remove the shortcuts you don't want from the All Users folder on your disk images.

Table 12-5   Components in Installed Components

Component	Subkey	StubPath
Address Book 6	{7790769C-0471-11d2-AF11-00C04FA35D02}	**"%ProgramFiles%\Outlook Express\setup50.exe" /APP:WAB /CALLER:WINNT /user /install**
Internet Explorer 6	{89820200-ECBD-11cf-8B85-00AA005B4383}	**%SystemRoot%\system32\ie4uinit.exe**
Internet Explorer Access	{ACC563BC-4266-43f0-B6ED-9D38C4202C7E}	**rundll32 iesetup.dll,IEAccessUserInst**
Microsoft Outlook Express 6	{44BBA840-CC51-11CF-AAFA-00AA00B6015C}	**"%ProgramFiles%\Outlook Express\setup50.exe" /APP:OE /CALLER:WINNT /user /install**
Microsoft Windows Media Player 6.4	{22d6f312-b0f6-11d0-94ab-0080c74c7e95}	**rundll32.exe advpack.dll,LaunchINFSection C:\WINDOWS\INF\mplayer2.inf, PerUserStub.NT**
Microsoft Windows Media Player 8	{6BF52A52-394A-11d3-B153-00C04F79FAA6}	**rundll32.exe advpack.dll,LaunchINFSection C:\WINDOWS\INF\wmp.inf, PerUserStub**
NetMeeting 3.01	{44BBA842-CC51-11CF-AAFA-00AA00B6015B}	**rundll32.exe advpack.dll,LaunchINFSection C:\WINDOWS\INF\msnetmtg.inf, NetMtg.Install.PerUser.NT**
Theme Component	{2C7339CF-2B09-4501-B3F3-F3508C9228ED}	**%SystemRoot%\system32\regsvr32.exe /s /n /i:/UserInstall %SystemRoot%\system32\themeui.dll**
Windows Desktop Update	{89820200-ECBD-11cf-8B85-00AA005B4340}	**regsvr32.exe /s /n /i:U shell32.dll**
Windows Messenger 4.0	{5945c046-1e7d-11d1-bc44-00c04fd912be}	**rundll32.exe advpack.dll,LaunchINFSection C:\WINDOWS\INF\msmsgs.inf, BLC.Install.PerUser**

> **Caution**   Be wary of preventing Windows XP Professional from configuring the Windows Desktop Update. This component is necessary to provide resiliency for Windows Installer–based applications. For example, when a user opens the shortcut of a Windows Installer–based application, the Windows Desktop Update passes it on to Windows Installer so that Windows Installer can check and repair the application, if necessary. If you prevent the operating system from configuring the Windows Desktop Update, you remove Windows Installer from the process. Even if you prevent Windows Installer from repairing broken shortcuts, it doesn't prevent Windows Installer from repairing components within an application.

AutoProf Profile Maker

The tools that this chapter describes will get the job done, but they aren't always cost-effective. In large organizations, you can end up with a mish-mash of batch scripts, *.vbs* scripts, *.reg* files, and other files that become difficult to manage. Auto-Prof (*http://www.autoprof.com*) publishes a settings-management product called Profile Maker (see Figure 12-9). In my office (and on job sites where I have the opportunity), I prefer using AutoProf Profile Maker to deploy user settings rather than using other techniques and products. In the following list, I describe some of the benefits of using Profile Maker to deploy settings (there are many other benefits, and I encourage you to visit the AutoProf Web site at *http://www.autoprof.com* to learn more about it):

- **Easy installation**   Profile Maker is easy to deploy and configure. It doesn't require a huge training commitment, and you can be proficient with it in minutes.

- **Familiar user interface**   Profile Maker has a user interface with which you're already familiar: Microsoft Management Console (MMC). It looks and feels like any of the Microsoft tools you have used in this environment.

- **Configure all your unmanaged settings in one place**   Profile Maker is robust enough to configure any setting you need to deliver. If Profile Maker doesn't support the setting directly, you can embed a batch or *.vbs* script in your configuration. You don't need lengthy logon scripts, *.reg* file collections, and so on. The types of settings you can configure are near-limitless, and they include the following:

- Transmission Control Protocol/Internet Protocol (TCP/IP) printer connections

- Shared printer connections

- Network drive mappings

- Outlook profiles and settings

- Settings for all versions of Office

- Settings for Internet Explorer versions 5 and 6

- Service Pack and hot-fix installations

- Windows Installer setup database installation

- Shortcut, file, and folder manipulation

- System policy

- Registry and *.ini* file settings

- **Common settings have user interfaces** Profile Maker provides a user interface for some of the most common settings, so you don't have to know where they are in the registry or file system. For example, the product provides a user interface for configuring Internet Explorer, Outlook profiles, printer connections, network drive mappings, and so on.

- **Extend Profile Maker with new capabilities** If Profile Maker doesn't provide a way to configure a particular setting or perform a particular task, you can add scripts to your configuration. For example, you can add VBScript, JScript, and batch scripts to your configuration, accomplishing almost any required task as part of your total configuration. You can also run any command, display message boxes, or prompt users for information as part of your configuration.

- **Filter settings using numerous criteria** Profile Maker allows you to filter individual or collections of settings using numerous criteria. For example, you can configure settings just for laptop computers, computers with a certain amount of memory, or computers that belong to a particular organizational unit. Another example is that you can use a combination of the file match and registry match filters to check for a certain version of a program file before applying a particular setting. Table 12-6 describes the different ways in which you can filter settings when using Profile Maker.

Table 12-6   Profile Maker Filters

Type	Filters
Hardware	■ Windows Management Instrumentation (WMI) query ■ Dial-up connection ■ Portable computer ■ Battery present ■ Personal Computer Memory Card International Association (PCMCIA) present ■ Central processing unit (CPU) speed ■ Disk space ■ Random access memory (RAM)available
Identity	■ Internet Protocol (IP) address range ■ Media Access Control (MAC) address range ■ Domain and workgroup ■ Organization unit ■ Site membership ■ Computer and *Domain Name Server (DNS)* name ■ Security group ■ User match
Software	■ Operating system ■ Terminal session ■ System/user language ■ File match ■ Registry match ■ Environment variable value
Other	■ Message box ■ Run once ■ Recurrence ■ Time range

- **Deliver settings in locked-down environments**   Profile Maker allows you to configure per-computer settings in locked-down environments, in which users are restricted and can't change those settings.

- **Support heterogeneous networks**   Profile Maker includes support for most versions of Windows, including the ubiquitous Windows 98. You can use one tool to deploy unmanaged settings to different versions of Windows, particularly as you're migrating to Windows XP Professional.

Figure 12-9   AutoProf Profile Maker greatly simplifies user profile deployment.

On the Resource Kit CD   To help you evaluate AutoProf Profile Maker and hopefully use it to deploy settings, I included a variety of configuration files on this book's companion CD. They are in the Samples\chap12 folder. After installing Profile Maker, simply drag and drop these files on to the Profile Maker Configurations node.

Best Practices

The following are best practices for creating and deploying default user profiles:

- **Avoid using default user profiles to customize settings, if possible.** Default user profiles aren't the most robust method for deploying user settings. If you have other technology available, such as AutoProf Profile Maker (*http://www.autoprof.com*), use it instead.

- **Use the right type of user profile.**   Use roaming user profiles in environments in which users frequently use different computers, and those computers have similar hardware and software. Otherwise, use local user profiles and redirect their My Documents folders to the network.

- **Customize default user profiles surgically, if possible.** The brute-force method for deploying user profiles carries with it a lot of baggage. Editing the existing Default User folder's Ntuser.dat file using Registry Editor is the simplest method. Otherwise, use the more precise methods of creating a default user profile that this chapter describes.

- **Customize the default user profile to run a configuration script on the network.** This method works primarily for simple configurations, but it gives you the flexibility to update settings later without having to update a default user profile: You simply update the script.

Part III

Distributing

Chapter 13

Unattended Setup

Most distribution methods, including unattended setup and disk imaging, rely on running Microsoft Windows XP Setup with the right combination of command-line options. This chapter describes the options for both versions of Windows XP Setup: Winnt.exe, which is the 16-bit version, and Winnt32.exe, the 32-bit version. It also gives examples of the best options to use in different scenarios.

Checklist

- Have you chosen between performing an upgrade or clean installation? If not, see Chapter 1, "Deployment Plan."

- Have you chosen a distribution method? If not, see Chapter 1, "Deployment Plan."

- Have you designed and built the Windows XP Professional answer file for use with Windows XP Setup? If not, see Chapter 6, "Answer Files."

- Have you designed and built the Windows XP Professional distribution point? If not, see Chapter 7, "Distribution Points."

- Have you specified and implemented default user and computer settings? If not, see Chapter 3, "Windows Configuration," Chapter 8, "Windows Settings," and Chapter 12, "User Profiles."

- Have you planned and designed any preinstallation tasks, such as partitioning and formatting computers' hard disks? See Chapter 3 for more information.

- If performing an unattended installation using Windows XP Setup, have you chosen the best methods for running the Windows XP Setup command on target computers? See the section "Distribution Methods."

- If performing clean installations, have you created a plan for backing up and restoring users' settings? If not, see Chapter 18, "User State Migration."

- If you're starting Windows XP Setup using MS-DOS, have you created startup media? For more information, see the section "Creating Startup Media," later in this chapter on page 383.

Distribution Methods

Unattended installations are usually performed from a network distribution point. However, there are instances when a distribution share is not appropriate and you need to use media, rather than a distribution point, to perform an unattended installation. This section helps you determine which method is more appropriate for your organization's needs.

More Info   See "Designing Unattended Installations," which is part of the Windows Server 2003 Deployment Kit's *Automating and Customizing Installations* book at *http://www.microsoft.com/technet/prodtechnol/windowsserver2003 /proddocs/deployguide/acicb_ui_overview.asp* for additional information about running Windows XP Setup.

On the Resource Kit CD   See "Unattended Installation Worksheet" in the file dist04.doc on this book's companion CD in the Aids folder. Use this worksheet to document the distribution methods you're using.

Distribution Points

A distribution point contains the Windows XP Professional source files, as well as any device drivers or other files that are required to customize the installation. Chapter 7 describes how to create distribution points. You typically create one distribution share for each operating system you are deploying. By using a network distribution point to perform an unattended installation, you can perform the following tasks:

- **Copy folders and files to target computers** A distribution point can contain special folders and files that Windows XP Setup copies to a computer's hard disk during an unattended installation. For example, if you want to create a Scripts folder on drive C of your target computers, you can add the Scripts folder to your distribution point, and Windows XP Setup will automatically copy them to your target computers during installation.

- **Copy device drivers to target computers** A distribution point contains folders for storing mass storage device drivers, HALs (Hardware Abstraction Layer), and Plug and Play device drivers. Windows XP Setup copies the contents of these folders to a computer's hard disk during an unattended installation. See Chapter 7 for more information about adding device drivers to a distribution point.

- **Copy a Sysprep folder to target computers** A distribution point can contain a Sysprep folder, which can be used to store Sysprep files and the Sysprep.inf file. This is useful if using image-based installations and you want to use unattended installation to create the disk images. In this case, you can add a Sysprep folder to the distribution point, and Windows XP Setup will automatically create the Sysprep folder on the disk image when you perform an unattended installation. For more information, see Chapter 15, "Disk Imaging with Sysprep."

Use a network distribution point to perform your unattended installation if you want to do the following:

- **Increase consistency** When you use a network distribution point, you create a single source for system files, device drivers, and customized installation files that Windows XP Setup copies to each target computer, which ensures that each unattended installation is consistent throughout your organization.

- **Reduce administrative costs** All system files, device drivers, and customized installation files are stored in a central location, which reduces the cost of updating and changing system files and device drivers. For example, if you need to upgrade an existing device driver or add new device drivers, you have to make the change only in the network distribution point. You do not need to create new answer files or create new floppy disks or CDs.

■ **Control access to your installation files**   You can secure a network distribution point by using file and folder permissions, which let you specify the users and groups who can gain access to your installation files. By default, in Windows Server 2003, the Everyone group is granted read-only permissions when you share a folder. Therefore, when you create a network distribution point, you need to grant write permissions to all the users who are responsible for configuring the distribution share.

In addition, network distribution points are useful if you are performing other types of automated installations, such as image-based or Remote Installation Services (RIS) installations. In these cases, you can use unattended installation with network distribution points to create consistent disk images that are easy to modify and update.

Despite the advantages, there are several disadvantages that might preclude you from using a network distribution point. If any of the following conditions are true, you probably do not want to use a distribution share to perform unattended installations:

■ **Slow network connections**   Accessing a distribution point across a slow network connection, such as a dial-up connection or a slow wide area network (WAN) connection, is overly time-consuming and impractical. I recommend that you do not use a network distribution point if your target computers use a slow network connection to reach it.

■ **Broadcast networks**   If the network uses hubs, the network traffic generated during an unattended installation might reduce bandwidth available to production applications. If upgrading to switches or using isolated network segments to perform the unattended installations is not possible, unattended installations from a network share might not be a good choice.

■ **Minimal file server capacity**   Network distribution points are typically stored on file servers. If your file servers do not have sufficient capacity to store all your distribution points, or if your file servers cannot handle an increase in file throughput during your rollout, you cannot use a network distribution point.

■ **Minimal number of unattended installations**   You need to create, test, and maintain network distribution points. If you're performing only a few unattended installations, it is probably not cost-effective or efficient to use them. However, if you are performing image-based or RIS installations and you're using unattended installations to create only a few disk images, distribution points are useful and cost-effective because they ensure consistency among disk images and make it easy to make configuration changes.

If you choose to use network distribution points, you can save them on multiple servers. This allows Windows XP Setup to copy files simultaneously from several servers, speeding up the file-copy phase of Windows XP Setup. In addition, you can use Distributed File System (DFS) to increase the availability of your network distribution points.

> **More Info** For more information about copying installation files from multiple servers, see the section "Running Winnt32.exe," later in this chapter on page 386. For more information about DFS, see the Windows Server 2003 Resource Kit.

Media Distribution

Media distribution is useful if you're deploying computers in remote locations that do not have high-speed network connections or in locations that do not have a local IT department available to set up and perform the unattended installation. Media distribution is also useful as an alternative installation method when network congestion limits your ability to access a network distribution point or when a target computer has a malfunctioning network adapter.

To use media distribution instead of a network distribution point, you use the Windows XP Professional CD to start the target computer. Then, you insert a floppy disk containing an answer file into the floppy disk drive. Windows XP Setup reads the answer file, copies the appropriate installation files from the operating system CD to the target computer's hard disk, and then configures the target computer based on the settings specified in the answer file. Using an operating system CD to perform an unattended installation has the following requirements (unless you've built a customized installation CD that alleviates these requirements):

- The target computer must have a floppy disk drive.

- The target computer must have a bootable CD-ROM drive, and the boot-order in the target computer's BIOS must list the CD-ROM drive before the hard disk.

- The answer file must be named Winnt.sif, and it must be saved on a floppy disk.

- The installation files must all be present on the operating system CD; you cannot access supplemental device drivers or files that are not on the CD.

- The answer file must have a *[Data]* section, and the entries within the *[Data]* section must be configured appropriately for an unattended installation that uses an operating system CD.

In addition, using an operating system CD to perform an unattended installation has the following limitations:

- You cannot use a Uniqueness Database (UDB) file to modify the answer file.

- You cannot use Dynamic Update to add updated installation files and device driver files during installation.

- You cannot perform an upgrade—only a clean installation. To perform an upgrade, you must have an operating system running on the target computer, which you don't have when you start a computer with the operating system CD.

- You cannot chain the installation of applications as described in Chapter 11, "Chaining Installations."

Despite the requirements and limitations, there are some advantages to performing an unattended installation with the operating system CD. Namely, you can configure the answer file to do the following:

- **Configure disks**   By using the *Repartition* setting in the *[Unattended]* section, you can delete all partitions on the target computer and create a new partition that is formatted with the NTFS file system.

- **Skip Mini-Setup**   By using the *UnattendSwitch* parameter in the *[Unattended]* section, you can prevent the Mini-Setup program from running when the target computer is started for the first time after unattended installation is completed.

- **Force BIOS startup**   By using the *UseBIOSToBoot* parameter in the *[Data]* section, you can force a target computer to use the BIOS to start, even if Windows XP Setup detects that it is more appropriate to use a device miniport driver to start the computer. The current generation of hardware uses the BIOS to start the computer, so this entry is rarely required. However, on computers with large drives that support extended int13 BIOS calls, this might not be the default behavior. Using the BIOS starts computers faster by eliminating possible delays caused by a miniport driver. Do not use this entry unless you are sure that the BIOS supports the extended int13 functions.

If you're using an operating system CD to perform an unattended installation, you need to configure settings in the *[Data]* section of the answer file. Listing 13-1 shows what this looks like. The Answer File Settings Worksheet (dist01.doc) on this book's companion CD in the Aids folder helps you document these settings. The following list describes each setting in more detail:

- `AutoPartition = 1`   Installs Windows XP Professional on the first available partition that has adequate space for a Windows XP Professional installation and does not already contain an installed version of Windows. Either omit the *AutoPartition* setting from your answer file or set the value of *AutoPartition* to *1*. If *AutoPartition* is set to *1*, the */tempdrive* option of Winnt32.exe is ignored by Windows XP Setup. If you do not set the value, the text-mode phase of Windows XP Setup installs Windows XP Professional on the partition where Win_nt.~ls is located (the location to which Windows XP Setup copies the source files during the text-mode phase).

- `MsDosInitiated = 0`   Informs Windows XP Setup that an unattended installation is running directly from the operating system CD. You must set this value to *0*. If you do not set the value to *0*, installation fails at the beginning of the GUI-mode phase of Windows XP Setup.

- `UnattendedInstall = Yes`   Informs Windows XP Setup that an unattended installation is running directly from the operating system CD. You must set this value to *Yes* if you are installing Windows XP Professional from the operating system CD.

- `UseBIOSToBoot = 0|1`   Specifies whether Windows XP Setup uses the BIOS to start the computer, even though Windows XP Setup might detect that it is best to use a device miniport driver to start the computer. If you want to use the BIOS to start the computer, you must set this value to *1*. The default setting is *0*. Do not use this entry unless you are sure that the BIOS supports the extended int13 functions.

- `Repartition = Yes|No`   Specifies whether to delete all partitions on the first drive of the target computer and to reformat the drive with NTFS. The default setting is *No*. Change this to *Yes* if you want Windows XP Setup to manually run the GUI-mode phase of Windows XP Setup (the text-mode phase of Windows XP Setup is automated, but the GUI-mode phase of Windows XP Setup is not). If you leave the default setting and Windows XP Setup detects a Windows installation on the first drive of the target computer, Windows XP Setup will stop during the text-mode phase of Windows XP Setup and ask you whether you want to delete the existing Windows installation.

- `UnattendSwitch = Yes|No`   Specifies whether Windows XP Setup skips Mini-Setup when installing Windows XP Professional. Use only with Winnt.exe. The default setting is *No*.

Listing 13-1   Media Distribution Answer Files

```
[Data]
AutoPartition=1
MsDosInitiated = 0
UnattendedInstall = Yes
UseBIOSToBoot = 1            ; Values are 0 or 1
[Unattended]
Repartition = Yes           ; Values are Yes or No
UnattendSwitch = Yes        ; Values are Yes or No
```

Setup Phases

Windows XP Setup runs in three phases:

- **File-copy mode**   In the file-copy phase, Windows XP Setup copies Microsoft Windows XP Professional source files to the target computer's hard disk. Windows XP Setup reboots the computer after copying the source files to the target computer. If additional files are included in the distribution point and you've set `OemPreinstall = Yes`, the file-copy phase also copies these to the target computer's hard disk.

- **Text mode**   In the text-mode phase, Windows XP Setup determines the computer's basic hardware configuration (CPU, motherboard, mass-storage controllers, file systems, and memory), installs the basic operating system necessary to continue, and creates the installation folders. This phase is distinguishable because the user interface is text-based. Windows XP Setup reboots the computer at the end of text mode.

- **GUI mode**   In the GUI-mode phase, Windows XP Setup configures the computer's hardware and network settings; sets the local Administrator password; and allows users to customize the installation (unless you've fully automated the installation by using an answer file). This phase is distinguishable because the user interface is graphical. Windows XP Setup reboots the computer at the end of GUI mode.

Preinstallation Tasks

You perform preinstallation tasks before installing Windows XP Professional. Preinstallation tasks can include the following:

- **Target analysis**   Before installing Windows XP Professional, you can analyze the target computer to ensure that it meets the requirements you specified in your deployment plan (see Chapter 1).

- **User state migration**   When you migrate user state, you save user settings and data to external media or a network location so you can restore those settings and data after installing Windows XP Professional. See the section "State Migration," later in this chapter on page 377.

■ **Disk configuration** Before performing a clean installation of Windows XP Professional, you can partition and format the hard disk. Chapter 3 helped you plan your disk configuration. For more information about this preinstallation task, see the section "Disk Configuration," later in this chapter on page 378.

■ **Dynamic Update** Dynamic Update downloads updated installation files and device drivers from the Windows Update Web site and installs them as part of your unattended installation. See the section "Dynamic Update," later in this chapter on page 380.

Traditionally, technicians visit each target computer to perform these preinstallation tasks. Preferably, you can automate these tasks so that they occur as part of the fully unattended Windows XP Professional installation process. Batch scripts can automate a large portion of these preinstallation tasks, but some tasks will require more advanced Windows Script Host scripts.

> **On the Resource Kit CD** See "Unattended Installation Worksheet" in the file dist04.doc on this book's companion CD in the Aids folder. Use this worksheet to document preinstallation requirements for the unattended installation.

State Migration

Chapter 1 and Chapter 18 help you create a user state migration plan. You must migrate local user state if you want to restore any of the following settings after installing Windows XP Professional:

■ User data that you want to be available to the end user. User data includes such things as documents, e-mail messages, spreadsheets, and databases.

■ User settings, such as desktop settings, shortcuts, and Internet Explorer Favorites.

■ Application settings, such as application-specific keyboard shortcuts, spell-checking options, and default file locations.

Microsoft provides two tools for migrating user data and settings. The tool you use depends on your environment:

■ **Files and Settings Transfer Wizard** Designed for home users and small office users, the wizard is also useful in a corporate network environment for employees who get a new computer and need to migrate their own files and settings without the support of an IT department or helpdesk.

■ **User State Migration Tool** Designed for IT administrators who perform large deployments of Windows XP Professional in a corporate environment, the User State Migration Tool provides the same functionality as the wizard, but on a large scale targeted at migrating multiple users. The User State Migration Tool gives administrators command-line precision for customizing specific settings, such as unique modifications to the registry. Chapter 18 describes how to use this tool in detail.

To account for this preinstallation task in your unattended installation, you run the command that exports user data and settings to external media or the network. You can automate this task by including the commands required to run it in the batch script that you use to run the installation process.

Disk Configuration

Chapter 5 helps you plan your disk configuration. You need to configure disks as a preinstallation task if you want to change the size of the system partition on target computers; repartition or reformat the system partition on target computers and you're not using an operating system CD to start Windows XP Setup; or you want to create and format extra partitions on target computers. You do not need to create a disk configuration plan in the following situations:

■ You want to extend the system partition; create and format extra partitions during or after the installation; or convert an existing system partition to NTFS. These tasks do not require substantial analysis and planning, and are relatively easy to perform by configuring answer file settings or running commands or scripts from the answer file.

■ You are using an operating system CD to perform an unattended installation, and you want to repartition and format the system partition on target computers. In this case, you can use the *Repartition* setting in the *[Unattended]* section of the unattended installation answer file to repartition and format the system partition before the unattended installation begins.

Even if your configuration plan specified how to partition and format the target computers' hard disks, it might not have specified which tools to use. The following tools are available for configuring target computers' hard disks:

■ **MS-DOS or Windows 98 disk configuration tools** You can start a target computer by using an MS-DOS or a Windows 98 boot disk, and then use the Fdisk.exe and Format.exe commands to partition and format the hard disk before you perform an unattended installation. This works only if you want to format your disks with the FAT or FAT32 file systems. If you want your hard disks formatted with NT file system (NTFS), you will have to use the Convert.exe command to convert the FAT or FAT32 file system to NTFS after you have installed the operating system onto the target computer, or you will have to use the Oformat.exe command.

> **On the Resource Kit CD** For more information about disk tools, including commands for configuring disks, see "Microsoft Windows Corporate Deployment Tools User's Guide" (Deploy.chm, which is in Deploy.cab in the Support\Tools folder of the Windows XP Professional CD).

- **Third-party disk configuration tools** Some third-party disk-management programs provide a bootable floppy disk or CD that allows you to partition and format hard disks. If you use a third-party program to partition or format a disk, be sure that the third-party program creates partitions that are compatible with NTFS 3.1, which is the version of NTFS that is used in Windows XP Professional. I tend to use Gdisk.exe, which comes with Symantec Ghost Corporate Edition (*http://www.symantec.com*), because I can use it to partition and format a disk from the command prompt quickly. Other vendors supply similar tools.

- **Windows Preinstallation Environment** You can start a target computer by using a Microsoft Windows Preinstallation Environment (Windows PE) and then use the Diskpart.exe command to partition the hard disk and the Format.exe command to format the hard disk. Windows PE is a bootable operating system that provides limited operating system functionality for performing preinstallation tasks. For more information about using Windows PE to configure disks, see Chapter 14, "Preinstallation Environment."

Each method for configuring disks has advantages and disadvantages. They boil down to two issues. The first is whether you must restart the computer before running Windows XP Setup. The first two options usually require that you restart the computer. You don't have to restart the computer after preparing it using Diskpart.exe and before running Windows XP Setup, however. In fact, the sample distribution point chap07 in the Samples folder on this book's companion CD contains batch scripts that automatically partition, format, and then run Windows XP Setup. The second issue is whether you can format the disk with NTFS or must first format it with FAT or FAT 32 and then convert it to NTFS later. Oformat.exe and Diskpart.exe both can format the disk with NTFS. Other utilities might not be able to format the disk with NTFS.

To account for this preinstallation task in your unattended installation, you can put the commands that partition and format the hard disk in the batch script that runs Windows XP Setup. If you must restart the computer after reformatting the hard disk, intervention is required; otherwise, if you're using Windows PE and Diskpart.exe to prepare the hard disk, you can run Windows XP Setup immediately after formatting the disk.

Dynamic Update

You can use Dynamic Update to update installation files and device drivers that are used by Windows XP Setup during an unattended installation. Dynamic Update does not replace Windows Update; it downloads only a small subset of Windows Update files and device driver files that prevent critical errors from occurring during the installation process. The files that Dynamic Update downloads include the following:

- **Updated installation files**   These can include system files, in-box device drivers (drives that come with the operating system), Setup information (*.inf*) files required during upgrades, DLL files used by the Winnt32.exe setup program, and file assemblies (*.asm* files). Dynamic Update downloads only replacements for existing installation files. It does not add new installation files to the setup process.

- **New device drivers**   These can include new device drivers that are critical to the setup process and are not on the operating system CD. New device driver files are not replacements for in-box device drivers. Replacements for in-box device drivers are considered updated installation files.

You can use Dynamic Update only if you are installing on target computers that have an existing connection to your network or the Internet. For example, you can use Dynamic Update if your target computer is running Microsoft Windows 2000 and it is connected to your network when you run Windows XP Setup. In addition, you can use Dynamic Update only with Winnt32.exe; you cannot use Dynamic Update with Winnt.exe. By default, Dynamic Update is disabled during an unattended installation of Windows XP Professional.

> **Note**   If you're upgrading a computer that is running Microsoft Windows 95 with Internet Explorer 4.01, you need to upgrade to Internet Explorer 5.0 or a higher version of Internet Explorer. The version of Secure Sockets Layer (SSL) in Internet Explorer 4.01 is not compatible with Dynamic Update and will cause Dynamic Update to fail.

To account for Dynamic Update in your unattended installation, you must complete three steps. The first is to identify and download dynamic updates. The second is to prepare the Dynamic Update files. Last is to configure the answer file and your Winnt32.exe command-line options to use Dynamic Update. The first two steps are manual processes that you complete before running Windows XP Setup. The last step is easily automated by customizing your answer file or Winnt32.exe command-line options.

More Info For more information about preparing Dynamic Update, see Chapter 19, "Software Update Services." For more information about customizing answer files for Dynamic Update, see Chapter 6. For more information about enabling Dynamic Update using the Winnt32.exe command-line options, see the section "Running Winnt32.exe," later in this chapter on page 386.

On the Resource Kit CD The companion CD contains the "Dynamic Update Worksheet" to help you plan for the Dynamic Update feature. It's the file dist05.doc in the Aids folder.

Running Winnt.exe

Winnt.exe is the 16-bit version of Windows XP Setup, and it works only on computers running legacy operating systems, such as MS-DOS, Microsoft Windows 3.1, or Microsoft Windows for Workgroups. Because none of these operating systems is on the upgrade path for Windows XP Professional, you can use Winnt.exe only for clean installations. Also, due to memory requirements, Microsoft recommends that you only use Winnt.exe from MS-DOS and not from 16-bit version of Windows.

On the Resource Kit CD Legacy operating systems don't support long filenames. If you start Windows XP Setup on computers running legacy operating systems, it will copy files from the distribution point or media using short (8.3) filenames. To restore long filenames during installation, create $$Rename.txt files in the distribution point. For more information about creating $$Rename.txt files, see Chapter 7, which provides the script rename.wsf. This script automatically detects long filenames and creates $$Rename.txt files for the distribution point. The script rename.wsf is on this book's companion CD in the Scripts folder.

You can use Winnt.exe to install Windows XP Professional from a distribution point on the network or media, such as a CD. For example, you can start the computer using MS-DOS and then run Winnt.exe from a network share that contains a distribution point or from a CD that contains the Windows XP Professional source files. In order to use Winnt.exe to connect to a distribution point on a network using

MS-DOS, you must create an MS-DOS boot disk that contains network support. In order to run Winnt.exe from a CD, you must create an MS-DOS boot disk that contains CD-ROM support. For more information, see "Creating Startup Media," later in this chapter on page 383. The following describes the syntax of Winnt.exe, and Table 13-1 describes each command-line option that Winnt.exe supports:

```
winnt [/s:[sourcepath]] [/t:[tempdrive]] [/u:[answer_file]]
[/udf:id [,UDB_file]] [/r:folder] [/rx:folder] [/e:command] [/a]
```

Table 13-1   Winnt.exe Command-Line Options

Option	Description
/s:sourcepath	Specifies the source location of the Windows XP Professional files. The location must be a full path of the form *x:\path* or *\\server\share\path*. The default is the current folder.
/t:tempdrive	Directs Windows XP Setup to place temporary files on the specified drive and to install Windows XP Professional on that drive. If you do not specify a location, Windows XP Setup attempts to locate a drive for you. If the computer contains multiple hard disks or multiple partitions, you must use **/t** to specify the disk or partition on which you want Windows XP Setup to install Windows XP Professional.
/u:answer_file	Performs unattended installation with an answer file. The answer file provides answers to some or all of the messages that the end user normally responds to during Windows XP Setup. If you use **/u**, you must also use **/s** to specify the location of the Windows XP Professional source files. For more information about creating answer files, see Chapter 6.
/udf:id [,UDB_file]	Indicates an identifier (*id*) that Windows XP Setup uses to specify how a UDB file modifies an answer file. The UDB file overrides values in the answer file, and the identifier determines which values in the UDB file Windows XP Setup uses. If no *UDB_file* is specified, Windows XP Setup prompts the user to insert a disk that contains the file $Unique$.udb. For example, **/udf:RAS_user, Our_company.udb** overrides settings specified for the identifier **RAS_user** in the file Our_company.udb. See the section "Using UDB Files," later in this chapter on page 393 for more information.
/r:folder	Specifies an optional folder in the distribution point or media's I386 folder to install. The folder remains after Windows XP Setup finishes installing Windows XP Professional.
/rx:folder	Specifies an optional folder in the distribution point or media's I386 folder to copy. The folder is deleted after Windows XP Setup finishes installing Windows XP Professional.
/e:command	Specifies a command to run after the GUI-mode phase of Windows XP Setup is finished.
/a	Enables accessibility options for use during Windows XP Setup.

On the Resource Kit CD   See "Unattended Installation Worksheet" in the file dist04.doc on this book's companion CD in the Aids folder. Use this worksheet to document the command-line options you require for running Winnt.exe.

More Info   For more information about running Windows XP Setup, see "Microsoft Windows Corporate Deployment Tools User's Guide," which is the file Deploy.chm in Deploy.cab on the Windows product CD in Support \Tools.

Creating Startup Media

To start Winnt.exe on a computer running MS-DOS, you must create startup media (boot disks). Startup media contain the system files and device drivers that are necessary to start the computer so that the computer's hard disk is accessible but not locked. It might also contain network support, CD and DVD device drivers, disk configuration tools, batch scripts, and so on. Here are the basic guidelines for creating startup media:

■ If you're installing Windows XP Professional from a network distribution point, your startup media must provide network support.

■ If you're installing Windows XP Professional from a CD, your startup media must provide CD-ROM support. You can start the computer using a floppy disk and then run Winnt.exe from the CD, or you can create a bootable CD from a floppy disk using a product such as Ahead Nero Burning ROM (*http://www.nero.com*).

■ If you're starting the computer with an MS-DOS boot disk, running Smartdrv.exe before starting Winnt.exe significantly improves the performance of the file-copy phase. Smartdrv.exe comes with MS-DOS, Microsoft Windows 98, and so on. The version of Smartdrv.exe you use must match the operating system on which you're running it.

■ If you've planned and designed preinstallation tasks, such as partitioning or formatting the disk, your startup media must include the tools necessary to perform those tasks. Alternatively, if your startup media has network support, you can run preinstallation tools from the network after starting the computer. If possible, script your preinstallation tasks so that you can automate it. For example, you can run many preinstallation tasks from an MS-DOS boot disk's autoexec.bat file. Partitioning and formatting the hard disk usually requires rebooting the computer before running Winnt.exe, however.

One source for MS-DOS boot disks with network or CD support that I use frequently is *http://www.bootdisk.com*. Another is Bart's Network Boot Disk at *http://www.nu2.nu/bootdisk/network*. Simply the most useful utility for creating startup media is Ghost Boot Wizard, which comes with Symantec Ghost Corporate Edition (*http://www.symantec.com*). Ghost Boot Wizard can create boot disks with network support for a large variety of network adapters. You can also create boot disks that support multiple network adapters. Ghost Boot Wizard can create boot disks with CD support, too. After you create an MS-DOS boot disk, I recommend that you archive it by using WinImage (see *http://www.winimage.com*).

For more information about creating startup media with network support, see the following Microsoft Knowledge Base articles (*http://support.microsoft.com*):

- **252448** How to Create an MS-DOS Network Startup Disk in Windows 2000
- **142857** How to Create a Network Installation Book Disk
- **128800** How to Provide Additional NDIS2 Drivers for Network Client 3.0
- **167685** How to Create an El Torito Bootable CD-ROM

Windows Preinstallation Environment

Installing Windows XP Professional using Winnt.exe has numerous limitations:

- MS-DOS doesn't recognize long filenames.

- You must build and maintain separate MS-DOS boot disks for each network adapter. In environments with varied network adapters, maintaining these different MS-DOS boot disks is a time-consuming, frustrating chore.

- You must restart the computer after partitioning and formatting the hard disk and before running Winnt.exe. This prevents you from fully automating the process.

- MS-DOS has a limited batch-scripting capability. This prevents you from fully automating the process, particularly preinstallation tasks.

For these reasons, I recommend that you use Windows PE to prepare the computer and run Windows XP Setup. It recognizes long filenames. It works out-of-the-box with most network adapters and is easy to configure for additional adapters. It doesn't require you to restart the computer after partitioning and formatting the hard disk but before running Winnt32.exe. And it provides a rich batch-scripting language as well as support for Windows Script Host. For more information, see Chapter 14.

Installing from MS-DOS

Before running Winnt.exe after starting a computer with an MS-DOS startup disk, verify the following:

- The target computer is connected to the network if you are using a network distribution point, and any peripheral devices—such as scanners, printers, and cameras—are connected to the target computer.

- Your MS-DOS boot disk contains the appropriate device drivers for network support, CD drives, and any other peripherals that your unattended installation requires. For example, if you are installing from a distribution point on the network, the target computer needs network connectivity. Likewise, if you are installing from the operating system CD, the target computer needs to load the drivers for the CD drive.

- The BIOS settings in your target computer list the floppy or CD drives, whichever is appropriate, as the first or second startup device.

- You have the proper permissions to access the distribution point on the network if you are installing from a network distribution point.

- Your answer file is on your network distribution point or media. If you're using the sample distribution point described in Chapter 7, the answer file is in *folder*\OEM*N*, where *folder* is the distribution point and OEM*N* is one of the configurations stored in the distribution point.

After verifying that the target computer and startup media are ready, do the following to install Windows XP Professional:

1. Analyze the target computer to ensure that it meets the hardware requirements that you defined in Chapter 1.

2. Perform the tasks in your user state migration plan. See Chapter 1 and Chapter 18.

3. Perform the tasks in your disk configuration plan. See Chapter 1 and Chapter 3.

4. Start the target computer using the startup media you created in the previous section. Also, if you're installing Windows XP Professional from a CD, insert the CD in the CD-ROM drive.

5. At the command prompt, run Winnt.exe with the command-line options that you documented in the Unattended Installation Worksheet (dist04.doc), which is on this book's companion CD in the Aids folder. For example, the following command installs Windows XP Professional from the network distribution point \\server\share\win2002.pro using the answer file Winnt.sif with the most common options: **winnt.exe /s:\\server\share\win2002.pro\i386 /t:c: /u:\\server\share\win2002.pro\OEM1\winnt.sif**.

> **Tip** Customize your MS-DOS boot disk's autoexec.bat file to automatically prepare the computer for installation and run Winnt.exe with the command-line options you documented in the Unattended Installation Worksheet (dist04.doc). Doing so automates a repetitive task and prevents human error. For an example, see Chapter 7. This batch script can automatically perform target analysis, save users' settings for later migration, partition and format the disk, and run Winnt.exe.

Running Winnt32.exe

Winnt32.exe is the 32-bit version of Windows XP Setup. You can start it on computers running Windows 95, Windows 98, Microsoft Windows Millennium Edition, Microsoft Windows NT with Service Pack 5 or later, Windows 2000, Windows XP Professional, and Windows PE. You can use Winnt32.exe for clean installations or upgrades. Not all of these Windows versions are on the upgrade path for Windows XP Professional, however, so you can only use Winnt32.exe for clean installations on those versions. Review Chapter 1 for the Windows XP Professional upgrade paths. The following describes the syntax of Winnt32.exe, and Table 13-2 describes each command-line option that Winnt32.exe supports:

```
winnt32 [/checkupgradeonly] [/cmd:command_line] [/cmdcons]
[/copydir:{i386|ia64}\folder_name] [/copysource:folder_name]
[/debug[level]:[filename]] [/dudisable] [/duprepare:pathname]
[/dushare:pathname] [/m:folder_name] [/makelocalsource] [/noreboot]
[/s:sourcepath] [/syspart:drive_letter] [/tempdrive:drive_letter]
[/udf:id [,UDB_file]] [/unattend[num]:[answer_file]]
```

Table 13-2   Winnt32.exe Command-Line Options

Option	Description
/checkupgradeonly	Checks the target computer for upgrade compatibility with Windows XP Professional. If you use this option with */unattend*, no user input is required. Otherwise, the results are displayed, and you can save them with a specified filename. The default filename is Upgrade.txt in the %SYSTEMROOT% folder.
/cmd:command_line	Instructs Windows XP Setup to execute a specific command before the final phase of the process. This occurs after the target computer has restarted and after Windows XP Setup has collected the necessary configuration information, but before it finishes.
/cmdcons	Installs the Recovery Console as a startup option on a functioning x86-based computer. The Recovery Console is a command-line interface from which you can perform tasks such as starting and stopping services and accessing the local drive (including drives formatted with NTFS). You can use the **/cmdcons** option only after installing Windows XP Professional on the PC.
/copydir:{i386|ia64} *folder_name*	Creates one or more folders in the folder where the Windows XP Professional source files are installed. *folder_name* refers to a folder that you have created to hold modifications just for your site.
	For example, for x86-based computers, create a **Private_drivers** folder in the i386 source folder for your installation and place driver files in the folder. Then type **/copydir:i386\Private_drivers** to have Windows XP Setup copy that folder to your newly installed computer, making the new folder location %SYSTEMROOT%\Private_drivers.
	Use */copydir* as many times as necessary to create more than one additional folder.
/copysource:folder_name	Creates one or more temporary folders in the folder where the Windows XP Professional source files are installed. *folder_name* refers to a folder that you have created to hold modifications just for your site.
	For example, create a **Private_drivers** folder in the source folder for your installation and place driver files in the folder. Then type **/copysource:Private_drivers** to have Windows XP Setup copy that folder to your newly installed computer and use its files during the installation, making the temporary folder location %SYSTEMROOT%\Private_drivers.
	Unlike the folders */copydir* creates, */copysource* folders are deleted after Windows XP Setup finishes.

Table 13-2   Winnt32.exe Command-Line Options

Option	Description
/debug[*level*]:[*filename*]	Creates a debug log at the *level* specified. For example: /*debug4:Debug.log*. The default log file is %SYSTEMROOT% \Winnt32.log, and the default debug level is 2. The log levels are as follows (each level includes the levels under it): ■ 0 logs severe errors. ■ 1 logs errors. ■ 2 logs warnings. ■ 3 logs information. ■ 4 logs detailed information for debugging.
/dudisable	Prevents Dynamic Update from running. Without Dynamic Update, Windows XP Setup runs only with the original Windows XP Professional source files. This option disables Dynamic Update even if you set *DUDisable* equal to *No* in the *[Unattended]* section of the unattended-setup answer file. For more information about Dynamic Update, see Chapter 19.
/duprepare:pathname	Carries out preparations on a distribution point so that it can be used with Dynamic Update files downloaded from the Windows Update Web site. This distribution point can then be used for installing Windows for multiple clients. For more information about Dynamic Update, see Chapter 19.
/dushare:pathname	Specifies a distribution point on which you previously downloaded Dynamic Update files (updated files for use with Windows XP Setup) from the Windows Update Web site and on which you previously ran /*duprepare:pathname*. When run on a client, this option specifies that the client installation uses the updated files on the distribution share specified in *pathname*.
/m:folder_name	Specifies that Windows XP Setup copies replacement files from an alternate location. Instructs Windows XP Setup to look in the alternate location first, and if files are present, to use them instead of the files from the default location.
/makelocalsource	Instructs Windows XP Setup to copy all installation source files to your local hard disk. Use **/makelocalsource** when installing from a CD to provide installation files when the CD is not available later in the installation.
/noreboot	Instructs Windows XP Setup not to restart the computer after the file-copy phase finishes, so that you can execute another command and then reboot the computer manually.
/s:sourcepath	Specifies the location of the Windows XP Professional source files. To simultaneously copy files from multiple servers, type the **/s:*sourcepath*** option multiple times (up to a maximum of eight). For example: **winnt32 /s:unc1 /s:unc2**. If you type the option multiple times, the first server specified must be available or Windows XP Setup fails.

Table 13-2   Winnt32.exe Command-Line Options

Option	Description
/syspart:drive_letter	On an x86-based computer, specifies that you can copy Windows XP Setup's startup files to a hard disk, mark the disk as active, and then install the disk into another computer. When you start that computer, it automatically starts with the next phase of Windows XP Setup.
	You must always use the /tempdrive option with the /syspart option. You can start Winnt32.exe with the /syspart option on an x86-based computer running Windows NT 4.0, Windows 2000, Windows XP Professional, or Windows PE. The computer cannot be running Windows 95, Windows 98, or Windows Millennium Edition.
/tempdrive:drive_letter	Directs Windows XP Setup to place temporary files on the specified partition. For a new installation, Windows XP Professional is installed on the specified partition. For an upgrade, the /tempdrive option affects the placement of temporary files only; the operating system is upgraded in the partition from which you run Winnt32.exe.
/udf:id[,UDB_file]	Indicates an identifier (**id**) that Windows XP Setup uses to specify how a UDB file modifies an answer file (see the /unattend entry). The UDB file overrides values in the answer file, and the identifier determines which values in the UDB file are used.
	For example, **/udf:RAS_user,Our_company.udb** overrides settings specified for the RAS_user identifier in the Our_company.udb file. If no UDB_file is specified, Windows XP Setup prompts the user to insert a disk that contains the $Unique$.udb file. See the section "Using UDB Files," later in this chapter on page 393 for more information.
	If you start from the Windows XP Professional CD and run an unattended installation, you cannot use the /udf command-line option for Winnt32.exe.
/unattend	Upgrades your previous version of Windows 98, Windows Millennium Edition, Windows NT 4.0, or Windows 2000 in unattended mode. Windows XP Setup downloads the Dynamic Update files from Windows Update and includes these files in the installation. All user settings are taken from the previous installation, so no user intervention is required during the installation process.

Table 13-2   Winnt32.exe Command-Line Options

Option	Description
/unattend[num]:[answer_file]	Performs a clean installation of Windows XP Professional in unattended mode. Windows XP Setup downloads the Dynamic Update files from the Windows Update Web site and includes these files in the installation. The specified *answer_file* provides Windows XP Setup with your custom settings.
	num specifies the number of seconds between the time that Windows XP Setup finishes copying the files and the time that it restarts the computer. You can use *num* on any computer running Windows 98, Windows Millennium Edition, Windows NT, Windows 2000, or Windows XP Professional.
	answer_file specifies the name of the answer file. By using the */unattend* command-line option to automate installation, you affirm that you have read and accepted the End-User License Agreement (EULA) for Windows XP Professional. Before using this command-line option to install Windows XP Professional on behalf of an organization other than your own, you must confirm that the end user (whether an individual or a single entity) has received, read, and accepted the terms of the Microsoft End-User License Agreement for Windows XP Professional.
	OEMs may not use this option on computers sold to end users.

On the Resource Kit CD   See "Unattended Installation Worksheet" in the file dist04.doc on this book's companion CD in the Aids folder. Use this worksheet to document the command-line options you require for running Winnt32.exe.

More Info   See "Microsoft Windows Corporate Deployment Tools User's Guide," which is the file Deploy.chm in Deploy.cab on the Windows product CD in Support\Tools, for more information about running Windows XP Setup.

Clean Installation from Windows

Before running Winnt32.exe to perform a clean installation, verify the following:

- The target computer is connected to the network and you have the proper permissions to access your distribution point if you are installing from a network distribution point.

■ Your answer file is saved on the media or in your distribution point. If you're using the sample distribution point described in Chapter 7, the answer file is in *folder*\OEM*N*, where *folder* is the distribution point and OEM*N* is one of the configurations stored in the distribution point.

After verifying that the target computer and startup media are ready, do the following to install Windows XP Professional:

1. Analyze the target computer to ensure that it meets the hardware requirements that you defined in Chapter 1.

2. Perform the tasks in your user state migration plan. See Chapter 1 and Chapter 18.

3. Perform the tasks in your disk configuration plan. See Chapter 1 and Chapter 3.

4. Start the target computer using the startup media you created in the previous section. Also, if you're installing Windows XP Professional from a CD, insert the CD in the CD-ROM drive.

5. At the command prompt, run Winnt32.exe with the command-line options that you documented in the Unattended Installation Worksheet (dist04.doc), which is on this book's companion CD in the Aids folder.

    For example, the following command installs Windows XP Professional from the network distribution point \\server\share\win2002.pro using the answer file Winnt.sif with the most common options: winnt32.exe /source: \\server\share\win2002.pro\i386   /tempdrive:c: /unattend:\\server\share \win2002.pro\OEM1\winnt.sif.

> **Tip** Automate the installation process using a combination of batch scripts and Windows Script Host scripts. For an example designed for use with Windows PE, see Chapter 7. You can automatically perform target analysis; save users' settings for later migration; partition and format the disk; and run Winnt32.exe.

Upgrade Installation from Windows

Before running Winnt32.exe to perform an upgrade installation, verify the following:

■ Your answer file is saved on the media or in your distribution point. If you're using the sample distribution point described in Chapter 7, the answer file is in *folder*\OEM*N*, where *folder* is the distribution point and OEM*N* is one of the configurations stored in the distribution point.

- If you are upgrading from Windows 98 or Windows Millennium Edition to Windows XP Professional, you have the following entries in your answer file (see Chapter 6 for more information):

```
[Unattended]
Win9xUpgrade=Yes
```

- If you are upgrading from Windows NT or Windows 2000, you have the following entries in your answer file (see Chapter 6 for more information):

```
[Unattended]
NtUpgrade=Yes
```

- You do not have the following entries in your answer file. Theses entries cannot be used if you are performing an upgrade unattended installation (see Chapter 6 for more information):

```
[Unattended]
OemPreinstall=Yes
```

Note Windows XP Setup reads only the following entries in an answer file during an unattended upgrade installation: *Win9xUpgrade*, *NtUpgrade*, *ProductKey*, *AutoActivate*, *DuDisable*, *DuShare*, and *DuStopOnError*.

After verifying that the target computer and startup media are ready, do the following to install Windows XP Professional:

1. Analyze the target computer to ensure that it meets the hardware requirements that you defined in Chapter 1.

2. At the command prompt or in the Run dialog box, run Winnt32.exe with the command-line options that you documented in the Unattended Installation Worksheet (dist04.doc), which is on this book's companion CD in the Aids folder.

    For example, the following command installs Windows XP Professional from the network distribution point \\server\share\win2002.pro using the answer file Winnt.sif with the most common options: winnt32.exe/source:\\server\share\win2002.pro\i386/unattend:\\server\share\win2002.pro\OEM1\winnt.sif.

Tip Automate the installation process using a combination of batch scripts and Windows Script Host scripts. For an example designed for use with Windows PE, see Chapter 7. You can automatically perform target analysis and run Winnt32.exe.

Checking for Compatibility First

Windows XP Setup can check a computer that's running Windows 98 to ensure that it meets the upgrade requirements. Run Windows XP Setup with the */checkugpradeonly* command-line option to check the computer and configuration for compatibility with Windows XP Professional. The result is an upgrade report that describes the hardware, device drivers, and software issues that might prevent Windows XP Professional from working properly.

You can use an unattended-setup answer file to run Windows XP Setup unattended, generating an upgrade report in a log file that you store on the network. You can create a log file for each computer on which you run Windows XP Setup, so that you can determine which computers are viable for upgrades and which aren't. To do so, use the */unattend* command-line option with Winnt32.exe to specify the path and filename of an unattended-setup answer file that automatically runs the upgrade check and writes the log file. The following shows the contents of the answer file:

```
[Win9xUpg]
ReportOnly = Yes
SaveReportTo = Path
```

Path is the path and filename of the log file you want Windows XP Setup to generate. It can be a UNC path, and it can include environment variables.

Using UDB Files

When creating a fully unattended installation of Windows XP Professional to numerous computers, some of the information that you provide in an answer file is unique to each computer. For example, the computer name must be unique. With Windows XP Professional, you can use a single answer file that contains information for all users and computers and then a Uniqueness Database (UDB) file that provides information specific to a single computer or a small group of computers.

UDB files contain replacement sections for or specific additional sections to an answer file. The replacement sections have formats similar to normal answer files. In essence, Windows XP Setup merges the UDB file with the answer file at the start of the GUI-mode phase, before the settings being merged are required by Windows XP Setup. This mechanism is completely transparent to the user. Listing 13-2 shows the general format of UDB files. The following sections describe this format in more detail.

Listing 13-2 UDB File Template

```
[UniqueIds]
id1 = section1,section2
id2 = section1,section2
id3 = section1,section3,section4
[id1:section1]
name=value
name=value
name=value
[id1:section2]
name=value
name=value
name=value
[id2:section1]
name=value
name=value
name=value
[id2:section2]
[id3:section1]
[id3:section3]
[id3:section4]
```

Note If you're seriously considering the use of UDB files, then I encourage you to think carefully about it first. In any organization of any size, UDB files are difficult to maintain, and they're never fully automatic (you must specify the computer's name on the Windows XP Setup command line). Instead, populate a database with each computer's MAC address and related facts, and then look up that information using a script. Chapter 6, "Answer Files," describes a sample script that this book's companion CD includes for this purpose. Then, you can use the script siftemp.wsf, also described in Chapter 6, to create individual answer files for individual computers. This scenario is more maintainable and more automatic than using UDB files. To improve matters more, Chapter 14, "Preinstallation Environment," describes how to look up settings in a database, and then generate a custom answer file just for that computer.

Creating UDB Files

The first section of a UDB file is the *[UniqueIds]* section, which lists all uniqueness IDs that are supported by this database. The format is `ID=section[,section]`. The left side is a uniqueness ID. The uniqueness ID is typically a computer name, but it can be any string that doesn't contain the asterisk (*), space ( ), comma (,), or equals (=) characters. The right side is a list of sections, each of which should match the name of a section in the answer file (see Appendix D). Listing 13-2 illustrates this format.

For example, if you were using computer names as the uniqueness IDs, this section might look like this:

```
[UniqueIds]
jerry1 = UserData, Unattended
jerry2 = UserData, Unattended
ferghus1 = UserData, Unattended
```

Following the *[UniqueIds]* section are the sections referenced in it. These section names can take either of two forms: They can be exactly like the section name in the answer file (*[Unattended]*), or the section name can be preceded with the uniqueness ID and a colon (*[jerry1:UserData]*). This allows you to create specialized replacement sections for each computer name. If both a general section (*[Unattended]*) and an ID-specific section (*[jerry1:Unattended]*) are available, Windows XP Setup uses the section for the uniqueness ID specified in the Winnt.exe or Winnt32.exe command-line option */udf*. The sections in the UDB file can contain any settings that the same-named sections could contain in the answer file. During installation, each setting specified in a referenced section overrides the value for the same setting in the answer file. Values are substituted as follows:

- If a setting is specified in the answer file but not in the UDB file for the specified uniqueness ID, the setting specified in the answer file is used.

- If a setting is specified in the UDB file section referenced by the uniqueness ID, the setting specified in the UDB file is used.

- If a setting is specified in the answer file and it appears in the UDB file section referenced by the uniqueness ID with no value to the right of the equals sign, the default value is used. This is equivalent to commenting out the setting in the answer file.

- If a setting is specified in the UDB file, but the value is left blank, no value will be used for that setting. This might result in the user being prompted for the information.

- If a section or setting is used in the UDB file, but there is no section by that name in the answer file, the section or setting will be created and used by Windows XP Setup.

- If a section is referenced in the *[UniqueIds]* section but does not exist, the user will be prompted to insert a floppy with a valid uniqueness database on it.

Listing 13-3 shows a sample UDB file. This file defines three uniqueness IDs: *jerry1*, *jerry2*, and *ferghus*. These are the indices into the UDB file. Following the *[UniqueIds]* section is the *[id:UserData]* section for each ID. The first is *[jerry1:UserData]*, which specifies a user and computer name for the uniqueness ID *jerry1*.

Following that are *[id:UserData]* sections for *jerry2* and *ferghus*. The next section, "Specifying UDB Files," describes how to specify the UDB file and uniqueness ID when running Winnt.exe or Winnt32.exe.

Listing 13-3   Sample UDB File

```
[UniqueIds]
jerry1 = UserData
jerry2 = UserData
ferghus = UserData

[jerry1:UserData]
UserName="Jerry Honeycutt"
ComputerName=jerry1

[jerry2:UserData]
UserName="Jerry Honeycutt"
ComputerName=jerry2

[ferghus:UserData]
UserName="Ferghus Honeycutt"
ComputerName=ferghus1
```

Specifying UDB Files

To specify a uniqueness ID during Windows XP Setup, you must run Winnt.exe or Winnt32.exe with the command-line option /**udf:***id*[,*udb_file*]. *id* is one of the uniqueness IDs specified in the UDB file's *[UniqueIds]*, and *udb_file* is the path and filename of the UDB file. The following list contains notes for using this command-line option:

- If you specify both the uniqueness ID and UDB filename, Windows XP Setup copies the UDB file to the local hard disk during the text-mode phase and uses it during the GUI-mode phase. This process is transparent to the user.

- If you specify only the uniqueness ID, Setup requires a floppy disk with a UDB file named $Unique$.udf. You must prepare this disk and make it available to the user in advance. Setup prompts the user for this disk during GUI-mode Setup.

- If the UDB file is corrupt or Setup can't locate the specified uniqueness ID in it, Setup prompts the user either to insert a floppy with the fixed UDB file or cancel. If the user chooses to cancel, Setup uses the settings in the answer file. These settings might not be appropriate for the computer.

Post-Installation Tasks

Post-installation tasks include any installation and configuration tasks that you need to perform after Setup installs Windows XP Professional. Post-installation tasks are usually described in your configuration plan, as described in Chapter 3. You usually perform these tasks by running a command, program, script, or batch file after Windows XP Setup is finished running.

You can use an answer file to automate only a limited number of installation and configuration tasks during installation. Many installation and configuration tasks must be performed after the operating system is installed and configured. Testing your unattended installations is the best way to determine whether an installation or configuration task must be performed after the operating system is installed. However, the following installation and configuration tasks always must be performed after the operating system is installed:

- Tasks that cannot be performed using a setting in an answer file. You cannot add any other sections or entries to an answer file that is used to perform an unattended installation. For more information about the settings you can use in an answer file, see Chapter 6.

- Tasks that rely on Active Directory directory service. For example, if a software installation program registers information in Active Directory or requires information from Active Directory, you must run the installation program after the operating system is installed and the computer is joined to a domain.

- Tasks that can be performed only while a user is logged on. For example, some software installation programs create shortcuts on the Start menu and the desktop. If you want these shortcuts applied to a specific user profile, then you need to run the installation program after the operating system is installed and the user is logged on.

You can automate post-installation tasks only if you can run the command, program, script, or batch file in quiet mode; if you can suppress all user prompts by supplying an answer file for the command, program, script, or batch file; or by emulating user input with tools such as Microsoft ScriptIt (*http://www.microsoft.com /technet/prodtechnol/winntas/downloads/scriptit.asp*), HiddenSoft AutoIt (*http://www.hiddensoft.com/AutoIt*), or VBScript SendKeys. For example, if you delete folders after you install the operating system, you need to use the **/q** parameter with the **rmdir** command. Likewise, if you install a Windows Installer-based application, you need to use the **/qb**, **/qn**, or **/qr** command-line options to install the program without user interaction. Alternatively, you can configure the user-interface level by customizing the application's Setup.ini file.

Two methods are available for running post-installation tasks: the *[GuiRunOnce]* section of an unattended-setup answer file and the Cmdlines.txt file. Chapter 11 describes these methods in detail.

Office 2003 Editions

When distributing Microsoft Office 2003 Editions during a desktop deployment, allowing user interaction isn't desirable. So I don't cover interactive installations in this chapter. How you distribute Office 2003 Editions largely depends on how you're distributing Windows XP Professional:

■ If you're using disk-imaging techniques to distribute Windows XP Professional, distributing Office 2003 Editions as part of your disk images is a good choice. For more information about including Office 2003 Editions on a Windows XP Professional disk image, see Chapter 15, "Disk Imaging with Sysprep." The same guidelines you read about in Chapter 15 apply if you're deploying Office 2003 Editions as part of a Remote Installation Service (RIS) disk image (see Chapter 16, "Remote Installation Service").

■ If you already have a software distribution infrastructure in place, such as Microsoft Systems Management Server (SMS), I recommend that you use it to deploy Office 2003 Editions. For more information about SMS, see Chapter 17, "Systems Management Server."

■ If you're business is small to medium-sized and you've deployed Active Directory, consider using Group Policy to deploy Office 2003 Editions. For more information, see Chapter 23, "Software Installation." You cannot take advantage of local installation sources if you deploy Office 2003 Editions from Active Directory, however, which means that users must maintain a connection to the Office 2003 Editions source files on the network to add or repair features.

■ If you're not using disk-imaging techniques, existing software distribution infrastructure, or Active Directory, you're down to installing Office 2003 Editions by running Office 2003 Setup on the target computer. The chapters following this describe how to install Office 2003 Editions using its setup program unattended. For more information about installing Office 2003 Editions in this scenario, see Chapter 23.

Best Practices

The following are best practices for running Windows XP Setup:

- **Document your command-line options.** Document the settings for Windows XP Setup in the Unattended Installation Worksheet (dist01.doc), which is in the Aids folder on this book's companion CD.

- **Use network distribution points.**   When possible, use network distribution points to install Windows XP Professional. Network distribution points help standardize configurations and are manageable.

- **Use distribution media for remote computers.**   Use distribution media to install Windows XP Professional on remote computers when a suitable connection to the network distribution point isn't available.

- **Run Windows XP Setup using Winnt32.exe.**   Use Winnt32.exe instead of Winnt.exe whenever possible. This precludes using MS-DOS to start computers and run Windows XP Setup; however, Windows PE is better suited to this purpose anyway (see Chapter 14).

- **Fully automate the Windows XP Professional installation.**   Fully automate the setup process to provide a consistent, standard configuration and eliminate human error. You can easily automate most preinstallation, installation, and post-installation tasks using batch scripts.

Chapter 14

Preinstallation Environment

Half the job of installing Microsoft Windows XP Professional or building disk images is starting the computer. Microsoft Windows Preinstallation Environment (Windows PE) is just another way to start computers; it is similar to using MS-DOS, only better. It allows you to more fully automate the installation process than using MS-DOS does. This chapter describes how to use, customize, and automate Windows PE for the purpose of installing Windows XP Professional in enterprise environments.

Checklist

- Have you designed and built the Windows XP Professional answer file for use with Windows XP Setup? If not, see Chapter 6, "Answer Files."

- Have you designed and built the Windows XP Professional distribution point? If not, see Chapter 7, "Distribution Points." This book's companion CD contains sample distribution points, customized for deploying Windows XP Professional by using Windows PE, in the folder Samples \chap14. The samples are based on the information from Chapters 7 and 9, most of which isn't repeated in this chapter.

- Have you planned and designed any preinstallation tasks, such as partitioning and formatting computers' hard disks? See Chapter 6 and Chapter 7 for more information. Also see the sections "Verifying Hardware Requirements" on page 424 and "Configuring the Hard Disks" on page 410.

- Have you planned and designed any post-installation tasks, such as restoring users' settings, configuring the operating system, and installing applications? See Chapter 3, "Windows Configuration," Chapter 6, and Chapter 7 for more information.

- Have you configured Remote Installation Service (RIS)? RIS is a convenient method of deploying Windows PE, which you learn about in Chapter 16, "Remote Installation Service."

- Do you have Windows PE? Windows PE is a benefit of Microsoft Software Assurance. For more information, see *http://www.microsoft.com /licensing/programs/sa/support/winpe.mspx*.

Bart's PE Builder

Trying to obtain Windows PE might lead you to nothing but frustration, assuming that your company isn't a Microsoft Enterprise Agreement customer or an original equipment manufacturer (OEM). A fellow named Bart Lagerweij provides a similar program, however. It's free to use in an enterprise environment; you just can't resell the product.

Bart's PE Builder builds the *Bart PE* CD from your original Windows XP Professional or Microsoft Windows Server 2003 product CD. Similar to Windows PE, Bart PE gives you a complete Win32 environment that includes network support; a graphical user interface (GUI); and access to the file allocation table (FAT), NT file system (NTFS), and CD-ROM File System (CDFS). You can use it as a preinstallation environment to test new computers, rescue files to a network share, and so on. Just like Windows PE, Bart PE replaces your plethora of MS-DOS boot disks, but Bart PE is much easier to get. Just keep in mind that Bart PE is in no way associated with Microsoft, and Microsoft does not support Bart PE.

In many ways, Bart PE is more flexible than Windows PE. For example, it includes a Start menu, you can build it from Windows XP Home Edition, and so on. For more information, see *http://www.nu2.nu/pebuilder*. You can download Bart's PE Builder from this Web site, and the documentation is good. Amazingly, countless companies and individuals have created *plug-ins* for Bart PE that expand its capabilities even more, and you can download most of them from the Web site.

Exploring Windows PE

Windows PE is a supercharged replacement for MS-DOS in your deployment processes. Windows PE is a minimal Windows system that provides limited services based on the Windows XP Professional or Windows Server 2003 kernel, depending on which version of Windows you used to build Windows PE. It also provides the minimal set of features required to run Windows XP Setup, install Windows XP Professional from networks, script basic repetitive tasks, and validate hardware. For example, with Windows PE, you can use more powerful batch scripts, Windows Script Host, and HTML Applications to fully automate computer preparation and Windows XP Professional installation, rather than the limited batch commands in MS-DOS. Here are examples of what you can do with Windows PE:

- Create and format disk partitions, including NTFS file-system partitions without rebooting the computer before installing Windows XP Professional on them. Formatting disks with NTFS by using an MS-DOS-bootable disk required third-party utilities. Windows PE replaces the MS-DOS-bootable disk in this scenario, allowing you to format disks with NTFS without using third-party utilities. Also, the file-system utilities that Windows PE provides are scriptable, so you can completely automate the setup-preparation process.

- Access network shares to run preparation tools or install Windows XP Professional. Windows PE provides network access comparable to Windows XP Professional. In fact, Windows PE provides the same network drivers that come with Windows XP Professional, allowing you to access the network quickly and easily. Customizing MS-DOS-bootable disks to access network shares was a time consuming and tedious process—no more.

- Use all the mass-storage devices that rely on Windows XP Professional device drivers. Windows PE includes the same mass-storage device drivers that Windows XP Professional provides, so you no longer have to customize MS-DOS-bootable disks for use with specialized mass-storage devices. Once again, Windows PE allows you to focus on important jobs rather than on maintaining MS-DOS-bootable disks.

- Customize Windows PE by using techniques and technologies that are already familiar to you. Windows PE is based on Windows XP Professional, so you are already familiar with the techniques and tools used to customize Windows PE. You can customize it for a variety of scenarios.

The following sections provide more detail about the features and limitations of using Windows PE. They focus specifically on using it in enterprise deployment scenarios, rather than in manufacturing environments.

Capabilities

Windows PE is a bootable CD that replaces the MS-DOS-bootable disk in most deployment scenarios (you can start it using RIS, too). It's a lightweight, 32-bit environment that supports the same set of networking and mass-storage device drivers that Windows XP Professional or Windows Server 2003 supports, and it provides access to similar features, including NTFS and standalone distributed file system (DFS). Windows PE includes the following features:

- **Hardware independence**   Windows PE is a hardware-independent Windows environment for both x86 and Itanium architectures. You can use the same pre-installation environment on all the desktop computers and servers in your company, without creating and maintaining different bootable disks for different hardware configurations. Kiss that collection of MS-DOS disks goodbye.

- **APIs and scripting capabilities**   Windows PE contains a subset of the Win32 APIs; a command interpreter capable of running batch scripts; and support for adding Windows Script Host (WSH), HTML Applications (HTAs), and Microsoft ActiveX Data Objects (ADO) to create custom tools or scripts. The scripting capabilities in Windows PE far exceed the capabilities of MS-DOS-bootable disks. For example, the command interpreter in Windows PE supports a more robust batch-scripting language than does MS-DOS, allowing you to use more advanced scripts.

- **Network access**   Windows PE uses Transmission Control Protocol/Internet Protocol (TCP/IP) to provide network access and supports standard network drivers for running Windows XP Setup and copying source files from the network to the computer. You can easily add or remove network drivers from a customized version of Windows PE. In contrast, customizing MS-DOS-bootable disks to access network shares is frustrating, mostly due to the need to build and maintain numerous disks. Windows PE alleviates this frustration by supporting the network drivers that Windows XP Professional supports, and Windows PE is easier to customize with additional network drivers.

- **Mass-storage devices**   Windows PE includes support for all mass-storage devices that Windows XP Professional supports. As new devices become available, you can easily add or remove drivers into a customized version of Windows PE. Customizing an MS-DOS-bootable disk to access atypical mass-storage devices requires tracking down and installing the 14-bit device drivers. However, Windows PE supports many of these mass-storage devices out of the box. And customizing Windows PE to support additional mass-storage devices is easier because it uses standard Windows device drivers that are readily available.

- **Disk management**   Windows PE includes native support for creating, deleting, formatting, and managing NTFS file system partitions. Also, Windows PE provides full unrestricted access to NTFS file systems. With Windows PE, you don't have to restart the computer after formatting a disk.

■ **Support for Preboot Execution Environment (PXE) protocol**   If the computer supports PXE, you can start it automatically from a Windows PE image located on RIS—and RIS doesn't install the Windows PE image on the computer's hard disk. Starting Windows PE from the network makes it a convenient tool to use in deployment scenarios, and you can easily customize a Windows PE directly on the RIS server.

> **Note**   You must build a custom Windows PE CD from the Windows PE source files as described in "Customizing Windows PE," later in this chapter on page 412.

Limitations

Windows PE has the following limitations:

■ Windows PE doesn't fit on floppy disks, but you can write a custom Windows PE image to a bootable CD.

■ Windows PE supports TCP/IP and NetBIOS over TCP/IP for network connectivity, but it doesn't support other protocols, such as Internetwork Packet Exchange/Sequenced Packet Exchange (IPX/SPX).

■ The Windows on Windows 32 (WOW32) subsystem allows 16-bit applications to run on the 32-bit Windows platform. The WOW32 subsystem isn't available in Windows PE, so 16-bit applications won't run in 32-bit versions of Windows PE. Similarly, in the Itanium version of Windows PE, the WOW64 subsystem is not available, so applications must be fully 64-bit compliant.

■ To reduce its size, Windows PE includes only a subset of the available Win32 APIs. Included are I/O (disk and network) and core Win32 APIs. The following categories of Win32 APIs aren't available in Windows PE (applications that require these APIs do not run in Windows PE):

  ▪ Active Directory Services Interfaces (ADSI)

  ▪ DirectX

  ▪ Microsoft .NET Framework

  ▪ OpenGL

  ▪ Power Options

  ▪ Printing and Print Spooler

  ▪ Still Image

  ▪ Tape Backup

- Terminal Services

- User Profile

- Window Station and Desktop

- Windows Management Instrumentation (WMI)

- Windows Multimedia

- Windows Shell

- Drive letter assignments aren't persistent between sessions. After you restart Windows PE, the drive letter assignments will be in the default order.

- Windows PE supports DFS name resolution to standalone DFS roots only.

- You can't access files or folders on a computer running Windows PE from another computer.

- Windows PE requires a VESA-compatible display device and will use the highest screen resolution it can determine is supported. If the operating system can't detect video settings, it uses a resolution of 640 by 480 pixels.

- You can build custom versions of Windows PE from Windows XP Professional and Windows Server 2003 products, but not Windows XP Home Edition.

- To prevent its use as a pirated operating system, Windows PE automatically reboots after 24 hours.

- Windows PE doesn't support the Microsoft .NET framework.

Using Windows PE as an Installation Platform

You probably used MS-DOS-bootable disks to handle system configuration, prepare computers for installation, and then install the operating system on the computer. MS-DOS-bootable disks are difficult to configure and maintain for this purpose because you must first track down the 16-bit device drivers required and then customize the disks to connect to the network. Each type of network adapter requires a unique disk, too, escalating the amount of work involved in maintaining these MS-DOS-bootable disks. Add to that the computer systems with atypical mass-storage devices that require you to customize disks with mass-storage device drivers, and the number of combinations that you maintain grows quickly. Even after all the time you spend building and maintaining MS-DOS-bootable disks, they are barely adequate to get the job done because MS-DOS provides minimal scripting capabilities—and the utilities it provides are the bare essentials. For example, after you start computers with an MS-DOS-bootable disk, you must usually perform many tasks manually before starting the Windows XP Professional installation instead of moving on to the next computer to install Windows XP Professional. After formatting a hard disk, you must usually restart the computer before installing Windows XP Professional.

Microsoft developed Windows PE specifically for deployment scenarios. Windows PE provides a lightweight, 32-bit environment that leverages the same device drivers as Windows XP Professional. You have access to a similar set of basic features that Windows XP Professional provides, including the NTFS file system and DFS shares. It supports long file names, too. And you can fully automate the installation process, so you can move on to the next computer or the next disk image faster. In deployment scenarios, there are a variety of ways you can use Windows PE, including the following examples:

- You can use the Windows PE bootable CD as is with no customizations to start computers (you must still build a Windows PE CD from Windows XP Professional or Windows Server 2003 source files, however). Then, you can connect to the network and install an operating system from a customized network share. Without customizations, the Windows PE bootable CD doesn't support WSH, HTA, or ADO.

- You can customize Windows PE in a variety of ways—such as adding device drivers, optional components, and other utilities—and then create a new Windows PE CD. You use the Windows PE CD to connect to the network and install an operating system from a customized network share. In this scenario, the user or technician starts the computer using the CD. Windows PE starts and then processes Startnet.cmd, which starts the networking connection. You can also customize this batch script to map a drive letter to the network share that contains the Windows XP Professional source files, verifies that the computer's configuration matches the required configuration, backs up the user's data to the network, runs Diskpart to partition the hard disk, formats the hard disk with the NTFS file system, and then runs Windows XP Setup fully unattended. Alternatively, the script can run a third-party disk-imaging utility to restore an operating-system image from the network share to the hard disk (See Chapter 15, "Disk Imaging with Sysprep," for a list of disk-imaging products that support Windows PE").

- You can create a Windows PE CD that contains both Windows PE and the operating system you're installing and then customize the CD so that it automatically installs the operating system when the CD starts. Because more powerful scripting capabilities are available with Windows PE than with MS-DOS, you're more able to completely automate the process. You can then distribute the CD to users or technicians so that they can automatically install the operating system. This scenario is much like the previous one, except that the CD contains the Windows XP Professional source files, so a network connection isn't necessary.

- In an Active Directory environment, you can customize and install Windows PE in RIS. Rather than starting computers with a CD, you can start Windows PE remotely by using RIS. This scenario is similar to using a Windows PE CD to start the computer and connect to the network, except that the user or technician starts the computer from the Windows PE image in RIS. Then, the custom scripts you add to Windows PE connect to the network, verify the computer's configuration, prepare the disk for installation, and then start Windows XP Setup. No floppy disks or CDs are required.

The following sections describe how Windows PE and your customizations enable these scenarios. They start with the basics, starting the computer. Then, they describe how to verify that the computer's configuration meets requirements, how to configure the computer's hard disk, and how to install Windows XP Professional.

Starting the Computer

To start the computer using a Windows PE CD, insert the CD into the computer's CD-ROM, configure the computer's BIOS to start from the CD before starting from the local hard disk (only if necessary), and then restart the computer. When prompted, press any key to start the computer from the CD. Windows PE loads and then runs the all-important Startnet.cmd batch script to configure the environment (Startnet.cmd serves a similar purpose to Autoexec.bat in MS-DOS). Windows PE runs Startnet.cmd every time it starts, making this file the central location from which to customize Windows PE for your scenarios.

There are two versions of Startnet.cmd that you might encounter, depending on when and from where you received Windows PE. The first version contains the line *factory –winpe*. This version relies entirely on Factory to configure the network connection. The second version contains the line *factory –minint*, followed by several other lines that configure the network connection. The first version is the default in newer versions of Windows PE, beginning with version 1.2. The second version is the default in older versions. I prefer the first version because it's much cleaner. You should use it, too. Listing 14-1 shows a slightly customized version of Startnet.cmd, and the following steps describe how it works:

1. *if exist oc.bat call oc.bat.* This command installs optional components only if they exist.

> **More Info**   See the section "Optional Components," later in this chapter on page 415.

2. *factory -winpe.* This command detects, installs, and configures network support for Windows PE. It first looks for the file Winbom.ini, as described in the sidebar "Finding Winbom.ini." When Factory finds a Winbom.ini, it looks in the file's *[Factory]* section for the *WinbomType* entry and checks that it is *WinPE*.

If not, it continues looking for another Winbom.ini file. After locating the Winbom.ini file, Factory configures the network connection as specified in the *[WinPE.Net]* section. It uses Plug and Play to install the network interface card and then configures the networking services and binds the network protocols.

3. *if exist a:\floppy.cmd a:\floppy.cmd.* This command runs the batch script called Floppy.cmd located on drive A, only if it exists. It provides an easy way to further customize Windows PE for different scenarios without requiring a separate copy of Windows PE for each. Instead, simply create a separate floppy for each scenario.

Listing 14-1 Startnet.cmd

```
@echo off
@rem startnet.cmd: configure Windows PE networking, etc.

  echo Installing optional components...

  if exist oc.bat call oc.bat

  echo Configuring network components...

  factory -winpe

  cls
  if exist a:\floppy.cmd a:\floppy.cmd

:end
```

Note Using Windows PE, you can accomplish many tasks three ways: answer files, batch scripts, or Winbom.ini. Winbom.ini is a simple Configuration Settings file that Windows PE uses when the command *factory –winpe* runs in Startnet.cmd. Using Winbom.ini to partition and format disks is often easier than using Diskpart, for example. Winbom.ini also gives you a moderate amount of control over how Windows PE starts.

More Info "Windows Preinstallation Environment User's Guide," which is Winpe.chm on the Windows PE CD in the Docs folder, contains a complete reference for the Factory command and Winbom.ini. I typically use batch scripts instead of Winbom.ini because they give me more control of the installation process.

Finding Winbom.ini

When you run the command *factory –winpe* in Startnet.cmd, Factory searches for Winbom.ini in the following order:

1. The path and filename specified by the registry key HKLM\SOFTWARE \Microsoft\Factory\Winbom.

2. The root of all removable media drives that are not CD-ROM drives, such as a floppy disk drive.

3. The root of all CD-ROM drives.

4. The location of Factory.exe, usually the %SYSTEMROOT%\System32 or %SYSTEMDRIVE%\Sysprep folders.

5. The root of %SYSTEMDRIVE%.

Configuring the Hard Disks

There are two ways to configure the target computer's hard disk using native Windows PE tools. The first is to use Diskpart to partition the disk and Format to format it. This is the method that the sample distribution points on this book's companion CD use because it provides the greatest amount of flexibility for scenarios in which you want to support various computer configurations from a single Windows PE CD or RIS image.

The second is using the *[DiskConfig]* section in Winbom.ini. Using this section, you describe the disk layout using settings such as *SizeN*, *PartitionTypeN*, and *FileSystemN*.

> **More Info**   Winbom.ini is predominately an OEM tool, and I prefer the flexi-
> bility of using batch scripts and Diskpart, so I'll refer you to "Windows Prein-
> stallation Environment User's Guide," which is Winpe.chm on the Windows
> PE CD in the Docs folder, for more information about using Winbom.ini to
> configure hard disks.

Listings 14-2 and 14-3 show how to use the first method. Listing 14-2 is Diskpart.txt, which is in the root of each sample distribution folder contained on this book's companion CD in the Samples folder. This file is a script for Diskpart that automatically configures the disk. It selects the first disk installed on the computer, removes its current partitions, creates a new primary partition using all the available space, assigns the drive letter C, and then marks the partition as active so that it'll boot. Listing 14-3 shows the command necessary to run Diskpart with Diskpart.txt as the script and then format the disk. The batch script setup32.cmd in each sample distribution folder contains these commands. The command to use diskpart.txt in Windows PE is *diskpart /s diskpart.txt*. Diskpart does not format the disk, so you must format the disk after partitioning it. The command *format c: /q /fs:ntfs /v:"" /y* quickly formats the newly partitioned disk with the NTFS file system and without a volume label. The command-line option */y* runs Format without prompting for input. You can run both commands within a batch script to automatically partition and format a disk, which is what you see happening in setup32.cmd in the next section.

Listing 14-2   diskpart.txt

```
select disk=0
clean
create partition primary
assign letter=c
active
```

Listing 14-3   setup32.cmd

```
diskpart /s diskpart.txt
format c: /q /fs:ntfs /v:"" /y
```

More Info   See Chapter 7 for a complete description of diskpart.txt and setup32.cmd, and how they fit into the installation process.

Installing Windows

After configuring the computer's hard disk and performing any other preinstallation tasks you've planned, you run Winnt32 (not Winnt) to start Windows XP Setup. Listing 14-4 shows winnt32.cmd from the sample distribution points included on this book's companion CD. This command shows how to run Winnt32 from Windows PE.

The important takeaway from Listing 14-4 is the command-line option */syspart:c:*. If you partition the disk using Diskpart and then format it using Format, Windows XP Setup fails without using the */syspart* command-line option. This option changes Windows XP Setup so that it simply copies the source files to the target computer and then prepares the disk so that Windows XP Setup continues after the computer restarts.

So how do you restart the computer in Windows PE from a batch script? I'm embarrassed to say that this one took a few tries for me to figure out. I first tried the Shutdown utility. Then I tried some third-party utilities. None of them worked. I tried a script. That didn't work. Then, out of frustration, I typed **exit** at the command prompt and, low and behold, Windows PE restarted the computer. So, that's the trick and that's why you see the line *exit* in the sample setup32.cmd batch scripts that you find on this book's companion CD.

Listing 14-4   winnt32.cmd

```
@..\i386\winnt32 /unattended:winnt.sif /syspart:c:
```

> **More Info**   See Chapter 7 for a complete description of setup32.cmd and winnt32.cmd, and how they fit into the installation process.

Customizing Windows PE

The uncustomized version of Windows PE is useful for preparing computers for installation, but you don't realize its full power until you customize it. You can add your own 32-bit command-line tools, scripts, optional components, and so on. To do that, you need the Windows PE source files and (*possibly but not always*) a Windows XP Professional product CD, both of which must have matching build numbers. You also need access to any command-line tools, scripts, and device drivers that you want to add to Windows PE. The Windows PE source files you received from Microsoft contain the following folders:

- ****   The root folder of the source files contains four files: Win51, Win51ip, Win51ip.sp1, and Winbom.ini. When you build a customized Windows PE CD, you must place these files at the root of the CD; otherwise, Windows PE will not start properly. For example, if Winbom.ini is missing, Windows PE hangs.

- **\Docs**   This folder contains the Windows PE documentation. In particular, "Windows Preinstallation Environment User's Guide," which is Winpe.chm on the Windows PE CD in the Docs folder, contains reference information that this chapter doesn't.

- **\I386**   This folder contains the Windows system files. You can usually use these files when customizing a Windows PE CD rather than starting from scratch. If you want to start from scratch, however, you can rebuild the I386 folder.

- **\Winpe**   This folder contains scripts and other files necessary to build an I386 folder and customized Windows PE CDs.

The first step in customizing Windows PE is simply to copy the Windows PE source files to your hard disk. If you received Windows PE on a CD, copy them from the CD. If you downloaded the files from Microsoft, keep the original files intact by making another copy. Make sure you copy the root folder that contains Win51,

Win51ip, sp1, and Winbom.ini—as well as the three subfolders Docs, I386, and Winpe. If you want, you can rebuild the I386 folder using the following steps:

1. Delete the existing I386 folder.

2. Turn off the read-only attribute of all files in the Winpe folder.

    The scripts in the Winpe folder overwrite certain files and can't do so with the read-only attribute set on those files.

3. Put the Windows XP Professional product CD in the CD-ROM drive, or make sure that a folder containing the Windows XP Professional source files is available on your local hard disk or on the network.

    If the files are on the network, map a drive to the share containing them, as it simplifies the command line.

4. Run the command **mkimg.cmd** *source destination* [*isoimage*] in the folder containing the Windows PE tools.

    Source is the path of the Windows XP Professional product CD or the folder containing the I386 folder. Don't use a trailing slash (C:\Winxp is good, but C:\Winxp\ is bad). *Destination* is the folder in which Mkimg.cmd will create the custom version of Windows PE. Mkimg.cmd will create this folder if it doesn't already exist. *Isoimage* is the path and filename of the International Organization for Standardization (ISO) image you want to create. You'll typically not use *Isoimage* because you want to create the ISO image after you've made other customizations. For example, if the Windows PE source files are in C:\MyWinpe, and the Windows XP Professional CD is in drive D, run the command **mkimg D: C:\MyWinpe\I386**.

    The process completes after several minutes. The result is the Windows PE files in the destination directory and optionally an ISO image that you can burn to a CD. If you're using Windows PE from RIS or from a hard disk image, you probably don't care about the ISO image. As well, you should wait to create the ISO image if you have additional customizations you want to make.

> **Note** You can create a custom version of Windows PE from any version of Windows XP or Windows Server 2003 except for Windows XP Home Edition or Windows Datacenter Server 2003.

The size of the 32-bit Windows PE image is about 120 MB. Your customizations will use additional space. Adding languages to the image also uses additional space. Regardless, there is usually enough room to copy the Windows XP Professional source files to the Windows PE CD so that you can more fully automate the Windows XP Professional installation process for users or technicians. If the Windows XP

Professional source files don't fit on the CD with your custom version of Windows PE, then you can reduce the size of Windows PE considerably. "Windows Preinstallation Environment User's Guide," which you find on the Windows PE CD in the file Winpe.chm, describes which files you can remove to reduce the size of Windows PE.

> **Tip**   To configure Windows PE to start from the CD every time without requiring the user to press a key, remove the file bootfix.bin from the I386 folder of the Windows PE directory structure before you create an .iso image. Bootfix.bin provides the Press Any Key To Boot From CD-ROM message.

Command-Line Tools

The following command-line tools are available when preinstalling an operating system or using Windows PE:

- **Diskpart**   Diskpart is a text-mode command interpreter that enables you to manage objects (disks, partitions, or volumes) by using scripts or direct input from a command prompt. With Diskpart, you can create and remove volumes, assign drive letters, and so on.

- **Factory**   Use Factory to update drivers, run Plug and Play enumeration, install applications, test, configure the computer with customer data, or make other configuration changes in your factory environment. For companies that use disk imaging (or cloning) software, efficient use of Factory can reduce the number of images you require.

- **Mkimg**   This command builds the file set for Windows PE from any Windows XP or Windows Server 2003 product CD except Windows XP Home Edition and Windows .NET Datacenter Server. It optionally creates an ISO image of the files. You can then burn that ISO file to a CD by using any CD-burning software that supports ISO-9660. The CD image-creation process takes several minutes and then the files are placed in the same location as where you run the *Mkimg* command.

- **Netcfg**   The network configuration tool configures network access. When you preinstall Windows, it is most commonly used in a script that runs when Windows PE boots. You don't need to use this tool if you're starting the network with the command *factory –winpe* in Startnet.cmd, which is the default.

- **Oscdimg**   This is a command-line tool that creates an ISO image file of a customized 32-bit or 64-bit version of Windows PE. You can then burn that ISO image file to a CD.

On the Resource Kit CD   See "Windows Preinstallation Environment User's Guide," which is Winpe.chm on the Windows PE CD in the Docs folder, for more information about these tools. Winpe.chm includes detailed documentation for each command-line option that these tools support. You find examples of using these tools in this chapter.

There are additional tools that would be useful to add to your Windows PE image, including the scripts that you create to automate redundant processes such as partitioning and formatting disks. You can place them anywhere within your Windows PE CD, but I recommend a subfolder in the I386 folder so that the tools will be available if you install Windows PE in RIS. Also, the following list describes tools that I like to include in a Windows PE image for installation preparation:

- Windiff.exe from the Windows Support Tools

- Depends.exe from the Windows Support Tools

- File Monitor (FileMon from Sysinternals at *http://www.sysinternals.com*)

- Registry Monitor (RegMon from Sysinternals at *http://www.sysinternals.com*)

Optional Components

You can add the following components to a customized Windows PE image:

- **ActiveX Data Objects**   ADO enables your client applications to access and manipulate data from a Microsoft SQL Server database through an OLE DB provider. Its primary benefits are ease of use, high speed, low memory overhead, and a small disk footprint. ADO supports key features for building client/server and Web-based applications. Windows PE doesn't support ADO access to Microsoft Access or Active Directory, though.

- **HTML Applications**   HTAs are full-fledged applications that are trusted and display only the menus, icons, toolbars, and title information that the Web developer creates. In short, HTAs pack all the power of Microsoft Internet Explorer—its object model, performance, rendering power, protocol support, and channel-download technology—without enforcing the strict security model and user interface of the browser. You can use the HTML and Dynamic HTML (DHTML) that you already know to create HTAs.

On the Resource Kit CD   This book's companion CD contains HTAs in the sample distribution points for this chapter. They are in the folder Samples \chap14.

■ **Windows Script Host**   WSH is a language-independent host that allows you to run any script engine on the Windows operating system. WSH is useful for scripting complex tasks that you can't easily do by using batch scripts.

Tip   If you intend to automate installations, you almost always want to include WSH and HTA in Windows PE. Size isn't a concern if you're installing Windows XP Professional from the network.

BuildOptionalComponents.vbs is the script you use to add support for optional component packages. This script is in the Windows PE Winpe folder. If you run this script without any command-line options, it creates a folder containing all the optional components. If you run this script with specific command-line options, the folder it creates contains only those components. After the script finishes, you simply copy the folder it creates over the I386 folder for your Windows PE image. The following describes syntax of BuildOptionalComponents.vbs, and Table 14-1 describes each command-line option:

```
BuildOptionalComponents [/S:location] [/D:location] /ADO /HTA /WSH /64 /Q /E
```

Table 14-1   BuildOptionalComponents.vbs Command-Line Options

/S:location	Specifies the source location of the Windows XP Professional source files.
/D:location	Specifies the destination location for the component files.
/ADO	Specifies to build ADO for Microsoft SQL Server connectivity.
/HTA	Specifies to build HTA.
/WSH	Specifies to build WSH.
/64	Specifies to build and check 64-bit version of Windows PE (requires Windows XP 64-Bit Edition).
/Q	Runs the script without prompting for inputs; returns any errors.
/E	Explores the resulting folder automatically when complete.

After you add optional components to Windows PE, customize Startnet.cmd to install them when Windows PE starts. BuildOptionalComponents.vbs creates the batch script oc.bat in %SYSTEMROOT%\System32, which installs the optional components. Call this batch script from Startnet.cmd, as shown in Listing 14-1.

Network Drivers

Although Windows PE supports network and mass-storage drivers, other types of device drivers don't function in Windows PE. Even if they appear to function, they're likely missing key dependencies that prevent them from working properly.

Windows PE supports all the network drivers included on the Windows product CD. When customizing a Windows PE image, you can add, remove, or replace network drivers as necessary. For example, you can remove unnecessary network drivers to reduce the size of the image and the time required to boot. After completing the following three steps, the Factory command in Startnet.cmd automatically identifies the network drivers that you add:

1. Copy the driver's *.inf* files to %SYSTEMROOT%\Inf (the matching catalog file isn't necessary).

2. Copy the driver's *.sys* files to %SYSTEMROOT%\System32\drivers.

3. Copy related *.dll*, *.exe*, or other files to %SYSTEMROOT%\system32.

In addition to adding, removing, and replacing network drivers, you can limit the number of network adapters that the factory command scans by using the *[netcards]* section of the Winbom.ini file. When this command runs from the Startnet.cmd batch file, it scans only for the network adapters in this section, resulting in a faster boot time. To add network adapters to this section, you must know the adapter's Plug and Play ID and the path of its .inf file. The following example shows the values necessary to specify the adapter's specific Plug and Play ID as well as its more generic ID, which ensures that it matches any network adapter supported by the driver:

```
[NetCards]
PCI\VEN_10B7&DEV_9200&SUBSYS_100010B7&REV_78\3&61AAA01&0&78=%systemroot%\|
nic\netel90b.inf
PCI\VEN_10B7&DEV_9200&SUBSYS_100010B7=%systemroot%\nic\netel90b.inf
```

Mass-Storage Drivers

Configuring a limited set of mass-storage drivers can reduce the boot time of Windows PE. Instead of loading the entire set of mass-storage drivers that the Windows product CD natively supports, Windows PE just loads the drivers that you specify in the Winpeoem.sif file, which is in %SYSTEMROOT%\System32. You can also configure this file to support additional mass-storage drivers that the Windows product CD doesn't natively support. The Winpeoem.sif file has the following three sections for controlling mass-storage drivers:

- *[MassStorageDrivers.Append]*   Specifies one or more third-party mass-storage drivers that a custom version of Windows PE loads in addition to the entire set of drivers that the Windows product CD supports. You copy the driver files to the %SYSTEMROOT%\System32\Drivers folder and copy supporting files to the appropriate locations as specified in the driver's .inf file.

- *[MassStorageDrivers.Replace]*   Specifies one or more third-party mass-storage drivers that a custom version of Windows PE loads instead of the entire set of drivers that the Windows product CD supports. You copy the driver files to the %SYSTEMROOT%\System32\Drivers folder and copy supporting files to the appropriate locations as specified in the driver's .inf file.

- *[OEMDriverParams]*   Specifies non-Plug and Play drivers for Windows PE to load in addition to the drivers that Windows XP Professional natively supports.

See "Windows Preinstallation Environment User's Guide," which is Winpe.chm on the Windows PE CD in the Docs folder, for detailed instructions about using this section.

Note   The F6 option to add mass-storage drivers still works when starting Windows PE.

Languages

Windows PE doesn't support multilanguage builds—only individual-language localized builds. Still, you can build Windows PE images in various languages without needing localized Windows PE tools for each language. In other words, you can use a single set of tools to build multiple localized Windows PE images.

You use the *[RegionalSettings]* section in the Config.inf file to add support for multiple languages. You must always match the Language value to the language of the Windows product CD that you're using to build the Windows PE image. Then, you use the *LanguageGroup* value to specify the languages of both the Windows PE tools and the Windows product CD. For a list of the specific languages that correspond to particular language groups, see the Microsoft Global Software Development Web site.

For example, to create a Japanese Windows PE image by using a Japanese Windows product CD, set **LanguageGroup=1,7** and **Language=0x0411** in the *[RegionalSettings]* section of Config.inf. The language group ID for Western Europe and United States is 1, and 7 is the language group ID for Japanese. The local ID (LCID) for Japanese is 0x0411, which matches the local of the Windows product CD. Adding 1 to the *LanguageGroup* value ensures that you can use the English preinstallation tools.

Starting Windows PE

Table 14-2 summarizes the three ways you can start Windows PE. You can create a bootable Windows PE CD or DVD, for example. You can install Windows PE in RIS. You can install Windows PE on a computer's hard disk so that the next time the computer starts, it logs on to the network, installs Windows XP Professional, and then deploys an image of that hard disk. The sections following this one describe how to create each of these three scenarios.

> **On the Resource Kit CD**   Notice the entry for 64-bit Windows in the table. You can create a 64-bit version of Windows PE from 64-bit Windows XP. The steps for creating this version of Windows PE are only slightly different from creating the 32-bit version, and they're well documented in the *Windows Pre-installation Environment User's Guide*, which you find on the Windows PE CD in the file Winpe.chm.

Table 14-2   Starting Windows PE

	Removable Media (CDs)	RIS	Non-removable Media (Hard Disks)
Disconnected PCs	Yes	No	Yes
Networked PCs	Not recommended	Yes	Not recommended
Active Directory	Not required	Required by RIS	Not required
64-bit Windows	Yes	No	Yes
Third-party tools	Not required	Not required	Useful

CD-Based Installation

When you build a custom Windows PE image (which you learned about in the section "Customizing Windows PE," earlier in this chapter on page 412), the result is an ISO image that you can burn to a CD using most popular CD-burning programs such as Ahead Nero Burning ROM (*http://www.ahead.com*). However, you might want to create an ISO image after customizing Windows PE further. In the folder that contains the Windows PE customization tools, Winpe, run the command **oscdimg –n –betfs-boot.com** *winpedestdir imagename*. *Winpedestdir* is the path of the customized version of Windows PE (the folder containing the I386 folder, Win51, Win51iP, Win51ip.sp1, and Winbom.ini). *Imagename* is the path and filename of the ISO image file that you want to create.

On the Resource Kit CD   Because this command and its command-line options are almost impossible to remember, I created the batch script winpecd.cmd on this book's companion CD in the Scripts folder. To use it, run the command **winpecd.cmd** *winpeimg isofile*, where *winpeimg* is the path of the folder to the Windows PE folder, and *isofile* is the path and name of the ISO file to create. You must make sure that oscdimg.exe is in the path or the same directory as the winpecd.cmd batch script.

Customizing Product CDs

You can use Oscdimg.exe to create customized CDs from the original Windows XP Professional or Windows Server 2003 CDs without Windows PE, too. For example, you can replace the file Winnt.sif in the product CD's I386 folder to customize installation. Here's an example using Windows XP Professional:

1. Copy a Windows XP Professional CD to a folder on your hard disk. For example, copy the entire CD to C:\Winxp.

2. Replace Winnt.sif in the I386 folder with a customized version that installs Windows XP Professional per your requirements.

3. In the Winpe folder, run the command *oscdimg.exe -n -bETFSBOOT.COM -lLabel Path Isopath*. The placeholder *Label* is the volume label of the original Windows XP Professional CD. The placeholder *Path* is the path of the folder containing the copy of the Windows XP Professional CD (C:\Winxp in step 1). The placeholder *Isopath* is the path and filename of the ISO image you want to create.

4. Burn the ISO image you created in step 3 to a new CD.

You can boot the computer using the customized Windows XP Professional product CD, and Windows XP Setup will use your customized Winnt.sif to install the operating system.

RIS-Based Installation

To speed the deployment process, you can start the target computer with Windows PE by using RIS. The benefit of starting Windows PE from the network is that you don't need to start the computer manually by using a bootable CD. This method is available for the 32-bit versions of Windows PE, but not for the 64-bit version.

> **More Info**   For more information about RIS, see Chapter 16.

To install Windows PE in RIS, you need either a Windows XP Professional product CD or an existing Windows XP Professional CD-based image. The Windows XP Professional product CD or existing Windows XP Professional CD-based image must be the same build number as Windows PE (otherwise, Windows PE might not start properly). You also need a properly configured RIS server, whether Windows 2000 Service Pack 2 or Windows Server 2003.

> **More Info**   Chapter 16 describes how to configure a Windows 2000 RIS server for use with Windows XP Professional.

Last, the client computer must support booting with PXE, or the RIS boot disk must support the NIC installed in the computer. With these requirements met, the following steps show how to install Windows PE in RIS:

1. Do one of the following:

   - Copy an existing Windows XP Professional CD-based image.

   - Create a new CD-based image using a Windows XP Professional product CD.

2. Copy the I386 folder from the CD or folder containing the Windows PE files over the I386 folder of the Windows XP Professional CD-based image you created in step 1. If Windows Explorer prompts you to overwrite folders or files, click Yes.

3. If your Windows PE files don't include a Winbom.ini file in %SYSTEMROOT% \System32, copy Winbom.ini from the root folder containing the files to the RIS image's I386\System32 folder.

If Factory doesn't find a Winbom.ini file that contains the setting *Restart=No* in the *[Winpe]* section, it prompts the user for whether to restart the computer, shut down the computer, or quit. The default Winbom.ini file that comes with Windows PE contains this setting, but you must copy the file to the image's System32 folder for Factory to find it when starting Windows PE from RIS.

4. In the CD-based image's Templates folder, open Ristndrd.sif in a text editor. Then, add the option **/minint** to the line that begins with *OSLoadOptions*.
Also change the description and help in the *[OSChooser]* section.

5. Start the RIS client and choose the operating system image that you created in the first step.
This procedure starts Windows PE from the network.

Disk-Based Installation

You can install a customized version of Windows PE on a hard disk, which is useful for preinstalling an operating system or creating a hard disk-based recovery solution, particularly for laptop computers. For example, you can install Windows PE on a small partition and the operating system on another partition. This configuration supports disaster-recovery scenarios by preventing the need for boot media to start the PC and source files for reinstalling the operating system, recovering data from the computer, or repairing the configuration. Here are the steps for installing Windows PE on a hard disk:

1. Boot the destination computer into Windows PE using a Windows PE CD.

2. Partition and format the computer's hard disk.
You can use Diskpart to quickly partition the disk and then use Format to format it. Don't forget to mark the disk as active.

3. On the active hard disk, create the directory C:\Minint and then copy the contents of the Windows PE CD's I386 folder to C:\Minint.
For example, use the command *xcopy d:\i386 c:\minint /s.*

4. Copy Ntdetect.com from the CD to the root of the hard disk.

5. Copy C:\Minint\setupldr.bin to C:\ntldr.

6. Restart the computer; it starts using Windows PE.

Automating Installations

So far in this chapter, you've learned how to customize Windows PE. You can add optional components such as WSH and HTA. You can add your own batch scripts and utilities to it. And after you complete your customizations, you can create a new CD or copy them to RIS. With a customized Windows PE CD, you can start each target computer in fine style, but you still have to manually configure disks, start Windows XP Setup, and so on. The power of Windows PE is its automation features. You can script most of the installation tasks you might need to perform. And when you do need to collect information from the user or technician, you can use HTA.

> **More Info**   For more information about creating HTAs, see HTML Goodies at *http://www.htmlgoodies.com/beyond/hta.html* and Microsoft MSDN at *http://msdn.microsoft.com/workshop/author/hta/hta_node_entry.asp*.

This book's companion CD contains sample distribution folders for deploying Windows XP Professional by using Windows PE in the Samples\chap14 folder. The subfolder win2002.pro prompts the user for information and uses it to generate an answer file. The subfolder win2002-db.pro is database-driven. Both samples require you to customize Windows PE with WSH and HTA. The subfolder win2002-db.pro requires you to customize Windows PE with ADO.

Both sample distribution points are based on the distribution folder you learned about in Chapter 7 and Chapter 11. Make sure that you read both chapters before trying to decipher the sample distribution points in this chapter. There are three key additions to the distribution folders in Samples\chap14 over what you learned about in Chapters 7 and 11, though (see setup32.cmd in each sample to learn how each of these scripts and HTAs fit together). The following sections describe these scripts.

> **Note**   In most environments, the sample scripts that you read about in this section and see in the Samples\chap14 on the companion CD aren't very useful without customization. They are examples only; you must customize them to suit your requirements. For example, the sample sifdata.hta prompts for settings such as the user's name; you probably need to collect different information. The sample distribution point in Samples\chap14 \win2002-db.pro looks up computer information in a local database, which isn't appropriate if you're storing configuration data in a SQL Server database. Use these sample scripts as starting points, and customize them to suit your project's requirements.

Verifying Hardware Requirements

The script verify.wsf verifies that the target computer meets the minimum hardware requirements as specified on the script's command line. If the computer meets the minimum hardware requirements, it returns an error level of 0, which is easy to test in a batch script (as shown in setup32.cmd in Samples\chap14\win2002.pro). A higher error level indicates that the computer fails the hardware requirements, and presumably installation should not continue.

There are a few caveats for using this script:

- You can run the script verify.wsf only by using the host Cscript.exe, which isn't a problem because you're running it in Windows PE.

- The script verify.wsf requires the file physmem.exe. Due to limitations in Windows PE, an external program is required to look up the physical memory installed on the target computer. Make sure that physmem.exe is in the same folder as the script verify.wsf.

On the Resource Kit CD   The script verify.wsf is on the companion CD in the Scripts folder. It's also in the folders Samples\chap14\win2002.pro and Samples\chap14\win2002-db.pro on the CD. For more information about this script's command-line options, type the command **cscript verify.wsf /?** at the command prompt. To see a sample of using it to verify the target computer's hardware requirements in Windows PE, see setup32.cmd in Samples\chap14\win2002.pro.

Prompting Users for Data

The HTA sifdata.hta displays a menu of configurations available in the distribution point, storing the user's choice in an environment variable. It looks in each of the distribution point's subfolders (two levels deep) for a specific target file (typically, winnt32.cmd). In the sample distribution points, each configuration (win2002.pro \OEM1, win2002.pro\OEM2, win2002.pro\OEMN) contains a batch file that starts Windows XP Setup for that configuration. That batch file is a perfect target for sifdata.hta. If a folder contains that target file, it adds the path to the menu. Storing the chosen path in an environment variable makes it easier to use batch scripts to start Windows XP Setup with the chosen configuration.

Also, the HTA sifdata.hta prompts users for information that is difficult to script without database support. Rather than allowing Windows XP Setup to prompt for the data, which requires the user or technician to hang around until Windows XP Setup gets to the GUI-mode phase, you can use sifdata.hta to prompt for the information up front and then store the user's input in the answer file using siftemp.wsf.

Examples of data that you can prompt users or technicians for include the full name, computer name, domain administrator account, and domain administrator password. The script siftemp.wsf substitutes variables (%FULLNAME% and so on) in an answer file with the data collected by sifdata.hta.

More Info   I described the script Siftemp.wsf in detail in Chapter 6.

On the Resource Kit CD   The HTA sifdata.hta is on the companion CD in the Scripts folder. It's also in the folders Samples\chap14\win2002.pro and Samples\chap14\win2002-db.pro on the CD. This HTA doesn't have any command-line options. You must run it by running sifdata.cmd, however. The batch script sifdata.cmd stores the results of the HTA as variables in the environment. Because the batch script sifdata.cmd calls clearenv.wsf, make sure that clearenv.cmd and clearenv.wsf are in the same folder as sifdata.cmd and sifdata.hta. To see a sample of using sifdata.hta, see setup32.cmd in Samples\chap14\win2002.pro.

Looking Up Database Records

In lieu of prompting users for information, you can store it in a database and then customize Windows PE with ADO so that you can extract the information from the database using the computer's Media Access Control (MAC) address as the key. The script dbrecord.wsf looks up a database record using a key and value you specify on the command line, and then returns the value of each field in the record.

For example, you populate a database with the information required to customize Windows XP Professional for each computer, adding each computer's MAC address to each record. Then, you can use the script dbrecord.wsf to look up the target computer's record based on its MAC address to retrieve data like the user's name, organization name, computer name, and so on. You use the script siftemp.sif to generate a customized answer file for the target computer based on the record returned by dbrecord.wsf.

More Info   I described the script Siftemp.wsf in detail in Chapter 6.

On the Resource Kit CD   The sample script dbrecord.wsf appears only in Samples\chap14\win2002-db.pro, and it supports comma-separated text files and Microsoft Excel spreadsheets. You can easily customize this script to add support for Microsoft SQL Server databases. For more information about this script's command-line options, use the command **cscript dbrecord.wsf /?** at the command prompt. To see a sample of using dbrecord.wsf, see setup32.cmd in Samples\chap14\win2002-db.pro.

Best Practices

The following are best practices for Windows PE:

- **Break the MS-DOS barrier.**   Forget everything you assumed about preparing computers for installation. To get the most out of Windows PE, you have to assume that there is a way to accomplish what you need.

- **Customize device drivers.**   Add the network and mass-storage device drivers required for your environment. But you can start Windows PE more quickly by limiting the device drivers it loads, as described in "Customizing Windows PE," earlier in this chapter on page 412.

- **Customize Windows PE with WSH and HTA.**   Half the power of Windows PE is the automation that's available. Unless you need the space when creating a distribution CD for Windows XP Professional, add the WSH and HTA components to Windows PE so you have full access to these features.

- **Fully customize installations by starting scripts from Startnet.cmd.** You can script most preinstallation, installation, and post-installation tasks using batch scripts, WSH, and HTAs. Launch these scripts from Startnet.cmd.

- **Use scripts and Diskpart instead of Winbom.ini in most cases.** Winbom.ini is predominantly a tool for system builders. For enterprise deployments, scripting installations using batch scripts, WSH, HTAs, and Diskpart is more flexible than using Winbom.ini.

- **Install Windows PE in RIS.**   If you have Active Directory and RIS, install Windows PE in RIS to make it more accessible as a deployment and troubleshooting tool. See the section "RIS-Based Installation," earlier in this chapter on page 421.

Chapter 15

Disk Imaging with Sysprep

Disk imaging is one of the most common techniques for deploying Microsoft Windows XP Professional and Microsoft Office 2003 Editions. Disk images deploy faster than other techniques. For a little more than the cost of deploying the operating system alone (bandwidth, disk space, man hours, and so on), you can include other applications and settings in your deployment. Finally, deploying disk images is a process that's straightforward to automate, reducing errors and user interaction. This chapter shows you how to create disk images using the Microsoft System Preparation tool and then describes the process of deploying them using third-party tools.

Checklist

- Have you determined which applications you want to include on your disk image? See Chapter 1, "Deployment Plan," for more information.

- Have you determined which settings you want to configure on your disk image? See Chapter 3, "Windows Configuration," for more information.

- Have you built a Windows XP Professional distribution point to install the operating system? See Chapter 6, "Answer Files," and Chapter 7, "Distribution Points," for more information.

- Have you selected third-party disk-imaging software? See the section "Disk-Imaging Tools" in this chapter on page 431.

- Have you planned a image-distribution method? See the section "Deploying the Disk Image" in this chapter on page 456.

Overview

Disk imaging is the fastest way to install Windows XP Professional on a large scale. To use this technique, you use third-party disk-imaging software or hardware disk duplicators. Disk-imaging software is more common because it's usually more flexible and provides more tools for managing the process. The Windows XP Professional deployment tools don't include disk-imaging software, so you must use third-party products, some of which I describe in the section "Disk-Imaging Tools" on page 431. The deployment tools do include software that helps you install Windows XP Professional and prepare it for duplication, however.

To deploy a disk image, you first set up a master installation (also called a source or sample installation), which is a computer with the operating system, applications, and settings that you want to install on destination computers in your organization. You already know how to complete this first step. Chapter 6, Chapter 7, Chapter 8, "Windows Settings," Chapter 11, "Chaining Installations," and Chapter 13, "Unattended Setup" show you how to automatically install Windows XP Professional, applications, and settings on any computer. After installing the operating system, applications, and settings on the sample computer, you run Sysprep, which prepares the master installation so that you can create a disk image that you can copy to multiple computers. Next, you use a third-party disk-imaging program to create the disk image of the master installation. Finally, you copy the disk image onto your destination computers.

On the Resource Kit CD Sysprep and its related files are on the
Windows XP Professional distribution media in Deploy.cab, which is in the
Support\Tools folder. For more information about using Sysprep, see
"Microsoft Windows Corporate Deployment Tools User's Guide," which is the
file Deploy.chm in Deploy.cab.

The tools are a given, but I'm jazzed about the documentation in the
file Deploy.cab—it's a huge improvement over the deployment documentation
for Windows 2000. First, Ref.chm describes how to build answer files and
includes a reference that describes all the settings you can use. Second,
Deploy.chm describes how to use the disk-imaging tools in Deploy.cab. It
also contains a complete reference for all the settings you can use in
answer files. This is the resource from which you're going to learn the most
about disk imaging.

You run Sysprep on the sample computer before you create an image of its
hard disk. Sysprep configures operating system settings on the sample computer to
ensure that every copy of the disk image is unique when you distribute it to a destination computer. Importantly, Sysprep configures the master installation so that
each destination computer has a unique security identifier (SID). Sysprep also configures the disk image so that every destination computer starts in Mini-Setup. Mini-
Setup is a shortened form of GUI-mode Setup that takes five or six minutes instead
of the usual 45 to 60 minutes, and it prompts the end user only for required and
user-specific information, such as accepting the End-User License Agreement
(EULA) and entering the product key, user name, and company name. After you
install a disk image on a destination computer, Mini-Setup runs the first time the destination computer starts.

Here's an overview of the entire disk-imaging process:

- Use the deployment tools to create a master installation of Windows XP
  Professional on a sample computer. Use the templates and techniques in Chapter
  6, Chapter 7, Chapter 8, Chapter 11, and Chapter 13 to automate the process.

- Run Sysprep using one of the following methods:

  - Start the installation and run Sysprep to prepare the disk image.

  - Add a command to your unattended-setup answer file that automatically
    runs Sysprep after installing Windows XP Professional on the sample
    computer. I prefer this method because the result is an automated process
    that leaves the sample computer in a state ready for cloning.

  - Use disk-imaging software to create an image of the master installation.

■ Transfer the image to your destination computers either across your network, by using a custom Windows Preinstallation Environment CD (see Chapter 14, "Preinstallation Environment"), or by transferring the image to a hard disk and installing the hard disk in the destination computer.

Note   Windows XP Professional supports two first-run experiences. The first is Windows Welcome, which is the typical experience that users have when they start a computer that they purchased from an original equipment manufacturer (OEM) or a store. The second is Mini-Setup, which is the typical experience that users have when they start a computer that IT prepares in a corporate environment. This chapter focuses on the Mini-Setup experience. For more information about Windows Welcome, see "Microsoft Windows Corporate Deployment Tools User's Guide," which is the file Deploy.chm in Deploy.cab. Deploy.cab is in the Support\Tools folder for the Windows XP Professional distribution media.

On the Resource Kit CD   For help planning and documenting a disk image, see "Disk Image Worksheet" on this book's companion CD. The file is diskimg01.doc in the Aids folder.

Sysprep Requirements

The following are key requirements for using Sysprep:

■ **Clean installation only**   You can use image-based installations only to install a clean version of the operating system and clean versions of software applications. You cannot use image-based installations to upgrade an operating system or software configuration.

■ **HAL compatibility**   You can perform an image-based installation only if the hardware abstraction layer (HAL) on the disk image is compatible with the hardware on the destination computer. In some cases, Windows XP Professional automatically upgrades the HAL that is on a disk image to suit the requirements of a destination computer, but this can occur only if the HAL on the disk image meets several requirements. For example, HAL APIC (Advanced Programmable Interrupt Controller) and HAL multiprocessor systems (MPs) are compatible, whereas the HAL programmable interrupt controller (PIC) is not compatible with either HAL APIC or HAL MPs.

■ **Limited configuration of some security settings**   You can't use image-based installations to deploy computers that contain any files that are encrypted using Encrypting File System (EFS). In addition, you cannot use image-based installations to deploy systems that you've already configured with NTFS security settings, such as file and folder permissions, unless the disk-imaging program supports the NTFS file system (most, including Symantec Ghost, do). You can use a script to configure these settings after installation is complete.

■ **Mass-storage controller compatibility**   The mass-storage controllers (Integrated Device Electronics [IDE] or Small Computer System Interface [SCSI]) must be identical types between the reference and destination computers. Windows XP Professional documentation also that the mass-storage controllers (IDE, SCSI, and the like) must be identical on the sample and target computers. This isn't necessarily so if you tell Sysprep in advance about the mass-storage controllers you're anticipating. (For more information, see the section titled, "Reducing Image Count," later in this chapter on page 438.) I've had good luck building images using one mass-storage controller and deploying to computers with completely different mass-storage controllers.

■ **Other hardware doesn't have to match**   Plug and Play (PnP) devices such as modems, sound cards, network adapters, video cards, and so on do not have to be the same on each destination computer. Device drivers not included in Drivers.cab should be included in the master installation before you run Sysprep. Alternatively, make sure that the uninstalled drivers are available on the destination computer at first run, so PnP can detect and install the drivers.

■ **Third-party disk-imaging software is required**   Third-party software or disk-duplicating hardware devices are required. These products create binary images of a computer's hard disk, and they either duplicate the image to another hard disk or store the image in a file on a separate disk.

■ **Hard disk size**   The size of the destination computer's hard disk must be at least the same size as the hard disk of the master installation. If the destination computer has a larger hard disk, the difference is not included in the primary partition. However, you can use the `ExtendOemPartition` entry in the Sysprep.inf file to extend the primary partition if it was formatted to use the NTFS file system.

Disk-Imaging Tools

The third-party disk-imaging software I use most often is Symantec Ghost. The product is easy to use and performs well with few problems. For more information about this product, see *http://www.symantec.com*. The following are mainstream disk-imaging products for you to evaluate.

- **Symantec Ghost**   See *http://www.symantec.com.*
- **PowerQuest DeployCenter**   See *http://www.powerquest.com.*
- **Altiris Deployment Solution**   See *http://www.altiris.com.*
- **Phoenix ImageCast**   See *http://www.phoenix.com.*

More Info   For a useful comparison of the mainstream disk-imaging products, see AppDeploy.com at *http://appdeploy.com/comparisons/imaging.*

Configuring Sysprep

For our purposes, Sysprep comprises three files, all of which you must put in the folder %SYSTEMDRIVE%\Sysprep on the sample computer:

- Sysprep.exe
- Setupcl.exe
- Sysprep.inf

When using Sysprep to prepare a disk image, you must copy all three files (Sysprep.exe, Setupcl.exe, and Sysprep.inf) to %SYSTEMDRIVE%\Sysprep. After copying the files to this folder, you can run Sysprep using its command-line options or its graphical user interface. After you deploy the disk image and the user finishes Mini-Setup, Mini-Setup removes the Sysprep folder. You can force Mini-Setup to leave this folder and its contents by setting FactoryMode=Yes in the [Unattended] section of Sysprep.inf. I don't recommend that you use this setting, however, because users can accidentally run Sysprep if it's exposed to them. It's very useful for testing and debugging purposes, though.

Creating Sysprep.inf

Sysprep.inf is an optional answer file that you can use to automate Mini-Setup fully or partially. Mini-Setup prompts the user for a few standard pieces of information required to configure the computer, such as time zone and keyboard settings. However, if Sysprep.inf is present and contains values for the required elements, Mini-Setup uses the information from Sysprep.inf instead of prompting the user. The syntax of Sysprep.inf is similar to the unattended-setup answer file. Sysprep.inf supports a subset of the sections and entries supported by regular answer files plus a few Sysprep-specific entries. When you run Sysprep.exe, the Sysprep.inf file is copied to %WINDIR%\System32\$winnt$.inf.

If Sysprep.inf is not used, Mini-Setup displays these screens:

- Welcome to Windows Setup
- License Agreement
- Product Key
- Regional and Language Options
- Personalize Your Software
- Computer Name and Administrator Password
- Date and Time Settings
- Networking Settings
- Workgroup or Computer Domain
- Completing Windows Setup

To bypass these pages and have Sysprep completely automate an installation, you can specify, at a minimum, the entries shown in Table 15-1.

Table 15-1   Fully Automating Mini-Setup

To Skip This Page	Add This Entry to Sysprep.inf
Welcome to Windows Setup	`[GuiUnattended]` `OemSkipWelcome=1`
License Agreement	`[Unattended]` `OemSkipEula=Yes`
Product Key	`[UserData]` `ProductKey=XXXXX`
Regional and Language Options	`[GuiUnattended]` `OemSkipRegional=1`

Personalize Your Software	`[UserData]`
	`FullName=Name`
	`OrgName=Name`

Computer Name and Administrator Password	`[UserData]`
	`ComputerName=Name`
	`[GuiUnattended]`
	`AdminPassword=Name`

Date and Time Settings	`[GuiUnattended]` `TimeZone=TZ`
Network Settings	`[Networking]`

Workgroup or Computer Domain	`[Identification]`
	`JoinWorkgroup=Workgroup`
	`or`
	`[Networking]`
	`[Identification]`
	`JoinDomain=Domain`
	`DomainAdmin=Name`
	`DomainAdminPassword=Password`

A typical Sysprep.inf file isn't complicated. Many times, Sysprep.inf can be as short as 10 lines. Listing 15-1 shows an example Sysprep.inf file, which is lengthy only because it's well-documented. You find this sample Sysprep.inf file on this book's companion CD in the Samples\chap15\win2002.pro folder. Look in each OEMΝ\$OEM$\\$1\Sysprep folder.

More Info See Chapter 6 and Appendix D, "Answer File Syntax," for more information about creating answer files, including Sysprep.inf.

Listing 15-1 Sysprep.inf

```
[Unattended]
    DriverSigningPolicy=Ignore
    ExtendOemPartition=1
    InstallFilesPath=\SYSPREP\I386

; Replace OemPnPDriversPath with the path of the third-party
; device drivers (separate folders with a semicolon):

    OemPnPDriversPath=\WINDOWS\DRIVERS

    OemPreinstall=Yes
    OemSkipEula=Yes

; If users won't have access to the source location from which
; you built the disk image, uncomment the following settings and
; set it to a network path containing the Windows XP Professional
; I386 folder:

;    ResetSourcePath=\\Server\Windows\win2002.pro

    UnattendMode=ReadOnly

[GuiUnattended]
    OemSkipRegional=1
    OemSkipWelcome=1

; Replace TimeZone with the correct time zone for the computer.
; See Ref.chm or Appendix D, "Answer File Syntax," for values:

    TimeZone=020

[UserData]

; Replace ComputerName, FullName, and OrgName with appropriate
; values. If any of these values is missing, the setup program
; will prompt the installer for the value:
```

```
;     ComputerName="Sample"
;      FullName="User Name"
     OrgName="Company Name"

; Replace ProductID with your product ID. If you don't provide
; a product key here, the setup program will prompt the installer:

     ProductKey=XXXXX-XXXXX-XXXXX-XXXXX-XXXXX

[TapiLocation]

; Replace AreaCode and CountryCode with appropriate values. See
; Ref.chm or Appendix D, "Answer File Syntax," for values:

     AreaCode=972
     CountryCode=1
     Dialing=Tone

[Identification]

; Replace DomainAdmin and DomainAdminPassword with the credentials
; of an account that can join the computer to the domain. The setup
; program will prompt the installer for these values if missing:

     DomainAdmin=Administrator
     DomainAdminPassword=Password

; Replace JoinDomain with the name of the domain to join:

     JoinDomain=DOMAIN

; Optionally, uncomment and replace MachineObjectOU with the LDAP
; path of the OU in which to create the computer account, if the
; account doesn't already exist:

;     MachineObjectOU="OU=Accounts,DC=honeycutt,DC=corp"

[Networking]

; This empty section is necessary if the answer file will include
; additional network settings described in Ref.chm. This answer
; file configures the computer with default networking components,
; including Client for Microsoft Networks, File and Printer Sharing
; for Microsoft Networks, QoS Packet Scheduler, and Internet Protocol
; (TCP/IP) configured to use DHCP.


[Sysprep]
     BuildMassStorageSection=Yes

[SysprepMassStorage]

;end
```

Changes to Sysprep.inf

The following are changes to Sysprep.inf that have occurred since the release of Microsoft Windows 2000 Professional:

- [Sysprep] section. This section is new.
- [GuiUnattended] section:
  - EncryptedAdminPassword is a new setting that allows Mini-Setup to install encrypted passwords for the Administrator account.
  - The value of AutoLogonCount is always used, even if the password is blank (AdminPassword=*).
- [Unattended] section:
  - TapiConfigured is a new setting that specifies whether to preconfigure Telephony Application Programming Interface (TAPI) settings on the installation.
  - The length of OemPnpDriversPath in Sysprep.inf is no longer limited to 255 characters.
  - If a path specified by OemPnpDrivesPath is already in the registry at HKLM\Software\Microsoft\Windows\CurrentVersion\DevicePath, Sysprep does not append the path in OemPnPDriversPath to the registry key a second time.
  - UpdateInstalledDrivers specifies whether to call PnP after Mini-Setup to re-enumerate all the installed drivers, and to install any updated drivers in the driver path.
  - UpdateUPHal refers to Hal.inf instead of Mp2up.inf.
  - AutoLogonAccountCreation is no longer supported. Instead, user accounts are created during Windows XP Setup.
  - EncryptedDomainAdminPassword is no longer supported.
- [UserData] section:
  - ProductID is now called ProductKey.

Cleaning After Sysprep

Sysprep will clean the critical device database, which is a registry listing of devices and services that have to start in order for Windows XP Professional to boot successfully. After Mini-Setup finishes, the devices not physically present in the system are cleaned out of the database, and the critical devices present are left intact. This improves the startup performance of Windows XP Professional.

To clean this database, you must run the command **sysprep –clean** after Mini-Setup finishes configuring the operating system. It's best to automate this step, as described in the section "Sysprep Configuration," later in this chapter on page 447.

> **More Info**   For more information about optimizing disk images, see the section "Optimizing Disk Images," later in this chapter.

Automating Mini-Setup

Fully automating Mini-Setup can be difficult. The culprits are `FullName` and `Computer-Name`, both in the `[UserData]` section, and `JoinDomain` in the `[Identification]` section. You can't set the first two values in Sysprep.inf because it replicates them to every computer on which you install the image. This isn't a hardship for the user name, but it's a no-go for the computer name, which must be unique for every computer on the network. There are three ways to handle this:

- **Set a default user name, such as "Valued Employee," and allow Mini-Setup to generate a computer name.**   By setting `ComputerName=*`, Mini-Setup generates a computer name based on the organization name and computer's Media Access Control (MAC) address.

- **Use a script to change the user name and computer name after Mini-Setup finishes.**   Like the previous option, set a default user name and allow Mini-Setup to generate a computer name. Also, don't join the computer to the domain. Then, create a Windows Script Host (WSH) script to look up the user's name and computer name in a database based on the computer's MAC address and then change both settings after Mini-Setup finishes. The script also joins the computer to the domain.

- **Use disk-image deployment tools to automatically update the user name, update the computer name, and join the computer to the domain.**   For example, Symantec Ghost Enterprise Console provides tools for changing user and computer names after installing a disk image on target computers.

You can set `JoinDomain` in Sysprep.inf, but you don't want to put a plain-text administrator password in the file. See the section called "Join Domain" in Chapter 6 for ways to mitigate this issue.

Reducing Image Count

You can reduce the number of images you maintain by creating one master image to install Windows XP Professional on destination computers that may use different mass-storage controllers. Table 15-2 describes example scenarios.

Table 15-2   Mass Storage Controller Scenarios

Controller Used to Create the Master Installation	Controller on the Computer	Sample Scenario
IDE	IDE	Created the master image on a computer that uses a PCI IDE controller; the destination computers use an Intel IDE controller.
IDE	SCSI	Created the master image on a computer that uses a PCI IDE controller; some of the destination computers start from a SCSI controller such as an Adaptec 7800.
SCSI	SCSI	Created the master image on a computer that uses an Adaptec 7800 controller; the destination computers use a Qlogic controller.
SCSI	IDE	Created the master image on a computer that uses an Adaptec 7800 controller; some of the destination computers start from an IDE controller.

Note   For the IDE-to-SCSI and the SCSI-to-SCSI scenarios, the hard disks on the destination computers must be accessible through extended INT13 basic input/output system (BIOS) functions for Sysprep to function properly. The computers must be able to start with a boot.ini that uses the `multi()` syntax instead of the `scsi()` or `signature()` syntax. To ensure that the `multi()` syntax is used, add `UseBiosToBoot` to the unattended-setup answer file that you use to install the operating system on the sample computer.

To ensure that your image works on as many hardware configurations as possible, you must identify the mass-storage controllers that you anticipate using in each configuration. Before running Sysprep on the master installation and creating your image, identify the different mass-storage controllers that you can install on each destination computer in the [SysprepMassStorage] section of the Sysprep.inf file. You can do this automatically by following the steps in the section called "Automated." Sysprep prepopulates the necessary driver information so that Windows XP

Professional can load the correct drivers when the operating system starts on a computer that uses one of the predefined mass-storage controllers. This capability is available only for PnP mass-storage controllers or controllers that use PnP miniports. Also, the computers' HALs between master and destination computers must still be compatible.

When you use the [SysprepMassStorage] section, Sysprep adds the devices listed in it to the critical devices database. This database is in the registry at HKLM\SYSTEM \CurrentControlSet\Control\CriticalDeviceDatabase. Each subkey corresponds to a device you added to [SysprepMassStorage] and contains a link to the actual device driver in the registry. Windows XP Professional tries to start each device in the database every time it boots. The problem is that this increases boot time significantly—something you don't want to inflict on users. The sections "Cleaning After Sysprep" and "Sysprep Configuration" describe how to remove unused device drivers from this database by running the **sysprep –clean** command.

The following sections ("Manually" and "Automated") show you how to identify mass-storage controllers in Sysprep.inf. Manual configuration is labor-intensive and error-prone, however; so I recommend that you use the automated process, even if it makes Sysprep take longer to finish. By using the automated process to identify mass-storage controllers in Sysprep.inf, you essentially set it and forget it, putting all the work back on to Sysprep.

On the Resource Kit CD   For help planning and documenting mass storage controllers, see "Mass Storage Controller Worksheet" on this book's companion CD. The file is diskimg02.doc in the Aids folder.

Manually

If you know the exact set of PnP IDs for the mass-storage controllers that you require, you may improve the boot time of the operating system if you manually create the [SysprepMassStorage] section in Sysprep.inf. To identify the potential mass-storage controllers on destination computers when the driver comes with Windows XP Professional, use these steps:

1. Generate a list of each of the hardware IDs for each of the mass-storage controllers that may be on the destination computers. For the best results, include in this list only the subset of PnP IDs that are required for your environment. Identifying unnecessary hardware IDs in this list causes longer start-up times than is normally required.

2. Compare the list generated in step 1 to the hardware IDs listed in the *.inf* files in %SYSTEMROOT%\Inf to determine which references are needed.

3. For mass-storage controllers that are provided on the Windows product CD, create a Sysprep.inf file with the syntax shown in Listing 15-2. In the listing, `hardware_id` is the PnP ID for the device as specified in the device's *.inf* file, and `path_to_device_inf` is the path to the *.inf* file that contains the PnP ID of the controller to install. Listing 15-3 shows an example that supports different IDE controllers included in Windows XP Professional.

Listing 15-2

```
[SysprepMassStorage]
hardware_id = path_to_device_inf
```

Listing 15-3

```
[SysprepMassStorage]
PCI\VEN_8086&DEV_1222 = "%WINDIR%\inf\mshdc.inf"
PCI\VEN_8086&DEV_1230 = "%WINDIR%\inf\mshdc.inf"
PCI\VEN_8086&DEV_7010 = "%WINDIR%\inf\mshdc.inf"
PCI\VEN_8086&DEV_7111 = "%WINDIR%\inf\mshdc.inf"
PCI\VEN_8086&DEV_2411 = "%WINDIR%\inf\mshdc.inf"
PCI\VEN_8086&DEV_2421 = "%WINDIR%\inf\mshdc.inf"
PCI\VEN_8086&DEV_7199 = "%WINDIR%\inf\mshdc.inf"
```

For mass-storage controllers that are not provided on the Windows product CD, use the following steps:

1. Copy the driver files for the mass-storage controllers on the destination computers to a folder on your computer—for example, to %SYSTEMROOT%\Drivers\Storage on the master computer's hard drive.

2. Add lines to the [SysprepMassStorage] section in the following format: *hardware_id* = "path_to_device_inf", "disk_directory", "disk_description", "disk_tag". `hardware_id` is the PnP ID for the device as specified in the device's *.inf* file, and `path_to_device_inf` is the path to the *.inf* file that contains the PnP ID of the controller to install. `disk_directory` is the name of the folder on the floppy disk provided by the OEM that contains the copy of the mass-storage driver. `disk_description` is the description of the floppy disk as specified in the Txtsetup.oem file provided by the OEM. Last, `disk_tag` is the disk tag of the floppy disk as specified in the Txtsetup.oem file provided by the OEM. The `disk_directory`, `disk_description`, and `disk_tag` values are required so that the repair process can distinguish between drivers that are included on the Windows XP Professional product CD and drivers that are not provided on the product CD.

3. Place the driver files in the location specified in the [SysprepMassStorage] section of Sysprep.inf. For example, to support a new Qlogic driver, if you copy the files to the %SYSTEMROOT%\Drivers\Storage folder, add the following to the [SysprepMassStorage] section (the following line is wrapped but should be one text line in your Sysprep.inf file):

```
[SysprepMassStorage]
PCI\VEN_1077&DEV_1080 = "C:\Windows\Drivers\Storage\qlogic\qlogic.inf",
"C:\Windows\Drivers\Storage\qlogic", "Qlogic Software Disk",
"C:\Windows\Drivers\Storage\qlogic\qlogic"
```

4. Create a Cmdlines.txt file that runs the command **Sysprep –clean**. This command disables all the mass-storage controllers that are not installed because they are not present on the destination computer. See the section titled "Preparing a Disk Image" on page 445 for more information about this command. If this command isn't added to Cmdlines.txt, the start-up process for the destination computers may be slower because the operating system attempts to load each controller driver each time the computer restarts.

Automated

The process described in the previous section is tedious and difficult to follow. You don't need to manually create the entries in the [SysprepMassStorage] section, though. Instead, include the [Sysprep] section in the Sysprep.inf file, and Sysprep automatically generates the entries in [SysprepMassStorage] from the PnP hardware IDs specified in Machine.inf, Scsi.inf, Pnpscsi.inf, and Mshdc.inf. In the [Sysprep] section, set the value of BuildMassStorageSection=Yes, as shown in Listing 15-4.

That's it! This works only for drivers that ship with Windows XP Professional. Also, the [SysprepMassStorage] section must be empty, or else the procedure fails.

Listing 15-4

```
[Sysprep]
BuildMassStorageSection=Yes

[SysprepMassStorage]
```

This technique may install more mass-storage drivers than you require, so it may increase the boot time of the computer. Running **sysprep –clean** after Mini-Setup finishes removes unused mass-storage drives, though. See the section "Preparing a Disk Image" on page 445 for more information about this command. Regardless, this technique is much less likely to generate errors.

> **Note**   When you build the [SysprepMassStorage] section automatically, Sysprep takes much longer to run. Rather than shutting down the computer after a few seconds, which is Sysprep's typical behavior, Sysprep grinds away for about 15 minutes while it builds this section. Be patient as long as you see hard disk activity and a spinning hourglass. Reducing image count is worth the wait.

Running Sysprep

You can run Sysprep from the command line or from the graphical user interface (GUI). When you run Sysprep from the command line, you can use various command-line parameters to control the way Sysprep runs. This chapter assumes you are running Sysprep from the command line, since you must use the command line to automate Sysprep. The following shows the syntax of the Sysprep command line, and Table 15-3 describes each command-line option:

```
sysprep [-bmsd] | { {[-factory] | [-reseal]} {[-clean] | [-activated]
[-audit] [-forceshutdown] [-mini] [-noreboot] [-nosidgen] [-pnp]
[-quiet] [-reboot]} }
```

Table 15-3 Sysprep Command-Line Options

Option	Description
-activated	Does not reset the grace period for Windows Product Activation. Use this option only if you've already activated the operating system.
-audit	Reboots the computer into Factory mode without generating new SIDs or processing any items in the [OEMRunOnce] section of Winbom.ini. Use this command-line option only if the computer is in Factory mode.
-bmsd	If the [Sysprep] section contains the entry BuildMassStorageSection=Yes, the [SysprepMassStorage] section exists in Sysprep.inf, and you run the command *Sysprep -bmsd*, Sysprep populates [SysprepMassStorage] with the entries Plug_and_Play_ID = path_to_device_inf_file corresponding to the PnP IDs of mass-storage devices specified in Machine.inf, Scsi.inf, Pnpscsi.inf, and Mshdc.inf. Sysprep builds the list of mass-storage devices; it does not install these devices in the critical device database or do any other processing. After using the *Sysprep –bmsd* command to generate the entries of the [SysprepMassStorage] section, you can delete items from this section before running *Sysprep -reseal* or *Sysprep -factory* on this installation. Installing a smaller number of items in the critical device database reduces the time required for this image to reboot into the operating system. Do not use the *-bmsd* command-line option with any other command-line options.
-clean	Clears unused mass storage drivers added by the [SysprepMassStorage] section of Sysprep.inf and removes phantom devices created by PnP. Do not use the *–clean* command-line option with any other command-line options.
-factory	Restarts in a network-enabled state without displaying Windows Welcome or Mini-Setup. This option is useful for updating drivers, running PnP enumeration, installing applications, testing, configuring the computer with customer data, or making other configuration changes in your factory environment. For companies that use disk imaging (or cloning) software, Factory mode can reduce the number of images required. When you have finished your Factory mode tasks, run *Sysprep -Reseal* option to prepare the computer for delivery.

Table 15-3   Sysprep Command-Line Options

Option	Description
-forceshutdown	Shuts down the computer after Sysprep finishes. Use this option with computers with an Advanced Configuration and Power Interface (ACPI) BIOS that do not shut down properly with Sysprep's default settings.
-mini	Configures Windows XP Professional to use Mini-Setup instead of Windows Welcome. If you don't use this command-line option, Mini-Setup doesn't run and it doesn't process Sysprep.inf.
-noreboot	Modifies registry keys (SID, OemDuplicatorString, and so on) without the system rebooting or preparing for duplication. This option is used mainly for testing, specifically to see whether the registry is modified properly. This option is not recommended because making changes to a computer after Sysprep has run may invalidate the preparation done by Sysprep. Do not use this option in a production environment.
-nosidgen	Runs Sysprep without generating new SIDs. You must use this option if you do not duplicate the computer or if the computer is a domain controller.
-pnp	Runs the full PnP device enumeration and installation during Mini-Setup. This command-line option has no effect if the first-run experience is Windows Welcome. Use **-pnp** to detect and install only legacy, non-PnP devices. Do not use *-pnp* on computers that use only PnP devices. Otherwise, you will increase the time required for the first-run experience without providing any additional benefit to the user.
-quiet	Runs Sysprep without displaying onscreen confirmation messages, which is useful if you automate Sysprep. For example, if you plan to run Sysprep immediately after unattended Setup, add *Sysprep -quiet* to the [GuiRunOnce], as described in the section "Sysprep Configuration," later in this chapter on page 447.
-reboot	Forces the computer to reboot automatically and then start Windows Welcome, Mini-Setup, or Factory mode, as specified. This is useful when you want to audit the system and verify that the first-run experience operates correctly.
-reseal	Clears the Event Viewer logs and prepares the computer for delivery to the customer. Windows Welcome or Mini-Setup is set to start at the next boot. If you run the command *Sysprep -factory*, you must seal the installation as the last step in your preinstallation process, either by running the command *Sysprep -reseal* or by clicking the Reseal button in the Sysprep dialog box.

Tip   Sysprep doesn't always shut down the computer properly. Sometimes it just reboots the computer. If Mini-Setup Wizard starts, however, you can't use the image. To prevent a surprise reboot, stick a blank floppy disk in drive A before running Sysprep. Thus, if the computer does restart, the computer will boot from the floppy disk and the Mini-Setup Wizard won't run.

New Sysprep Features

Sysprep has several new features that are useful for image-based installations in corporate environments:

- **Cancel Restart Support**   A Sysprep parameter that prevents a computer from restarting after you run Sysprep. This parameter is mainly used for testing, especially to check if the registry was modified correctly after you perform installation tasks.

- **Countdown Timer Setting For Product Activation**   A Sysprep parameter that prevents a reset of the countdown timer for product activation. By default, the countdown timer for product activation is reset when you run Sysprep. This parameter is useful if you activate a computer before you deliver it to an end user. This setting is not relevant if you have a volume license.

- **Mass Storage Support**   A Sysprep parameter (*-bmsd*) and an answer file entry that instructs Sysprep to build a list of drivers for mass storage controllers. This prevents you from having to enter device driver information manually in the Sysprep answer file if an image supports more than one type of mass storage controller.

- **Device Driver Cleanup Support**   A Sysprep parameter that clears unused mass storage drivers added by the [SysprepMassStorage] section of Sysprep.inf and removes phantom devices created by PnP.

- **Audit Support**   A Sysprep parameter that lets you verify software and hardware installation without generating new SIDs or processing any items in the Factory mode answer file (Winbom.ini). You can use audit support only with the new Factory mode feature.

- **Factory Mode**   A Sysprep parameter that restarts a computer in a network-enabled state without running Mini-Setup. Factory mode is useful for updating drivers, running PnP enumeration, installing applications, testing, configuring the computer with customer data, or making other configuration changes before you deliver a computer to an end user. The Factory mode answer file, Winbom.ini, allows you to automate many installation tasks.

- **Forced Shutdown Support**   A Sysprep parameter that forces a computer to shut down after you run Sysprep. This parameter is useful if a computer has an ACPI BIOS and it does not shut down properly when you run Sysprep.

■ **Reseal Support**   A Sysprep parameter that clears the Event Viewer logs and prepares the computer for delivery to the customer. Typically, you use the *-reseal* parameter after you perform installation and auditing tasks in Factory mode.

In addition, the Sysprep answer file (Sysprep.inf) has several changes that affect the way you perform an image-based installation. For more information about the changes in Sysprep.inf, see the section "Changes to Sysprep.inf" on page 436.

Preparing a Disk Image

There are two ways to build a disk image. You can sit in front of a sample computer, install the operating system and applications manually, configure settings manually, and then run Sysprep manually. This is an error-prone process that's difficult to repeat if you must rebuild the disk image. I advise against any manual steps when building disk images.

The second method is to automate the process so that you run Windows XP Setup on the sample computer, walk away, and return to find that the disk is ready to duplicate. Keep the following in mind about automated disk-imaging when you're deciding between manual and automated methods:

■ **Stores master installation files in a central location**   Installation files are transferred from operating system CDs, file shares, and floppy disks to a centralized distribution share. Installation to the sample computer is from the distribution share, ensuring that you use the right files each time you build a disk image from the distribution files.

■ **Requires a fast network connection between the file server and master computers**   Network connectivity is necessary to transfer installation files from the distribution share on a file server to a master computer.

■ **Simplifies updating and modifying disk images**   Master installations are updated at a single location and then automatically installed on master computers before new disk images are created.

■ **Simplifies testing**   Errors can be fixed on the distribution share and then each master computer can be automatically updated.

■ **Doesn't require record-keeping to track installation and configuration information for each disk image**   The answer files in each configuration set provide installation and configuration information for each disk image.

- **Complements unattended installations** The distribution share you use to create your master installations can be used to perform your unattended installations.

- **Ensures consistency every time you make a change to a master installation** Changes are made to configuration sets on a centralized distribution share, which lessens the potential for inconsistency and errors.

The following sections describe how to prepare an automated disk-imaging process. You must first design a Windows XP Professional installation. Then create a way to copy additional files to the sample computer and install applications and settings. You can also install Office 2003 Editions to the master computer. Last, after installing the operating system, applications, and settings, you configure Sysprep and then run it to prepare the disk for duplication. Automate even this last step, as described in the section "Sysprep Configuration" on page 447.

On the Resource Kit CD This book's companion CD includes a sample distribution point that you can use to build a disk image. It's in the folder Samples\chap15. The section "Starting with a Template" describes how to use this sample. You must expand Deploy.cab from the Support\Tools folder on the Windows XP Professional distribution media in to the sample distribution point's Tools folder. Also, copy Sysprep.exe and Setupcl.exe from the Tools folder to OEM*N*\$OEM$\$1\Sysprep in the distribution point. I didn't provide the Sysprep files on the companion CD in order to ensure that you were using the most recent versions.

Windows Installation

The first step is to build a Windows XP Professional distribution point that automatically installs the operating system with no user intervention. This includes any device drivers that the installation requires for the hardware to which you're deploying the operating system. It also includes any applications that you want to install on the disk image, such as Office 2003 Editions. See Chapter 6, Chapter 7, Chapter 11, and Chapter 13.

Office 2003 Editions

There are a few considerations you must take if you're installing Office 2003 Editions on a disk image. First, I suggest that you use a local installation source (compressed CD image) to install Office 2003 Editions instead of an administrative installation. This ensures that users have access to the Office 2003 Editions source files, regardless of their network connectivity or location. For more information about local installation sources, see Chapter 7.

If you're using an administrative installation to install Office 2003 Editions, make sure that you define a source list for Office 2003 Editions by using Custom Installation Wizard to create a transform.

Last, set the NOUSERNAME property to True. This prevents Office 2003 Setup from defining a user name during installation, allowing users to enter their own names the first time they run an Office 2003 Editions program. You can set the property using the Modify Setup Properties page, Setup.ini, or the Office 2003 Setup command line. For more information about setting this property, see Chapter 9, "Office Settings."

To prevent user-specific information from appearing on the hard disk image, do not start any Office 2003 Editions programs on the sample computer. Starting an Office 2003 Editions program writes user-specific information to the Windows XP Professional registry, which is then duplicated to all users. All your Office 2003 Editions customizations and settings should be defined in your transform.

Sysprep Configuration

There are four key steps you must complete to automate the image-building process beyond just installing Windows XP Professional and applications on the sample computer. To fully automate the process, you must configure Sysprep, automatically run Sysprep, and then clean up the computer after Mini-Setup finishes. The following list describes these tasks:

1. You must create a Sysprep.inf file that customizes Mini-Setup.

    The section "Creating Sysprep.inf," earlier in this chapter on page 432 describes this file. If you're using the sample distribution folder in Samples\chap15 on the companion CD, customize Sysprep.inf to suit your requirements. (See the documentation I provided in the sample Sysprep.inf file for settings that you should customize.)

2. You must automatically create a Sysprep folder at the root of %SYSTEM-DRIVE%, which is typically drive C.

This folder includes three files: Sysprep.exe, Setupcl.exe, and Sysprep.inf. Sysprep.exe and Setupcl.exe are part of the Windows XP Professional deployment tools, which is Deploy.cab in the Support\Tools folder of the Windows XP Professional distribution CD. (These files aren't on this book's companion CD.) To create the Sysprep folder automatically, you add the folder and files to the OEM\$1 folder on your distribution point, as shown in the sample in Samples\chap15 on the companion CD. For example, to automatically create C:\Sysprep on the sample computer when you install Windows XP Professional to it, create the folder OEM\$1\Sysprep in your distribution point and then copy Sysprep.exe, Setupcl.exe, and Sysprep.inf files to it.

3. To fully automate the image-building process, you must automatically run Sysprep after Windows XP Setup finishes installing the operating system.

    The easiest way to do that is to execute the Sysprep command line from the [GuiRunOnce] section of the unattended-setup answer file that you're using to install the operating system on the sample computer. Listing 15-5 shows winnt.sif, a sample unattended-setup answer file that automatically runs Sysprep after installing the operating system. This answer file is part of the sample in the Samples\chap15 folder.

4. After deploying the disk image and Mini-Setup finishes, you want to run the command **Sysprep —clean** to remove unused device drivers from the computer's configuration.

To run this command, set `InstallFilesPath=\SYSPREP\I386` in Sysprep.inf and then create the file Cmdlines.txt in the I386\OEM subfolder of the Sysprep folder. This file should contain the following lines (the sample distribution point in Samples\chap15 on the companion CD already contains this file):

```
[Commands]
\Sysprep\Sysprep.exe -clean
```

Listing 15-5   winnt.sif

```
[Unattended]
    DriverSigningPolicy=Ignore
    FileSystem=ConvertNTFS

; Replace OemFilesPath with path to the $OEM$ folder:

    OemFilesPath=\\Server\Share\win2002.pro\OEM1\$OEM$

; Replace OemPnPDriversPath with the path of the third-party
; device drivers (separate folders with a semicolon):

    OemPnPDriversPath=\WINDOWS\DRIVERS
```

```
OemPreinstall=Yes
OemSkipEula=Yes
Repartition=No
TargetPath=\WINDOWS
UnattendMode=ReadOnly
UnattendSwitch=Yes
```

[GuiRunOnce]

```
; The following command starts runinst.vbs, which runs all of
; the packages contained in $OEM$\$$\APPS\RUNONCE. Then, it runs
; Sysprep to prepare the computer's disk for duplication.

    "%SYSTEMROOT%\APPS\runinst.vbs %SYSTEMROOT%\APPS\RUNONCE"
    "%SYSTEMDRIVE%\SYSPREP\sysprep.exe -mini -quiet -reseal -forceshutdown"

; Add commands this this section that you want Windows XP
; to run the first time a user logs on to it (enclose each
; command in quotation marks). See AdminPassword, AutoLogon,
; and AutoLogonCount in the [GuiUnattended] section.
```

[GuiUnattended]

```
; The following settings automatically log on to the computer as
; local Administrator one time. Doing so ensures that the commands
; listed in [GuiRunOnce] execute, which includes Sysprep. Note that
; AdminPassword must equal *, which is a blank password.

    AdminPassword=*
    AutoLogon=Yes
    AutoLogonCount=1

    OemSkipRegional=1
    OemSkipWelcome=1

; Replace TimeZone with the correct time zone for the computer.
; See Ref.chm or Appendix D, "Answer File Syntax," for values:

    TimeZone=020
```

[UserData]

```
; Replace ComputerName, FullName, and OrgName with appropriate
; values. If any of these values is missing, the setup program
; will prompt the installer for the value:

    ComputerName="Sample"
    FullName="User Name"
    OrgName="Company Name"

; Replace ProductID with your product ID. If you don't provide
; a product key here, the setup program will prompt the installer:
```

```
            ProductKey=XXXXX-XXXXX-XXXXX-XXXXX-XXXXX

[TapiLocation]

; Replace AreaCode and CountryCode with appropriate values. See
; Ref.chm or Appendix D, "Answer File Syntax," for values:

    AreaCode=972
    CountryCode=1
    Dialing=Tone


[Identification]

; Don't join this computer to a domain before running Sysprep.
; Instead, join it to a workgroup, as shown below, and then
; join it to a domain by using Sysprep.inf or a script.

    JoinWorkgroup=SAMPLE

[Networking]

; This empty section is necessary if the answer file will include
; additional network settings described in Ref.chm. This answer
; file configures the computer with default networking components,
; including Client for Microsoft Networks, File and Printer Sharing
; for Microsoft Networks, QoS Packet Scheduler, and Internet Protocol
; (TCP/IP) configured to use DHCP.

[Components]

; Uncomment and set each of the following components to On to install
; it or Off to not install it (see Ref.chm or Appendix D, "Answer File
; Syntax," for more information about each component). These settings
; don't necessarily correspond to the operating system defaults:

;    accessopt=On
;    calc=On
;    certsrv=Off
;    certsrv_client=Off
;    certsrv_server=Off
;    charmap=On
;    chat=Off
;    deskpaper=On
;    dialer=On
;    fax=Off
;    fp_extensions=Off
;    fp_vdir_deploy=Off
;    freecell=On
;    hearts=On
;    hypertrm=On
;    IEAccess=On
;    iis_common=Off
```

```
;    iis_ftp=Off
;    iis_htmla=Off
;    iis_inetmgr=Off
;    iis_nntp=Off
;    iis_nntp_docs=Off
;    iis_pwmgr=Off
;    iis_smtp=Off
;    iis_smtp_docs=Off
;    iis_www=Off
;    iis_www_vdir_printers=Off
;    iis_www_vdir_terminalservices=Off
;    iisdbg=Off
;    indexsrv_system=Off
;    media_clips=On
;    media_utopia=Off
;    minesweeper=On
;    mousepoint=On
;    mplay=On
;    msmq_ADIntegrated=Off
;    msmq_Core=Off
;    msmq_HTTPSupport=Off
;    msmq_LocalStorage=Off
;    msmq_MQDSService=Off
;    msmq_RoutingSupport=Off
;    msmq_TriggersService=Off
;    msmsgs=On
;    msnexplr=On
;    mswordpad=On
;    netcis=Off
;    netoc=On
;    objectpkg=On
;    OEAccess=On
;    paint=On
;    pinball=On
;    rec=On
;    reminst=Off
;    rstorage=Off
;    solitaire=On
;    spider=On
;    templates=On
;    TerminalServer=Off
;    TSClients=Off
;    TSWebClient=Off
;    vol=On
;    wms=On
;    wms_admin_asp=On
;    wms_admin_mmc=On
;    wms_server=On
;    zonegames=On

;end
```

Starting with a Template

This book's companion CD contains a sample distribution point that you can use to create your own disk image. It uses all the techniques that this chapter describes to completely automate the image-building process. Here's how to use the sample to create your own distribution point for building Windows XP Professional images:

1. Copy Samples\chap15\win2002.pro from this book's companion CD to your development server, and do one of the following:

    - If you're creating a disk image for Windows XP Professional, leave the folder named win2002.pro (I use the convention *version.edition* for naming distribution folders).

    - If you're creating a disk image for Windows XP Table PC Edition, name the folder win2002.tab.

2. Do one of the following:

    - If you're creating a disk image for Windows XP Professional, copy the I386 folder from your Windows XP media to win2002.pro. The result should be the folder win2002.pro\I386.

    - If you're creating a distribution point for Windows XP Tablet PC Edition, copy the I386 folder from your Windows XP media to win2002.tab; then copy the CMPNENTS folder from the second CD to win2002.tab.

3. Create a folder in win2002.pro or win2002.tab to store original device drivers, such as win2002.pro\Drivers. Within that folder, create a subfolder for each device driver that you download from OEMs and expand.

4. Determine how many configurations you want to create (the sample folder includes OEM1, OEM2, and OEMN). Create additional OEM*N* folders if necessary or remove unused OEM*N* folders. For example, if you need only two configurations, delete the folder win2002.pro\OEMN. If you need four configurations, copy win2002.pro\OEMN to OEM3 and OEM4.

5. In each OEM*N* folder under win2002.pro or win2002.tab, update drivers.txt to point to each device driver's *.inf* file that you want to include. If you examine the drivers.txt file, you'll find an example of the file's syntax.

6. In each OEM*N* folder under win2002.pro or win2002.tab, update winnt.sif, which is the unattended-setup answer file. In particular, you must update the following settings (see the sample winnt.sif file for more settings that you must replace when customizing a distribution point):

- `OemFilesPath`. Set this property to the Universal Naming Convention (UNC) path of the OEM folder. For example, if you're editing winnt.sif in win2002.pro\OEM2 and the UNC path of the distribution point will be \\Server\Windows, add `OemFilesPath=\\Server\Windows\win2002.pro\OEM2 \$OEM$` to the `[Unattended]` section of winnt.sif.

- `OemPnPDriversPath`. Update this property with the path of each folder that contains third-party device drivers. This path is relative to the folders on the target computer. So, if you have files in OEM \DRIVERS,OEM \DRIVERS\LAN, and OEM\DRIVERS\VIDEO, add `OemPnPDriversPath= \WINDOWS\DRIVERS;\WINDOWS\DRIVERS\LAN;\WINDOWS\DRIVERS\VIDEO` to the `[Unattended]` section.

> **Tip** Often, device drivers that you download from a vendor's Web site aren't suitable for deployment. They install from package files, so you can't easily extract the device driver files and then figure out which files are necessary and which aren't. You can almost always get the latest device drivers from Windows Update, though, and these device drivers are in a suitable format for deployment through an answer file and on a disk image. The trick is to use the Windows Update Catalog. In Internet Explorer, click Tools, Windows Update. On the Web page's left pane, click Personalize Windows Update. In the right pane, select Display The Link To The Windows Update Catalog Under See Also and click Save Settings. Now you'll see the Windows Update Catalog link on left pane of the Windows Update Web site and you can search for and download device drivers that are packaged ready for deployment.

7. In win2002.pro or win2002.tab, run drivers.cmd, which copies the device driver files described by the *.inf* files in drivers.txt to the distribution point. It also runs rename.wsf to create $$Rename.txt files for long filenames.

8. Do the following:

   - Add packages that you want to install after Setup finishes but before it runs Sysprep to the OEM*N*\$OEM$\$$\APPS\CMDLINES folder. These are typically hotfixes, settings, and so on.

   - Add packages that you want to install after Windows XP Setup finishes to the folder OEM*N*\$OEM$\$$\APPS\RUNONCE. These are typically applications.

9. In each OEM*N*\$OEM$\\$1\Sysprep folder under win2002.pro or win2002.tab, update Sysprep.inf, which is the answer file for Mini-Setup. See the sample Sysprep.inf file for settings that you must replace when customizing it.

10. Copy to each OEM*N*\$OEM$\\$1\Sysprep folder the files Sysprep.exe and Setupcl.exe. These files are in the Deploy.cab file on your Windows XP Professional product CD. For your convenience, you should copy all of the files from Deploy.cab to the distribution point's Tools folder.

I customized this sample as described in the previous section, "Sysprep Configuration." It contains Sysprep.inf. It automatically creates the Sysprep folder on the sample computer. It automatically runs Sysprep after Windows XP Setup finishes. And Mini-Setup runs **Sysprep –clean** after it finishes. All you have to do in order to use this template is customize the sample as described in this section.

Installing the Configuration

After you create the distribution point described in the previous section, installing the configuration on a sample computer is straightforward. Run Windows XP Setup from the distribution point, including the */unattended* command-line option to use the unattended-setup answer file that runs Sysprep after installing the operating system. To simplify running Windows XP Setup, I've created two batch scripts in the distribution point that run it with the appropriate command-line options:

■ **Setup32.cmd**   Run this batch script if you're running Windows XP Setup from a 32-bit environment, such as Windows Preinstallation Environment.

■ **Setup.bat**   Run this batch script if you're running Windows XP Setup from a 16-bit environment, such as MS-DOS.

Both batch scripts accept a single command-line option, which is the name of the configuration you want to install: OEM1, OEM2, OEM*N*, and so on. For more information about these batch scripts and configurations, see Chapter 7.

> **Tip**   Whether it's superstition or has some basis in fact, I usually build custom computers for the express purpose of building disk images. I use the most generic hardware I can find and I leave out any unnecessary devices (sound cards, and so on). My thinking, and what I want to pass on to you, is that by using generic hardware, I have a better chance of producing a disk image that works on many different configurations. The goal, of course, is to manage fewer disk images.

Windows Product Activation

Windows Product Activation (WPA) is an anti-piracy technology designed to verify that the product has been legitimately licensed.

Windows XP Professional upgrade licenses acquired through a Microsoft volume licensing agreement, such as Microsoft Open License, Enterprise Agreement, or Select License, do not require activation. Installations of Windows XP Professional made with volume licensing media and volume license product keys (VLKs) have no activation, hardware checking, or limitations on installation or imaging.

A VLK is a product key issued to a specific customer under a specific license agreement. Each VLK is associated with a specific customer and type of product that the customer is licensed for. For Select License Agreement, Enterprise Agreement, School Agreement or Campus Agreement customers, one VLK is issued per enrollment agreement per product family. For Microsoft Open License customers, the VLK is provided on the Open License order confirmation. These VLKs are to be used when prompted by the product at installation or when a custom image is created. A VLK must be used with volume licensing media. VLKs cannot be used with retail full-packaged product or OEM CD media.

Use the `ProductKey` entry of Sysprep.inf to automate product key entry into network and custom CD install images so that end users are never prompted to enter a product key during product installation.

Creating the Disk Image

After you run Sysprep on a master installation, you can create the disk image by using a third-party program. Microsoft does not provide a disk-imaging program. The section "Disk-Imaging Tools," earlier in this chapter on page 431 describes four of the more popular disk-imaging products, however. Regardless, disk imaging typically involves the following steps:

1. Start the master computer by using a removable disk or starting it from the network (Windows Preinstallation Environment). The third-party disk-imaging product might include a startup disk that contains the software.

2. Run the third-party disk-imaging program to create an image of the master installation.

3. Save the image in a shared folder or write the image directly to a CD or DVD.

4. Shut down the master computer.

The disk-imaging process might vary depending on the disk-imaging software you use. Refer to the documentation that came with your disk-imaging software to design your disk-imaging process.

> **Caution** After you use Sysprep to prepare a master installation, you must not reset SIDs or perform other system preparation tasks by using third-party disk-imaging programs. Doing so after you run Sysprep can damage your master installation and make your disk image unusable. Furthermore, resetting SIDs by using a third-party tool is not supported.

Deploying the Disk Image

Image delivery is the process of creating, managing, and distributing disk images. The image-delivery process begins after you configure your master computer and it ends after you copy a disk image onto a destination computer. To design an effective image-delivery process, perform the following tasks:

- Choose a disk-imaging program that you will use to create and manage disk images.

- Choose an image-distribution method that you will use to store and transfer disk images to destination computers.

Your disk-imaging program must be compatible with the operating system and file system you are deploying, and your distribution method must be compatible with your organization's networking and hardware capabilities.

The following sections describe the two methods available for distributing disk images: network and media distribution. Each method of distributing disk images has advantages and disadvantages. Table 15-4 summarizes the advantages and disadvantages of each distribution method. You can use Table 15-4 to identify which distribution method is best suited for each of your disk images and your organization.

Table 15-4 Comparing Distribution Methods

Feature	Network Distribution	Media Distribution
Can be used to deploy disk images in remote offices that do not have fast network connections.	No	Yes
Can be used to deploy disk images to computers that do not have network connectivity.	No	Yes
Requires a file server with adequate capacity to store disk images.	Yes	No

Table 15-4   Comparing Distribution Methods

Feature	Network Distribution	Media Distribution
Requires software-based security to prevent unauthorized access to disk images (permissions, user rights).	Yes	No
Requires physical security to prevent unauthorized access to disk images (locks on doors, locks on office desks).	No, but it is a good idea	Yes
Accommodates disk images of any size without special file-splitting or disk-spanning software.	Yes	No
Requires CD or DVD recording hardware and media.	No	Yes

Choose network distribution if all the following statements are true:

- You are deploying computers that are connected to a fast network (> 4 Mbps).

- You have a file server with sufficient capacity to store all your disk images.

- You have a disk-imaging program that supports network distribution of disk images.

Choose media distribution if all the following statements are true:

- You are deploying computers that are connected to a slow network or you are deploying computers that are not connected to a network.

- You have CD or DVD recording hardware.

- You have a disk-imaging program that supports disk-to-disk or disk-to-CD copying.

Disk-Imaging Programs

Microsoft does not provide disk-imaging software; you must purchase a third-party disk-imaging program to create a disk image of a master computer's hard disk. See the section "Disk-Imaging Tools" on page 431 for help in choosing a program. Not all disk-imaging programs are compatible with Windows XP Professional. When you evaluate disk-imaging programs, make sure that you choose a program that supports the following Windows XP Professional features:

- **Long filenames**   Be sure that your disk-imaging program supports long filenames. (Long filenames can be up to 255 characters and can contain spaces, multiple periods, and special characters that are not allowed in MS-DOS filenames.) Most commercial third-party disk-imaging programs can handle long filenames, but some shareware and freeware disk-imaging programs cannot.

■ **NTFS 3.1**   Be sure that your disk-imaging program supports NTFS 3.1, which is the version of NTFS used by Windows XP Professional. Although many disk-imaging programs support NTFS, these programs do not necessarily support the new features in NTFS 3.1, such as the clean shutdown flag.

In addition to these required features, consider choosing a disk-imaging program that supports the following optional features:

■ **Network share support**   Some disk-imaging programs can copy disk images to and from network shares. This feature is essential if you distribute disk images across a network.

■ **CDR-RW support**   Some disk-imaging programs can write the disk image directly to a writable CD. This feature is useful if you distribute disk images on CDs.

■ **Large-file support (also known as file splitting or disk spanning)**   Some disk-imaging programs can copy an image onto multiple CDs or other media. This feature is useful because a typical disk image of Windows XP Professional does not fit on one CD.

■ **Standalone support**   Some disk-imaging programs provide a mechanism for booting a computer that is not connected to a network and then copying an image from removable media without using a network connection. This feature is useful if you distribute your disk images on CD or DVD.

■ **Multicast image deployment**   Some disk-imaging programs have a multi-cast server feature that lets you simultaneously copy a disk image onto multiple computers over a network connection. This feature is useful for large-scale rollouts in which you want to automate and control the disk-copy process.

■ **Image management**   Some disk-imaging programs have image-management features that let you view, add, and remove files and folders from a disk image. This feature is useful for updating a disk image without having to reconfigure a master computer and create a new disk image.

Some disk-imaging programs can create, resize, or extend a partition before you copy a disk image onto a destination computer. Although these features might be useful, not all disk-imaging programs can perform these tasks; in fact, some programs might cause a STOP 0x7B error (INACESSIBLE_BOOT_DEVICE). If you want to create a partition on a destination computer's hard disk before you perform an image-based installation, you need to be sure that the disk-imaging program is compatible with the file systems used by Windows XP Professional. If you want to resize or extend a partition before you copy a disk image onto a destination computer, use the `ExtendOemPartition` setting in the Sysprep.inf file.

More Info For more information about Stop 0x7B errors, see article Q257813, "Using Sysprep May Result in 'Stop 0x7B (Inaccessible Boot Device)' on Some Computers," in the Microsoft Knowledge Base. To find this article, see the Microsoft Knowledge Base at *http://support.microsoft.com*.

Network Distribution

To distribute disk images across a network, you need the following:

- **High-speed network connectivity** You must have a network connection to every destination computer that you are deploying. Ethernet local area networks (LANs) and Token Ring LANs are well-suited for distributing disk images across a network. Wide area networks (WANs) are generally not fast enough, unless the LAN segments that make up the WAN are connected with a fast T-Carrier service (T2 or higher). Digital Subscriber Line (DSL), cable modem, Integrated Services Digital Network (ISDN), and dial-up modem connections are not suitable for network distribution. Table 15-5 shows disk image transfer times based on connection type and network speed. Image transfer times are based on optimum network speeds only and are calculated for a 2.5 gigabyte (GB) disk image. File server performance is not factored into the disk image transfer times. You can use Table 15-5 as a rough guide to help you determine whether your network is suitable for network distribution.

Table 15-5   Network Bandwidth

Connection Type	Network Speed	Transfer Time (2.5 GB Disk Image)
Fast Ethernet	100 megabits per second (Mbps)	3 minutes, 25 seconds
Fast Token Ring	16 Mbps	21 minutes, 22 seconds
Ethernet	10 Mbps	34 minutes, 9 seconds
T2	6.312 Mbps	54 minutes, 6 seconds
Token Ring	4 Mbps	1 hour, 25 minutes
T1	1.544 Mbps	3 hours, 41 minutes

- **Adequate file server capacity** You must have a file server configuration that can handle large file transfers. Several factors determine whether a file server is adequate for large file transfers. The disk type (IDE or SCSI), disk access speed, network adapter settings, disk rotation speed, bus speed, and protocol type can all influence the performance of a file server. Many hard disk manufacturers provide applications that measure your disk performance.

- **A disk-imaging program that supports network distribution**   You must have a third-party disk-imaging program that supports network deployment or transfer of disk images. Many disk-imaging programs can copy a disk image directly to a network share. Others can copy a disk image only onto a hard disk on the same computer you are imaging, which means you must manually copy the disk image to a network share. Some programs also provide network deployment features, such as a multicast feature that you can use to deploy images simultaneously to multiple destination computers and a subnet selection feature that you can use to distribute images to selected subnets. Although these features are not required for network distribution, they can make an image-based deployment faster and easier.

- **A network boot disk**   You must have a network boot disk (floppy or CD) to transfer disk images across the network. You use the boot disk to start the destination computer you are deploying and connect the destination computer to a network. Some third-party disk-imaging programs provide a network boot disk (floppy). You can also create one yourself. For more information about creating a network boot disk, see Chapter 13.

Network distribution might also require additional administrative overhead, such as network configuration and troubleshooting, file server configuration and management, and security configuration. For example, you might have to configure network settings or troubleshoot network issues if a destination computer cannot access the network. Likewise, you might have to add storage capacity to your file servers and address performance issues to ensure that your file servers are optimally configured for handling disk images. You might also have to configure permissions, security policies, or user rights on your file servers so that unauthorized users do not download or copy your disk images.

Media Distribution

To distribute images on media, you need CD or DVD recording hardware, a disk-imaging program that supports media distribution, a file-splitting or disk-spanning program, and a boot disk with CD or DVD support.

Media distribution might also require additional administrative overhead. The most common administrative tasks associated with media distribution include configuring and troubleshooting CD-ROM drives, maintaining and updating disk images, and managing security. For example, you might have to configure or troubleshoot CD-ROM or DVD drives if your boot disk fails to load the appropriate CD-ROM or DVD device drivers on a destination computer. Likewise, you might have to record new CDs or DVDs (and destroy old CDs and DVDs for security purposes) every time you make a change to your disk image. You will also spend administrative time ensuring that the CDs and DVDs are physically secure and not available to unauthorized users.

The following are requirements for distributing disk images using media:

- **You must have a CD or DVD recorder to distribute images on media.** You can use any type of CD or DVD recording device (for example, CD-R or CD-RW). However, you must make sure that the CD-ROM drives in your destination computers can read the media you create.

- **You must have a disk-imaging program that allows you to copy a disk image directly onto a hard disk, CD, or DVD on the same computer.** Some disk-imaging programs do not support standalone disk-image creation (for example, disk-to-disk or disk-to-CD). This feature is necessary if your master computers are not connected to a network or if you want to create distribution media immediately after you create a disk image.

- **Most disk images of Windows XP Professional or Windows Server 2003 do not fit on a single CD, so you need a file-splitting or disk-spanning tool that splits a disk image into several files.** Some disk-imaging programs provide this functionality, but most do not. To find vendors and shareware Web sites that offer file-splitting or disk-spanning programs, search the Web by using the keywords "file splitting" or "disk spanning."

- **You must have a boot disk to start the destination computer.** The boot disk can be the CD or DVD that contains the disk image or it can be a separate floppy disk. The boot disk must also include the device drivers for the CD-ROM or DVD drive that is in the destination computer. Some third-party disk-imaging programs provide a network boot disk (floppy). You can also create one yourself.

Optimizing Disk Images

You must see AppDeploy.com at *http://www.appdeploy.com/articles/imaging-bp.shtml* for a variety of techniques you can use to optimize disk images. The following suggestions may help you to reduce the size of your image and decrease the time required to image your master installation onto the destination computers:

- Use in-box drivers whenever possible to minimize the number of driver files copied to every destination computer.

- If you include additional drivers, use a common set of drivers that is used across multiple product lines. Install this common set on all computers as part of the master installation, reducing the time required to locate and install a specific custom driver before you deliver the destination computer to the customer.

- Limit the number of devices listed in the `[SysprepMassStorage]` section of Sysprep.inf.

- If you include a blank `[SysprepMassStorage]` section in the Sysprep.inf file and if you set `BuildMassStorageSection=Yes` in the `[Sysprep]` section, Sysprep automatically generates the entries in `[SysprepMassStorage]` from the PnP hardware IDs specified in Machine.inf, Scsi.inf, Pnpscsi.inf, and Mshdc.inf.

- Minimize the number of additional applications that you install.

- If a particular application is included on most of your computers, consider including a staged version of the application in the master installation. To stage an application means having all the files available locally. In this case, the application setup is required only to make the relevant changes in the registry, eliminating time-consuming file copying. If you do not want to include this application on the destination computer, you can detach (or delete) the files.

- The CD Boot method does not support staged applications.

- Use the Diskpart and Format command-line tools to create a single NTFS partition at the beginning of the preinstallation process. Using Diskpart removes a reboot between fdisk and format, which is required in MS-DOS.

- Use a small image to install Windows XP Professional on a small partition and then use `ExtendOemPartition` if you install to an NTFS file system partition.

- Delete Hiberfil.sys and Pagefile.sys from the master installation before creating the image. Use the command **del /a:sh hiberfil.sys** to delete Hiberfil.sys. Windows XP Professional automatically re-creates these files if necessary. The Pagefile.sys file is as large as the available RAM on the computer. Make sure that at least this much free space exists on the %SYSTEMDRIVE% partition on the destination computer so that Mini-Setup can properly regenerate the file.

- Delete the contents of the %WINDIR%\System32\Dllcache folder before you create an image of the master installation. You must leave the empty Dllcache folder on the system for Windows File Protection (WFP) to function properly.

Note   To delete files from an image, you must have tools that can edit the image or access the disk to delete the files. You cannot delete files from a Windows XP Professional installation while that installation of Windows is running.

Mapping Sysprep Settings

When you run Sysprep, it modifies hundreds if not thousands of registry settings to prepare the computer's hard disk for duplication. Table 15-6 describes the settings that relate directly to Sysprep. These settings prepare the Mini-Setup wizard to run the next time Windows XP Professional starts. I tracked them down by comparing snapshots of the registry before and after running Sysprep. I divided this table into sections, with each key in a different section. The first column is the value, and the second column is the value's type. The third column describes how Sysprep configures each value and the value's purpose.

Table 15-6   Sysprep Registry Settings

Value	Type	Description
HKLM\SOFTWARE\Microsoft\Sysprep		
SidsGenerated	REG_DWORD	Sysprep sets this value to 0x01, indicating that it removed the computer's SID, and Setupcl.exe will regenerate it.
CriticalDevicesInstalled	REG_DWORD	Sysprep sets this value to 0x01, indicating that it created the critical devices database.
HKLM\SOFTWARE\Microsoft\Windows\CurrentVersion\Setup		
SourcePath	REG_DWORD	Sysprep sets this to the value of InstallFilesPath in Sysprep.inf, which indicates to the setup program where to find installation files.
HKLM\SOFTWARE\Microsoft\Windows\CurrentVersion\Setup\OOBE		
RunWelcomeProcess	REG_DWORD	Sysprep sets this value to 0x00, which disables the Windows Welcome out-of-box experience.
HKLM\SYSTEM\CurrentControlSet\Control\Lsa\Kerberos\SidCache		
MachineSid	REG_BINARY	Sysprep deletes this value to remove the computer's SID.
HKLM\SYSTEM\CurrentControlSet\Control\Session Manager		
SetupExecute	REG_MULTI_SZ	Setup adds Setupcl.exe to this value. This runs Setupcl.exe when Windows XP Professional restarts so that Setupcl.exe can regenerate the computer's SID and run the Mini-Setup Wizard.
HKLM\SYSTEM\Setup		
BootDiskSig	REG_DWORD	Sysprep stores the signature of the boot disk in this value.

Table 15-6   Sysprep Registry Settings

Value	Type	Description
CloneTag	REG_MULTI_SZ	Sysprep stores the date and time that you prepared the disk in this value.
Cmdline	REG_SZ	Sysprep stores the setup command-line *setup -newsetup -mini* in this value. This is the command that runs the Mini-Setup Wizard.
MiniSetupInProgress	REG_DWORD	Sysprep sets this value to 0x01, indicating that the Mini-Setup Wizard is in the process of running.
SetupType	REG_DWORD	Sysprep sets this value to 0x01.
SystemSetupInProgress	REG_DWORD	Sysprep sets this value to 0x01.

Sysprep changes other settings that I don't describe in Table 15-6. The settings that it changes depend on the computer's configuration. For example, it disables Remote Desktop and Remote Assistance. It configures System Restore to create an initial system checkpoint the next time Windows XP Professional starts. It also resets the computer's digital ID and resets the WPA timer.

Last, if you're using [SysprepMassStorage], Sysprep fills the critical devices database and configures the device drivers for each device. The changes that Sysprep makes to the registry are numerous, but the following list summarizes some of the most significant that I found while sniffing out the changes that it makes:

- Sysprep resets the event system. These settings are in HKLM\SOFTWARE \Microsoft\EventSystem.

- Sysprep removes certificate templates and certificates from the keys HKLM\SOFTWARE\Microsoft\Cryptography and HKLM\SOFTWARE \Microsoft\EnterpriseCertificates.

- Sysprep resets the configuration of Group Policy in the key HKLM\SOFTWARE \Microsoft\Windows\CurrentVersion\Group Policy.

- Sysprep removes the computer from the domain, if it's a domain member, by deleting the appropriate values from the keys HKLM\SOFTWARE\Microsoft \Windows NT\CurrentVersion\Winlogon, HKLM\SOFTWARE \Microsoft \Windows NT\CurrentVersion\Winlogon\DomainCache, and elsewhere.

- Sysprep removes policies from the key HKLM\SOFTWARE\Policies.

- Sysprep removes networking components from the keys HKLM\SYSTEM \CurrentControlSet\Control, HKLM\SYSTEM\CurrentControlSet\Enum, and HKLM\SYSTEM\CurrentControlSet\Services.

- Sysprep resets the application compatibility data in HKLM\SYSTEM \CurrentControlSet\Control\Session Manager\AppCompatibility.

- Sysprep resets power management settings in the key HKLM\SYSTEM \ControlSet\Control\Session Manager\Power.

- Sysprep configures the Netlogon service to load on demand instead of automatically in HKLM\SYSTEM\CurrentControlSet\Services\Netlogon.

- Sysprep adds the devices specified in [SysprepMassStorage] to the critical devices database. This database is in the key HKLM\SYSTEM \CurrentControlSet\Control\CriticalDeviceDatabase.

- Sysprep installs and configures device drivers for the devices listed in the [SysprepMassStorage] section. It configures these device drivers in the key HKLM\SYSTEM\CurrentControlSet\Services.

Best Practices

The following are best practices for deploying disk images with Sysprep:

- Fully automate the image-building process to reduce errors and add consistency.

- Use the [SysprepMassStorage] section to create a disk image that works on multiple hardware configurations.

- If you're using Sysprep and disk images to deploy Windows XP Professional, design in to it a method for migrating users' settings and data, as described in Chapter 18, "User State Migration."

- Follow the guidelines in Knowledge Base article 240126 at *http://support .microsoft.com* for using Sysprep with NTFS volumes.

- See *http://www.appdeploy.com/articles/imaging-bp.shtml* at AppDeploy.com for a variety of disk-imaging best practices and tips (If this link is unavailable, open *http://www.appdeploy.com*, click Articles).

Chapter 16

Remote Installation Service

Remote Installation Services (RIS) is a disk-imaging service that comes with Microsoft Windows 2000 Server and Windows 2003 Server. Using RIS is similar to using other disk-imaging products, as described in Chapter 15, "Disk Imaging with Sysprep." It has the benefit of not requiring third-party products, however, because RIS is built into the server operating system. This chapter describes how to customize RIS and how to use it to deploy Windows XP Professional with applications and settings.

Checklist

■ Have you determined which applications you want to include on your disk image? See Chapter 1, "Deployment Plan," for more information.

■ Have you determined which settings you want to configure on your disk image? See Chapter 3, "Windows Configuration," for more information.

■ Have you built a Windows XP Professional distribution point to install the operating system? See Chapter 6, "Answer Files," and Chapter 7, "Distribution Points," for more information.

Overview

RIS is one of the highly touted features of Windows 2000 Server. It's a component of IntelliMirror. Using RIS, you can perform remote automated installation of Windows 2000 Professional. Windows 2003 Server adds enhancements to RIS, too.

RIS allows you to support on-demand image-based or script-based clean operating system installations over a network connection from a RIS server to a RIS client. RIS is included in Windows Server 2003, Standard Edition; Windows Server 2003, Enterprise Edition; and Windows Server 2003, Datacenter Edition operating systems. RIS allows you to standardize client operating system installations, control the end-user installation experience, and choose the software distribution media you use. RIS supports large-scale deployments of Windows XP Professional and can also serve as an operations and recovery tool.

RIS uses Preboot Execution Environment (PXE) technology to enable client computers without an operating system to boot remotely to a RIS server that performs installation of a supported operating system over a Transmission Control Protocol/Internet Protocol (TCP/IP) network connection. Just about any network card these days will support PXE; make sure to check with the original equipment manufacturer (OEM) to confirm that your network interface cards (NICs) are supported. You can create different sets of RIS images to accommodate various configurations of different groups of client computers. You can also use Group Policy settings to limit the installation options that RIS presents to clients. You can use RIS to provide interactive operating system installations that require user input or provide fully automated installations that require no user input other than logon credentials.

It is recommended that you use RIS when you have a large number of clients that need clean installations of an operating system and when you have an idea of the software configurations you want to deploy in your organization. To deploy RIS, your network infrastructure must be able to support RIS-based installations. The following sections describe the server and client requirements for using RIS.

Window 2003 Server has some capabilities added over Windows 2000 Server:

- Deployment of Windows 2000 Professional, Windows 2000 Server, Windows XP Professional, and the Windows Server 2003 family operating systems

- Automation of the Client Installation Wizard (CIW) using the Autoenter feature

- Enhanced cross-domain functionality

- Increased security by adding a masked double-prompt Administrator password

- Automatic Dynamic Host Configuration Protocol (DHCP) authorization with Risetup.exe

- Autodetection of the target system hardware abstraction layer (HAL) type to allow filtering of images from the CIW

- Support for the Recovery Console and support for Windows Preinstallation Environment

- Support for Microsoft Windows XP 64-Bit Edition Version 2003 and the 64-bit versions of the Windows Server 2003 family

- Support for the Uniqueness Database in .sif files

- Support for Secure Domain Join

- Support for NTLM version 2 (NTLMv2)

- Support for encrypted local Administrator password entries

> **More Info**   Wes Miller of Microsoft gave a comprehensive webcast about the enhancements for RIS in Windows Server 2003. In addition to his webcast, he answered many questions about the latest version of RIS. I recommend that you see the transcription at *http://support.microsoft.com /default.aspx?scid=%2Fservicedesks%2Fwebcasts%2Fen%2Fwc072502%2F wct072502.asp*. If you can't find the webcast at this address, search support for the keywords *Wes, Miller*, and *webcast*.

Server Requirements

Before you can begin using RIS, there are a number of requirements that must be met. RIS requires you to have Windows 2000 Server or Windows Server 2003 with *Domain Name Server (DNS)*, DHCP, and Active Directory configured, as described in the following list:

- **DNS**   RIS servers rely on DNS to locate the required Active Directory servers to facilitate domain operations. If you use Windows Server 2003 DNS, you have the benefit of dynamic updates for your DNS server. However, it is not a requirement to use Windows Server 2003 DNS for RIS to function. Whichever DNS server you use, it must support the SRV-RR record type and the dynamic update protocol specified in Requests for Comments (RFCs) 2052 and 2136.

- **DHCP**   RIS servers require a DHCP server on the network that is authorized and has an activated scope. Remote boot-enabled clients must receive an Internet Protocol (IP) address from a DHCP server before they can contact a RIS server to request an operating system installation. You can install Windows Server 2003 DHCP or you can use existing DHCP services provided with Windows 2000 Server. You can use a third-party DHCP server.

■ **Active Directory** You must install RIS on a computer running Windows Server 2003 or Windows 2000 Server in an Active Directory domain. For best results, configure this computer as a member server. Although you can install RIS on a domain controller, the heavy traffic load generated by RIS can impact the performance of the domain controller. RIS uses Active Directory to locate RIS clients and other RIS servers. You can administer the RIS server from the Active Directory Users And Computers snap-in (dsa.msc) located on the RIS server. For more information about Active Directory, see the Directory Services Guide of the Windows Server 2003 Resource Kit (or see the Directory Services Guide on the Web at *http://www.microsoft.com/windows/reskits*).

Argon RIS Menu Editor

Are you tired of carrying around boot disks for MS-DOS and other operating systems? Add them to a RIS server as maintenance tools, and you can leave the boot disks in your bottom desk drawer. In addition to operating system installation, RIS supports starting maintenance and troubleshooting tools from the network. The name is a bit misleading, though. These are really bootable images that you load into RIS and then start when you boot from the network. For example, you can add an image of an MS-DOS boot disk to the RIS maintenance and troubleshooting tools, and then you can start that disk by booting the computer from the network and choosing the boot-disk image you added. You can restrict these maintenance and troubleshooting tools to administrators, so you needn't worry about restricted users accessing them.

You can add to RIS any disk that you can configure to start the computer. That includes an MS-DOS boot disk that logs on to the network and installs UNIX or some other operating system. That also includes an MS-DOS boot disk that logs on to the network and installs Microsoft Windows 98. I typically maintain all my various boot disks in RIS so that they're quickly accessible from any workstation. I particularly like to configure a RIS server in lab environments and then add the variety of boot disks I use in the lab to the RIS server. This makes using the lab environment much more convenient.

So, the trick is how you add the disk images to RIS. For that, you use a product from Argon called RIS Menu Editor (RISme). You can learn more about RISme at *http://www.argontechnology.com*. I've used this product for years with great success. It's a necessary addition to any RIS server. And even if you're not using RIS to deploy Windows XP Professional, you should still consider configuring a RIS server with RISme just to make all your boot disks convenient to access.

On the Resource Kit CD   This book's companion CD contains the worksheet "Planning for RIS Servers" (Ris02.doc) in the Aids folder. This worksheet helps you document your RIS server configurations.

Client Requirements

You must examine your existing network clients to ensure that they meet the requirements for using RIS. If you are planning to install the operating system through RIS, you need to do the following:

- **Evaluate whether your client computers meet the minimum hardware requirements for Windows XP Professional**   Before you begin creating images of Windows XP Professional, you must make sure your hardware is compatible. There are a couple ways of doing this; to verify whether your existing client hardware is compatible with Windows XP Professional, see the Hardware Compatibility List (HCL) at *http://www.microsoft.com /whdc/hcl/default.mspx*. You can also use the Windows Catalog and the Upgrade Advisor, both of which you learn about at *http://www.microsoft.com /windowsxp/pro/howtobuy/upgrading/checkcompat.asp*.

- **Determine whether your client computers utilize the same HAL as the master computer (for Riprep images only)**   RIS Server allows you to create and customize images much like Symantec Ghost can: You create a master image and load software and configure the workstation to meet your organization's requirements; you can then capture that image using Riprep.exe. Before you can do that, you must make sure that the master image's HALs are compatible. For example, if the master computer on which you run Riprep.exe has an Advanced Configuration and Power Interface (ACPI) HAL, the client computers you designate to receive operating system images generated from that master computer must also have an ACPI HAL (if not, the image does not work properly). The HAL type is indicated by the original filename of the file Hal.dll. There are a number of different ways to determine what types of HALs are in your environment:

  - Use a management tool such as Microsoft Systems Management Server (SMS) to obtain your client inventory, from which you can determine the HAL types. For more information about SMS, see Chapter 17, "Systems Management Server."

  - View the properties of Hal.dll to determine the HAL types. This file is in %SYSTEMROOT%\System32. Right-click it and then click Properties. On the Version tab, click Original File Name. The original filename that displays in the Value list (such as Halacpi.dll or Hal.dll) indicates the HAL type.

By default, the HAL autodetect feature of Riprep.exe causes the CIW to filter images based on the HALs of the client computer. The CIW will list only the computers that are compatible.

■ **Evaluate the remote boot capabilities of RIS clients (whether they are PXE-enabled or if they require a RIS boot floppy disk)** For a client to use RIS, the client must connect to a RIS over the network. There are two ways that a client can do this. The best way to facilitate the remote boot is to use a PXE-enabled RIS client, which means that both the network adapter and basic input/output system (BIOS) of the RIS client support PXE.

If a RIS client does not have a PXE-enabled network adapter and supporting BIOS, you can emulate PXE support by using a Peripheral Component Interconnect (PCI)–based network adapter that boots from a RIS boot floppy disk. The RIS boot floppy disk is a startup disk that simulates the PXE startup process for computers that do not have a remote boot-enabled BIOS. By using the RIS boot floppy disk to emulate PXE support, you can enable RIS-based operating system installations on non-PXE-compliant client systems. The Remote Boot Floppy Generator (RBFG) utility allows you to generate RIS boot floppy disks for use with RIS clients that are not PXE-enabled. Remember that the remote boot floppy generator does not support Windows XP 64-bit Editions or the Windows 2003 64-bit Editions.

To determine whether your NICs are PXE-enabled, you can do one of the following:

■ Verify that your RIS clients have PCI, Mini-PCI, or CardBus type network adapters. RIS clients can perform a remote boot only from these types of network adapters.

■ Verify that the BIOSs of your RIS clients are capable of using the network adapter as the primary boot device. A read-only memory (ROM) BIOS that is at least version .99n satisfies this requirement.

More Info Laptop computers have typically been at odds with RIS, particularly older laptop computers that don't have built-in PCI network adapters that support RIS. Argon Technology sells a CardBus network adapter that does support RIS, however. For more information, see *http://www.argontechnology.com/nics/cardbus/index.shtml*.

Most computers these days conform to the Net PC or PC 98 specifications and have PXE remote boot-enabled network adapters and remote-enabled BIOSs. You can also obtain this information by using the SMS if you have it in your environment or you could go to each system and inspect it manually. However, it might be easier for you to use a remote script to determine whether the BIOS of client computers in a specified domain supports PXE-enabled remote booting. To do this, you can use the BIOS Information script, which is on this book's companion CD in the Samples\chap16 folder (GetRIS-BIOSInfo.vbs). To return the BIOS information, run this script at the command line and specify the Active Directory domain name and the **getallbios** command. The returned information verifies whether the BIOS of client computers supports PCI adapters and selectable booting. If so, the BIOS supports remote booting from a network adapter.

This script uses Active Directory Service Interface and the Windows Management Instrumentation (WMI) to query the computer accounts in the computer container to obtain the information on the BIOS. For the script to function properly, you must have WMI installed on both the computer running the script and the computers that you query with the script. In addition, you must have Active Directory Service Interface (ADSI) installed on the computer running the script.

For RIS clients that are not PXE-enabled, you need to determine whether they can use a RIS boot floppy disk. To use a RIS boot floppy disk, these clients must have a PCI-type network adapter because RIS boot floppy disks do not support Personal Computer Memory Card International Association (PCMCIA), CardBus, Industry Standard Architecture (ISA), universal serial bus (USB), or other non-PCI network adapters. You can generate the RIS boot floppy disks for these clients by running the Rbfg.exe utility. This is on the RIS server in the following directory: *RISServerName*\RemoteInstall\Admin\i386\Rbfg.exe. This disk will allow you to install the operating system on portable computers, but remember that it will not work with PCMCIA network cards—it is not supported.

- Audit existing client computers so you can inventory software and hardware configurations.

- Decide whether you want to prestage RIS computer objects in Active Directory for more secure RIS-based operating system installations.

- Evaluate operating system configurations.

On the Resource Kit CD   This book's companion CD contains the worksheet "Planning for RIS Clients" (Ris01.doc) in the Aids folder. This worksheet helps you document your client computers and their readiness for RIS.

RIS Components

There are several key components that RIS uses when installed. The key components start services and provide the means for the installation of the client operating system. After you install RIS, you will see new services, as follows:

- **Remote Installation Service (BINLsvc)** This service detects PXE-initiated DHCP requests from RIS clients and facilitates a response to those requests. Remote Installation also directs clients to files on the RIS server that initiate the installation process and then services CIW requests. In addition, Remote Installation checks Active Directory to verify client credentials, determines whether a client can be serviced, and confirms whether to create a new computer account object or reset an existing account on behalf of the client.

- **Trivial File Transport Protocol (TFTP) Daemon** A RIS server uses TFTP to download the CIW and the initial files needed to start the remote installation process on the client computer. The first file that downloads is Startrom.com, which is a small bootstrap program that displays the Press F12 For Network Boot prompt to the client. If the user presses F12 within three seconds, the CIW downloads to the client so the installation process can begin. The file Startrom.com is located on your RIS server in the directory path *ServerName* \RemoteInstall\OSChooser\i386\.

- **Single Instance Store Service (SIS)** SIS consists of an NT file system (NTFS) filter driver and a groveler agent that interacts with RIS images. The SIS service reduces the hard-disk storage requirements for RIS images. SIS does this by monitoring the RIS server partition for duplicate files. Whenever the groveler agent finds a duplicate file, SIS copies the original file into a directory and an NTFS reparse point containing the current location, size, and attributes of the original file. This way, SIS retains only a single instance of the file while replacing duplicate files with links to the single instance. This enables SIS to store the duplicate files it finds in RIS images and reduce disk space usage on your RIS server. Remember that if you are backing up your RIS server, you must have software that is SIS-aware. The backup software that comes with Windows 2003 Server supports SIS.

Installing RIS

To install a RIS server, use the following steps:

1. If you have not already installed Remote Installation Services through control panel or through an unattended-setup answer file, open Add Or Remove Programs and use Add/Remove Windows Components to install the RIS component.

2. Open the Remote Installation Services Setup Wizard.

3. In the wizard, click Next; the wizard then prompts you for the following information:

   - **Remote Installation Services Drive And Directory**   Enter the disk drive and directory where you want to install RIS. The disk should be dedicated to the RIS server and contain enough space to store as many client images as you plan to host with this server. The recommended minimum amount of space is 4 gigabytes.

   - **Initial Settings**   Select Respond to client computers requesting service if you want the RIS server to begin responding to client computers as soon as you finish the wizard. Select Do Not Respond To Unknown Client Computers If You Want The RIS Server To Respond Only To Prestaged Client Computers In Active Directory. You can change these settings later.

   - **Source Path**   Enter the location of the client images. This location can be either the compact disc or a shared folder that contains the installation files.

   - **Friendly Description And Help Text**   Enter the friendly description for the client computer installation. This description will be displayed to users or clients of this server. The Help text describes the operating system installation choices to users or clients of RIS.

   To install RIS on the server, you must be a part of Enterprise Admin Group or delegated permission. You can also manage a RIS server through Remote Desktop on Windows XP Professional or install the Administration Tool Kit. RIS does not currently support the Encrypting File System (EFS). The distributed file system (DFS) is not supported as a target location. You can, however, run RIS on a computer that is also running DFS. After RIS is installed, check to make sure that all the services have started successfully, open Event Viewer, and review the entries for System Log and Application Log.

On the Resource Kit CD   This book's companion CD contains the worksheet "Designing the RIS Server Configuration" (Ris09.doc) in the Aids folder. This worksheet helps you plan the configuration of your RIS servers.

Authorizing a RIS Server

Authorization prevents unauthorized RIS servers, ensuring that only RIS servers authorized by administrators can service clients. If an attempt is made to start an unauthorized RIS server on the network, it will be automatically shut down and thus unable to service client computers. A RIS server must be authorized before it can service client computers. Use DHCP Manager to authorize a RIS Server:

1. Click Start, point to Programs, point to Administrative Tools, and click DHCP. The DHCP Manager snap-in appears.

2. Right-click DHCP in the upper-left corner of the DHCP screen and select Manage Authorized Servers.

3. If your server is not already listed, click Authorize and enter the IP address of the RIS server.

4. Click Yes when prompted to verify that the address is correct.

Configuring a RIS Server

There are a number of ways to configure a RIS server for many different environments, so you have to decide the best way to configure your environment. One of the nice things about RIS is that it can accommodate just about any environment, from 50 users to 5000 users. If you are using RIS in a large environment, be careful because if there are some performance issues that must be considered:

- Where to place RIS servers on the network to minimize the impact of RIS traffic

- Where RIS clients are located in proximity to the RIS servers that service them

- How many clients you intend to service

- How you distribute different operating system images to various user groups

- What security methods you apply to ensure secure operating system installations

- How you configure your Active Directory infrastructure to support RIS

Remember that a RIS server will generate a lot of traffic on the network when it responds to the client. The number of RIS servers you have will be determined by the number of RIS clients you have. In corporate environments, you need to design a RIS server configuration that provides secure responses to clients requesting service. To do this, you need to set specific RIS server properties, provide security for nonprestaged clients, and secure the operating system images that you distribute to clients. You can also include prestaging RIS client computer accounts in Active Directory as part of your design, to maximize the security of RIS-based operating system installations. The following sections describe these considerations.

Network Configuration

When designing your RIS server configuration, the RIS servers are dependent on how your network is configured, which will determine how they perform. Depending on how you place and configure your RIS servers, one operating system image can support multiple Active Directory sites, domains, and organizational units; or you can provide multiple customized images that you distribute to clients from strategically placed RIS servers.

If you have a large number of clients, you might want to consider using a load-balancing technique known as a server referral of client installations. RIS server can accommodate only a limited number of requests at once, so by having multiple RIS servers, each loaded with different sets of images, you can offload some of the clients to designated servers. The client boots up and requests the installation of an operating system. The request is passed to the RIS referral server, which is configured with the Do Not Respond To Unknown Clients option (allowing only prestaged clients to be acknowledged by the RIS referral server). The RIS referral server checks Active Directory to verify whether the client has a prestaged computer account and whether it is configured to receive service from a specific RIS install server. If it finds a prestaged computer account and a designated RIS install server, the RIS referral server passes the request to the appropriate RIS install server, and the operating system gets installed.

Prestaging a computer account is the process of creating a valid computer account object within the Active Directory directory service. Prestaging a computer for use with Remote OS Installation allows the administrator the ability to deliver a blank computer directly to the user for OS installation. By prestaging the computer account in Active Directory, the administrator can configure the RIS servers to respond only to prestaged computers. This ensures that only those computers that have been prestaged as Authorized users are allowed to install an operating system from the RIS server. Prestaging can save both time and money by reducing, and in some cases eliminating, the need to fully preinstall the computer.

The number of RIS servers you will need is impacted by the demand for new, upgraded, or custom operating system installations. As a result, you need to determine your needs prior to deploying a standard desktop configuration of Windows XP Professional or other operating systems to your clients. After you determine your needs, you can calculate how many RIS servers to deploy. You can base your estimate on the following metric for best-case scenarios: One RIS server can send multiple operating system images over the network for up to 75 clients simultaneously.

Hardware and bandwidth will play a role in determining how many servers you will need. If bandwidth is slow and hardware is old, of course, you have to add more servers to make up for performance losses in those areas.

As a general guideline when deciding where those servers should go, place RIS servers in close physical proximity to the client computers they service rather than making connections across a wide area network (WAN) link. However, it might be necessary for your clients to locate a RIS server across a router or domain. If so, make sure that your router can pass DHCP traffic, and it must be another trusted domain in order for RIS to work.

> **On the Resource Kit CD**   This book's companion CD contains the worksheet "Planning the RIS Network Configuration" (Ris04.doc) in the Aids folder. This worksheet helps you document your network configuration for RIS.

Server Properties

When configuring RIS server properties, there are many things that have an impact on performance and functionality. You configure the RIS server in Active Directory. Right-click the RIS server, click Properties, and then click the Remote Install tab. You can configure the following:

- **Client support**   Consists of options that allow you to determine which clients the RIS server responds to.

- **Computer naming format**   Consists of various options that determine how computer account objects will be named.

- **Computer account location**   Consists of options that determine where the computer account objects will be placed in Active Directory.

Table 16-1 shows the settings that you can configure for the properties of RIS server.

Table 16-1   RIS Server Properties

Properties	Description
Client Support Options	You need to configure the way RIS servers respond to clients requesting installation service.
Respond To Client Computers Requesting Service	You want a RIS server to acknowledge all clients requesting service, including prestaged and nonprestaged clients, to whom the server makes its operating system images available. Use it when maximum security is unnecessary or when you are setting up a RIS referral server.
Do Not Respond To Unknown Client Computers	You want a RIS server to acknowledge only clients with prestaged computer accounts in Active Directory, to whom the server makes its operating system images available. Use it when you want to maximize the security applied to RIS clients so unauthorized clients cannot receive an operating system installation.

Table 16-1   RIS Server Properties

Properties	Description
Client Computer Naming Format Options	You configure the Automatic Setup option in Group Policy, so you can apply the computer naming format to nonprestaged clients and to Custom Setup clients that do not provide input for computer name and Active Directory location.
User Name	You want to name the client computer requesting RIS service based on the user name of the operating system installer. This is the default setting.
NP Plus MAC Address	You want to name the client computer requesting RIS service based on the Media Access Control (MAC) address of the client network adapter.
Custom Naming Scheme	You want to name the client computer requesting RIS service based on a custom naming format that you specify.
Other Name Variations	You want to name the client computer requesting RIS service based on name variations such as first name, last name, initial, and so on.
Client Account Location Options	You want to define the default Active Directory container for all client computer accounts prior to installation.
Default Directory Service Location	You want to specify that the client computer account object is created in the Computers container by default when the client joins the domain. Use it when you want the client computer to become a member of the same domain as the RIS server handling the client-installation process.
Same Location As That Of The User Setting Up The Client Computer	You want to specify that the client computer account object is created within the same Active Directory container as the user account of the user setting up the computer, for example, in the Users container.
The Following Directory Service Location	You want to predetermine where client computer account objects are created in Active Directory. Use it when you want to configure an account location for all client computers installed from a RIS server.

The Remote Install tab on the RIS server also allows you to perform and modify the following by clicking Advanced:

- **Associate new answer files with existing images by clicking Advanced on the Remote Install tab of the RIS server Properties dialog box**   You can define answer file associations on your RIS server. For example, from the Images tab, you can associate answer files with existing operating system images. This process allows you to provide custom operating system installations based on answer files that you create and tailor for specific user needs.

■ **Set security permissions on answer files after you associate the answer file with an image**   You can set permissions on the answer file to enable specific users to access the image associated with it.

■ **Add new Risetup images to the RIS server from the Image tab of RIS server Properties**   You can add new Risetup images to your RIS server based on an operating system CD that you provide. If you click the Add button on the Images tab, a dialog box displays with an option that starts the Risetup Wizard.

■ **Removing tools from the Tools tab allows you to remove tools or view the properties of system maintenance and troubleshooting tools provided by third parties**   You cannot add tools to your RIS server from the Tools dialog box.

■ **Set security permissions on the RIS server computer account object in Active Directory**   If you decide to delegate administration of your RIS server, you can set permissions on your RIS server computer account in Active Directory from the Security tab of RIS server Properties.

Security Configuration

There are a number of different ways to configure a secure way to deploy operating systems to clients. There are four areas that need to be addressed when configuring RIS security:

■ To provide secure responses from your RIS server to clients, with load balancing you can control how a RIS server responds to remote boot-enabled clients that request service; set Client support options on the RIS server Properties dialog box. Available settings include the following:

   ■ Respond To Client Computers Requesting Service. The RIS server responds to all clients requesting service. This is the least secure setting because the RIS server does not distinguish between authorized and unauthorized clients.

   ■ Do Not Respond To Unknown Client Computers. The RIS server only responds to clients that have a prestaged computer account object in Active Directory. This is the most secure setting for your network because it enables you to limit access to only authorized clients that are prestaged in Active Directory.

   If you configure a RIS server with the Respond To All Clients Requesting Service option, you designate that server to handle all client requests for RIS services. This is not the recommended configuration; all clients, including unauthorized ones, will get a response back from the RIS server. However, you can enhance security by configuring the RIS server to respond only to prestaged clients using the Do Not Respond To Unknown Client Computers option. By configuring this option, you have greater control over which computer accounts get installed and which server it will use.

■ To provide security for non-prestaged RIS clients, you can control which users can create computer accounts in Active Directory by delegating control over who has the preassigned right to join into the domain. This provides the user with Create/Delete Computer object permissions.

■ You can optimize network security for RIS services by prestaging computer accounts in Active Directory and then configure the RIS server to respond only to those prestaged clients. Also, you can configure your users with read, write, and reset or change password permissions on the prestaged computer account objects.

■ Providing authorization for your RIS servers must be done for RIS to work. By authorizing a RIS server, it makes it available in Active Directory. This will ensure that the clients can respond to necessary RIS server.

The easiest way to authorize RIS on a computer running Windows Server 2003 is to use the Verify Server feature on the Remote Install tab of the RIS server Properties dialog box. You can also type the following command at the command line: **Risetup /Check**. Or you can run the authorization function in the Managed Servers dialog box in the Windows Server 2003 DHCP snap-in.

On the Resource Kit CD   This book's companion CD contains the worksheet "Planning RIS Server Security" (Ris05.doc) in the Aids folder. This worksheet helps you document your RIS security configuration.

Customizing the Client Installation Wizard

When you connect to a RIS server, you get a client installation page that shows up. This page is designed to help your client perform the installation through RIS. This page be left as default, or you can customize it to accommodate your organization with such things as technical support numbers, e-mail addresses, or policies and procedures. This page is designed to help and control the end users' installation of the images.

The CIW uses the Remote Installation service (BINLsvc), which listens for DHCP requests. The Remote Installation service directs the client to the files that are required to start the installation. RIS also checks Active Directory to verify the credentials; it also determines whether the client needs the remote operating system installation service; and whether or not to create a new computer account object on behalf of the client request or reset an existing computer account object.

The default screens that are used during the client logon process and the installation of the operating system are the following, which are in the OSChooser folder of the RIS installation folder:

- **Welcome.osc**   Displays a welcome screen to the user.

- **Login.osc**   Requires the user to log on.

- **Choice.osc**   Displays setup options to the user: Automatic, Custom, Restart, Maintenance, and Tools. The degree to which this screen and its options are displayed is controlled through RIS Group Policy settings:

  - Automatic is the default installation option enabled for all users of the CIW.

  - Custom Setup allows you to override the automatic computer name assignment, as well as the computer account-creation mechanism. You are prompted to manually enter a computer name or the Active Directory location in which the computer account should be created. This also can be used to prestage clients in Active Directory.

  - Restart A Previous Setup provides the ability to restart a failed setup attempt. If you started to install the OS and for some reason lost your connection to the RIS server, you can reboot the client computer, press F12 when prompted for a network service boot, and choose Restart A Previous Setup Attempt.

  - Maintenance And Troubleshooting provides access to third-party independent software vendor (ISV) and OEM pre-OS maintenance and troubleshooting tools.

- **OSAuto.osc**   Determines whether a computer account object already exists in Active Directory that has the same globally unique identifier (GUID) as the computer that is running the CIW. If a duplicate GUID is found, DupAuto.osc is displayed. If no duplicate GUID is found, OSChoice.osc is displayed. (This screen is not displayed to users.)

- **DupAuto.osc**   Indicates that a duplicate GUID was found and instructs the user to contact the network administrator.

- **OSChoice.osc**   Displays the list of operating system images that are available to the user who is logged on to the RIS server.

- **Warning.osc**   Warns the user that the drive will be formatted.

- **Install.osc**   Displays a summary page to the user.

When the Remote Installation Setup Wizard (RISetup.exe) is run, a default set of the CIW screens is installed at RemoteInstall\Oschooser*language*.

The Oschooser folder in the RIS installation folder contains the .osc files. If multiple languages are installed, there is a subdirectory for each language that the server supports. All of the files that the CIW uses are in this directory, with the exception of Welcome.osc and Multiling.osc. The Welcome.osc file is the first screen that every user sees, no matter what language the server uses; the screen displays the languages that are supported. When the user connects to the server, he or she can select the appropriate language.

These files are HTML 2.0 files. Here is a list of all the tags that can be configured when customizing any .osc file:

- *<OSCML></OSCML>*
- *<META SERVER ACTION="server side action">*
- *<META KEY= F1 | F3 | ENTER | ESC HREF="screen name">*
- *<META ACTION="LOGIN">*
- *<TITLE> Title </TITLE>*
- *<FOOTER> Footer </FOOTER>*
- *<BODY [LEFT="left margin"] [RIGHT="right margin"]>*
- *<PRE [LEFT="left margin"] [RIGHT="right margin"]> </PRE>*
- *<FORM ACTION="screen name"> </FORM>*
- *<INPUT [NAME="osc var name"] [TYPE="TEXT | PASSWORD"] [VALUE="starting value"] [SIZE="display size"] [MAXLENGTH="max length"]>*
- *<SELECT [MULTIPLE] [NOAUTO] [NAME="osc var name"] [SIZE="height"]> [<OPTION.....> <OPTION.....>] </SELECT>*
- *<OPTION [SELECTED] [TIP="help text"] [VALUE="return value"]> Item description*
- *<SELECT>*
- *</SELECT>*
- *
*
- *<P [LEFT="left margin"] [RIGHT="right margin"] > </P>*
- *<BOLD> text </BOLD>*
- *<FLASH> text </FLASH>*
- *<TIPAREA [LEFT="left margin"] [RIGHT="right margin"] [SIZE="height"]>*
- *<OPTION VALUE="OSAUTO" TIP="Text">*

> **On the Resource Kit CD**   This book's companion CD contains the docu-
> ment "SCML and Client Installation Wizard Variables" (Ris13.doc) in the
> Aids folder. This document describes the syntax of the *.osc* files and how to
> customize them.

Using CD-Based Images

You use a CD-based image if you want to distribute the network equivalent of CD-
based installation functionality. This type of image is a replica of an operating system CD file structure, located across the network on a remote RIS server. You create
CD-based images by running the Risetup wizard on a RIS server and using an operating system CD to create the image. This works much like an unattended install as
described in Chapter 13, "Unattended Setup." You can't have a fully configured
clone image using Risetup, but you can certainly distribute software and drivers by
creating OEM folders.

You always have at least one CD-based image. When you install remote installation services on your RIS server, it automatically creates one CD-based image of
the operating system and stores it under the Images folder within the RIS directory
structure. This image is available to remote boot-enabled clients; these clients can
access this CD-based image from a remote server if you configure them to do so.
You can make additional CD-based images using operating system CDs for Windows 2000 Professional, Windows 2000 Server and Windows 2000 Advanced Server,
Windows XP Professional, and Windows Server 2003. To create a CD-based image,
place the CD in the drive of your RIS server and run **Risetup-add**. You can also start
the wizard by clicking Advanced on the Remote Install tab of the RIS server's Properties dialog box.

After the image is complete, you can add software and device drivers to that
image by adding those specific files to the distribution point in RIS. When RIS is
installed, the RemoteInstall directory is automatically shared as Reminst, so those
drivers and applications are available through the RIS clients.

You can create and associate multiple answer files with Risetup images, which
allows you to customize the applications and drivers you want to install with each
image. However, you cannot include preconfigured application or desktop configurations with a CD-based image. Also, CD-based images take longer to install than an
equivalent-sized mirror image.

There are four areas that need to be considered when designing a Risetup
image:

- The operating systems you want to image

- The software applications you want to include on your distribution share

- The special hardware drivers you want to include on your distribution share
- The operating system configuration settings or components you want to provide

> **On the Resource Kit CD**   This book's companion CD contains the worksheet "Defining RISETUP Images" (Ris07.doc) in the Aids folder. This worksheet helps you document CD-based RIS images.

Templates

The directory RemoteInstall\Setup\English\Images\win2002.pro\i386\templates on the RIS server contains the templates associated with the image. Each template in this directory appears in CIW's OS Choices screen, which means that the same CD-based image can appear in CIW more than one time for each template associated with it. After installing RIS, you see one template, Ristndrd.sif, which is the default.

Templates are answer files that contain placeholders. RIS uses templates, which have the .sif extension. Windows XP Setup uses answer files. Prior to starting the setup program, RIS replaces a template's placeholders with actual values and then uses the resulting answer file to run the setup program. For example, it replaces every occurrence of the placeholder *%USERNAME%* in a template with the user's actual name when it generates the answer file.

In general, you won't need to customize RIS templates much. The exception is to copy the OEM folders to the target computer and then specify the location of device drivers by using the *OemPnPDriversPath* settings. Listing 16-1 shows a sample RIS template that I use for CD-based images. It's only slightly customized. First, it sets *DriverSigningPolicy=Ignore* and *OemPnPDriversPath* to the path of third-party device drivers on the target computer. It also sets *OemPreinstall=Yes* to copy the OEM folder to the target computer.

Listing 16-1   Ristndrd.sif

```
[Data]
    AutoPartition=1
    Floppyless=1
    MsdosInitiated=0
    LocalSourceOnCD=1
    OriSrc="\\%SERVERNAME%\RemInst\%INSTALLPATH%\%MACHINETYPE%"
    OriTyp=4
    UnattendedInstall=Yes

[SetupData]
    OsLoadOptions="/noguiboot /fastdetect"
    SetupSourceDevice="\Device\LanmanRedirector\%SERVERNAME%\RemInst
\%INSTALLPATH%"

[Unattended]
```

```
          DriverSigningPolicy=Ignore
          FileSystem=ConvertNTFS
          InstallFilesPath="\\%SERVERNAME%\RemInst\%INSTALLPATH%\%MACHINETYPE%"
          OemPnPDriversPath=\WINDOWS\DRIVERS
          OemPreinstall=Yes
          OemSkipEula=Yes
          Repartition=No
          TargetPath=\WINDOWS
          UnattendMode=ReadOnly
          UnattendSwitch=Yes

      [GuiUnattended]
          AutoLogon=Yes
          AutoLogonCount=1
          OemSkipRegional=1
          OemSkipWelcome=1
          TimeZone=%TIMEZONE%

      [UserData]
          ComputerName=%MACHINENAME%
          FullName="%USERFIRSTNAME% %USERLASTNAME%"
          OrgName="%ORGNAME%"
          ProductID=XXXXX-XXXXX-XXXXX-XXXXX-XXXXX

      [Display]
          AutoConfirm=1
          BitsPerPel=16
          Xresolution=1024
          Yresolution=768

      [TapiLocation]
          AreaCode=972
          CountryCode=1
          Dialing=Tone

      [Identification]
          CreateComputerAccountInDomain=No
          DoOldStyleDomainJoin=Yes
          JoinDomain=%MACHINEDOMAIN%
          MachineObjectOU="OU=Accounts,DC=honeycutt,DC=corp"

      [Networking]
          InstallDefaultComponents=Yes

      [RemoteInstall]
          Repartition=Yes
          UseWholeDisk=Yes

      [OSChooser]
          Description="Microsoft Windows XP Professional"
          Help="Automatically installs Windows Professional without
      prompting the user for input. This build includes Service Pack 2."
          LaunchFile="%INSTALLPATH%\%MACHINETYPE%\templates\startrom.com"
          ImageType=Flat

      ;end
```

> **On the Resource Kit CD**   This book's companion CD contains the document "Reserved OSC Variables" (Ris12.doc) in the Aids folder. This document describes the predefined OSC variables that you can use in .osc files and templates.

Template Permissions

You control which templates users see in CIW by setting permissions on them. If users have permission to read a template, that template shows up in the list of operating system choices. If users don't have permission to read a template, that template doesn't show up in the list of choices.

OEM Folder

Unlike the distribution points you learned to create in Chapter 7, you must copy the OEM folder to the RIS installation folder on the same level as the I386 folder. That is, if you have a CD-based image in the RIS installation folder in RemoteInstall\Setup\English\Images\win2002.pro\i386, create your OEM folder in RemoteInstall\Setup\English\Images\win2002.pro\OEM.

You use the same techniques that you learned in Chapter 7 and Chapter 11, "Chaining Installations," to add third-party device drivers and applications to your CD-based images. The structure and content of the OEM folder are the same, only the location of the OEM folder is different.

Creating RIS Images

After your RIS servers, you must decide how to distribute the operating system. There are two ways to do that. You can perform a CD-based installation or you can perform a mirror installation, which is cloning computers. You've already configured the RIS server for CD-based installations. This section describes how to create mirror-image installations.

Use Riprep.exe to create mirror images. Riprep.exe allows you to create customized images to install on your client operating system. The first thing you need is a master image with all the applications and configurations; this becomes the referenced computer that you will use to make a master image. After you configure the master installation, you run Riprep, which is on the server at the following location: *servername*\reminst\admin\i386\riprep. This converts the master installation into a remote installation image—a functionally identical replica of the master computer disk—that you can install on multiple destination computers. Riprep also replicates the image to a RIS server, where it is available for installation on remote boot-enabled client computers.

The recommended way to install the master image is through an unattended install, which gives you the flexibility to add components, drivers, and legacy applications to the install. After you configure the master installation, you run Riprep, which is on the server at the following location: *servername*\reminst\admin \i386\riprep. This converts the master installation into a remote installation image—a functionally identical replica of the master computer disk—that you can install on multiple destination computers. Riprep also replicates the image to a RIS server, where it is available for installation on remote boot-enabled client computers.

Riprep configures various operating system settings on the master computer to ensure that every copy of the master computer's disk image is unique when you install it on destination computers. This includes resetting the security identifiers (SIDs) and access control lists (ACLs). Riprep also configures the master installation image so that after the initial installation of the image, every destination computer starts in a special setup mode known as Mini-Setup. This mode is similar to Sysprep, which you learned about in Chapter 15.

There are number of requirements that must be met by the master image:

- You must have at least one CD-based image stored on the RIS server that matches the operating system on the master computer from where you create the Riprep image. The answer file (Riprep.sif) that Riprep generates for the image refers the client computer to the RIS server to obtain drivers that start the text-mode portion of the CIW during installation of the operating system image.

- The image on the server must have the same language and the first two numbers of the same SKU in order to work. This is to make sure that it is the same as the master image. Example: a 5.1.2600.0 image will work for a 5.1.2600.1106 version of the same SKU.

- During image installation, Mini-Setup uses Plug and Play to detect hardware differences between the master and destination computers. Therefore, identical hardware is not needed except for the HAL type. You can perform a RIS-based installation only if the HAL in the RIS (Riprep) image is compatible with the HAL on the destination computer.

- The Riprep wizard supports preparation and replication of images only from the system partition (C:\ system partition) on the master computer. The master computer cannot have a partition greater than that of the target machine.

Each time the client uses the CIW to choose an operating system image, the installation processes the information contained in the *.sif* file. By modifying the contents of a *.sif* file associated with an installation image, you can predefine the configuration settings for that image. This is particularly important if you need to change any aspect of that image for new clients.

There are five main decisions that you must make before you begin creating the Riprep image:

- **The operating systems you want to image**   When choosing an operating system, you should document what the operating system is, the name that corresponds to it, and the version number that can be found under the properties of the file Ntdll.dll located in the i386 folder on the operating system CD.

- **The software applications you want to install and configure in the master installation**   Software applications that you want to install on the master images should be defined before you begin. Any Microsoft Office 2003 Editions programs or in-house line of business applications should all be tested on the master machine before you deploy the image. It is also a good idea to have all the latest and greatest service packs and hotfixes in your master image. Because of the length of time that each service pack takes to install, you should include it in the master before you capture the image.

- **The special hardware drivers you want to include in the master installation**   Hardware configurations with other images have to be considered when creating images. You do not have to have an image for each specific piece of hardware. You could use one image across various types of hardware, but there might be some computers that have specific hardware that will not be detected by Plug and Play, in which case it would be an option to create another image. To ensure that the drivers for this hardware are properly detected, you need to add the drivers and any support files to your Riprep image. You can perform a RIS-based installation only if the HAL in the RIS (Riprep) image is compatible with the HAL on the destination computer. See Chapter 7 to learn more about adding third-party device drivers to a distribution point. The only difference with RIS is that you copy the OEM folder to the directory that contains the I386 folder.

- **Operating system and software settings you want to provide** Operating system and software settings that you might want to change or configure on the master images are as follows:

  - Local policy settings, such as Group Policy Administrative Template settings

  - Control Panel settings, such as power options, sound scheme settings, system startup and recovery options, system performance settings, and accessibility options

  - Internet Explorer settings, such as the default home page, security and privacy settings, and connection settings

  - Optional Windows components settings, such as network monitoring tools, Remote Storage, and Services for NetWare

  - Services settings, such as startup type, logon accounts, and recovery actions

  - Desktop settings, such as desktop shortcuts, folder options, and fonts

  - Display appearance and settings

  - Microsoft Word or Microsoft Excel settings, such as view, edit, save, and spelling options

- **Whether to reuse the master installation to create new images with differing operating system and application configurations** To use Riprep to capture images you must complete the following steps:

  1. Install the CD-based Windows XP Professional image from an available RIS server on a supported client computer.

  2. Install any applications locally on the client computer. Configure the client computer with any specific corporate standard desktop settings. Be sure that the client installation is exactly as you want it to be. After the image is replicated to the RIS server, you cannot alter its configuration. You can completely automate this process by using the techniques described in Chapter 7 and Chapter 11.

  3. Run Riprep by typing ***RISservername*\Reminst\Admin\I386\RIPrep.exe** in the Run dialog box or at the command prompt. The Remote Installation Preparation Wizard starts, and you are presented with a welcome screen that describes the feature and its functionality. Click Next.

  4. Click Next to accept the default RIS server.

  5. Type the name of the folder you want to create for the image. The folder is created under \remoteInstall\setup\OS Language\Images. Click Next.

6. Type a friendly description and help text that describe the image. The friendly description and help text are displayed to users of the CIW during image selection. Provide enough information so that a user can distinguish between images. Click Next.

7. The wizard displays a summary screen of your selections. After you have reviewed them, click Next.

The image preparation and replication process begins. The system is prepared, and files are copied to the RIS server specified. After the replication of the image completes, any remote boot-enabled client computer can select the image for a local installation.

Restricting CIW Choices

Using Group Policy is how you control which choices are available to users. To restrict the client installation options for users of RIS within your organization, apply the appropriate Group Policy settings for the RIS servers on your network.

1. Create and edit a new Group Policy Object (GPO).

2. Under User Configuration, Windows Settings, click Remote Installation Services.

3. Double-click the Choice Options in the right pane. Each Choice Option configures the menu option as follows:

- Allow. If this option is selected, the users that this policy is applied to are offered the installation option.

- Don't Care. If this option is selected, the administrator accepts the policy settings of the parent container. For example, if the administrator for the entire domain has set RIS-specific policy, and the administrator of this container has chosen the Don't Care option, the policy that is set on the domain is applied to all users who are affected by that policy.

- Deny. If this option is set, the users affected by this policy are not allowed to access that installation option within the CIW.

On the Resource Kit CD This book's companion CD contains the worksheet "Designing the RIS Deployment Mode and CIW Process" (Ris08.doc) in the Aids folder. This worksheet helps you document which users are granted or denied access to images and which options are available to users in CIW.

Best Practices

The following are best practices for using RIS:

- Make sure that you determine the right amount of RIS servers for your network.

- Install RIS on a physical disk separate from the one on which the operating system is installed.

- Learn how to control the number of installation options and operating system choices a user can access within the CIW.

- Use the Remote Installation Preparation (RIPrep) wizard image format to deploy a standard corporate desktop configuration across different types of client hardware throughout your organization.

- Use RIS with computers that contain the PXE-based remote boot ROM.

- When using the CIW, use standard ASCII characters for user name, password, and domain name information.

Chapter 17

Systems Management Server

Microsoft Systems Management Server (SMS) provides tools that help you deploy Microsoft Windows XP Professional in an enterprise environment. This chapter assumes you have expertise with using SMS, and your SMS infrastructure is already in place; or you have plans for deploying an SMS infrastructure prior to deploying Windows XP Professional.

Checklist

- Have you built and tested a Windows XP Professional distribution point? If not, see Chapter 6, "Answer Files"; Chapter 7, "Distribution Points"; and Chapter 13, "Unattended Setup," for more information about customizing and installing Windows XP Professional.

- Have you created an unattended-setup answer file that installs Windows XP Professional without user intervention? See Chapter 6 and Appendix D, "Answer File Syntax," for guidance.

■ Do you have an SMS infrastructure in place or have plans to implement an SMS infrastructure prior to deploying Windows XP Professional? See the Systems Management Server Administrator's Guide for more information.

■ Have you installed Service Pack 2 for SMS 2.0? If not, download and install Service Pack 2 from *http://www.microsoft.com/smserver /default.asp.*

SMS Overview

Deploying Windows XP Professional on a large scale is easier when you use automated installation. Regardless, there are many tasks involved when you use automated techniques to deploy the operating system throughout your organization. SMS helps you with all these tasks:

■ Selecting computers that meet the requirements for Windows XP Professional

■ Distributing Windows XP Professional source files to all sites, including remote sites and sites without technical support staff

■ Monitoring the distribution to all sites

■ Preparing computers for an installation in locked-down environments

■ Launching the installation automatically while allowing users to control timing

■ Resolving problems related to the distributions or installations

■ Reporting on the rate and success of deployment

Note   SMS provides tools for upgrading your current computers, but not for installing new computers that do not have an operating system already installed (clean installations). To use SMS software distribution, you must install SMS client components on the target computers. These SMS components require that the computer already have a properly configured operating system.

SMS software distribution is based on multiple components and tasks, which allow you to completely control the process. The following sections describe SMS packages, distribution, and advertising.

Packages

SMS software distribution starts with an SMS *package*, which is the basic unit of software distribution. It contains the installation source files and instructions that direct the software distribution process.

Each package contains at least one SMS *program*, which is a command that runs on each targeted computer to control the execution of the package. Programs can direct the installation of software or contain any other command to run at each targeted computer, like an operating system upgrade. Most packages also contain source files, such as installation source files, that the program uses when it runs.

You can create a package by using Packages in the SMS Administrator console, or you can create or obtain a package definition file and use Create Package from the Definition Wizard. A *package definition file* is an alternative, noninteractive way to create a package. It is a formatted text file that contains all the information necessary to create the package. You can download package definition files at *http://www.microsoft.com/smserver/downloads/20/tools/winpdf.asp*. You can also use SMS tools and wizards to create packages from package definition files with minimal user interaction. After you create a package, use the SMS Manage Distribution Points Wizard to choose the distribution points.

More Info   Some installations, like Windows XP Professional, provide extensive options for automatic installation. Others don't. If the installation you want to distribute doesn't provide unattended operation, you can use SMS Installer to prepare your installation for software distribution. SMS Installer can generate attended and unattended installation scripts that you can customize. Although this kind of scripting is not appropriate for a Windows XP Professional upgrade, it's useful for preinstallation and post-installation tasks. For more information about SMS Installer, see "Creating Self-Extracting Files with SMS Installer 2.0" in the Systems Management Server Administrator's Guide.

Distribution

You control the distribution of a package by using distribution points, which is under the package definition in the SMS Administrator console, under Packages. Packages contain information about software distribution, such as the location of the package's source files. And distribution points are shares on SMS site servers where packages' source files are copied for access by client computers.

Packages also include information about how and when to update distribution points. For ease of administration, you can group distribution points into distribution point groups. And when SMS needs to propagate package files to other sites, SMS compresses these files for replication between sites. You can also create and use a compressed copy of a package's source files within the originating site.

Advertising

After you create a Windows XP Professional package, you advertise one or more of the package's programs to your users by creating an advertisement. You create an advertisement by using Advertisements in the SMS Administrator console. An *advertisement* specifies what program is available to client computers, which computers will receive it, and its installation schedule. Figure 17-1 illustrates the distribution process.

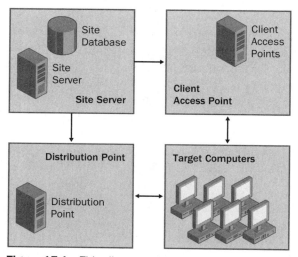

Figure 17-1   This diagram shows an overview of the SMS 2.0 software distribution process.

When an SMS client receives an advertisement, the user can still have some control over the scheduling of the SMS program. You can run the advertisement in a special privileged mode so that you need not give administrative privileges to users. You can also run the advertisement so that it operates without any user intervention.

Packaging Windows XP

When you use SMS to deploy Windows XP Professional, you must put the Windows XP Professional source files in an SMS package. For each SMS program, SMS obtains the files from a distribution folder. You must also include all the custom files required to complete the upgrade, such as device drivers and answer files (see Chapter 7). You can even include standard applications, language packs, and service packs (see Chapter 11, "Chaining Installations").

Each Windows XP Professional SMS package definition also contains SMS programs. Each program is a different combination of command-line options that you create for installing the Windows XP Professional package. For example, your default program might be to install Windows XP Professional with no user intervention. If you want to allow power users to choose options, they need a different program. All these SMS programs must be compatible with the set of files for the package available at the distribution folder. For example, you must provide the different unattended-setup answer files required for each SMS program in the package.

> **Note** If you are not using an answer file, Windows XP Setup will prompt users to enter a product key during installation. To avoid this prompt, see the section "Answer Files," later in this chapter on page 502.

Package Definition

Listing 17-1 shows a package definition file for Windows XP Professional. Copy it to a text file named winxp.sms. Alternatively, you can download sample package definition files from *http://www.microsoft.com/smserver/downloads/20/tools/winpdf.asp*.

Listing 17-1 winxp.sms

```
[PDF]
Version=2.0
[Package Definition]
Language=English
Publisher=Microsoft
Name=Windows XP Professional
Programs=unattended32bitx86, manual32bitx86
MIFPublisher=Microsoft
MIFName=Windows NT
MIFVersion=5.0
[unattended32bitx86]
Name=Automated upgrade from Win98/98SE/ME, Windows 2000 Pro, NTW 4.0 (x86 SP6)
CommandLine=i386\winnt32.exe /UNATTEND30 /BATCH /NOREBOOT
EstimatedDiskSpace=1500MB
EstimatedRunTime=60
AfterRunning=SMSRestart
CanRunWhen=AnyUserStatus
SupportedClients=Win 9x, Win NT (i386)
Win 9x MinVersion1=4.10.1998
Win 9x MaxVersion1=4.10.9999.9999
Win NT (i386) MinVersion1=4.0.1381.0
Win NT (i386) MaxVersion1=4.00.9999.9999
Win NT (i386) MinVersion2=5.00.0000.0
Win NT (i386) MaxVersion2=5.00.9999.9999
[manual32bitx86]
Name=Manual upgrade from Win98/98SE/ME, Windows 2000 Pro, NTW 4.0 (x86 SP6)
CommandLine=i386\winnt32.exe /NOREBOOT
EstimatedDiskSpace=1500MB
EstimatedRunTime=60
AfterRunning=SMSRestart
CanRunWhen=UserLoggedOn
UserInputRequired=True
```

```
AdminRightsRequired=True
SupportedClients=Win 9x, Win NT (i386)
Win 9x MinVersion1=4.10.1998
Win 9x MaxVersion1=4.10.9999.9999
Win NT (i386) MinVersion1=4.0.1381.0
Win NT (i386) MaxVersion1=4.00.9999.9999
Win NT (i386) MinVersion2=5.00.0000.0
Win NT (i386) MaxVersion2=5.00.9999.9999
```

Windows XP Setup supports the */unattend30* and */batch* command-line options. The option */unattend30* means that you will do an unattended upgrade and that all the required information is to be taken from the current installation. The computer will restart 30 seconds after Windows XP Setup completes the first phase, copying files to the computer. Windows XP Setup doesn't use an answer file. The */batch* command-line option specifies that Windows XP Setup not display any error messages. This is appropriate when you are sending the package to users whom you do not want involved in the process or if you are running the upgrade when no one is at the computer. However, if there are problems with the upgrade, such as a lack of disk space, they are not readily apparent because Windows XP Setup doesn't display an error message. However, you can find error information in the SMS status messages generated as a result of the operation and also in the log files in the %WINDIR% folder on the target computer. If you encounter problems in your testing and the status messages are insufficient, remove the */batch* option to allow Windows XP Setup to display errors during package testing. Also, with the */batch* option, if the user clicks Cancel during the first phase of Windows XP Setup, the user will not be asked to confirm that they want to stop the installation.

The estimated disk space and run time values included in Listing 17-1 are estimates that might not be realistic for your environment. You might want to increase them. These values are informational only and for the benefit of the user.

If you include an answer file in the command line of the package program, you can specify many of the options for your upgrade. For example, you can specify on which disk to install Windows XP Professional, or whether an upgrade or clean installation needs to be done.

> **Note** Listing 17-1 runs Windows XP Setup with administrative rights securely provided by SMS. This is an important benefit when you are upgrading target computers running Microsoft Windows NT or upgrading Microsoft Windows 2000 to Windows XP Professional. This feature means that you do not have to give administrative privileges to users.

Upgrade Packages

The following procedure describes how to set up a typical upgrade package for Windows XP Professional. The first step is to set up the location of the package source files for distributing Windows XP Professional:

1. Copy a customized and tested Windows XP Professional distribution point to a disk on the SMS site server or to a network share on the network.

    For more information about creating Windows XP Professional distribution points, see the following chapters:

    ■ See Chapter 6 for more information about answer files.

    ■ See Chapter 7 for more information about building and customizing Windows XP Professional distribution points.

    ■ See Chapter 11 for more information about adding installations and settings to a Windows XP Professional distribution point.

2. Customize the Windows XP Professional distribution point to run the command %LOGONSERVER%\NETLOGON\smsls.bat after Windows XP Setup finishes.

    This step ensures that Windows XP Professional runs the SMS client setup program as soon as possible in order to replace the Windows 98– and Windows Me–specific SMS client components with Windows XP SMS client components. Chapter 11 describes how to run commands after Windows XP Setup finishes. The place to run this command is from the *[GuiRunOnce]* section of the answer file. This batch script exists only if you set up SMS Logon points. For more information, see "Using Logon Scripts and Logon Points" in the Systems Management Server Administrator's Guide.

3. Create the package definition file winxp.sms, as described in the section "Package Definition."

    You can use the samples that you download from Microsoft at *http://www.microsoft.com/smserver/downloads/20/tools/winpdf.asp.*

4. In the SMS Administrator console, click Packages. On the Action menu, point to New, choose Package From Definition (as shown in Figure 17-2), and then click Next.

5. Click Browse, and then choose the file you created in step 3. In the package definition list, click Windows XP Professional; then, on the Source Files tab, click Create A Compressed Version Of The Source, and click Next.

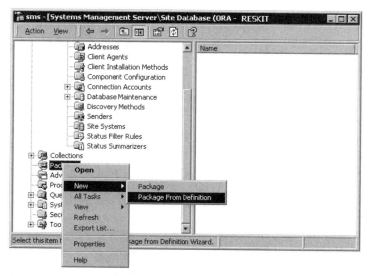

Figure 17-2   Create packages using the Package From Definition Wizard.

6. In the Source directory box, enter the path to the package source files that you created in step 1, click Next, and then click Finish. If the site server is extremely low on disk space, on the Source Files tab, you can choose the Always Obtains Files From A Source Directory option. In addition to saving disk space, this ensures that there are source files in an alternate location for disaster recovery should the SMS site server be lost for some reason. However, this slows future distributions of the software, and you must ensure that the source directory is always available.

7. Click Programs under your new package.

8. In the right pane, double-click Automated Upgrade From Win98/98SE/ME, Windows 2000 Pro, NTW 4.0 (X86 SP6), do the following, and click OK:

- Verify that the command line is the correct setup command for your needs. See Chapter 13 for more information about running Windows XP Setup.

- In the Comment box, type a comment for the program. The user can see your comments, so make them descriptive. Include contact information for the help desk, for example.

- On the Requirements tab, adjust the Estimated Disk Space and Estimated Run Time to values that are appropriate for the upgrade you are doing. These values are information for your users.

- On the Environment tab, verify that Program Can Run is set to Whether Or Not A User Is Logged On. This setting ensures that the program is run with administrative rights, which is necessary to upgrade Microsoft Windows NT and Microsoft Windows 2000 to Windows XP Professional.

9. To ensure that users do not upgrade their computers before you are ready to deploy Windows XP Professional, click Access Accounts under your new package; then delete the Guests and Users accounts in the right pane. Later, you'll have to give access to users who are authorized to upgrade to Windows XP Professional.

> **More Info**   If you want to use security to control the users who can adjust or deploy the package, see the chapter "Distributing Software" in the Systems Management Server Administrator's Guide.

If you require multiple unattended-setup answer files to accommodate variations in your upgrades, you must create additional programs for the package in the SMS Administrator console. Each program will specify a different answer file. You can use separate answer files to upgrade different groups of computers in different ways while still using just a single package. For more information about creating answer files, see Chapter 6.

Allowing User Input

Many SMS administrators consider a best practice to not allow user input during package installations. When users install software by themselves, the setup program generally prompts for responses, such as on which disk to install the software or which options to install. Every user interaction introduces the opportunity for error that can later cause problems. Users might not understand the implications of the answers they provide. If even a small percentage of users make mistakes, the number of help desk calls can be overwhelming at a time when you are upgrading thousands of computers.

Another reason to prevent user input during an upgrade is to allow the installation to occur while no one is present at the computer so that you minimize the inconvenience to users. Finally, providing all the answers in an answer file ensures that you maintain configuration standards. When you follow those standards, you simplify future computer maintenance and support by reducing the number of variables that could be relevant to a problem.

Chapter 6 described how to create answer files for Windows XP Professional. Chapter 13 described how to specify answer files to Windows XP Setup by using the command-line option */unattend*. To use an answer file, you must edit the package to use the */unattend* command-line option to specify it.

Answer Files

Chapter 6 described how to create unattended-setup answer files for Windows XP Professional. When deploying Windows XP Professional by using SMS, there are other settings you should consider adding to your answer files. For more information about the settings that this section describes, see Appendix D.

A new requirement for Windows XP Professional is the product-activation process. If a computer running Windows XP Professional is not activated within 30 days after installation, it will become unusable. This requirement is in addition to the product key. To enable automatic product activation, you can add the *AutoActivate=Yes* setting to the *[Unattended]* section of the answer file. In addition, it might be necessary to add *ActivateProxy* to your answer file if Windows XP Professional will go through a proxy server to reach the Internet for product activation.

> **More Info**   For more information about these settings, see Appendix D.

When upgrading computers that are running Microsoft Windows 98 or Microsoft Windows Me to Windows XP Professional, you must account for the lack of prior domain participation. Computers running Windows 98 or Windows Me have not been members of a domain, even if the users using them have been logging on to a domain, and have not had local accounts (although they can have local profiles and password list files). Also, the SMS client must be upgraded from the version run on Windows 98 or Windows Me before it can run successfully on Windows XP Professional. Therefore, relevant details must be specified in the answer file, such as *JoinDomain*, *DomainAdmin*, *DomainAdminPassword*, and *ProductKey* values.

> **More Info**   See Appendix D for more information about these settings.

A computer that is upgraded from Windows 98 or Windows Me to Windows XP Professional is given a local Administrator account, which requires a password. You can specify that password in the *[GuiUnattended]* section of the answer file or let the user be prompted for it at the end of the upgrade. This password can be read from the answer file by anyone who can access the SMS package share, though. This is not an immediate security risk because computers running Windows 98 and Windows Me were not secure before the upgrade, due to the nonsecure nature of those operating systems. You can encrypt this password as described in Chapter 6, however.

You might want to set the Administrator account password to a secure value and begin enforcing limited user privileges. You can do this after the upgrade by running a program that changes the password from the temporary value specified in the answer file and that could be seen by unauthorized people to a value shared only with authorized staff. The password is compiled within the program and is not available to unauthorized staff. You can easily create such programs by using common programming languages or scripting tools, such as SMS Installer. You can distribute the program with SMS, or you can invoke the program at the end of the Windows XP Professional upgrade by specifying appropriate values in the answer file. Another alternative is to use the Cusrmgr.exe utility from the Windows XP Resource Kit to change the password to a random (and unknown) value or disable the local Administrator account altogether. In that case, you must be sure to first add Domain Admins or a similar group to the local Administrator group so that someone can still manage that computer.

A better alternative is to encrypt the password for the administrative account in the answer file. You must use Windows Setup Manager provided on the Windows XP Professional product CD to create an unattended-setup answer file. Setup Manager (Setupmgr.exe) is on the product CD in Deploy.cab in the folder Support\Tools. In the Administrator Password dialog box, select the Encrypt Administrator Password In Answer File check box. Setup Manager will create an answer file with the following lines in the *[GuiUnattended]* section:

```
AdminPassword=encrypted password
EncryptedAdminPassword=Yes
```

Use these lines in the *[GuiUnattended]* section of the package answer file to assign a local Administrator password. Users who see the file cannot determine the password because it will be encrypted.

Last, the answer file must also specify that you want to upgrade the computers that are running Windows 98 or Windows Me. Do this by including the setting *Win9xUpgrade=Yes*. Without this line, Windows XP Setup does a clean installation of Windows XP Professional rather than an upgrade.

Caution   Answer files can be read by unauthorized users, so you need to consider security issues when you create them—particularly when specifying a user account and password for joining a computer to the domain. It is unlikely that people would gain access to the files from an SMS distribution point because the distribution points are hidden, and people must know where to look for these details. An appropriate precaution, however, is to use an administrative account whose only right is Add Workstations To Domain. Chapter 6 describes this technique.

Preparing for Distribution

Before you distribute Windows XP Professional packages, there are several tasks you must perform to ensure that your SMS infrastructure is ready to receive them. The following sections describe each of these tasks.

Site Servers

Windows XP Professional is a large operating system that requires considerable disk space. Not only are copies of the Windows XP Professional source files required, but SMS also make copies of the files as it moves the package between servers. Therefore, you must review your site servers and distribution points to ensure that they have enough disk space. The easiest way to do this is to go to System Status in the SMS Administrator console, click Site Status, and click Site System Status for each site, as shown in Figure 17-3. The right pane displays the distribution points and their free disk space. Depending on your SMS configuration, you may need to have enough space for two to three times the package size available on your SMS Site server.

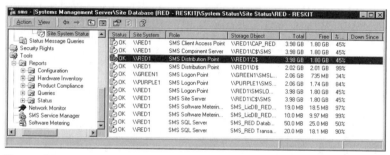

Figure 17-3   Use Site System Status to view the available disk space on each distribution point.

Distribution Points

You might want to limit the number of Windows XP Professional upgrades that you perform concurrently at each site. Upgrades can create a heavy load on the local network and distribution points. Before you upgrade, you need to experiment in a lab or run a pilot. When you test, use servers that are typical of your distribution points and a typical network, which enables you to judge how many clients you can comfortably upgrade at one time. If you find that your network is not a bottleneck for the upgrades but that your distribution points are a bottleneck, consider adding more distribution points at the site.

> **More Info**   For more information about how to add distribution points, see "Distributing Software" in the Systems Management Server Administrator's Guide.

Distribution Point Groups

Because a Windows XP Professional package is large and you will use it extensively, you may want to dedicate distribution points for it. You can refer to these distribution points as a group. You can create a distribution point group for your Windows XP Professional distribution points to reduce the number of administrative tasks.

You can create distribution point groups (and add or remove distribution points from the groups) when you are creating or adjusting distribution points. Then, during distribution, you can specify the distribution point groups at the same places that you specify distribution points.

> **More Info**   For more information about distribution point groups, see "Managing Distribution Point Groups" in the Systems Management Server Administrator's Guide.

Sender Controls

If a Windows XP Professional package is sent to any site that does not have adequate sender controls in place, it can overload the network link at a time when it may interfere with other business functions. Therefore, check the sender controls to be sure they are properly set.

The SMS Administrator console includes SMS address definitions for each site with which it directly communicates. SMS addresses include the SMS site server name, security details for accessing that site, and network transport details (if required). The addresses also include a schedule to specify when high-, medium-, and low-priority transfers can be executed; and how much of the network link can be used at any time of the day.

Fan-Out Distribution

SMS 2.0 has a feature called *fan-out distribution*, which allows child sites to distribute software to lower sites. This reduces the workload on the site that you use to initiate the software distribution because the software does not need be distributed from the initiating site to all sites. This also reduces the workload on the network link between the initiating site and the rest of the sites, which is often the most significant issue. When you are distributing a package to many sites, copying Windows XP Professional over the network many times from any site can cause an unacceptably heavy load.

Figure 17-4 illustrates the difference between software distribution with fan-out and without fan-out distribution. Fan-out distribution occurs automatically if the initiating site does not have an SMS address for the destination site. Therefore, you must use the SMS Administrator console to review the SMS addresses for each site and make sure that the site has addresses only for direct parent and direct child sites.

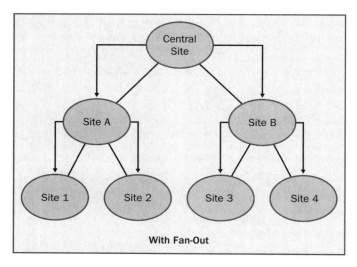

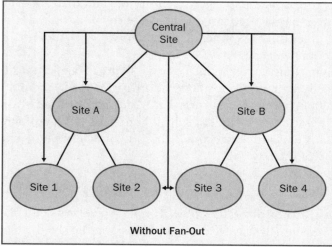

Figure 17-4 Fan-out distribution reduces the load on the site server.

Test Site

To ensure that your plan is complete, distribute the Windows XP Professional package to a test site or a small number of sites before sending it to your entire organization. This procedure enables you to quickly correct problems and to minimize their impact. The test site or sites should be as typical as possible, but at least one site should also represent a high-risk scenario. Examples of such a scenario include deploying with a site server or distribution points that have very little disk space to spare, or having a network link that is particularly slow or unreliable.

A best practice for this level of testing is to start with small sites that do not have complex requirements. An ideal test site has a support staff ready to assist you, if needed, and users who are willing to run your test software distribution. At such sites, you can identify solutions for any problems that you might not have built into your contingency plans during deployment planning. As your confidence in your procedures increases, expand your testing to sites that are larger, more complex, or more difficult to support.

During the distribution phase, your Windows XP Professional deployment needs to be transparent to your users because you have not yet run the upgrades on their computers. Caution is appropriate now, but is more critical later in the deployment process.

More Info For more information about the tasks presented in this section, see the Systems Management Server Administrator's Guide.

Distributing the Packages

This section describes the basic steps for distributing packages. When you perform this task, note that all distribution points for all sites are listed, so you can select all the intended distribution points at one time. However, make sure that you first distribute the package to a small number of sites so that you can test your SMS infrastructure and procedures. As your confidence increases and capacity allows, you can include additional distribution points at other sites.

More Info For more information about this procedure, see "Distributing Software" in the Systems Management Server Administrator's Guide.

Here's how to distribute a Windows XP Professional package:

1. In the SMS Administrator console, click Packages, click the Windows XP Professional package, and then click Distribution Points.

2. On the Action menu, point to New, Distribution Points to start the New Distribution Points Wizard and then click Next.

3. Select the distribution points you want to use. If this is a test distribution, select the distribution points that you planned. Also, if you're using distribution point groups, select them now.

    Note that all distribution points for all sites are listed, so you can select all the intended distribution points now. However, you might do a limited number of distribution points at one time to better manage network traffic.

4. Click Finish to start the distribution.

Caution   As soon as you click Finish, the distribution process begins. You might notice a short delay, due to system processing, package priorities, or sender schedules; however, be prepared for immediate SMS activity.

More Info   For more information about the flow of a package after you initiate distribution, see "Software Distribution Flowcharts" in the Systems Management Server 2.0 Resource Guide.

The Windows XP Professional files are compressed into a single file that is then sent to child sites with distribution points that you selected. At each site, the package might then be sent to other child sites if they have distribution points for this package.

Testing the Distribution

As SMS distributes Windows XP Professional packages, verify that they are arriving properly at the distribution points. The section "Monitoring the Distribution," later in this chapter on page 509, describes how you can verify that the packages have arrived at all distribution points and how you can quickly identify any problems. However, you also need to test the distributions to ensure that they are complete and that the directory trees are properly laid out. You do not need to test all distribution points at this level, but make sure to spot-check a few distribution points to confirm that the production distribution is working as you intended.

Expanding the Distribution

When the first distribution of the package has been completed successfully, you can distribute the package to additional sites and distribution points. The procedure is exactly the same, except that you might want to send to more distribution points at a greater frequency and with less monitoring. You should make sure that the package has reached the new sites before advertising the package to clients at those sites. SMS does not make the advertisement available to the clients until a distribution point is available.

Using the Courier Sender

Network links to some of your sites might be slow or unreliable, or they might already be fully utilized by other traffic. Therefore, sending a large package such as Windows XP Professional over the network links might not be acceptable. SMS 2.0 includes an alternate sender, called the Courier Sender, which you can use to provide all the benefits of SMS software distribution, but without the network overhead normally involved in getting packages to sites.

With the Courier Sender, you copy the SMS package to a CD or similar media, and then send it through mail or by courier to your sites. At the sites, someone puts the CD into the site server and runs a simple program. From this point on, the software distribution carries on as it normally would. The advertisements, status information, and other information will flow over the network at the times you specify; however, this traffic is small relative to the traffic that the package itself would have required if you had sent the package over the network.

> **More Info**   For more information about Courier Sender, see the Systems Management Server Administrator's Guide.

Monitoring the Distribution

Distributing Windows XP Professional in an organization with many SMS sites takes some time to complete. Some sites take longer than others due to the speed of the wide area network (WAN) links, the reliability of those links, sender scheduling, and other variables. There is also the possibility that, despite good preparations, some sites or distribution points might have inadequate disk space by the time the package arrives. For these reasons, it is important to give the Windows XP Professional distribution adequate time to complete. Monitor it closely to determine whether there are any issues to resolve, and make sure that the distribution of the package is complete at all sites. The following sections describe how to monitor the status of your distribution.

System Status Subsystem

SMS 2.0 includes a powerful System Status subsystem for monitoring the distribution. The SMS Administrator console includes a System Status node, in which you can obtain summary and detailed results from the System Status subsystem. You can also obtain the status of the package distribution from the Package Status node.

When you create a package, the definition of that package is immediately distributed to all child sites; however, the actual files for that package, if any, are not distributed at that time. The same package definition is re-sent when the package definition is updated. Status information for the package definition distribution is then available. Therefore, when reviewing package status, make certain that you distinguish between the distribution of the package definition and the package files.

Software distribution status is summarized at several levels, as described in the following list:

- **Package Status For All Packages**   When you select Package Status (under System Status), you can see how many distribution points have been targeted for each package and how many have been installed, are retrying, or have failed. This level is useful to identify how many distribution points, if any, might need intervention. Note the size difference between the original package and the compressed package. The package identification number might also be useful for other purposes, such as troubleshooting. At this level, there are no status messages to query.

- **Package Status For A Specific Package**   Below the package status for all packages, you can select each package. At this level, you can see which sites should or should not have the package, and which ones might need intervention. You can also verify that all sites have the same package version, as indicated by the Source Version column. At this level, you can click Show Messages, All on the Action menu to see all the status messages for the package from all sites and distribution points. This can be a lot of messages; therefore, it is better to review the messages at each site individually.

- **Package Status At The Sites**   Below the package status for a specific package, you can select each site. This level of status checking allows you to see which specific distribution points within a site might be having problems with the distribution. At this level, you can click Show Messages, All on the Action menu to see all the status messages for the package from this site and all its distribution points. The following sequence of messages is typical (the distribution point–specific messages are listed in the next section):

    - 30000 or 300001—package created or modified
    - 30003—program created

- 2300, 2310, and 2311—Distribution Manager preparing the package

- 2339—Distribution Manager initiating schedule and sender to send the package information (not the package files)

- 30009—distribution point assigned

- 2333—preparing to send compressed image of package

- 2335—Distribution Manager–initiated scheduler and sender to send the package files to the sites

- 2315—Distribution Manager deleted the compressed image of the package

- When reviewing status messages, notice that each sequence of Distribution Manager activities ends with the message 2301, which indicates that the sequence was successful. This message appears whenever Distribution Manager completes any activities. Distribution Manager is the SMS component that distributes packages from the site server to the SMS distribution points and that initiates the sending of the package to other sites.

- **Package Status At A Distribution Point**   At the package status at each site, you can select each distribution point. At this level, you can click Show Messages, All on the Action menu to see all the status messages for the package at this distribution point. The following sequence of messages is typical:

    - 2317—Distribution Manager is refreshing the package on distribution point (not seen the first time the package is sent to the distribution point)

    - 2322—Distribution Manager decompressed the package to the temporary directory (if applicable)

    - 2329—Distribution Manager copied the package from the temporary directory or package source to the distribution point

    - 2330—Distribution Manager successfully distributed the package to the distribution point

    - 2342—Distribution Manager is starting to distribute the package to the distribution point

> **More Info**   For a list of all status messages and their complete message text, see Chapter 26, "Status Messages," in the Systems Management Server 2.0 Resource Guide.

Reporting Distribution Status

You might want to produce a report of the package distribution status, either for easy reference or to address your own specific requirements. You can perform queries of the package distribution status classes and incorporate the responses in the reporting tool of your choice as is done with other SMS reporting tools. Table 17-1 lists the relevant classes and the category of status information that you can find in each. Creating reports can be a complex operation and is beyond the scope of this chapter. For more information, see the Advanced Systems Management Server 2.0 Reporting technical paper at *http://www.microsoft.com/smsmgmt/techdetails/AdvReport.asp*.

Table 17-1   WMI Package Distribution Status Classes

Class	Status Information
SMS_PackageStatus	Overall summary information about the status of packages on the distribution points.
SMS_PackageStatus RootSummarizer	Information about the status of a given package. Maps to Package Status in the SMS Administrator console.
SMS_PackageStatus DetailsSummarizer	Detailed information about the status of a given package by site code. Maps to the package console tree under Package Status (in the SMS Administrator console).
SMS_PackageStatus DistPointsSummarizer	Detailed information about the status of a given package at a given site. Maps to the site code under the package console tree (under Package Status in the SMS Administrator console).

Troubleshooting Distributions

Monitoring the software distributions can indicate whether a software distribution has encountered problems at some point. Typically, this is due to lack of disk space, network link difficulties, or server problems. The status message text indicates such problems.

Isolating the problem is the first step in solving any technical problem. When you know which component failed, you can concentrate your efforts on the appropriate issues. Using the monitoring techniques described earlier will help you to isolate the problem. Also, the chapter "Software Distribution Flowcharts" in the Systems Management Server 2.0 Resource Guide includes graphics that show the typical flow of the software distribution process. If you find indications that your software distribution did not make it to a certain point in the flow, there is a good chance that the failure occurred at the previous point in the flowchart.

After you isolate the particular component, understanding how it works can provide clues as to why it failed. The flowcharts can also help you gain an understanding of the process. In addition, the related log files can show what is happening with the component at a very low level and, therefore, what might not be working. The logs are enabled by using the SMS Service Manager.

> **More Info** For troubleshooting tips for software distribution, see the chapter titled "Software Distribution Flowcharts" in the Systems Management Server 2.0 Resource Guide.

Advertising the Packages

Computers can be upgraded to Windows XP Professional when they receive the appropriate advertisement. The advertisements give descriptive information about the package to end users, and they include the details necessary for SMS to run the programs. The advertisements can even be assigned to run at specific times so that the user cannot block the upgrade or so that the upgrade can occur while the user is away from the computer. The following sections describe how to advertise a Windows XP Professional package.

Selecting Computers

An advertisement tells SMS to make available to an SMS collection a specific program within a package. A *collection* is a flexible definition of computers, users, or user groups. In the case of a Windows XP Professional software distribution, you would initially use collections that are a small number of computers used for testing purposes. Later, you would use collections that are all computers that are ready for Windows XP Professional. You might subdivide the collection by site or information collected from SMS Inventory.

Query-based collections have the additional benefit of being dynamic; as time goes on, you can add computers to a collection, and the advertisements that are available to that collection automatically become available to those additional computers. If the collection is based on the memory capacity of computers, for example, computers are added to the collection as their hardware is upgraded for Windows XP Professional. If you install additional memory in a computer, the SMS hardware inventory detects this and records it within SMS. This computer is automatically included in the collection; therefore, the Windows XP Professional upgrade is made available to the computer. Other than physically adding the memory to the computer, this is all automatic. The following steps describe how to create collections:

- Create a query containing the systems that are ready to receive the Windows XP Professional installation.

- In the SMS Administrator console, click Collections.

- On the Action menu, click New, Collection; then type a name for the collection in the Collection Properties dialog box and do one of the following:

  - On the Membership Rules tab, click the New Query Rule button. In the Query Rule Properties box, click the Browse button and then select the appropriate query. For example, use a query that you have made to report on the computers that are available to be upgraded to Windows XP Professional. You might have other queries that you prefer to use, such as All Windows 98 Systems, or queries that you have defined to include all computers at specific sites. Add additional query rules or direct membership rules as necessary.

  - On the Membership Rules tab, click the New Direct Rule button and then use the Create Direct Membership Rule Wizard to specify the computers that you want to upgrade. This choice might be your best option during testing, especially if you have a small number of arbitrarily chosen computers that you want to run the package on.

An issue to consider is that SMS 2.0 allows collections to include computers, users, or user groups. Including domain users or user groups might not be appropriate because users can often log on to different computers. Therefore, each computer that a user logs on to could be upgraded, especially if the advertisement is assigned and runs whether or not the user chooses it. However, the computers that they log on to might not be ready for the upgrade, or the users that usually use the computer might not be trained to use Windows XP Professional.

Preparing Computers

The computers to which you are going to advertise need to be ready for the advertisement. During the Windows XP Professional upgrade, the computer needs to restart several times. If this can occur automatically, the entire upgrade can be accomplished without user intervention.

Some users put a boot password on their computer. This password is required by the computer itself and therefore cannot be circumvented by software. Until this password is entered, the computer will not restart, and the Windows XP Professional upgrade cannot continue. Therefore, make sure to advise users to temporarily disable their boot passwords. If this is not possible, someone must be present during the upgrade. The same issue holds true if the computer stops for confirmation during restart because of hardware configuration changes or other issues.

I recommend that you give users advance notice of the upgrade so that they can be sure to close all documents. If users know that the upgrade is imminent, they will also be more inclined to get any training they require, perform backups, and prepare any programs they are responsible for.

If you're advertising the package with an assignment to run overnight or over a weekend, any client computers running Windows 98 or Windows Me need a user logged on in order for the advertisement to start automatically. These users might want to use a secure screen saver to prevent others from using their computer while they are away. Target computers running Windows NT or Windows 2000 do not require a user to be logged on for the advertisements to start.

Advertising the Packages

You now have a Windows XP Professional package ready to distribute, you have the right computers selected, and you have the computers ready for the upgrade. The next step is to initiate the process. Do this by creating an advertisement as shown in the following steps:

1. In the SMS Administrator console, click Advertisements.

2. On the Action menu, point to New and then choose Advertisement.

3. In the Name box, type a name for your advertisement that helps you to identify it.

4. In the Package list, click the name of the package you're advertising: Microsoft Windows XP Professional.

5. In the Program list, click the name of the program: Automated Upgrade From Win98/98SE/ME, Windows 2000 Pro, NTW 4.0 (X86 SP6).

6. Click Browse and then select the collection to which you're advertising the program.

7. If you want to set the advertisement to run at a specific time, click the Schedule tab and then click the New button to add a schedule.

Caution Assigned advertisements run only once for each target computer to which they're advertised. If the advertisement fails at the target computer, the client does not attempt to automatically run it again. This ensures that computers are not caught in an infinite loop of trying to run an assigned advertisement, failing, restarting, and then trying again. Therefore, you might also want to select Allow Users To Run The Program Independently Of Assignments. This allows users to run the program ahead of schedule or to run it afterward if the program fails the first time. Alternatively, you can create a new advertisement at a later time for the computers that failed to upgrade.

As with the previous phases of Windows XP Professional software distribution, start the advertising on a limited scale and expand as it proves successful. This is especially true now because end users are definitely affected by the software distribution. You can expand the advertising by creating additional advertisements, each aimed at different collections, or by adjusting the collection that the advertisement is based on so that it includes more and more computers. Separate advertisements might be necessary to advertise different programs to appropriate collections. For example, the Windows 98 upgrade program should be advertised only to the computers in the Windows 98 collection.

Expanding Security

If you restricted access to the package on the distribution points when you created the package, you must now open that access. Do this by following the steps in this section. If you are using SMS to run the program with administrative privileges, add the client network connection accounts used in the SMS site as your package access accounts. Here's how to open security for the Windows XP Professional package:

1. In the SMS Administrator console, click Packages.

2. Click the Windows XP Professional package and then click Access Accounts.

3. On the Action menu, click New, Windows NT Access Account.

4. In the Access Account Properties dialog box, click Set.

5. In the Windows NT Account dialog box, enter the domain and user or group, specify the Account Type, and then click OK.

6. In the Access Account Properties dialog box, verify that the Permissions are Read.

7. Repeat steps 1 through 6 to add additional users or groups.

Upgrading Computers

When you have Windows XP Professional on a distribution point in the same site as the computers to be upgraded, and the advertisement is available at the computers, you can do the following:

■ **Schedule the upgrade for a time that is convenient for the user.**   Distribution to all users can be done with SMS at a time that you believe is convenient to them. However, you can give users the option to adjust the date and time, as shown in Figure 17-5, to coincide with a time when they are not using their computers. You can also make the upgrade mandatory at a certain date and time so that users cannot postpone the upgrade indefinitely.

■ **Report the status of the upgrade.** When the first and final phases of the Windows XP Professional upgrade are completed at the computer, SMS produces status files that are propagated up the SMS hierarchy. You can use this information to report on the overall progress of the upgrade project or to investigate the status of an individual computer, as discussed in the next section. You can produce customized status files to indicate specific details relating to the status of the upgrade, if desired. The programs that create these status files are invoked as part of the package execution and therefore must be included in its definition. For example, you might want to include such status files if you have Windows XP Setup initiate post-upgrade tasks.

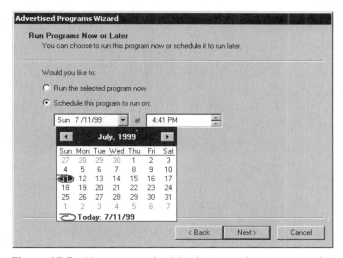

Figure 17-5 Users can schedule the upgrade at a convenient time.

Many organizations do not give their end users full privileges on client computers, which helps to minimize problems that are caused by users making uninformed or unintentional computer changes. However, this lack of privileges would normally stop users from initiating a Windows XP Professional upgrade for their computers. SMS avoids this problem by doing the Windows XP Professional upgrade in the context of a special SMS security account when Windows XP Setup is set to run with administrative rights.

Monitoring Advertisements

The SMS status message that reports the progress of the upgrade at each computer can also be used to report the progress of the Windows XP Professional deployment as a whole. The number of computers ready to be upgraded, those successfully upgraded, and the locations of failures can all be reported. You can then intervene where any problems have occurred.

SMS 2.0 includes a powerful System Status subsystem that allows you to readily monitor the distribution. The SMS Administrator console includes a System Status node in which you can obtain summary and detailed results from the System Status subsystem. There is an Advertisement Status node that allows you to obtain the status of the advertisements:

- **Status For All Advertisements**   When you select Advertisement Status under System Status in the SMS Administrator console, you can view the following:

  - How many systems have received the advertisement

  - How many systems have experienced general failures processing the advertisement

  - How many times the advertised program has been started

  - How many times the program has run to completion or failed

  - Various advertisement details

- **Status For A Specific Advertisement**   Below the advertisement status for all advertisements you can select each advertisement. At this level, you can view the following:

  - Which sites have clients that have received the advertisement

  - Which sites contain clients that experienced a general failure while processing the advertisement

  - How many times the advertised program has run at each site

  - How many times it ran to completion or failed

- **Status At A Site**   At the advertisement status level, you can select each site. On the Action menu, click Show Messages, All to see the status messages for the advertisement at this site. The following sequence of messages is typical:

  - 30006—advertisement created

  - 3900—advertisement processed within a site (distributed to client access points)

  - 10002—advertisement received at a client

  - 10005—program started

  - 10007—program failed

    The message indicates why this has occurred. Common reasons are that the user canceled the program or otherwise forced it to stop, or the client computer did not have enough disk space.

- 10008—program completed successfully

- 10009—program completed successfully and a status Management Information Format (MIF) file was generated

  At this point, the SMS part of the upgrade is done. This corresponds with the end of the first phase of Windows XP Setup.

- **Reporting Advertisement Status**   You might want to produce a report of the advertisement status, either for easy reference or to address your own specific requirements. You can perform queries of the SMS advertisement status subsystem and incorporate the responses in the reporting tool of your choice, as is done with other SMS reporting functions. Table 17-2 lists the relevant class and the category of status information that can be found in the class.

Table 17-2   WMI Advertisement Status Class

Class	Status Information
SMS_AdvertisementStatusSummarizer	Displays detailed advertisement status information grouped by site code. You can locate maps to the advertisement items under Advertisement Status (in the SMS Administrator console).

> **Note**   Windows XP Professional without a service pack produces a status MIF with the MIFVersion property set to 5.0. This is the same value that Windows 2000 used. If you are deploying both Windows 2000 and Windows XP Professional at the same time, advertisement status reporting could be inaccurate for this reason. When deploying Windows XP Professional with SP1 (or later) slipstreamed, the MIFVersion should be set to 5.1. Confirm this is the correct value in your testing.

Troubleshooting

You can use the advertisement-monitoring process to isolate problems, hopefully before the users report problems. Typical problems include lack of disk space, user interference, or package definition errors. The texts of the status messages indicate such problems. Also make sure to verify that the package is available on at least one distribution point at the site.

Isolating the problem is the first step in solving any technical problem. If you know which component failed, you can concentrate your efforts on the appropriate issues. Using the monitoring techniques listed previously will help you to isolate the problem.

More Info   For graphics that show the typical flow of the software distribution process on the server side, see the chapter "Software Distribution Flowcharts" in the Systems Management Server 2.0 Resource Guide. For graphics that show the flow on the client side, see the chapter "Client Features Flowcharts" in the Systems Management Server 2.0 Resource Guide.

If you find indications that your software distribution did not make it to a certain point in the flow, there is a good chance that the failure occurred at the previous point in the flowchart.

After you isolate the component, understanding how it works can provide clues about why it failed. The flowcharts can help you gain an understanding of the process. In addition, the related log files can show what is happening with the component at a very low level, which can help you see what might not be working. You enable server logs by using the SMS Service Manager, and client logs are always enabled.

SMS has several features that can help you resolve problems on client computers:

- Remotely control the client computer.

- Transfer files to the computer to replace files that need updating.

- Restart the computer.

- Obtain computer details, either based on the routine inventory or on real-time remote control tools. The routine inventory is available even when the client is offline.

- Upgrade incompatible application software.

There will be situations in which manual intervention is needed, such as when an upgrade makes it impossible to restart the computer or to connect a computer to the network, or when the SMS client components become inoperative.

Distributing Office 2003

The process of deploying Microsoft Office 2003 Editions and Microsoft Office 2003 Multilingual User Interface Packs (MUI Packs) is similar to that for deploying Windows XP Professional. When you use SMS to install and maintain Office 2003 Editions and MUI Packs, you can help to set a precise control over the deployment process. For example, by using SMS, you can query client computers for software requirements before you install Office 2003 Editions, and you can target the installation only to computers that meet your criteria.

The steps necessary to deploy Office 2003 Editions using SMS are no different from those for deploying Microsoft Office XP. Office 2003 Editions requires SMS Service Pack 2. And, you'll need new package definition files, however. You can install the package definition files (.pdf files) from the Office 2003 Editions Resource Kit. Package definition files contain the information required for Systems Management Server to create a software distribution package. The files for Office 2003 Editions are consolidated into two files: Office11.sms (for all Office 2003 editions) and MUI11.sms (for Office MUI Packs). You can download both package definition files from *http://www.microsoft.com/office/ork/2003*.

> **More Info** See the white paper "Using SMS 2.0 to Deploy Microsoft Office XP" at *http://www.microsoft.com/technet/prodtechnol/sms/deploy/depopt /smsoffxp.asp* for more detailed information about deploying Office 2003 Editions using SMS. Although this white paper covers Office XP, the process and considerations are the same for deploying Office 2003 Editions.

Best Practices

The following are best practices for deploying Windows XP Professional by using SMS:

- **Learn the two phases of deploying Windows XP Professional by using SMS.** With large software distributions, such as Windows XP Professional, it is important to note the two phases of SMS 2.0 software distribution: distribution and advertising. Distribution gets the software close to the computers that you want to upgrade. Advertising lets the clients know that the upgrade is available.

- **Use an answer file to automate Windows XP Setup.** Without an answer file, Windows XP Setup requires user intervention. Use an unattended-setup answer file to fully automate the installation process.

- **Check the available disk space on your distribution points.** With a package as large as Windows XP Professional, the distribution phase consumes a great deal of resources, and problems could arise due to lack of disk space. Therefore, make sure to plan and monitor the distribution phase carefully. After you have successfully completed the distribution phase, begin the advertising phase.

- **Place distribution points near the target computers.** Installing Windows XP Professional on target computers can cause significant amounts of network traffic as Windows XP Setup runs. To reduce the risk of incomplete installations and to minimize elapsed time to install software, you should ensure that all clients have distribution servers available across high-availability, high-bandwidth network links.

- **Test your implementation by starting with limited distributions.**   Test your distribution by first distributing Windows XP Professional to only one site. Also, you should send the initial advertisement of the package to only a few clients at that site, which allows you to test your SMS infrastructure and procedures on a limited scale. As your confidence increases and as capacity allows, you can distribute the package to more sites and increase the scope of the advertisement to include more clients and sites until you eventually include your entire organization.

- **Monitor the health and status of packages and distribution points.** Package Status provides a summary report of the health of packages and distribution points in your site. In many organizations, administrators distribute multiple packages concurrently to multiple destinations. Package Status allows you to monitor when packages arrive at distribution points. A package must arrive at a distribution point before a client can access, install, or run an advertisement.

- **See "SMS Site Design Best Practices" for more best practices.**   The help file Bstprac.chm at *http://www.microsoft.com/smsmgmt/deployment/bstprac.asp* contains more best practices for SMS infrastructures.

Chapter 18

User State Migration

User state migration is often overlooked when migrating to a new operating system. If you're upgrading to Microsoft Windows XP Professional from an earlier version of Windows, Windows XP Setup will automatically migrate users' settings; but if you're cleanly installing Windows XP Professional, you must plan for and migrate users' existing data and settings. This chapter describes user state migration, including the tools that Microsoft and third-party vendors supply.

Checklist

- Have you decided whether to migrate users' settings? See Chapter 1, "Deployment Plan," Chapter 3, "Windows Configuration," and Chapter 4, "Office Configuration."

- Do users store their documents on the network? See Chapter 3 for more information about folder redirection.

- Have you determined which documents and settings you must migrate? If not, see the section "Planning Migration," later in this chapter on page 524.

- Do you have a test lab in which to test user state migration? If not, see Chapter 1.

- Do you already have a relationship with an independent software vendor (ISV) that includes migration tools as part of its deployment packages? If not, see the section "Using Third-Party Tools," later in this chapter on page 537.

Planning Migration

User state migration is the process of migrating the current *state* of the user's environment to the new operating system. This is often called *personality transfer*. User state migration is backing up users' data and settings before installing a new operating system and then restoring those settings after installing a new operating system. Examples of settings that you might want to migrate include drive mappings, printer connections, and so on.

User state is any data, operating-system settings, and application settings. And, in some cases, applications themselves that are part of users' configurations and must be available after migration are part of user state. Here's a partial list of what could be included in your user state information:

- **Application data**   Any data generated by a Microsoft application or other applications.

- **Application settings**   Any configuration setting that a user may be able to configure. This might be a setting stored in the registry, a private .ini file, or a special data file associated with the application.

- **Windows settings**   Settings such as desktop settings: background picture, color scheme, mouse settings.

- **Network settings**   Mapped drives, printer connections, shared resources.

- **Internet settings**   Favorites, cookies, and passwords for Web sites.

It is a critical part of your deployment to consider whether and how you will migrate users' state. In the planning process, consider the following questions:

- What data are you interested in assuring makes it to the new desktop?

- What data are you not interested in transferring to the new desktop?

- Which applications will be part of the migration?

- Which applications will not be part of the migration?

- Which operating-system settings do you want to be part of the migration?

- Which operating-system settings will you specify in the deployment or post-deployment, and thus do not want to migrate?

- Which network settings do you want to migrate?

- Which network settings are changing and thus you do not want to migrate?

- Will different groups within your organization require you to migrate different settings and applications (executives versus task-oriented workers)?

The tools that are available for user state migration range from scripted tools that you develop yourself to enterprise tools designed to migrate settings for thousands of computers. Microsoft offers two tools that are designed for either one-to-one migrations or domain-based scripted migrations. The two tools that Microsoft has made available for user state migration have different designs and intended purposes.

The Files And Settings Transfer Wizard is meant to assist in transferring user state from one PC to a new PC, such as when you receive a new computer. It is also useful for migrations on mobile computers that are disconnected from a network.

The second tool is the User State Migration Tool (USMT), which is designed for enterprise migrations within a Windows NT, Windows 2000, or Windows 2003 domain.

> **More Info**   See "Deploying Windows XP Part I: Planning" at *http: //www.microsoft.com/technet/prodtechnol/winxppro/deploy/depovg/depxpi.asp* and "User State Migration in Windows XP" at *http://www.microsoft.com /windowsxp/pro/techinfo/deployment/userstate/modifying.asp* for more information about planning user state migration.

Using Files And Settings Transfer Wizard

The Files And Settings Transfer Wizard (fastwiz.exe) is on the Windows XP Professional product CD. After inserting the CD in the drive, click Perform Additional Tasks, Transfer Files And Settings. This runs Fastwiz.exe. You can also start the Files And Settings Transfer Wizard from the Windows XP Professional Start Menu. Click Start, All Programs, Accessories, System Tools, Files And Settings Transfer Wizard.

The Files And Settings Transfer Wizard is designed for ease of use and is typically used when you migrate a single machine from an earlier version of Windows to Windows XP Professional. It's also useful for transferring personality from one computer running Windows XP Professional to another. Although it is not the typical tool that you would use in an enterprise migration, it would be useful for mobile computers such as laptops or telecommuting users' desktops. It's also useful in one-off scenarios in which you're replacing a users' computer. The easiest way to use the Files And Settings Transfer Wizard is to run it while both machines are connected over a network or with an Ethernet crossover cable. Other options that are available are direct cable connection; floppy or other removable media; or a removable drive or network folder. The important thing to consider is that the destination computer needs to be available when you use one of the direct connections such as Ethernet cable or needs to have access to the same media capabilities such as a CD player if your original computer has a CD-RW drive. The general steps to use the wizard are simple and are documented in the Microsoft Knowledge Base article 293118 (*http://www.microsoft.com/support*).

Like User State Migration Tool, the actual data that the Files And Settings Transfer Wizard is able to transfer is determined by settings in an *.inf* file: Migwiz.inf. For more information about this file, see the section "Deploying User State Migration Tool."

When you run the tool the first time, you tell it whether you are running it on the new or old computer. The *old* computers can be running Windows 95, Windows 98, Windows 98 Second Edition, Windows Millennium Edition, Windows NT 4.0, Windows 2000, or Windows XP Professional (32-bit). After you choose the old computer and click Next, it asks how you want to transfer the data, as shown in Figure 18-1. (By default, the wizard migrates the settings shown in the figure.) As shown in Table 18-1, this is a large amount of data, so you must make sure that your destination has enough space available for it.

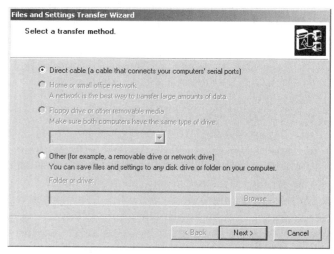

Figure 18-1   Using the Files And Settings Transfer Wizard, the user chooses how to transfer the data.

Table 18-1   Migrated Data and Settings

Category	Settings
Settings	■ Accessibility ■ Command Prompt Settings ■ Display Properties ■ Internet Explorer Settings ■ Microsoft Messenger ■ Microsoft NetMeeting ■ Mouse And Keyboard ■ MSN Explorer ■ Network Printer And Drives ■ Outlook Express ■ Regional Settings ■ Sounds And Multimedia ■ Taskbar Options ■ Windows Media Player ■ Windows Movie Maker
Folders	■ Fonts ■ My Documents ■ My Pictures ■ Shared Desktop ■ Shared Documents
File Types	■ *.asf (Windows Media Audio/Video file) ■ *.asx (Windows Media Audio/Video shortcut) ■ *.AU (AU format sound) ■ *.avi (video clip) ■ *.cov (fax cover page file) ■ *.cpe (fax cover page file) ■ *.doc (WordPad document) ■ *.eml (Internet e-mail message) ■ *.m3u (M3U file) ■ *.mid (MIDI sequence) ■ *.midi (MIDI sequence) ■ *.mp2 (Movie File MPEG) ■ *.mp3 (MP3 Format Sound) ■ *.mpa (Movie File MPEG) ■ *.mpeg (Movie File MPEG) ■ *.MSWMM (Windows Movie Maker Project) ■ *.nws (Internet News Message) ■ *.rtf (Rich Text Format) ■ *.snd (AU Sound Format) ■ *.wav (Wave Sound) ■ *.wm (Windows Media Audio/Video file) ■ *.wma (Windows Media Audio file) ■ *.wri (Write document)

More Info   See "Step-by-Step Guide to Migrating Files and Settings" at *http://www.microsoft.com/technet/prodtechnol/winxppro/deploy/mgrtfset.asp* for step-by-step instructions for migrating user state.

Deploying User State Migration Tool

The USMT is the tool that you use in enterprise deployments of Windows XP Professional to migrate users' data and settings. It is designed to be run in a batch file or script to assist in automating your deployment. Using USMT lessens the impact of deploying disk images or installing Windows XP Professional cleanly on users' computers. The following steps show the typical deployment scenario:

1. Run Scanstate.exe, which is part of USMT, on the user's desktop to capture state information. You can run this from user's logon scripts.

2. Back up the user's entire desktop using your preferred imaging product.

3. Install your Windows XP Professional disk image on the user's computer.

More Info   For more information about building Windows XP Professional disk images, see Chapter 15, "Disk Imaging with Sysprep."

4. Run Loadstate.exe, which is part of USMT, to restore the user's data and settings to the desktop. You can run this from users' logon scripts. Don't run this by using your answer file's *[GuiRunOnce]* section, however, as the program would run once per computer and not necessarily target the user correctly.

Note   USMT is on the Windows XP Professional product CD in the \Valuadd\Msft\Usmt folder. An updated version is found the Windows Server 2003 product CD in the same folder. (I expect the Windows XP Professional Service Pack 2 CD to contain the updated version.) The new version contains updated documentation that describes the contents of the various INF files and how to customize them to help fine-tune your deployment. (The filename of that document is Usmtinfcommands.doc.) Before using USMT, you *must* read this document. Also, if you're going to use USMT, I strongly recommend that you use the version that comes with the Windows Server 2003 or Windows XP Professional Service Pack 2 product CDs.

As you learned, USMT contains two primary files: Scanstate.exe and Load-state.exe. Use Scanstate.exe to capture information. Use Loadstate.exe to restore it. In addition to the two files, USMT contains four INF files: Migapp.inf, Migsys.inf, Miguser.inf, and Sysfiles.inf. You learn more about these files later in this section. Scanstate.exe creates another INF file, migration.inf, which contains information that allows Loadstate.exe to determine what settings to transfer.

Planning State Migration

State migration isn't as daunting as the name sounds. In the planning stages of your deployment, you have three decisions to make. The first and most important is to plan what settings you want to migrate from earlier versions of Windows to Windows XP Professional. If you're using the USMT, you can use the *.inf* files and the documentation it provides to plan which settings you need to migrate and which you don't.

The second big planning decision is to decide at what part in the process you want to save users' state. You must decide not only when, but how. For example, do you want to save users' state by running a script in their logon scripts? This is a logical place for this task because you must save each user's state individually. (Some third-party products don't have this requirement.) The problem is that users must actually log on to their computers using their accounts in order for this to succeed.

The last big planning decision is to decide at what part in the process you want to restore users' state. At first glance, running a script in the *[GuiRunOnce]* section of the Windows XP Professional answer file sounds like a great idea, but it's not. You must load each user's state individually, so doing so from their logon script is a better choice.

These choices apply to the USMT that you learn about in this chapter. Some of the third-party products that you also learn about in this chapter simplify the process. For example, some of them allow you to save and restore users' state remotely. They allow you to save and restore multiple users' state in one sitting so that you don't have to rely on users' logging on to their computers. If these are your requirements, see the section "Using Third-Party Tools," later in this chapter on page 537.

Running Scanstate.exe

The following shows the syntax of Scanstate.exe, and Table 18-2 describes each command-line option:

```
scanstate.exe \\server\sharing\folder [/?] /i filename.inf [/l logfile.txt]
[/v verbosity] [/x] [/s] [/f] [/u] [/c] [/p] [/md domain] [/mu user] [/o]
```

Table 18-2 Scanstate.exe Command-Line Options

Option	Description
/?	Displays help.
/i filename.inf	Specifies an .inf file containing rules that define what state to migrate. Use multiple **/i** command-line options to specify multiple .inf files.
/l logfile.txt	Specifies a path and filename of the log file. By default, the log is saved in %USERPROFILE%\Local Settings\Application Data\scanstate.log.
/v verbosity	Specifies the level of detail used in the log. The value of verbosity can be one of the following:
	0. Least detail
	7. Most detail
/x	Specifies that no settings or files will be migrated by default.
/s	Specifies that settings listed in the .inf files be migrated. System elements are also migrated. These elements are Network Printers, RAS Connections, and Cookies.
/f	Specifies that files listed in the .inf files will be migrated.
/u	Enables collection of the entire HKEY_CURRENT_USER registry key by default.
/c	Specifies to continue when encountering an error that can be ignored. Scanstate.exe still returns an error code.
/p	Prescans the system to determine how much storage space will be needed. It generates a space estimate file (USMTsize.txt) instead of an actual store. The file is a tab-delimited file with two columns. The first column is block size, and the second is how many bytes are required at that block size. The first line of the file is the numbers for the store location indicated on the command-line.
/md domain	Provides an easy way to change the domain name during migration. If after the migration the user will be part of a different domain, this is an easy way to provide the domain the user should be created in.
/mu user	Provides an easy way to change the user's logon name during migration. If after the migration the user will have a new logon name, this is an easy way to change it so the user is created with the correct logon name.
/o	If there is already a migration store at the indicated target location, the store is overwritten without warning.

If /x, /f, /s, and /u are not used, the default command-line options are /f /s /u. Also, Scanstate.exe ignores /x if you use /f /s /u.

It is typical that Scanstate.exe would either be located on a mapped network drive or run from a shared location to which the user has read and execute access. One interesting note is that the migrated data comes from the currently logged-on user's information store. If multiple users have access to a machine, you need to run Scanstate.exe for each of the users' accounts so that all users' data is saved. The most common way to run Scanstate.exe is within a batch file or VBS script that captures the currently logged-on user's name (%USERNAME%) and uses that name to uniquely store the data. You can run this from users' logon scripts.

Running Loadstate.exe

The following shows the syntax of Loadstate.exe, and Table 18-3 describes each command-line option:

```
loadstate.exe \\server\sharing\folder [/?] /i filename.inf [/l logfile.txt]
[/v verbosity] [/x] [/s] [/f] [/u] [/c] [/md domain] [/mu user] [/q]
```

Table 18-3 Loadstate.exe Command-Line Options

Option	Description
/?	Displays help.
/i filename.inf	Specifies an .inf file containing rules that define what state to migrate. Use multiple /i command-line options to specify multiple .inf files.
/l logfile.txt	Specifies a path and filename of the log file. By default, the log is saved in %USERPROFILE%\Local Settings\Application Data\loadstate.log.
/v verbosity	Specifies the level of detail used in the log. The value of *verbosity* can be one of the following:
	0. Least detail
	7. Most detail
/x	Specifies that no settings or files will be migrated by default.
/s	Specifies that settings listed in the .inf files be migrated. System elements are also migrated. These elements are Network Printers, RAS Connections, and Cookies.
/f	Specifies that files listed in the .inf files will be migrated.
/u	Enables collection of the entire HKEY_CURRENT_USER registry key by default.
/c	Specifies to continue when encountering an error that can be ignored. Loadstate.exe still returns an error code.
/md domain	Provides an easy way to change the domain name during migration. If after the migration the user will be part of a different domain, this is an easy way to provide the domain the user should be created in.

Table 18-3   Loadstate.exe Command-Line Options

Option	Description
/mu user	Provides an easy way to change the user's logon name during migration. If after the migration the user will have a new logon name, this is an easy way to change it so the user is created with the correct logon name.
/q	Loads migrated settings to the current user. The migrated user is not created, and administrator rights are not required. This will have slightly different results than running from administrator mode. For example, security can prevent some settings or files from being restored. Also, the /md and /mu switches are ignored.

If /x, /f, /s, and /u are not used, the default command-line options are /f /s /u. Also, Loadstate.exe ignores /x if you use /f /s /u.

Using Migsys.inf

Migsys.inf file contains settings related to the operating system. The default settings that this file migrates include the following:

- Accessibility Options
- Classic Desktop
- Display Properties
- Folder Options
- Fonts
- Internet Options
- Localization/International Settings
- Mouse and Keyboard
- ODBC Data Source Names
- Outlook Express
- Screen Saver Selection
- Sounds and Multimedia
- Taskbar

All these settings are listed in a section of the file labeled *[System Settings]*. If you want to disable some portion of the standard migration, you simply use the semicolon (;) to comment out a section of the file. For example, if you were going to manage screen saver information via group policies post-deployment, you could just comment out the screen saver settings in the default Migsys.inf file. Listing 18-1 shows an example of this.

If you do not want to migrate any of the settings in this file, you simply do not include it on the Scanstate.exe command line. This is the same with any of the other *.inf* files. You specify which information to capture by using the */i* switch followed by the name of the *.inf* file.

Listing 18-1   Migsys.inf Example

```
[System Settings]
Accessibility, %accessibility%
Fonts,, dir, %csidl_fonts%
Mouse and Keyboard, %mouse_and_keyboard%
Browser, %internet_settings%
International, %International%
Multimedia, %Multimedia%
Outlook Express, %outlook_express%
Display, %display%
;ScreenSaver, %screensaver%
FolderOptions, %folderoptions%
TaskBar, %taskbar%
Classic, %classic%
```

Using Miguser.inf

Miguser.inf contains settings related to users' data rather than operating-system settings. The default data that is specified by the contents of this file include the following:

- Desktop

- Favorites

- My Pictures

- My Documents

- Shared Desktop

- Shared Documents

- Shared Favorites

- Shared Start Menu Items

- Start Menu Items

This information is the actual user's data that you usually do want to capture, but there may be some information that you do not want to transfer. So again, you can simply comment out the information that you did not want to migrate. Listing 18-2 shows an example of commenting out the Favorites so that the data will not be migrated. If you do not want to migrate any of this data, you simply do not specify the file Miguser.inf on the Scanstate.exe command line.

Listing 18-2 Miguser.inf Example

```
[User Settings]
Desktop Items,, dir,%csidl_desktopdirectory%
Shared Desktop Items,, dir,%csidl_common_desktopdirectory%
Start Menu Items,, dir,%csidl_startmenu%
Shared Start Menu Items,, dir,%csidl_common_startmenu%
;Favorites,, dir,%csidl_favorites%
Shared Favorites,, dir,%csidl_common_favorites%
My Pictures,, dir,%csidl_mypictures%
My Documents,, dir,%csidl_personal%
Shared Documents,, dir,%csidl_common_documents%
```

Using Migapps.inf

Another very important *.inf* file is Migapps.inf. This file is very complicated and specifies application information that will be migrated. It includes information that is used to identify a given application, registry settings that are migrated, and even in some cases actual files that will be migrated. By default, Migapps.inf migrates data and settings related to the following 58 applications:

- Access 2000
- Access 97
- Access XP
- Acrobat Reader 4.0
- Acrobat Reader 5.0
- Adobe Photoshop Suite 6
- AIM
- BattleCom
- Command Prompt
- CuteFTP
- Eudora 5
- Excel 2000
- Excel 97
- Excel XP
- FrontPage XP
- FrontPage 2000
- GameVoice 1
- GetRight 4

- GoZilla
- ICQ
- Lotus SmartSuite
- Microsoft Office
- Money 2001
- MSN Messenger
- MSN Zone
- MSN Explorer
- Music Match Jukebox
- Netmeeting
- Odigo
- Outlook 97 and Outlook 98
- Outlook XP
- Outlook 2000
- PhotoDraw 2000
- PowerPoint 97
- PowerPoint XP
- PowerPoint 2000
- Prodigy Internet
- Publisher 2000
- Publisher XP
- Quicken 2001
- Quicken 2001 Home & Business
- QuickTime Player 5
- RealJukebox 2
- RealPlayer 8 Basic
- RogerWilco
- Sonique
- WinAmp
- Windows Media Player
- Windows Messenger

- Windows Movie Maker

- WinZip

- Word 2000

- Word 97

- Word XP

- WordPerfect Office 2000

- Works 2001

- WS_FTP LE 5

- Yahoo Messenger

> **Note**   Applications' program files are not migrated by Scanstate.exe. Only application settings and application data are actually migrated. You need to install any application that you want to be part of your deployment. Some third-party migration tools can migrate entire applications, however. See the section "Using Third-Party Tools" for some products you can evaluate.

This is an extensive list that expectedly includes a large number of Microsoft applications, but includes many third-party applications as well. And if you want to avoid migrating settings for a certain application, you can simply comment out the appropriate section of the Migapps.inf file. Listing 18-3 shows a fragment of the Migapps.inf file in which we commented out the CuteFTP application.

Listing 18-3   Migapps.inf Example

```
[Applications]
Acrobat Reader 40, %acroread40%
Acrobat Reader 50, %acroread50%
Adobe Photoshop Suite 6, %photoshop6%
AIM, %AIM%
BattleCom, %battlecom%
CmdExe, %cmdexe%
;CuteFTP 4, %cuteftp4%
```

Using Sysfiles.inf

Another *.inf* file that ships as part of USMT is the Sysfiles.inf file. This file lists files that should not be migrated. The files are operating system files that if migrated could cause conflicts with newer versions of the same files in Windows XP Professional. There is usually no need to edit this file unless you know of specific files that you may not want to migrate.

> **Note**   If you chose to edit any of the default *.inf* files, make sure that you carefully document which changes were made. Another method is to copy and rename the original files and edit your copies instead of using the original files.

> **More Info**   See "User State Migration Tool: INF Commands," which is the file USMTINFCOMMANDS.DOC on the Microsoft Windows Server 2003 CD in the folder Valueadd\Msft\Usmt, for information about customizing the Microsoft User State Migration Tool. The Windows XP Professional Service Pack 2 product CD should contain this file in the same folder.

Using Third-Party Tools

The migration of user data is such a primary part of any deployment that it has been one area in which third-party vendors have found a fruitful area to augment. There are a number of tools, none of which I recommend over another, but all of which may be useful in your scenario. I recommend that you give these tools a serious look if you're not comfortable with customizing USMT's *.inf* files, but the default *.inf* files don't meet your requirements. Prices range from single-use applications to enterprise solutions. The tools that this section describes include the following:

- Eisenworld PC-Relocator (also known as AlohaBob PC Relocator)
- PowerQuest DeployCenter Library 2.0
- Altiris eXpress Migration Suite
- Miramar Desktop DNA

Eisenworld PC-Relocator

Formally known as AlohaBob, Eisenworld PC-Relocator is one of the oldest and most well regarded migration products. In addition to migrating user settings, PC-Relocator selectively migrates applications. Other tools, including Microsoft's own tools, only migrate application settings, but you still have to reinstall the application itself from original media after the tool has completed. PC-Relocator comes in versions appropriate for single users with a new PC and allows transfers from the original PC to the new one over a USB, parallel, or network cable to a version appropriate for a large enterprise in which migrations are handled remotely from a central console.

If you choose to install the centralized administrator's console, and thus be able to migrate data from a remote location, you will actually be installing three components:

■ You install the server component to host the main program components, store migration data, and control the migration of data.

■ The console can be installed on the same machine that the server components are installed on or on another machine convenient to the technician who is managing the migrations.

■ An agent is remotely installed on each client machine that you want to migrate data from. PC-Relocator allows selectively choosing exactly which data, settings, and applications that you want to migrate, and the console provides drag-and-drop convenience.

The Stand-Alone installation is useful for laptop users, telecommuters, and similar standalone machines because it also supports moving data, settings, and applications. The migration can be scripted using a built-in scripting language to automate standalone processes. Like most other migration solutions, PC-Relocator can store its interim data (known as a Digital Moving file) on local or removable media, network locations, USB drives, and so on.

On the Resource Kit CD   See *http://www.eisenworld.com* to download the latest version or learn more about the product.

PowerQuest DeployCenter Library 2.0

PowerQuest provides a range of tools targeted at enterprise backup and restore, desktop deployment, and data migration. The new DeployCenter Library is a combination of the most popular tools from the many tools that they have available. PowerMigration DNA is the tool that is used to migrate user state. As one piece of an entire set of solution tools, it has capabilities similar to the migration capability of USMT or Eisenworld's products; unlike USMT, it does provide for migration of whole applications. It is similar to Miramar's tool (because it is licensed by Power-Quest from Miramar).

PowerMigration DNA was licensed from Miramar by PowerQuest for use in the DeployCenter Library. It is virtually identical to the Miramar tool, but has been enhanced to work well within the overall DeployCenter product suite. For example, a migration can be started from the central DeployCenter console.

Unlike USMT, when a computer supports multiple users, PowerMigration DNA allows you to migrate multiple users' state in one operation, instead of needing to log on as each user to migrate their settings. This is a huge advantage to this tool, as this process makes it easier for a technician to migrate a multiple-user workstation. Also, you can choose to migrate any and all installed applications as well as the settings for the applications and the operating system. PowerMigration DNA also supports direct machine-to-machine migrations that are similar to those performed by the Files And Settings Transfer Wizard and Eisenworld PC-Relocator. Individual migrations can be scheduled to complete without user intervention during a convenient time, such as overnight or on a weekend.

More Info   For more information about PowerMigration DNA and to download a trial version, see *http://www.powerquest.com*.

Altiris eXpress Migration Suite

The Altiris eXpress Migration Suite is a complete migration solution for migrating to Windows XP Professional. The suite provides pre-migration hardware and software assessment, OS deployment, software installation, personality restoration, and post-migration status reporting. As a full end-to-end to solution, it is relatively expensive; but because it replaces other similar end-to-end solutions or cobbled-together solutions, it may be very cost-effective in the long run. The tools that are included cover all aspects of a deployment similar to PowerQuest's DeployCenter Library. Tools are included to support all of the following:

- Software and hardware upgrade assessment
- Computer personality backup (user state migration)
- Computer cloning and network configuration (imaging)
- Software installation
- Personality restoration (user state migration)
- Post-migration status

Note   The eXpress Migration Suite was previously marketed by Altiris as the Migration Toolkit. For more information about this product and to download a trial version, see *http://www.altiris.com*.

PC Transplant Pro is the migration tool. It is responsible for individual migrations as well as the detailed configuration of multiple migrations. It's also available as a standalone product if you have other software to support the rest of your deployment.

Miramar Desktop DNA

Miramar has a patent on its migration technology. There are two migration products: Desktop DNA Enterprise Edition and Desktop DNA Professional. The Professional product is targeted at single-machine migrations, such as home computers, and mobile computers, such as laptops or tablet PCs. This product migrates application settings, operating-system settings, and data such as the contents of the My Documents folder. It is very similar to the Files And Settings Transfer Wizard in its capabilities.

The Desktop DNA Enterprise Edition is the tool that you would use in an enterprise deployment, but also includes the standalone features of the professional product. It is identical to the PowerMigration DNA product from PowerQuest because PowerQuest licensed the technology from Miramar.

> **Tip**   An interesting feature of both Miramar's and PowerQuest's DNA products is called *Muscle Migration*. This feature gives the capability to individually choose each application that you want to migrate in addition to core applications such as Microsoft Office 2003 Editions. In the Miramar product, muscle migrations are not enabled by default; you have to copy a .dll file from an Extras folder into the main product folder to enable these migrations. Details are in the product documentation.

Using Scripted Tools

In many cases, USMT and other, more expensive tools are more than is required. For example, an organization that just wants to migrate users' network drive mappings and printer connections will find the process of using USMT more work than necessary and the expense of third-party products unnecessary. Instead, you can script simple migrations using Windows Script Host.

The script usrcnx.wsf on this book's companion CD in the Scripts folder is one such example. This script exports users' network drive mappings and printer connections to a file. Then, after refreshing the desktop' with clean images, you run the script again to import the users' network drive mappings and printer connections. This script is easily customized to include additional settings, even registry settings. The following shows the syntax of the script usrcnx.wsf, and Table 18-4 describes each option:

`usrcnx.wsf [/?] [/O `*`filename`*` | /I `*`filename`*`]`

Table 18-4   Usrcnx.wsf Command-Line Options

Option	Description
/?	Displays help.
/O filename	Saves the user's network drive mappings and printer connections to the file *filename*.
/I filename	Loads the user's network drive mappings and printer connections from the file *filename*.

Best Practices

The following are best practices for user state migration:

- **Plan user state migration early.**   Identify early the applications, data, and settings you must migrate. Also decide when, where, and how you want to save and restore users' state.

- **Use User State Migration Tool if possible.**   Evaluate User State Migration Tool before third-party user state migration tools because the tool is very easy to use and costs nothing more than time and effort to use. Only if you decide that you can't reasonably meet your requirements by using this tool (difficulty, limitations, and so on) should you look at third-party products.

- **Evaluate third-party migration tools in the lab.**   If you're using a third-party user state migration tool, evaluate each one in a lab environment that accurately reflects typical configurations in your environment.

- **Estimate space requirements in advance.**   Test different configurations to accurately estimate how much space is required on the server for migration files.

Part IV

Managing

Chapter 19

Software Update Services

Microsoft Software Update Services (SUS) helps you collect, approve, and distribute critical operating system patches to resolve known security vulnerabilities and stability issues. You can use these services on computers running Microsoft Windows 2000, Microsoft Windows XP, and Microsoft Windows Server 2003. This chapter describes how to design SUS servers and deploy SUS in your enterprise.

Checklist

- Can you dedicate a server for running SUS? If not, see the section "Server Component" later in this chapter on page 548 for information about the applications that can run on the same server as SUS.

- Is high availability a priority for your SUS servers? If so, see the section "Network Load Balancing" later in this chapter on page 555 to learn how to enhance availability of your SUS servers by using Network Load Balancing.

- Do your client computers already have the new Automatic Updates client? Windows 2000 SP3, Windows XP SP1, and Windows Server 2003 have the version of Automatic Updates that supports SUS; for all other versions of Windows, you must deploy an update client, as described in the section "Automatic Updates Deployment," later in this chapter on page 567.

SUS Overview

Prior to SUS, administrators had to continually check the Windows Update Web site for operating system patches and then download, test, and distribute patches manually. SUS streamlines and automates these processes for you. By using SUS, you can download the latest patches to an intranet server, test the patches in your operating environment, select the patches you want to deploy to specific computers, and then deploy the patches in a timely and efficient manner. SUS provides dynamic notification of critical updates to Windows-based computers, whether or not they have Internet access, and it provides a simple automatic solution for distributing critical updates to networked clients and servers.

On the Resource Kit CD   This book's companion CD contains tools for planning an SUS deployment. See "Scaling an SUS Deployment" (sus01.doc), "Deploying the Server Component" (sus02.doc), and "Deploying Automatic Updates" (sus03.doc). These tools are in the CD's Aids folder.

Many organizations don't want their users downloading and installing critical or security updates from an Internet source without an administrator testing and approving them. SUS allows you to install a server component on an internal server running Windows 2000 Service Pack 2 or later, or Windows Server 2003. Both operating systems can download critical updates and security patches as soon as they are published on the Windows Update Web site. After a patch is downloaded, you can safely test and stage its content before deploying it to production environments.

You begin by determining the Internet connectivity, security requirements, and scale of your SUS server deployment. After deploying and testing the server configuration, deploy and configure Automatic Updates on the client computers that will connect to your servers that run SUS for critical updates. At the completion of these steps, you're ready to deploy critical patches by using SUS. This chapter guides you through each of these steps.

Tip   Microsoft Systems Management Server (SMS) with the SUS Feature Pack provides an alternative to SUS for deploying and managing software patches. See *http://www.microsoft.com/smserver/evaluation/overview /featurepacks/suspack.asp* for more information. Also see Chapter 17, "Systems Management Server."

Patch Analysis

Microsoft provides several tools for analyzing client computers and determining what patches their operating systems need. Those tools include Microsoft Baseline Security Analyzer (MBSA), Windows Update, SUS, Automatic Updates, and SMS:

- **MBSA**   MBSA is a scanning tool that runs on Windows 2000 and Windows XP operating systems to look for missing patches and service packs in Windows operating systems, Internet Information Services (IIS), and Microsoft SQL Server. MBSA can scan computers running Windows NT 4.0, Windows 2000, and Windows XP operating systems. For more information about the MBSA tool, see Chapter 22, "Patch Management."

- **Windows Update**   Windows Update scans a Windows-based computer, searching for all applicable critical, important, or moderate Windows updates. The Windows Update Web site can evaluate a computer running Windows against a known list of applicable updates to determine which updates are needed for that computer. You can install those updates from the Web site. In Windows 2000, Windows XP, and Microsoft Windows Millennium Edition, the Automatic Updates features are added to the Windows Update program that allow you to configure computers to automatically visit Windows Update and download critical updates. Automatic Updates retrieves all critical updates and Microsoft Security Response Center security updates that are classified as moderate or important. For more information about configuring Automatic Updates, see "Automatic Updates Deployment," later in this chapter on page 567.

- **SUS**   SUS is a server component. When you install it on a server running Windows 2000 or Windows Server 2003, it allows small- and medium-size enterprises to bring critical updates from Windows Update inside their firewalls to distribute to computers running Windows 2000 and Windows XP. The same Automatic Updates component that can direct Windows 2000 and Windows XP computers to Windows Update can direct them to an SUS server inside your firewall for installing critical updates.

- **Automatic Updates**   Automatic Updates is a client component that scans only for critical updates, but if the server running SUS contains updates other than critical ones, Automatic Updates downloads and applies those as well. SUS receives critical and moderate security updates.

- **SMS**   SMS 2.0 is already used by many large enterprises as the tool to distribute software updates to desktops and servers. SMS 2.0 has been extended with the SMS 2.0 Software Update Services Feature Pack to integrate with supported Microsoft scanning tools for Windows and Microsoft Office security patches. Using it, you can scan an entire enterprise regularly and store the results as an inventory. Then, the SMS administrator can automatically go to the Microsoft download center to get critical patches and deploy them across your enterprise.

> **Note**   You can use Automatic Updates or Windows Update in combination
> with MBSA. For example, after using Automatic Updates to deploy updates,
> run MBSA to check the update status. Multiple scans performed on the
> same computer can show different results, depending on the tool you use.
> MBSA finds all missing updates; Windows Update finds missing critical,
> important, and moderate updates; and Automatic Updates finds missing
> critical updates only.

Update Categories

The Microsoft Security Response Center rates the severity of an update as
critical, important, moderate, or low as follows:

- **Critical**   A vulnerability with an exploitation that can allow the propa-
  gation of an Internet worm without user action.

- **Important**   A vulnerability with an exploitation that can result in compromise of the confidentiality, integrity, or availability of users' data; or
  of the integrity or availability of processing resources.

- **Moderate**   Exploitability is mitigated to a significant degree by factors
  such as default configuration, auditing, or difficulty of exploitation.

- **Low**   A vulnerability that is extremely difficult to exploit or has minimal
  impact.

Server Component

You install the server component of SUS on Windows 2000 Server SP2 or later, or
Windows Server 2003. It requires IIS 5.0 or later and Internet Explorer 5.5 or later.
You must install SUS on a partition that uses the NT file system (NTFS), and the system partition on your server must also use NTFS. The minimum requirements for a
server computer running SUS support approximately 15,000 clients that use one
server running SUS. The number of clients per server can be greater, depending on
the hardware used. The following list describes the minimum requirements for a
server computer running SUS:

- Pentium III 700 MHz processor or greater

- 512 MB of RAM

- 6 GB of free disk space for setup and security packages

The server running SUS synchronizes with the Windows Update Web site for operating system patches. The server component contains an SUS Administration Web page for administering SUS. The IIS Web site responds to update requests from Automatic Updates clients. And the Windows Update Synchronization Service is a synchronization service that downloads content to the servers running SUS. It also synchronizes data among multiple servers running SUS and distribution points within the intranet.

> **Note** The server component of SUS is available in English and Japanese. These languages are for the administration and installation of SUS only. Both the English and Japanese versions of SUS support clients of any locale supported by Windows.

You can configure servers running SUS to synchronize content from an SUS content distribution point, a second-tier server on the intranet that's also running SUS, or a server running SUS that retrieves updates directly from an external Web site. And you can use SUS to perform staged deployments that involve multiple servers. For example, you can configure one server in a test environment to publish updates to test clients and then review the results. If the results are satisfactory, you can configure other servers running SUS to publish those updates to the enterprise.

The recommended configuration is to install SUS on a dedicated server because other applications that rely on IIS might be configured in ways that are not compatible with SUS. If your organization requires that you maximize the use of each server by loading additional applications onto it, be sure that you know what changes are made to IIS when SUS is installed and how those changes might affect your other applications. The following applications have been tested and can be safely used on the same server with SUS:

- Microsoft FrontPage Server Extensions 2002

- Microsoft Windows SharePoint Services

- Active Server Pages .NET (ASP.NET) applications

- Server Component Requirements

Client Component

Automatic Updates checks the local server running SUS to determine which updates are needed. It then downloads your approved updates and installs the updates on client computers. You create schedules for downloading updates and determine which server each Windows-based computer connects to. You define the rules governing the behavior of Automatic Updates by using Group Policy in an Active Directory environment. In a non–Active Directory environment, you must edit the registry directly. Automatic Updates supports the following:

- Download of approved content from a server running SUS

- Scheduled installations of downloaded content

- Administrator-configurable options using either Group Policy or the registry

- Installation of critical patches with elevated privileges

- Windows 2000 operating systems

This client component, Automatic Updates, is supported on Windows XP, Windows 2000 Professional, Windows Server 2003, and Windows 2000 Server SP2 or later. You do not need to install Automatic Updates on Windows-based computers that run Windows 2000 SP3 or later, Windows XP SP1 or later, or Windows Server 2003 because those operating systems already have an SUS-compatible version of Automatic Updates. On all other intranet Windows-based servers and clients, Automatic Updates must be installed for them to connect to a server running SUS. That includes Windows XP prior to Service Pack 1. To update clients that don't have an SUS-compatible version of Automatic Updates, you can install the standalone Windows Installer package, as described in the section "Deploying Automatic Updates," later in this chapter on page 567. Automatic Updates can download packages from either a local server running SUS or from the Microsoft Windows Update Web site (a public Web site). Typically, you'll want to use the former method because it provides a greater degree of security for clients. Last, Automatic Updates requires no particular hardware configuration.

Security Features

The administration of servers running SUS is completely Web-based. You can administer the server by using either a standard HTTP connection or a Secure Sockets Layer (SSL)-enabled HTTPS connection. SUS benefits from the inherent security of NTFS because SUS must be installed on a hard disk that is formatted with NTFS. Also, if you configure a proxy password, SUS stores it securely as a Local Security Authority (LSA) Secret.

The server running SUS contains all the synchronization service and administrative tools for managing updates. Using the Hypertext Transfer Protocol (HTTP) protocol, it responds to requests for approved updates made by the client computers connected to it. SUS can download packages from either the public Microsoft Windows Update servers or from another intranet server running SUS. During these downloads, no server-to-server authentication is carried out. All content is checked to verify that it has been correctly signed by Microsoft. Any content that is not correctly signed is not trusted and not applied. Automatic Update also checks the cyclical redundancy check (CRC) on each update to confirm that it was not tampered with en route.

After you run SUS Setup, you must install and configure the IIS Lockdown Tool and the Urlscan Security Tool for servers running Windows Server 2000. For servers running Windows Server 2003, these tools are automatically installed and run. See *http://www.microsoft.com/technet//security/tools/tools/locktool.asp* for more information about the IIS Lockdown Tool. For more information about the Urlscan Security Tool, see *http://www.microsoft.com/technet/security/tools/tools/urlscan.asp*.

SUS Server Design

Security and scalability are the most significant issues when designing your SUS server deployment. You must determine your Internet connectivity and project the scale of service. You make these decisions by reviewing your current Internet connectivity policies; analyzing your security, connectivity, and scope of service needs; and then selecting the deployment model that best fits in your environment and requirements.

The presence or absence of Internet connectivity affects your SUS design and deployment in the following ways:

- **No intranet connection to the Internet**   If your networked Windows-based computers are not connected to the Internet, set up an internal server running SUS, as shown in Figure 19-1. In this example, a server is created that is connected to the Internet but isolated from the intranet. After you download, test, and approve the patches on this server, you can hand-carry media to servers running SUS and to distribution points within the intranet. Although Figure 19-1 describes this design in its simplest form, it can be scaled to any size deployment.

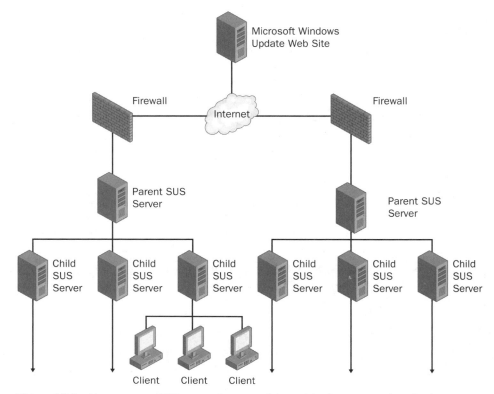

Figure 19-1 You can use SUS even when your intranet isn't connected to the Internet.

- **Intranet connected to the Internet** If your Windows-based, networked computers are connected to the Internet, you can set up a server running SUS inside the firewall of your organization. This server synchronizes content directly with the external public Web site, as shown in Figure 19-2. Each client downloads updates from the SUS server.

SUS deployments like those shown in Figure 19-1 and Figure 19-2 can handle about 15,000 clients. Those models are sufficient to cover the needs of most small-to medium-size organizations. Enterprises with larger or more complex networked systems, however, will likely require multiple SUS servers. For optimal performance and security, large enterprises, highly secure organizations, or organizations with users spread across sites and WAN links should deploy multiple SUS servers. Some common reasons to deploy multiple servers include the following.

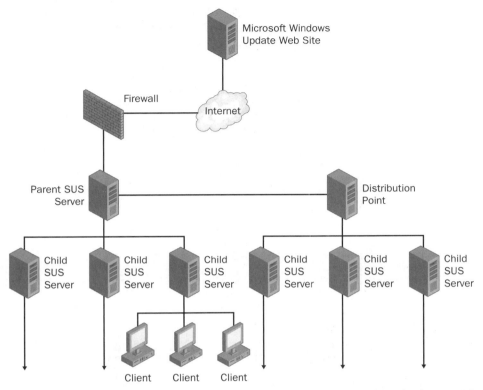

Figure 19-2 Implementing SUS on an intranet that's connected to the Internet is straightforward.

- You have more clients to service than one server can handle efficiently.

- Your clients are geographically dispersed.

- You must avoid the risk of a single point of failure (high reliability).

You can scale out your SUS implementation by deploying multiple independent servers or multiple internally synchronized servers. You can also use Network Load Balancing (NLB) to enhance availability. For example, you can deploy multiple servers that are configured so that each server is managed independently, with each server synchronizing its content to a public Web site, as shown in Figure 19-3. This design is an extension of the single-server model shown in Figure 19-2. The deployment method shown in Figure 19-3 is appropriate for situations in which different LAN or WAN segments are managed independently, such as branch offices. It is also appropriate in cases where one server running SUS is configured to deploy patches only to clients running a certain operating system (such as Windows 2000) while another server is configured to deploy patches only to clients running another operating system (such as Windows XP). In these situations, the two servers do not need to synchronize content. The following sections describe how to deploy SUS using multiple synchronized servers, with and without NLB.

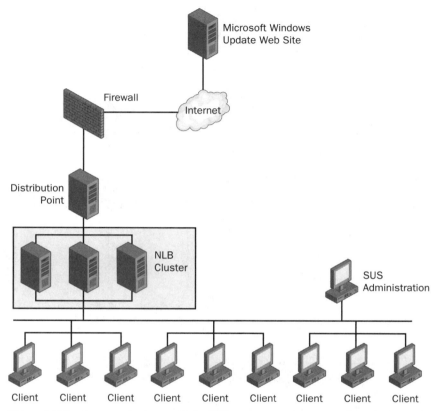

Figure 19-3 You can deploy multiple SUS servers and manage them independently.

Synchronized Servers

You can deploy multiple servers running SUS that synchronize all content within your organization's intranet. In this case, one server is set up as the parent server. It's the source with which the other servers synchronize. Additional servers running SUS are child servers. They synchronize content from the parent server or from a manually configured content distribution point. The child servers can perform manual or automatic synchronizations, and the synchronizations can include updates along with the list of approved updates or updates only without the list. When applicable, the servers can be located throughout a geographically dispersed network to provide the best connectivity to all clients.

As you see in Figure 19-4, you can design the deployment of multiple internally synchronized servers to expose a single server to the Internet (an expanded version of Figure 19-1), or you can completely isolate your intranet from the Internet by scaling out the design, as shown in Figure 19-2.

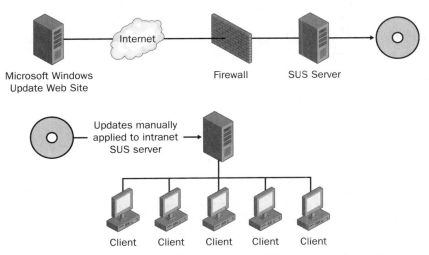

Figure 19-4   You can deploy multiple servers and then synchronize their content.

Network Load Balancing (NLB)

If you have good network connectivity to a large number of clients, consider creating a central store of servers running SUS in combination with NLB, as shown in Figure 19-5. You can use NLB to distribute Transmission Control Protocol/Internet Protocol (TCP/IP) traffic to multiple servers running SUS. NLB partitions client requests among the servers by using one or more virtual Internet Protocol (IP) addresses. Using NLB, you can configure a large number of clients to access a single location for updates and have multiple servers transparently sharing the load.

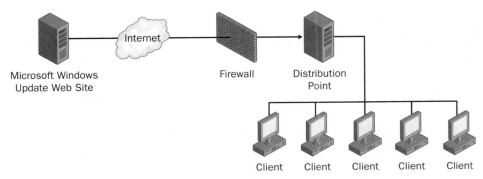

Figure 19-5   Using NLB, you can deploy a single client configuration but share the load among multiple servers running SUS.

SUS Server Deployment

After you've identified the server model that best suits your needs and have installed the necessary hardware, you're ready to deploy the SUS server component. This process consists of downloading, installing, customizing, and securing the SUS server software. After completing these tasks, you need to create any necessary additional software distribution points and child servers before testing and staging content. Here's an overview of the process:

1. Install the SUS server software.
2. Configure the SUS server.
3. Create distribution points.
4. Secure SUS administration.
5. Configure SUS for use with NLB.
6. Synchronize content.
7. Approve updates.
8. Stage content.

Installing the Server Software

Retrieving and installing the SUS server software follows the same process, whether you deploy one or multiple servers. First, install the SUS server component on the appropriate computer, maintaining the default configuration. You can then configure the SUS server software. For more information, see "Configuring the Server" below.

To download and install the SUS server component from Microsoft, go to *http://www.microsoft.com/downloads* (search for the keywords Software Update Services). Run the setup program you download to install it. The setup program puts a shortcut for the SUS Administration Web page on the Start menu in the Administrative Tools folder.

Configuring the Server

The default server settings for the SUS server component don't apply in all cases. On the SUS Administration site, you can customize the SUS settings, configure the Domain Name System (DNS) or Windows Internet Naming Service (WINS) name, and then select the appropriate content synchronization options. Here is the default configuration for SUS and how to change those settings:

- Software updates are downloaded from the Windows Update Web site instead of an intranet server running SUS.

- You can synchronize content on your intranet server from the external Windows Update servers, from another internal server that runs SUS, or from a distribution point. To configure the option to synchronize content, click Set Options in the left pane of the SUS Administration Web page, and then select the check box next to your preference under Select Which Server To Synchronize Content From:

    - Synchronize Directly From The Microsoft Windows Update Servers. In the box, type the name of the server from which to synchronize content.

    - To synchronize content from another intranet server running SUS or from a distribution point, select Synchronize From A Local Software Update Services Server. In the box, type the name of the server from which to synchronize content.

- **The proxy server configuration is set to Automatic**   SUS detects whether or not you use a proxy server. If you do use a proxy server, it must support auto-configuration. If it doesn't, you must manually configure the name and port. To change the default SUS settings, click Set Options in the left pane of the SUS Administration Web page, and then select the check box to indicate whether or not you use a proxy server. If you do, configure it as described in the following list:

    - If your network supports automatic proxy server configuration, select Automatically Detect Proxy Server Settings.

    - If your network does not support automatic proxy server configuration, select Use The Following Proxy Server To Access The Internet.

    - To bypass the proxy server for local addresses, select the Bypass Proxy Server For Local Addresses check box.

    - If your proxy server requires a user ID and password to access the Internet, select the Use The Following User Credentials To Access The Proxy Server check box, and then enter the proxy authentication user ID and password.

    - If your proxy server requires credentials but uses basic authentication, also select the Allow Basic Authentication When Using Proxy Server check box.

- **Downloaded content is stored locally**   The two types of data included during the synchronization of the server running SUS are the actual packages and the metadata. Actual packages contain the updates. During synchronization, SUS downloads the AUCatalog.cab file. The actual packages are not downloaded unless you select the Actual packages option. *Metadata*, also called *dictionary objects*, describes the available packages and their applicability. This information is located in a file named AUCatalog.cab. If you do not download the actual packages to a local folder, they remain on the external Windows Update servers. Using this configuration, computers running the Automatic Updates client connect to the intranet server running SUS, read the list of approved packages, and then download the approved packages from the public Windows Update Web site. In this way, you can take advantage of the Windows Update servers for global scaling while maintaining local control of which updates clients install. If you download the packages to a local folder, the packages are stored on your intranet Server running SUS. In this configuration, computers running Automatic Updates connect to the server running SUS, read the list of approved packages, and then download them directly from that server. To configure where to store packages, click Set options in the left pane of the SUS Administration Web page. Select one of the following options and then select the check box next to each language that you support:

    - Maintain The Updates On A Microsoft Windows Updates Server.

    - Save The Updates To A Local Folder.

- **Content is downloaded in all languages that SUS supports**   Configure the list of locales, as described in the previous item. If you change the list of locales, synchronize immediately to ensure that the appropriate packages for the additional locales are downloaded. Similarly, if you modify your server running the SUS configuration from Maintain The Updates On A Microsoft Windows Update Server to Save The Updates To A Local Folder, immediately perform a synchronization to download the necessary packages. If you download content in all locales, the initial server synchronization with the Windows Update servers is approximately 600 MB of data. If you select only one or two locales to download, the initial synchronization will be approximately 150 MB. Selecting the locales that you want to support determines only which packages are downloaded to the server running SUS. It does not determine which locales can be serviced. For example, if a computer that runs its native operating system in Japanese connects to a server that runs SUS, it retrieves a list of approved packages. If the server running SUS maintains content locally and does not support Japanese, it will fail to download the approved packages because they will not be available.

- **Patches that are approved by the SUS administrator and later updated on the public Windows Update Web site are not automatically reapproved for distribution**   You must manually reapprove updated patches. In addition to the new content that is posted to the external Microsoft Windows Update servers, previously posted content is sometimes updated. If you approve content for distribution and it is then updated before the distribution takes place, the content is marked on the Approve Updates page as Updated. To customize the behavior of updated content, click Set Options in the left pane of the SUS Administration Web page, and then select one of the following:

  - Automatically Approve New Versions Of Previously Approved Updates.

  - Do Not Automatically Approve New Versions Of Previously Approved Updates. I Will Manually Approve These Later.

- **Clients access the SUS server by using the NetBIOS server name**   If your network requires DNS, you must configure the DNS name that clients use to locate and access the server running SUS. By giving the DNS name to the server, SUS returns a Uniform Resource Locator (URL) to the clients containing the DNS name. To configure a DNS name, click Set Options in the left pane of the SUS Administration Web page, and then type the DNS name under Specify The Name Your Clients Use To Locate This Update Server.

When SUS is installed on a computer running Windows Server 2003, its setup program runs the IIS Lockdown Tool and installs and configures the Urlscan Security Tool. Table 19-1 shows the settings that make IIS more secure. If SUS is installed on a computer running Windows 2000 Server, you must manually install and run these two programs separately.

Table 19-1   IIS Security Settings for Use with SUS

Option	SUS Setting
Remove Script Mappings: ASP	Enable .ASP files
Remove Script Mappings: IDQ	Disable
Remove Script Mappings: SHTML, SHTM, STM	Disable
Remove Script Mappings: IDC	Disable
Remove Script Mappings: printer	Disable
Remove Script Mappings: HTR	Disable
Remove Sample Web Files	Remove
Remove Scripts Virtual Directory	Remove
Remove MSDAC Virtual Directory	Remove
Disable WebDAV	Disable WebDav
Prevent IIS Anonymous User From Executing System Utilities	Prevent
Prevent IIS Anonymous User Account From Writing Web Content	Prevent

The SUS setup program makes the changes shown in Table 19-2 to the IIS metabase. It makes these changes whether the server operating system is Windows 2000 or Windows Server 2003. And because IIS runs in a secure mode by default on servers running Windows Server 2003, IIS Lockdown is not applied when you install SUS on them. However, the SUS setup program sets a property in the IIS metabase to enable asp.dll. The following ISAPIRestrictionList setting disables all script mappings except asp.dll: ISAPIRestrictionList: = "0" , "asp.dll".

Table 19-2   IIS Metabase Changes

Property	Value	Result
w3svc/AspProcessorThreadMax	1	Ensures that IIS does not start more than one thread per process.
w3svc/AspThreadGateEnabled	True	Throttles the number of threads based on CPU usage.

At the end of installation, SUS stops any Web site running on that server. And for security purposes, SUS disables several Internet Server Application Programming Interface (ISAPI) handlers when SUS is installed on the host IIS server. This can disable existing functionality for sites that rely on ASP.NET, FrontPage Server Extensions, or Windows SharePoint Services. If you have Web sites that rely on any of these technologies, you must re-enable the necessary ISAPI handlers after SUS setup is completed. For FrontPage Server Extensions and Windows SharePoint Services, enable admin.dll, fpadmdll.dll, author.dll, owssvr.dll, and shtml.dll.

Creating Distribution Points

When you install SUS, the setup program creates a distribution point on the server. When you synchronize the server with a parent server or with an external Web site, all the content on the Web site is downloaded to the distribution point. If SUS downloads new updates, it updates the distribution point. The SUS setup program creates the distribution point in a virtual root named Content. If you choose to maintain content on the public Web site instead of downloading the patches to the local server running SUS, this distribution point is empty except for the AUCatalog.cab file. AUCatalog.cab defines the updates that have been approved for deployment to clients.

You can also create a distribution point on a server that is not running SUS. Such a server must be running IIS 5.0 or later. You can download and test packages on to servers running SUS, and then copy approved and tested packages to distribution points for client access. If your SUS design includes distribution points, perform the following tasks to create a distribution point:

1. Confirm that IIS is running.

2. Create a folder named \Content.

3. Copy all of the following items from the source server running SUS to the newly created \Content folder:

   - *SUSserver*\Aucatalog1.cab

   - *SUSserver*\Aurtf1.cab

   - *SUSserver*\approveditems.txt

   - All the files and folders under the \Content\cabs

4. Create an IIS virtual root called http://*IISserver*/Content that points to the \Content folder.

Securing Administration

You can administer a server that runs SUS by running Internet Explorer from a remote computer. By default, all administration is done over HTTP by using the URL *http://SUSserver/SUSAdmin*. Only users with local administrator credentials on the SUS server can use the SUS Administration Web site. By using HTTP, you send all communications in plain text over the network without any encryption during your administrative session. You have two choices for securing SUS administration:

- Administer the server locally only and never from a remote computer.

- Use secure HTTPS/SSL for server administration.

Before using Hypertext Transfer Protocol Secure (HTTPS) for secure remote administration, you must obtain and install a valid digital certificate for server authentication from your organization. For more information about installing digital certificates, see "Installing and configuring a certification authority" in Help and Support Center for Windows Server 2003, or talk to your security administrator. Here's how you turn on HTTPS for SUS:

1. Start the IIS MMC snap-in.

2. On the SUS Properties page, set the SSL port to **443**.

3. On the Directory Security tab, start the Web Server Certificate Wizard by clicking Server Certificate.

4. Follow the wizard instructions to assign the digital certificate for SSL authentication for SUS. Store the digital certificate for SSL in the local computer store of the server that you want to administer.

And here's how you turn on SSL for SUS folders:

1. Right-click the administration folder (\autoupdate\administration) in the navigation pane and then click Properties.

2. Click the Directory Security tab and then click Edit.

3. Select the Require Secure Channel (SSL) and the Require 128-bit Encryption check boxes.

4. Repeat steps 1 through 3 for each of the following additional folders:

   - \autoupdate\dictionaries
   - \shared\content\EULA

Note   The \Content\EULA folder does not exist until SUS performs a successful synchronization.

Configuring for NLB

If your deployment consists of multiple servers in a central location, NLB can help balance the flow of incoming and outgoing TCP/IP traffic between these servers and their clients. To configure this load-balancing model, perform the following tasks:

1. Create a manually configured content distribution point. For more information, see "Creating Distribution Points," earlier in this chapter on page 560.

2. Make sure that this content distribution point contains content for all the locales you need to support for all clients.

3. Configure each server running SUS to do the following:

   - Store content locally.
   - Synchronize from the appropriate content distribution point.
   - Synchronize the list of approved items from the same content distribution point.

4. Install and configure NLB on each server that is part of the cluster. For more information about deploying NLB, see "Deploying Network Load Balancing" in the Windows Server 2003 Deployment Kit.

5. Configure your clients to point to this cluster for its updates by using either the cluster's virtual IP address or its DNS or WINS name.

It is recommended that you install NLB in Unicast mode with a single network interface card (NIC) in each server because all the servers involved are on the same intranet. After you install and configure the NLB service on each server running SUS, you have a virtual IP address that you can use to access the cluster. You can register this IP address with a friendly name on your DNS or WINS servers. When running NLB in unicast mode with a single network card in each server, keep the following in mind:

- Each server in the NLB cluster synchronizes content from the manually configured content distribution point.

- The NLB service determines which host in the cluster will respond to each client request.

- You cannot access resources on one server from another server in the cluster.

- To administer any servers in the cluster, you must be at the console of that server or use a remote client outside of the cluster.

Synchronizing Content

You can synchronize a server running SUS with the public Windows Update servers, with another server running SUS, or with an SUS distribution point. Synchronizing from another server running SUS or distribution point is useful in these scenarios:

- You have multiple servers running SUS and you do not want all of them to go to the Internet to synchronize content.

- You have physical sites that do not have Internet access.

- You want to test content in a controlled environment and put the testing content on a distribution point from which the production servers running SUS synchronize.

You synchronize content immediately by using the SUS Administration page:

1. Click Synchronize Server in the left pane of the SUS Administration Web page.

2. Click Synchronize Now.

Click View Synchronization Log in the left pane of the SUS Administration page to check the synchronization log. This synchronization log contains the following:

- The time that the last synchronization occurred

- Success and failure information for the overall synchronization operation

- Time of the next synchronization if scheduled synchronization is enabled

- The update packages that have been downloaded or updated since the last synchronization

- The update packages that failed synchronization

After the initial synchronization, you can create a synchronization schedule. To create, modify, or turn off synchronization schedules, click Synchronize Server in the left pane of the SUS Administration Web page. In the Synchronization Schedule dialog box, select the settings you want.

In addition to synchronizing content, SUS can synchronize the list of approved packages with another server that runs SUS or with an SUS distribution point. If you have multiple servers running SUS or distribution points, you can approve a list of packages on a parent server. Child servers and distribution points then synchronize to the parent server for the list of approved packages. In this case, the list of approved items cannot be modified on the child server or distribution point. All changes to the approved list must occur on the parent server. To synchronize the list of approved items with the content, select the Synchronize List Of Approved Items Update From This Location (Replace Mode) check box on the Set Options page of the Software Update Services Administration page.

Approving Updates

As an administrator, you have complete control over which updates are downloaded to which client computers. You control this by using the SUS Administration page. For each item on the Approval Page, SUS displays the item status in the right corner of the item description (see Table 19-3).

Table 19-3   Update Types

Status	Explanation
New	The update that was recently downloaded has not been approved and will not be offered to any clients that query the server.
Approved	The update has been approved by an administrator and is available to clients that query the server.
Not Approved	The update has not been approved and is not available to clients that query the server.
Updated	The update has been changed during a recent synchronization.
Temporarily Unavailable	One of the following conditions exists: ■ The associated update package is not available. ■ A dependency required by the update is not available.

Here's how to obtain more information about a particular update:

1. Click Approve Updates in the left pane of the SUS Administration Web page.

2. Under the update name, click Details.

3. Select the information you want from the list, which includes the following:

    ■ The .cab files associated with the package

    ■ The locale for each .cab file

    ■ The platform for each .cab file

    ■ A link to the actual .cab file that was used to install the package and any command-line setup options necessary to install the package

    ■ A link to the Read More page about the update

After reviewing and testing each update, approve it by using the following steps:

1. Click Approve Updates in the left pane of the SUS Administration Web page.

2. Select the updates that you want to distribute to your clients.

3. Do one of the following:

    ■ Click Approve.

    ■ To disapprove updates, clear the check boxes next to all updates, and then click Approve.

When you disapprove the updates, current packages are not available to any of your clients. You are notified whether the approval is successful. For more information about the updates you have approved, click View Approval Log in the left pane of the SUS Administration Web page. The synchronization and approval logs are stored in XML files that you can view with a text editor in a folder accessible to administrators on the server running SUS. The filename of the approval log is history_Approve.xml. The filename of the synchronization log is historySync.xml. Both files are in the SUS installation folder in AutoUpdate\Administration. New information is continually appended to these files, so it is recommended that you regularly remove out-of-date information.

You can check the functionality of the server running SUS by using the Monitor Server page, which is accessible on the SUS Administration Web page. This is stored in RAM and needs to be occasionally refreshed. The synchronization service also generates an event log message whenever it synchronizes, if it encounters a major error, or if you change the list of approved updates. An approval log is maintained on each server running SUS to track the content that has been approved or not approved. The approval log contains the following information:

- A record of each time the list of approved packages was changed

- The list of items that changed

- The new list of approved items

- A record of who made the change—either the server administrator or the synchronization service

Staging Content

Before you distribute patches to your enterprise, test them thoroughly. Before deploying the client component of SUS, you need to have a staging and testing plan in place. You have two options for staging content:

- Option one for staging content is the following:

  1. Set up one server running SUS for testing.

  2. Download and test the content on the test server running SUS and on at least one test client for each operating system.

  3. After you test the content, approve it on a production server running SUS.

     The production server synchronizes with the public Web site for the approved content, and the clients retrieve the approved patches during their next polling cycle.

- Option two for staging content is the following:

  1. Set up one server running SUS for testing.

  2. Download and test the content on the test server running SUS and on at least one test client for each operating system.

  3. After you test the content, copy the list of approved items and the tested content to a distribution point.

  4. Configure the production server running SUS to download the content and the list of approved items to clients and child servers from the distribution point.

  5. Download the content.

Caution   The first option has the risk of approving content that is changed before the clients actually begin downloading it. The second option prevents this risk because it copies content as well as the approved list to the distribution point server.

Automatic Updates Deployment

The following versions of Windows already contain the version of Automatic Updates that supports SUS, so you don't have to deploy a client:

■ Install Windows 2000 SP3

■ Install Windows XP SP1

■ Install Windows Server 2003

For all other versions of Windows, SUS requires the installation of Automatic Updates, a feature that allows Windows-based computers to receive content from the SUS server. There are several ways you can deploy Automatic Updates to your client computers, depending on your operating environment. After you deploy Automatic Updates, you can centrally control its configuration on the clients. Automatic Updates is packaged as a Windows Installer database, which makes it simple to deploy for updating computers that run Windows 2000 and Windows XP. If your client computer is running Windows 2000 SP2 or Windows XP, deploy Automatic Updates by following the instructions to download and run the client software you find on the Software Update Services Client Web site.

Deploying Automatic Updates

To centrally deploy Automatic Updates, create a network distribution point that contains the WUAU22.msi file for clients to access. After creating the distribution point, you can centrally control Automatic Updates deployments by using any of the following methods:

■ **Group Policy Software Distribution**   Use this method if your network uses Active Directory and Windows 2000 or later.

■ **SMS**   Use this method if you are running SMS on your network.

■ **A logon script**   Use this method if Active Directory is not part of your operating environment. A logon script is appropriate only for users who are administrators.

For example, to deploy automatic Updates by using Group Policy in Active Directory environments, use the following steps:

1. Create a Group Policy object (GPO) and edit it.

2. Under Computer Configuration Or User Configuration, expand Windows Settings.

3. Double-click Scripts.

4. Double-click the type of script you want to deploy (Startup or Shutdown for computers or Logon or Logoff for users).

5. Create a script that does the following: If the version of %SYSTEM-ROOT%\System32\wuaueng.dll is earlier than 5.4.3630.11, the script installs wuau22.msi. This can be done with VBScript by using the `GetFileVersion` method on the `Scripting.FileSystemObject` object.

   Be sure to allow sufficient time for the policies to replicate throughout the domain and then restart the client computers.

6. Restart the client computers. When you restart the client computers, the packages are installed, and the policies are processed.

   Because the application is installed on the local computers, be sure that authenticated users have the appropriate permissions to open source folders.

Automatic Updates self-upgrades when a newer version is posted on the server that it checks for updates. Each time Automatic Updates checks the public Web site or internal server that runs SUS for updates, it also checks for a newer version of Automatic Updates. To confirm that the Updated Automatic Updates installed successfully, check that %SYSTEMROOT%\System32\wuaueng.dll is version 5.4.3630.11 or higher.

Using Automatic Updates

Automatic Updates downloads critical updates based on the configuration options that the user selects by using the Automatic Updates tool in Control Panel or by reading the policy settings that you configure. Every 22 hours minus a random offset, Automatic Updates polls the server running SUS for approved updates. If any new updates need to be installed, the client downloads them. After the new updates are downloaded, Automatic Updates polls the server running SUS again for the list of approved packages to confirm that the packages it downloaded are still valid and approved. This means that if you remove updates from the list of approved updates while Automatic Updates is downloading updates, only the updates that are still approved are actually installed.

If you configure Automatic Updates to notify users of updates that are ready to download, it sends the notification to the System event log and to a logged-on administrator of the computer. If no administrator is logged on, Automatic Updates waits for an administrator to log on before displaying the notification. You can manipulate the notification options, as described in the following list:

- If Automatic Updates is configured to notify the user of updates that are ready to install, the notification is sent to the System event log and to the notification area of the server running SUS.

- When a logged-on administrator clicks the notification area icon, Automatic Updates displays the available updates to install. The user must then click the Install button to install them. A message appears if the update requires the computer to be restarted to complete the update. Until the system is restarted, Automatic Updates cannot detect additional updates.

- The Remind Me Later button provides a way for the installation to be deferred. The options are 30 minutes, 1 hour, 2 hours, 4 hours, 8 hours, tomorrow, and in 3 days.

If Automatic Updates is configured to install updates on a set schedule, applicable updates are downloaded and marked as ready to install. A logged-on administrator is notified by the notification-area icon, and an event is logged to the system Event Log. This indicates that the updates can be installed. If the user clicks the notification, a dialog box appears in which the Remind Me Later option is unavailable. At the scheduled day and time, Automatic Updates installs the update and restarts the computer if necessary, even if there is no local administrator logged on. If a local administrator is logged on, Automatic Updates displays a warning that an installation is about to begin. If the updates require the computer to restart, and any user is logged on, a similar countdown dialog box is displayed, warning the logged-on user about the impending restart.

Administering Automatic Updates

Group Policy is the preferred method for configuring your client computers because of its precise control. You can also set policies by using Windows NT 4.0 System Policy or by editing the registry directly. Here's how to configure the behavior of Automatic Updates clients by using Group Policy:

1. Using the Group Policy Management Console (GPMC), create a new GPO or edit an existing GPO to which you want to add this setting.

2. Expand Computer Configuration, expand Administrative Templates, expand Windows Components, and then click Windows Update.

3. On the Windows Update template, double-click Configure Automatic Updates, enable the policy, and then select one of the following options in the Configure Automatic Updating list:

    - **Notify For Download And Notify For Install.**   This option notifies a logged-on administrative user prior to the download and prior to the installation of the updates.

    - **Auto Download And Notify For Install.**   This option automatically begins downloading updates and then notifies a logged-on administrative user prior to installing the updates.

- **Auto Download And Schedule The Install.** Typically, if Automatic Updates is configured to perform a scheduled installation, the recurring scheduled installation day and time are also set.

4. On the Windows Update template, double-click Specify Intranet Microsoft Update Service Location, enable the policy, and then do the following:

   - In the Set The Intranet Update Service For Detecting Updates box, type the URL of the SUS server to which you want to direct clients. If the policy is disabled or not configured, Automatic Updates gets its updates from the public Windows Update service.

   - In the Set The Intranet Statistics Server box, type the URL of the computer to which you want to send statistics. The statistics server must be running IIS. The statistics sent to the server are stored in the IIS logs. The same server can host both SUS and the statistics.

> **Note**   See the Explain tab for the Reschedule Automatic Update scheduled installations and the No Auto-Restart For Scheduled Automatic Update installation options to see how those settings best suit your environment.

Policies for Automatic Updates always take precedence of users' settings. Automatic Updates options in Control Panel options are disabled on the target computer when you define Automatic Updates policies. In test environments, apply policy settings by using the Local Group Policy object. In production environments, it's more efficient to set policies at the organizational unit (OU) or domain level. Be aware that some Group Policy settings have an effect on other settings, such as removing access and links to Windows Update features:

- **Remove Access To Use All Windows Update Features**   If this policy is enabled, Automatic Updates is disabled for that user. Because this policy is a per-user setting, it makes a local administrator appear as a non-administrator. With this policy enabled, Automatic Updates still runs, and scheduled installations can still occur. This setting is available only in Windows XP. Use this policy if you do not want some users to receive updates from SUS.

- **Remove Links And Access To Windows Update**   If this policy is enabled, Automatic Updates receives updates from your server that runs SUS. Users who have this policy set cannot get updates from a Windows Update Web site that you have not approved on your server that runs SUS. If this policy is not enabled, the Windows Update icon remains on the Start menu for local administrators to visit the Windows Update Web site. Local administrators can use it to install unapproved software from the public Windows Update Web site. This happens even if you have specified that Automatic Updates must get approved updates from your server that runs SUS.

In a non–Active Directory environment, you can configure Automatic Updates by modifying the registry, by editing the registry directly or by deploying registry settings using System Policy, such as with Windows NT 4.0. The settings are in HKLM\SOFTWARE\Policies\Microsoft\Windows\WindowsUpdate\AU. The values you can set are shown in Table 19-4. See Chapter 8, "Windows Settings," for help with deploying these settings.

Table 19-4   Automatic Updates Registry Values

Name	Values	Type
NoAutoUpdate	<ul><li>*0*—Automatic Updates is enabled (default)</li><li>*1*—Automatic Updates is disabled</li></ul>	REG_DWORD
AUOptions	All of the following options notify the local administrator:<ul><li>*2*—Notify of download and installation</li><li>*3*—Automatically download and notify of installation</li><li>*4*—Automatic download and scheduled installation</li></ul>	REG_DWORD
ScheduledInstallTime	Set to *N*, where *N* is a military hour from 0 to 23	REG_DWORD
UseWUServer	Set this to *1* to enable Automatic Updates to use the Windows Update server as specified in WUServer (Table 19-5)	REG_DWORD
ScheduledInstallDay	<ul><li>*0*—Every day</li><li>1 through 7—The days of the week from Sunday (1) to Saturday (7)</li></ul>	REG_DWORD
RescheduleWaitTime	Set to *N*, where *N* is a number of minutes from 1 to 60	REG_DWORD
NoAutoRebootWith LoggedOnUsers	<ul><li>*0*—Automatically reboot the computer</li><li>*1*—Allow the logged-on user to choose whether to reboot the computer or not</li></ul>	REG_DWORD

To specify the server running SUS that you want your clients and servers to connect to for their updates, you need to add two entries to the registry in the subkey HKLM\Software\Policies\Microsoft\Windows\WindowsUpdate. For the required entries, see Table 19-5.

Table 19-5   Automatic Updates Server Selection Registry Values

Name	Values	Type
WUServer	The HTTP name for the Windows Update intranet server (for example, http://intranetsus)	REG_SZ
WUStatusServer	The HTTP name for the Windows Update intranet server (for example, http://intranetsus)	REG_SZ

Best Practices

The following are best practices for deploying SUS in your enterprise:

- **In enterprises that already use SMS, use Microsoft Systems Management Server (SMS) with the SUS Feature Pack to deploy updates.**   For more information about SMS, see Chapter 17, "Systems Management Server."

- **Deploy the SUS server component on a dedicated server.**   Other applications might configure IIS in ways that are compatible with SUS.

- **On WANs, use multiple synchronized or independent servers for SUS.**   By using multiple synchronized servers or independent servers, you avoid transferring updates across slow links.

- **Use HTTPS and SSL to secure the SUS Administration Web page.**   Without securing the SUS Administration Web page, the Web browser exchanges all information, including passwords, using plain text. For more information, see the section "Securing Administration," earlier in this chapter on page 561.

- **Consider using NLB for SUS.**   When servicing a large number of clients, you increase availability by creating a central store of servers running SUS with NLB. For more information, see the section "Network Load Balancing," earlier in this chapter on page 555.

- **Configure Automatic Updates using Group Policy.**   Group Policy is the preferred method for configuring Automatic Updates for Windows 2000, Windows XP, and Windows Server 2003. For other versions of Windows, edit the registry directly or use System Policy.

Chapter 20

Policy Management

Group Policy is the best way to manage computers running Microsoft Windows XP Professional. This chapter describes policies for most desktop deployment scenarios and suggests best practices for configuring many of them.

Checklist

- Have you planned the security polices, such as password policies, you want to deploy? See Chapter 3, "Windows Configuration," for more information.

- Have you identified any legacy applications that won't run in the security context of a restricted user? See the section "Security Settings" on page 575 to learn how to cope with these applications without putting users in the Administrators group.

- Do you intend to redirect users' documents to a central network location, making it easier to back up their important files? See the section "Folder Redirection" on page 592.

■ Do you want to manage settings for which no policy actually exists? See the section "Administrative Templates" on page 599 to learn how to build your own polices. Also see the section "AutoProf Policy Maker" to learn more about a product that extends Group Policy with many new features.

■ Are you aware of the Group Policy tools that are available to help you better configure and manage policies? See the section "Using the Group Policy Tools" on page 607 for a description of these tools.

Overview

This chapter describes policies for deploying and managing Windows XP Professional and Office 2003 Editions on networks running Windows Server 2003. Although this chapter doesn't explicitly cover Windows 2000 Professional, the information it contains applies equally well with few exceptions. For example, Windows XP Professional supports more policies than Windows 2000 Professional.

Designing, deploying, and managing Active Directory with Group Policy is a book unto itself. As a result, this chapter doesn't cover how to use Group Policy, which is a skill that most of you already possess, anyway. If you're in need of a Group Policy primer, however, I've included a few of the best on this book's companion CD. Although this chapter doesn't describe using Group Policy, it does describe most of the useful policies for deploying and managing Windows XP Professional, beginning with security settings and ending with creating your own policy settings using templates.

Common Questions

There are some common questions about Group Policy in desktop deployment scenarios, including the following:

■ **Do users have to log on to the domain in order for Group Policy Objects (GPOs) to apply?**   The answer isn't a straight yes or no. If the computer is joined to the domain, computer policies will apply to the computer when it starts. If the user's account is in the domain, user policy will also apply. If the user's account is local, however, user Group Policy will not apply. That leads to situations in which you can have computers receiving policies while users aren't. This also means that a user who brings his own laptop PC to work and connects it to the network will not receive computer policies because the computer isn't a domain member.

> ■ **If users take their corporate-issued laptop PCs home, does Windows XP Professional still apply GPOs?**   If users log on to their laptop PCs with cached credentials, the operating system applies cached policies to the computer. If they log on by using local accounts, then the operating system only applies local policies to the computer.
>
> See the Group Policy FAQ at *http://www.activedir.org/gp_faq.htm* for answers to other common Group Policy questions.

Security Settings

Other than administrative templates, which you learn about in the section "Administrative Templates" on page 599, security settings are the most common and necessary policies for Windows XP Professional. By using policies, you can require the use of strong passwords, prevent dictionary attacks, and restrict group membership. See the following sections for more information:

- Password Security
- Account Lockout
- Audit Policy
- User Rights
- Security Options
- Restricted Groups
- System Services
- Registry ACLs
- File System ACLs
- Software Restriction

Password Security

Password security is a fundamental pillar of desktop security. What good are the firewalls, authentication protocols, and so on if passwords are easy to crack? Group Policy provides security settings that enforce password security, though.

In a GPO, password policies are in Computer Configuration\Windows Settings\Security Settings\Account Policies\Password Policy. Not leaving anything to chance, Windows Server 2003 defines default settings for these policies in the

Default Domain Policy, which is applied to each domain in Active Directory. Table 20-1 describes the default settings for each of these policies. These default settings when paired with an account lockout policy are generally sufficient to protect passwords. The default settings for Windows 2000 Server weren't as strict, however. If you're using Windows 2000 Server or migrating to Windows Server 2003, you should consider updating these policies to the more restrictive default values that Windows Server 2003 uses.

Table 20-1   Default Password Policies

Policy	Default Value
Enforce Password History	24 passwords remembered
Maximum Password Age	42 days
Minimum Password Age	1 day
Minimum Password Length	7 characters
Passwords Must Meet Complexity Requirements	Enabled
Store Passwords Using Reversible Encryption	Disabled

Most of the settings you see in Table 20-1 are self-explanatory. By setting the Enforce Password History Policy to 24, for example, you prevent users from repeating the same few passwords over and over again. The Minimum Password Age policy prevents users from cycling through passwords in quick succession so that they can once again use their favorite passwords. The settings for the Minimum Password Age policy and Enforce Password History policy shown in Table 20-1 mean that users can't reuse a password for at least 24 days.

To prevent password hacking, you must also make passwords as complex as possible because longer and more-complex passwords prevent attackers from hacking them. The Passwords Must Meet Complexity Requirements policy requires passwords to meet the requirements defined by the default password filter (Passfilt.dll) included with Windows Server 2003:

- Passwords are not based on the users' account name.

- Passwords are the minimum required length (Minimum Password Length policy).

- Passwords contain characters from three of the following four categories:

    - Uppercase alphabetic characters (A–Z)

    - Lowercase alphabetic characters (a–z)

    - Arabic numerals (0–9)

    - Non-alphanumeric characters (!, @, #, and so on)

> **Note** For domain accounts, there can be only one account policy. Account policies include password policy, account lockout policy, and Kerberos policy. The account policy must be defined in the Default Domain policy and is enforced by the domain controllers that make up the domain. A domain controller always obtains the account policy from the Default Domain Policy Group Policy object, even if there is a different account policy applied to the organizational unit (OU) that contains the domain controller. By default, workstations and servers joined to a domain (such as member computers) will also receive the same account policy for their local accounts. However, local account policies can be different from the domain account policy, such as when you define an account policy specifically for the local accounts.

Account Lockout

Inexplicably, both Windows 2000 Server and Windows Server 2003 don't define account lockout policies in the Default Domain Policy. These policies will certainly generate a small amount of Help Desk traffic when users forget their passwords, but they also prevent password hacks such as dictionary attacks. You can minimize Help Desk traffic while still preventing dictionary attacks by setting the threshold high enough for most users to finally discover their passwords while preventing hackers from trying the thousands of inevitable combinations before doing the same.

In a GPO, account lockout policies are in Computer Configuration\Windows Settings\Security Settings\Account Policies\Account Lockout. Table 20-2 describes the settings I recommend for each of these policies. The following list describes each of these policies in more detail:

- **Account Lockout Duration** This setting allows you to define the length of time that the account will be locked after exceeding the number of logon attempts specified by the Account Lockout Threshold policy. Values range from 1 to 99,999 minutes, after which time Active Directory automatically unlocks the account. If the duration is 0, the administrator must manually unlock the account.

- **Account Lockout Threshold** This setting specifies the number of logon attempts that can fail before Active Directory locks a user's account. Values range from 1 to 999. Set the value high enough to prevent Help Desk calls when users inevitably mistype their passwords but low enough to prevent dictionary attacks.

- **Reset Account Lockout After** This setting specifies the number of minutes after a failed logon attempt before Active Directory resets the threshold counter. Values range from 1 to 99,999 minutes. This value must be less than or equal to the account lockout duration.

Table 20-2 Recommended Account Lockout Policies

Policy	Default Value
Account Lockout Duration	30
Account Lockout Threshold	5
Reset Account Lockout Count After	30

Audit Policy

You use audit policies to monitor the success and failure of security events. They're in Computer Configuration\Windows Settings\Security Settings\Local Policies\Audit Policy. Settings include the following:

- **Audit Account And Logon Events** Tracks user logon and logoff events on computers used to authenticate an account. You can choose to audit successes, failures, or both.

- **Audit Account Management** Tracks changes to the Security Accounts database. You can choose to audit successes, failures, or both.

- **Audit Directory Service Access** Audits users' access to Active Directory objects that have their system access control list (SACL) defined. You can choose to audit successes, failures, or both.

- **Audit Logon Events** Tracks users who have logged on, logged off, or made a network connection. Also records the type of logon requested (interactive, network, or service). This option differs from the Audit Account Logon Events policy in that it records where the logon occurred versus where the logged-on account exists. You can choose to audit successes, failures, or both.

- **Audit Object Access** Tracks unsuccessful attempts to access objects such as directories, files, and printers. Individual object auditing is not automatic and must be enabled in the object's properties. You can choose to audit successes, failures, or both. Avoid object auditing because it significantly degrades performance.

- **Audit Policy Change** Tracks changes in security policy, such as assignment of privileges or changes in the audit policy. You can choose to audit successes, failures, or both.

- **Audit Privilege Use** Tracks unsuccessful attempts to use privileges. Privileges indicate rights assigned to users. Tracks all user rights except Bypass Traverse Checking, Debug Programs, Create A Token Object, Replace Process Level Token, Generate Security Audits, Back Up Files And Directories, and Restore Files And Directories. You can choose to audit successes, failures, or both. Avoid privilege auditing because it significantly degrades performance.

- **Audit Process Tracking** Tracks events such as program activation and exits. You can choose to audit successes, failures, or both. Avoid process tracking because it significantly degrades performance.

- **Audit System Events** Tracks events that affect the entire system or the audit log. Records events such as restart or shutdown. You can choose to audit successes, failures, or both.

User Rights

User rights assignment determines what a user or group can and can't do in Windows XP Professional. Rights assignment is typically specified by group because specifying rights by individual user is inefficient and error-prone. The Default Domain Policy doesn't specify any rights assignments and in most cases, you don't need to, either. Windows XP Professional does configure rights assignments in the local GPO, however, and you can create GPOs that modify the following rights as required. Table 20-3 describes each right and the groups that have each right by default.

Table 20-3   Default Rights Assignments

Right	Description	Default Assignments
Access This Computer From The Network	Allows a user to connect over the network to the computer.	■ Administrators ■ Backup Operators ■ Everyone ■ Power Users ■ Users
Act As Part Of The Operating System	Allows a process to perform as a secure, trusted part of the operating system.	
Adding Workstations To Domains	Allows a user to join a computer to the domain.	
Adjust Memory Quotas For A Process	Determines which accounts can use a process with Write Property access to another process to increase the processor quota assigned to the other process.	■ Administrators ■ LOCAL SERVICE ■ NETWORK SERVICE
Allow Logon Through Terminal Services	Specifies which users and groups can log on to the computer by using Remote Desktop.	■ Administrators ■ Remote Desktop Users
Back Up Files And Directories	Allows users to back up files and directories. This right supersedes file and directory permissions.	■ Administrators ■ Backup Operators

Table 20-3   Default Rights Assignments

Right	Description	Default Assignments
Bypass Traverse Checking	Allows users to change directories and access files and subdirectories, even if the user has no permission to access parent directories.	■ Administrators ■ Backup Operators ■ Everyone ■ Power Users ■ Users
Change The System Time	Allows users to set the time for the internal clock of the computer.	■ Administrators ■ Power Users
Create A Page File	Allows users to create new page files for virtual memory and change the size of a page file.	■ Administrators
Create A Token Object	Allows processes to create access tokens that can be used to access local resources. Only the Local Security Authority should be allowed to create this object.	
Create Permanent Shared Objects	Allows users to create special permanent directory objects, such as \\Device, which are used within the Windows XP Professional object manager.	
Debug Programs	Allows users to debug various low-level objects such as threads.	■ Administrators
Deny Access To This Computer From The Network	Prevents specific users and groups from accessing the computer via the network. This setting supersedes the Access This Computer From The Network right if an account is subject to both policies.	■ Guest ■ SUPPORT_*N*
Deny Logon As A Batch Job	Prevents specific users and groups from logging on as a batch job. This setting supersedes the Logon As A Batch Job right if an account is subject to both policies.	
Deny Logon As A Service	Prevents specific service accounts from registering a process as a service. This setting supersedes the Log On As A Service right if an account is subject to both policies.	

Table 20-3 **Default Rights Assignments**

Right	Description	Default Assignments
Deny Logon Locally	Prevents specific users and groups from logging on directly at the computer. This setting supersedes the Log On Locally right if an account is subject to both policies.	■ Guest ■ SUPPORT_*N*
Deny Logon Through Terminal Services	Determines which users and groups are prohibited from logging on as a Terminal Services client. This right is used for Remote Desktop users.	
Enable Computer And User Accounts To Be Trusted For Delegation	Allows users to set the Trusted For Delegation setting on a user or computer object. The user granted this right must have write access to the account control flags on the computer or user object.	
Force Shutdown From A Remote System	Allows users to shut down a Windows XP Professional computer from a remote location on the network.	■ Administrators
Generate Security Audits	Allows accounts to log security audits.	■ LOCAL SERVICE ■ NETWORK SERVICE
Increase Scheduling Priority	Allows users to boost the execution priority of a process. This can be performed via the Task Manager user interface.	■ Administrators
Load And Unload Device Drivers	Allows users to install and remove device drivers. This right is necessary for Plug and Play device driver installation.	■ Administrators
Lock Pages In Memory	Allows users to lock pages in physical memory so they cannot be paged out to a virtual memory on disk.	
Log On As A Batch Job	Allows users to log on by means of a batch-queue facility. In Windows XP Professional, the Task Scheduler automatically grants this right as necessary.	■ SUPPORT_*N*

Table 20-3   Default Rights Assignments

Right	Description	Default Assignments
Log On As A Service	Allows processes to register with the system as a service. Some applications such as Microsoft Exchange Server 2003 require a service account, which should have this right. Review the users and groups assigned this right on the system prior to applying the security templates in order to determine which assignments are necessary.	■ NETWORK SERVICE ■ SYSTEM
Log On Locally	Allows users to log on at a system's console.	■ Administrators ■ Backup Operators ■ Guest ■ Power Users ■ Users
Manage Auditing And Security Log	Allows users to view and clear the security log and specify what types of object access, such as file and registry key access, are audited.	■ Administrators
Modify Firmware Environment Values	Allows users to modify system environment variables stored in nonvolatile RAM on systems that support this type of configuration.	■ Administrators
Perform Volume Maintenance Task	Allows users to run volume-maintenance tasks, such as Disk Cleanup and Disk Defragmenter.	■ Administrators
Profile System Performance	Allows users to perform profiling (performance sampling) on the system.	■ Administrators
Remove Computer From Docking Station	Allows users to undock a laptop from a docking station.	■ Administrators ■ Power Users ■ Users
Replace A Process Level Token	Allows services to modify a process's security access token. This is a powerful right used only by the system.	■ LOCAL SERVICE ■ NETWORK SERVICE
Restore Files And Directories	Allows users to restore backed-up files and directories. This right supersedes file and directory permissions. If the network makes use of a group to restore backups, assign this right to that group.	■ Administrators ■ Backup Operators

Table 20-3   Default Rights Assignments

Right	Description	Default Assignments
Shut Down The System	Allows users to shut down Windows XP Professional.	■ Administrators ■ Backup Operators ■ Powers Users ■ Users
Synchronize Directory Service Data	Allows users and groups to synchronize directory service data; also known as Active Directory Synchronization.	
Take Ownership Of Files Or Other Objects	Allows users to take ownership of files, directories, printers, and other objects on the computer. This right supersedes permissions protecting objects.	■ Administrators

Security Options

In Windows Server 2003, Group Policy provides numerous options for configuring security. You can disable or rename the local Administrator account. You can disable the Guest account. Windows Server 2003 provides more options than Windows 2000 Server, too. In a GPO, security options are in Computer Configuration\Windows Settings\Security Settings\Local Policies\Security Options. The following list describes some of the more useful and interesting security options in Group Policy (see the GPO editor for more):

- **Accounts: Administrator Account Status**   This policy allows you to explicitly enable or disable the local Administrator account. Some organizations prefer to disable the local Administrator account rather than deal with securing it during deployment. I recommend that you secure the local Administrator account with an encrypted password rather than disabling the account, though. See Chapter 6, "Answer Files," for more information.

- **Accounts: Guest Account Status**   This policy allows you to explicitly enable or disable the local Guest account. It serves the same purpose as the previous policy. Windows XP Professional disables the guest account by default, however.

- **Accounts: Rename Administrator Account**   Use this policy to rename the local Administrator account. You can use this policy at any time without changing the SID (security identifier). In other words, this affects only the account name that you type in the logon dialog box. I tend to use this policy only on forward-facing servers to make it more difficult for hackers to break in to them.

- **Accounts: Rename Guest Account**   Use this policy to rename the local Guest account, similar to the previous policy. If you will enable the Guest account, you should at least rename the account to protect it from intrusion.

- **Devices: Prevent Users From Installing Printer Drivers**   Enabling this policy allows only accounts in the local Administrators or Power Users groups to install a printer driver when adding a network printer. Disabling this setting allows any user to install a printer driver when adding a network printer.

- **Devices: Unsigned Driver Installation Behavior**   This policy is similar to the *DriverSigningPolicy* setting in answer files. (See Appendix D, "Answer File Syntax".) By configuring this policy, you specify how the operating system behaves when users try to install an unsigned device driver: Silently Succeed, Warn But Allow Installation, Do Not Allow Installation. If you're concerned about preventing the installation of unverified device drivers, don't allow their installation by using this policy. On the other hand, if unsigned device drivers are common and acceptable in your environment, allow their installation.

- **Interactive Logon: Do Not Display Last User Name**   This is a common request. By enabling this policy, you prevent Windows XP Professional from displaying the name of the last user who logged on to it in the logon dialog box. Enable this policy in environments when privacy is a requirement and it's inappropriate for a person to know who the last user was who logged on to a computer.

- **Interactive Logon: Message Text For Users Attempting To Log On**   Enabling this policy displays a disclaimer that users must read each time they log on to their computers. For example, you can use this policy to display your organization's Acceptable Usage policy each time users log on to their computers.

- **Interactive Logon: Message Title For Users Attempting To Log On**   This policy specifies the title for the message in the previous policy.

- **Interactive Logon: Prompt User To Change Password Before Expiration**   This policy specifies how many days in advance to warn users that their passwords are expiring. With this advance warning, the user has time to construct a password that is sufficiently strong. It's also "procrastinator-friendly."

- **Network Access: Do Not Allow Storage Of Credentials Or .Net Passwords For Network Authentication**   This policy is more appropriate for kiosk scenarios. Enabling this policy prevents Windows XP Professional from prompting users to save their passwords. They must type their passwords every time they log on to a server, Web site, mail server, and so on.

Restricted Groups

Restricted groups allow you to strictly control group membership. This is a powerful capability that answers the need that many administrators have to manage group membership. For example, you can create a specialized group called Local Administrators and then automatically add that group to the local Administrators group in Windows XP Professional. You can automatically add the Domain Users group to the local Power Users group (not recommended). For each group that you restrict, you can define the following:

- **Members**   You can define the users and groups that are members of the specific group. Any users or groups not explicitly permitted membership are automatically removed from the group and denied membership.

- **Members Of**   You can define the groups to which the specific group belongs.

In a GPO, restricted groups are in Computer Configuration\Windows Settings \Security Settings\Restricted Groups. To add a group, right-click Restricted Groups and then click Add Group. For example, to add the local Administrators group, click Add Group, type **Administrators**, and then click OK. Figure 20-1 shows the Administrators Properties dialog box. Click Add to add users and groups to the member list. In the example shown in the figure, I added the local Administrator, the Domain Admins group, and the Local Admins groups.

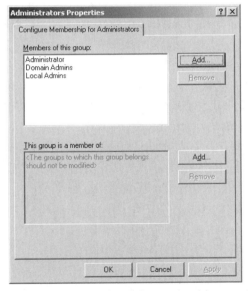

Figure 20-1   Restricted Groups enables you to define group membership as a policy.

Note   An empty Members list means that the restricted group has no members; an empty Members Of list means that the groups to which the restricted group belongs are not modified.

System Services

System Services gives you an ability that most administrators have always wanted: You can specify the status of services as a policy. Most administrators have pet services that they adamantly disable during deployment. They typically rely on registry hacks or customize disk images to disable certain services. Using System Services, you can specify whether a service starts automatically, starts manually, or is disabled altogether. A typical example is the Indexing service, which many IT professionals prefer to disable.

Configure System Services is in Computer Configuration\Windows Settings \Security Settings\System Services. Double-click a service and then select the Define This Policy Setting check box to configure its startup mode. Click Edit Security to change the service's access control list (ACL).

Service security is important. If compromised, a service can offer access to system resources that users can hack. To mitigate this risk, keep the following points in mind when configuring System Services:

- Only run services that are needed. If you do not have an FTP server or use Telnet, disable those services. Disabling these services closes holes that hackers exploit.

- Restrict the users who have access to each service.

- If you're not using a service, set the startup mode to disable, which ensures that the particular service does not start when the operating system starts.

- If you are configuring either the startup mode or ACLs, change one and then change the other. If you set a service's startup mode to disable, make sure that you change the ACL to give only Administrators and System full control.

- Run all services with the fewest number of privileges needed.

Registry ACLs

At first glance, most IT professionals skip by the Registry node in the GPO editor. Imagine that you have a legacy application that won't run in your locked-down environment, however. The reason it won't run is that the application requires permission to write a registry value in HKLM that restricted users can only read. The first thought many administrators have is to put users in the local Administrators group so they can run the application. That's a terrible idea because it gives users unrestricted control of the computer, and there is a simple solution available. Instead, you can configure the ACL for the subkey containing that value to give users permission to write values in it. You do that using the Registry node, which is in Computer Configuration\Windows Settings\Security Settings\Registry.

To add a subkey to a GPO, right-click Registry and then click Add Key. In the Select Registry Key dialog box, either type the path of a key or click it in the Registry list. If the key doesn't exist on the local computer, you must type it. If you do type it, keep in mind that you type **CLASSES_ROOT** for HKCR, **MACHINE** for HKLM, and **USERS** for HKCU. Generally, you don't need to define ACLs for HKCU unless you're trying to prevent users from changing settings in their user profile. You'll commonly change settings in HKLM to allow users to change settings that they normally can't change, though. After adding the subkey, you'll see the Database Security For *Subkey* dialog box. In this dialog box, configure the ACL for the subkey. The steps are the same as configuring a subkey's ACL in Registry Editor, so I won't cover them here. Only Full Control, Read, and Special Permissions appear in the Permissions list. Click Advanced to define granular permissions.

File System ACLs

You can configure file system ACLs similar to configuring registry ACLs, as described in the section "Registry ACLs" on page 586. Doing so requires that you deploy Windows XP Professional with the NT file system (NTFS). To continue the example from the previous section, a legacy application you're deploying might require write access to a file that restricted users can only read. Instead of dumping users in to the Administrators group, you can create a GPO that configures the ACL for that file or folder. You do that using the Registry node, which is in Computer Configuration\Windows Settings\Security Settings\File System.

To add a file or folder to a GPO, right-click File System and then click Add File. In the Add A File Or Folder dialog box, either type the path of a file or folder or click it in the list. If the file or folder doesn't exist on the local computer, you must type it. After adding the file or folder, you'll see the Database Security For *File* dialog box. In this dialog box, configure the ACL for the file or folder. The steps are the same as for configuring a file or folder's ACL by using Windows Explorer, so I won't cover them here.

Software Restriction

When you use software-restriction policies, you specify software that is or isn't allowed to run so that you can protect your organization from untrusted programs (and prevent users from distractions, too). You can define a default security level of Unrestricted or Disallowed for a GPO so that software is either allowed or not allowed to run by default. Then you create exceptions to the default security level for specific programs. For example, you can disallow all programs but a few specific ones to run—a common scenario for managing task-based workers. Group Policy supports the following types of rules:

■ **Hash rules** Programs are identified by the program file's hash value, which enables Group Policy to identify the program without regard to the program's path name or filename.

- **Certificate rules**   Programs are identified by their digital certificate. You can allow program files that are signed with a particular certificate to run.

- **Path rules**   Programs are identified by the path name and filename.

- **Internet zone rules**   Programs are identified by their locations, which correspond to Internet Explorer security zones.

A software-restriction policy is made up of the default security level plus the rules defined in the GPO. This policy can apply to all the computers or to individual users. Software-restriction policies provide a number of ways to identify software, as described in the previous list, and they provide a policy-based infrastructure to enforce decisions about whether the software can run. With software-restriction policies, users must follow the guidelines that are set up by administrators when they run programs. For example, you can apply a policy that does not allow certain file types to run in the e-mail attachment folder of your e-mail program if you are concerned about users receiving viruses through e-mail.

To use software-restriction policies, you must add them to the GPO. Restriction policies that you add to the Computer Configuration node of a GPO apply to the computer and all its users. To add per-computer software-restriction policies, go to Computer Configuration\Windows Settings\Security Settings\Software Restriction Policies. Right-click Software Restriction Policies and then click New Software Restriction Policies. Restriction policies that you add to the User Configuration node of a GPO apply to the users that the GPO covers. To add per-user software-restriction policies, go to User Configuration\Windows Settings\Security Settings\Software Restriction Policies. Right-click Software Restriction Policies and then click New Software Restriction Policies. After you create the polices, see the following sections for more information about configuring them.

> **Tip**   You can prevent restriction policies from applying to administrators. In Software Restriction Policies, double-click Enforcement. Under Apply Software Restriction Policies To The Following Users, click All Users Except Local Administrators. If your users are members of the local Administrators group, you might not want to turn on this setting because it defeats restrictions for these users.

Default Security Level

The default security level specifies whether programs that don't have specific rules are allowed or not allowed to run. In the details pane, the current default security level is indicated by a black circle with a check mark in it. Here's how to configure the default security level:

1. In Software Restriction Policies, click Security Levels.

2. Right-click either Disallowed or Unrestricted, and then click Set as Default.

> **Caution**   In certain folders, if you set the default security level to Disallowed, you can adversely affect your operating system.

Rules are created to specify exceptions to the default security level. When the default security level is set to Unrestricted, rules specify software that is not allowed to run. When the default security level is set to Disallowed, rules specify software that is allowed to run. At installation, the default security level of software-restriction policies on all files on your computer is set to Unrestricted.

Certificate Rules

Certificate rules allow or disallow programs to run based upon a digital certificate. For example, you can add a rule that allows programs with a particular certificate to run. Here's how to create a certificate rule:

1. In Software Restriction Policies, right-click Additional Rules and then click New Certificate Rule.

2. Click Browse and then select a certificate.

3. Select a security level: Disallowed or Unrestricted.

4. In the Description box, type a description for this rule and then click OK.

The only file types that are affected by certificate rules are those that are listed in Designated File Types. There is one list of designated file types that is shared by all rules. Finally, for software-restriction policies to take effect, users must update policy settings by logging off from and then logging on to their computers.

Hash Rules

Hash rules allow or disallow programs to run based upon the program file's hash value, which Group Policy calculates when you select the program file. For example, you can add a rule that restricts programs with a particular hash value from running. A file that is renamed or moved to another folder still results in the same hash, but any change to a file results in a different hash. Here's how to create a hash rule:

1. In Software Restriction Policies, right-click Additional Rules and then click New Hash Rule.

2. Click Browse to select a file from which to calculate the hash value, or paste a precalculated hash value in the File Hash box.

3. In the Security Level list, click a security level: Disallowed or Unrestricted.

4. In the Description box, type a description for this rule and then click OK.

The only file types that are affected by certificate rules are those that are listed in Designated File Types. There is one list of designated file types that is shared by all rules. Finally, for software-restriction policies to take effect, users must update policy settings by logging off from and then logging on to their computers.

> **Tip** You can create a hash rule for a known virus or a Trojan horse to prevent the malicious software from running. If you want other users to use a hash rule so that a virus cannot run, calculate the hash of the virus by using software-restriction policies and then e-mail the hash value to other users. Never e-mail the virus itself. If a virus has been sent through e-mail, you can also create a path rule to prevent users from running mail attachments (see the section "Path Rules" on this page for more information).

Internet Zone Rules

Internet zone rules allow or disallow programs to run based upon their location. For example, you can add a rule that prevents programs in the Internet zone from running. Here's how to create an Internet zone rule:

1. In Software Restriction Policies, right-click Additional Rules and then click New Internet Zone Rule.

2. In the Internet Zone list, click an Internet zone: Internet, Local Computer, Local Intranet, Restricted Sites, or Trusted Sites.

3. Select a security level: Disallowed or Unrestricted.

4. In the Description box, type a description for this rule and then click OK.

Zone rules apply to Windows Installer packages only. The only file types that are affected by certificate rules are those that are listed in Designated File Types. There is one list of designated file types that is shared by all rules. Finally, for software-restriction policies to take effect, users must update policy settings by logging off from and then logging on to their computers.

Path Rules

Path rules allow or disallow programs to run based upon their path name and filename. For example, you can add a rule that prevents programs that are in the temporary folder from running (many mail clients extract attachments to the temporary folder when users open them). If you create a path rule for a program with a security level of Disallowed, a user can still run the software by copying it to another location. Here's how to create a path rule:

1. In Software Restriction Policies, right-click Additional Rules and then click New Path Rule.

2. In Path, type a path or click Browse to find a file or folder. The wildcard characters that are supported by the path rule are the asterisk (*) and the question mark (?).You can use environment variables such as %PROGRAMFILES% or %SYSTEMROOT% in your path rule.

3. Select a security level: Disallowed or Unrestricted.

4. In the Description box, type a description for this rule and then click OK.

> **Caution** IOn certain folders, such as %SYSTEMROOT%, setting the security level to Disallowed can adversely affect the operation of your operating system. Make sure that you do not disallow a crucial component of the operating system or one of its dependent programs.

The only file types that are affected by certificate rules are those that are listed in Designated File Types. There is one list of designated file types that is shared by all rules. Finally, for software-restriction policies to take effect, users must update policy settings by logging off from and then logging on to their computers.

Registry Path Rules

Registry path rules are special path rules based on registry keys. You don't always know the exact path that contains a program, but you do know where in the registry the path is indicated. The most common location for these paths is the App Paths key in HKLM\SOFTWARE\Microsoft\Windows\CurrentVersion. By using registry path rules, you make your software-restriction policies robust enough to handle different installation locations for a program. Here's how to create a registry path rule:

1. In Registry Editor, right-click the subkey for which you want to create a rule and then click Copy Key Name. Note the value name in the right pane.

2. In Software Restriction Policies, right-click Additional Rules and then click New Path Rule.

3. In Path, paste the subkey name and value name. Enclose the entire path in percent signs. For instance, to stop Outlook Express from running, type **%HKEY _LOCAL_MACHINE\SOFTWARE\Microsoft\Windows\CurrentVersion \App Paths\msimn.exe\Path%**. Do not use the abbreviations for root keys, such as HKLM or HKCU.

4. Select a security level: Disallowed or Unrestricted.

5. In the Description box, type a description for this rule and then click OK.

The registry path rule can contain a suffix after the closing percent sign (%). Do not use a backslash (\) in the suffix. You can use the following registry path rule: %HKEY_CURRENT_USER\Software\Microsoft\Windows\CurrentVersion\Explorer \Shell Folders\Cache%OLK*, for example.

The only file types that are affected by certificate rules are those that are listed in Designated File Types. There is one list of designated file types that is shared by all rules. Finally, for software-restriction policies to take effect, users must update policy settings by logging off from and then logging on to their computers.

Folder Redirection

Group Policy make it possible to control where users store data by using the Folder Redirection feature, which allows you to redirect users' folders to a location on a network server. You can redirect the Application Data, My Documents, Start Menu, and Desktop folders from users' profiles to a network location. There are two big benefits of using Folder Redirection. The first is that it removes typically large folders from roaming user profiles and stores them centrally, making the logon process much faster because the roaming user profile contains less data. The second is that it gives users access to all of their documents from any computer, even if you don't deploy roaming user profiles on your network. See Chapter 12, "User Profiles," for more information about roaming user profiles.

As you'll learn in this section, Folder Redirection in Windows Server 2003 is many times more powerful, more flexible, and less error-prone than its counterpart in Windows 2000 Server. Windows Server 2003 provides four options for basic Folder Redirection:

- **Create A Folder For Each User Under The Root Path**   You specify a Universal Naming Convention (UNC) path, such as \\Server\Folders, and Folder Redirection automatically creates subfolders for each user to which the policy applies. In most cases, this is the easiest and least error-prone option to use.

- **Redirect To The User's Home Directory**   This option is for organizations that have implemented home folders and need to maintain compatibility with the current folder structure that is in place. This option is particularly useful in scenarios where you support applications that aren't compatible with Folder Redirection because they will default to the user's home folder.

- **Redirect To The Following Location**   Use this option to redirect folders to locations other than users' home folders; otherwise, this option is similar to the previous. You'd use an environment variable for the user's folder in the path, such as \\Server\Folders\%USERNAME%.

- **Redirect To The Local User Profile Location** Use this option to redirect folders to the default locations in users' local profiles.

You configure Folder Redirection in a GPO. Folder Redirection is in User Configuration\Windows Settings\Folder Redirection. Immediately under Folder Redirection, you see the four folders that you can redirect: Application Data, Desktop, My Documents, and Start menu. When you redirect the My Documents folder, you can optionally redirect the My Pictures folder as well. The primary tasks for configuring Folder Redirection include the following, and the next few sections describe how to complete these tasks:

- Creating or selecting a GPO for Folder Redirection.

- Selecting Basic or Advanced Folder Redirection options. Advanced Redirection allows you to apply the redirection to users that belong in a specified security group.

- Identifying the target folder location. You can redirect folders to any of the following locations:

    - The root of a network file share

    - A folder on a network share

    - A local folder

    - A home directory (applicable only if you have existing home directories in your environment)

- Setting permissions for root folders and users' folders.

Note To get the best performance from Folder Redirection, it is recommended that you create the root share on the server and let the system create the users' folders, synchronize files at logoff when you use Folder Redirection with Offline Files, and follow the guidelines in the following sidebar "Folder Redirection Guidelines." If you allow Folder Redirection to create the redirected folders on a specified network, the folders that are created in this way have proper permissions assigned to them. If you must create folders for users, make sure that you set the correct permissions. Then, clear the Grant Exclusive Rights To check box on the Settings tab of the Folder Redirection Properties page. If you do not clear this check box, Folder Redirection first checks pre-existing folders to determine whether the user is the owner. If the administrator previously created the folder, the check fails, and redirection is cancelled. Folder Redirection logs an event in the Application event log, indicating that redirection failed and that the new directories for the redirected folder cannot be created due to not being able to assign a security ID as the owner of the folder (Event ID 101).

Folder Redirection Guidelines

The following suggestions for redirecting the My Documents folder are appropriate for most deployments and can provide a faster and simpler deployment:

- Redirect My Documents to a network share.

- Allow Folder Redirection to create folders for you. When setting redirection policy for a group, use the path to the share, such as *server* *share*. Folder Redirection then appends the user name and the folder name when the policy is applied.

- Allow Folder Redirection to perform all the moving of folders and files when you select a folder for redirection or change the target network share to which you redirect the folder. The Folder Redirection client not only moves files to the appropriate network share, but it also sets proper folder security and renames entries in the Offline Files cache database so that they continue to link to the correct target folders and files. Any files pinned by the user in the Offline File Cache stay pinned.

- Combine Folder Redirection with Offline Files to provide the user access to My Documents, even when the user's workstation is temporarily disconnected from the network. This is particularly useful for people who use portable computers.

- Include redirected folders, particularly My Documents, in routine server backups. Performing backups of user data that is located on network shares is simpler and more reliable because it requires no action on the part of the user or interaction with the workstation.

- Use Group Policy to set profile quotas and disk quotas to establish limits on the disk space that is used by users' data and settings.

- Redirect user-specific data from the hard disk that holds the operating system files. This data can be redirected to a different hard disk on the user's local computer or to a network share. This simplifies system maintenance by separating system files from user files.

- Centralize storage on large shares to reduce workstation hardware and maintenance costs. Pooling disk space more than offsets the cost of increasing server disk capacity.

- Do not use the Redirect to home folder policy setting unless you have already deployed home folders in your organization.

- Leave the My Pictures folder located in the My Documents folder.

> When you redirect My Documents, the Recycle Bin size for My Documents defaults to a percentage of the size of the server partition in which the redirected My Documents resides. You can manually change this size in one-percent increments. Because a Recycle Bin can grow large, encourage users to empty their Recycle Bins periodically.

Root Folder

In most cases, you should redirect special folders to a root folder instead of a specific location because this appends the correct paths for you, including %USERNAME%. Here's how to redirect special folders to a root folder:

1. Open a GPO that is linked to the site, domain, or OU that contains the users whose special folders you want to redirect.

2. Under User Configuration\Windows Settings\Folder Redirection, double-click Folder Redirection to display the special folder that you want to redirect.

3. Right-click the special folder that you want to redirect (such as Desktop or My Documents) and then click Properties.

4. Click the Target tab and then select Basic - Redirect Everyone's Folder To The Same Location in the Settings box.

5. Under Target folder location, select Create a Folder For Each User Under The Root Path.

6. In the Root Path box, type a UNC path, such as **servername****sharename**, and then click OK.

7. In the Properties dialog box for the special folder, click OK.

8. The user name and folder name are appended to the UNC path automatically.

Specific Path

Here's how to redirect special folders to a specific path:

1. Open a GPO that is linked to the site, domain, or OU that contains the users whose special folders you want to redirect.

2. Under User Configuration\Windows Settings\Folder Redirection, double-click Folder Redirection to display the special folder that you want to redirect.

3. Right-click the special folder that you want to redirect and then click Properties.

4. In the Setting box on the Target tab, select Basic - Redirect Everyone's Folder To The Same Location.

5. Under Target folder location, select Redirect To The Following Location. In the Root Path box, type a UNC path, such as **\\servername\sharename**; or type a locally valid path, such as **C:\Folder**, and then click OK.

Local Profile Location

Here's how to redirect special folders to their default local profile location:

1. Open a GPO that is linked to the site, domain, or OU that contains the users whose special folders you want to redirect.

2. Under User Configuration\Windows Settings\Folder Redirection, double-click Folder Redirection to display the special folder that you want to redirect.

3. Right-click the special folder that you want to redirect (such as Desktop or My Documents) and then click Properties.

4. In the Setting box on the Target tab, select Basic - Redirect Everyone's Folder To The Same Location.

5. Under Target folder location, select Redirect To The Local User Profile Location and then click OK.

Home Directory

Typically, it is recommended that you do not redirect to a home directory unless you have already deployed home directories in your organization. However, if you have home directories and want to transition your users to use My Documents while maintaining compatibility with the home directory environment, you can redirect a user's My Documents folder to the user's home folder. The Redirect To Home Folder policy setting is intended only for organizations in which home folders are already in place. Redirect only the My Documents folder to the home folder. Windows 2000 Professional does not support this type of folder redirection.

When a folder is redirected to the home folder, security and ownership are not checked, and permissions are not changed. Folder Redirection behaves as if the administrator has set directory security correctly. This relaxed security is the reason that redirection to the home folder is not recommended if the home folder structure is not already in place and if you have not updated your configuration. Typically, folder redirection fails if a user is not the owner of the folder to which the My Documents folder is redirected. Because redirection to the home folder is intended for an earlier environment, Folder Redirection does not check for proper folder ownership. Instead, ownership check is left to the administrator.

Users must have the home folder property set correctly on their user object in Active Directory. The client computer gets the path for the user's home folder from the user object in Active Directory when the user logs on. User accounts that have redirected folders must have this path set correctly, or else Folder Redirection fails.

The following steps show how to configure this type of Folder Redirection:

1. Open a GPO that is linked to the site, domain, or OU that contains the users whose My Documents folders you want to redirect.

2. Under User Configuration\Windows Settings\Folder Redirection, double-click Folder Redirection to display the special folder that you want to redirect.

3. Right-click My Documents and then click Properties.

4. On the Target tab of the Setting box, select Basic - Redirect Everyone's Folder To The Same Location.

5. Under Target folder location, select Redirect To The User's Home Directory and then click OK.

Domain administrators have full control over the users' My Documents folder when you redirect My Documents to the home directory. This is the case even if you select the Grant The User Exclusive Rights To My Documents option on the Settings tab in the My Documents Properties dialog box.

AutoProf Policy Maker

Group Policy doesn't do everything that every IT professional needs it to do. In fact, even Microsoft folks will admit that there are holes in the coverage that Group Policy provides. That's why Microsoft made Group Policy extensible. To date, however, very few companies have stepped forward and extended Group Policy with useful tools that help you better manage users and computers.

Policy Maker from AutoProf (*http://www.autoprof.com*) is a new product that fills this void. If you've ever wished that your GPOs could do more, I recommend that you evaluate Policy Maker, shown in Figure 20-2. It seamlessly adds new features to every GPO you create, such as:

■ **Network drive mappings**   You can assign network drives. For example, you can create a GPO that maps drive M: to the network share containing the accounting department's data files, and then assign that GPO to the accounting department's OU.

- **Shared printer connections**   You can assign printer connections (shared and TCP/IP). In a classroom environment, for example, you can assign GPOs to each classroom's OU that connects to the printer in that classroom.

- **Creating, changing, and removing shortcuts**   You can create GPOs that add shortcuts to Internet Explorer, the Start menu, the Quick Launch toolbar, the desktop, and so on. You can also remove shortcuts by using a GPO, such as shortcuts to distracting programs that are difficult to remove from Windows XP Professional. A practical application that I've used is to update existing shortcuts by using a GPO. For example, you can add command-line options to existing shortcuts.

- **Configuring environment variables**   You can create GPOs that define system and user environment variables. I've assigned environment variables via GPOs, and then relied on those environment variables in logon and other scripts. Doing so makes scripts less sensitive to change.

- **Configuring registry settings**   Instead of creating your own administrative templates for use with Group Policy, Policy Maker allows you to add, change, or remove any setting in the registry. This is handy when no policy exists for a setting that you want to manage, but you know the location of the setting in the registry.

- **Copying and removing files**   You can create a GPO that copies and removes files on the computer. For example, you can copy network shortcuts to the users' Nethood folders. You can create a GPO that automatically adds certain shortcuts to the SendTo folders.

- **Managing files and folders, even attributes**   You can create GPOs that manage files and folders. For example, you can remove temporary folders through a GPO. Another example is creating a GPO that changes the attribute of Internet Explorer's Links folder so that it doesn't show up on the Favorites menu. There are many practical applications for managing files and folders through a GPO, and Policy Maker gives you numerous and flexible options for doing so.

- **Configuring Microsoft Office**   You can almost completely configure Microsoft Office by using a GPO. Policy Maker even presents you with similar dialog boxes that Office presents, making it easier to configure Office in a GPO.

- **Building Outlook user profiles**   You can use a GPO to create Outlook user profiles. Creating Outlook user profiles has always been a tedious chore, but Policy Maker makes doing it a no-brainer.

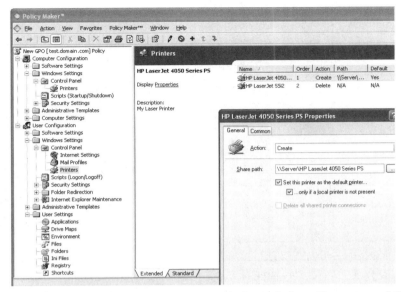

Figure 20-2   AutoProf Policy Maker extends Group Policy with many capabilities that Group Policy doesn't provide.

Policy Maker is easy to install, with installation usually taking just a few minutes. And using Policy Maker is straightforward for any IT professional with basic knowledge of using the Group Policy editor. That's because Policy Maker fits seamlessly into the Group Policy editor (refer to Figure 20-2). The client-side extension supports Windows 2000, Windows XP Professional, and Windows Server 2003; and it supports reporting by using Resultant Set of Policy (RSoP). Profile Maker also supports all versions of Office and Outlook.

Administrative Templates

Registry-based policies and *administrative templates* are two names for the same thing. They are registry settings that override users' preferences, and users can't change them for good reasons that you'll learn about in this section. Other policies, including security settings, might or might not be registry settings. In the GPO editor, you find registry-based policies in the Administrative Templates folder under Computer Configuration or User Configuration.

Figure 20-3 shows the workflow using registry-based policies. You define policies using the GPO editor. Administrative templates, files with the *.adm* extension, define the policies you can set. Administrative templates and policy templates are the same thing, and you frequently see the short name *ADM files*. These templates describe the user interface for collecting settings from the administrator and their locations in the registry. When the administrator defines policies, the editor stores them in a file called Registry.pol. Windows XP Professional loads the settings contained in the file Registry.pol when the operating system starts, when users log on to it, and at regular intervals. The next section describes where in the registry Windows XP Professional stores policies and where you find the Registry.pol file.

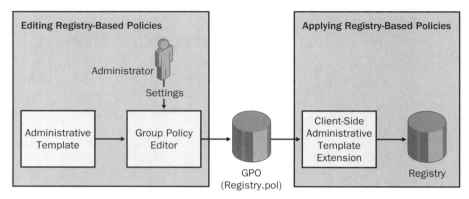

Figure 20-3   Registry-based policies start with administrative templates, which define the settings that are available and the location where they are stored in the registry.

The following components combine to implement registry-based policy:

- The Administrative Templates extension, which you use to edit policy settings. This extension is the Administrative Templates folder in the editor, which creates the Registry.pol file based on settings that the administrator defines.

- A built-in registry client-side extension, which processes policies and creates their corresponding values in the registry (available only in Windows 2000 or later). Although the client-side extension is responsible for reading settings from the Registry.pol file and writing them to the registry, Windows XP Professional and other applications must look for and use these settings to give them meaning.

Windows XP Professional comes with administrative templates that define all the proper policies that the operating system supports. If you want to use policies for an application, such as one in Office 2003 Editions, you must load the administrative templates for it. In fact, the Office 2003 Editions Resource Kit comes with a big handful of administrative templates that help you better manage the entire productivity suite. Windows XP Professional provides the following administrative templates:

- **System.adm**   Core settings and primary template file, defining most of the settings you see in Administrative Templates

- **Wmplayer.adm**   Windows Media settings

- **Conf.adm**   NetMeeting conferencing software

- **Inetres.adm**   Internet Explorer

All registry-based policies can be in one of three states: Enabled, Disabled, or Not Configured. *Enabled* explicitly turns on the setting by adding the setting to the registry with a value of 0x01. *Disabled* explicitly turns off the setting by adding the setting to the registry with a value of 0x00 or removing the value altogether. The *Not Configured* option removes the setting from the registry altogether, which yields to the user's preference. Many policies collect additional settings, as shown in Figure 20-3.

When setting a policy, pay particular attention to the language to ensure that you get the result you want. Some policies are positive, so enabling the policy turns on the feature. Other policies are negative, however, so turning on those policies actually disables those features. To make things more confusing, outside of Windows XP Professional, you frequently see policies that you have to enable and then turn the setting on or off. In other words, to turn on a setting, you have to enable the policy and then select or clear a second check box to turn the setting on or off. The Office 2003 Editions policy templates are notorious for this extra level of indirection. All this just illustrates that you have to pay close attention to the names of policies when setting them. Read their names out loud, prefixing the sentences with the words enable or disable—just to be sure.

On the Resource Kit CD   Prior to configuring policies by using administrative templates, you must plan them. This book's companion CD contains a tool called Policies.xls, which is located in the Aids folder, that can help you plan the settings that you want to deploy. This spreadsheet, which contains most of the known administrative policies for Windows XP Professional, indicates where the operating system stores the setting in the registry. Use this as a list from which to choose and then record your required setting by any you choose to configure.

Group Policy Storage

Where does Windows XP Professional store policies in the registry and on the disk? The branch \Software\Policies is the preferred branch for registry-based policies. This branch in HKLM contains per-computer policies, and the branch in HKCU contains per-user policies. Another branch, inherited from earlier versions of Windows, is \Software\Microsoft\Windows\CurrentVersion\Policies. Policies in this branch tend to tattoo the registry, which means they make permanent changes to the registry that you must explicitly change. What prevents users from changing these keys, and thus the policies they enforce, are their ACLs. The Users and Power Users local groups do not have permission to change values in these keys. An administrator can overwrite these keys directly and change the policy, however.

That covers the location of policies in the registry; now for their location on the file system. The local GPO is in %SYSTEMROOT%\System32\GroupPolicy. This is a super-hidden folder. To show it in Windows Explorer, click Tools, Options; on the Folder Options dialog box's View tab, select the Show Hidden Files And Folders option and then clear the Hide Protected Operating System Files check box. It contains the following subfolders and files (our focus is the file Registry.pol):

- **\Adm**   Contains all the ADM files for the local GPO.

- **\User**   Includes the file Registry.pol, which contains registry-based policies for users. When users log on to the computer, Windows XP Professional applies these to HKCU.

- **\User\Scripts**   Contains the local GPO's per-user scripts. The scripts in \Logon run when users log on to Windows XP Professional and the scripts in \Logoff run when they log off of the operating system.

- **\Machine**   Includes the file Registry.pol, which contains registry-based policies for the computer. When Windows XP Professional starts, it applies these settings to HKLM.

- **\Machine\Scripts**   Contains the local GPO's per-computer scripts. The scripts in \Startup run when Windows XP Professional starts, and the scripts in \Shutdown run when the operating systems shuts down.

If you're familiar with System Policy and the file Ntconfig.pol, you're probably wondering whether the files Registry.pol and Ntconfig.pol use similar formats. They don't. Both are binary files, but Registry.pol is much simpler. It contains a simple list of settings—including their value names, type, and data—in a binary format. Ntconfig.pol is actually a registry hive file that you can load and browse in Regedit. Unfortunately, you can't do the same with Registry.pol.

Extending Registry-Based Policy

You can extend registry-based policy by customizing existing administrative templates or by creating new ones. Windows XP Professional provides administrative templates for its policies. Other applications, such as Office 2003 Editions, also provide templates. When you install the Office 2003 Editions Resource Kit, it adds the Office 2003 Editions policy templates to %SYSTEMROOT%\Inf. You should never customize these templates. You might want to create your own templates that extend registry-based policy, though.

First, the caveats: Extending registry-based policy is generally something that developers do to give administrators more control over users' applications. Remember that a registry-based policy requires developers to add code to their applications that read policies and enforce those settings. If developers added policies to their code, they almost certainly created policy templates for them, so you don't have to. On the other hand, if no code enforces a policy setting, creating an administrative template for it is useless. It almost sounds as if extending registry-based policy is futile. But there are still times when it's useful and other times that are extremely valuable:

- **Repairing broken policies** I don't run across broken policies often, but when I do, the only way to fix them is to create a custom template for them. For example, during the Windows XP Professional beta, the screen saver policy stored the timeout period incorrectly in the registry. My simple fix was to create a custom template for it. Likewise, the policy templates that the Office 2003 Editions Resource Kit provides have a couple of broken policies.

- **Creating custom administrative templates** Windows XP Professional supports hundreds of policies, as does Office 2003 Editions. Hunting for policies is sometimes frustrating. You can create a custom administrative template that assembles all the policies you're deploying in one place, making the job a bit easier. You can also rephrase the language of a policy with easier-to-understand descriptions.

- **Customizing Windows XP Professional** Many of the registry settings you can use to customize Windows XP Professional have no user interface. You can build a user interface for them by creating an administrative template and changing those settings with the Group Policy editor. This goes against one of the primary features of Group Policy, however, because settings you change outside the normal policy branches in the registry will tattoo the registry.

You can use any text editor to create an administrative template. Administrative templates have a language all their own (you learn about that language in Appendix C, "Administrative Template Syntax"). The GPO editor is very good about displaying useful error messages when a template file contains an error. It gives you the line number, the keyword that's in error, and more information.

In summary, do the following:

- Create an administrative template using the language you learn about in Appendix C. The template file is a text file with the *.adm* extension.

- Load the template file in the Group Policy editor as you learn to do in the section "Deploying Registry-Based Policy" on page 604.

- Edit the settings that the administrative template defines.

More Info   The tool Regtoadm helps you build administrative templates faster than creating them by hand. Yizhar Hurwitz graciously provides this tool—among many other useful utilities—at *http://www.new-ofek.co.il /yizhar*. Download and run this tool; then click File, Import to import an existing *.reg* file. Regtoadm automatically generates an *.adm* file, which you see in the right pane. You can edit the file and then save it by clicking File, Save ADM Template.

On the Resource Kit CD   On this book's companion CD in the Samples \chap20 folder, I provided you with numerous sample *.adm* files that you can use to get started. Simply edit the file to your requirements and then import it in to the Group Policy editor. The comments that each template file contains describes what you need to change in order to use it. The name of the file describes the type of setting that you can configure with it. For example, the file called boolean.adm is an administrative template for setting a registry value either on or off. You can combine multiple templates in a single file, but keep in mind the syntax of these files, as described in Appendix C.

Deploying Registry-Based Policy

To use an administrative template, whether you created it or an application such as Office 2003 Editions provides it, you must load it in the Administrative Templates extension. You load template files into each GPO in which you want to use them. If you use a template with Active Directory, you'd have to load it in each GPO in which you want to use it, though. Here's how to load a template in the local GPO:

1. Right-click Administrative Templates under Computer Configuration Or User Configuration and then click Add/Remove Templates.

2. In the Add/Remove Templates dialog box, click Add.

3. In the Policy Templates dialog box, type the path and filename of the administrative template you want to load in to the local GPO.

Group Policy Improvements

Windows XP Professional includes improved policy management, enabling you to fine-tune, manage, or simply turn off features you don't want users to access. Here's a brief list of the improvements you find in Windows XP Professional:

- Windows XP Professional supports all 421 Windows 2000 policies.

- Windows XP Professional adds 212 new policy settings, and Windows 2000 ignores them.

- The Group Policy editor uses Web view to display useful information about policies that IT professionals use to assess and verify settings.

- The Group Policy editor includes integrated help that makes learning and tracking down policies easier.

- Windows XP Professional doesn't wait for the network to fully initialize before presenting the desktop, using cached credentials in the meantime and allowing users to get to work faster. It applies policies in the background when the network is ready.

These improvements are big advantages. However, you'll be happy to know that the big picture doesn't change much. You use roughly the same tools in the same ways to configure and manage user settings. If you're already familiar with Windows 2000 Professional Group Policy, you're equally familiar with Windows XP Professional Group Policy.

The Windows XP Professional policy templates are fully compatible with Windows 2000 Server and its version of Active Directory. You have to load them in each GPO in which you want to use them, though, and the steps for doing that are the same as you learned in the previous sections. You can avoid having to load the Windows XP Professional administrative templates in each GPO by copying them to %SYSTEMROOT%\Inf on the server. Just copy all the files with the *.adm* extension from %SYSTEMROOT%\Inf on a computer running Windows XP Professional to the same folder on the server. The server operating system automatically updates each GPO when you open it for editing. If you're uncomfortable with replacing your Windows 2000 Professional administrative templates, you should continue loading the Windows XP Professional templates in GPOs where you want to use them. I've replaced my Windows 2000 administrative templates with Windows XP Professional administrative templates, however, and haven't felt any pain. Windows Server 2003 includes the Windows XP Professional administrative templates by default.

Consider these best practices when using Windows XP Professional administrative templates in Windows 2000 Server:

- In a mixed environment, use Windows XP Professional template files to administer your GPOs. Windows 2000 ignores Windows XP Professional–specific settings.

- Apply the same policy settings to both Windows XP Professional and Windows 2000 to give roaming users a consistent experience.

- Test interoperability of the various settings before deployment.

- Configure policy settings only on client machines using GPOs. Do not try to create these registry values by other methods.

Tattoos on the Registry

Group Policy and System Policy, policies that versions of Windows earlier than Windows 2000 Professional use, handle changes differently. Windows XP Professional automatically removes a GPO's settings from the registry when the GPO no longer applies to the user or computer. Also, Group Policy doesn't overwrite users' preferences. So if you delete a GPO from Active Directory, Windows XP Professional removes that GPO's settings from the registry and reverts back to users' preferences. Likewise, if you remove an individual policy from a GPO, Windows XP Professional removes that setting from the registry and restores users' existing preferences. Group Policy doesn't make permanent irreversible changes to the registry.

System Policy does make permanent, irreversible changes to the registry, though. In other words, it tattoos the registry. Removing System Policy leaves all the policies it contained in the registry. The only way to restore users' preferences, assuming that these policies don't overwrite their preferences, is to manually remove the policy from the registry or explicitly change the setting in System Policy. One of the nastier incarnations of this behavior can occur when you upgrade from an earlier version of Windows to Windows XP Professional. When you upgrade, policies in the registry are permanent, and you must manually remove them from the registry; Windows XP Professional doesn't remove them automatically.

Using the Group Policy Tools

The Group Policy tools in Windows XP Professional and Windows Server 2003 contain a lot of improvements. The sections following this one describe each of these tools and how to use them. Some of these enhancements deserve special mention, though. First is Group Policy Update Tool (Gpupdate.exe). Group Policy refreshes policies every 90 minutes by default. In Windows 2000, if you change a policy and want to see the results immediately, you had to use the commands **secedit /refreshpolicy user_policy** and **secedit /refreshpolicy machine_policy**. Gpupdate.exe replaces both of these commands in one easy-to-use command.

Second is RSoP. Windows XP Professional includes new tools for seeing which policies the operating system is applying to the current user and computer and the location in which they originated. One of the toughest parts of administering Group Policy on a large network is tracking down behaviors that result from combinations of GPOs that you didn't intend or didn't know were occurring. These tools help you track down these behaviors much faster than you could with Windows 2000 because they give you a snapshot of how the operating system is applying them and where they originated.

Gpresult

The Group Policy Result Tool displays the effective policies and RSoP for the current user and computer. The following describes the command's syntax, and Table 20-4 describes each command-line option:

```
gpresult [/s Computer [/u Domain\User /p Password]]
[/user TargetUserName] [/scope {user|computer}] [/v] [/z]
```

Table 20-4   Gpresult Command-Line Options

Option	Description
/s Computer	This option specifies the name or Internet Protocol (IP) address of a remote computer (don't use backslashes). It defaults to the local computer.
/u Domain\User	This option runs the command with the account permissions of the user specified by *User* or *Domain\User*. The default is the permissions of the current console user.
/p Password	This option specifies the password of the user account that the */u* option specifies.
/user TargetUserName	This option specifies the user name of the user for whom you want to display RSoP.
/scope {user|computer}	This option displays either user or computer results. Valid values for the */scope* option are *user* or *computer*. If you omit the */scope* option, Gpresult.exe displays both user and computer settings.
/v	This option specifies that the output display verbose policy information.

Table 20-4   Gpresult Command-Line Options

Option	Description
/z	This option specifies that the output display all available information about Group Policy. Because this option produces more information than the /v option, redirect output to a text file when you use this parameter: **gpresult /z >policy.txt**.
/?	This option displays help.

The following are examples of using this command:

```
gpresult /user jerry /scope computer
gpresult /s camelot /u honeycutt\administrator /p password /user jerry
gpresult /s camelot /u honeycutt\administrator /p password /user jerry /z >policy.txt
```

Gpupdate

The Group Policy Update Tool (Gpupdate.exe) refreshes local and network policy settings, including registry-based settings. As I mentioned, this command replaces the obsolete command secedit /refreshpolicy. The following describes this command's syntax, and Table 20-5 describes each command-line option:

```
gpupdate [/target:{computer|user}] [/force] [/wait:value] [/logoff] [/boot]
```

Table 20-5   Gpresult Command-Line Options

Option	Description
/target:{computer |user}	This option processes only the computer settings or the current user settings. By default, both the computer and user settings are processed.
/force	This option ignores all processing optimizations and reapplies all settings.
/wait:value	This option is the number of seconds that policy processing waits to finish. The default is 600 seconds. 0 means don't wait, and -1 means wait forever.
/logoff	This option logs the user off after the refresh has completed. This is required for those Group Policy client-side extensions that do not process on a background refresh cycle but that do process when the user logs on, such as user Software Installation and Folder Redirection. This option has no effect if there are no extensions called that require the user to log off.
/boot	This option restarts the computer after the refresh is finished. This is required for those Group Policy client-side extensions that do not process on a background refresh cycle but that do process when the computer starts up, such as computer Software Installation. This option has no effect if there are no extensions called that require the computer to be restarted.
/?	This option displays help.

The following are examples of using this command:

```
gpupdate
gpupdate /target:computer
gpupdate /force /wait:100
gpupdate /boot
```

Help and Support Center

Although of limited use for IT professionals because you can't use it remotely, users can run Help and Support Center's RSoP reports on their own computers to check policy settings. This tool provides a user-friendly, printable report of most policies in effect for the computer and console user. Here's how to use this tool:

1. Click Start and then click Help And Support Center.

2. Under Pick A Task, click Use Tools To View Your Computer Information And Diagnose Problems.

3. Click Advanced System Information and then click View Group Policy Settings Applied.

Resultant Set of Policy

Although Help and Support Center's RSoP report isn't suitable for use by IT professionals, the RSoP snap-in is suitable because you can use it to view RSoP data for remote computers. You use this tool to predict how policies work for a specific user or computer, as well as entire groups of users and computers. Sometimes, GPOs applied at different levels in Active Directory conflict with each other. Tracking down these conflicting settings is difficult without a tool like this snap-in.

The RSoP snap-in checks Software Installation for applications associated with the user or computer. It reports all other policy settings, too, including registry-based policies, redirected folders, Internet Explorer maintenance, security settings, and scripts. You've already seen two tools that report RSoP data: Gpresult.exe and Help and Support Center. The RSoP snap-in is almost as easy to use in Windows XP Professional (your account must be in the computer's local Administrators group to use this tool):

1. Click Start, Run, and type **mmc**.

2. Click File, Add/Remove Snap-in and then click Add.

3. In the Available Standalone Snap-ins dialog box, select Resultant Set Of Policy and then click Add.

4. Click Next in the Resultant Set Of Policy Wizard; and click Next again.

5. On the Computer Selection page, click Another Computer, type the name of the computer you want to inspect, and then click Next.

6. On the User Selection page, select the user for which you want to display RSoP data, and then click Next.

7. Click Next and then click Finish to close the wizard.

Figure 20-4 shows the results. In this example, you see the password policies applied to the computer. For each setting, you see the GPO that's the source for it.

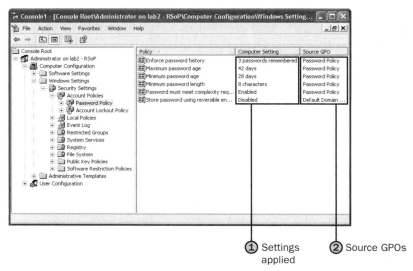

① Settings applied   ② Source GPOs

Figure 20-4   The RSoP snap-in is the best tool for figuring out the source of policy settings when multiple GPOs apply to a computer.

Group Policy Management Console

Group Policy Management Console (GPMC) is a new tool that allows you to manage and maintain enterprise environments in a more cost-effective and efficient way. It consists of a new Microsoft Management Console (MMC) snap-in and a set of scriptable interfaces for managing Group Policy. This tool makes managing Group Policies easier by providing a single place to manage all aspects of your Group Policy design. Microsoft created this tool based on the following customer feedback:

■ A user interface (UI) that makes Group Policy much easier to use

■ Backup/restore of GPOs

■ Import/export and copy/paste of GPOs and Windows Management Instrumentation (WMI) filters

- Simplified management of Group Policy–related security

- HTML reporting of GPO settings and Resultant Set of Policy (RSoP) data

- Scripting of policy-related tasks that are exposed within this tool (not scripting of settings within a GPO)

To run this tool, you must have the following operating requirements:

- Windows Server 2003 (Windows 2000 Server isn't supported).

- Windows XP Professional with Service Pack 1 (SP1) and the Microsoft.NET Framework. In addition, a post-SP1 hotfix (QFE Q326469) is required.

    This QFE updates your version of gpedit.dll to version 5.1.2600.1186, which is required by GPMC. This QFE is included with GPMC, and GPMC setup will prompt you to install it. However, if the language of GPMC does not match the language of your operating system, GPMC will not install the QFE, and you will need to separately obtain and install this QFE. This QFE will be included in Windows XP Professional Service Pack 2.

By using this tool, you can achieve the following:

- Group Policy Management Console Overview Creating and Editing GPOs

- Scoping GPOs

- Group Policy Inheritance

- Delegating Group Policy

- Reporting on GPO Settings

- GPO Details

- GPO Operations (Backup, Restore, Copy, Import, and Migration Tables)

- WMI Filters

- Searching for GPOs

- Group Policy Modeling

- Group Policy Results

- Platform Dependencies

- GPMC Options

- Internet Explorer Enhanced Security Configuration Considerations

- Scripting Group Policy–Related Tasks

For more information about GPMC and to download it, see *http://www.microsoft.com/windowsserver2003/gpmc/gpmcwp.mspx*. Installing GPMC is simple: Just double-click the file you downloaded. Upon completion of the installation, the Group Policy tab that appeared on the Property pages of sites, domains, and OUs in the Active Directory snap-ins is updated to provide a direct link to GPMC. The functionality that previously existed on the original Group Policy tab is no longer available because all functionality for managing Group Policy is available through GPMC.

To open the GPMC snap-in directly, use any of the following methods:

- Run gpmsc.msc.

- Click the Group Policy Management shortcut in the Administrative Tools folder on the Start Menu or in the Control Panel.

- Create a custom MMC console and add the Group Policy Management snap-in.

GPMC integrates the existing Group Policy functionality exposed in these tools into a single unified console, along with several new capabilities. Built-in to GPMC is support for managing multiple domains and forests, making it possible for administrators to easily manage Group Policy across an enterprise. Administrators have complete control of which forests and domains are listed in GPMC, making it possible to display only pertinent parts of an environment. There are a number of operations that can be performed by using the GPMC which adds benefits to any administrator that is using GPOs. Some of them are as follows:

- **Backup**   Transfers the contents of a GPO from Active Directory to the file system; this provides a means to back them up and export or import to other domains. This is extremely important when building the GPOs in a test lab: It allows you to test them first and then import them into your production environment.

- **Restore**   Returns a GPO to the state when it was backed-up. A restore operation can only restore a GPO to the original domain in which the GPO was created because it restores the original GPO ID, policy settings, and ACLs.

- **Import**   Transfers the policy settings from a backed-up GPO in the file system to a GPO in Active Directory. The source GPO can be any backed-up GPO in the file system. The destination GPO must be an existing GPO in Active Directory.

- **Copy**   Transfers the policy settings from an existing GPO in Active Directory to a new GPO in Active Directory. The copy operation creates a new GPO with a new GPO ID and copies the policy settings from the source GPO to the new GPO. Please note that import and copy are similar; but in a copy operation, the source GPO must be in the Active Directory and the operation creates a new GPO with a new GPO ID. In an import operation, the source GPO must be in the file system, and the destination GPO must be an existing GPO in the Active Directory.

Best Practices

The following are best practices for managing Windows XP Professional by using Group Policy:

- Use the best mix of technologies depending on your client operating systems:
  - Homogeneous networks with Windows 2000 Professional and Windows XP Professional: Use Group Policy exclusively to manage user and computer settings.
  - Heterogeneous networks with Active Directory: Use Group Policy to manage Windows 2000 Professional and Windows XP Professional settings; and use System Policy and third-party tools to manage all other versions of Windows.
  - Networks without Active Directory: Use System Policy and third-party tools to manage all versions of Windows.
- In networks using Windows 2000 Server and Active Directory, update the password policies in the Default Domain Policy to the more restrictive default values that Windows Server 2003 uses. See the section "Password Security" on page 575 for more information.
- Configure account lockout policies to prevent dictionary attacks.

Chapter 21

Desktop Management

Deploying standard desktop configurations and managing users' computers and settings reduces the time required to support computer users in your company. Microsoft Windows XP Professional includes desktop management technologies (Microsoft IntelliMirror) that allow you to centrally manage the desktop and ensure that users' data, software, and settings are available to them when they move from one computer to another. Most IntelliMirror features rely on Group Policy, which requires the Microsoft Active Directory directory service. You can use many of these tools and features to manage desktop computers in non-Active Directory environments, though.

Checklist

- Have you designed a standard desktop configuration? See Chapter 1, "Deployment Plan," for more information.

- Have you built and tested your Windows XP Professional distribution points? See Chapter 6, "Answer Files," Chapter 7, "Distribution Points," and Chapter 11, "Chaining Installations," for more information.

- Have you implemented a technique for managing user profiles? See Chapter 12, "User Profiles," for more information.

■ Have you implemented Group Policy in your Active Directory environ-
ment? See Chapter 20, "Policy Management," for more information.
Although most features in this chapter require Active Directory and
Group Policy, many don't.

Management Overview

The desktop management tools available for managing Windows XP Professional
clients differ depending on whether the operating system is running in an Active
Directory environment or in other network environments. IntelliMirror relies on
Group Policy, and most also require Active Directory; both are available in Microsoft
Windows 2000 Server and Microsoft Windows Server 2003 environments. Group
Policy requires Active Directory.

In an environment without Active Directory, you can use a variety of tools,
such as Microsoft Systems Management Server (SMS) for managing software distribution, the Internet Explorer Administration Kit (IEAK) for managing Internet
Explorer settings, and System Policy for managing registry-based settings. In addition, each local computer has its own local Group Policy Object (local GPO), regardless of whether it participates in a domain. Although it is possible to set a variety of
settings via the local GPO, System Policy scales more easily to a large number of clients. The local GPO can be useful if you need to apply only certain settings to a small
number of Windows XP Professional clients in a Windows NT 4.0 or other domain.

For Windows XP Professional desktops operating in other environments, such
as Microsoft Windows NT version 4; UNIX or Novell; or in a mixed environment, the
desktop management tools differ. Table 21-1 summarizes the differences in desktop
management tools between Active Directory and other environments.

Table 21-1   Desktop Management Overview

Task	Active Directory	Other
Configure registry-based settings for computers and users	■ Administrative templates deployed by using Group Policy ■ Administrative templates, deployed via local GPO	■ System Policy ■ Local GPO
Manage local, domain, and network security	■ Security Settings deployed via Group Policy ■ Security Settings deployed via local GPO	■ Local GPO
Centrally install, update, and remove software	■ SMS ■ Group Policy–based software distribution	■ SMS

Table 21-1 **Desktop Management Overview**

Task	Active Directory	Other
Manage Internet Explorer configuration settings after deployment	■ Internet Explorer Maintenance in the Group Policy Microsoft Management Console (MMC) snap-in ■ Internet Explorer Maintenance deployed via local GPO ■ IEAK	■ Local GPO ■ IEAK
Apply scripts during user logon/logoff and computer startup/shutdown	■ Logon/logoff and startup/shutdown scripts can be centrally configured via Group Policy or independently through the local GPO	■ Local GPO
Centrally manage users' folders and files on the network	■ Folder Redirection in conjunction with Offline Files and Folders	■ System Policy ■ Manipulation of registry settings
Centrally manage user settings on the network	■ Roaming User Profiles	■ Roaming User Profiles (for Windows domains)

You can also manage Windows XP Professional desktops on UNIX and Novell networks by using standards-based protocols such as TCP/IP, Simple Network Management Protocol (SNMP), Telnet, and Internetwork Packet Exchange (IPX). To enable policy-based administration on UNIX and Novell networks, use a local Group Policy object or System Policy.

Active Directory Environments

When you use Windows XP Professional in Active Directory environments, you can take full advantage of IntelliMirror and Group Policy management features. If you're managing Windows XP Professional desktops on networks without Active Directory, see the section "Non-Active Directory Environments," later in this chapter on page 625. IntelliMirror allows you to manage desktops from a central location, saving you significant time while improving manageability. It ensures that users' data, software, and personal settings are available when they move from one computer to another, whether or not their computers are connected to the network.

IntelliMirror has four components: user data management, user settings management, computer settings management, and Group Policy–based software installation and maintenance. These components are based on Group Policy, roaming user profiles, and Offline Files. These components help you do the following:

- Centrally create and manage the configuration of each user's desktop.

- Enable users to access files from any location at any time by using roaming user profiles and Folder Redirection in combination with Offline Files.

- Manage the way software is deployed and installed on computers to ensure that users have the software they need to perform their jobs. Large organizations that need advanced software distribution and inventory capabilities should consider SMS. See Chapter 17, "Systems Management Server," for more information.

- Manage and enforce centralized data storage, which helps you back up important corporate data.

- Save time when replacing computers by using Remote Installation Services (RIS) and Group Policy–based software installation and maintenance to easily replace applications, roaming user profiles to recover user profiles, and Folder Redirection to centrally manage files. You can also use Group Policy to manage RIS by centrally setting client configuration options.

More Info   See Chapter 16, "Remote Installation Service," and Chapter 20 for more information.

Active Directory and Group Policy provide the foundation for implementing IntelliMirror. The following sections describe the IntelliMirror features. Without Active Directory, you can't take full advantage of IntelliMirror for managing clients.

More Info   The section "Non-Active Directory Environments" on page 625 describes the tools you can use for managing Windows XP Professional clients. Chapter 20 provides detailed information about Group Policy. For more information about planning and implementing Active Directory, see the Windows Server 2003 Deployment Kit.

Active Directory and Group Policy

Active Directory stores information about all physical and logical objects on the network. This information is automatically replicated across the network to simplify finding and managing data, no matter where the data is located in the organization. The Active Directory structure you create determines how you apply Group Policy settings. In an Active Directory environment, Group Policy allows you to define and control the state of computers and users in an organization. Group Policy allows you to control more than 600 customizable settings that you can use to centrally configure and manage users and computers.

Depending on the size of your organization, managing desktops, users, and their permissions can be a very complex task, especially because changes constantly happen. For example, users join and leave organizations, get promoted and transferred, and regularly change offices. Similarly, printers, computers, and network file shares are frequently added, removed, and relocated. When implemented in a Windows 2000 Active Directory infrastructure, Group Policy–based IntelliMirror features greatly simplify managing these ongoing changes. Once set, Group Policy automatically maintains the state you design without requiring further intervention.

User Data Management

Files that users create are user data. Examples are word processing documents, spreadsheets, or graphics files. User data belongs to the user and is located on the user's computer or on a network share to which the user has rights. Less-obvious forms of user data include Microsoft Internet Explorer cookies and Favorites and customized templates. User data is usually hard to re-create, such as a template that that a user has customized. With IntelliMirror, users can transparently access their data from any computer on the network that's running Windows XP Professional, regardless of whether or not that computer is their primary computer. IntelliMirror technologies that support user data management include these:

- **Folder Redirection** You can redirect user data to a network share, where it can be backed up as part of routine system maintenance. You can do this so that the process is transparent to the user. I recommend that you train users to store all user data in My Documents and then redirect the folder to a network share. This capability helps you to enforce corporate policy such as storing business-critical data on servers that are centrally managed by the IT staff. If users are in the habit of storing documents on their desktop, you should also consider redirecting the desktop. Although you can redirect the Application Data folder, this is generally recommended only in the following cases:

- To reduce the size of the profile, decreasing logon time on multiuser computers where you have enabled a Group Policy setting to delete cached profiles. This gives users access to their application data, but without the need to download possibly large files every time they log on to the computer.

- To reduce the size of the profile in situations in which keeping initial logon time short is a top priority, such as on terminals.

- For Terminal Services clients.

- **Offline Files and Synchronization Manager**   By using Offline Files and Synchronization Manager, you can ensure that the most up-to-date versions of a user's data reside on both the local computer and on the server. You can use Offline Files in conjunction with Folder Redirection to make available offline those folders that have been redirected to a server. Users can manually configure which files and folders are available offline, or you can configure them through Group Policy. The file is stored on a server, and the file on the local computer is synchronized with the network copy. Changes made while offline are synchronized with the server when the user reconnects to the network. With Windows XP Professional, Offline Files supports Distributed File System (DFS) and Encrypting File System (EFS).

- **Roaming User Profiles**   Although profiles are commonly used as a method of managing user settings (such as a user's shortcuts and other customizations of their environment), the profile also contains user data, including Favorites and Cookies. When roaming user profiles are enabled, users can access this data when they log on to any computer on the network. Windows XP Professional Group Policy settings allow the profile to roam correctly and free up system memory.

User Settings Management

With the user settings management tools in Windows XP Professional, you can centrally define computing environments for groups of users, and grant or deny users the ability to further customize their environments. You can reduce support calls by providing a preconfigured desktop environment appropriate for the user's job. You can save time and costs when replacing computers by automatically restoring the user's settings. You can help users be more efficient by automatically providing their desktop environment, no matter where they work.

The primary IntelliMirror features that support user settings management are roaming user profiles and administrative templates. To learn about using administrative templates, see Chapter 20. The settings in administrative templates control the desktop with pre-defined configurations. A user profile contains the per-user hive file, which contains the user's settings, and a set of profile folders that store files, like desktop icons, links, and so on. See Chapter 12 for more information.

By default, user profiles are on the local computer; Windows XP Professional creates one profile for each user who has logged on to that computer. By configuring user profiles to roam, you can ensure that Windows XP Professional copies the settings in users' profiles to a network server when they log off from their computers and are available to them no matter where they next log on to the network. Although useful for roaming users, roaming user profiles are also beneficial for users who always use the same computer. For these users, roaming user profiles provide a transparent way to back up their profile to a network server, protecting the information from individual system failure. If a user's primary workstation needs to be replaced, the new computer receives the user's profile from the server as soon as the user logs on.

Some folders in a user profile cannot be configured to roam; these folders are in the Local Settings folder and include the subfolders Application Data, History, Temp, and Temporary Internet Files. These folders contain application data that is not required to roam with the user, such as temporary files, noncritical settings, and data too large to roam effectively. This data is not copied to and from the server when a user logs on or logs off.

As an example of using roaming and nonroaming folders, you might configure Internet Explorer to store a user's Favorites in the roaming portion of the user profile and store the temporary Internet files in the local, nonroaming portion of the user profile. By default, the History, Local Settings, Temp, and Temporary Internet Files folders are excluded from the roaming user profile. You can configure additional folders to not roam by specifying them in Group Policy: User Configuration\Administrative Templates\System\User Profiles\Exclude directories in roaming profile.

Computer Settings Management

Group Policy allows you to customize and restrict desktop computers on your network. For optimal control, use GPOs in an Active Directory network to centralize computer management. However, if you aren't using Active Directory, you can control security on a computer-by-computer basis by using the local GPO. Each computer has one local GPO that you can use to manage the computer outside of an Active Directory environment. If you configure desktop security this way, make sure to set workstation security to match corporate policy. You can configure these policies on a disk image, too.

The Computer Configuration tree in the Group Policy MMC snap-in includes the local computer-related Group Policy settings that specify operating system behavior, desktop behavior, application settings, security settings, computer-assigned application options, and computer startup and shutdown scripts. Computer-related Group Policy settings are applied when the operating system starts up and during periodic refresh cycles. You can also customize computer configuration settings by using the Group Policy MMC snap-in, thus simplifying individual computer setup.

Group Policy Desktop Management

Group Policy is the primary tool for defining and controlling how programs, network resources, and Windows XP Professional behave for users and computers in an organization. Group Policy settings are contained in Group Policy objects (GPOs) created by using the Group Policy MMC snap-in.

Using Group Policy in an Active Directory environment, you can specify a user or computer configuration once and then rely on Windows XP Professional to enforce that configuration on all affected client computers until you change it. After you apply Group Policy, the system maintains the state without further intervention.

You can define configurations by implementing Group Policy settings from a central location for hundreds or even thousands of users or computers at one time. For example, you might use Group Policy to install Microsoft Office 2003 Editions on all computers used by members of the Sales department, prevent temporary employees from accessing Control Panel, or manage access to adding or removing hardware.

Don't confuse Group Policy settings with preferences. You configure Group Policy settings, and Windows XP Professional enforces them automatically. Preferences are system settings and configuration options, such as a screen saver or the view in My Documents that users set and alter without an administrator's intervention. Group Policy settings take precedence over preferences.

Group Policy Software Distribution

Although the advanced software deployment and management features of SMS offer distinct advantages in enterprise-sized organizations—such as inventory, diagnosis, and monitoring—Group Policy provides some capability to deploy software to workstations and servers running Windows XP Professional. With Group Policy–based software deployment, you can target groups of users and computers based on their location in the directory. Group Policy–based software deployment uses Windows Installer as the installation engine on the local computer.

The Software Installation and Maintenance component allows you to efficiently deploy, patch, upgrade, and remove software applications without visiting each desktop. This gives users reliable access to the applications that they need to perform their jobs, no matter which computer they are using. Group Policy–based software distribution enables you to do the following:

- Centrally deploy new software, upgrade applications, deploy patches and operating system upgrades, and remove previously deployed applications that are no longer required.

- Ensure that users have the software they need to be productive without an administrator or technical support person having to visit each computer.

- Create a standard desktop operating environment that results in uninterrupted user productivity and straightforward administration.

- Maintain version control of software for all desktop computers in the organization.

- Identify and diagnose Group Policy setting failures by using Resultant Set of Policy (RSoP) in logging mode.

- Deploy in combination with Windows Installer 64-bit applications as well as 32-bit applications.

Using the Software Installation extension of the Group Policy MMC snap-in, you can centrally manage the installation of software on a client computer, either by assigning applications to users or computers or by publishing applications for users. The following choices are available, as Chapter 20 describes and Table 21-2 shows:

- **Assign software to users** As an administrator, you can install applications assigned to users the first time they log on after deployment, or you can have the application and its components install on demand as the user invokes that functionality.

- **Assign software to computers** When you assign an application to a computer, the installation occurs the next time the computer starts up, and the application is available for all the users on that computer.

- **Publish software for users** You can publish applications for users only. Those users can choose to install the software from a list of published applications located in Add Or Remove Programs in Control Panel. Add Or Remove Programs includes an active Web link that is associated with each application that provides users with the support information they need to install certain applications.

Table 21-2   Assigning and Publishing Software

Situation or Condition	Publish	Assign to User (Install on Demand)	Assign to User (Full Install)	Assign to Computer
After the administrator deploys the software, it is available for installation:	The next time the user, to whom this application's Group Policy setting applies, logs on. It is also immediately visible in Add Or Remove Programs.	The next time the user, to whom this application's Group Policy setting applies, logs on. It is also immediately visible in Add Or Remove Programs.	The next time the user logs on. It is also immediately visible in Add Or Remove Programs.	The next time the computer is started.
The software is installed:	By the user from Add Or Remove Programs or, optionally, by opening an associated document (for applications deployed to auto-install).	By the user from the Start menu or a desktop shortcut or by opening an associated document.	Automatically when the user logs on.	Automatically when the computer is started.
The software is not installed, and the user opens a file associated with the software:	The software installs only if Auto-Install is selected.	The software installs.	Does not apply. The software is already installed.	Does not apply. The software is already installed.
The user wants to remove the software by using Add Or Remove Programs:	The user can uninstall the software, and subsequently choose to install it again by using Add Or Remove Programs.	The user can uninstall the software, but it is reassigned the next time the user logs on. It is available for installation again from the typical software distribution points.	The user can uninstall the software, but it is reassigned the next time the user logs on. It is available for installation again from the typical installation points.	Only the local administrator and the network administrator can remove the software.

Non-Active Directory Environments

On a network not running the Active Directory directory service, you can implement the following IntelliMirror and Group Policy features to manage Windows XP Professional:

- Roaming user profiles and logon scripts
- Folder Redirection
- Internet Explorer Maintenance
- System Policy
- Local GPO

Roaming User Profiles

In a Windows NT 4.0 domain, you can use both roaming user profiles and logon scripts to manage user settings.

> **More Info** For more information about each topic, see Chapter 12.

My Documents Redirection

In a Windows NT 4.0 domain, you can redirect My Documents and its subfolders Application Data, Desktop, and the Start menu to a local or network location by using the following methods:

- You can use System Policy to redirect these folders, which provides only limited functionality compared with true Folder Redirection because you can't actually move folder contents or set access control lists (ACLs).
- Users can manually redirect the My Documents folder by changing the target folder location in the My Documents Properties page.
- Manipulation of registry settings.

> **Note** You can't configure Folder Redirection by using a local GPO.

Internet Explorer Maintenance

Instead of using Group Policy to control Internet Explorer settings, you can use the IEAK to apply settings to Internet Explorer clients by using autoconfiguration packages. You can download IEAK from Microsoft's Web site at *http://www.microsoft.com /downloads.*

> **More Info** For more detailed information about using IEAK, see Chapter 10, "Internet Explorer Settings."

System Policy

Like Active Directory–based Group Policy objects, System Policy can define a specific user's settings or the settings for a group of users. The resulting policy file contains the registry information for all users, groups, and computers that will use the policy file. Separate policy files for each user, group, or computer are not necessary.

Group Policy includes the functionality from Windows NT 4.0 System Policy. It also provides additional policy settings for scripts, Software Installation and Maintenance, security settings, Internet Explorer maintenance, and folder redirection. Table 21-3 compares Group Policy and Windows NT 4.0 System Policy.

Table 21-3 Comparison of Group Policy and System Policy

Comparison	Group Policy	System Policy
Tool used	MMC Group Policy snap-in	System Policy Editor (Poledit.exe)
Number of settings	More than 150 security-related settings and more than 620 registry-based settings	72 settings
Applied to	Users or computers in a specified Active Directory container (site, domain, or organizational unit [OU]) or local computers and users	Domains or local computers and users
Security	Secure	Not secure
Extensible by	Using MMC or .adm files	Using .adm files
Persistence	Does not leave settings in the users' profiles when the effective policy is changed	Persistent in users' profiles until the specified policy is reversed or until you edit the registry
Defined by	User or computer membership in security groups	User membership in security groups

Table 21-3   Comparison of Group Policy and System Policy

Comparison	Group Policy	System Policy
Primary uses	■ Implementing registry-based settings to control the desktop and user ■ Configuring many types of security settings ■ Applying logon, logoff, startup, and shutdown scripts ■ Implementing IntelliMirror Software Installation and Maintenance ■ Implementing IntelliMirror data and settings management ■ Optimizing and maintaining Internet Explorer	Implementing registry-based settings that govern the behavior of applications and operating system components such as the Start Menu

Note   System Policy settings applied to computers that have been upgraded to Windows XP Professional are persistent in ("tattoo") the registry. Applying Group Policy to a computer with persistent registry-based System Policy settings might have unpredictable results. It is recommended that you remove these settings from computers before applying GPOs.

Windows XP Professional clients in an Active Directory environment can process Group Policy, but can't process Windows NT 4.0 System Policy. Windows NT 4.0 policies are persistent in user profiles. This means that after a registry-based setting is applied by using Windows NT 4.0 System Policy, the setting persists until the specified policy is reversed or until you edit the registry to remove the corresponding entry. The effect of persistent registry-based settings can cause conflicts when a user's group membership changes. If the Windows XP Professional computer account object or user account object that you manage exists in a Windows NT 4.0 domain, you can still use certain System Policy tools to manage them.

More Info   For detailed information about configuring and deploying System Policy, see Chapter 20.

Local Group Policy Object

In addition to setting System Policy, you can configure settings in the local GPO for any computer, whether or not it participates in an Active Directory domain. Although System Policy scales more easily to a large number of clients, the local GPO can be useful if you need to apply only certain settings to a small number of Windows XP Professional clients in a Windows NT 4.0 or other domain.

The local GPO is in %SYSTEMROOT%\System32\GroupPolicy. Not all Group Policy extensions are available for the local GPO. Each Group Policy extension snap-in queries the Group Policy engine to get the GPO type and then determines whether the GPO is to be displayed. To set the local GPO, use the Group Policy snap-in focused on the local computer.

Table 21-4 shows which Group Policy snap-in extensions open when the Group Policy snap-in is focused on a local GPO.

Table 21-4   Local GPO Extensions

Group Policy Snap-in Extension	Available In Local GPO
Software Installation	No
Scripts	Yes
Security Settings	Yes
Administrative Templates	Yes
Folder Redirection	No
Internet Explorer Maintenance	Yes
RIS	No

UNIX and Novell Environments

You can use local GPOs and System Policy to manage Windows XP Professional in Novell and UNIX environments. You can also perform typical desktop-management tasks that are based on industry-standard protocols, such as Telnet and SNMP, a standards-based TCP/IP network management protocol that is implemented in many environments. For more information about using local GPOs and System Policy, see "Non-active Directory Environments," earlier in this chapter on page 625.

Standards-Based Management

Windows XP Professional provides full support for SNMP, allowing you to easily manage systems that run Windows XP Professional by using a UNIX-based SNMP management suite available from independent software vendors.

Telnet Client and Server

You can use Telnet to remotely log on to and execute commands on Windows XP Professional. The Telnet client included with Windows XP Professional is character- and console-based, and is enhanced for advanced remote management capabilities. The Windows XP Professional Telnet client also provides NTLM authentication support. With this feature, a Windows XP Professional Telnet client can log on to a Windows XP Professional Telnet server that uses NTLM authentication.

Novell NetWare IPX Network

IPX is the native NetWare protocol used on many earlier Novell networks. You can integrate Network Connections clients into a NetWare IPX network, with the exception of clients running Microsoft Windows XP Professional 64-Bit Edition. The client must run a NetWare redirector to see a Novell NetWare network. This redirector is called Client Service for NetWare (CSNW).

A remote access server is also an IPX router and Service Advertising Protocol (SAP) agent. Once configured, remote access servers enable file and print services and the use of Windows Sockets programs over IPX on the NetWare network for Network Connections clients. Remote access servers and their Network Connections clients use the Point-to-Point (PPP) IPX Control Protocol (IPXCP), as defined in RFC 1552, "The PPP Internetwork Packet Exchange Control Protocol (IPXCP)," to configure the remote access line for IPX.

Network Connections clients are always provided an IPX address by the remote access server. The IPX network number is generated automatically by the remote access server, or a static pool of network numbers is given to the remote access server for assignment to Network Connections. For automatically generated IPX network numbers, the remote access server uses the NetWare Router Information Protocol (RIP) to determine an IPX network number that is not in use in the IPX network. The remote access server assigns that number to the connection. Configure a connection by selecting NWLink IPX/SPX/NetBIOS Compatible Transport Protocol on the General tab of Local Area Connection Properties.

Novell ZENworks

To use Novell ZENworks, you must register Windows XP Professional with ZENworks. A workstation record can then be imported into the Novell Directory Services (NDS) database of a Novell NetWare network. The workstation is registered by running Wsreg32.exe either from the command line or from a logon script. The following is an example of the logon script code that detects Windows XP Professional and runs the correct registry program:

```
IF " %PLATFORM" =" WINDOWS_NT" THEN BEGIN
    #F:\PUBLIC\WSREG32.EXE
END
```

After the workstation is registered, you can import it into NDS by using Nnwadmn32.exe. You can administer Windows XP Professional–based clients by using the standard ZENworks tools.

Standardized Desktop Configurations

IntelliMirror and Group Policy allow you to manage desktops with great efficiency. To take full advantage of these benefits, it is recommended that you define and set up standard configurations. You must carefully adapt a standard configuration to the target users' applications, tasks, and locations. It can also increase productivity by preventing users from making system changes that could cause downtime. Because standard configurations are easier to troubleshoot or replace, they can also reduce support costs.

IntelliMirror and Group Policy are designed for use in environments in which administrators need to centralize tasks such as the following:

- Creating managed desktops
- Managing mobile users
- Managing new users
- Managing multiuser desktops
- Replacing computers

Creating Managed Desktops

The managed desktop contains settings that can lower the cost of ownership of a desktop for any user. This configuration can reduce help desk costs and user downtime by providing users with just the applications and tools they need to perform their jobs. The user is permitted to install approved applications and make extensive customizations of applications and the desktop environment.

At the same time, the managed desktop configuration can keep users from making potentially harmful changes to configuration settings, such as adding or disabling hardware devices; or changing system or user environment settings, such as the location of the My Documents folder; and can restrict access to such features as the MMC administration snap-ins and some hardware-configuration items in Control Panel. The user for this configuration does not usually require access to Network Connections. Table 21-5 shows the desktop management features used to create a typical managed desktop configuration.

Table 21-5   Features of a Managed Desktop Configuration

Feature	Specifics	Explanation
Multiple Users	Per-user logon accounts	Users might share this computer during different shifts. Each user has a unique logon account.
Roaming User Profiles	Yes	Makes user settings available from any computer and enables administrators to easily replace computers without losing user configuration.
Folder Redirection	My Documents folder	User data is saved on server shares and Group Policy prevents users from storing data locally.
Ability For User To Customize	Most	Allows users to personalize their work environment while preventing changes to critical system settings.
Assigned Applications	Multiple	Core applications are automatically installed before the user logs on.
Published Applications	Multiple	All required applications are available for users to install locally.
Group Policy Settings	Yes	Group Policy settings are used to create the managed environment.

Managing Mobile Users

Many organizations have mobile users—traveling employees who use a portable computer. Mobile users have unique needs because, although these users usually log on to the same computer, they sometimes connect through a high-speed line and sometimes through a low-speed line, and some mobile users never have a fast connection. Such users fall into two main categories:

- **Users who spend the majority of time away from the office or have no fixed office** Typically, these users connect by using slow links, although they might have occasional LAN access to their logon server, data servers, and application-delivery servers.

- **Users who spend most of their time in an office, but occasionally work at home or in another location** The majority of their network access is at LAN speed, but they occasionally use the Routing and Remote Access service or remote network links.

Despite the apparent differences between these two types of users, you can generally accommodate them with a single configuration. However, you might want to consider creating a slightly different GPO for users who spend the majority of their time out of the office.

Mobile users are often expected to provide much of their own computer support because on-site support is not available. For this reason, you might want to grant them more privileges than equivalent users on a desktop computer (for example, so they can install printers). You might, however, decide to restrict mobile users from making system changes that might damage or disable their systems. For example, you might restrict mobile users from altering certain Internet Explorer settings or adding unapproved hardware devices. Although these users might need access to some of the MMC administration snap-ins, you can make available only a restricted set.

Mobile users expect transparent access to the most critical parts of their data and settings, regardless of whether the portable computer is connected to the network. They roam to desktop computers while their portable computer is in use; for example, to read mail while they are in a remote office. Finally, mobile users frequently disconnect their portable computer from the network without logging off and shutting down. This is more likely to happen with the hibernate and standby features of Windows XP Professional.

IntelliMirror provides several tools that greatly simplify managing mobile users. User data and settings management tools allow users to work on files offline and automatically update network versions of those files when they later reconnect to the network. The Offline Files feature allows users to work on network files when they are not actually connected to the network. Synchronization Manager coordinates synchronization of any changes between the offline version of a file and the network version. Synchronization Manager also helps manage multiuser network files. If multiple users modify the same network file, Synchronization Manager notifies the users about the conflict and offers several resolution methods. The users can save the network version, their local version, or both versions. If both are to be kept, the user is asked for a new filename to store one of the versions so that uniqueness is maintained.

Note   If users are likely to disconnect from the network without logging off, it is recommended that you set Offline Files to periodically synchronize in the background. If Offline Files is set to synchronize only when users log off, users' files might not be up to date. You might also want to educate users to manually synchronize their data before disconnecting from the network to ensure that all files are up to date.

Software installation for the mobile user requires some additional planning. You can make sure that all important software components, defined by you or the user, are completely installed initially. This allows the user access to necessary software even when he or she is not connected to the network. Thus, prior to these users leaving the office, you must ensure that all relevant features within the application are installed locally and are not just advertised. For example, make sure that the spelling checker for Microsoft Office 2003 Editions is locally installed so that the user does not trigger on-demand installation of this feature while offline.

It is not recommended that you publish software for mobile users who connect over slow links. Additionally, when mobile users connect over a slow link, user-assigned software effectively behaves the same as if you published it for these users. If you set the Group Policy slow-link detection setting to the default in the user interface, the software does not install on demand. However, you can define the connection speed that is considered to be a slow link in the Group Policy setting for slow-link detection. Treat any link that is slower than local area network (LAN) speed as a slow link. If you determine that it is appropriate for mobile users to download software from a remote location and they experience difficulty staying connected when downloading the software, you can verify that the connection speed and Group Policy settings are set appropriately in the Group Policy slow-link detection setting in Computer Configuration/Administrative Templates/System/Group Policy or User Configuration/Administrative Templates/System/Group Policy.

Typically, a mobile user has a single portable computer and does not roam between portable computers (unless the computer is replaced). However, roaming user profiles are useful to give some measure of protection against mobile computer failure or loss and to allow roaming to desktop computers when the mobile user is often connected to a fast network. When the mobile user is not often connected to a fast network, it is best not to use roaming user profiles.

Data accessed by the mobile user often falls into one or more of the following categories:

- Data that resides on a network server that users want to access while not connected to the network. Users typically own this data (for example, their home directory), but shared data can also be stored on the local computer.

- Data that resides only on the network server (either not needed offline or volatile shared data that is inappropriate for storing offline).

- Data that resides only on the portable computer local disk. Examples are policy manuals or other read-only items or large document sets that are needed offline by the user, but the performance overhead of synchronizing precludes storing them on a file server. (In this case, a suitable backup mechanism is definitely needed.) Other examples might be large database files or other data items that have their own synchronization mechanism, such as the offline storage feature in Microsoft Office Outlook.

Table 21-6 summarizes desktop management features you can use to create a mobile user configuration.

Table 21-6   Features of a Mobile User Configuration

Feature	Specifics	Explanation
Number Of Users	One	Each user has a local logon account.
Roaming User Profiles	Yes, depending on connection type and frequency	Provides centralized storage of user state to help administrators replace computers without losing user configuration. Also facilitates roaming.
Folder Redirection	My Documents folder	Allows users to access centrally stored data and documents from anywhere. Redirected folders are automatically made available offline to provide access when users are not connected to the network.
Ability For User To Customize	Within certain guidelines	Allows users to personalize their work environment while preventing changes to critical system settings.
Assigned Applications	Multiple	Core applications are installed on all laptops.
Published Applications	Multiple	Optional applications are available for users to install locally.
Group Policy Settings	Yes	Policy settings are used to create the managed environment.

More Info   For more information about supporting mobile users, see Appendix A, "Mobile Scenarios."

Managing New Users

IntelliMirror, Group Policy, Windows Installer, and RIS greatly streamline adding new users and their computers to your network. You might use these technologies as follows to add a new managed user.

A new user logs on to a new computer and finds shortcuts to documents on the desktop. These shortcuts link to common files, data, and URLs such as the employee handbook, the company intranet, and appropriate departmental guidelines and procedures. Desktop options, application configurations, Internet settings, and so on are configured to the corporate standard. As the user customizes his or her environment (within boundaries defined by the administrator), these changes are added to the initial environment. For example, the user might change the screen resolution for better visibility and might add shortcuts to the desktop.

In this situation, a default domain profile and Group Policy are used to configure the new user's environment based on job requirements. The advantage of using a default domain profile is that all new users start from a common, administrator-defined configuration in an existing domain structure. You create a customized domain profile that applies to all new domain users the first time they log on, and they receive the customized settings from this profile. Then, as the user personalizes desktop settings and items, these settings are saved in the user's profile that is stored locally; or, in the case of a roaming user profile, in a predetermined location on the network. By implementing a default domain profile in conjunction with roaming user profiles, the administrator provides users with the necessary business information as a starting point and also allows them to access their settings whenever and wherever needed. Finally, the administrator uses Folder Redirection to redirect the user's My Documents folder to a network location, so that the user's documents are safely stored on a network server and can be backed up regularly.

The administrator uses the Software Installation and Maintenance extension of Group Policy to assign Microsoft Word to a user or a specific group of users. The new user logs on for the first time and sees that the software, required to do his job, is listed in the Start menu. When the user selects Microsoft Word from the Start menu or double-clicks a Word document, Windows Installer checks to see whether the application is installed on the local computer. If it is not, Windows Installer downloads and installs the necessary files for Word to run and sets up the necessary local user and computer settings for an on-demand installation.

Managing Multiuser Desktops

A multiuser desktop is managed but allows users to configure parts of their own desktops. The multiuser desktop is ideal for public shared access computers, such as those in a library, university laboratory, or public computing center. The multiuser desktop experiences high traffic and must be reliable and unbreakable while being flexible enough to allow some customization.

Users can change their desktop wallpaper and color scheme. Because many different people use the computers and security must be maintained, they cannot control or configure hardware or connection settings. The computers often require certain tools, such as word processing software, spreadsheet software, or a development studio. Students might need access to customized applications for instructional purposes and need to be able to install applications that the network administrator has published.

With the multiuser desktop configuration, users can do the following:

- Modify Internet Explorer and the desktop
- Run assigned or published applications
- Configure some Control Panel options

However, users cannot do the following:

- Use the Run command in the Start menu or at a command prompt
- Add, remove, or modify hardware devices

In the multiuser environment, turnover is high and a user is unlikely to return to the same computer. Therefore, local copies of roaming user profiles that are cached on the computer are removed after the user logs off if the roaming user profile settings were successfully synchronized back to the server. Roaming user profiles use the My Documents and Application Data folders that are redirected to a network folder. However, users can log on even if their network profile is not available. In this case, the user receives a new profile based on the default profile.

The multiuser computer is assigned a set of core applications that is available to all users who log on to that particular computer. In addition, a wide variety of applications is available by publishing for user or assigning to users. Due to security risks, users cannot install from a disk, CD-ROM, or Internet location. To conserve disk space on the workstation, most applications must be configured to run from a network server. Start menu shortcuts and registry-based settings are configured when the user selects an application to install, but most of the application's files remain on the server. The shares that store the applications can be configured for automatic caching for programs so that application files are cached at the workstation on first use.

Table 21-7 shows the desktop management features used to create a multiuser computing environment.

Table 21-7 Features of a Multiuser Desktop Configuration

Feature	Specifics	Explanation
Multiple Users	Per-user logon accounts	Users share this computer during different shifts. Each user has a unique logon account.
Roaming User Profiles	Yes	Makes user settings available from any computer and enables administrators to easily replace computers without losing their configuration. When the user logs off, the local cached version of the profile is removed to preserve disk space.
Folder Redirection	My Documents and Application Data	User data is saved on server shares and Group Policy prevents users from storing data locally.
Ability For User To Customize	Some	Most of the system is locked down, but some personal settings are available.
Assigned Applications	Multiple	Core applications that are common to all users are assigned to the computer. Other applications are available for on-demand install by means of user assignment.

Table 21-7   Features of a Multiuser Desktop Configuration

Feature	Specifics	Explanation
Published Applications	Multiple	Applications are available for users to install from Add Or Remove Programs in Control Panel.
Group Policy Settings	Yes	Group Policy settings are used to create the managed environment.

Replacing Computers

When a user receives a new or different computer, it can cause a time-consuming interruption in productivity. It is extremely important that such users regain productivity in the shortest possible time and with a minimum of support. This can be accomplished by storing user data and settings independently of any specific computer. By using the Group Policy features, roaming user profiles, and Folder Redirection, you can assure that the user's data, settings, and applications are available wherever the user logs on to the network.

To further simplify setting up a new managed computer on your network, use RIS to create standardized operating system configurations. RIS allows you to create a customized image of a Windows XP Professional or Windows 2000 Professional desktop from a source computer. Then you can save that desktop image to the RIS server. The image can include the operating system alone or a preconfigured desktop image, including the operating system and a standard, locally installed desktop application. You can use that preconfigured image to set up multiple desktops, saving valuable time. Create as many standard desktop images as you need to meet the needs of all types of users in your organization. For more information about using RIS, see Chapter 16.

These technologies might work together as follows:

1. A user's computer suddenly undergoes a complete hardware failure. The user calls the internal support line. Shortly, a new computer, loaded only with the Windows XP Professional operating system, arrives. Without waiting for technical assistance, the user plugs in the new computer, connects it to the network, starts it, and can immediately log on.

2. Because roaming user profiles are enabled, the user finds that the desktop takes on the same configuration as the computer it replaced: the same color scheme; screen saver; and all the application icons, shortcuts, and favorites are present. Because folder redirection and software installation are enabled, the user can seamlessly access data files on the server using the necessary productivity applications after they automatically install.

Best Practices

The following are best practices for managing Windows XP Professional desktop:

- **Create standardized desktop configurations.**   Standard desktop configurations reduce deployment costs, support costs, and deployment errors.

- **In Active Directory environments, use Group Policy to manage settings.**   Group Policy is available in Active Directory environments, and it's the preferred technology for managing user and computer settings.

- **In non-Active Directory environments, use System Policy and local GPOs to manage settings.**   Both System Policy and local GPOs are available for networks that aren't using Active Directory. Use System Policy to deploy settings to large numbers of computers and local GPOs for small numbers of computers.

Chapter 22

Patch Management

Keeping Microsoft Windows XP Professional and Microsoft Office 2003 Editions updated is important to your organization's success. Not only is it important for the obvious reasons of keeping your computers healthy and maintaining application compatibility, but keeping Windows XP Professional and Office 2003 Editions updated with current service packs and hotfixes protects your organization's security by closing vulnerabilities in both products.

Checklist

- Have you evaluated the latest service pack to determine whether you need to deploy it or not? For more information, see the Microsoft Knowledge Base at *http://support.microsoft.com*.

- Do you have an inventory of which computers are current and which aren't? See Chapter 17, "Systems Management Server," for more information about using it to inventory your environment.

- Do you have computers that are already running the current version of Windows XP Professional that require updating to the current service pack? If so, consider using the update installation as described in the section "Deploying Service Packs," later in this chapter on page 645.

■ Are you deploying Windows XP Professional to your desktop computers and want to include the latest service pack in that distribution? If so, consider using the integrated installation as described in the section "Slipstreaming Service Packs," later in this chapter on page 649.

■ Do you have a method in place for deploying hotfixes and security fixes as they come from Microsoft? See "Deploying Hotfixes," later in this chapter on page 651. Also, see Chapter 17 and Chapter 19, "Software Update Services."

Obtaining Service Packs

Windows XP Professional service packs come from Microsoft in two forms. You can receive the service pack on a CD or from *http://www.microsoft.com/downloads*. Only the full versions of service packs are available on CDs, but there are two options for installing service packs from the Web site:

■ **Express installation** This installation option detects the components installed on the destination computer and installs only those files that are necessary to update the destination computer. This method ensures that the entire service pack is loaded on your system and is recommended for end users who want to reduce their download time.

■ **Network download** This installation option downloads all the service pack files. This is an ideal download mechanism for administrators who want to set up a network share for deployment. For our purposes, I'll consider only this option in this book because it's the only option appropriate for desktop deployment.

The actual name of the service pack file depends on the version of Windows and the service pack number. Table 22-1 describes the service packs that Microsoft has released for Microsoft Windows 2000 and Windows XP Professional. Windows XP Professional service packs have names like XPsp*n*.exe.

Table 22-1   Service Pack Files

Windows Version	Service Pack Number	Filename
Windows 2000	SP1	W2Ksp1.exe
Windows 2000	SP2	W2Ksp2.exe
Windows 2000	SP3	W2Ksp3.exe
Windows XP Professional	SP1	XPsp1.exe
Windows XP Professional	SP1a	XPsp1a.exe

> **More Info**   For more information about Windows XP Professional service
> packs, see "Microsoft Windows XP Service Pack 1 Installation and Deploy-
> ment Guide" at *http://www.microsoft.com/WindowsXP/pro/downloads*
> */servicepacks/sp1/spdeploy.asp.*

Extracting Service Packs

Windows XP Professional service packs are self-extracting, compressed files. You
can install service packs directly from those files, but that's not the best practice.
Doing so extracts the contents of the service pack on each client computer. Instead,
extract the file's contents to a network share and then install the service pack using
Update.exe, which is in the share. You extract the file's contents using the command
filename *–x*. The service pack starts and then prompts you for the location in which
you want to extract the files.

Using Command-Line Options

You can use the same command-line options with the service pack file (XPsp1.exe,
XPsp1a.exe, and so on) or Update.exe after extracting the contents of the service
pack file. The following shows the command-line syntax of both, and Table 22-2
describes each command-line option:

```
update.exe [/u] [/f] [/n] [/o] [/z] [/q] [/l] [/s:folder]
spname [/u] [/f] [/n] [/o] [/z] [/q] [/l] [/s:folder] [/x[:folder]]
```

Table 22-2   Update.exe Command-Line Options

/u	Installs unattended. If you use this option, only critical error prompts will appear onscreen during the installation process.
/f	Forces other applications to close at shutdown.
/n	Does not back up files for removing the service pack.
/o	Overwrites original equipment manufacturer (OEM) files without prompting.
/z	Does not restart the computer after the installation is completed.
/q	Uses quiet mode (the same as unattended mode, but with the user interface hidden from view). If you use this option, no prompts appear onscreen during the installation process.
/l	Lists installed hotfixes.
/s:folder	Combines original Windows XP Professional source files with the service pack in a shared distribution folder for an integrated installation. This is also known as *slipstreaming*.
/x[:folder]	Extracts service pack files without starting Update.exe. You are prompted to provide the path for the folder to which you want to extract the service pack unless you specify folder.

> **Tip**   The Microsoft Knowledge Base at *http://support.microsoft.com* contains a full description of the fixes in each service pack. Check these descriptions to determine whether you need to deploy each service pack. Regardless of whether you find specific fixes that you need, it's a best practice to update Windows XP Professional with current service packs to close security vulnerabilities. Also, some applications require a certain service pack level before you install them. If you're deploying Windows XP Professional, update the source files by slipstreaming the latest service pack into them prior to deployment. Doing so ensures that you're deploying the latest bits.

Planning Deployment

To ensure a successful service-pack deployment, prepare by assessing the methods and tools available by completing these important planning tasks:

- Choose an installation method.
- Identify the deployment tools and files.
- Check the space requirements.
- Test the deployment.

The following sections describe these planning tasks in more detail.

Deployment Methods

Windows XP Professional service packs support the following installation methods:

- **Update installation**   The update-installation method installs the service pack on a computer that's already running Windows XP Professional.

> **More Info**   See the section "Deploying Service Packs" on page 645 for more information about using this method.

- **Integrated installation (slipstreaming)**   The integrated installation combines the original Windows XP Professional source files with the service pack. The integrated-installation method allows you to install Windows XP Professional with the service pack already integrated into the source files. I highly recommend this method for new installations of Windows XP Professional.

More Info See the section "Slipstreaming Service Packs" on page 649 for more information about using this method.

Note A combination installation installs a service pack with a variety of other components. It uses a combination of the update and integrated installation methods. For more information about combination installations, see "Microsoft Windows XP Hotfix Installation and Deployment Guide" at *http://www.microsoft.com/WindowsXP/pro/downloads/servicepacks /sp1/hfdeploy.asp.*

Deployment Tools

This section provides an overview of the common service pack deployment tools and files. For more detailed information about using these tools to deploy service packs, see the sections "Deploying Service Packs" and "Slipstreaming Service Packs," later in this chapter on page 645 and page 649. Depending on the scenario you choose, you might need one or more of the following deployment tools and files:

- **Microsoft Windows Installer** You can deploy Windows XP Professional service packs using the Windows Installer database Update.msi. For more information, see the section "Windows Installer," later in this chapter on page 648.

- **Microsoft Systems Management Server** Systems Management Server (SMS) provides a variety of tools to help you deploy service packs in your organization. You can automatically upgrade all the SMS client computers in your organization with the new service pack. See Chapter 19 for more information about using this tool.

- **Unattended-setup answer file** You can use an unattended-setup answer file to automate the installation of an integrated installation, just as you learned how to do in Chapter 13, "Unattended Setup," and throughout this book.

- **Other methods** Any other method that's available to you for pushing a command to the desktop is a viable way to deploy a Windows XP Professional service pack. You can use management products other than SMS, including AutoProf ProfileMaker (*http://www.autoprof.com*), which has the built-in capability to deploy Windows XP Professional service packs to client computers. For that matter, if you need to install a service pack or hotfix on a remote computer, you can use a tool such as Sysinternals Psexec to automatically copy the file to the remote computer and run it with elevated privileges. For additional suggestions on methods to run commands on client computers with elevated privileges, see Chapter 23, "Software Installation."

Space Requirements

Table 22-3 shows the disk-space requirements for the current Windows XP Professional service packs. It compares them to the first three Windows 2000 service packs.

Table 22-3   Service Pack Space Requirements

Service Pack	Service Pack Files Only	Uninstallation Files	Total
Windows 2000 SP1	10 MB	205 MB	215 MB
Windows 2000 SP2	20 MB	250 MB	270 MB
Windows 2000 SP3	20 MB	175 MB	195 MB
Windows XP Professional SP1	145 MB	233 MB	378 MB
Windows XP Professional SP1a	145 MB	233 MB	378 MB

Testing the Deployment

Although Microsoft has a high degree of confidence in each service pack, the company cannot test all possible hardware configurations and line-of-business (LOB) applications that might be present in your environment. Instead, I recommend that you test the service pack in your environment before deploying it. Testing the service pack in your environment includes the following procedure:

1. Take a cross-section of the types of computers used in your environment that should receive the service pack. Make sure that the computers you are using for the test are equipped with the software and the hardware devices that are typically used in your business.

2. Install the service pack on each of these computers in the same way that you expect to do in your specific environment. Make sure that you perform each of the following actions:

   - Update existing computers that are running Windows XP Professional to the service pack.

   - Upgrade existing computers that are running earlier versions of Windows to the integrated Windows XP Professional source files and service pack.

   - Install Windows XP Professional integrated with the service pack to a computer with no previous or existing operating system (clean installation).

   - Verify that the software and hardware continue to work as expected for the various scenarios.

3. If you are installing Windows XP Professional for the first time in your organization, consider setting up a pilot group to help test your deployment and verify that it works in your environment as expected.

Forget Reinstalling Service Packs

The Update.exe program for Windows XP Professional no longer needs to reapply the service pack after every system state change. Windows XP Professional includes the file Driver.cab, which contains all the Plug and Play driver files that come with the operating system. Windows XP Setup and other components in the system use this file to install the drivers for new devices without requiring access to the Windows XP Professional product CD or the network.

The service pack does not update the Driver.cab file itself; instead, the Update.exe program installs an additional driver cabinet file, such as Sp1.cab. This file contains only updated versions of drivers that exist in the original Driver.cab file. In addition to the Sp1.cab file, the Update.exe program installs a new Drvindex.inf file that points to Sp1.cab for all of the updated drivers and also points to Driver.cab for all of the remaining drivers.

Update.exe also installs a Layout.inf file. Layout.inf ensures that proper binaries are installed following the removal and addition of services that results in a change to the operating system. For example, after you remove TCP/IP from Microsoft Windows NT 4.0 and then try to reinstall it on Windows NT 4.0, you must first reinstall the service from the original CD and then reapply the service pack. This is unnecessary in Windows XP Professional. The Layout.inf file is updated to determine whether the binary must be installed from the original Windows XP Professional product CD or from the service pack and then prompts for the appropriate media.

For more information on this issue, see the Knowledge Base article Q274215 in the Microsoft Knowledge Base at *http://support.microsoft.com*.

Deploying Service Packs

The following sections provide instructions for installing service packs in Windows XP Professional. You can either update computers already running Windows XP Professional or install an integrated Windows XP Professional and the service pack together. This section describes using an update installation to update computers that are already running Windows XP Professional. The section "Slipstreaming Service Packs," later in this chapter on page 649 describes the second option.

During the update installation, the service pack is installed on a computer that is already running Windows XP Professional. When you run the Update.exe program or deploy the Update.msi Windows Installer database, it installs the updated system files and makes the necessary registry changes. After the computer is restarted, the installation is complete and Windows XP Professional runs with an updated set of files.

This section describes the steps involved in using the following tools:

- **Local installation**   Installing the service pack using local service pack files
- **Shared installation**   Installing the service pack using shared service pack files
- **SMS deployment**   Deploying the service pack using SMS
- **Windows Installer**   Deploying the service pack using Active Directory

Important   If a system file on a computer becomes corrupted or needs to be replaced, you will need the service pack source files to replace that system file. This means that if you deploy a service pack from a shared installation, you need to maintain that share to ensure that users' computers continue to function normally.

Tip   When you deploy a new service pack, don't forget to update your deployment tools and support tools. These are in the Support\Tools folder on your updated Windows XP Professional CD. In particular, if you're using Sysprep to create disk images, make sure you're using the latest version of Sysprep.

Local Installation

Using a local installation, you set up a shared distribution folder on a network so that users can upgrade their computers from a central point and store their system backup files locally. You do this by starting the service pack program with whatever command-line options are appropriate (XPsp1a.exe for Windows XP Professional). You can also create logon scripts for users, which will ensure that they can upgrade to the service pack when they next use their computers.

Here's how to install a service pack:

1. Copy the service pack file to a shared folder on the network.

2. Before beginning the installation, stop any real-time virus scanners that are running on the computers that you'll be upgrading.

    Real-time virus scanners can cause problems with the installation if they are running. For each computer you plan to upgrade, back up the files and close any open programs before you continue (unless you plan to force programs to close during the installation).

3. To install the service pack from the distribution folder, run the command *server**share**spfile.exe*, including any command-line options you need.

    For example, to force the service pack to close running programs when it starts, include the */f* option on the command line.

> **More Info**   For more information about the command-line options available, see "Using Command-Line Options," earlier in this chapter on page 641.

4. The service pack displays the progress of the installation as it verifies and extracts files. As soon as this process is complete, Setup Wizard opens.

    Follow the instructions given by Setup Wizard. When you are prompted to select whether to archive files, I suggest that you select the Archive Files option to ensure that you can remove the service pack later if necessary (surprises do happen occasionally).

5. After the installation is completed, Setup Wizard gives you the option to restart the computer now or later.

    I recommend that you immediately restart the computer because the changes won't take effect until you do so.

6. Remember to restart any real-time virus scanners.

Shared Installation

A shared installation stores the service pack source files in a shared distribution folder rather than extracting them to the local computer. Because the service pack source files are kept remotely on the network, this method is suitable only for computers that are permanently connected to the network. For example, this method is not suitable for upgrading laptops.

Shared distribution folders for service pack source files must be permanent to ensure that all the files a computer might need to replace are available. Extracting the files from service pack files can be useful if you want to use the distribution folder as the folder that contains the service pack source files. This saves disk space on local computers because the installation would point to the distribution folder for service pack files rather than creating this folder locally. The service pack files folder is needed whenever Windows XP Professional requires a service pack file, such as when Windows File Protection needs to restore a corrupted or tampered-with file or when an optional component is configured. If you move the shared distribution folder, see article Q271484, "Files and Folders Are Added to Your System After Service Pack Is Installed," in the Microsoft Knowledge Base for more information.

Here's how to deploy a service pack from a shared installation:

1. Create a network share for the distribution folder. Then, type the command *spfile.exe /x:folder /u* where *folder* is the folder you created, to extract the service pack files into the shared distribution folder.

2. For each computer you plan to upgrade, stop any real-time virus scanners, back up the files, and close programs before you continue (unless you plan to force programs to close during the installation).

3. To install the service pack from the shared distribution folder, run the service pack update using Update.exe: *\\server\share\Update\Update.exe*.

4. The installation continues, as described in the section "Local Installation, on page 646."

SMS Deployment

To install a service pack using SMS, you must have SMS 2.0 with Service Pack 4 installed. See Chapter 17 for more information about using SMS to distribute packages. Here's how to install a service pack using SMS:

1. Create the SMS package by importing the package definition file for the service pack. In the package, provide the path to the service pack source files.

2. Distribute the SMS package to the distribution points.

3. Create the advertisement to notify SMS clients about the service pack.

Windows Installer

Deploying a service pack using Windows Installer and Active Directory is new for Windows XP Professional. The Windows Installer database Update.msi contains all the information that Windows Installer requires to install or remove the service pack. This package file describes the relationships among service pack features, components, and resources. The package file also contains an installation database, a summary information stream, and data streams for various parts of the service pack installation.

The Windows Installer database gets around one of the major issues with service pack deployment: deploying service packs to restricted users. In most enterprise environments, users aren't members of the local Administrators group, so they can't install service packs. Distribution tools such as SMS are sometimes used in cases like these. So are tools such as AutoProf ProfileMaker. When you deploy a service pack using the Windows Installer database, though, the database automatically installs with elevated privileges. In fact, the database installs the next time the computer restarts and before the user logs on to it.

You can use the Software Installation and Maintenance feature in Active Directory to deploy Update.msi for all the computers and to install the service pack. The Software Installation and Maintenance feature uses a Group Policy object (GPO) to deploy the package (on networked computers) within Active Directory containers, such as sites, domains, and organizational units (OUs) that are associated with the GPO. Microsoft requires that you use the machine-assigned distribution method when using Update.msi. There are no other methods available.

> **More Info**   For more information, see article Q278503, "Best Practices for Using Update.msi to Deploy Service Packs," in the Microsoft Knowledge Base. See Chapter 23, "Software Installation," for more information about deploying Windows Installer databases using Active Directory.

After you assign the package, Windows Installer automatically installs the service pack the next time the computer starts. The user does not have to log on to the computer as local Administrator to install the service pack (it installs prior to the user logging on to the computer). Only a network administrator or a user logged on to the computer as local Administrator can remove the service pack.

Here's how to assign a service pack to computers using Active Directory:

1. Create a shared network distribution folder as described in "Shared Installation," earlier in this chapter.

2. Create a Group Policy object for the service pack.

3. Assign the service pack's Update.msi file to the computer.

4. When the computers are restarted, they will be upgraded to the service pack.

Slipstreaming Service Packs

You can apply service packs directly to the Windows XP Professional source files to create an integrated installation. Because an integrated installation replaces individual files, the space requirements for this installation type are practically identical to the space requirements for the original Windows XP Professional source files. Also, you can usually continue to use your existing answer files and OEM folders. You cannot remove a service pack that you installed together with Windows in an integrated installation. Here's how to create an integrated installation of Windows XP Professional and the service pack:

1. Create a Windows XP Professional distribution folder as described in Chapter 7, Distribution Points. This is essentially a copy of the Windows product CD's I386 folder on a shared network folder.

2. Do one of the following:

    ■   Run the command *spfile.exe /x:folder /u*, in which *spfile.exe* is the service pack file and *folder* is the distribution folder you created in the previous step, to extract the service pack files and integrate them into your distribution point.

    ■   Extract the service pack files to a shared network folder and then run the command *spfolder\Update\Update.exe /x:folder /u*, where *spfolder* is the path of the shared network folder and *folder* is the distribution folder that you created in step 1.

3. Setup Wizard displays the progress of your installation and informs you when the installation is completed.

You can now deploy Windows XP Professional to multiple computers from the shared distribution folder as described in Part III, "Distributing." During the typical installation process, Windows XP Setup installs the updated operating system with the service pack already applied.

Important   When you run the Update.exe program, as described earlier for an integrated installation, a Svcpack.log file is created automatically in %SYSTEMROOT% on the computer that is running the Update.exe program. If you plan to update more than one version of Windows XP Professional on this computer, rename the Svcpack.log file after you update each version. This ensures that you do not overwrite the current log file when you update additional versions of Windows XP Professional.

On the Resource Kit CD   This book's companion CD contains the batch script, Spapply.cmd, which integrates a service pack with a Windows XP Professional distribution point. The command-line syntax is *spapply.cmd pack folder*, where *folder* is the distribution point containing an I386 folder, and *pack* is either the pathname and filename of the service pack file or the path of the folder containing a service pack that you've already expanded. This script is in the Scripts folder on the CD.

Deploying Hotfixes

Hotfixes are files or collections of files that fix specific problems in Windows XP Professional. Microsoft provides hotfixes as self-extracting, self-installing cabinet files (*.exe*). Hotfixes that you install appear in Add Or Remove Programs, so you can remove them if necessary.

You can usually recognize a hotfix by its unique naming scheme. Hotfix names use the format Q######_WXP_SP*X*_*ARCH*_*LLL*.exe. In this chapter, I call them Q*hotfix*.exe, with *hotfix* representing *######_WXP_SPX_ARCH_LLL*. Here's a description of each placeholder you see in this name:

- **######** The number of the related Microsoft Knowledge Base article.
- **X** The service level for the hotfix.
- **ARCH** The processor architecture for the hotfix: X86 or IA64.
- **LLL** The language for the hotfix. This is not always present.

Similar to service packs, hotfixes support two types of installations: update installations and combination installations. Use update installations to install hotfixes on computers that are already running Windows XP Professional. Use combination installations to perform unattended installations of Windows XP Professional, the service pack, or both.

> **Note** Hotfixes are applied only to software that is already installed when you apply the hotfixes. For example, if you remove a component and later reinstall it, you must reinstall any hotfixes that apply for that component. In addition, if you add further components to your computer that require this hotfix, you must install the hotfix again. Fixes included in a service pack do not work the same way. After you install a service pack, fixes are applied to all components you add or reinstall without you having to reinstall the service pack.

Update installations apply Windows XP Professional hotfixes to computers that are already running the operating system. The updater automatically installs and updates system files, and makes related changes to the registry. After the computer restarts (which is required only to replace some system files during installation), the installation is finished and Windows XP Professional is running with updated system files.

You install hotfixes by running the updater, Q*hotfix*.exe. This program extracts the hotfix files and runs the Update.exe hotfix installation program. Update.exe then checks the service pack version that the computer is using. If the service pack version of the computer was released prior to the hotfix and the language is identical, Update.exe installs the hotfix files. If the service pack was released after the hotfix or the language is incorrect, Update.exe displays an error message. If your service pack version was released after the hotfixes, and you use the **/u** or **/q** command-line options to install the hotfix unattended, the installation fails silently. Update.exe registers the hotfixes it installs in the following registry keys:

- HKLM\SOFTWARE\Microsoft\Windows NT\CurrentVersion\Hotfix\Q*hotfix*, where *hotfix* is a hotfix number.

- HKLM\SOFTWARE\Microsoft\Updates\Windows XP\SP*N*\Q*hotfix*, where *N* is a service pack number and *hotfix* is a hotfix number.

During the installation, information for removing hotfixes is in a hidden folder named %SYSTEMROOT%\$NtUninstallQ*hotfix*$, where *hotfix* is the hotfix number.

You can remove hotfixes using Add Or Remove Programs. If you install multiple hotfixes that replace the same files and you want to return your computer to its original state, you must remove the most recently installed hotfix first. For example, if you installed hotfix A before installing hotfix B, and both hotfixes replace the same file, you just remove hotfix B before hotfix A. You can remove only hotfixes that you install using the update-installation method; you can't remove hotfixes that you deploy using the combination-installation method.

More Info   See "Microsoft Windows XP Hotfix Installation and Deployment Guide" at *http://www.microsoft.com/WindowsXP/pro/downloads /servicepacks/sp1/hfdeploy.asp* for more information about deploying Windows XP Professional hotfixes.

On the Resource Kit CD   This book's companion CD contains two scripts to help you determine the hotfixes installed on a computer. Both scripts are in the Scripts folder. First, the script hasfix.wsf checks a list of computers for a particular hotfix. The command-line syntax of this script is *hasfix.wsf /Q:hotfix [COMPUTER1, …]*. Second, the script hotfixes.wsf lists the hotfixes installed on each of a list of computers. The command-line syntax of this script is *hotfixes.wsf [COMPUTER1, …]*.

Update Installations

The same update-installation methods are available for hotfixes that are available for service packs. These include running Update.exe manually with a combination of options, using SMS, using Windows Installer, or using products such as AutoProf ProfileMaker. And like service packs, you can install hotfixes from a network share or by downloading the hotfixes from Microsoft's Web site. This chapter focuses on network distribution because installing hotfixes from Microsoft's Web site is a method primarily for consumers, not enterprises.

The following shows the command-line syntax of Update.exe, and Table 22-4 describes each command-line option that it supports:

```
update.exe [/u] [/f] [/n] [/o] [/z] [/q] [/l]
Qhotfix.exe [/u] [/f] [/n] [/o] [/z] [/q] [/l] [/x:folder]
```

Table 22-4   Update.exe Command-Line Options

/u	Installs unattended. If you use this option, only critical error prompts will appear onscreen during the installation process.
/f	Forces other applications to close at shutdown.
/n	Does not back up files for removing the hotfix.
/o	Overwrites OEM files without prompting.
/z	Does not restart the computer after the installation is completed.
/q	Uses quiet mode (the same as unattended mode, but with the user interface hidden from view). If you use this option, no prompts will appear onscreen during the installation process.
/l	Lists installed hotfixes.
[/x:folder]	Extracts service pack files without starting Update.exe. You are prompted to provide the path for the folder to which you want to extract the service pack unless you specify *folder*.

To install a Windows XP Professional hotfix on a single computer, you run the hotfix program on the computer you want to update: Q*hotfix*.exe. To deploy hotfixes to multiple computers, create a network distribution folder and then copy each hotfix you want to deploy to the folder. After copying the hotfixes to the distribution folder, run the hotfix program on each computer using the methods that are available to you for pushing command lines. For example, you can use software distribution tools to run the hotfix program on each computer. After installing hotfixes, you must restart each computer to ensure the hotfixes are installed properly.

You can install multiple hotfixes from a single batch script and install them as a unit. As a result, you do not need to restart the computer after installing each hotfix. You use the /z and /q command-line options to install the hotfix without restarting the computer and to install the hotfix silently. After installing multiple hotfixes using the /z and /q command-line options, restart the computer to complete their installation. For example, Listing 22-1 shows how to install a series of hotfixes and then restarts the computer after installing the last.

Listing 22-1   Chaining Hotfixes

```
@echo off
@rem hotfixes.cmd: install hotfixes on local computer

setlocal enableextensions
set HOTFIXES=\\Server\Updates

    %HOTFIXES%\Q123456_Wxp_sp2_x86.exe /Z /Q
    %HOTFIXES%\Q123321_Wxp_sp2_x86.exe /Z /Q
    %HOTFIXES%\Q123789_Wxp_sp2_x86.exe /Z /Q

    rem Shutdown.exe comes with Windows XP
    rem /i shows the user interface
    rem /r restarts the computer
    rem /t waits 30 seconds before restarting
    rem /c displays a message to the user
    rem /f forces running applications to close

    shutdown /i /r /t 30 /c "This computer must restart." /f

:end
```

> **More Info**   The batch script in Listing 22-1 tries to install the hotfixes every time it runs. If you want to install hotfixes from users' logon scripts, you don't want to use this batch script as is. Instead, you want to run batch scripts one time only. Chapter 8, "Windows Settings," and Chapter 12, "User Profiles," describe a technique for running portions of batch scripts one time only. They use a Windows Script Host (WSH) script to run the commands if a given globally unique identifier (GUID) is missing from the registry, and after running the commands, the script stores the given GUID in the registry to prevent the commands from running again.

Combination Installations

Combination installations allow you to install Windows XP Professional integrated with the latest service pack and post-service pack hotfixes from a single network distribution point. You create a combination installation by including the components you want to install with the hotfixes as entries in the file Svcpack.inf. You can also install a service pack at the same time as the hotfixes. In other words, you don't need to install Windows XP Professional, the latest service pack, or the hotfixes separately. Do them all together.

The first step is building a Windows XP Professional distribution point as described in Chapter 6, "Answer Files," Chapter 7, "Distribution Points," and Chapter 11, "Chaining Installations." This includes the distribution point's I386 and OEM folders (the distribution folder will contain an IA64 folder instead of an I386 folder if you're deploying Windows XP 64-Bit Edition). If your Windows XP Professional source files don't already have the latest service pack integrated into them, perform an integrated installation of the service pack, as described in the section "Slipstreaming Service Packs," earlier in this chapter on page 649. After you have a distribution point that contains Windows XP Professional integrated with the latest service pack, use the following steps to add your hotfixes:

1. Add to *folder*\I386\Dosnet.inf, where *folder* is the pathname and filename of your distribution point, the entry svcpack to the [OptionalSrcDirs] section.

2. Create the folder *folder*\I386\svcpack, and copy each hotfix file to it. You must rename each hotfix file so that it uses 8.3 filenames, however. For example, if you're installing the hotfix Q123456_Wxp_sp2_x86.exe, rename the file Q123456.exe (the renaming parts of the filename are no longer necessary at this point because you know the operating system, service pack level, and processor architecture of the distribution point).

3. Expand the hotfix file to a temporary folder. The command to expand it is *folder*\I386\svcpack\Q*hotfix*.exe /x:*tempfolder*, where *tempfolder* is the path of the empty temporary folder into which you want to expand it. After expanding the hotfix file, copy the following files as described here:

   ■ Copy the .*cat* file from the temporary folder to *folder*\I386\svcpack. The .*cat* file is a catalog file that contains the hotfix's digital signature.

   ■ For each binary file in the temporary folder, delete the corresponding file in *folder*\I386. Although the binary files in the temporary folder might have extensions like .*exe*, .*dll*, and .*sys*, the files in the distribution point's I386 folder will have extensions like .*ex_*, .*dl_*, and .*sy_*. The files that end with an underscore (_) are compressed versions of those same files. After deleting the binary files from the distribution point, copy the binary files and any subfolders from the temporary folder to the I386 folder. For example, you must copy the folder I386\uniproc in the temporary folder to *folder*\I386\uniproc, where *folder* is the network distribution point. You don't need to copy Update.exe, Update.inf, Spmsg.dll, SPcustom.dll, SPuninst.exe, Update.ver, or any of the symbols files.

4. Delete the file *folder*\I386\Svcpack.in_, where *folder* is the distribution point, and create a new Svcpack.inf file in *folder*\I386 that looks like Listing 22-4. If you're deploying multiple hotfixes, add an entry for each hotfix under both [ProductCatalogsToInstall] and [SetupHotfixesToRun].

Caution   Some of the hotfixes you install will contain duplicate binary files. Before replacing any file in the I386 folder with a file from a hotfix, compare the file versions. Keep only the file with the higher file version. For example, if you already copied a file called sample.dll with a version of 5.1.2600.1100 to *folder*\I386, and another hotfix contains the same file with a version of 5.1.2600.1106, don't replace the file.

Listing 22-2   Svcpack.inf

```
[Version]
Signature="$Windows NT$"
MajorVersion=5
MinorVersion=1
BuildNumber=2600

[SetupData]
CatalogSubDir="\I386\svcpack"

[ProductCatalogsToInstall]
Q######.cat
Q######.cat
Q######.cat
Q######.cat

[SetupHotfixesToRun]
Q######.exe /Q /N /Z
Q######.exe /Q /N /Z
Q######.exe /Q /N /Z
Q######.exe /Q /N /Z
```

You install the customized distribution point containing Windows XP Professional, an integrated service pack, and hotfixes as described in Chapter 13. Windows XP Setup installs the operating system and automatically applies the hotfixes.

Note   Windows XP Professional Service Pack 1 and all post–Service Pack 1 hotfixes have Qchain.exe functionality built into them. You can install Service Pack 1 and then install any number of post–Service Pack 1 hotfixes without having to restart the computer in-between each hotfix. For more information about how the Qchain.exe tool works, see article Q296861, "Use Qchain.exe to Install Multiple Hotfixes with Only One Reboot," in the Microsoft Knowledge Base.

AutoProf Software Update

Policy Maker Software Update is a product from AutoProf (*www.autoprof.com*) that provides features similar to Microsoft Software Update Services. In my opinion, however, Policy Maker Software Update is a better tool to use for deploying hotfixes. The key difference between the two is the simplicity of using Policy Maker Software Update. Policy Maker Software Update integrates into Group Policy, as shown in Figure 22-1. If you already know how to use Group Policy, then you already know much of how to manage patches by using Policy Maker Software Update. For more information about Policy Maker Software Update, see *http://www.autoprof.com*.

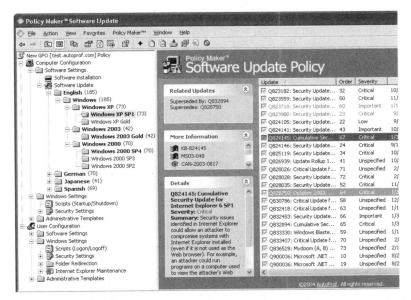

Figure 22-1 Policy Maker Software Update is an effective solution to deploying hotfixes for Windows XP Professional.

Patching Microsoft Office

Microsoft Office 2003 Editions service packs and product updates improve the security, performance, and reliability of Office applications. Similar to Windows XP Professional service packs, Office 2003 Editions service packs typically update the entire product package and represent a new baseline version of the product. Also like Windows XP Professional, Microsoft might release interim updates between

Office 2003 Editions service packs. These updates respond to emerging issues such as virus attacks and bug fixes. They tend to update specific applications or features, and require the most recent baseline version of Office 2003 Editions (service packs don't require the most recent baseline version of Office 2003 Editions). The last thing you must know about interim updates is that they're cumulative; that is, each interim update includes all of the updates for it.

You can download Office 2003 Editions service packs and updates from the Office 2003 Editions Resource Kit. The address is *http://www.microsoft.com /office/ork.*

Deploying service packs and updates is easier with Office 2003 Editions than with earlier versions of Office. For example, administrators can now install Office 2003 Editions from a compressed CD image on the network, creating a local installation source on users' computers and distributing binary client patches to users' computers. Because users always have access to the local installation source, they can apply the smaller client patches. Because the original network distribution point remains at the baseline version, client configurations never become out of sync with an update version. But if you choose to install Office 2003 Editions from an uncompressed network distribution point, you can continue to use the full-file administrative versions of each update. As with previous versions of Office, administrative updates are files with the *.msp* extension that you apply to the administrative installation on the network and then users reinstall Office 2003 Editions from the network distribution point.

After you choose a method for distributing updates, stick with it. The strategy you choose for updating Office 2003 Editions on users' computers depends on the following factors:

- **Deployment method**   The method you use to deploy Office 2003 Editions in the first place determines your options for updating clients later. If you want to distribute binary patches throughout your organization, for example, deploy Office 2003 Editions from a compressed CD image and take advantage of the local installation source, which Office 2003 Setup creates by default on users' computers.

- **Management practices**   If your organization maintains strong centralized control over software deployment (for example, if you use SMS to manage software distribution), you can more reliably keep clients synchronized with an updated administrative installation point.

- **Network capacity**   Recaching and reinstalling Office from an updated administrative image requires considerably more network bandwidth than distributing binary updates.

- **Client hard disk capacity**   Caching all installation files on the local computer requires approximately 240 MB of hard disk space in addition to the space required by a typical installation of Office 2003 Editions.

> **More Info**   For more information about the two types of distribution methods, see Chapter 7.

Client Patches

Client patches, which apply directly to each client computer, update Office 2003 Editions files instead of replacing them. By maintaining a baseline installation CD image of Office 2003 Editions in a network distribution point and then distributing client patches, client computers always remain synchronized with the installation image because the Windows Installer database's file version remains the same on both the source and client. Even after updating client computers by using Detect And Repair or Install On First Use, client computers that you update with binary patches continue to work properly with the original source.

Client patches are usually smaller than administrative patches and are easier than administrative patches to distribute to client computers. There are two caveats, however. First, when you install Office 2003 Editions from the baseline CD image, you must change all previously distributed client patches to the installation. This gradually increases the time it takes to install Office 2003 Editions. Second, even with client updates, users almost always need access to the network distribution point. If you intend to update Office 2003 Editions using client updates, you should deploy Office 2003 Editions from a compressed image of the CD on the network and take advantage of the local installation source.

Use client updates if any of the following are true:

- You had synchronization problems between client computers and administrative installations in the past.

- You distribute software updates to different groups at different times. Because the original installation image always remains at the same level, it can support clients with different patches installed. In other words, you don't have to maintain different distribution points for different client computers.

- Your environment has bandwidth limitations. Client patches are smaller than full-file patches and require less network bandwidth.

- You support users who have limited or unreliable access to the network, such as mobile users who don't frequently connect to the network.

To use client patches, you must be using an edition of Office 2003 Editions that supports Custom Installation Wizard and other administrative tools. The retail editions of Office 2003 Editions don't support these tools. You must also create a compressed installation source, such as a copy of the Office 2003 Editions CD, on a read-only network share with the creation of local installation source enabled. Last, users must be local administrators of their computers or you must have a distribution method in place that you can use to install software with elevated privileges. For example, you can distribute Office 2003 Editions with SMS or Active Directory, and the product will install with elevated privileges.

Deploying Office 2003 Editions client patches to computers on which you've already installed Office 2003 Editions is similar to applying Windows XP Professional hotfixes to client computers that are already running the operating system. You can use the same tools, such as SMS, to deploy them. Just store the client patch on a network distribution point and run it for each user. If users are local administrators, you can run the client patch from their logon scripts; otherwise, you must use a distribution method that can install the patch with elevated privileges. You can also use the standalone version of the OHotFix utility to extract the client patch from the *.exe* file that contains it and then apply the patch to the computer. The OHotFix utility is available from the Office 2003 Editions Resource Kit Toolbox at *http://www.microsoft.com/office/ork.*

When you install Office 2003 Editions for the first time, you must chain to the installation all the current patches to ensure that the new client computer has the latest client updates. You can chain any number of client patches to the Office 2003 Editions installation. Just keep in mind that Office 2003 Editions patches are cumulative, so you need to install only the latest patches for each application to install all the fixes included in earlier client patches. You chain client patches to the Office 2003 Editions installation just as you'd chain any other installation: Add *[ChainedInstall_N]* sections to the Office 2003 Editions Setup.ini file. See Chapter 11 to learn more about chaining installations with Office 2003 Editions. And you can use either the OHotFix utility or Windows Installer to install the patch:

- To use the OHotFix utility to chain client patches, extract each patch file (*.msp)* from the client update (*.exe).* Modify the OHotFix.ini file to run in quiet mode and to apply the patches. In the Office 2003 Editions Setup.ini file, chain OHotFix.exe to the core Office installation.

- To use Windows Installer to install the patch, extract each binary patch (*.msp)* from the corresponding client update (*.exe).* In the Office 2003 Editions Setup.ini file, chain Msiexec.exe to the core Office 2003 Editions installation, creating a separate *[ChainedInstall_N]* section for each patch.

Administrative Patches

Office 2003 Editions administrative patches perform full-file replacement. You apply them to network distribution points and then recache and reinstall Office 2003 Editions on users' computers. Reinstalling the files replaces any previously cached files on users' computers, overwriting older versions with newer versions. And new client computers that you install from the administrative installation automatically get the updated versions of the files; you don't need to chain each client patch.

In an ideal world, you'd recache and reinstall an updated administrative installation on all your client computers in a timely manner. If there is a delay between the time you update an administrative installation and recaching Office 2003 Editions on client computers, however, the client computers become out of sync with the administrative installation. Operations that rely on the client computer and administrative installation remaining synchronized can fail. These operations include Install On First Use and Detect And Repair. Thus, using administrative patches can require you to maintain two administrative installations: an unpatched administrative installation that works on computers to which you haven't reinstalled Office 2003 Editions and a patched administrative installation that works on computers to which you have reinstalled it.

Use administrative patches if any of the following is true:

- You maintain strong, centralized control of software deployment and lock down users' configurations. For instance, if you use SMS or Group Policy to distribute Office 2003 Editions, creating and maintaining administrative installations might be the best method for keeping client computers current.

- You support users who have consistent and reliable network access.

- You support users who are not local administrators, and you can't easily give them elevated privileges for installing a client patch.

- You allow users to run any Office 2003 Editions applications from the network. You can't use the Run From Network feature from a compressed CD image.

Using administrative patches to distribute Office 2003 Editions updates requires that you use an edition of Office 2003 Editions that supports the Custom Installation Wizard and other administrative tools. The retail editions of Office 2003 Editions don't support them. Your network must also have enough bandwidth to recache and reinstall Office 2003 Editions.

Warning Before you update an administrative installation, make sure that no clients are using the network distribution point. If a file on the distribution point is in use during the upgrade process, a newer version of that file is not copied to the administrative installation.

Here's how to patch an administrative installation and then recache and reinstall the updated version of Office 2003 Editions on client computers:

1. Download the administrative patch from the Office 2003 Editions Resource Kit and extract the patch (*.msp*) file from the self-extracting executable file.

2. Apply the administrative patch to the administrative installation. The command is *msiexec /a admininstall /p patchfile SHORTFILENAMES=1*, where *admininstall* is the pathname and filename of the Windows Installer database (*.msi* file) to patch, and *patchfile* is the pathname and filename of the patch file (*.msp*). You must have permission to change files in *admininstall*.

3. Do one of the following:

    ■ Run Office 2003 Setup from the administrative installation on each client computer. Office 2003 Setup automatically detects the updates and then recaches and reinstalls Office 2003 Editions.

    ■ Run *setup.exe REINSTALL=featurelist REINSTALLMODE=vomu /qb* on each client computer, where *featurelist* is a list of features to reinstall. For service packs, *featurelist* is usually *ALL*. Microsoft includes with each update a list of all the features to which the update applies. You can reduce the time and bandwidth required to update client computers by setting *REINSTALL* to just the list of features that the update modifies. The names of these features are case-sensitive, so mind the typing. Office 2003 Setup doesn't use the *REINSTALLMODE* property by default, so it's safer to explicitly include this property on the command line, setting it to *vomu*. For more information about this property, see the Knowledge Base article 826530.

Warning   If you originally deployed Office 2003 Editions from an administrative installation, you must use an administrative patch to update it. If you update it with a client patch, the client computer and administrative installation become out of sync, causing future updates to fail. To synchronize a computer to which you applied a client update with an administrative installation, you must first uninstall Office 2003 Editions and then reinstall it from an updated administrative installation.

Best Practices

The following are best practices for chaining packages to a Windows installation:

- **Read all the documentation that comes with each service pack before deploying it.**   The documentation describes fixes, new service pack deployment features, and any issues about which you should be aware.

- **Test each service pack in your own environment before deploying it.** Although Microsoft tries to test each service pack thoroughly, only you can test it in your particular environment for compatibility with your hardware and software.

- **Maintain the latest service packs on each desktop computer.**   Doing so helps keep Windows health and closes security vulnerabilities that Microsoft has found.

- **Deploy the full version of each service pack.**   Express installations aren't appropriate in a business environment. Instead, download and deploy the full version of each service pack.

- **Deploy local installations to laptop computers and shared installations to desktop computers.**   Local installations extract the service pack files to the local computer so that those files are available for replacement when the computer isn't connected to the network. Shared installations leave the service pack files on the network so that they don't use space on every desktop computer in your company.

Chapter 23

Software Installation

Part of a Microsoft Windows XP Professional deployment project is often application installation, particularly on disk images. There are many tools available for deploying applications to existing computers, some of which Microsoft provides (Systems Management Server [SMS], Group Policy, Terminal Services, and so on). This chapter focuses on preparing applications for installation by using the application-deployment tools at your disposal or including them on your disk image. It does refer you to information about using various deployment tools, but it doesn't cover them individually.

Checklist

- Have you planned the applications that you're deploying as part of your new Windows XP Professional configuration? See Chapter 1, "Deployment Plan."

- Have you tested the applications you're deploying for compatibility? See Chapter 2, "Application Compatibility," for more information.

- Are you deploying Microsoft Office 2003 Editions? For help planning an Office 2003 Editions deployment, see Chapter 4, "Office Configuration."

- Are you including applications in your Windows XP Professional distribution point or disk image? See Chapter 11, "Chaining Installations."

- Do you use Microsoft Systems Management Server (SMS) for application deployment? See Chapter 17, "Systems Management Server," for more information.

Overview

Application deployment isn't quite as simple as running the setup programs. There are two issues confronting you when installing software on disk images or existing computers running Windows XP Professional:

- **Privileges**   Unlike Microsoft Windows 98, in which users have complete control of the computers they use, Windows XP Professional is secure. In locked-down environments in which user accounts are not members of the Administrators group, deploying software automatically is tricky because they don't have the necessary privileges to install applications.

- **Interaction**   Whether you're installing software on a disk image or deploying it to existing computers, the setup program must run silently without user interaction. During the disk-imaging process, this is necessary to build disk images using an automated process. While deploying software to existing computers, you don't usually want users to interact with the setup program because they don't always know the proper settings or policies regarding software installation.

These are complex issues. Privilege is a particularly difficult issue if you don't have a software distribution infrastructure already in place. Although this chapter gives you an overview of these issues and how to address them, I don't have the space necessary to cover them in the depth that the following resources provide:

- **AppDeploy.com at *http://www.appdeploy.com***   This Web site provides comprehensive information about deploying applications that are packaged using a variety of technologies.

- **SourceForge at *http://unattended.sourceforge.net***   This nondescript Web site contains a wealth of information, including information about automating the installation of many earlier installers.

- **Real Men Don't Click at *http://isg.ee.ethz.ch/tools/realmen***   Don't let the name distract you. This Web site describes how to automate a variety of processes, including software installation.

- **InstallShield at** *http://www.installshield.com/microsite/packaging_ebook1*   This Web page contains the e-book "The Administrator Shortcut Guide to Software Packaging for Desktop Migrations." This guide is an excellent resource to learn about packaging applications for deployment.

> **More Info**   For more information about deploying software in a managed environment, see "Deploying a Managed Software Environment" in the Microsoft Windows Server 2003 Deployment Kit at *http://www.microsoft.com /resources/documentation/WindowsServ/2003/all/deployguide/en-us /Default.asp?url=/resources/documentation/WindowsServ/2003/all /deployguide/en-us /dmebe_swi_overview.asp.*

User Privileges

The following are methods for installing applications with elevated privileges in locked-down environments where users are not members of the Administrators group:

- **SMS**   SMS is Microsoft's software distribution infrastructure. In addition to its many capabilities, it can install software on locked-down computers by installing the software using an alternative security context, such as the Administrator account. A variety of third-party products provide similar feature sets. For more information about SMS, see Chapter 17. For some third-party products to evaluate, see the section "Third-Party Distribution Products," later in this chapter on page 687.

- **Security Configuration Editor**   Even after successfully installing some applications, they refuse to run in a locked-down environment. These programs access files and registry settings that locked-down users don't have permission to access. A good solution is to use Security Configuration Editor to create a security template that you deploy via Group Policy or apply directly to a disk image. The template would loosen security just enough to allow the application to run without requiring you to dump the user in to the local Administrators group out of frustration. See Chapter 20, "Policy Management," for more information.

- **Group Policy**   You can deploy Windows Installer–based software by using Group Policy. And Group Policy automatically installs software with elevated privileges.

■ **Nefarious Hacks**   In the absence of a formal software distribution infrastructure, you can use a variety of *hacks* to install applications with elevated privileges. These include using Scheduled Tasks, AutoLogon, and so on. The section "Elevating Installation Privileges," later in this chapter on page 688, gives examples.

User Interaction

When distributing software, limit user interaction. First, an automated disk-imaging process requires it. A setup program that requires user interaction means that you have to attend the image-building process and increases the likelihood of errors. Second, to deploy software when users aren't at their desks (at night, on weekends, and so on), you must automate the installation so that it occurs without interaction. Last, user interaction is generally bad because users don't usually know how to configure the applications you install for use in your environment.

Windows Installer-based applications are easy to install silently. You simply use the */qb* or */qn* command-line options. The */qb* command-line option installs a setup database with a progress indicator but without user interaction. The */qn* command-line option installs a setup database silently in the background (nothing on the display and no user interaction). Other installer technologies, including legacy installers, often provide some means for silent installation. Some of them even allow you to configure responses to setup questions; others don't. The section "Automating Legacy Installers" on page 683 describes how to use them.

Windows Installer

Windows Installer is a component of Windows XP Professional that simplifies the application installation process. It manages the installation and removal of applications by applying a set of centrally defined setup rules during the installation process. You can also use this service to modify, repair, or remove an existing application. Windows Installer technology consists of the Windows Installer service for the operating system and the package (*.msi*) file format that contains information about application setup and installation.

Windows Installer is an integral part of Microsoft IntelliMirror and a core component of the Group Policy–based change and configuration management technology. (See Chapter 21, "Desktop Management.") By using the IntelliMirror technologies, Group Policy, and change and configuration management, administrators can approve certain applications, specifying that all configuration operations on those applications (installation, removal, and repair) run as the local system account. The administrator has control and management of the file system and registry, and Windows Installer performs user-initiated software installations. Only applications that are approved by the administrator run with elevated privileges.

Administrators use Active Directory directory service, IntelliMirror, and Group Policy to assign and publish applications to groups of users or computers within the enterprise. Active Directory is a secure, distributed, partitioned, and replicated directory service that provides management services. These services include a standardized method of locating resources within the enterprise and applying Group Policy to objects managed by Active Directory.

Features

Windows Installer can perform the following tasks:

- **Restores original computer state upon installation failure** Windows Installer keeps track of all changes made to the system during the application-installation process. If the installation fails, Windows Installer can restore, or roll back, the system to its initial state.

- **Helps prevent inter-application conflicts** Windows Installer enforces installation rules that help to prevent conflicts with shared resources between existing applications. Such conflicts can be caused when an install operation makes updates to a dynamic-link library (*.dll*) shared by an existing application or when an operation deletes a *.dll* shared by another application.

- **Reliably removes existing programs** Windows Installer can reliably uninstall any program it previously installed. It removes all the associated registry entries and application files, except for those shared by other installed software. You can uninstall an application at any time after a successful installation. (Removal should not be confused with rollback, which restores a computer to its initial state when an installation failure has occurred.)

- **Diagnoses and repairs corrupted applications** An application can query Windows Installer to determine whether an installed application has missing or corrupted files. If any are detected, Windows Installer repairs the application by recopying only those files found to be missing or corrupted.

- **Supports on-demand installation of application features** Windows Installer can be configured to initially install a minimal subset of an application. Later, additional components can be automatically installed the first time the user accesses features that require those components. This is known as advertising. For example, Windows Installer could install Microsoft Word 2003 with a minimal set of features. The first time the user tried to access a mail merge function (not included with the original installation), Windows Installer would automatically install the mail merge component. Similarly, Windows Installer can also purge components that go unused in an application. For example, Windows Installer can remove the mail merge component if it goes unused for 60 days.

- **Supports unattended application installation**   Installation packages can be configured to require no installation process interaction from the user. During the installation process, Windows Installer can query the computer for desktop attributes, including determining whether any applications were previously installed by Windows Installer.

- **Supports 32-bit and 64-bit applications**   32-bit applications can be installed on 64-bit machines.

- **Supports Microsoft .NET Framework**   The Microsoft .NET Framework is a new platform for building integrated, service-oriented applications that gather information from and interact with a wide variety of sources, regardless of the platforms or languages in use. The .NET Framework and the common language runtime can deliver write-once, compile-once, run-anywhere application development. Specifically, the .NET Framework delivers code reuse, code specialization, resource management, multilanguage development, security, deployment, and administration.

- **Integrated with side-by-side components**   This feature eliminates *.dll* version conflicts by permitting an application to be bound to the version of the component it was designed and tested with, regardless of the computer that hosts the application. Side-by-side components support the simultaneous execution of multiple versions of each component.

- **Integrated with software restriction policies**   This feature provides virus-protection support, including protection from Trojan horse viruses and worms propagated through e-mail and the Web. Software restriction policies make the simple, point-and-click, active context user experience safe. Group Policy implements them as part of the list of trusted applications, and Windows Installer operates with applications permitted by these software restriction policies.

Technology

Windows Installer technologies are divided into two parts that work in combination: a client-side installer service (Msiexec.exe) and a package file (*.msi* file). Package files are also called *setup databases*. Windows Installer uses the information contained within a package file to install the application. The following list describes the Windows Installer technologies:

- **Installer service**   Windows Installer is an operating system service that allows the operating system to manage the installation process.

- **Installer program**   The Msiexec.exe program is a component of Windows Installer. This program uses a dynamic-link library (DLL), Msi.dll, to read the package files (*.msi*), apply transforms (*.mst*), and incorporate command-line options. The installer performs all installation-related tasks: copying files onto the hard disk, making registry modifications, creating shortcuts on the desktop, and displaying dialog boxes to query user installation preferences when necessary. Windows Installer associates the *.msi* file extension with Msiexec.exe. When a user double-clicks a file with the *.msi* extension, the operating system runs the Msiexec.exe application to install the package.

- **Installation package file** Each package (*.msi*) file contains a relational type database that stores all the instructions and data required to install (and uninstall) the program across many installation scenarios. A package file can contain instructions for installing an application when a prior version of the application is already installed. The package file can also contain instructions for installing the software on a computer in which that application has never been present.

- **Transforms** The installation process can be manipulated by applying transforms (*.mst*) to the installation database. A transform makes changes to elements of the database. For example, Windows Installer can use a transform file to change the language in the user interface of an application. Windows Installer transform files modify the installation package file at installation time and can therefore dynamically affect the installation behavior. Customization transforms, much like patches, remain cached on the computer. These transforms are applied to the base package file whenever Windows Installer needs to perform a configuration change to the installation package. Transforms are applied only at initial installation and not to an application that has already been installed.

Using Windows Installer

Msiexec.exe supports numerous command-line options. Rather than describing them all at one time, the following sections describe various combinations for achieving tasks.

Installing a Package

Table 23-1 describes the command-line options for installing a package, and the following describes the syntax:

```
msiexec /i {Package | ProductCode}
```

Table 23-1 Installing a Package

Option	Description
/i	Installs or configures a product.
Package	Specifies the name of the Windows Installer package file.
ProductCode	Specifies the globally unique identifier (GUID) of the Windows Installer package.

Creating Administrative Installations

Table 23-2 describes the command-line options for creating administrative installations, and the following describes the syntax:

```
msiexec /a Package
```

Table 23-2   Creating Administrative Installations

Option	Description
/a	Applies the administrative installation option.
Package	Specifies the name of the Windows Installer package file.

Repairing a Package

Table 23-3 describes the command-line options for repairing a package, and the following describes the syntax:

```
msiexec /f [p][o][e][d][c][a][u][m][s][v]{Package | ProductCode}
```

Table 23-3   Repairing a Package

Option	Description
P	Reinstalls missing files but doesn't check version.
o	Reinstalls missing files or files that are from an earlier version.
e	Reinstalls missing files or files that are from the same or earlier version.
d	Reinstalls missing files or files that aren't from the same version.
c	Reinstalls missing files or files that are corrupt. This option repairs only files that have a checksum in the package file.
a	Reinstalls all files regardless of their versions or checksums.
u	Rewrites the essential registry values described in the package file. This includes values in the per-user branches HKU and HKCU.
m	Rewrites essential registry values described in the package file. This includes values in the per-computer branches HKLM and HKCR.
s	Reinstalls all shortcuts and overwrites existing icons.
v	Recaches the source package locally.
Package	Specifies the name of the Windows Installer package file.
ProductCode	Specifies the GUID of the Windows Installer package.

Uninstalling a Package

Table 23-4 describes the command-line options for uninstalling a package, and the following describes the syntax:

```
msiexec /x {Package | ProductCode}
```

Table 23-4 Uninstalling a Package

Option	Description
/x	Uninstalls a product.
Package	Specifies the name of the Windows Installer package file.
ProductCode	Specifies the GUID of the Windows Installer package.

Advertising a Package

Table 23-5 describes the command-line options for advertising a package, and the following describes the syntax:

```
msiexec /j [{u | m}] Package
msiexec {u | m} Package /t TransformList
msiexec {u | m} Package /g LanguageID
```

Table 23-5 Advertising a Package

Option	Description
/j	Advertises the product.
/ju	Advertises to the current user.
/jm	Advertises to all users of the computer.
Package	Specifies the Windows Installer package file.
/t TransformList	Applies transform to advertised package.
/g LanguageID	Identifies the language.

Logging Results

Table 23-6 describes the command-line options for logging results, and the following describes the syntax:

```
msiexec /L [i][w][e][a][r][u][c][m][p][v][+][!]LogFile.txt
```

Table 23-6 Logging Results

Option	Description
i	Logs status messages.
w	Logs nonfatal warnings.
e	Logs all error messages.
a	Logs startup of actions.

Table 23-6   Logging Results

Option	Description
r	Logs action-specific records.
u	Logs user requests.
c	Logs initial user interface parameters.
m	Logs out-of-memory errors.
p	Logs terminal properties.
v	Logs verbose output. To use this option, specify **/L*v**.
+	Appends to existing file.
!	Flushes each line to the log.
*	Logs all information except for the v option. This is a wildcard.
Logfile.txt	Specifies the name and path of the text log file.

Applying a Patch

Table 23-7 describes the command-line options for applying a patch, and the following describes the syntax:

```
msiexec /p PatchPackage
```

Table 23-7   Applying a Patch

Option	Description
/p	Applies a patch.
PatchPackage	Specifies a specific patch.

Installing a Transform

Table 23-8 describes the command-line options for installing a transform, and the following describes the syntax:

```
msiexec /i Package TRANSFORMS=TransformList
```

Table 23-8   Installing a Transform

Option	Description
/i	Installs or configures a product.
Package	Specifies the Windows Installer package file.
TRANSFORMS=	Specifies the property used to specify which transform (.mst) files should be applied to the package.
TransformList	Specifies the list of paths separated by semicolons.

Advertising with a Transform

Table 23-9 describes the command-line options for advertising with a transform, and the following describes the syntax:

```
msiexec /i Package /j[u][m] /t TransformList
```

Table 23-9   Advertising with a Transform

Option	Description
/i	Installs or configures a product.
Package	Specifies the name of the Windows Installer package file.
/j	Advertises a product. This option ignores any property values entered on the command line.
/ju	Advertises to the current user.
/jm	Advertises to all users of this computer.
/t	Applies transform to the advertised package.
TransformList	Specifies the list of paths separated by semicolons.

Setting a User Interface Level

Table 23-10 describes the command-line options for setting a user interface level, and the following describes the syntax:

```
msiexec /q{n | b | r | f | n+ | b+ | b-}
```

Table 23-10   Setting a User Interface Level

Option	Description
n	Displays no user interface.
b	Displays a basic user interface.
r	Displays a reduced user interface with a modal dialog box displayed at the end of the installation.
f	Displays the full user interface with a modal dialog box displayed at the end.
n+	Displays no user interface, except for a modal dialog box displayed at the end.
b+	Displays a basic user interface with a modal dialog box displayed at the end.
b-	Displays a basic user interface with no modal dialog boxes.

Managing Windows Installer

Windows Installer provides a number of policies for managing how it installs applications and interacts with users:

- **User Configuration\Administrative Templates\Windows Components \Windows Installer (HKCU\Software\Policies\Microsoft\Windows \Installer)**

  - Always Install With Elevated Privileges (AlwaysInstallElevated)

  - Directs Windows Installer to use system permissions when it installs any program on the system. You must also set the per-computer version of this policy for it to work.

- **Search Order (SearchOrder)**   Specifies the order in which Windows Installer searches for installation files. In other words, you can specify the order in which it looks at network, local media, and Web locations for installation files.

- **Prohibit Rollback (DisableRollback)**   Prohibits Windows Installer from generating and saving the files it needs to reverse an interrupted or unsuccessful installation. This is useful when you know that the disks won't have enough space to hold the rollback files. It's dangerous, however, because Windows Installer can't restore the computer if the installation fails.

- **Prevent Removable Media Source For Any Install (DisableMedia)**   Prevents users from installing programs from removable media. Using this policy is a nifty way to prevent users from installing applications themselves, circumventing IT policies. This controls only Windows Installer-based applications, though.

- **Computer Configuration\Administrative\Templates\Windows Components \Windows Installer (HKLM\Software\Policies\Microsoft\Windows\Installer)**

  - Disable Windows Installer (DisableMSI)

  - Disables or restricts the use of Windows Installer. Use this policy to limit Windows Installer to managed applications. Your choices are to allow users to install Windows Installer-based applications, to never allow them, or to allow users to install only managed applications.

- **Always Install With Elevated Privileges (AlwaysInstallElevated)**   Directs Windows Installer to use system permissions when it installs any program on the system. You must also set the per-user version of this policy for it to work.

- **Remove Browse Dialog Box For New Source (DisableBrowse)**   Prevents users from searching for installation files when they add features or components to an installed program. By default, if Windows Installer can't find the application's source files, it displays a dialog box allowing them to browse for the files.

- **Prohibit Patching (DisablePatch)** Prevents users from using Windows Installer to install patches. Prevents users from patching their applications to protect them from malicious code.

- **Disable IE Security Prompt For Windows Installer Scripts (SafeFor Scripting)** Allows Web-based programs to install software on the computer without notifying the user.

- **Enable User Control Over Installs (EnableUserControl)** Permits users to change installation options that typically are available only to system administrators. Use this policy only in environments that don't lock down, and carefully control configurations because it bypasses some of the security features built in to Windows Installer.

- **Enable User To Browse For Source While Elevated (AllowLockdown Browse)** Allows users to search for installation files during privileged installations. By default, Windows Installer doesn't allow users to browse for installation source files when it's running with elevated privileges.

- **Enable User To Use Media Source While Elevated (AllowLockdown Media)** Allows users to install programs from removable media, such as floppy disks and CD-ROMs, during privileged installations. By default, Windows Installer doesn't allow users to install applications from local media when it's running with elevated privileges.

- **Enable User To Patch Elevated Products (AllowLockdownPatch)** Allows users to upgrade programs during privileged installations. By default, Windows Installer doesn't allow users to patch applications when the installation program is running with elevated privileges.

- **Allow Admin To Install From Terminal Services Session (EnableAdminTS Remote)** Allows Terminal Services administrators to install and configure programs remotely. Windows Installer allows administrators to install applications only when they are console users. This policy allows them to install applications using Terminal Services.

- **Cache Transforms In Secure Location On Workstation (Transforms Secure)** Saves copies of transform files in a secure location on the local computer. Windows Installer stores transforms in users' profile folders so that transforms follow them from computer to computer. Users can change the transforms, however. This policy causes Windows Installer to store transforms in a secure location, preventing users from changing them, but the transforms don't follow users.

- **Logging (Logging)**   Specifies the types of events that Windows Installer records in its transaction log for each installation. The log, Msi.log, appears in the Temp directory of the system volume.

- **Prohibit User Installs (DisableUserInstalls)**   Allows IT professionals to prevent user installs. This policy has three choices. Allow Per-User Installations (the default), and Windows Installer favors per-user installations over per-computer. Hide Per-User Installations, and Windows Installer favors per-computer installations over per-user. Prohibit User Installations, and Windows Installer prevents applications from installing per-user. The last option is desirable to ensure a standard configuration that's available to all users on all computers.

- **Turn Off Creation Of System Restore Checkpoints (LimitSystemRestore Checkpointing)**   Prevents Windows Installer from creating System Restore checkpoints. System Restore enables users to restore their computers to a previous state without losing personal data files in the event of a problem. By default, Windows Installer automatically creates a System Restore checkpoint each time an application is installed, so that users can restore their computer to the state it was in before installing the application.

Installing with Elevated Privileges

The policy *AlwaysInstallElevated* installs Windows Installer-based applications with elevated privileges. Microsoft documentation often calls this a privileged installation. This policy is one way to enable users to install applications that they couldn't otherwise install because they're in restricted groups or you've locked down the desktops in your enterprise. A better way is to deploy those applications through Active Directory or by using something like SMS. If neither product is available to you, consider using this policy, but keep in mind that the consequences of doing so can be severe because the users can take advantage of this policy to gain full control of their computers. Potentially, users could permanently change their privileges and circumvent your ability to manage their accounts and computers. In addition, this policy opens the door to viruses disguised as Windows Installer package files. For these reasons, this isn't a setting that I recommend in any but the most dire situations (in which there's no method available other than tossing users in the local Administrators group).

For this policy to be effective, you must enable both the per-computer and per-user versions of it at the same time. In other words, enable it in Computer Configuration as well as User Configuration.

Caching Transforms in a Secure Location

Transforms are essentially answer files for Windows Installer-based applications. When you install an application using a transform, Windows Installer stores the transform with an *.mst* extension in the Application Data folder of the user profile. Windows Installer needs this file to reinstall, remove, or repair the application. Keeping it in the user profile ensures that the file is always available. For example, if users have roaming user profiles, the transform follows them from computer to computer. This is not secure, however. When you set the TransformsSecure policy, Windows Installer saves transforms in %SYSTEMROOT% instead—where users don't have permissions to change files. But because Windows Installer requires access to the transform used to install an application, the user must use the same computer on which they installed the application or have access to the original installation source to install, remove, or repair the software. The idea behind this policy is to secure transforms in enterprises when IT professionals can't risk users maliciously changing the files.

Locking Down Windows Installer

Table 23-11 describes the policies that provide the most security for Windows Installer-based applications and Windows XP Professional in general. The first part of the table contains per-user policies, and the second part contains per-computer policies. In the Setting column, Not Configured means that you don't define the policy. Enabled speaks for itself.

Table 23-11   Secure Windows Installer Settings

Policy	Setting
User Configuration	
Always Install With Elevated Privileges	Not Configured
Prevent Removable Media Source For Any Install	Enabled
Computer Configuration	
Always Install With Elevated Privileges	Not Configured
Enable User To Browse For Source While Elevated	Not Configured
Enable User To Use Media Source While Elevated	Not Configured
Enable User To Patch Elevated Products	Not Configured
Remove Browse Dialog Box For New Source	Enabled
Disable Windows Installer	Enabled For Non-Managed Apps Only
Prohibit Patching	Enabled
Enable User Control Over Installs	Not Configured
Disable IE Security Prompt For Windows Installer Scripts	Not Configured
Cache Transforms In Secure Location On Workstation	Enabled

Removing Windows Installer Data

If you thought that manually removing legacy applications was difficult, try removing a Windows Installer-based application manually. More than once I've broken Windows Installer-based applications so badly that I couldn't remove them, repair them, or reinstall them. In these cases, I had to manually remove the application's Windows Installer data from the registry or reinstall Windows XP Professional. Tools are available that automate this process, and you learn about them in this chapter.

Before I introduce the tools, I will point you to the location in the registry where Windows Installer stores data about the applications it installs. Don't modify these settings using Registry Editor (Regedit) because doing so will likely inflict pain on you. Straightening out the relationships between all the different bits of data that Windows Installer stores in the registry is difficult. This is just good information to have available.

On the Resource Kit CD   The tools you learn about in the next two sections come with Windows Support Tools. You install the tools from \Support\Tools on your Windows XP Professional CD.

Msizap.exe

Msizap is a tool that removes most of the data that Windows Installer maintains for an application. It doesn't remove the application's files or settings from the hard disk, however; you have to clean those up yourself. You can focus this utility on a single application or you can make sweeping changes to the Windows Installer data. I've had good luck using Msizap to remove a single application's Windows Installer data from the registry, but I don't trust it to make huge changes, such as allowing it to remove all the Windows Installer folders and registry keys.

The following examples show the different forms of the Msizap program's command line. The first two forms are the most useful. In the first case, you specify the product code, which is the product's unique GUID. You're not likely to know the product code off the top of your head, so you'll want to use the second form, in which you specify the path and name of the package file. Then Msizap will look up the product code for you.

An example is in order. Assuming that you've installed Microsoft Office XP and can't remove it using Add Or Remove Programs, you'd type **msizap T!** ***path*\proplus.msi** in the Run dialog box. *Path* is the path containing the package file Proplus.msi. After Msizap finishes removing the application's Windows Installer data from the registry, you'll still have plenty of cleaning to do. You'll want to get rid of the application's files and other settings that it might have stored in the registry. For example, you'll still see the application's shortcut on the Start menu, but when you click it, you'll see an error message telling you that the application isn't installed.

The following describes the syntax of the Msizap.exe command, and Table 23-12 describes its command-line options:

```
msizap T[A!] productcode
msizap T[A!] packagefile
msizap *[A!] ALLPRODUCTS
msizap PSA?!
```

Table 23-12   Msizap.exe Command-Line Options

Option	Description
*	Removes all Windows Installer folders and registry keys, adjusting shared DLL counts and stopping the service.
T	Removes all Windows Installer information for a product.
P	Removes the in-progress key.
S	Removes rollback information.
A	Gives administrators full control to targeted folders and keys instead of removing them.
W	Applies changes for all users instead of just the current user.
G	Removes cached Windows Installer files that are orphaned.
!	Automatically responds Yes to all prompts.
?	Displays help.

Tip   I'm not comfortable with manually removing a program's files and registry settings after using Msizap. Most large applications store settings in the registry beyond the typical HKU\Software\Vendor\Product\Version keys. For example, they register components in HKCR, and you might not get rid of them all. My solution seems odd, but it works well. Zapping a program's Windows Installer data from the registry should enable me to reinstall it. So I reinstall the application and then use Add Or Remove Programs to remove it. Windows Installer is likely to do a much cleaner job than I can of removing the application.

Msicuu.exe

Windows Installer Clean Up (Msicuu.exe in the Windows Support Tools) puts a graphical user interface on Msizap.exe. If you're sitting at the computer, use this tool instead of using Msizap at the command prompt. It's less error-prone.

1. In the Run dialog box, type **Msicuu** and click OK.

2. In the Windows Installer Clean Up dialog box, shown in Figure 23-1, click the application for which you want to remove Windows Installer data from the registry and then click Remove.

3. Confirm that you want to remove the application's Windows Installer data from the registry by clicking OK.

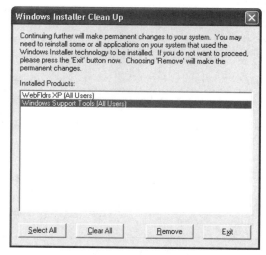

Figure 23-1   Windows Installer Clean Up is a friendly interface for Msizap.

Installing Office 2003

Most of the information that this chapter contains applies to installing Office 2003 Editions on users' computers. Office 2003 Editions is more complex to deploy than your typical utility or program, however, so this section contains additional information about installing it.

In Windows XP Professional, different groups of users have different levels of rights and permissions. In these environments, default users have limited access to system areas of the computer. Because Office 2003 Setup writes to system areas of the operating system and the registry, a user must have administrator rights to the local computer to install Office 2003 Editions. Users without administrator rights cannot install Office 2003 Editions. To install Office 2003 Editions on computers in which users lack administrator rights, you must run Office 2003 Setup with elevated privileges. After Office 2003 Editions is installed, users without administrator rights can run all installed features, including installing features on demand, provided that the initial installation was performed in an elevated context.

In organizations in which users are not the administrators of their computers, there are three methods of elevating the Office 2003 Editions installation:

- Log on to the computer as an administrator and install Office 2003 Editions.

- Assign, publish, or advertise Office 2003 Editions programs using Group Policy. You can use Group Policy software installation and maintenance to assign or publish Office 2003 Editions. You can also log on to the computer as an administrator and run Office 2003 Setup with the */j* command-line option to advertise Office 2003 Editions.

- Use a software management tool, such as SMS, in an administrative context.

Because all the core Office 2003 Editions programs are installed as Windows Installer packages, any of the preceding methods grants users elevated privileges and allows them to install Office 2003 Editions and any chained packages. When the initial installation is performed with elevated privileges, all subsequent installations—including install on demand and automatic repair of features—are also automatically elevated.

 More Info For more complete information about installing Office 2003 Editions, see the Office 2003 Editions Resource Kit at *http://www.microsoft.com /office/ork/2003/two/ch5/default.htm*.

Automating Legacy Installers

To achieve a fully unattended and automated installation, the packages you install must support unattended installation. Many setup programs support an */s* or */q* command-line option for such a thing; others don't.

Often, you can find out whether the package supports unattended installation by typing **setup /?** at the command prompt, where *setup* is the file name of the setup program. If the setup program doesn't provide clues, you need to know which vendor's product was used to create the package. You can usually tell by running the setup program and looking for logos, for example. Armed with that information, the following sections describe how to install packages created by different packaging software unattended. Table 23-13 summarizes the necessary commands.

Table 23-13   Unattended Package Installation

Package Type	Unattended Installation
Windows Installer	`msiexec.exe /i package.msi /qn ALLUSERS=2`
InstallShield	`setup.exe /s /sms`
	To create the Setup.iss file necessary to run setup silently, type **setup.exe /a /r** to create a Setup.iss from your responses to the setup program's dialog boxes and then copy Setup.iss from %SYSTEMROOT% to the folder containing the package.
InstallShield PackagefortheWeb	`setup.exe /a /s /sms`
	To create the Setup.iss file necessary to run setup silently, type **setup.exe /a /r** to create the Setup.iss based on your responses and then copy Setup.iss from %SYSTEMROOT% to the folder containing the package.
Wise Installation System	*setup.exe /s*

More Info   Don't see an application's installer in this chapter? SourceForge maintains information about a variety of installers and how to automate them. For more information, see *http://unattended.sourceforge.net /installers.html*. For an exhaustive list of applications and how to automate their installation, see ApplyDeploy.com at *http://www.appdeploy.com* (click the Packages link).

Windows Installer

The number of applications packaged as Windows Installer databases is multiplying rapidly. And what often looks like a self-contained, self-extracting setup program with a file name such as Setup.exe is often a file that decompresses to a Windows Installer database. You can usually extract the database by using a tool such as WinZip (from WinZip Computing at *http://www.winzip.com*) or by running the setup program and looking in the %USERPROFILE%\Local Settings\Temp folder for the package file. Windows Installer databases have the *.msi* file extension.

To install Windows Installer databases unattended using Msiexec.exe, use the */qb* command-line option for a basic user interface or the */qn* command-line option for no user interface. Also, to ensure that the package installs for use by all users, add the *ALLUSERS=2* property. For example, the command *msiexec.exe /i* *program.msi /qn ALLUSERS=2* installs the package file program.msi with no user interaction and for use by all users who share the computer.

InstallShield

Packages created by InstallShield (*http://www.installshield.com*) usually have the file name Setup.exe. To create an unattended installation for an InstallShield package, you need to create an InstallShield script, which has the *.iss* file extension. Many applications come with such a file, but they're easy to create if they don't:

1. Run the setup program using the */r* command-line option. This creates a Setup.iss file based on how you configure the installation as you step through the setup program. The result is the file Setup.iss in %SYSTEMROOT%.

2. Copy Setup.iss from %SYSTEMROOT% to the folder containing the package. If you're using the distribution folder described in this chapter, you'll want to create a subfolder in OEM*N*\$OEM$\APPS\RUNONCE for the package and then start the setup program from a batch file that you put in OEM*N*\$OEM$\APPS \RUNONCE. This avoids duplicate file names.

3. Run the setup program using the */s* command-line option. The setup program runs silently using the responses provided by the Setup.iss file.

> **Tip** Packages created by InstallShield will spawn a separate process and then return immediately to the calling program. This means that the setup program runs synchronously, even if you start the setup program using *setup /wait*. You can add the */sms* command-line option to force the setup program to pause until installation is finished, however, making the process synchronous.

PackagefortheWeb

PackagefortheWeb is an InstallShield-packaged application contained in a self-contained, self-extracting file. Create a Setup.iss file (using it is almost the same as described in the previous section). The difference is that you must use the */a* command-line option to pass the command-line options to the setup program after the file extracts its contents. For example, a file that you downloaded called Prog.exe will expand its contents into the temporary folder and then run Setup.exe when finished. To pass command-line options to Setup.exe, you must use the */a* command-line option. Here's how this extra option changes the steps:

1. Run the setup program using the */a /r* command-line options: *setup.exe /a /r*. This creates a Setup.iss file based on the way you configure the installation as you step through the setup program. The Setup.iss file is in %SYSTEMROOT%.

2. Copy Setup.iss from %SYSTEMROOT% to the folder containing the package. If you're using the distribution folder described in this chapter, you'll want to create a subfolder in OEM*N*\\$OEM$\APPS\RUNONCE for the package and then start the setup program from a batch file that you put in OEM*N*\\$OEM$\APPS \RUNONCE. This avoids duplicate file names.

3. Run the setup program using the */a /s* command-line options: *setup.exe /a /s*. The setup program runs silently using the responses in the Setup.iss file.

Wise Installation System

Packages created using Wise Installation System (*http://www.wise.com*) recognize the **/s** command-line option for unattended installation. There isn't a tool available to script the installation, however.

Repackaging Legacy Applications

Some legacy installers don't support silent installations, and some that do support silent installations don't provide a way to script settings. No legacy installers provide the management capabilities that Windows Installer provides.

In these cases, you can consider repackaging an application that uses a legacy installer. Repackaging an application is part art and part science. The topic is too large to cover in this chapter, so I'll serve you better by referring you to some exceptional sources of information on the topic:

- **Wise for Windows Installer at *http://www.wise.com***   Wise for Windows Installer is the packaging tool that I use most. It's easy to use, and I get very good results almost every time I use this product.

- **The Definitive Guide to Windows Installer Technology for System Administrators at *http://www.wise.com/ebook***   This free e-book describes Windows Installer in depth, including how to repackage legacy applications using Wise for Windows Installer.

- **AppDeploy.com at *http://www.appdeploy.com***   This Web site provides useful articles about repackaging. It also provides a forum in which you can get guidance from other people. One item on this Web site that is valuable is a list of files and registry keys that you can exclude from your packages.

- *http://www.microsoft.com/windows2000/techinfo/planning/management/veritas.asp*   This is a step-by-step guide to repackaging applications using Veritas WinINSTALL LE, which comes with Microsoft Windows 2000. It's a good tutorial on how to use most packaging tools.

- **The Administrator Shortcut Guide to Software Packaging for Desktop Migrations** at *http://www.installshield.com/microsite/packaging_ebook1*   This e-book is an excellent resource to learn about packaging applications for deployment.

- **Administrator's Introduction to Application Repackaging and Software Deployment Using Windows Installer (InstallShield Press, 2003)**   This book, which is available through most booksellers, is a valuable resource for serious repackaging work.

Third-Party Distribution Products

The following list describes some third-party products that I've used before to distribute software:

- **Executive Software SiteKeeper** at *http://www.executive.com*   SiteKeeper is a distribution tool for small businesses that installs software on computers with elevated privileges. It's a good product to use in shops that don't have Active Directory available because it provides some of the same distribution features. Shops that are using Active Directory should use Group Policy, however.

- **AutoProf Profile Maker** at *http://www.autoprof.com*   Profile Maker is a versatile tool for centrally configuring user and computer settings. In addition to configuring computers, Profile Maker can run commands with elevated privileges and includes features specifically designed for installing applications in locked-down environments.

More Info   AppDeploy.com provides information on more than 150 software distribution tools at *http://www.appdeploy.com/tools*. Many of these products have reviews posted to help you make an informed decision when evaluating them.

Elevating Installation Privileges

Privileges are a nasty little paradox. On the one hand, you don't want to add users to the local Administrators group. Restricting users is a best practice that prevents human error, senseless distractions, opportunistic viruses, and so on. On the other hand, deploying software to restricted users is difficult because they don't have the privileges necessary to install most applications, such as Office 2003 Editions. What I want to show you in this chapter is how to run processes elevated, so you can perform many of the tasks I've described in locked-down environments.

The sections following this one go from elegant to dodgy. Group Policy, specifically the *AlwaysInstallElevated* policy, is one way to allow restricted users to install Windows Installer-based applications. You can also use the Secondary Logon feature or Scheduled Tasks. The section "AutoLogon," later in this chapter on page 691, describes a method that SMS uses, and I tend to like this solution. The last two methods I describe in this section are very dodgy and can be used against you if you're not careful.

Group Policy

The policy *AlwaysInstallElevated* installs Windows Installer-based applications with elevated privileges. This policy is one way to allow users to install Windows Installer-based applications that they couldn't otherwise install because their accounts are in restricted groups or you've locked down the desktops.

Keep in mind the consequences of using this policy. Users can take advantage of this policy to gain full control of their computers. Potentially, users can even permanently change their privileges and circumvent your ability to manage their accounts and computers. Not only that, this policy opens the door to viruses disguised as Windows Installer package files. For these reasons, this isn't a setting that I recommend in any but the most necessary scenarios—when there's no other method available other than to toss users in the local Administrators group.

For this policy to be effective, you must enable both the per-computer and per-user versions of it at the same time. In other words, enable it in Computer Configuration as well as User Configuration. If you're going to use this policy, I recommend that you enable it for each rollout unit just prior to deploying software to it. Deploy your package and then immediately remove the policy for that unit. You can at least limit your exposure to the perils that this policy creates.

Note If you have Active Directory and Group Policy, you shouldn't consider using the *AlwaysInstallElevated* policy. The only reason you'd use this policy is in lieu of a software management infrastructure. You'd set this policy and then find some clever method for launching the setup program on the remote computer. If you have Active Directory and Group Policy, however, you have at your disposal an elegant solution for small and medium businesses: Software Installation and Maintenance. This feature allows you to deploy software through Group Policy objects (GPOs). The best part is that you can deploy Windows Installer-based software to restricted users and locked-down desktops because applications you deploy through Group Policy install with elevated privileges. The paper "Understanding Software Installation" is an excellent walk-through of the subject. The URL is *http://www.microsoft.com/resources/documentation/windows/xp/all /proddocs/en-us/sag_adeconcepts_01.mspx.*

Caution Setting the Windows Installer policy Always Install With Elevated Privileges allows a user without administrator rights to the computer to install any Windows Installer package. Similarly, setting the policy Enable User To Use Media Source While Elevated allows users without administrator rights to install programs from a CD. The installation runs with elevated privileges, and the user has unlimited access to system files and the registry. Setting either of these policies leaves the computer highly vulnerable, potentially allowing an attacker to run malicious code on the computer. Using these policies to elevate a software installation is not recommended.

Secondary Logon

Secondary Logon, also called *Run As*, enables users to run programs in the contexts of accounts other than their own. For example, if I'm logged on to the computer using the account Jerry, which is in the Power Users group, but I need to run a program as an administrator, I hold down the Shift key, right-click the program's shortcut icon, click Run As, and then type the Administrator account's name and password. The program runs under the Administrator account. Because Secondary Logon relies on users knowing the credentials, which they won't know, it's not a really useful tool for software deployment, unless you give users a temporary set of credentials with which to use Secondary Logon. I include it here to answer the inevitable question about whether you can use it for that purpose.

You can use Secondary Logon from the command prompt, too. The following shows you the syntax for this command, and Table 23-14 describes each option:

```
runas [ [/noprofile | /profile] [/env] [/netonly] ] /user:Username Program
runas [ [/noprofile | /profile] [/env] [/netonly] ] /smartcard
[/user:Username] Program
```

Table 23-14   Runas.exe Command-Line Options

Option	Description
/noprofile	Specifies that Runas should not load the user profile. Programs load faster but often don't work properly.
/profile	Specifies that Runas should load the user profile.
/env	Uses the current environment instead of the user's environment.
/netonly	Specifies that the credentials are for remote access only.
/savecred	Uses the credentials previously saved by the user.
/smartcard	Specifies that the credentials are provided by a smart card.
/user:Username	Specifies the account name to use; it should be in the form of user@domain or domain\user.
Program	Specifies the command to execute.

Scheduled Tasks

One thing I like about Scheduled Tasks is that you have remote access to the Scheduled Tasks folder on each computer. Also, you can include an account name and password in each task. You're not relying on users to provide the credentials necessary to run a job, such as installing software. For this reason, Scheduled Tasks beats Secondary Logon. In My Network Places, find the computer on which you want to add a task. Open the computer's Scheduled Tasks folder; right-click in the folder; click New, Scheduled Task; and then rename the task. Configure the task as described in the following list:

- In the Task tab's Run box, type the command you want to execute. Remember to keep the command's path relative to the computer on which you're running it.

- In the Task tab's Run As box, type the account in which you want to run the task and then click Set Password to set the matching password. Type the account in the form domain\username.

- On the Schedule tab, configure the task's schedule. In the scenarios that I've described (deploying software and settings), you'd want to schedule the task to run once.

- On the Settings tab, configure Windows XP Professional to remove the task from the Scheduled Tasks folder after it runs. No reason to leave behind artifacts.

Note Be careful not to schedule tasks that require user interaction. Users won't see the task running unless they look in Windows Task Manager and view tasks for all users. For example, if you schedule a task to run on a computer as the local administrator and the user Jerry is the current console user, Jerry won't be able to interact with the task. If the task requires user interface, it'll hang. Many programs, particularly setup programs, have command-line options that run them quietly. Install Office 2003 Editions with no user interaction by using the */qn* command-line option, for example. Also, use this method to install software or run programs that don't interact with the current console user's profile because this method will affect the profile only of the user you typed in the Run As box. In other words, install applications that support per-computer installations or run programs that interact with *HKLM*.

AutoLogon

This is my favorite method when I don't have a software management infrastructure available for deploying software. I use AutoLogon. This is the same capability that you can configure in answer files (as described in Chapter 6, "Answer Files"), but you can use it after deployment. Table 23-15 describes the settings you need to configure for AutoLogon. To enable this feature, you must set the REG_SZ value AutoAdminLogon to 1. Then, you set the REG_SZ value DefaultUserName to the account that you want to use and set the REG_SZ value DefaultPassword to the account's password. If the user name doesn't include the domain, set the REG_SZ value DefaultDomainName to the name of the domain authenticating the account. Just remember that you must add the account to one of the local groups in order to log on to Windows XP Professional using that account. The domain administrator is already a member of the local Administrators group, but I don't recommend using the domain administrator account with this technique. Instead, you can use the local Administrator account, which is always available. The last value you set is the REG_DWORD value AutoLogonCount. Set this value to the number of times you want to automatically log on to Windows XP Professional.

Here's how it works. If the AutoAdminLogon value is 1, and the AutoLogonCount value is not 0, Windows XP Professional automatically logs on to the computer using the credentials provided in the values DefaultUserName, DefaultDomainName, and DefaultPassword. The operating system then decrements the value in AutoLogonCount. When AutoLogonCount reaches zero, Windows XP Professional removes the values AutoLogonCount and DefaultPassword from the registry and no longer logs the user on to it automatically.

Table 23-15   Configuring AutoLogon

Setting	Name	Type	Data
HKLM\SOFTWARE\Microsoft\Windows NT\CurrentVersion\Winlogon			
Enable AutoLogon	AutoAdminLogon	REG_SZ	0 | 1
User Name	DefaultUserName	REG_SZ	Name
User Domain	DefaultDomainName	REG_SZ	Domain
User Password	DefaultPassword	REG_SZ	Password
Number Of Times To Log On To Windows XP Professional	AutoLogonCount	REG_DWORD	N
HKLM\SOFTWARE\Microsoft\Windows\CurrentVersion\RunOnce			
Program To Run	Name	REG_SZ	Command

The last step is to put the command you want to run in HKLM\SOFTWARE\Microsoft\Windows\CurrentVersion\RunOnce. Because you're putting this command in the RunOnce key, Windows XP Professional runs this command one time and then removes the value from the registry. Each value in RunOnce is a command. The name of each REG_SZ value doesn't matter, but you store the command line that you want to execute in it.

An example will tie everything together for you. Suppose that I want to deploy an application to a computer, but the users in my organization are restricted and can't install it. I'd configure the values described in Table 23-15 so that when the current user logs out or when Windows XP Professional restarts, the operating system automatically logs the domain Administrator on to the computer. I know that the application reboots the computer one time during the installation process, so I have to set AutoLogonCount to 2. The first time Windows XP Professional logs the user on to it, it starts the setup program, and the second, it continues the setup program. The script shown in Listing 23-1 shows a way to automatically configure Windows XP Professional for this scenario.

Listing 23-1

```
[Version]
Signature=$CHICAGO$
[DefaultInstall]
AddReg=Reg.Settings
[Reg.Settings]
HKLM,SOFTWARE\Microsoft\Windows NT\CurrentVersion\Winlogon,AutoAdminLogon,0,"1"
HKLM,SOFTWARE\Microsoft\Windows NT\CurrentVersion\Winlogon,DefaultUserName,0,
    "Administrator"
HKLM,SOFTWARE\Microsoft\Windows NT\CurrentVersion\Winlogon,DefaultDomainName,0,
    "HONEYCUTT"
HKLM,SOFTWARE\Microsoft\Windows NT\CurrentVersion\Winlogon,DefaultPassword,0,
    "PASSWORD"
```

```
HKLM,SOFTWARE\Microsoft\Windows
NT\CurrentVersion\Winlogon,AutoLogonCount,0x10001,0x02
HKLM,SOFTWARE\Microsoft\Windows\CurrentVersion\RunOnce,Setup,0,
"\\Server\Share\Setup.exe"
```

The last thing that you should know about this technique is that after Windows XP Professional automatically logs the user on to it and the task completes, you'll want to log the account off of the computer. Otherwise, you leave Windows XP Professional vulnerable because anybody wandering by the computer has access to the account you used. The Windows Support Tools, which you install from the Windows XP Professional CD in the Support\Tools folder, contains a utility called Shutdown. After installing the application, run the command *shutdown -l* to log the user off of Windows XP Professional. To restart the computer, run *shutdown −r*. To chain the application's setup program to the Shutdown command, use a batch file and the Start command with the */wait* command-line option, which enables you to run programs synchronously, one after the other. To see the command-line options for the Shutdown command, type **shutdown /?** at the command prompt. Type **start /?** to see the options for the Start command.

Sysinternals Psexec

You can use Sysinternals Psexec to install software on remote computers. To download Psexec, see *http://www.sysinternals.com*. Also, this book's companion CD contains batch scripts that you can use to automate this command for a list of computers. For more information about these batch scripts, see Appendix E, "Batch Script Syntax." In particular, use the batch script forlist.cmd to run Psexec for a list of computers contained in a text file or forcmd.cmd to run Psexec for a list of computers generated by the command *net view*.

Before using Psexec to install software on remote computers, you must attend to a few details first. You need to make sure that you can install the application silently—either by using an answer file or by specifying the appropriate command-line options (see the section "Automating Legacy Installers"). Then, you need to copy the installation package to the target computer. The easiest way to do that is to copy the package to a subfolder of the admin$ share on the target computer, which happens to be the %SYSTEMROOT% folder. Then, you can use Psexec to launch the program locally. Incidentally, Psexec does have a command-line option that copies the program file to the target computer for you, but this assumes that the entire package is included in a single file. For example, if you have a program that's packaged as Setup.exe and requires the */s* command-line option to run silently, you can use the command *psexec \\target −u username −p password −c setup.exe /s* to install it on the remote computer *target* using the account *username* and password *password*. Of course, using Psexec to run programs on remote computers requires that the account you use have the appropriate credentials.

On the Resource Kit CD   This book's companion CD contains wrappers for Psexec in the form of batch scripts. Remexec.cmd and Remsetup.cmd are in the Scripts folder. Remexec.cmd executes a command for a list of computers that you specify on the command line. The program file must exist on the target computer, however. Remsetup.cmd copies a program file to a target computer and then executes it. You must run the batch scripts using an account that has appropriate permissions on the target computer, and Psexec.exe must be in the current path.

Best Practices

The following are best practices for installing software on computers running Windows XP Professional:

- Configure installations so that they don't require user interaction.

- In locked-down environments, use distribution tools that allow you to install applications with elevated privileges.

- Repackage applications as Windows Installer-based applications to take advantage of the management features in Windows Installer.

Part V

Appendixes

Appendix A

Mobile Scenarios

For organizations that support mobile users, important considerations are hardware, power management, and security on portable computers. In addition, some administrative concerns are relevant to roaming users in organizations that use roaming user profiles or Folder Redirection. You can configure and manage Microsoft Windows XP Professional to provide support for mobile users and include features and tools that are designed specifically for portable computer users.

Overview

Windows XP Professional offers several new features for mobile users. In addition, several Microsoft Windows NT 4 and Microsoft Windows 2000 features, as well as processes such as starting, hibernating, standby, and resuming, are enhanced in Windows XP Professional in order to increase functionality for mobile users. The following list describes these new features:

- **Fast system startup** Windows XP Professional provides improved system boot and resume performance, resulting in fast system startup. The standby feature reduces power consumption by turning off the display, hard disk, and other system components while preserving the contents of memory. Standby also allows you to return to work quickly after waking the system. The hibernate feature saves the entire system state to the hard disk and turns off the computer. When the system restarts from hibernation, the desktop and all applications are restored to their previous state.

- **Folder Redirection** Folder Redirection allows the administrator to direct the contents of special shell folders, such as My Documents, to an alternate location on a server or a network share. When Folder Redirection is applied to these special folders, the redirection is transparent to users; they can continue to work with documents on the server as if the documents are on their local drives. Folder Redirection is best used in conjunction with Offline Files.

- **Offline Files** The Offline Files feature allows users to disconnect from the network and work as if they are still connected. When the computer is offline, files and folders appear in the same directory in which they appear online. By using Offline Files, users can continue to work with copies of files that are available on a network when they are not connected to the network. Offline Files stores the data in the computer's cache to make network files available offline. When users reconnect to the network, Offline Files synchronizes the files stored on the local drive with the files on the network.

- **Hibernation** The hibernation feature allows the Windows XP Professional desktop to be restored quickly after a computer is shut down. When a computer is put into hibernation, the current system state is saved to the hard disk before the computer is turned off. Then, when a user restarts the computer, Windows XP Professional restarts any programs that were running when the computer entered hibernation and restores all previous network connections.

- **ACPI and APM support** Windows XP Professional supports the Advanced Configuration and Power Interface (ACPI) specification for robust power management and system configuration. Windows XP Professional also provides some power management features for portable computers with a legacy Advanced Power Management (APM) version 1.2–based basic input/output system (BIOS).

- **Enhanced battery life** Windows XP Professional provides several new features to enhance battery life. Windows XP Professional automatically dims a laptop's display when it is switched to battery power, and turns off the display panel when the laptop's lid is closed. In addition, Windows XP Professional features intelligent processor throttling to reduce central processing unit (CPU) power consumption. Windows XP Professional also provides more accurate estimates of remaining battery life.

- **Processor performance control** Windows XP Professional provides native support for processor performance control technologies such as Intel Speed-Step Technology, AMD PowerNow!, and Transmeta LongRun. Windows XP Professional also features an adaptive processor performance control algorithm that dynamically balances system performance and power consumption, based on the current CPU workload and remaining battery life.

- **Battery and processor metrics** Windows XP Professional displays information about processor performance and battery activity in System Monitor. The processor performance data available includes the current processor frequency and power consumption. Battery information provided includes the charge and discharge rates, voltage, and remaining capacity.

- **Wake-on-critical battery** Windows XP Professional supports wake-on-critical battery for portable computers that implement this feature. This feature allows a computer to awaken from standby when battery power becomes critically low and switch to hibernation to prevent data loss.

- **Dynamic configuration of hot added devices** When you insert and remove devices such as CardBus cards or universal serial bus (USB) devices, Windows XP Professional detects and configures them without requiring you to restart the computer.

- **Hot and cold docking or undocking** With your portable computer fully powered, you can dock to a docking station and undock from a docking station without shutting down the computer.

Table A-1 shows the new or enhanced features in Windows XP Professional that support mobile users and indicates which of these features are available in Microsoft Windows 95, Microsoft Windows 98, Microsoft Windows NT Workstation 4, and Microsoft Windows 2000 Professional.

Table A-1   Mobile Features in Windows XP Professional

Feature	Windows 95	Windows 98	Windows NT 4	Windows 2000	Windows XP
Offline Files				Yes	Yes
Folder Redirection				Yes	Yes
Roaming User Profiles			Yes	Yes	Yes
Briefcase	Yes	Yes	Yes	Yes	Yes
Hibernation	Yes	Yes		Yes	Yes
Power management	Yes	Yes		Yes	Yes
ACPI support		Yes		Yes	Yes
APM support	Yes	Yes		Yes	Yes
Standby (APM and ACPI only)	Yes	Yes		Yes	Yes
Battery management (APM and ACPI only)		Yes		Yes	Yes
Dynamic configuration of PC Cards	Yes	Yes		Yes	Yes
Hot and cold docking or undocking	Yes	Yes		Yes	Yes
Hot insertion and removal of devices in hot swappable module bays		Yes		Yes	Yes

Preparation

Before you can make use of mobile computing in your organization, you need to identify the critical operating system components, properties, and features that you will need to configure on your portable computers. You must also ensure that you address critical configuration issues that are specific to portable computers:

- **Check BIOS Compatibility**   Windows XP Professional supports the ACPI specification, which enables reliable system configuration and power management features. If a portable computer has an ACPI-compliant BIOS, use the Hardware Compatibility List (HCL) to verify that it is compatible with Windows XP Professional. If it is not, upgrade the BIOS to the latest available version. If you upgrade to an ACPI-based BIOS on your portable computer after you install Windows XP Professional, and your old BIOS was either not ACPI-compliant or not compatible with Windows XP Professional, you must reinstall Windows XP Professional in order to enable ACPI and the power-management features that it supports. For more information about hardware compatibility, see the HCL at *http://www.microsoft.com/whdc/hcl/default.mspx*. If a portable computer has an APM-based BIOS, run the Apmstat.exe support tool to determine whether the BIOS has any known problems. If the APM BIOS is known to be compatible with Windows XP Professional, APM power management is enabled by default. Apmstat.exe is part of the Windows Support Tools, which are in the Support\Tools folder on the Windows XP Professional product CD.

- **Grant Installation and Configuration Rights**   If you configure a portable computer for a user who travels frequently, add this user to the Power Users group. The user can then install, uninstall, and configure software. If a hardware device fails or needs to be reinstalled while not connected to the network, a member of the Power Users group can reinstall the device, but only if the driver package meets the following conditions:

    - It is present on the system (that is, it does not need to be installed from removable media, such as a CD provided by a vendor).

    - It is digitally signed.

    - It can be installed without any user interface.

- If a user must be able to add hardware even if the driver package does not meet these conditions, add this user to the Administrators group. All other types of users should be members of the Users group, which does not allow them to install, uninstall, or configure software and hardware, except when the above-mentioned three conditions are true. In general, no Users should be members of the Administrators group unless they need to install, uninstall, and configure non–Plug and Play (PnP) hardware and drivers.

- **Verify Hardware Configuration**   After you install new hardware on a portable computer, you need to verify that all devices function when the computer is both docked and undocked. Log on in turn as a member of the Power Users and the Users groups to test the devices, as well as the docking and undocking functionality. This testing is necessary because some hardware can be fully installed only by a member of the Administrators group. When members of the Power Users or Users group add the devices, the driver packages might not be installed. Windows XP Professional uses one hardware profile to load drivers when the portable computer is docked (the Docked Profile) and another when the computer is undocked (the Undocked Profile). Verify that the properties are set correctly for both the Docked Profile and the Undocked Profile.

- **Configure Power Management Options**   Windows XP Professional power management is based on the concept of power schemes. A power scheme is a group of preset power options that is passed to the operating system to control a computer's power management behavior. Power schemes are presented to the user in the Power Options Control Panel option. The power policy used when the computer is powered by AC (utility) power can be different from the policy that is used when the computer is powered by a battery. Verify that the power schemes that are available are appropriate for the target user environments. The most useful power schemes for portable computers are Portable/Laptop, Presentation, and Max Battery. Using the default power scheme settings might not always be the best configuration. You might need to explore the best configuration for the user's needs.

- **Install Applications**   All software and software components must be installed locally and run locally on portable computers (this includes Microsoft Office 2003 Editions). You must therefore make sure that you do not have any partially installed programs or distributed programs installed on a portable computer that is frequently used offline. Only Administrators can install software for personal digital assistants (PDAs) because some PDA software cannot be installed by members of the Power Users group. Also, only members of the Administrators group can use the Internet Connection Wizard to configure an Internet connection.

- **Configure Offline File Storage**   If you have files and folders that you want to make available offline for mobile users, enable and configure file-storing settings on the server or network share. This is particularly important for folders such as My Documents that have been redirected to a network share or a server. Also, make sure that you have configured all offline files settings, including synchronization settings, on the portable computer. If a user uses an e-mail program or a Web browser, be sure to configure the e-mail program and the Web browser for offline content.

- **Configure Security** Because portable computers are vulnerable to theft, you must ensure that they are configured securely. Format all hard disks as NTFS and apply the appropriate permissions to files and folders that contain sensitive data. Also, encrypt files and folders that contain sensitive data, and require users to use strong passwords for logging on both locally and on the network. You might also want to encrypt the Offline Files cache, so that any network files made available offline are also encrypted.

- **Configure Roaming User Profiles and Folder Redirection** If you're supporting roaming desktop users or portable computer users who are connected directly to a network most of the time, configuring roaming user profiles and Folder Redirection can provide a number of advantages, such as fast computer replacement and the storage of backup copies of data on the network. If portable computers in your organization are rarely connected to the network or are connected remotely most of the time, however, do not use roaming user profiles or Folder Redirection. For more information about roaming user profiles and Folder Redirection, see the section "User Profiles and Folder Redirection" later in this appendix on page 715.

Hardware Management

The PnP support in Windows XP Professional allows devices to be configured on the system without the computer having to be restarted. You can therefore add or remove a device from the computer while it is running, and Windows XP Professional will automatically allocate resources, install or uninstall the appropriate device drivers, and enable or disable the device. Full PnP support is useful for portable computers because the device configuration on portable computers changes frequently to accommodate the user's environment (docked or undocked) and the user's needs (such as working remotely online or working offline). For portable computers that are ACPI-enabled, PnP makes the following functionality possible:

- Dynamic configuration of devices, such as PC Cards and CardBus.

- Hot swapping of Integrated Drive Electronics (IDE) devices in device bays, such as hard disks, floppy drives, and CD-ROM drives.

- Hot docking and undocking.

Note Full PnP support is possible only if both the device and the device drivers support PnP, and the computer is ACPI-based.

Hardware Profile Creation

Windows XP Professional uses hardware profiles to determine which drivers to load when the system hardware changes. Hardware profiles are an important feature for portable computers that use a docking station. Windows XP Professional uses one hardware profile to load drivers when the portable computer is docked (the Docked Profile) and another (the Undocked Profile) when the computer is undocked. Windows XP Professional creates these two hardware profiles for portable computers when the computer is docked and undocked.

The hardware profiles are created when Windows XP Professional queries the BIOS for a dock serial ID and then assigns names for the docked and undocked configurations. You do not need to reconfigure the Docked Profile or the Undocked Profile if your system is PnP-compliant. If a portable computer is fully PnP-compliant, you need only these hardware profiles, and you do not need to designate which profile to use when the computer starts. The computer detects the docked or undocked state and uses the appropriate profile.

If a portable computer is not fully PnP-compliant, you might need to create a new hardware profile. You can then configure the profile by enabling and disabling devices. For more information about configuring hardware profiles, see Windows XP Professional Help and Support Center.

Dynamic Device Configuration

With dynamic device configuration, portable computer users can add or remove PC Cards, CardBus cards, USB and IEEE 1394 devices, and so forth without restarting the computer. The device and the device drivers must support PnP in order for users to take advantage of dynamic configuration.

Caution   Some ACPI-enabled computers might not be fully ACPI-compliant or support hot addition and removal of devices in hot swappable module bays. Removing such devices on these computers without first shutting down the system can physically damage the device.

Docking and Undocking

Docking and undocking of portable computers can be done either hot or cold. In a cold dock or undock, the computer is shut down before it is inserted into or removed from the docking station. In a hot dock or undock, the computer is running, with or without programs and documents open, when it is inserted into or removed from the docking station. Computer manufacturers can design the docking stations and BIOS of their mobile computers in different ways, resulting in different docking and undocking behaviors. For specific information about the docking and undocking behavior of your portable computers, see the manufacturer's documentation.

Hot docking and hot undocking can be performed only on computers that are ACPI-enabled. To hot dock a system, insert the fully powered system into the docking station. To hot undock a system, click Eject PC on the Start menu before removing the system from the docking station. The Eject PC command appears only if a computer is ACPI-enabled. Some portable computer manufacturers support other methods of hot undocking. See manufacturer documentation for details about a given system.

Removing a portable computer without using the Eject PC command is not recommended. Use the Eject PC command to perform a hot undock. Note that undocking a portable computer while it is in standby or hibernation is not recommended. If a system is in standby or hibernation, first resume the system and then follow the hot undock procedure.

> **Caution**   Data loss or system instability can occur if a user does not use the Eject PC command before undocking in a fully powered state or from standby or hibernation.

You can use Group Policy to disable hot undocking, in which case the Eject PC command does not appear on ACPI-enabled computers. For more information about using Group Policy to control undocking privileges, see the section "Undocking Portable Computers" later in this appendix on page 725.

Cold docking takes place when the computer is completely shut down before it is docked or undocked. It is recommended that you use cold docking and undocking if you have an APM-based system or other non-ACPI-based computer. To perform a cold dock, insert the computer into the docking station while the computer is shut down. To perform a cold undock, shut down the computer, and then remove or eject it from the docking station. When you shut down the computer before a cold dock or undock, you must use the shut down command. Do not use the hibernate or stand by commands.

ACPI and APM

Configuring power management allows you to control how a computer consumes energy. Windows XP Professional supports the ACPI specification. The ACPI architecture is designed to provide for Operating System-Directed Power Management (OSPM). Windows XP Professional also supports the legacy APM version 1.2 BIOS architecture; however, APM provides only limited power management support.

If you do not have an APM-based or ACPI-based computer, it is still possible to manage some aspects of power consumption. For example, depending on the capabilities of your hardware, you can reduce the power consumed by the computer by setting timers to turn the display or disk drives off.

ACPI Power Management

Using features supported by ACPI, Windows XP Professional directs and manages power usage on a system-wide basis. The operating system's power policy determines what devices to turn off and when to put the computer into a low-power state. Power policy is based on a combination of application requirements, the user's preferences, and the computer's hardware capabilities. To conserve energy and prolong battery life, when the computer is idle the operating system can turn off devices such as the display panel or hard disk drive, or put the computer into a low-power sleep state such as standby or hibernation.

Each device class on the computer has a power policy owner. The policy owner for a particular device class is the component that is best aware of how the device is used. Typically, this is the device class driver. Each policy owner must manage power appropriately for its class and work consistently with the operating system's policy for putting the computer into a low-power state. For example, a network adapter might sense that no network cable is plugged in, and therefore request that the operating system put the adapter in a low-power state because it is not being used.

In order to use the ACPI power-management features in Windows XP Professional, your computer must have an ACPI-compliant BIOS that is compatible with Windows XP Professional. During installation, Windows XP Professional determines which HAL to install on the computer. If the computer has an ACPI-compliant BIOS, an ACPI HAL is installed and you can use ACPI power-management features. If the computer does not have an ACPI-compliant BIOS, a non-ACPI HAL is installed and ACPI power-management features are not available. The HAL directs information from the operating system and device drivers to specific devices. In order to determine which HAL to install, Windows XP Professional performs the following process during installation:

1. Windows XP Professional checks the ACPI BIOS tables during startup. These tables list the devices that are installed on the computer and their power management capabilities. If this information is missing, or if the information is in the wrong form, a non-ACPI HAL is installed.

2. If the tables are correct, Windows XP Setup determines whether the computer's BIOS is known to be incompatible with the ACPI standard. If the BIOS is on the incompatible list, a non-ACPI HAL is installed.

3. If the BIOS is not on the incompatible BIOS list, Windows XP Setup checks the BIOS date. If the BIOS is not on the incompatible BIOS list, and the BIOS date is later than 1/1/99, an ACPI HAL is installed.

4. If the BIOS is not on the incompatible BIOS list, and the BIOS date is earlier than 1/1/99, Windows XP Setup determines whether the BIOS is known to be compatible with Windows XP Professional. If the BIOS is compatible, an ACPI HAL is installed. If the BIOS is not compatible, an earlier HAL is installed.

More Info   For more information about BIOS compatibility, see the HCL at *http://www.microsoft.com/whdc/hcl/default.mspx*.

You can use Device Manager to determine whether your computer is operating in ACPI mode. Here's how to determine whether Windows XP Professional is running in ACPI mode:

1. In Control Panel, click Performance And Maintenance and then click System.

2. In the System Properties dialog box, click the Hardware tab and then click Device Manager.

3. In the details pane, click Computer.

4. If Advanced Configuration and Power Interface (ACPI) PC is listed under Computer, the computer is operating in ACPI mode.

If you have an ACPI BIOS, but Windows XP Professional is not installed in the ACPI mode, your ACPI BIOS might be noncompliant. Check with your computer manufacturer to see if a more recent ACPI-compatible BIOS is available. If Windows XP Professional is installed in non-ACPI mode on your computer, and you upgrade to a new BIOS version, you must reinstall Windows XP Professional to enable ACPI mode.

APM Power Management

Windows XP Professional support of APM power management is intended to provide compatibility with legacy notebook computers. The APM power management system is not designed to run on desktop computers, as power management support for the APM system is limited to battery status, suspend, resume, and auto-hibernate functions. APM does not work with every APM-compatible system running Windows XP Professional. Microsoft has tested APM-capable systems to determine how well each system and BIOS combination supports APM. Mobile systems can support APM if they meet the following criteria:

- Hardware must meet basic Windows XP Professional requirements.

- An ACPI-compliant BIOS is not available for end-user system upgrade.

- The APM 1.2–compliant BIOS is not on the Disable APM List for a particular BIOS version number and date.

- All user-defined CMOS power control features are disabled or minimized, time-outs are set to Off or to the longest possible time allowed, and the APM BIOS is enabled.

To use APM-based power management features with Windows XP Professional, the APM-based BIOS on your computer must be compatible with Windows XP Professional. Windows XP Professional supports APM version 1.2 on portable computers. The portable computer, however, must have an APM-compatible BIOS for APM features to work properly. Windows XP Professional determines whether a BIOS is APM-compatible during installation, and does one of the following on the basis of this determination:

- Installs APM support (Ntapm.sys and Apmbatt.sys) and enables APM if the computer's BIOS is found on the auto-enable APM list.

- Doesn't install or enable APM support if the computer's BIOS is found on the disable APM list. APM on these systems does not work reliably, and data loss might occur if used.

- Installs APM support but does not enable APM support if the computer's BIOS is not on the auto-enable APM list or the disable APM list. APM might work properly, but you must enable APM in the Windows XP Professional graphical user interface (GUI).

> **Note** APM must be enabled in the BIOS before Windows XP Professional is installed. If APM is disabled in the BIOS before installation, Windows XP Professional does not install power management support even if the APM BIOS is on the auto-enable APM list.

If APM is not enabled after you install Windows XP Professional, either the computer's BIOS is on the disable APM list or it is not on the auto-enable APM list. You can determine whether either of these is the case by using the Apmstat.exe tool, which is included with the Windows Support Tools on the Windows XP Professional operating system CD in the Support\Tools folder. To determine APM BIOS compatibility by using Apmstat.exe, type **apmstat** at the command prompt. If Apmstat.exe reports that an APM BIOS is known to be incompatible or that an APM BIOS is known to have problems, do not attempt to circumvent Windows XP Setup by forcing it to install APM support. This might cause a computer to behave erratically and even lose data. Also, if an APM BIOS is known to be incompatible, make sure that APM is disabled in the BIOS. If Apmstat.exe reports that an APM BIOS is not known to be compatible and it is not known to be incompatible, you might still be able to use APM, but you must enable and configure APM so that it works properly on your computer.

Here's how to verify that APM support is installed on a computer:

1. In Control Panel, click Performance And Maintenance, and then click System.

2. Click the Hardware tab and then click Device Manager.

3. On the View menu, click Show hidden devices.

4. If NT APM/Legacy Support is listed in the details pane, APM support is installed.

Here's how to enable APM:

1. In Control Panel, click Performance And Maintenance and then click Power Options.

2. Click the APM tab.

3. Under Advanced Power Management, select the Enable Advanced Power Management Support check box.

> **Note**   The APM tab is present only if an APM BIOS is detected that is either APM 1.2–compliant or that might work with APM even if it is not APM 1.2–compliant. It is not recommended that you enable APM support on a computer that has a BIOS that is not APM-compliant. If problems occur after you enable APM support, disable APM and contact the computer manufacturer for an updated BIOS. The APM tab is not present if a computer has multiple processors because Windows XP Professional does not install APM support on multiprocessor computers.

To utilize APM power management on your system, you must configure an APM-based BIOS so that power management works properly with Windows XP Professional. This might involve configuring the APM BIOS in the following way:

- **Set BIOS timeouts to the maximum time or disable them.**   This process allows the operating system (instead of the BIOS) to control time-outs. Because some APM BIOSs turn off or refuse to function if all timeouts are disabled, you might want to set timeouts to the maximum allowed time instead of disabling them.

- **Make sure that screen blanking is turned off in the BIOS.**   Typically, you can turn off screen blanking in the BIOS by disabling the timeout for the display or by setting the timeout to the maximum value. Screen blanking reduces power to the display, which causes the computer to appear to be shut down.

- **Activating a pointing device typically wakes the system and restores power to the display.**   USB and other external pointing devices do not wake the system or restore power to the display, however.

- **Do not use a supplemental video card with a portable computer if you use APM.**   Use only the video card included with the portable computer. The APM BIOS might not detect a video card that is added to the system or a video card that is in a docking station. If the adapter is not discovered by the APM BIOS, the suspend feature does not work.

Power Management Options

Whether you have an ACPI-based or an APM-based computer, several power-management options are available for you to configure. These options include choosing and configuring a power scheme, enabling the battery status indicator, configuring the power and sleep buttons, and setting low-battery alarms.

Power Schemes

Using power schemes, you can configure how and when a computer turns off devices, enters a suspend state, or changes processor performance levels on mobile systems that support this function. You can configure these settings according to the power source in use—whether the computer is plugged into a wall outlet or powered by battery. Depending on the hardware capability, you might be able to configure some of these settings even if the computer is not ACPI- or APM-enabled.

The following default power schemes are available in Windows XP Professional: Home/Office Desk, Portable/Laptop, Presentation, Always On, Minimal Power Management, and Max Battery. You can customize any scheme, or add or delete new schemes to fit a specific situation. For more information about configuring the standby feature and the hibernate feature, see the section "Hibernation and Standby" on the following page.

The default power scheme on portable computers is Portable/Laptop; the Home/Office Desk scheme does not optimize battery power. You might need to change the power scheme based on how the computer is used. For example, you might choose the Presentation scheme to prevent the computer from turning off the display during a presentation. Here's how to configure a power scheme:

1. In Control Panel, click Performance And Maintenance, and then click Power Options.

2. Click the Power Schemes tab.

3. Select a power scheme. You can then change the settings in the power scheme to best meet your needs.

Hibernation and Standby

When a computer enters hibernation, the current state of the computer is saved to disk, and the power to the computer is turned off. When a computer wakes from hibernation, it reads the current state data from the disk and restores the system to the state it was in before it entered hibernation. All programs that were running are restarted, and network connections are restored. Hibernation is enabled by default. All ACPI-compatible and most APM-compatible computers can be set to enter hibernation. Because the contents of the computer's memory are written to disk when the computer enters hibernation, you must have at least as much available disk space as you have memory.

Here's how to disable hibernation:

1. In Control Panel, click Performance And Maintenance, and then click Power Options.

2. Click the Hibernate tab.

3. Clear the Enable Hibernation support check box.

> **Note**   You must have the proper hardware to use hibernation. If the Hibernate tab is not available, the computer does not support hibernation.

When a computer enters standby, the computer's state is saved to memory, and most circuitry and devices are turned off. When a computer resumes from standby, the state is restored from memory, and power is restored to all devices. If power is interrupted when the computer is in standby, data might be lost. All installed devices and device driver software must properly support power management in order for standby to be available.

To provide security, you can have the computer prompt the user for a user name and password after it resumes from hibernate or standby. Password protection is enabled by default. Here's how you can disable password protection when a computer resumes from standby:

1. In Control Panel, click Performance And Maintenance, and then click Power Options.

2. Click the Advanced tab.

3. Clear the Prompt For Password When Computer Resumes From Standby check box.

> **Note**   When you must turn off your portable computer to comply with airline regulations, you must shut down the computer, rather than allowing it to remain in standby. While in standby, the operating system can reactivate itself to run preprogrammed tasks or to conserve battery power. For more information about shutting down a computer, see Windows XP Professional Help and Support Center.

Group Policy Refresh Interval

You can configure the refresh interval by using Group Policy, which controls how often policies are applied on the computer. By default, the refresh interval is 90 minutes, but it can be set to any value between 0 and 64,800 minutes. You can also set an interval offset, which is a random period of time that is applied to the refresh interval. Randomizing the refresh interval prevents clients with the same refresh interval from overloading the server by simultaneously requesting policy updates. By default, the interval offset is 30 minutes, meaning that a random time between 0 and 30 minutes is applied to the refresh interval.

In some cases, Group Policy refresh settings can prevent a computer from entering hibernation or standby because a policy update resets the hibernation or standby timer (as moving the mouse or pressing a key does). For example, if a computer is set to enter hibernation or standby after being idle for 45 minutes, but the Group Policy refresh interval is set at 30 minutes, the hibernation or standby timer never reaches 45 minutes. To ensure that the standby timer reaches 45 minutes (or whatever time you set), set the Group Policy refresh interval so that it is greater than the hibernation setting or standby setting in Power Options. You can also configure Group Policy so that it does not apply settings while the computer is being used. Here's how to change the Group Policy refresh interval and the interval offset for using local policy:

1. In the Run dialog box, type **gpedit.msc**.

2. Do one of the following:

    - In the details pane of Group Policy, under User Configuration, open the Administrative Templates folder and then open the System folder.

    - In the details pane of Group Policy, under Computer Configuration, open the Administrative Templates folder and then open the System folder.

3. Click Group Policy.

4. In the details pane, double-click Group Policy refresh interval for users.

5. Click Enabled.

6. Change the settings for the refresh interval and the interval offset.

Here's how to disable policy updates while a computer is running by using local policy:

1. In the Run dialog box, type **gpedit.msc**.

2. In the details pane of Group Policy, under Computer Configuration, open the Administrative Templates folder and then open the System folder.

3. Click Group Policy.

4. In the details pane, double-click Disable Background Refresh Of Group Policy.

5. Click Enabled.

Battery Monitoring and Management

Windows XP Professional allows you to monitor and manage a portable computer's battery by using Power Meter. Windows XP Professional can also monitor multiple batteries. Battery monitoring and management are available only on ACPI-enabled and APM-enabled computers.

By default, the battery status icon will appear on the taskbar whenever the computer is operating on battery power. You must enable the battery status icon to make it appear on the taskbar at all times. This icon gives users direct access to the power meter feature, allows selection of the current power scheme, and offers direct access to power properties by means of the Power Options Control Panel option. Here's how to add the battery status icon to the taskbar:

1. In Control Panel, click Performance And Maintenance and then click Power Options.

2. Click the Advanced tab.

3. Select the Always Show Icon On The Taskbar check box.

> **Note**   The display icon changes from a battery to a plug depending on the computer's power source—battery power or wall outlet. The display also changes to indicate that the battery is charging or fully charged and shows the remaining battery capacity when the computer is operating on battery power.

If your portable computer uses multiple batteries, you can also configure the battery meter to display the status of multiple batteries:

1. In Control Panel, click Performance And Maintenance, and then click Power Options.

2. Click the Power Meter tab.

3. Click Show Details for each battery.

You can set alarms to indicate low-battery and critical-battery levels. You can select visual and audible alarm notifications; specify an action to take, such as making a change in power state (standby, hibernation, shutdown); and specify the execution of a program to be run:

1. In Control Panel, click Performance And Maintenance, and then click Power Options.

2. Click the Alarms tab.

3. Set the battery activation levels that you want.

4. Click Alarm Action to configure the behaviors of an activated alarm.

Button and Switch Behavior

ACPI-enabled mobile computers can have up to three buttons for controlling system power: a Power button, a Sleep button, and a Lid Switch. Windows XP Professional allows you to configure the action of each button as follows:

- Do Nothing
- Ask Me What To Do
- Sleep
- Hibernate
- Shut Down

Here's how to configure power system button functionality:

1. In Control Panel, click Performance And Maintenance, and then click Power Options.

2. Click the Advanced tab.

3. Do the following:

   - Under When I Close The Lid Of My Portable Computer, select a lid-switch action.

   - Under When I Press The Power Button On My Computer, select a power-button action.

   - Under When I Press The Sleep Button On My Computer, select a sleep-button action.

Wake-On-LAN, Etc.

On ACPI-compatible systems, Windows XP Professional can enable some devices to wake the system from the hibernation or standby. Windows XP Professional supports wake events such as modem wake-on-ring, wake-on-LAN, and wake-on-critical battery. Windows XP Professional also supports wake-on-LAN for CardBus network adapters. In order for the wake features to function, they must be supported by the appropriate computer hardware. Here's how to enable a device to wake the computer:

1. In Control Panel, click Performance And Maintenance, and then click System.

2. Click the Hardware tab and then click Device Manager.

3. Select the device that you want to wake the system and then double-click to open the Properties dialog box.

4. On the Power Management tab, click Allow This Device To Bring The Computer Out Of Standby.

Control Panel Policy

You can prevent users from configuring power options by specifying Control Panel settings in Group Policy. You can disable Control Panel entirely, hide specific Control Panel tools, and show specific Control Panel options. Hiding Power Options can be beneficial if you have configured the power options and you do not want users to change those options. However, if you hide Power Options, users have no means to reconfigure power management settings if they need to be changed while they are away from the office. For example, portable computer users frequently use the Portable/Laptop power scheme. When they use the portable computer for a presentation, however, it is recommended that they switch to the Presentation scheme to prevent the portable computer from turning off the display or entering standby or hibernation during the presentation. Users cannot change power schemes or any other power option if Power Options is not available.

Here's how to hide Power Options by using local policy:

1. In the Run dialog box, enter **gpedit.msc**.

2. In the Group Policy console tree, under User Configuration, open Administrative Templates.

3. Click the Control Panel folder.

4. In the details pane, double-click Hide Specified Control Panel Applets.

5. In the Hide Specified Control Panel Applets Properties dialog box, click Enabled and then click Show.

6. Click Add.

7. Type **power options**.

8. Typically, Power Options appears in the Show Contents dialog box under List Of Disallowed Control Panel Applets.

Here's how to disable Control Panel by using local policy:

1. In the Run dialog box, type **gpedit.msc**.

2. In the Group Policy console tree, under User Configuration, open the Administrative Templates folder.

3. Click the Control Panel folder.

4. In the details pane, double-click Disable Control Panel.

5. Click Enabled.

> **Note**   Disabling Control Panel in Group Policy prevents Control.exe from starting. This removes Control Panel from the Start menu and removes the Control Panel folder from My Computer.

User Profiles and Folder Redirection

A user profile is a group of settings and files that defines the environment that the system loads when a user logs on. For more information about user profiles, see Chapter 12, "User Profiles." The following guidelines can be used when planning profile configurations for users of mobile computers:

- If the user regularly connects to the network via fast link, consider using a roaming user profile.

- If the user rarely connects via fast link, use a local profile. By default, roaming user profiles do not roam over slow links. For example, if a user in the field generally connects via a dial-up connection, but comes into the office twice a year and connects via the LAN, a roaming profile offers little advantage because the server copy would be up-to-date on only those two occasions.

- If the user roams to LAN-connected computers in the domain and also has a laptop computer, use a roaming user profile for the user. For the laptop computer, enable the Group Policy setting Only Allow Local User Profiles. A Computer Configuration Group Policy setting takes precedence over a User Configuration setting, so the user will receive his or her User setting on desktop computers, but will receive the Computer setting on the laptop computer.

Roaming User Profiles

Windows XP Professional includes new Group Policy settings, support for Windows XP Professional fast network logon, and more robust roaming. These features increase the usability, resilience, and performance of roaming user profiles. The Group Policy settings that you use to manage user profiles have been moved to their own folders in the Group Policy snap-in, under *Computer Configuration\Administrative Templates\System\User Profiles* and *User Configuration\Administrative Templates\System\User Profiles*. In addition, three new Computer Configuration settings are available with Windows XP Professional:

- **Prevent Roaming-Profile Changes From Propagating To The Server**   Determines whether changes users make to their roaming profiles are merged with the server copy of the profile. If this policy is set, users receive their roaming profiles when they log on, but any changes they make to their profiles will not be merged to their roaming profiles when they log off.

- **Add The Administrators Security Group To Roaming User Profiles**   In Windows XP Professional, the default file permissions for newly generated roaming profiles are full control for the user and no file access for the Administrators group. By default, an administrator must take ownership of a user's profile folder in order to gain access to it. Because taking ownership is an audited event, this increases the security of the profile folder. This policy allows the Administrators group to have full control of the user's profile directories, as in Windows NT 4. See Knowledge Base article 327462 at *http://support.microsoft.com* for important changes to how Windows XP Professional Service Pack 1 verifies permissions on existing roaming user profiles.

- **Only Allow Local User Profiles**   Determines whether roaming user profiles are available on a particular computer. By default, when a roaming profile user logs on, his or her roaming profile is copied from the server to the local computer. If the user has already logged on to this computer in the past, the roaming profile is merged with the local profile. Similarly, when the user logs off this computer, the local copy of his or her profile, including any changes that have been made, is merged with the server copy.

Folder Redirection with Roaming

The Folder Redirection feature of IntelliMirror allows an administrator to redirect the location of certain folders in the user profile to a network location. See Chapter 21, "Desktop Management," for more information about Folder Redirection. Combining Folder Redirection with roaming user profiles allows you to decrease logon and logoff times for roaming and mobile users. A common practice is to redirect My Documents and My Pictures, and allow Application Data, Desktop, and Start Menu to roam with the profile. In addition to the benefits of improved availability and secure backup that having the data on the network provides, users also realize performance gains over low-speed network connections and in subsequent logon sessions. Because only some of their documents are copied, performance is improved when users' profiles are copied from the server. Not all the data in the user profile is transferred to the desktop each time the user logs on—only the data that user accesses during a session.

> **Note** When implementing roaming user profiles or Folder Redirection for users of laptop computers, keep in mind that the user must log on at least once (sometimes twice) over a fast link in order for these features to apply. If an administrator configures the laptop in the office, he or she should make sure that the user of the laptop logs on to it while still connected via fast link before taking it into the field. An alternative is to use Group Policy to change the slow link speed temporarily.

Offline Files

By using Offline Files, users can disconnect from the network and work as if still connected. When the computer is offline, the files and folders appear in the same directory that they appear in online—as if they are still in the same location on the network. This allows the user working offline to edit files. The next time the user connects to the network, the offline changes are synchronized with the network share. Any changes that were made while the user was working offline are updated to the network.

Offline Files is especially useful for mobile users with portable computers because they can use it to access their files when they are not connected to the network. Thus users can always open, update, and work with current versions of network files when they are not connected to the network. Offline Files stores the data in the computer's cache to make network files available offline. The cache is a portion of disk space that a computer accesses when it is not connected to the network. The view of shared network items that you make available offline is the same as the view online, even if users lose a connection to the network or remove a portable computer from the docking station. Users have the same access permissions to those files and folders that they have when they are connected to the network.

If two users on the network make changes to the same file, they can save their own version of the file to the network, keep the other user's version, or save both.

You can make shared files or folders available for offline use from any computer that shares files by using Server Message Block (SMB)–based file and printer sharing, which includes any computer running Windows 2000, Windows 95, Windows 98, or Windows NT 4. The Offline Files feature is not available on Novell

NetWare networks. When configuring a shared folder, you have the option to choose whether all the files in the folder are automatically available offline, or whether a user must explicitly mark a file to be available offline.

Offline Files is a standalone technology, which means that you do not need to pair it with Folder Redirection and set up and configure network shares. However, pairing the two technologies works well. By default, any folder that is redirected is available offline as well. In Windows XP Professional, all the files in a redirected folder, including subfolders, are automatically made available offline. You can disable automatic caching of redirected folders by using the Group Policy setting Do Not Automatically Make Redirected Folders Available Offline under User Configuration\Administrative Templates\Network\Offline Files.

> **Note**   In Windows 2000, redirected folders are not automatically made available offline. To make folders available offline, administrators use the policy setting Administratively Assigned Offline Files, or the users manually make all files available offline.

Files on a Network Share

Before you can have offline access to the files on a shared network folder, you must specify how the files in the folder are stored in a cache on the client computer—in this case, the user's portable computer. For non-executable files, such as word processing documents, spreadsheets, and bitmaps, there are two options for storing files: automatic caching and manual caching:

- **Automatic Caching**   Automatic caching makes a file available offline by creating a locally stored copy of the file when a user opens the file on a portable computer. Automatically stored files might not always be available in the cache because Offline Files might remove, or purge, them when the cache becomes full. Offline Files will purge files based on frequency of use. Automatic caching is most useful when you have an unreliable or unpredictable network connection. For example, if a user is working on an automatically stored file, and the portable computer is disconnected from the network, the user can continue working on the file without interruption. To make a file available offline at all times, you can use My Computer to mark the file as Always Available Offline.

- **Manual Caching**   Manual caching makes a file or a folder available offline, but only when it is pinned; that is, manually marked on the user's computer. A manually stored file or folder that is not pinned on the user's computer is not available offline. Manual caching is useful for users who need access to a file or folder all the time or for users who need access to entire folders, especially folders that contain documents created by or modified by other users. For example, manual caching works well for users who frequently use a portable computer away from the office without a network connection but still need access to many files on the network. In this case, you can manually pin folders on the user's portable computer to make those folders available to the user when away from the office. Automatic caching is not ideal in this case because the files in the network folder are not locally stored unless the portable computer user opens each file while the portable computer is connected to the network share.

Here's how to configure automatic or manual caching on a shared network folder:

1. Right-click the shared folder that you want to configure, click Properties, and then click the Sharing tab.

2. In the Properties dialog box, click Caching.

3. In the Setting list, select a type of storing.

In the Setting list, you can also choose Automatic Caching Of Programs And Documents, which is useful if a user runs programs from the network. This option stores a copy of a network program on the user's hard disk so the user can run the program offline. However, users of portable computers must be careful when using this feature because only the program files that are executed are stored on the local computer. For example, if you run Microsoft Word from a network share, but you do not use the spelling checker, the spelling checker is not stored. If you then run Word offline and try to run the spelling checker, the tool is not available. To avoid this problem, you can load all programs and associated tools locally on a portable computer and not use the Automatic Caching Of Programs And Documents option.

Synchronization for Offline Files

Synchronization ensures that any changes made to offline files and folders are propagated back to the network, and any changes that have occurred on the network are propagated to the user's computer. Some synchronization features and options relate specifically to portable computers.

In order for synchronization to occur, the hard disk on a user's portable computer must be turned on so that files can be copied from the network to the local cache, and files in the local cache can be copied to the network. Synchronization might not be an optimum use of power for a portable computer running on battery power. However, certain options allow you to set synchronization to occur when a computer runs on battery power. You can also use Group Policy to synchronize all offline files before logging off.

To ensure that all offline files are fully synchronized, you must enable the policy setting, Synchronize All Offline Files Before Logging Off, in the Administrative

Templates\Network\Offline Files folder. When this Group Policy setting is enabled, all files in the user's redirected folder are available when the user is working offline. If this setting is not enabled, the system performs only a quick synchronization, and as a result only files that were used recently are cached. This setting appears in the Computer Configuration and User Configuration folders. If both settings are configured, the setting in Computer Configuration takes precedence over the setting in User Configuration.

By default, offline files are not synchronized when a computer is in an idle state and using battery power because portable computers rely on a low-power idle state to conserve battery power, and you might not want to use battery power to synchronize files. You can change the default so that synchronization occurs when the computer is on idle and running on battery power:

1. In All Programs, point to Accessories, click Synchronize and then click Setup.

2. In the Synchronization Settings dialog box, click the On Idle tab and then click Advanced.

3. In the Idle Settings dialog box, clear the Prevent Synchronization When My Computer Is Running On Battery Power check box.

You can schedule synchronization to occur on specific days and at specific times. Because a scheduled synchronization is often a low-priority task that consumes power, Windows XP Professional allows you to prevent scheduled synchronization from occurring when a computer is running on battery power. Here's how to prevent scheduled synchronization from occurring when a computer is running on battery power:

1. In All Programs, point to Accessories, click Synchronize, and then click Setup.

2. In the Synchronization Settings dialog box, click the Scheduled tab.

3. Click a scheduled task and then click Edit.

4. On the Settings tab, under Power Management, select the Don't Start The Task If The Computer Is Running On Batteries check box.

If a scheduled synchronization is in progress, and a portable computer is switched from alternating current to battery power, you can have Windows XP Professional cancel synchronization. This might occur if scheduled synchronization starts on a docked portable computer that is using a wireless network connection, and the user performs a hot undock. Here's how to stop scheduled synchronization when the computer is running on battery power:

1. In All Programs, point to Accessories and then click Synchronize.

2. In the Items to Synchronize dialog box, click Setup.

3. Click the Scheduled tab.

4. Click a scheduled task and then click Edit.

5. On the Settings tab, under Power Management, select the Stop The Task If Battery Mode Begins check box.

Automatic Connection for Scheduled Synchronization

If a computer is not connected to a network when synchronization is scheduled to start, you can configure Windows XP Professional to connect so that synchronization can occur. In this case, Windows XP Professional attempts to connect to the designated network, detects that the computer is not connected to the network, and then informs the user that the network is not available. By default, Windows XP Professional does not connect if there is no network connection at the time of synchronization. Although you might use this option for portable computer users who are normally connected to the network, you might not want to enable it for users who frequently use the portable computer while it is disconnected from the network. Here's how to enable automatic connection for scheduled synchronization:

1. In All Programs, point to Accessories, click Synchronize, and then click Setup.

2. On the Scheduled tab, under Current Synchronization Tasks, click a scheduled task and then click Edit.

3. On the Synchronization Items tab, select If my computer is not connected when this scheduled synchronization begins, automatically connect for me.

Synchronization Over a Slow Link

Windows XP Professional does not provide a system-wide definition or threshold for a slow link. Instead, it allows every system component to define a slow link according to its own capabilities and requirements. For example, one component might define a slow link as 28.8 kilobits per second (Kbps), whereas another might define it as 56 Kbps. For Offline Files and synchronization in a Windows 2000 Active Directory environment, you can use Group Policy settings to define file synchronization behavior over a slow link. The default slow link threshold value is 64 Kbps. A slow-link connection affects synchronization by preventing the following:

■ Automatic transition of shared network folders from an offline to an online state

■ The copying of newly added files from the network share to the user's computer

In Windows XP Professional and Windows 2000 Server, you can use the Configure Slow Link Group Policy setting located in Computer Configuration\Administrative Templates\Network\Offline Files to define the threshold value at which Offline Files considers a network connection to be slow.

After a network share has been offline to a user—for example, if a server goes offline and is then brought back online, or if a user undocks a portable computer and then docks it—the share becomes available online for the user if the following three conditions are true:

- No offline files from that network share are open on the user's computer.

- None of the offline files from that network share have changes that need to be synchronized.

- The network connection is not considered a slow link.

When these conditions are true, and a user opens a file on the network share, the user is working online on that network share. Any changes that the user makes are saved to both the file on the network share and the file stored in the Offline Files folder. If any one of the conditions is not true, and a user opens a file on the network share, the user is still working offline even though the network share is available. Any changes that the user makes are saved only to the offline version of the file.

When a user first connects to a network over a slow-link connection, the user is only working offline on any shared network folders even if the online folders are available. To start working online with a shared network folder, the user must synchronize the shared network folder. Synchronization shifts the folder to an online state and pushes any offline files that have changed to the shared network folder. To pull files from the shared network folder to the Offline Files folder, the user must perform a second synchronization, which pulls files that have changed from the network share to the Offline Files folder.

Note   When you use a slow-link connection, a second synchronization does not pull newly created files from the network share to the Offline Files folder. To make new files on the network share available offline during a slow-link connection, you must pin the files.

Slow-link connections can prevent a network share from coming online even though the network share is available. Although you can bring the network share online by synchronizing it, this method might not be ideal. For example, when a user's portable computer is disconnected from the network, and the user requires access to a file on a shared network folder that has been made available offline, a file to which the user has made several changes offline might not be ready to synchronize with the network share. Or, the user might be in a hurry and does not want to take the time to synchronize files. The user wants only to connect to the network, get the new file from the network share, and then log off. Windows XP Professional provides a way for the user to make a folder available online without synchronizing offline files.

Here's how to make a folder available online without synchronizing offline files:

- In the notification area, click the Offline Files icon to open the Offline Files Status dialog box.

- Select Work online without synchronizing changes.

Offline Files Security

Windows XP Professional provides several methods of protection for offline files. The Offline Files folder, including the Offline Files database and the stored offline files, is secured against unauthorized access by administrator permissions. Additionally, the same user rights that protect their network counterparts protect offline files and folders. Windows XP Professional also supports encryption of offline files.

Offline files are stored (cached) in the Offline Files folder. Each computer has only one Offline Files folder, even if the computer is shared by multiple users, and all offline files are stored in this folder. By default, this folder is protected by administrator permissions so that unauthorized users cannot view the contents. However, these permissions are applied to the folder only if the folder is located on a drive that is formatted to use NTFS. Windows XP Professional notifies you of this limitation when you first cache an offline file on a file allocation table (FAT) or FAT32 drive.

In addition to the protection afforded by the permissions on the actual Offline Files folder, offline files and folders retain the permissions set for them on the network share. This type of security is important if multiple users share a single computer. For example, if a user creates a file on a network share, changes its permissions so that only that user has access to the file, and then makes the file available offline, another user who tries to open the offline version of the file on the user's computer is denied access, just as if the second user tried to open the file directly on the network share.

This type of security is applied to offline files regardless of the formatting of the user's hard disk. Thus, if you set permissions on a file on a network share that is formatted to use NTFS, and you make that file available offline on a computer that has a FAT or FAT32 drive, the permissions carry over to the offline version of the file, even if the drive is formatted to use FAT or FAT32.

You can secure data on portable computers by encrypting the offline files. Windows XP Professional provides Encrypting File System (EFS) support for Offline Files. The local cache of Offline Files can be encrypted if the cache directory resides on an NTFS volume. When the cache is encrypted, the local copy of a cached file is automatically encrypted. Here's how to encrypt offline files:

1. In Folder Options, click the Offline Files tab.

2. Select the Encrypt Offline Files To Secure Data check box.

You can also use Group Policy to apply this option to groups of users. In the Group Policy snap-in, go to Computer Configuration\Administrative Templates\Network\Offline Files. Offline files stored on local hard disks are secured by EFS; however, the files are encrypted in the system context, and the encryption applies to all users of the local computer. If both the local computer and the remote computer in which the files are stored are encrypted, files are encrypted at all times. If the local computer is encrypted, but the remote location of the files is not, the files are encrypted while they are stored locally. If the remote location is encrypted and the local computer is not, however, you are warned when you try to make a file available offline that it will not be encrypted on the local computer. You can override the default and make the files available; when you attempt to synchronize the files, the local copy will be deleted.

Reinitializing Offline Files Folder

Portable computer users who frequently work offline might accumulate hundreds of files in the Offline Files folder on their hard disk. Because many of these files might be out of date, rarely used, or no longer needed offline, you might want to delete them from the Offline Files folder (the cache) to maximize the available disk space. Users might also want to delete files in the Offline Files folder if a network share has been deleted or is no longer available. In addition to deleting individual files, you can reinitialize the Offline Files cache, which deletes the entire contents of the Offline Files folder and resets the Offline Files database. Reinitializing the Offline Files cache is useful when you transfer a computer to a new user or when a user has been working offline with sensitive or proprietary documents and you want to ensure that they are no longer available offline or that they are not in the cache.

You can safely remove offline files from the cache without affecting network files or folders by deleting files from the Offline Files folder or by reinitializing the cache. Do not delete or move any files directly from the %SYSTEMROOT%\CSC folder. Here's how to reinitialize the Offline Files folder:

1. In Windows Explorer, click Tools and then click Folder Options.

2. Click the Offline Files tab.

3. Press CTRL+SHIFT and then click Delete Files.

4. Restart the computer.

Laptop Security

Because portable computers are vulnerable to theft, it is important that you provide security for portable computers and the data that is stored on them. You can do this by formatting hard disks to use NTFS so that permissions can be set and encryption can be enabled on files and folders by means of EFS. You can also add portable computer users to the Power Users group so that they have maximum control of the portable computer without having full control of the system. Ensuring that users use strong passwords to log on to their portable computers and that administrators use strong passwords for the local administrator account is another important security measure. Also, Group Policy settings can be used to restrict access to the computer and any data that is stored on it.

Undocking Portable Computers

Portable computers can be undocked in two ways, depending on the type of docking station, the type of portable computer, and the permissions and Group Policy settings that have been implemented on the computer. A portable computer can be undocked in the following circumstances:

- While the portable computer is shut down and the power is off, a user physically ejects it or removes it from the docking station (a cold undock).

- While the portable computer is running, a user uses the Eject PC command in Windows XP Professional to eject the computer from the docking station, before physically removing the computer (a hot undock).

To prevent an unauthorized user from undocking a portable computer from a docking station, the portable computer or docking station must include some type of physical lock. Portable computers might simply use a keyed lock that must be manually unlocked to prevent undocking by unauthorized users. Docking stations can include a lock as well, some of which can be programmatically controlled. For example, some docking stations allow administrators to require that an authorized user log on and select Eject PC before freeing the lock and allowing physical removal of the portable computer from the docking station.

You can choose a Group Policy setting that controls who has undocking privileges on a portable computer. If a user has undocking privileges, he or she is able to use the Eject PC command. If the user does not have undocking privileges, the Eject PC command is not available. However, any program can call the application programming interface (API) that controls the Eject PC command, which means that any program can have its own button or menu item that tries to eject a portable computer. If a user tries to use such a button or menu item and does not have undocking privileges, the command fails. By default, undocking permissions are granted to a user during a clean installation of Windows XP Professional and during an upgrade from Windows 95, Windows 98, or Windows NT 4. To prevent a user from undocking, you must use Group Policy to set undocking privileges:

1. In the Run dialog box, enter **gpedit.msc**.

2. In the details pane of Group Policy, under Computer Configuration, open Windows Settings, Security Settings, and the Local Policies; and open the User Rights Assignment folder.

3. In the details pane, right-click Remove Computer From Docking Station, and then click Properties.

4. In the Properties dialog box, click Add to add users and groups to the list. Alternatively, Click Remove to remove users and groups from the list.

Note Restricting undock privileges offers no security benefits if the docking station in question does not provide a programmatically controlled locking mechanism.

BIOS Security

Some computers allow you to implement system security or device security at the BIOS level. Typically, equipment manufacturers implement this type of security by requiring a password at startup while the BIOS is loading. If the user enters an incorrect password, the BIOS does not finish loading, and the computer does not start; or the BIOS might finish loading, but it does not transfer control of the computer to Windows XP Professional. Although this type of security is designed to control access to the computer at startup, it might also control access when the computer resumes from a low-power state such as standby or hibernation. In these cases, users might have to enter the BIOS password when the system resumes from either standby or hibernation.

To implement BIOS security on a portable computer, contact the portable computer manufacturer to verify that it operates properly with the standby and hibernate features of Windows XP Professional. Also be aware that BIOS security can supersede Windows XP Professional security by preventing Windows XP Professional from taking control of the computer or other devices.

Wireless Networking

With the rapid growth of wireless networking, users can access data from anywhere in the world, using a wide range of devices. Wireless networks offer additional benefits by reducing or eliminating the high cost of laying expensive fiber and cabling and by providing backup functionality for wired networks. Windows XP Professional provides extensive support for wireless networking technology so that businesses can extend the capabilities of their enterprise networks to wireless devices.

The primary wireless Local Area Network (WLAN) solution is IEEE 802.11, which is the WLAN standard developed by the Institute of Electrical and Electronics Engineers (IEEE). The IEEE 802.11b specification, recently created and adopted, adds to the groundwork laid by IEEE 802.11. IEEE 802.11a, currently in development, will make further improvements to 802.11b. The IEEE 802.11–defined Media

Access Control (MAC) is also used for the 802.11 extensions 802.11b and 802.11a. To achieve higher data rates, 802.11b and 802.11a define different physical layer specifications. The following list provides an overview of the current standards:

- **802.11** IEEE 802.11 is a shared WLAN standard using the carrier sense multiple access MAC protocol with collision avoidance. The standard allows for both direct sequence and frequency-hopping spread spectrum transmissions at the physical layer. The original 802.11 specification defines data rates of 1 Mbps and 2 Mbps and uses a radio frequency of 2.45 GHz.

- **802.11b** The major enhancement to IEEE 802.11 by IEEE 802.11b is the standardization of the physical layer to support higher bandwidth. IEEE 802.11b supports two additional speeds, 5.5 Mbps and 11 Mbps, using the same frequency of 2.45 GHz. A different modulation scheme is used to provide the higher data rates of 5 Mbps and 11 Mbps. Direct sequence spread spectrum (DSSS) is the physical layer defined in the 802.11b standard.

- **802.11a** The latest standard, IEEE 802.11a, is currently being developed. This wireless standard operates at a data transmission rate as high as 54 Mbps and uses a radio frequency of 5.8 gigahertz (GHz). Instead of DSSS, which 802.11b uses, 802.11a uses Orthogonal Frequency Division Multiplexing (OFDM), which allows data to be transmitted by subfrequencies in parallel. This provides greater resistance to interference and provides greater throughput. This higher-speed technology allows wireless networking to perform better for video and conferencing applications. Because they are not on the same frequencies as Bluetooth or microwave ovens, OFDM and IEEE 802.11a will provide both a higher data rate and a cleaner signal.

Windows XP Professional has improved and built upon the wireless support provided in Windows 2000. Windows XP Professional includes support for automatic switching between different access points when roaming, auto detection of a wireless network, and automatic wireless configuration—allowing for zero client configuration. Additional security is also provided by the inclusion of an 802.1x client implementation in Windows XP Professional and the inclusion of wireless device authentication support in the Windows Remote Authentication Dial-In User Service (RADIUS) server, Internet Authentication Service (IAS).

Roaming

Windows 2000 includes technologies that allow wireless devices to detect the availability of a network and act appropriately. Windows XP Professional enhances this technology to accommodate the transitional nature of a wireless network. The media sense feature of Windows 2000 is enhanced in Windows XP Professional to allow for detection of a move to a new access point, thus forcing reauthentication to ensure appropriate network access. Media sense also allows the detection of changes in the Internet Protocol (IP) subnet, so that an appropriate address can be used in order to ensure optimum resource access.

Multiple IP address configurations (Dynamic Host Configuration Protocol [DHCP]–assigned or static) can be made available on a Windows XP Professional system and the appropriate configuration automatically chosen. When an IP address change occurs, Windows XP Professional allows for additional reconfiguration to occur, if necessary. For example, information engineering (IE) proxy settings can be redetected. By means of Windows Sockets extensions, applications that can be configured to be network-aware (such as firewalls or browsers) can be notified of changes in network connectivity and can update their behavior based on these changes. The auto-sensing and reconfiguration effectively negates the need for a mobile IP to act as a mediator and solves most of the problems users face when roaming between networks.

When a station is roaming from access point to access point, information about the state of the station, as well as other information, must be moved along with it. This includes station location information for message delivery and other attributes of the association. Rather than re-create this information upon each transition, one access point can pass the information to the new access point. The protocols to transfer this information are not defined in the standard, but several wireless LAN vendors have jointly developed an Inter-Access Point Protocol (IAPP) for this purpose, further enhancing multivendor interoperability.

Zero Client Configuration

Automatic wireless network configuration and 802.1x authentication are selected by default. When automatic wireless configuration is enabled on your computer, you can roam between different WLANs without having to reconfigure the network connection settings on your computer for each location. These Windows XP Professional technologies allow for zero client configuration.

Zero configuration is a client-based user identification method that allows wireless devices to work in different modes without the need for configuration changes after the initial configuration. The zero configuration initiative automatically provides the IP address, the network prefix, the gateway router location, the Domain Name Server (DNS) server address, the address of a RADIUS or IAS server, and all other necessary settings for the wireless device. It also provides security features for the client.

Zero configuration allows a wireless device to function in different environments—such as work, the airport, and home—without any user intervention. Zero configuration uses the Windows XP Professional user interface when attempting to connect wireless devices. The order of preference for zero configuration IEEE 802.11 connection using IEEE 802.1x authentication is infrastructure before ad hoc mode and computer authentication before user authentication. You can change the default settings to allow guest access, for example, which is not enabled by default.

Wired Equivalent Privacy (WEP) authentication attempts to perform an IEEE 802.11 shared key authentication if the network adapter has been preconfigured with a WEP shared key. In the event that authentication fails or the network adapter is not preconfigured with a WEP shared key, the network adapter reverts to the open system authentication.

The IEEE 802.1x security enhancements are available in Windows XP Professional. Wireless network adapters and access points must also be compatible with IEEE 802.1x for an IEEE 802.1x deployment.

Network Adapter Support

Microsoft partnered with 802.11 network adapter vendors to improve the roaming experience by automating the process of configuring the network adapter to associate with an available network.

The wireless network adapter and its Network Driver Interface Specification (NDIS) driver need to do very little beyond supporting some new NDIS object identifiers (OIDs) used for the querying and setting of device and driver behavior. The network adapter scans for available networks and passes those to Windows XP Professional. The Windows XP Professional Wireless Zero Configuration service then takes care of configuring the network adapter with an available network. If there are two networks covering the same area, the user can configure a preferred network order, and the computer will try each network in the order defined until it finds one that is active. It is even possible to limit association to only the configured, preferred networks.

If an 802.11 network is not found nearby, Windows XP Professional configures the network adapter to use ad hoc networking mode. It is possible for the user to configure the wireless network adapter either to disable or be forced into ad hoc mode. These network adapter enhancements are integrated with security features so that if authentication fails, another network will be located to attempt association with.

Automatic Wireless Configuration

Automatic wireless configuration supports the IEEE 802.11 standard for WLANs and minimizes the configuration required to access WLANS. When automatic wireless configuration is enabled on your computer, you can roam between different WLANs without having to reconfigure the network connection settings on your computer for each location. Whenever you move from one location to another, automatic wireless configuration scans for an available WLAN in the new location, configures your network adapter card to match the settings of that WLAN, and attempts to access that WLAN. When several WLANs are available in the same location, you can create a list of preferred WLANs and define the order in which access to each is attempted. You can also specify that if an access attempt to a preferred WLAN fails, an attempt will be made to access any visible (available) WLAN of the same type. Here's how to set up automatic wireless configuration:

1. Open Network Connections.

2. Right-click the connection for which you want to set up automatic wireless network configuration and then click Properties.

3. On the Wireless Networks tab, do one of the following:

   ■ To enable automatic wireless network configuration for this connection, select the Use Windows To Configure My Wireless Network Settings check box. This check box is selected by default.

   ■ To disable automatic wireless network configuration for this connection, clear the Use Windows To Configure My Wireless Network Settings check box.

4. The list of available wireless networks detected by automatic wireless network configuration appears under Available networks. To make changes to the Preferred networks list, do the following:

   ■ To add an available wireless network to the Preferred networks list for this connection, under Available networks, click the network that you want to add and then click Configure.

   ■ To add a new wireless network to the Preferred networks list for this connection, under Preferred networks, click Add, and in Wireless Network Properties, specify the network name (Service Set Identifier), wireless network key (Wired Equivalent Privacy) settings, and whether the network is a computer-to-computer (ad hoc) network.

   ■ To change the order in which connection attempts to preferred networks are made for this connection, under Preferred networks, click the wireless network that you want to move to a new position on the list and then click Move Up or Move Down.

   ■ To remove a wireless network from the list of preferred networks for this connection, under Preferred networks, click the wireless network that you want to remove and then click Remove.

5. To refine the type of wireless network to access, click Advanced and then click the network type you want. For example, if you want to make a computer-to-computer (ad hoc) connection, and if both computer-to-computer and access point (infrastructure) networks are within range of your computer, click Computer-to-computer (AdHoc) networks only.

Here's how to set up 802.1x authentication:

1. Open Network Connections.

2. Right-click the connection for which you want to enable or disable IEEE 802.1x authentication and then click Properties.

3. On the Authentication tab, do one of the following:

    ■ To enable IEEE 802.1xx authentication for this connection, select the Network Access Control Using IEEE 802.1X check box. This check box is selected by default.

    ■ To disable IEEE 802.1xx authentication for this connection, clear the Network Access Control Using IEEE 802.1X check box.

4. In EAP Type, click the Extensible Authentication Protocol type to be used with this connection.

5. If you select Smart Card or other Certificate in EAP type, you can configure additional properties if you click Properties and, in Smart Card or other Certificate Properties, do the following:

    ■ To use the certificate located on your smart card for authentication, click Use My Smart Card.

    ■ To use the certificate located in the certificate store on your computer for authentication, click Use A Certificate On This Computer.

    ■ To verify that the server certificate presented to your computer is still valid, select the Validate Server Certificate check box, specify whether to connect only if the server is located within a particular domain, and then specify the trusted root certification authority.

    ■ To use a different user name when the user name in the smart card or certificate is not the same as the user name in the domain to which you are logging on, select the Use A Different User Name For The Connection check box.

6. To specify whether the computer attempts authentication to the network if a user is not logged on and/or if the computer or user information is not available, do the following:

    ■ To specify that the computer attempt authentication to the network if a user is not logged on, select the Authenticate As Computer When Computer Information Is Available check box.

    ■ To specify that the computer attempt authentication to the network if user information or computer information is not available, select the Authenticate As Guest When User Or Computer Information Is Unavailable check box.

Here's how to connect to an available wireless network:

1. Right-click the network connection icon in the notification area and then click View Available Wireless Networks.

2. In Connect to Wireless Network, under Available Networks, click the wireless network that you want to connect to.

3. If a network key is required for WEP, do one of the following:

    ■ If the network key is automatically provided (for example, the key is stored on the wireless network adapter given to you by your administrator), leave Network Key blank.

    ■ If the network key is not automatically provided for you, in Network key, type the key.

4. Click Connect.

5. To configure additional wireless network connection settings, or if you are having difficulty making a connection to the wireless network that you selected, click Advanced and then configure the settings in the Wireless Networks tab.

For more information about zero client configuration for wireless network clients in Windows XP Professional, see "Wireless Networking" in Windows XP Professional Help and Support Center.

Appendix B

Multilingual Scenarios

A large number of corporations do business internationally, have employees or customers who communicate using more than one language, or have a need to create a single global corporate desktop image or a single code base to develop and test applications. To meet the needs of today's global business environment, Microsoft Windows XP Professional includes desktop configurations and application support designed to ensure multilingual compatibility.

Multilingual Overview

Windows XP Professional supports companies that need to allow users (employees or customers) to work in more than one language. Typically, these companies do the following:

- Operate internationally and must support different regional options, such as time zones, currencies, or date formats.

- Have employees or customers who speak different languages or require language-dependent keyboards or input devices.

- Develop internal line-of-business applications that must run internationally or in more than one language.

Table B-1 presents an overview of the most common problems that multilingual and international organizations face and outlines the possible solutions that you can apply to your Windows XP Professional deployment.

Table B-1   Multilingual Issues

Problem	Solution
Users need to edit documents that contain multiple languages.	All versions of Windows XP Professional contain support for editing documents in multiple languages. Some versions might require the installation of additional language collections. For advanced multilingual support, such as localized language user interface elements, dictionaries, and proofing tools, deploy Microsoft Windows XP Professional Multilingual User Interface (MUI) Pack together with the Microsoft Office 2003 Editions with MUI Pack.

Table B-1 Multilingual Issues

Problem	Solution
Regional offices need automatic operating system deployments with the correct language and regional options, such as the default input language, date, time, and currency formats.	Determine each office's language and regional needs to help reduce the number of unique setup scripts. For each unique setup script, specify the appropriate *[RegionalSettings]* values in the answer file; use new keywords to set the default standards and formats and input language/keyboard layout combination for the default user account for new users.
Roaming users need to log on anywhere in their native languages.	Consider using Windows XP Professional MUI Pack for desktops if roaming users must log on in a native language user interface. Use Active Directory directory service and Group Policy to publish MUI Pack language packages to users so that they can install the correct user interface language wherever they log on.
Multiple users need to log on to the same computer in different languages.	Consider using Windows XP Professional MUI Pack for desktops if users must log on in a native language user interface. Use the Terminal Services Client to support different language sessions for different users sharing computers connected to a Microsoft Windows 2000 Server MultiLanguage version-based computer running Terminal Services.
Users need language-specific keyboards, Input Method Editors, or alternative input devices.	Windows XP Professional contains built-in support for a variety of keyboard layouts and input methods and devices. Install additional language collections and input languages as needed. Place the On-Screen Keyboard on desktops in which the physical keyboard might not match the operating system language version in use.
Existing line-of-business applications must accommodate language and regional differences.	Ensure proper code page support for applications developed under older operating systems; test applications by changing the Language For Non-Unicode Programs and default input languages.
Application developers want to create single code-based applications that run in the correct local language.	Deploy Windows XP Professional MUI Pack internationally as the desktop standard; develop applications in Unicode that support the multilingual user interface. Write applications that check for the default user interface language and follow world-ready software development guidelines.
Sites on the corporate intranet must account for language and regional differences.	Use the Location setting to configure desktop browsers to receive appropriate local content, such as local weather or news.
IT wants to do simultaneous worldwide rollouts of hotfixes, patches, and Service Packs.	Deploy Windows XP Professional MUI Pack as the global desktop standard.

Table B-1 Multilingual Issues

Problem	Solution
Users need to share folders or files containing text in other languages.	Ensure that only Unicode characters are used for Active Directory and other folder and filenames; install the Complex Script and Right-To-Left or East Asian Language Collections as needed.

Windows XP Professional includes technologies that enhance your company's ability to do business in multiple languages and/or across multiple regions:

- **Support for 135 locales** Versions of Microsoft Windows earlier than Windows XP Professional support up to 126 locales. Windows XP Professional adds support for nine additional locales: Galician, Gujarati, Kannada, Kyrgyz, Mongolian (Cyrillic), Punjabi, Divehi, Syriac, and Telugu.

- **Built-in language support** Each language version of Windows XP Professional provides built-in support for editing documents in hundreds of languages, grouped into three language collections. The Basic Language Collection, which is always installed, supports most Western languages. The Complex Script and Right-To-Left Language Collection can be installed to support languages such as Arabic, Hebrew, Indic, or Thai; and the East Asian Language Collection can be installed to support Simplified or Traditional Chinese, Japanese, or Korean. Users can change input languages, keyboard layouts, and other regional options (except for the language for non-Unicode programs) without restarting the computer for the changes to take effect. Administrators can customize the desktop with new tools, such as the Language Toolbar, to simplify switching languages, keyboard layouts, and other regional options.

- **Redesigned Regional and Language Options Control Panel** The Control Panel for regional and language options has been redesigned to make it easier to add and change input languages and keyboard layouts; change standards and formats for displaying dates, amounts, and currencies; set the default location for Web content; and change the language for non-Unicode programs. The most frequently used options are now easier to find and use.

- **New, simplified terminology** The terminology used in versions of Windows earlier than Windows XP Professional has been updated to simpler, more descriptive terms:

    - Standards And Formats, which determines the formats used to display dates, times, currency, numbers, and the sorting order of text—was previously called the UserLocale.

    - Input Language, which specifies the combination of the language and keyboard layout used to enter text, was previously called the Input Locale.

■ Language For Non-Unicode Programs, which specifies the default code pages and fonts for running non-Unicode programs, was previously called the SystemLocale.

■ **Additional answer file and installation options**   Windows XP Professional includes four new language settings that you can use in the *[RegionalSettings]* section of unattended-setup answer files. These settings make it easier for you to customize language settings, such as the default input language for new user accounts. Other features provide more options for customizing unattended mode installations and silent configurations after setup.

■ **Updated multilingual troubleshooter**   The Multilingual Document Consultant in Windows XP Professional Help And Support Center can assist you in diagnosing and resolving problems with displaying or entering different languages.

■ **Improved Windows XP Professional MUI Pack**   The Windows XP Professional MUI Pack ensures that most of the operating system user interface—including the Start and Programs menus, alerts and dialog boxes, and the Windows XP Professional Help And Support Center—appears in the localized language that has been selected as the default. (In Microsoft Windows 2000 Professional MultiLanguage version, for example, a user who switches the user interface language to German might still find some user interface elements displayed in English.) Although it is based on the code of the Microsoft Windows XP Professional International English language version, the MUI Pack also includes more-localized components that make it easier to develop multilingual applications. New Windows Installer MUI language packages reduce storage space requirements on network servers or CD images and make it easier for administrators to set up, and users to install, additional user interface languages. The MUI Pack also includes improved local drivers, makes roaming easier, and simplifies remote administration over a corporate network.

Multilingual Features

This section introduces some of the key features, concepts, and terms you need to understand as you work with a multilingual or international deployment of Windows XP Professional. Included are discussions of basic concepts, such as language collections; the use of alternative keyboard layouts, Input Method Editors, and Unicode; and descriptions of new terms introduced with Windows XP Professional.

Built-In Language Support

Each language version of Windows XP Professional supports hundreds of languages through 17 language groups, which are organized into three separately installable language collections, as shown in Table B-2.

Table B-2 Language Support

Language Collection	Installation Status	Language Group ID and Name
Basic	Always installed on every language version.	1 Western Europe, United States
		2 Central Europe
		3 Baltic
		4 Greek
		5 Cyrillic
		6 Turkic
Complex Script and Right-To-Left	Always installed on the Arabic language version and the Hebrew language version; optionally installed on all other language versions.	11 Thai
		12 Hebrew
		13 Arabic
		14 Vietnamese
		15 Indic
		16 Georgian
		17 Armenian
East Asian	Always installed on the Simplified Chinese, Traditional Chinese, Japanese, and Korean language versions; optionally installed on all other language versions.	7 Japanese
		8 Korean
		9 Traditional Chinese
		10 Simplified Chinese

Note In Windows XP Professional—unlike Microsoft Windows 2000 Professional—you cannot install individual language groups. You must install the appropriate language collection as described previously, which includes support for all the language groups in that language collection.

Support for Locales

A locale is a collection of Windows XP Professional operating system settings that reflects a specific region's language and cultural conventions. For example, the English (Canadian), English (United Kingdom), and English (United States) locales reflect different regions that share a common language but use different dialects, currencies, and so on. Windows XP Professional supports a total of 135 locales.

Standards And Formats

The Standards And Formats section of the Regional And Language Options Control Panel in Windows XP Professional, formerly called the UserLocale, determines the formats used to display dates, times, currency, numbers, and the sorting order of text. On a given computer, each user account can have its own unique Standards And Formats setting. The Standards And Formats setting does not affect any language settings, other than the language used to display the names of days and months, and time and date formats.

For example, an English-speaking salesperson from the Boston office logs on to a desktop in the Milan office. The Milan desktop uses the International English language version of Windows XP Professional. The salesperson selects a Standards And Formats setting of Italian (Italy), which immediately changes the currency to Lira and the date format to dd/MM/yyyy—without restarting the computer.

Input Method Editors and Keyboard Layouts

For a computer to support a given language, the computer must be able to display the language onscreen using the correct alphabet, characters, and fonts. The computer must be able to accept input typed on a specific language keyboard or specialized input device. The appropriate language collection must be installed, and the default input language and keyboard layout determine how characters entered on the keyboard will be displayed on the screen.

Languages such as Japanese use an Input Method Editor (IME), so that a user can enter Asian text in programs by converting the keystrokes into Asian characters. The IME interprets the keystrokes as characters and then gives the user the opportunity to insert the correct interpretation into the program being worked in. Windows XP Professional contains IMEs for Simplified Chinese, Traditional Chinese, Japanese, and Korean.

The Input Language setting of the Regional And Language Options Control Panel, formerly called an Input Locale, specifies the combination of the language being entered and the keyboard layout, IME, speech-to-text converter, or other device being used to enter it. Input languages are added to a computer user by user; each user can add multiple input languages, enabling multiple-language document editing, viewing, and printing. When you change input languages, some programs (such as Microsoft Office 2003 Editions) offer additional features, such as fonts or spelling checkers designed for different input languages. For example, a user in the Tokyo office who wants to write an e-mail message in both Japanese and Russian would need to install Russian as an input language to enter and display the Russian language using a Japanese keyboard. The user can then change between the Japanese and Russian languages while composing the message.

Each input language that Windows XP Professional supports has a default keyboard layout associated with it. Some languages also have alternative keyboard layouts. For example, a standard U.S. English language keyboard has 101 keys; whereas a typical keyboard for the Japanese localized language version of Windows XP Professional has 106 keys. In these situations—in which the physical keyboard might not match the language being entered or a difference in the number of characters and keys makes it difficult to type—administrators or users can add layouts for additional keyboards. Also, by using the On-Screen Keyboard, users can enter text by selecting characters on the appropriate language version On-Screen Keyboard.

> **Tip** Administrators can make it easier for users to change input languages and keyboard layouts by placing the Language Toolbar on the desktop or in the Taskbar, or by enabling keyboard sequences or hot keys. For more information, see "Multiple Language Access" later in this appendix on page 751.

Unicode and Code Pages

Unicode is an international standard for representing the characters in common use in the most widely used languages. Unicode provides a universal character set that can accommodate most known scripts, meaning that the text used in documents, files, and applications created in one operating system language (such as Japanese) display correctly in a different operating system language (such as English). Windows XP Professional supports Unicode as its base character encoding.

Windows XP Professional supports code pages to ensure backward compatibility and comprehensive language support for legacy documents and applications. A code page is an ordered set of characters in which a numeric index (code point) is associated with each character of a particular writing system. There are separate code pages for different writing systems, such as Western European and Cyrillic. In a code page–based environment, each set of characters from a specific language has its own table of characters.

Because a code page is a much smaller ordered set of characters than Unicode, code pages have limited capabilities to display the characters of another code page's language. Documents based on the code page of one operating system rarely transfer successfully to an operating system that uses another code page, resulting in unintelligible text or characters. For example, if someone in Boston using the International English language version of Microsoft Windows 98 with the Latin code page opens a file created in the Japanese language version of Windows 98, the code points of the Japanese code page are mapped to unexpected or nonexistent characters in the Latin script.

To ensure that new applications being written for Windows XP Professional can function in any language, use Unicode as the base character encoding. Do not use code pages.

Language for Non-Unicode Programs

The Language For Non-Unicode Programs, previously called the SystemLocale, specifies the default code pages and associated bitmap font files for a given computer and affects all of that computer's users. The default code pages and fonts enable non-Unicode applications to run as they do on a system localized to the language of the Language For Non-Unicode Programs. If an application displays question marks (???) instead of the expected alphanumeric characters, the Language For Non-Unicode Programs probably needs to be switched to the language in which the application was developed. Switching the Language For Non-Unicode Programs to match an older application's language affects other operating system settings that will improve overall application and system compatibility.

For example, assume that a data entry clerk in the Tokyo office is using the International English language version of Windows XP Professional. If the clerk wants to run a non-Unicode accounting application designed for the Japanese localized language version of Windows 98, the clerk needs to change the Language For Non-Unicode Programs of the computer to Japanese and restart the computer. Otherwise, Kanji characters would be displayed as question marks.

> **Note**   Changing the Language For Non-Unicode Programs alone does not change the language of the Windows XP Professional user interface elements, such as the system menus and dialog box display languages. Only the Windows XP Professional MUI Pack allows a user to change the language of the user interface.

User Interface Language Options

Using the Windows XP Professional MUI Pack, users can change the language of the user interface—such as the names of menu options, choices in dialog boxes, and Help system—to any of the localized language versions of Windows XP Professional.

Administrators can specify the default user interface language by using setup scripts or silent configurations, and also can restrict users' abilities to change the user interface language by using Group Policy settings.

Windows XP Language Versions

Windows XP Professional includes three different language versions: International English, individual localized language versions, and the MUI Pack. Understanding the differences between the language versions that are available will help you to choose the language version that best meets your company's specific language and international needs.

- **Windows XP Professional International English version** The International English version of Windows XP Professional is designed for companies that do business mostly in English, but have some users with additional language needs. This version provides complete language and regional support for more than 135 locales, allowing users to read and write documents in almost any language. The Windows XP Professional user interface, however, is in English. If you require the user interface to appear in a language other than English, a localized language version or the MUI Pack is a more appropriate choice.

- **Windows XP Professional Localized Language versions** Each localized language version of Windows XP Professional contains the same language and regional support that is included in the International English version, meaning that users can read and write documents in almost any language. However, the operating system user interface appears only in the localized language instead of English. A localized language version contains more extensive application compatibility than the International English version of Windows XP Professional, as well as extra local drivers, and legacy DOS and basic input/output system (BIOS) support. If your company, or a particular office or division of your company, operates primarily in a language other than English or requires that the operating system user interface be in a language other than English, a localized language version of Windows XP Professional is an appropriate choice.

- **Windows XP Professional MUI Pack** The Windows XP Professional MUI Pack allows users to change the language of the operating system user interface to any of the supported localized language versions (including English). This version is well-suited for companies that do the following:

  - Want to deploy and maintain a single operating system standard or desktop image worldwide

  - Want to maintain a single code base for international application development

  - Want to do single, simultaneous, worldwide rollouts for hotfixes, patches, and Service Packs

  - Have multilingual offices in which different language speakers must share computers

  - Have users who need to be able to log on anywhere in any language

  The MUI Pack is based on the International English version of Windows XP Professional. Although the user interface can be switched to any of the supported languages, compared to a localized language version of Windows XP

Professional, some parts of the operating system are not localized in the MUI Pack:

- 16-bit code
- Bitmaps
- Some registry keys and values
- INF files
- Some system components, including:
  - Narrator
  - MSN Explorer
  - NetMeeting
- Internet Connection Wizard

Table B-3 shows the user needs that each language version supports.

Table B-3 Differences Between Language Versions

User Needs	International English Version of Windows XP Professional	Localized Language Versions of Windows XP Professional	Windows XP Professional MUI Pack
Ability to read and write documents in multiple languages	Yes	Yes	Yes
Language and regional support for more than 135 locales	Yes	Yes	Yes
Language and regional support for supported localized language versions			Yes
Localized language user interface		Yes	Yes
Ability to transact business primarily in one or more languages besides English		Yes	Yes
Ability to transact business mostly in English, but have access to additional languages	Yes	Yes	Yes
Extensive support for localized language applications compatibility		Yes	Yes
Extensive support for localized language drivers		Yes	Yes
Legacy DOS and BIOS support		Yes	

Table B-3   Differences Between Language Versions

User Needs	International English Version of Windows XP Professional	Localized Language Versions of Windows XP Professional	Windows XP Professional MUI Pack
Single code base for application development	Yes	Yes	Yes
Single code base for application testing in different user interface languages			Yes
Ability to log on anywhere in any language			Yes
Single, simultaneous, worldwide rollouts for hotfixes, patches, and Service Packs			Yes

Deployment Planning

To deploy the appropriate language versions of Windows XP Professional and configure regional support based on your organization's current geographic and IT infrastructure, you need to determine your language and regional requirements, as well as your hardware requirements and limitations. You also need to take into account the needs of roaming users in your organization, and whether you are upgrading an earlier localized language version of Windows. Also, consider whether your organization requires a single global image, and whether you will require specific regional builds for different offices in your organization.

Language Requirements

If you do business in multiple languages or have multilingual office environments, you need to know which languages or dialects your organization must support, and whether these languages require IMEs or alternative keyboards or input devices.

If you do business internationally, you need to know which countries and regions your organization must support, and which languages or dialects are used in each. You must determine whether currency, time zone, or calendar formats vary between the different countries and regions. Additionally, you must determine which line-of-business applications you have that must accommodate such regional differences. A four-column planning table can help you determine your language and regional needs. You can organize the table as follows:

- In column 1, list your offices or divisions.

- In column 2, list the languages or dialects used in those offices or divisions.

- In column 3, note the corresponding Windows XP Professional language collections and locales that support those languages or dialects.

- In column 4, note any special standards and formats settings, input language support, or default languages for non-Unicode programs required for your offices or divisions.

> **Tip** You can use the resulting worksheet to plan your physical deployment and complete the *[RegionalSettings]* section of your answer files. For more information about completing your answer file, see "Unattended Installations" later in this appendix on page 753.

Hardware Requirements

Supporting multiple languages can impact your hardware requirements in two areas:

- **Hard disk space**   Some languages require more hard-disk storage space than others. The more languages installed on a computer, the more hard-disk space consumed. In addition, the Windows XP Professional MUI Pack requires more disk space for each user interface language to be installed or supported.

- **Specialized hardware devices**   Some languages or users require special keyboards, IMEs, or alternative input devices.

> **Note**   Installing a language collection enables you to view text in those languages in a document, on a Web page, and so on. However, to input text in a given language, you must also add that language as an input language. For more information about adding input languages, see "Configuring Desktops" later in this appendix on page 748.

If a workstation needs to support users who speak multiple languages, that workstation must have enough space on the hard disk for the appropriate language resources. The amount of disk space that you need depends, in part, on the Windows XP Professional language version that you deploy. Every language version of Windows XP Professional comes with support for all the languages in the Basic Language Collection, which is installed by default. Table B-4 lists the estimated hard drive space that you need to install additional language support.

Table B-4   Disk Space Requirements for Language Support

Language Collection	Installation Status	Space Required in Megabytes (MB)
Basic	Always installed on every language version.	N/A
Complex Script and Right-To-Left	Always installed on the Arabic language version and the Hebrew language version; optionally installed on all other language versions.	10
East Asian	Always installed on the Simplified Chinese, Traditional Chinese, Japanese, and Korean language versions; optionally installed on all other language versions.	230

The Windows XP Professional MUI Pack contains Windows Installer packages that allow users to install the user interface languages on demand. Because they are compressed, Windows Installer packages require less storage space on a network server or CD image. Providing on-demand installation also saves storage space on desktops because users can install only the user interface languages that they need, when they need them. For a list of the storage space required on a client computer for each user interface language that is installed, see "Locales & Languages" at *http://www.microsoft.com/globaldev/DrIntl/faqs/Locales.mspx*. For more detailed information about using Windows Installer packages with the Windows XP Professional MUI Pack, see "Using Windows Installer Packages" later in this appendix on page 763.

> **Tip**   If your organization uses regional or customized builds or a CD-based deployment, include the appropriate Windows Installer packages on the custom image or CD to ensure that support for those user interface languages is available. This ensures that the specific user interface languages that each office needs are available either for unattended installations during deployment or for on-demand installations by users post-deployment.

If your language requirements require you to use special keyboards, IMEs, or alternative input devices, your hardware must meet minimum hardware compatibility requirements. You can find the minimum hardware compatibility requirements on the Hardware Compatibility List (HCL) at *http://www.microsoft.com/hcl*.

Roaming User Needs

If you have many roaming users who need to log on from different locations and edit documents in several languages, you must ensure that the appropriate language files are either installed or installable on demand on those users' workstations. You can also install Terminal Services so that users can sign on to unique Terminal Services sessions in different languages.

If your roaming users need to log on from different locations in their native language user interface version of the operating system, you must install the Windows XP Professional MUI Pack as appropriate.

> **Tip** If you have deployed a Windows 2000 Server MultiLanguage version, you can extend the life cycles of old desktops and functionality of thin clients for use as multilingual workstations. By installing Terminal Services on clients connected to a computer running Windows 2000 Server MultiLanguage version, you effectively permit the client to function as a Windows XP Professional MUI Pack–based workstation that allows users to change user interface languages easily.

Upgrade Paths

A localized language version of a Windows-based client cannot be upgraded to a different language version of Windows XP Professional or to the Windows XP Professional MUI Pack. For example, you cannot upgrade a Japanese localized language version of Windows 2000 Professional to either the International English language version or MUI Pack of Windows XP Professional. You can upgrade to the Windows XP Professional MUI Pack only from an International English language version of Windows or from the Microsoft Windows 2000 Professional MultiLanguage version.

Table B-5 shows which of these earlier versions of Windows clients can be upgraded to the Windows XP Professional MUI Pack.

> **Note** To replace any other language versions of Windows with the Windows XP Professional MUI Pack, you must remove the previous Windows version and perform a clean installation of the Windows XP Professional MUI Pack.

Table B-5   Upgrade Matrix for Windows XP Professional MUI Pack

International English or MultiLanguage Version of Windows	Windows XP Professional MUI Pack
Microsoft Windows NT Workstation 3.51	
Windows NT Workstation 4.0	Yes

Table B-5   Upgrade Matrix for Windows XP Professional MUI Pack

International English or MultiLanguage Version of Windows	Windows XP Professional MUI Pack
Windows 98	Yes
Windows Millennium Edition (Me)	Yes
Windows 2000 Professional	Yes
Windows 2000 Professional MultiLanguage version	Yes
Windows XP Home Edition	

Single Global Images

The Windows XP Professional MUI Pack enables a global organization's IT department to deploy and maintain a single global desktop image. In this way, your company can create a single build that includes user interface language support for all of the languages in which you do business. The build can also include world-ready applications such as Office 2003 Editions.

For example, if your company supports user interfaces in English, French, Italian, Spanish, Japanese, Simplified Chinese, and Traditional Chinese, you can create a single global image that includes user interface support for those seven languages. You can also make support for those languages available for on-demand installation after deployment by using Windows Installer packages.

> **Tip**   Deploying and maintaining a single global image can significantly improve IT efficiency and help lower many costs. It enables single code base application development and testing, simplifies releasing hotfixes and service patches, and reduces end user support calls.

Regional Builds

You can further customize Windows XP Professional deployments by creating specific regional builds tailored to each office's multilingual and international needs. For each office or site, you can create a regional build that specifies the appropriate language version of the operating system, the default input language, and the standards and formats appropriate to that region. You can also include the appropriate localized language versions of third-party applications, such as virus-checking utilities, as well as other specialized drivers and applications required by that office. For example, you might create the following four unique regional builds for North America:

- Two Canadian builds for the Vancouver, B.C. and Montreal offices to deploy the International English version of Windows XP Professional, with English and French (Canada) set as the default input languages, and Canada set as the default for Standards And Formats. English is the default input language in Vancouver, and French is the default input language in Montreal.

- A U.S. English build so that users in Seattle and other U.S. locations can install the International English version of Windows XP Professional, with English (U.S.) set as the default input language and optional support for the East Asian Language Collection, which includes the font files, font linking, and registry settings needed for Simplified Chinese and Traditional Chinese, Japanese, and Korean language support.

- A Boston regional build that installs the U.S. English build along with optional support for the East Asian Language Collection.

    The regional build for the Tokyo office, by contrast, might install the Japanese localized language version of Windows XP Professional, as well as the Japanese localized language versions of virus checking and accounting applications.

Using the Windows XP Professional MUI Pack, global organizations can also take a hybrid approach combining a single global core image, which contains the baseline operating system and applications, with additional regional core images that include localized language applications, settings, and so on. The global IT department develops and maintains the global core; individual countries/regions are responsible for building and maintaining their own regional cores. Local offices can also add a third-tier customization core image for custom stationery or templates, printer drivers, and so on.

Configuring Desktops

Using Windows XP Professional, you can customize desktops to support your company's specific language and regional needs. You can configure desktops with specific Regional And Language Options, such as a default input language or keyboard layout. You can also configure the browser to receive localized, regional content, and you can add toolbars and keyboard shortcuts to simplify switching between input languages.

Windows XP Professional enables administrators to specify the appropriate input language and keyboard layout combination and standards, and formats settings for the default user account on a computer. All subsequent new user accounts created on that computer inherit the specified defaults; existing user accounts are not affected. Administrators can specify these default settings through the user interface or by using answer files. For more information about specifying the default settings through the user interface, see the following section, "Regional and Language

Options." For more information about specifying the default settings through the answer files, see "Unattended Installations" later in this appendix on page 753.

Regional and Language Options

You can use the Regional And Language Options settings in Control Panel to configure input languages for user accounts, and for the MUI Pack, to specify or change the default user interface language, or to install or remove user interface language packs. Here's how to install the Complex Script and Right-To-Left Collection or East Asian Language Collection:

1. In Control Panel, click Regional And Language Options.

2. Click the Languages tab, and then under Supplemental Language Support, select the check boxes of the language collections that you want to install.

   Here's how to change the Language For Non-Unicode Programs:

1. Log on as an Administrator.

2. In Control Panel, click Regional And Language Options.

3. Click the Advanced tab, and then under Language For Non-Unicode Programs, select the language for which the application was developed.

Regional and Language Support

Some language versions of Windows XP Professional might require installing the Complex Script and Right-To-Left Language Collection or the East Asian Language Collection, as well as the appropriate input languages, to properly input and display all characters. Administrators can specify which input languages are available for user selection at the Windows logon screen, and which are applied to new user accounts, by adding the appropriate input languages to the default user account:

1. In Control Panel, click Regional And Language Options.

2. Click the Languages tab, and then under Text Services And Input Languages, click Details.

3. Under Installed Services, click Add.

4. In the Input Language box, click the input language that you want to add to enable users to input text in that language.

   This installs the input language with the default keyboard layout/IME listed in the Keyboard Layout/IME box.

Here's how to add an alternative keyboard layout and IME for an input language:

1. In Control Panel, click Regional And Language Options.

2. Click the Languages tab, and then under Text Services And Input Languages, click Details.

3. Under Installed Services, click Add.

4. In the Keyboard Layout/IME box, click the alternative keyboard layout or IME that you want to add to enable users to input text in the specified input language.

Here's how to specify the default input language for the current user:

1. In Control Panel, click Regional And Language Options.

2. Click the Languages tab, and then under Text Services And Input Languages, click Details.

3. Under Default Input Language, select the appropriate input language.

Here's how to add an input language for the default user account:

1. Log on as an Administrator.

2. In Control Panel, click Regional And Language Options.

3. Click the Languages tab, and then under Text Services And Input Languages, click Details.

4. Under Installed services, click Add.

5. In the Input Language box, click the input language that you want to add to enable users to input text in that language and then click OK. If you want to add more than one input language, repeat this step for each language that you want to add.

6. Click OK or Apply to close the Text Services And Input Languages dialog box.

7. Click the Advanced tab and then select the Apply All Settings To The Current User Account And To The Default User Profile check box.

User Interface Language

The Windows XP Professional MUI Pack allows users to change user interface languages, as long as support for additional user interface languages has been installed and Administrators have not locked down the desktop by using Group Policy settings:

1. In Control Panel, click Regional And Language Options.

2. Click the Languages tab, and then under Language Used In Menus And Dialogs, select the language that you want to use.

Here's how to specify the user interface language for the default user account:

1. In Control Panel, click Regional And Language Options.

2. Click the Languages tab, and then under Language Used In Menus And Dialogs, select the language that you want to use.

3. Click the Advanced tab, and then select the Apply All Settings To The Current User Account And To The Default User Profile check box.

Localized Content

You can configure the default location to ensure that a user or group of users receives the appropriate local content, such as news and weather, from Internet or intranet content providers. You can change the default location without impacting other multilingual settings, such as the default standards and formats used for currency, sorting, dates, and so on.

The Location setting of the Regional And Language Options Control Panel enables Web content providers to redirect users to more appropriate regional sites when they visit a generic site. For example, users in the Milan office would want the default location set to Italy to ensure that they connect to the appropriate servers, content providers, and so on. Here's how to configure localized browser content:

1. In Control Panel, click Regional And Language Options.

2. Click the Regional Options tab, and then under Location, click the region or location for which you want customized content.

Multiple Language Access

Administrators can configure desktops to simplify working in multiple languages. For example, you can add a language toolbar to the desktop or a language icon to the Taskbar, making it easier for users to change between different input languages when they need to compose documents in multiple languages. You can also enable specific key sequences that let users quickly change between installed input languages and alternative keyboard layouts/IMEs. Here's how to add the Language bar to the desktop or Taskbar:

1. In Control Panel, click Regional And Language Options.

2. Click the Languages tab, and then under Text services and input languages, click Details.

3. In the Text Services and Input Languages dialog box, under Preferences, click Language Bar.

4. In the Language Bar Settings dialog box, select the check boxes that correspond to the language bar and Taskbar options you want to enable.

Here's how to enable or change key sequences for switching input languages or keyboard layouts and IMEs:

1. In Control Panel, click Regional And Language Options.

2. Click the Languages tab, and then under Text Services And Input Languages, click Details.

3. In the Text Services and Input Languages dialog box, under Preferences, click Key Settings.

4. In the Advanced Key Settings dialog box, select the options that correspond to the key sequences and actions you want to use to enable a user to change between installed input languages or keyboard layouts/IMEs.

5. If you want to use the On-Screen Keyboard to input text in a different language, change to the appropriate input language before enabling the On-Screen Keyboard.

Here's how to display the On-Screen Keyboard:

1. From the Start menu, point to All Programs, point to Accessories, and then point to Accessibility.

2. Click On-Screen Keyboard.

Special Characters (Code Points)

Users can input characters that are not on the keyboard by pressing and holding the Alt key and then typing the appropriate decimal code value for that character on the numeric keypad:

- If the first digit typed is 0, the value is recognized as a code point in the current input language. For example, pressing and holding the Alt key while typing 0163 produces £, the pound sign (U+00A3 in the format for Unicode encoding), if the default input language is English (U.S.).

- If the first digit typed is any number between 1 and 9, the value is represented as a code point in the operating system's original equipment manufacturer (OEM) code page. For example, pressing and holding the Alt key while typing 163 produces ú (U+00FA) if the code page is 437 (MS-DOS Latin US).

Group Policy Settings

Windows XP Professional enables administrators to automate different users' Regional And Language Options, such as the default input language or standards and formats, by using a Group Policy logon script. When a given user logs on to a computer, the Group Policy logon script silently calls the Regional And Language Options Control Panel to specify the correct settings for that user.

For more information about using a Group Policy logon script to silently configure desktop settings, see the following section, "Unattended Installations." The Windows XP Professional MUI Pack allows administrators to use Group Policy settings to control users' abilities to change the user interface language.

Unattended Installations

Windows XP Professional contains keywords and options that simplify creating unattended installations of new computers and silent configuration of existing computers. For unattended installations of any language version of Windows XP Professional, you may need to specify additional options for running Winnt32 or Winnt. Also, you must specify certain keywords and values in your Unattend.txt or Sysprep.inf answer file. There are also special considerations for performing unattended installations of the Windows XP Professional MUI Pack.

Running Windows XP Setup

If your organization requires the installation of East Asian language and locale support, you must specify **/copysource:*lang*** or **/rx:*lang*** to copy the necessary language files. If you do not, and if the *[RegionalSettings]* section of your answer file contains East Asian values, Windows XP Setup will ignore everything in the *[RegionalSettings]* section of your answer file. If you install one of the East Asian localized language versions of Windows XP Professional, you do not need to specify the **/copysource** or **/rx** command-line options because East Asian language and locale support are installed by default.

For Winnt32, the appropriate syntax is **winnt32.exe /unattend:*unattend.txt* /copysource:*lang* /s:*source***. To run Winnt from a 16-bit, MS-DOS network startup disk, the appropriate syntax is **winnt.exe /u:*unattend.txt* /rx:*lang* /s:*source***.

> **Note**   For the MUI Pack, you must specify certain options to run Winnt32. You cannot run Winnt. For more information about specifying options for the MUI Pack, see "Installing the MUI Pack" later in this appendix on page 757.

Defining Settings in Answer Files

For unattended installations of Windows XP Professional, you can customize the following sections of the answer file to address specific language and other regional needs:

- *[RegionalSettings]* Options

- *[GuiUnattended]* Options

- *[TapiLocation]* Options

If you are creating an answer file for a localized language version of Windows XP Professional other than International English, create the answer file using that localized language version. Otherwise, change the Language For Non-Unicode Programs to that of the localized language version, and save the answer file as ANSI text using the appropriate text encoding method for the language version that you are installing. For example, if you are creating an answer file to install the Russian localized language version on a desktop, use the Russian localized language version of Windows XP Professional to create the answer file. Otherwise, change the Language For Non-Unicode Programs to Russian and use the Cyrillic OEM code page to author the answer file.

The *[RegionalSettings]* section of the answer file specifies multilingual and international settings such as the language collections installed, the input languages installed, and the language for non-Unicode programs. All of the *[RegionalSettings]* values can be specified in either Unattend.txt or Sysprep.inf. Listing B-1 shows an example of the *[RegionalSettings]* section.

Note Any [RegionalSettings] values specified in Sysprep.inf will override any values set in Unattend.txt. In addition, if you use Sysprep, all the appropriate additional language files specified must already be installed on the computer.

Listing B-1   *[RegionalSettings]*

```
[RegionalSettings]
Language="locale ID"LanguageGroup="language group ID","language group ID"...
SystemLocale="locale ID"UserLocale="locale ID"InputLocale="locale
ID:keyboard layout ID", "locale ID:keyboard layout ID", ...
UserLocale_DefaultUser="locale ID"
InputLocale_DefaultUser="locale ID:keyboard layout ID", ...
```

Table B-6 describes the *[RegionalSettings]* keys and identifies the corresponding settings in the Regional And Language Options Control Panel. For a complete listing of valid values for these keys, see "Locales & Languages" at *http://www.microsoft.com/globaldev/DrIntl/faqs/Locales.mspx*.

Table B-6   *[RegionalSettings]* **Keys**

Setting	Description	Regional And Language Options Control Panel Settings
Language	Specifies the language installed. If this setting is specified, the SystemLocale, UserLocale, and InputLocale keys are ignored.	Standards and Formats. Input Language. Language for Non-Unicode Programs.
LanguageGroup	Specifies the language groups installed on the computer. Installing one language group also installs support for all of the other language groups in the same language collection. For example, if you install the Korean language group (8), Windows XP Professional installs support for all the other language groups in the East Asian Language Collection (i.e., Japanese [7], Traditional Chinese [9], and Simplified Chinese [10]). For a list of the language groups installed under each language collection, see "Built-In Language Support" earlier in this appendix on page 736.	Same effect as: Installing support for Complex Script and Right-To-Left languages. Installing support for East Asian languages.
SystemLocale	Enables non-Unicode applications to run and display menus and dialog boxes in the localized language.	Language for Non-Unicode Programs.
UserLocale	Controls settings for sorting numbers, time, currency, and dates.	Standards and Formats.
InputLocale	Specifies input language and keyboard layout combinations. The first keyboard layout specified becomes the system default. Specified combinations must be supported by one of the languages defined by using either the LanguageGroup setting or the default language for the language version of Windows XP Professional being installed. If an available language does not support the specified combination, the default combination is used. This setting is ignored if the Language setting is specified.	Input Language(s).
1UserLocale_DefaultUser	Controls the formats for numbers, time, currency, and dates for the default user. The specified setting must be supported by one of the languages specified using the LanguageGroup setting or the default language for the language version of Windows XP Professional being installed.	Same effect as: Setting Standards And Formats. Selecting Apply All Settings To The Current User Account And To The Default User Profile check box on the Advanced tab.

Table B-6 *[RegionalSettings]* **Keys**

Setting	Description	Regional And Language Options Control Panel Settings
1InputLocale_DefaultUser	Sets the input language and keyboard layout combinations for the default user.	Same effect as: Specifying Input Languages. Selecting Apply All Settings To The Current User Account And To The Default User Profile check box on the Advanced tab.

> **Note** If you specify a Language setting, the value associated with it overrides all the values specified in the InputLocale, SystemLocale, and UserLocale keys. Typically, using the Language setting is the preferred method for specifying input languages because it prevents the occurrence of incompatible values in the InputLocale, SystemLocale, and UserLocale keys and installs locales appropriate for the specified language and locale combinations.

You must specify the time zone of the computer by using the *TimeZone* setting in the *[GuiUnattended]* section of your answer file. If the *TimeZone* setting is not present in your answer file, the user is prompted for a time zone during installation. To preset time zones, add Listing B-2 to the *[GuiUnattended]* section in your answer file. Index specifies the time zone of the computer. For a list of valid Time Zone indices, see Ref.chm in Support\Tools\Deploy.cab on the Microsoft Windows XP Professional operating system CD.

Listing B-2 *TimeZone* Setting

```
[GuiUnattended]
TimeZone="index"
```

> **Note** If you specify *OemPreinstall=Yes* in the *[Unattended]* section of your answer file, you may want to add *OemSkipRegional=1* to the *[GuiUnattended]* section to ensure that Windows XP Setup does not prompt the user for regional information during the GUI-mode phase.

You can specify dialing rules specific to your country or region by using the *[TapiLocation]* section of your answer file. These dialing rules specify the default country code and area code that a modem uses when dialing the phone. The *[TapiLocation]* keys described here are supported in both Unattend.txt and Sysprep.inf, and are valid only for computers with modems. To preset telephone dialing rules, in your answer file, specify the appropriate values in the *[TapiLocation]* section, as shown in Listing B-3. For a complete list of country codes to use for telephony, search on the Internet for "ISO 3166" or see the International Telecommunication Union website at *http://www.itu.int/home/index.html*.

Listing B-3   *[TapiLocation]*

```
[TapiLocation]
CountryCode="CountryCode"AreaCode="AreaCode"
```

In Listing B-4, an International English language version of Windows XP Professional is configured with additional support for the East Asian Language Collection installed. English (U.S.) is the default for both the Language For Non-Unicode Programs (the SystemLocale) and the Standards And Formats (the UserLocale). Additional input languages and keyboard layouts are also installed for Japanese, Chinese (Taiwan), Chinese (People's Republic of China), Korean, and German. The telephone country code is set to U.S. and the area code is 425. The time zone is Redmond (U.S.) Pacific Standard Time.

Listing B-4   Sample Regional Settings

```
[GuiUnattended]
TimeZone="020"

[RegionalSettings]
LanguageGroup="1","7","8","9","10"SystemLocale="0409"UserLocale="0409"
InputLocale="0409:00000409","0411:e0010411","0404:00000404","0804:00000804",
"0412:E0010412","0407:00000407"[TapiLocation]
CountryCode="US"AreaCode="425"
```

Installing the MUI Pack

Unattended installation of the Windows XP Professional MUI Pack is slightly different from that of the Windows XP Professional International English or localized language versions for the following reasons:

■ Because the Windows XP Professional MUI Pack requires the use of files from several CD-ROMs, you should carefully review how this affects different deployment methods, including network installation, creating custom images on multiple CD-ROMs using Sysprep, or a combination of CD-ROM and network installation.

■ You must specify *OemPreinstall=Yes* and *OemFilesPath=source* in the *[Unattended]* section of your answer file to point to the location of the user interface language files. If you are installing the MUI Pack from the default location of \i386\OEM, you do not need to specify an *OemFilesPath* value.

- The *[Commands]* section of Cmdlines.txt must be used to specify the execution of Muisetup.exe, the program that installs the user interface languages.

The MUI Pack requires special attention to ensure consistency within the *[RegionalSettings]* section of the answer file. You must specify the language groups and locales to install to support the appropriate user interface languages and applications. The other settings that you specify in the *[RegionalSettings]* section depend on your workstation configurations:

- **For single-user systems** Set locales to the same value as the default user interface language (specified when running Muisetup). For example, if German is set as the default user interface language, specify one of the German locales in the answer file.

- **For shared workstations and in Terminal Services environments** Set the default user interface language and the Language For Non-Unicode Programs to English, the administrative language of the MUI Pack. You can set the input language according to individual preferences or requirements. Or, if specified by using the Language setting, restrict the input language to be the same as the language for non-Unicode programs.

> **Note** Install the appropriate language groups to ensure support for both the locales and the user interface languages specified. For example, if you install the Japanese (Japan) user interface language, you must also install the East Asian Language Collection to ensure Japanese language and locale support.

The example in Listing B-5 installs support for the East Asian Language Collection. English (U.S.) is the default for both the Language For Non-Unicode Programs (the SystemLocale) and Standards And Formats (the UserLocale). Additional input language and keyboard layouts are also installed for Japanese, Chinese (Taiwan), Chinese (People's Republic of China), Korean, and German. In addition to the *[RegionalSettings]* options, you must specify the following settings in the *[Unattended]* section when installing the MUI Pack. The *OemFilesPath* setting points to the installation share that you create to contain the MUI user interface language files. If you are installing the MUI Pack from the default location of \i386\OEM, you do not need to specify an *OemFilesPath* value. The *[GuiUnattended]* section of the answer file lets you disable the OEM Regional prompt that would otherwise be displayed during Windows XP Setup. Because you specified *OemPreinstall=Yes* in the

[Unattended] section of your answer file, you may want to add *OemSkipRegional=1* to the *[GuiUnattended]* section to ensure that Windows XP Setup does not prompt the user for regional information during the GUI-mode phase.

Listing B-5   Sample Regional Settings

```
[Unattended]
OemPreinstall="Yes"
OemFilesPath=source

[GuiUnattended]
OemSkipRegional=1

[RegionalSettings]
LanguageGroup="1","7","8","9","10"SystemLocale="0409"UserLocale="0409"
InputLocale="0409:00000409","0411:e0010411","0404:00000404","0804:00000804",
"0412:E0010412","0407:00000407"
```

For unattended installations of the Windows XP Professional MUI Pack, you must copy all the MUI files from CD2 into a temporary directory below the top-level directory on a network share or CD. In the following example, the computer name is \\MUICORE, the share name is OEM, and the temporary directory is MUIINST: \MUICORE\OEM\MUIINST.

> **Tip**   For CD-based deployments, if the MUI Pack files are located on the CD (and not on a network share), the user may need to change CDs to complete the installation. This would require user intervention to change CDs, effectively preventing a fully unattended installation.

For the Windows XP Professional MUI Pack, you must create a Cmdlines.txt file in the top level of your temporary directory. Cmdlines.txt must contain a *[Commands]* section that executes the Muisetup program using the appropriate command-line options and values, as shown in Listing B-6.

> **Note**   You must use quotation marks around the command, and the path to Muisetup must specify the temporary directory you created in the installation source.

Listing B-6   Sample Cmdlines.txt

```
[Commands]
".\temporary directory name\MUISETUP.exe [/i LangID LangID...]
[/d LangID] /r /s"
```

Table B-7 describes the Muisetup command-line options.

Table B-7   Muisetup Command-Line Options

Command-Line Option	Description
/i	Specifies the user interface language(s) to be installed. Typically, languages are entered in four-digit hexadecimal LangID values.
/d	Specifies the default user interface language (applied to all new user accounts and used in places such as the Winlogon screen).
/r	Specifies that the restart message not be displayed.
/s	Specifies that the installation complete message not be displayed.

Listing B-7 specifies that Muisetup install the Japanese (Japan) and German (Germany) user interface languages, and sets Japanese (Japan) as the default user interface language used for the Winlogon screen and applied to all new user accounts.

Listing B-7   Sample Cmdlines.txt

```
[Commands]
".\MUIINST\MUISETUP.exe /i 0411 0407 /d 0411 /r /s"
```

You can use Windows Installer (*.msi*) packages to install additional MUI user interface language support. To do this, you must copy the *.msi* files for those user interface languages to the installation share and then invoke Windows Installer in your Cmdlines.txt file to install the user interface languages on the computer. To install multiple user interface languages, repeat the msiexec invocation, specifying the appropriate *.msi* file for each additional user interface language that you want to install.

In Listing B-8, the German (Germany) user interface language is silently installed from the German *.msi* package, and the Japanese (Japan) user interface language is silently installed from the Japanese *.msi* package.

Listing B-8   Sample Cmdlines.txt

```
[Commands]
"msiexec.exe /i 0407.msi /q"
"msiexec.exe /i 0411.msi /q"
```

When installing Windows Installer packages, you can choose whether to set a particular user interface language for the current user, the default user, or both. You can also specify whether a user interface language can be uninstalled by any user. Table B-8 describes these properties and how to use them. For more information about these options, see Chapter 23, "Software Installation."

Table B-8   Windows Installer Package Properties

Property	Description
CURRENTUSER=1	Sets the user interface language being installed as the user interface language for the current user. If this is not specified, the user interface language will be installed without changing the current user's user interface language.
DEFAULTUSER=1	Sets the user interface language being installed as the user interface language for the default user account, which affects the logon screen and all new user accounts. If this is not specified, the user interface language will be installed without changing the default user account's user interface language.
ALLUSERS=1	Specifies that the user interface language can be uninstalled by any user of that computer.

In Listing B-9, the German (Germany) and Japanese (Japan) user interface languages are silently installed, and the current user and default user accounts are set to Japanese. In addition, the German *.msi* package is to be installed per computer, allowing all users of the computer to remove it.

Listing B-9   Sample Cmdlines.txt

```
[Commands]
"msiexec.exe /i 0407.msi allusers=1 /q""msiexec.exe /i 0411.msi
defaultuser=1 currentuser=1 /q"
```

> **Caution**   Use the *ALLUSERS=1* property carefully because it allows any user to remove a user interface language from a computer—even if that user interface language might be required by another user of the same computer. If you install a given user interface language by using the *CURRENTUSER=1* and *DEFAULTUSER=1* properties, do not specify the *ALLUSERS=1* property for the same user interface language.

Using Silent Configurations

You might want to change a computer's Regional And Language Options silently after the initial installation. For example, if your organization locks down the desktop to prevent a group of users from accessing the Control Panel, you can update that group's Regional And Language Options by using a Group Policy–applied logon script. In these situations, you can use Rundll32.exe to call the Regional And Language Options Control Panel with an answer file that specifies the appropriate settings.

The syntax for calling Rundll32 from the command line is as follows: Rundll32 shell32,Control_RunDLL intl.cpl,,/f:***unattend.txt***. The answer file specified in ***unattend.txt*** must contain a *[RegionalSettings]* section that specifies the appropriate regional and language settings.

Changing Language and Regional Options

The format of the answer file specified in a silent configuration is exactly the same as that used during Windows XP Setup. This means that all the *[RegionalSettings]* options can be changed silently after the initial installation.

Listing B-10 is an example of a silent configuration that does the following:

- Adds the "German-German" input language for the current user

- Adds the "German-Swiss German" input language to the list of input languages for the default user

- Configures the Language For Non-Unicode Programs to German

Listing B-10   *[RegionalSettings]*

```
[RegionalSettings]
InputLocale="0407:00000407"
InputLocale_DefaultUser="0407:00000807"
SystemLocale="0407"
```

If you specify multiple input languages for the *InputLocale* and *InputLocale_DefaultUser* settings, as shown in Listing B-11, the first value specified will be set as the default for that particular user. In the following example, the *InputLocale* will set "German-German" as the default input language for the current user while also making "German-Swiss German" available as an input language.

Listing B-11   *[RegionalSettings]*

```
[RegionalSettings]
InputLocale="0407:00000407", "0407:00000807"
```

Changing MUI Pack Defaults

The Windows XP Professional MUI Pack contains two new keywords that you can use after running Windows XP Setup to perform silent configurations. These keywords are intended for silent configuration after installation, when the specified user interface language has already been installed on the computer. Table B-9 describes these additional *[RegionalSettings]* keys.

For a complete listing of valid values for these keys, see "Locales & Languages" at *http://www.microsoft.com/globaldev/DrIntl/faqs/Locales.mspx*.

Table B-9 *[RegionalSettings]* **Keys for Silently Configuring MUI Pack Defaults**

Setting	Description
MUILanguage	Sets the user interface language for the current user.
MUILanguage_DefaultUser	Sets the user interface language for the default user account, including the logon screen and the user interface language applied to all new user accounts.

Using Windows Installer Packages

The Windows XP Professional MUI Pack includes Windows Installer packages that allow users to install user interface languages on demand. For companies that support one global image, on-demand installation enables smaller and faster installations and images. If you do regional builds or CD-based deployments, include on a CD or network share the Windows Installer package for each specific user interface language your company needs to support.

To enable on-demand installations, you can publish a Windows Installer (*.msi*) package for each user interface language that your company supports on the appropriate Active Directory servers. The Windows Installer packages are then listed as additional user interface languages in the appropriate users' Add Or Remove Programs Control Panel. If you publish the *.msi* packages with the Maximum UI option, users can choose whether to install and set a specific user interface language for the current user, the default user, or both. Alternatively, to set the user account settings automatically, you can publish the *.msi* packages with the Basic UI option and then apply transforms to the packages.

For example, assume that your company supports 12 different languages worldwide. Your IT department publishes those 12 Windows Installer user interface language packages in the global Active Directory. A clerk in the Boston office, using Windows XP Professional MUI Pack with English (U.S.) as the default user interface language, can then install Italian and Japanese user interface language support when it is needed. All that the user needs to do is open the Add Or Remove Programs Control Panel and select the Italian and Japanese user interface language support packages.

Appendix C

Administrative Template Syntax

You manage registry-based policies using the Group Policy Object (GPO) editor. *Administrative templates*, text files with the *.adm* extension, define the policies you can manage. Administrative templates and *policy templates* are the same thing, and you frequently see the short name *ADM files*. These templates describe the user interface for collecting settings from you and their locations in the registry.

This appendix describes the syntax for creating and customizing administrative templates. It doesn't describe the process of adding templates to the GPO editor, though. For more information about using the templates you create with the aid of this appendix, including samples of complete templates, see Chapter 20, "Policy Management." The information in this appendix applies to Microsoft Windows NT 4.0, Microsoft Windows 2000, and Microsoft Windows XP Professional.

Comments

Comments are useful and necessary to document the contents of your administrative templates. You can add comments to templates in two different ways. Precede the comment with a semicolon (;) or two forward slashes (//). Place comments on lines by themselves. You see examples of comments throughout this appendix; I documented each example using them. Listing C-1 shows examples of valid comments. I prefer using // for comments.

Listing C-1

```
; This is a comment
// This is also a comment

// Per-user settings
CLASS USER

; Per-computer settings
CLASS MACHINE
```

Strings

In a one-off, quick-and-dirty administrative template, don't feel bad about hard-coding strings. That means adding the string where you need it and repeating the same string as often as necessary. If you're creating enterprise-class templates or if you're managing the templates over time, use string variables, which makes it easier to maintain templates that use the same strings more than once. More important, it makes the localization of templates far easier and much less error-prone.

Define strings at the end of your administrative template in the *[strings]* section. The format of each string is *name="string"*. You must enclose the string in double quotes. To use string variables in your template, use the format *!!name*. Each time the GPO editor sees *!!name*, it substitutes the string for the name. Incidentally, the *!!* makes searching templates for strings easy—just search the file for the double-exclamation marks. Listing C-2 is an example of how you use strings and string variables in administrative templates:

Listing C-2

```
POLICY !!Sample
  SUPPORTED "At least Microsoft Windows XP"
  EXPLAIN !!Sample_Explain

...

[strings]
Sample="Sample Policy"
Sample_Explain="This sample policy doesn't do much of anything."
```

> **Note**   In this appendix, I tend not to use string variables for clarity. Doing so prevents you from looking up each string as you're wading through the listings. Keep in mind that you want to use string variables if you plan on localizing your files.

CLASS

The first entry in an administrative template is the keyword *CLASS*, which defines whether the policies following it are per-user or per-computer. That is, it specifies where in the GPO editor you see the policy User Configuration Or Computer Configuration. You can use multiple *CLASS* keywords in a template. When the Windows XP Professional client-side extensions process the policies, it merges the settings defined in the *CLASS USER* sections and does the same for the settings defined in all the *CLASS MACHINE* sections. Then it loads the settings defined in the *CLASS USER* sections into HKEY_CURRENT_USER and the settings defined in the *CLASS MACHINE* sections into HKEY_LOCAL_MACHINE.

Syntax

```
CLASS Name
```

Parameters

Name   This must be *MACHINE* or *USER*. *MACHINE* specifies that the policies following the *CLASS* keyword are per-computer policies, and *USER* specifies that the policies following the keyword are per-user policies. This keyword persists until you change it by using additional *CLASS* keywords.

Example

Listing C-3

```
CLASS MACHINE

// Policies here are per-computer policies

CLASS USER

// Policies here are per-user policies

CLASS MACHINE

// Policies here are per-computer policies
```

CATEGORY

After defining whether policies appear under the Computer Settings Or User Settings branch of the GPO editor by using the *CLASS* keyword, use *CATEGORY* keywords to create subfolders in that branch. The policy editor displays your settings in those folders. Just as you can create subfolders within folders in the file system, you can create subcategories within categories by nesting *CATEGORY* keywords. All the *CATEGORY* keyword does is create subfolders.

Categories can include zero or more policies. Categories that contain no policies usually contain one or more subcategories at a minimum. You define the registry key in which the GPO editor creates settings for that category using the *KEYNAME* keyword, which you learn about in the next section. Using the *KEYNAME* keyword here is optional if you're defining the key elsewhere. Last, you end a category with *END CATEGORY*.

Syntax

```
CATEGORY Name
  [KEYNAME Subkey]

  Policies

END CATEGORY
```

Parameters

Name   This is the folder name you want to see in the GPO editor. Use a string
            variable or a string enclosed in quotes.

Subkey   This is an optional subkey of HKEY_LOCAL_MACHINE or
            HKEY_CURRENT_USER to use for the category. Do not include either
            root key in the path, though, because the preceding *CLASS* keyword
            specifies which of these root keys to use. If you specify a subkey, all
            nested categories, policies, and parts use it unless they specifically
            provide their own subkey. Enclose names that contain spaces in dou-
            ble quotes.

Example

Listing C-4

```
// Settings are per-user in HKEY_CURRENT_USER
CLASS USER

CATEGORY "Desktop Settings"
  KEYNAME "Software\Policies\System"

  // Add policies for the Desktop Settings category here

  CATEGORY "Custom Application Settings"
    KEYNAME "Software\Policies\CustomApps"

    // Add policies for the custom applications subcategory here

  END CATEGORY
END CATEGORY
```

Keywords

The valid keywords you can use within a *CATEGORY* section are the following:

- *CATEGORY*
- *END*
- *KEYNAME*
- *POLICY*

KEYNAME

Use the *KEYNAME* keyword within a category to define which subkey of
HKEY_CURRENT_USER or HKEY_LOCAL_MACHINE (depending on the *CLASS* keyword) contains the value you're changing. Do not include a root key in the path

because the *CLASS* keyword defines it. If the name contains spaces, you must enclose the string in double quotes. The example in the previous section, "CATE-GORY," shows how to use the *KEYNAME* keyword.

POLICY

Use the *POLICY* keyword to define a policy that you can change using the GPO editor. The policy editor displays the policy and its controls in a dialog box that you use to change the policy's state and settings. You can include multiple *POLICY* keywords in a single category, but you don't need to include the *KEYNAME* keyword before each *POLICY* keyword. The most recent *KEYNAME* keyword applies for each policy. You end a policy with *END POLICY*.

Each policy contains a *VALUENAME* keyword to associate a registry value with it. By default, the GPO editor assumes that it's a REG_DWORD value and stores 0x01 in it when you enable the policy. The policy editor also removes the value when you disable the policy. You must use the *VALUEON* and *VALUEOFF* keywords if you don't want the policy editor to remove the value when you disable the policy. You don't have to use any keywords other than *VALUENAME* to get this behavior. You can include optional *PART* keywords that specify additional options, however, such as drop-down list boxes, check boxes, text boxes, and so on. You see these controls in the bottom part of the policy's dialog box.

Syntax

```
POLICY Name
[KEYNAME Subkey]
EXPLAIN Help
VALUENAME Value

   [Parts]

END POLICY
```

Parameters

Name	This is the name of the policy as you want to see it in the GPO editor. Use a descriptive but short name.
Subkey	This is an optional subkey of HKEY_LOCAL_MACHINE or HKEY_CURRENT_USER to use for the policy. Do not include either root key in the path, though, because the preceding *CLASS* keyword specifies which of these root keys to use. If you specify a subkey, all nested policies and parts use it unless they specifically provide their own subkey. Enclose names that contain spaces in double quotes.
Help	This is the string that the GPO editor displays in the Explain tab and in the Extended tab of the policy's dialog box.

Value

This is the registry value to modify. Enabling the policy sets the REG_DWORD value to 0x01. Select the Not Configured option or disable the policy, and the GPO editor removes the value from the registry. To specify values other than the default 0x01, use the *VALUEON* and *VALUEOFF* keywords directly following the *VALUENAME* keyword:

```
VALUEON [NUMERIC] Enabled
VALUEOFF [NUMERIC] Disabled
```

When you use these keywords, the GPO editor sets the registry value to *Enabled* when you enable the policy and sets the value to *Disabled* when you disable the policy. The default value type is REG_SZ, but you can change it to REG_DWORD by prefixing the value with the keyword *NUMERIC*. Regardless, setting the policy to Not Configured removes the value altogether.

Example

Listing C-5

```
CLASS MACHINE

CATEGORY "Disk Quotas"

  KEYNAME "Software\Policies\MS\DiskQuota"
  POLICY "Enable disk quotas"
    EXPLAIN "Enables and disables disk quotas management."
    VALUENAME "Enable"
    VALUEON NUMERIC 1
    VALUEOFF NUMERIC 0
  END POLICY

END CATEGORY
```

Keywords

The valid keywords within a *POLICY* section include the following:

- *ACTIONLISTOFF*

- *ACTIONLISTON*

- *END*

- *KEYNAME*

- *PART*

- *VALUENAME*

- *VALUEOFF*

- *VALUEON*

- *HELP*

- *POLICY*

> **Note** Additional keywords are available for policies, but they are for developers creating policy extensions. For example, *CLIENTEXT* associates a client-side extension with a policy via the extension's globally unique identifier (GUID). I'm not covering these keywords because they don't fit our purposes here.

EXPLAIN

The *EXPLAIN* keyword provides help text for a specific policy. In Windows 2000 and more recent versions of Windows, each policy's dialog box includes an Explain tab, which provides details about the policy. You also see this help text on the Extended tab of the GPO editor's right pane in Windows XP Professional or later. Each policy you create for Windows 2000 or later should contain one *EXPLAIN* keyword followed by a full description of the policy and its settings. Although I don't show this in my examples (trying to keep them simple), you should enclose this keyword between *#if version >=3* and *#endif* to prevent the Windows NT 4.0 System Policy Editor from choking on this keyword, as shown in Listing C-6.

Listing C-6

```
#if version >= 3
  EXPLAIN "Enables and disables disk quotas management."
#endif
```

VALUENAME

The *VALUENAME* keyword identifies the registry value that the GPO editor modifies when you enable or disable the policy. The syntax is *VALUENAME Name*. You saw an example of this keyword in the section "POLICY." Unless you set the *VALUEON* and *VALUEOFF* keywords, described in the next section, the GPO editor creates the policy as a REG_DWORD value:

- **Enabled** Sets the value to 0x01
- **Disabled** Removes the value
- **Not Configured** Removes the value

VALUENAME, VALUEON, and *VALUEOFF* describe the value that enables and disables the policy. If you want to define additional settings that enable you to collect additional values to refine the policy, you must use the *PART* keyword. Settings in a *PART* section are in the bottom part of the policy's dialog box.

VALUEON and VALUEOFF

You can use the *VALUEON* and *VALUEOFF* keywords to write specific values based on the state of the policy. The section "POLICY" contains an example of how these keywords are used. The syntaxes are *VALUEON [NUMERIC] Enabled* and *VALUEOFF [NUMERIC] Disabled*. By default, the GPO editor creates the value as a REG_SZ value; if you want it to create the value as a REG_DWORD value, prefix it with the *NUMERIC* keyword. For example:

```
// Created as a REG_SZ value containing "0"
VALUEON 0

// Created as a REG_DWORD value containing 0x01
VALUEOFF NUMERIC 1
```

ACTIONLIST

The *ACTIONLIST* keyword enables you to group settings together. Think of it as a list of values you want the GPO editor to change when you change a policy. The following two variants of the *ACTIONLIST* keyword are the most commonly used:

- **ACTIONLISTON**   A list of values to change when the policy is enabled
- **ACTIONLISTOFF**   A list of values to change when the policy is disabled

Syntax

```
ACTIONLIST
  [KEYNAME Subkey]
  VALUENAME Value
  VALUE Data
END ACTIONLIST
```

Parameters

Subkey	This is an optional subkey of HKEY_LOCAL_MACHINE or HKEY_CURRENT_USER to use for the action list. Do not include either root key in the path, though, because the preceding *CLASS* keyword specifies which of these root keys to use. Enclose names that contain spaces in double quotes.
Value	This is the registry value to modify. Enabling the policy sets the REG_DWORD value to 0x01. Select the Not Configured option, and the GPO editor removes the value from the registry. To specify values other than the default 0x00 and 0x01, use the *VALUE* keyword.
Data	This is the data to which you want to set the value. The default value type is REG_SZ, but you can change it to REG_DWORD by prefixing the value with the keyword *NUMERIC*. If you follow the keyword *VALUE* with the keyword *DELETE (VALUE DELETE)*, the GPO editor removes the value from the registry. Regardless, setting the policy to Not Configured removes the value altogether.

Example

Listing C-7

```
POLICY "Sample Action List"
  EXPLAIN "This illustrates action lists"
  ACTIONLISTON
    VALUENAME Sample1 VALUE 1
    VALUENAME Sample2 VALUE 1
  END ACTIONLISTON

  ACTIONLISTOFF
    VALUENAME Sample1 VALUE 0
    VALUENAME Sample2 VALUE 0
  END ACTIONLISTOFF
END POLICY
```

PART

The *PART* keyword enables you to specify various options, including drop-down lists, text boxes, and check boxes, in the lower part of a policy's dialog box. For simple policies that you only need to enable or disable, you won't need to use this keyword. In fact, only a relative few of the policies in Windows XP Professional use the *PART* keyword.

You begin a part with the *PART* keyword and end it with *END PART*. The syntax of the *PART* keyword is *PART Name Type*. Name is the name of the part, and Type is the type of part. Each policy can contain multiple *PART* keywords, and the GPO editor displays them in the dialog box using the order that it found them in the administrative template. This section gives you the overall syntax of the *PART* keyword, and the sections following this one describe how to create the different types of parts.

Syntax

```
PART Name Type

  Keywords

  [KEYNAME Subkey]
  [DEFAULT Default]
  VALUENAME Name
END PART
```

Parameters

Name

This specifies the name of the setting as you want to see it in the policy's dialog box. Enclose the name in double quotes if it contains spaces. This is the setting's prompt.

Type

This can be one of the following types:

- **CHECKBOX**   Displays a check box. The REG_DWORD value is 0x01 if you select the check box or 0x00 if you clear it.
- **COMBOBOX**   Displays a combo box.
- **DROPDOWNLIST**   Displays a combo box with a drop-down list. The user can choose only one of the entries supplied.
- **EDITTEXT**   Displays a text box that accepts alphanumeric input. The value is either REG_SZ or REG_EXPAND_SZ.
- **LISTBOX**   Displays a list box with Add and Remove buttons. This is the only type that can be used to manage multiple values in one key.
- **NUMERIC**   Displays a text box with an optional spin control that accepts a numeric value. The value is a REG_DWORD value.
- **TEXT**   Displays a line of static text. It stores no data in the registry and is useful for adding help to the dialog box.

Keywords

This is information specific to each type of part. See the sections following this for more information about these keywords.

Subkey

This is an optional subkey of HKEY_LOCAL_MACHINE or HKEY_CURRENT_USER to use for the part. Do not include either root key in the path, though, because the preceding *CLASS* keyword specifies which of these root keys to use. If you specify a subkey, all nested parts use it unless they specifically provide their own subkey. Enclose names that contain spaces in double quotes.

Default

This is the default value for the part. When you enable the policy, the GPO editor fills the control with the default value. Use a default value that's appropriate for the part's type.

Value

This is the registry value to modify. The value type and data depend entirely on the part's type.

Example

Listing C-8

```
CATEGORY "Sample Part"
  EXPLAIN "This illustrates parts"
  KEYNAME "Software\Policies"
  POLICY "Sample Policy"
    EXPLAIN "This is a sample policy including parts."
    VALUENAME "Sample"
    PART test EDITTEXT
```

```
      DEFAULT "This is the default text"
      VALUENAME Sample
   END PART
 END POLICY
END CATEGORY
```

Keywords

The valid keywords within a *PART* section are the following:

- *CHECKBOX*

- *COMBOBOX*

- *DROPDOWNLIST*

- *EDITTEXT*

- *END*

- *LISTBOX*

- *NUMERIC*

- *PART*

- *TEXT*

CHECKBOX

The *CHECKBOX* part displays a check box. In the registry, it's a REG_SZ value. By default, the check box is cleared, and the settings it writes to the registry for each of its states are as follows:

- **Checked**   Writes 1 to the REG_SZ value

- **Cleared**   Writes 0 to the REG_SZ value

Include the keyword *DEFCHECKED* within the part if you want the check box selected by default. Otherwise, the check box is cleared by default.

Syntax

```
PART Name CHECKBOX
  DEFCHECKED
  VALUENAME Value
END PART
```

Parameters

Name   This specifies the name of the setting as you want to see it in the pol-
                              icy's dialog box. Enclose the name in double quotes if it contains
                              spaces. You see the name next to the check box.

Value

This is the registry value to modify. Enabling the policy sets the REG_SZ value to 1. Set the Not Configured option, and the GPO editor removes the value from the registry. To specify values other than the default 0 and 1, use the *VALUEON* and *VALUEOFF* keywords following the *VALUENAME* keyword:

```
VALUEON [NUMERIC] Enabled
VALUEOFF [NUMERIC] Disabled
```

When you use these keywords, the policy editor sets the registry value to Enabled when you enable the policy and sets the value to Disabled when you disable the policy. The default value type is REG_SZ, but you can change it to REG_DWORD by prefixing the value with the keyword *NUMERIC*. Regardless, setting the policy to Not Configured removes the value altogether. You can also use the *ACTIONLISTON* and *ACTIONLISTOFF* keywords to associate multiple values with a check box.

Example

Listing C-9

```
CLASS USER

CATEGORY "Sample Policies"
  EXPLAIN "These are sample policies that illustrate parts."

  POLICY "Sample Policy"
    SUPPORTED "At least Microsoft Windows XP Professional"

    EXPLAIN "This is a sample policy that illustrates a part."
    KEYNAME "Software\Policies"

    PART Sample1 CHECKBOX
      VALUENAME Sample1
    END PART

    PART Sample2 CHECKBOX
      DEFCHECKED
      VALUENAME Sample2
      VALUEON NUMERIC 11
      VALUEOFF NUMERIC 12
    END PART

  END POLICY

END CATEGORY
```

Keywords

The valid keywords within a *CHECKBOX* section include the following:

- *ACTIONLISTOFF*
- *ACTIONLISTON*

- *DEFCHECKED*

- *END*

- *KEYNAME*

- *VALUENAME*

- *VALUEOFF*

- *VALUEON*

COMBOBOX

The *COMBOBOX* keyword adds a combo box to the policy's dialog box. It has one additional keyword you must use: *SUGGESTIONS*. This creates a list of suggestions that the GPO editor places in the drop-down list. Separate the items in this list with white space and enclose items containing spaces within double quotes. End the list with *END SUGGESTIONS*.

A few keywords modify the behavior of the combo box:

- **DEFAULT**   Specifies the default value of the combo box

- **EXPANDABLETEXT**   Creates the value as a REG_EXPAND_SZ value

- **MAXLENGTH**   Specifies the maximum length of the value

- **NOSORT**   Prevents the GPO editor from sorting the list

- **REQUIRED**   Specifies that a value is required

Syntax

```
PART Name COMBOBOX
  SUGGESTIONS
    Suggestions
  END SUGGESTIONS
  [DEFAULT Default]
  [EXPANDABLETEXT]
  [MAXLENGTH Max]
  [NOSORT]
  [REQUIRED]
  VALUENAME Value
END PART
```

Parameters

Name	This specifies the name of the setting as you want to see it in the policy's dialog box. Enclose the name in double quotes if it contains spaces. You see the name next to the combo box.
Suggestions	This is a list of items to put in the drop-down list. Separate each suggestion with white space (line feeds, tabs, spaces, and the like), and enclose any suggestion that includes a space in double quotes.

Default	This is the default value for the part. When you enable the policy, the GPO editor fills the control with the default value. Use a default value that's appropriate for the part's type.
Max	This is the maximum length of the value's data.
Value	This is the registry value to modify. The GPO editor creates this in the registry as a REG_SZ value and fills it with any text that you typed or selected in the combo box.

Example

Listing C-10

```
CLASS USER

CATEGORY "Sample Policies"
  EXPLAIN "These are sample policies that illustrate parts."

  POLICY "Sample Policy"
    SUPPORTED "At least Microsoft Windows XP Professional"

    EXPLAIN "This is a sample policy that illustrates creating a part."
    KEYNAME "Software\Policies"

    PART Sample COMBOBOX
      SUGGESTIONS
        Sample1 Sample2 "Another Sample"
      END SUGGESTIONS
      VALUENAME Sample
    END PART

  END POLICY

END CATEGORY
```

Keywords

The valid keywords within a *COMBOBOX* section are the following:

- *DEFAULT*
- *END*
- *EXPANDABLETEXT*
- *KEYNAME*
- *MAXLENGTH*
- *NOSORT*
- *REQUIRED*
- *SUGGESTIONS*
- *VALUENAME*

DROPDOWNLIST

The *DROPDOWNLIST* keyword adds a drop-down list to the policy's dialog box. It has one additional keyword you must use: *ITEMLIST*. This creates a list of items that the GPO editor places in the drop-down list. Define each item within the *ITEMLIST* section using the syntax *NAME* Name *VALUE* Value. Enclose items containing spaces within double quotes. End the list with the *END ITEMLIST*.

A few keywords modify the behavior of the combo box:

- **DEFAULT**   Specifies the default value of the drop-down list

- **EXPANDABLETEXT**   Creates the value as a REG_EXPAND_SZ value

- **NOSORT**   Prevents the GPO editor from sorting the list

- **REQUIRED**   Specifies that a value is required

Syntax

```
PART Name DROPDOWNLIST
  ITEMLIST
    NAME Item VALUE Data
  END ITEMLIST
  [DEFAULT Default]
  [EXPANDABLETEXT]
  [NOSORT]
  [REQUIRED]
  VALUENAME Value
END PART
```

Parameters

Name	This specifies the name of the setting as you want to see it in the policy's dialog box. Enclose the name in double quotes if it contains spaces. You see the name next to the drop-down list.
Item	This is the name of each item in the list and the text you'll see in the drop-down list; it isn't the value that the GPO editor stores in the registry
Data	This is the data you want the GPO editor to store in the value when you select the associated item.
Default	This is the default value for the part. When you enable the policy, the GPO editor fills the control with the default value. Use an item defined in *ITEMLIST*.
Value	This is the registry value to modify. The GPO editor creates this in the registry as a REG_SZ value and fills it with the value of Data associated with the selected item.

Example

Listing C-11

```
CLASS USER

CATEGORY "Sample Policies"
  EXPLAIN "These are sample policies that illustrate parts."

  POLICY "Sample Policy"
    SUPPORTED "At least Microsoft Windows XP Professional"

    EXPLAIN "This is a sample policy that illustrates creating a part."
    KEYNAME "Software\Policies"

    PART Sample DROPDOWNLIST
      ITEMLIST
        NAME Sample1 VALUE 0
        NAME Sample2 VALUE 1
        NAME "Another Sample" VALUE 2
      END ITEMLIST
      VALUENAME Sample
    END PART

  END POLICY

END CATEGORY
```

Keywords

The valid keywords within a *DROPDOWNLIST* section are the following:

- *DEFAULT*

- *END*

- *EXPANDABLETEXT*

- *KEYNAME*

- *NOSORT*

- *REQUIRED*

- *ITEMLIST*

- *VALUENAME*

EDITTEXT

The *EDITTEXT* part type enables you to input alphanumeric text in a text box. The GPO editor stores the text in a REG_SZ value. A few keywords modify the behavior of the text box:

- **DEFAULT**   Specifies the default value of the text box

- **EXPANDABLETEXT**   Creates the value as a REG_EXPAND_SZ value

- ***MAXLENGTH***   Specifies the maximum length of the value
- ***REQUIRED***   Specifies that a value is required

Syntax

```
PART Name EDITTEXT
  [DEFAULT Default]
  [EXPANDABLETEXT]
  [MAXLENGTH Max]
  [REQUIRED]
  VALUENAME Value
END PART
```

Parameters

Name	This specifies the name of the setting as you want to see it in the policy's dialog box. Enclose the name in double quotes if it contains spaces. You see the name next to the text box.
Default	This is the default value for the part. When you enable the policy, the GPO editor fills the control with the default value. Use a default value that's appropriate for the part's type.
Max	This is the maximum length of the value's data.
Value	This is the registry value to modify. The GPO editor creates this in the registry as a REG_SZ value and fills it with any text that you typed.

Example

Listing C-12

```
CLASS USER

CATEGORY "Sample Policies"
  EXPLAIN "These are sample policies that illustrate parts."

  POLICY "Sample Policy"
    SUPPORTED "At least Microsoft Windows XP Professional"

    EXPLAIN "This is a sample policy that illustrates creating a part."
    KEYNAME "Software\Policies"

    PART Sample EDITTEXT
      VALUENAME Sample
    END PART

  END POLICY

END CATEGORY
```

Keywords

The valid keywords within an *EDITTEXT* section are the following:

- *DEFAULT*

- *END*

- *EXPANDABLETEXT*

- *KEYNAME*

- *MAXLENGTH*

- *REQUIRED*

- *VALUENAME*

LISTBOX

The *LISTBOX* part type adds a list box with Add and Remove buttons to the policy's dialog box. This is the only type of part that you can use to manage multiple values in one key. You can't use the *VALUENAME* option with the *LISTBOX* part because it doesn't associate just a single value with it. Use the following options with the *LIST-BOX* part type:

- **ADDITIVE**   By default, the content of list boxes overrides values already set in the registry. That means that the Windows XP Professional client-side extensions remove values before setting them. When you use this keyword, the client-side extensions do not delete existing values before adding the values set in the list box.

- **EXPLICITVALUE**   This keyword makes you specify the value name and data. The list box shows two columns, one for the name and one for the data. You can't use this keyword with the *VALUEPREFIX* keyword.

- **VALUEPREFIX**   The prefix you specify determines value names. If you specify a prefix, the GPO editor adds an incremental number to it. For example, a prefix of *Sample* generates the value names *Sample1*, *Sample2*, and so on. The prefix can be empty (""), causing the value names to be 1, 2, and so on.

By default, without using either the *EXPLICITVALUE* or *VALUEPREFIX* keywords, only one column appears in the list box. For each entry in the list, the GPO editor creates a value using the entry's text for the value's name and data. For example, the entry Sample in the list box creates a value called *Sample* whose data is Sample. The default behavior is seldom the desirable result.

Syntax

```
PART Name LISTBOX
  [EXPANDABLETEXT]
```

```
    [NOSORT]
    [ADDITIVE]
    [EXPLICITVALUE | VALUEPREFIX Prefix]
END PART
```

Parameters

Name   This specifies the name of the setting as you want to see it in the pol-
                            icy's dialog box. Enclose the name in double quotes if it contains
                            spaces.

Prefix   This is the prefix to use for incremental names. If you specify a prefix,
                            the GPO editor adds an incremental number to it. For example, a pre-
                            fix of *Sample* generates the value names *Sample1*, *Sample2*, and so on.
                            The prefix can be empty (""), causing the value names to be 1, 2, and
                            so on.

Example

Listing C-13

```
CLASS USER

CATEGORY "Sample Policies"
  EXPLAIN "These are sample policies that illustrate parts."

  POLICY "Sample Policy"
    SUPPORTED "At least Microsoft Windows XP Professional"

    EXPLAIN "This is a sample policy that illustrates creating a part."
    KEYNAME "Software\Policies"

    PART Sample LISTBOX
      EXPLICITVALUE
    END PART

  END POLICY

END CATEGORY
```

Keywords

The valid keywords within a *LISTBOX* section are the following:

- *ADDITIVE*

- *END*

- *EXPANDABLETEXT*

- *EXPLICITVALUE*

- *KEYNAME*

- *NOSORT*

- *VALUEPREFIX*

NUMERIC

The *NUMERIC* part type enables you to input alphanumeric text using a spinner control that adjusts the number up and down. The GPO editor stores the number in a REG_DWORD value, but you can change the value's type to REG_SZ using the *TXT-CONVERT* keyword. A few other keywords modify the behavior of the text box:

- **DEFAULT**   Specifies the initial value of the text box.

- **MAX**   Specifies the maximum value. The default is 9999.

- **MIN**   Specifies the minimum value. The default is 0.

- **REQUIRED**   Specifies that a value is required.

- **SPIN**   Specifies the increment to use for the spinner control. The default value is 1, and using 0 removes the spinner control.

- **TXTCONVERT**   Writes values as REG_SZ values rather than REG_DWORD.

Syntax

```
PART Name NUMERIC
  [DEFAULT Default]
  [MAX Max]
  [MIN Min]
  [REQUIRED]
  [SPIN]
  [TXTCONVERT]
  VALUENAME Value
END PART
```

Parameters

Name	This specifies the name of the setting as you want to see it in the policy's dialog box. Enclose the name in double quotes if it contains spaces. You see the name next to the text box.
Default	This is the default value for the part. When you enable the policy, the GPO editor fills the control with the default value. Use a default value that's appropriate for the part's type.
Max	This is the maximum value. The default is 9999.
Min	This is the minimum value. The default is 0.
Value	This is the registry value to modify. The GPO editor creates this in the registry as a REG_DWORD value, setting it to the value that you specify in the dialog box. To change the value's type to REG_SZ, use the *TXTCONVERT* keyword.

Example

Listing C-14

```
CLASS USER

CATEGORY "Sample Policies"
  EXPLAIN "These are sample policies that illustrate parts."

  POLICY "Sample Policy"
    SUPPORTED "At least Microsoft Windows XP Professional"

    EXPLAIN "This is a sample policy that illustrates creating a part."
    KEYNAME "Software\Policies"

    PART Sample NUMERIC
      DEFAULT 11
      MIN 10
      MAX 20
      VALUENAME Sample
    END PART

  END POLICY

END CATEGORY
```

Keywords

The valid keywords within a *NUMERIC* section are the following:

- *DEFAULT*

- *END*

- *KEYNAME*

- *MAX*

- *MIN*

- *REQUIRED*

- *SPIN*

- *TXTCONVERT*

- *VALUENAME*

TEXT

The *TEXT* part adds static text to the bottom part of the policy's dialog box.

Syntax

```
PART Text TEXT
END PART
```

Parameters

Text   This is the text you want to add to the dialog box.

Example

Listing C-15

```
CLASS USER

CATEGORY "Sample Policies"
  EXPLAIN "These are sample policies that illustrate parts."

  POLICY "Sample Policy"
    SUPPORTED "At least Microsoft Windows XP Professional"

    EXPLAIN "This is a sample policy that illustrates creating a part."
    KEYNAME "Software\Policies"

    PART "This is sample text added to the dialog box." TEXT
    END PART

  END POLICY

END CATEGORY
```

Appendix D

Answer File Syntax

Answer files are the very basic components of most Microsoft Windows XP Professional desktop deployment methods. Chapter 13, "Unattended Setup," describes the format of answer files; tells you how to create and use them; and gives you a list of sections and entries required for a fully unattended installation. In addition, see Chapter 13 for many examples of complete answer files that you can use in your own project. This appendix describes the syntax of the most common sections and entries in typical answer files, particularly the entries I use most in this book. Throughout this book, I describe additional less-often-used sections and entries, though.

This appendix applies to unattended-setup answer files as well as Sysprep.inf. Fewer sections and entries apply to Sysprep.inf, and some are unique to Sysprep.inf. This appendix indicates which type of answer files each section and entry applies.

 More Info For more information about Sysprep.inf, see Chapter 15, "Disk Imaging with Sysprep." Chapter 15 contains a table that describes all the sections and entries that work in Sysprep.inf. It also contains several examples that you can use in your own disk imaging projects.

Many more sections and settings are available than I describe in this appendix. The compiled help file Ref.chm describes them all in detail. This file is on your Windows XP Professional product CD in the Support\Tools folder in the cabinet file Deploy.cab. This is a great resource that you'll want to keep handy, and you'll want to get the latest version of Ref.chm after Microsoft ships Windows XP Professional Service Pack 1 (SP1) because it might add a few settings to your repertoire.

[Components]

The *[Components]* section applies to unattended-setup answer files.

The *[Components]* section describes which components to install. This section applies to Windows XP Professional and Microsoft Windows Server 2003. Each entry in this section is a component's name. *Name=On* installs the component, and

Name=Off does not install the component. Table D-1 describes each component. The following describes the syntax and possible values for each entry.

Syntax	*Name = On	Off*
Values	■ *On* Installs the component
	■ *Off* Does not install the component
Default Value	*On*
Example	*AccessOpt = On*
Registry Subkey	HKLM\Software\Microsoft\Windows\CurrentVersion\Setup\OC Manager\Subcomponents

Table D-1   *[Components]* Section Entries

Entry	Description
accessopt	Specifies whether to install the Accessibility Wizard.
appsrv_console	Specifies whether to install the Application Server Console.
aspnet	Specifies whether to install the ASP.NET Web development platform.
autoupdate	Specifies whether to install AutoUpdate.
bitsserverextensionsisapi	Specifies whether to install Internet Server Application Programming Interface (ISAPI) for Background Intelligent Transfer Service (BITS) server extensions on client computers.
bitsserverextensionsmanager	Specifies whether to install the Microsoft Management Console (MMC) snap-in, administrative application programming interfaces (APIs), and Active Directory Service Interfaces (ADSI) extensions for BITS server extensions.
calc	Specifies whether to install the Calculator feature.
certsrv	Specifies whether to install the Certificate Services components.
certsrv_client	Specifies whether to install the Web client components of Certificate Services.
certsrv_server	Specifies whether to install the server components of the Certificate Services feature for the Windows Server 2003 family only.
charmap	Specifies whether to install the Character Map feature that inserts symbols and characters into documents.
chat	Specifies whether to install the Chat feature.
clipbook	Specifies whether to install the clipboard viewer.
cluster	Specifies whether to install the Cluster service.
complusnetwork	Specifies whether to enable network COM+ access.

Table D-1 *[Components]* **Section Entries**

Entry	Description
deskpaper	Specifies whether to install a desktop background on the computer desktop.
dialer	Specifies whether to install the Phone Dialer feature.
dtcnetwork	Specifies whether to enable Microsoft Distributed Transaction Coordinator (MS DTC) network access.
fax	Specifies whether to install the Fax feature.
fp_extensions	Specifies whether to install Microsoft FrontPage server extensions.
fp_vdir_deploy	Specifies whether to install Visual InterDev rapid application development (RAD) Remote Deployment Support.
freecell	Specifies whether to install the Freecell game.
hearts	Specifies whether to install the Hearts game.
hypertrm	Specifies whether to install the HyperTerminal feature.
ieaccess	Specifies whether to install visible entry points to Internet Explorer.
iis_asp	Specifies whether to install Active Server Pages for Internet Information Services (IIS).
iis_common	Specifies whether to install the common set of files required by IIS.
iis_ftp	Specifies whether to install the File Transfer Protocol (FTP) service.
iis_inetmgr	Specifies whether to install the MMC-based administration tools for IIS.
iis_internetdataconnector	Specifies whether to install the Internet Data Connector.
iis_nntp	Specifies whether to install the Network News Transfer Protocol (NNTP) service for the Windows Server 2003 family.
iis_serversideincludes	Specifies whether to install server-side includes.
iis_smtp	Specifies whether to install the Simple Mail Transfer Protocol (SMTP) service for the Windows Server 2003 family.
iis_webadmin	Specifies whether to install the Web user interface (UI) for Web server administration (Remote Administration Tools).
iis_webdav	Specifies whether to install WebDAV publishing.
iis_www	Specifies whether to install the World Wide Web (WWW) service.
iis_www_vdir_scripts	Specifies whether to create the optional scripts directory on the default Web site.

Table D-1 *[Components]* **Section Entries**

Entry	Description
indexsrv_system	Specifies whether to install the Indexing Service files.
inetprint	Specifies whether to install Internet Printing.
licenseserver	Specifies whether to turn Terminal Services licensing on.
media_clips	Specifies whether to install sample sound clips on the computer.
media_utopia	Specifies whether to install the Utopia Sound Scheme on the computer.
minesweeper	Specifies whether to install the Minesweeper game on the computer.
mousepoint	Specifies whether to install all the available mouse pointers distributed with the Windows XP Professional or Windows Server 2003 family.
msmq_adintegrated	Specifies whether to integrate Message Queuing (also known as MSMQ) with Active Directory if the computer belongs to a domain.
msmq_core	Specifies whether to set up the Message Queuing components and provide functionality for any dependent clients.
msmq_httpsupport	Specifies whether to enable the sending and receiving of messages using the Hypertext Transfer Protocol (HTTP) protocol.
msmq_localstorage	Specifies whether to store messages locally, so the computer can send and receive messages even when not connected to a network.
msmq_mqdsservice	Specifies whether to provide access to Active Directory and site recognition for downstream clients.
msmq_routingsupport	Specifies whether to provide efficient routing.
msmq_triggersservice	Specifies whether to associate the arrival of incoming messages at a queue with functionality in a Component Object Model (COM) component or a standalone executable program.
msnexplr	Specifies whether to install MSN Explorer.
mswordpad	Specifies whether to install the WordPad feature on the computer.
netcis	Specifies whether to install Microsoft COM Internet Services.
netoc	Specifies whether to install additional optional networking components.
objectpkg	Specifies whether to install the Object Packager feature (packager.exe) on the computer.

Table D-1 *[Components]* **Section Entries**

Entry	Description
oeaccess	Specifies whether to install visible entry points to Outlook Express.
paint	Specifies whether to install the Microsoft Paint feature on the computer.
pinball	Specifies whether to install the Pinball game on the computer.
pop3admin	Specifies whether to install the optional Web UI for the Remote Administration Tools on the computer.
pop3service	Specifies whether to install the main POP3 service on the computer.
pop3srv	Specifies whether to install the root POP3 component on the computer.
rec	Specifies whether to install the Sound Recorder feature on the computer.
reminst	Specifies whether to install Remote Installation Services (RIS), which enables you to install an operating system remotely onto a computer with either a new PXE-based remote boot read-only memory (ROM) or a network card supported by the remote installation boot floppy disk.
rootautoupdate	Specifies whether to turn on the Optional Components Manager (OCM) Update Root Certificates.
rstorage	Specifies whether to install the Remote Storage feature that enables the use of tape libraries as extensions of NTFS file system volumes.
solitaire	Specifies whether to install the Solitaire game on the computer.
spider	Specifies whether to install the Spider Solitaire game on the computer.
templates	Specifies whether to install Document Templates on the computer.
terminalserver	Specifies whether to install Terminal Server (Terminal Services for multiple users) on the computer.
tswebclient	Specifies whether to install the ActiveX control and sample pages for hosting Terminal Services client connections over the Web.
vol	Specifies whether to install the Volume Control feature on the computer.
wbemsnmp	Specifies whether to install the Windows Management Instrumentation (WMI) Simple Network Management Protocol (SNMP) Provider components.

Table D-1 *[Components]* **Section Entries**

Entry	Description
wmaccess	Specifies whether to install visible entry points to Windows Messenger.
wmpocm	Specifies whether to install visible entry points to Windows Media Player.
wms	Specifies whether to install the core Windows Media Server components.
wms_admin_asp	Specifies whether to install the Windows Media Services Web-based administrative components.
wms_admin_mmc	Specifies whether to install the Windows Media Services MMC-based administrative components.
wms_isapi	Specifies whether to install the Windows Media Services Multicast and Advertisement Logging Agent components.
wms_server	Specifies whether to install the Windows Media Services server components.
zonegames	Specifies whether to install the Microsoft Gaming Zone Internet games on the computer.

[Data]

The *[Data]* section applies to unattended-setup answer files.

The *[Data]* section contains entries for starting directly from the Windows XP Professional product CD when performing an unattended setup (booting from the product CD). This section isn't necessary when running Setup from a network share or from the MS-DOS command prompt. The *[Data]* section contains the following entries:

- **AutoPartition** Installs Windows XP Professional to the first available partition that has adequate space for a Windows XP Professional installation and does not already contain an installed version of Windows.

- **DisableAdminAccountOnDomainJoin** Disables the local Administrator account immediately after the RIS client successfully joins the domain.

- **MsDosInitiated** Informs the Windows Setup Loader that an unattended Setup is running directly from the Windows XP Professional product CD.

- **UnattendedInstall** Informs the Windows Setup Loader that an unattended Setup is running directly from the Windows XP Professional product CD.

- **UseBIOSToBoot** Specifies whether Setup uses the basic input/output system (BIOS) to start the computer, even though Windows Setup might detect that it is best to use a device miniport driver to start the computer.

AutoPartition

AutoPartition installs Windows XP Professional to the first available partition that has adequate space for a Windows XP Professional installation and does not already contain an installed version of Windows.

Syntax	*AutoPartition = 1*
Value	*1*
Example	*AutoPartition = 1*
Notes	■ Either omit the *AutoPartition* entry from your answer file or set the value of *AutoPartition* to 1.
	■ If *AutoPartition = 1*, the **/tempdrive** command-line option of Winnt32.exe is ignored during Setup.
	■ If you do not set the value, text-mode Setup installs Windows XP Professional on the partition where the directory WIN_NT.~LS is located.

DisableAdminAccountOnDomainJoin

DisableAdminAccountOnDomainJoin disables the local Administrator account immediately after the RIS client successfully joins the domain.

Syntax	*DisableAdminAccountOnDomainJoin = 1*
Value	*1*
Default Value	*1*, if Windows XP Professional is installed using RIS.
Example	*DisableAdminAccountOnDomainJoin = 1*
Notes	The value must always be set to 1. If you do not want the local Administrator account to be disabled after the RIS client joins the domain, you must completely remove the *DisableAdminAccountOnDomainJoin* entry from the unattended installation file.

MsDosInitiated

MsDosInitiated informs the Windows Setup Loader that an unattended Setup is running directly from the Windows XP Professional product CD.

Syntax	*MsDosInitiated = 0*
Value	*0*
Example	*MsDosInitiated = 0*
Notes	The value must always be set to 0. If an unattended Setup is running directly from the product CD and you do not set the value to 0, Setup fails at the beginning of GUI-mode Setup.

UnattendedInstall

UnattendedInstall informs the Windows Setup Loader that an unattended Setup is running directly from the Windows XP Professional product CD.

Syntax	*UnattendedInstall = Yes*
Value	*Yes*
Example	*UnattendedInstall = Yes*
Notes	■ The value must always be set to *Yes* if you preinstall Windows XP Professional by using the CD Boot method. If *UnattendedInstall* is *Yes*, set *MsDosInitiated* to *0*.
	■ The *UnattendedInstall* entry is not the same as the *UnattendSwitch* entry in the *[Unattended]* section of the answer file. *UnattendSwitch* controls Windows Welcome; *UnattendedInstall* does not.

UseBIOSToBoot

UseBIOSToBoot specifies whether Setup uses the BIOS system to start the computer, even if Windows Setup might detect that it is best to use a device miniport driver to start the computer.

Syntax	*UseBIOSToBoot = 0	1*
Values	■ *0* Setup uses the default behavior to start the computer.
	■ *1* Setup uses the BIOS to start the computer.
Default Value	*0*
Example	*UseBIOSToBoot = 1*
Notes	■ On computers with large drives that support extended int13 BIOS calls, using the BIOS starts computers faster by eliminating possible delays caused by a miniport driver.
	■ Do not use this entry unless you are sure that the BIOS supports the extended int13 functions.
	■ The current generation of hardware uses the BIOS to start the computer, so this entry is rarely required.

[Display]

The *[Display]* section applies to unattended-setup answer files and Sysprep.inf.

The *[Display]* section contains entries for specifying display settings for graphics devices. If the specified settings are not valid for the graphics device, Setup finds the closest match to the selected settings to configure the device.

> **Note**   If the monitor plugged into the computer is a Plug-and-Play device and is capable of displaying a screen resolution of 800 x 600 x 16m, the display resolution must be at least 800 x 600 x 16m. Setup uses the 640-by-480-pixel screen size only if the monitor is unable to display an 800-by-600-pixel screen.

Sysprep.exe configures the operating system to use the video settings in the *[Display]* section of Sysprep.inf. If there are no display settings or if Setup does not use Sysprep.inf, Sysprep.exe uses the video settings in the registry. If you configure the display settings manually, set them in the unattended-setup answer file or use the defaults; then Sysprep retains those settings. If you define the screen resolution in both the *[Display]* section of Sysprep.inf and in the *[ComputerSettings]* section of Winbom.ini, the operating system uses the settings in Sysprep.inf.

The *[Display]* section contains the following entries:

- ***BitsPerPel***   Specifies the valid bits per pixel for the graphics device.
- ***Vrefresh***   Specifies a valid refresh rate for the graphics device.
- ***Xresolution***   Specifies a valid x resolution for the graphics device.
- ***Yresolution***   Specifies a valid y resolution for the graphics device.

BitsPerPel

BitsPerPel specifies the valid bits per pixel for the graphics device.

Syntax	*BitsPerPel* = valid_bits_per_pixel
Value	valid_bits_per_pixel
Example	For example, a value of 8 implies 256 colors, and a value of 16 implies 65,536 colors.

Vrefresh

Vrefresh specifies a valid refresh rate for the graphics device.

Syntax	*Vrefresh* = valid_refresh_rate
Value	valid_refresh_rate
Example	*Vrefresh* = 75

Xresolution

Xresolution specifies a valid x resolution for the graphics device.

Syntax	*Xresolution* = valid_x_resolution
Value	valid_x_resolution
Example	*Xresolution = 1024*

Yresolution

Yresolution specifies a valid y resolution for the graphics device.

Syntax	*Yresolution* = valid_y_resolution
Value	valid_y_resolution
Example	*Yresolution = 768*

[GuiRunOnce]

The *[GuiRunOnce]* applies to unattended-setup answer files and Sysprep.inf.

The *[GuiRunOnce]* section contains commands to execute the first time an end user logs on to the computer after GUI-mode Setup completes. Commands called in the *[GuiRunOnce]* section run synchronously: Each application runs in the order listed in this section, and each command must finish before you run the next command. Each line specifies a command that the *[GuiRunOnce]* registry entry, HKLM\Software\Microsoft\Windows\CurrentVersion\Runonce, executes.

> **Tip**   You must put each command line in quotation marks.

Commands run using the *[GuiRunOnce]* section in the context of the currently logged-in end user. If the end user does not have the permissions necessary to run the command completely, the application fails. Because this application runs in the context of a logged-in end user instead of as a service, the registry entries that the application creates are for the current end user instead of the default user. (Setup propagates default user registry settings to new end users.) If you want any settings and updates to appear only for the specifically logged-in end user, this might be appropriate. Otherwise, Cmdlines.txt is a better approach to running commands and installing applications because it runs as a system service.

[GuiUnattended]

The *[GuiUnattended]* section applies to unattended-setup answer files, and Sysprep.inf. Sysprep.inf supports only a subset of this section's entries.

The *[GuiUnattended]* section for unattended-setup answer files contains entries for preparing the graphical user interface (GUI) for unattended Setup. It supports the following entries:

- **AdminPassword**   Sets the Administrator account password.

- **Arguments**   Indicates that arguments or entries accompany the custom program that runs concurrently with the Setup program.

- **AutoLogon**   Configures the computer to log on once with the Administrator account.

- **AutoLogonCount**   Specifies the number of times that the computer automatically logs on with the specified Administrator account and password.

- **DetachedProgram**   Indicates the path of the custom program that runs concurrently with the Setup program.

- **EMSBlankPassword**   Enables the use of a blank administrator password in unattended installations to Expanded Memory Specificaction (EMS) servers.

- **EncryptedAdminPassword**   Enables Setup to install encrypted passwords for the Administrator account.

- **OEMSkipRegional**   Enables unattended Setup to skip the Regional and Language Options page in GUI-mode Setup and Mini-Setup.

- **OEMSkipWelcome**   Enables unattended Setup to skip the Welcome page in GUI-mode Setup and Mini-Setup.

- **ProfilesDir**   Specifies the location of Windows XP Professional or Windows Server 2003 family profiles.

- **ServerWelcome**   Specifies whether to install the Web UI for Remote Administration at first logon on a member of the Windows Server 2003 family.

- **TimeZone**   Specifies the time zone of the computer.

AdminPassword

AdminPassword sets the Administrator account password.

Syntax	*AdminPassword* = "*password*"	*
Values	■ **password** The password may contain as many as 127 characters. Passwords are case-sensitive and must be enclosed in quotes. End users cannot change or specify their own passwords in Mini-Setup. You can enter a new password in the appropriate dialog box, but the password does not change.
	■ * The administrator password is blank or null.
Example	*AdminPassword* = "*YhJ##3*"
Registry Subkey	HKLM\Software\Microsoft\Windows\CurrentVersion \WinLogon\DefaultPassword
Notes	■ If you specify a password in the Administrator account, you cannot use *AdminPassword* in the Sysprep.inf file to change it; the administrator password remains the same. However, if the administrator password was initially blank (either manually or through unattended Setup), you can use *AdminPassword* to change it to a nonblank password.
	■ Security breaches can occur if you use a common, nonblank administrator password for all computers provided to end users. Prior to running Sysprep, I recommend that you use an automation process to set the administrator password to blank. End users can then specify their own passwords after receiving the computers.

Arguments

Arguments indicates that arguments or entries accompany the custom program that runs concurrently with the setup program.

Syntax	*Arguments* = string
Value	string
Example	*Arguments* = /n/s
Notes	This entry is required if you are using *DetachedProgram*.

AutoLogon

AutoLogon configures the computer to log on once with the Administrator account.

Syntax	*AutoLogon* = Yes	No
Values	■ *Yes* Configures the computer to log on once with the Administrator account.
	■ *No* Does not automatically log on to the computer.
Default Value	No
Example	*AutoLogon* = Yes

Registry Subkey	HKLM\Software\Microsoft\Windows NT\CurrentVersion \WinLogon\AutoAdminLogon
Notes	■ The entry is not valid on upgrades.
	■ If you specify a password in the *AdminPassword* entry, Setup uses that password when you log on automatically to the computer. After the installation finishes, Setup deletes the password from the copy of the answer file left on the computer.
	■ Encrypting the Administrator password in the *EncryptedAdminPassword* entry disables *AutoLogon*.
	■ To skip Windows Welcome, set *UnattendSwitch* to *Yes* in the *[Unattended]* section of the answer file.
	■ If you want to log on automatically after running Sysprep in factory mode, set *AuditAdminAutoLogon* to *Yes* in the *[ComputerSettings]* section of Winbom.ini.

AutoLogonCount

AutoLogonCount specifies the number of times that the computer automatically logs on with the specified Administrator account and password.

Syntax	*AutoLogonCount* = integer
Value	integer
Example	*AutoLogonCount* = 5
Registry Subkey	HKLM\Software\Microsoft\Windows\CurrentVersion\WinLogon \AutoLogonCount
Notes	■ The value decrements after each logon, and WinLogon disables the feature after the specified number of logon attempts.
	■ Requires *AutoLogon* = *Yes* and *AdminPassword* = password in the answer file. If *AutoLogon* = *Yes*, WinLogon checks the value of *AutoLogonCount*. If the number for *AutoLogonCount* is greater than 0, WinLogon decrements the count and then checks *AdminPassword*. If *AdminPassword* = password, WinLogon uses this password to log on automatically. If *AdminPassword* = *, the user must enter a password.
	■ If *AutoLogonCount* = *0*, WinLogon deletes *AutoAdminLogon*, *AutoLogonCount*, and *DefaultPassword* from the registry. During the next reboot, the user must log on manually.
	■ The function of this entry has changed slightly between Windows 2000 Professional and Windows XP Professional. Please review this entry carefully before using it in your answer file.
	■ Make sure that the password for the master installation (that you plan to duplicate onto one or more destination computers) is blank.
	■ You must reboot the computer to decrement the value of *AutoLogonCount*.

DetachedProgram

DetachedProgram indicates the path of the custom program that runs concurrently with the Setup program.

Syntax	*DetachedProgram* = detached_program_string
Value	detached_program_string
Example	*DetachedProgram* = "%SYSTEMDRIVE%\extras\install.exe"
Notes	If the program requires any arguments, you must specify them in the *Arguments* entry.

EMSBlankPassword

EMSBlankPassword enables the use of a blank administrator password in unattended installations to EMS servers.

Syntax	*EMSBlankPassword* = Yes | No
Values	■ *Yes* Enables the use of * with *AdminPassword* when preinstalling to EMS servers. ■ *No* Disables the use of * with *AdminPassword* when preinstalling to EMS servers.
Default Value	*No*
Example	*EMSBlankPassword* = Yes
Notes	Applies only to the Windows Server 2003 family. By default, blank administrator passwords (*AdminPassword* = "*") are not allowed in unattended installations of any member of the Windows Server 2003 family to EMS servers.

EncryptedAdminPassword

EncryptedAdminPassword enables Setup to install encrypted passwords for the Administrator account.

Syntax	*EncryptedAdminPassword* = Yes | No
Values	■ *Yes* Instructs Setup to install the encrypted Administrator account password. ■ *No* Instructs Setup to keep the Administrator account password as clean text.
Default Value	*No*
Example	*EncryptedAdminPassword* = Yes
Notes	■ To encrypt your Administrator passwords, use Setup Manager on the Windows OPK CD (in Tools) and in Deploy.cab. ■ If you use this key to install an encrypted Administrator password during an unattended installation, Setup disables *Autologon*.

OEMSkipRegional

OEMSkipRegional enables unattended Setup to skip the Regional and Language Options page in GUI-mode Setup and Mini-Setup.

Syntax	*OEMSkipRegional = 0	1*
Values	■ *0* Displays the Regional and Language Options page in GUI-mode Setup and Mini-Setup.
	■ *1* Skips the Regional and Language Options page in GUI-mode Setup and Mini-Setup.
Example	*OEMSkipRegional = 0*
Dependency	*OEMPreinstall = Yes*
Notes	If you set *OEMPreinstall* to *Yes* and provide values for the *[Regional-Settings]* section in the *[Unattended]* section, set *OEMSkipRegional* to *1* to ensure that Setup completes without prompting the end user for regional information.

OEMSkipWelcome

OEMSkipWelcome enables unattended Setup to skip the Welcome page in GUI-mode Setup and Mini-Setup.

Syntax	*OEMSkipWelcome = 0	1*
Values	■ *0* Displays the Welcome page in GUI-mode Setup and Mini-Setup.
	■ *1* Skips the Welcome page in GUI-mode Setup and Mini-Setup.
Example	*OEMSkipWelcome = 0*
Dependency	*OEMPreinstall = Yes*
Notes	■ If *OEMPreinstall* in the *[Unattended]* section of the unattended-setup answer file is set to *Yes*, unattended Setup automatically stops on the Welcome page. To avoid this pause in your factory or testing environment, set *OEMSkipWelcome = 1*. Do not ship any computer with *OEMSkipWelcome = 1*. Instead, change *OEM-SkipWelcome* in the *[GuiUnattended]* section of Sysprep.inf to *0* before delivering the computer to the customer.

ProfilesDir

ProfilesDir specifies the location of Windows XP Professional or Windows Server 2003 family profiles.

Syntax	*ProfilesDir* = path_to_profile_folder
Value	path_to_profile_folder
Default Value	*"%SYSTEMDRIVE%\Documents and Settings"*

Example	*ProfilesDir = "%SYSTEMROOT%\Profiles"*
Notes	■ This entry is useful if you require new installations to use the same profile folder as Windows NT 4.0 or Windows 2000 Professional. This entry is valid only on clean installations of the Windows XP Professional or Windows Server 2003 family. Setup ignores this entry during upgrades.
	■ The specified directory can contain an environment variable such as %SYSTEMDRIVE% or %SYSTEMROOT%. Enclose path_to_profile_folder in quotation marks if it is a long filename or if it contains an environment variable.

ServerWelcome

ServerWelcome specifies whether to install the Web UI for Remote Administration at first logon on a member of the Windows Server 2003 family.

Syntax	*ServerWelcome = Yes	No*
Value	■ *Yes* Displays the Web UI for Remote Administration.
	■ *No* Does not display the Web UI for Remote Administration.
Default Value	*Yes*
Example	*ServerWelcome = Yes*
Notes	■ On the Windows Server 2003, Web Edition, if this entry is set to *Yes*, Sasetup.msi will be run from the hard drive on first logon, the Web UI for Web server administration will be added to the Startup program group for the Administrator account, and the Web UI will be launched.
	■ On Windows Server 2003, Standard Edition, Windows Server 2003, Enterprise Edition, Microsoft Small Business Server, and Windows Server 2003, Datacenter Edition, if this entry is set to *Yes*, the Configure Your Server Wizard will be run on first user logon. If this parameter is set to *No*, the Configure Your Server Wizard will not be run.
	■ This parameter will not be utilized during a Sysprep (Sysprep.inf) install.

TimeZone

TimeZone specifies the time zone of the computer.

Syntax	*TimeZone* = index

Value	*index*. Index value corresponding to each time zone. The following list shows the numeric values corresponding to the time zones:

- *000*. Dateline Standard Time (Greenwich Mean Time [GMT]-12:00) International Date Line West
- *001*. Samoa Standard Time (GMT-11:00) Midway Island, Samoa
- *002*. Hawaiian Standard Time (GMT-10:00) Hawaii
- *003*. Alaskan Standard Time (GMT-09:00) Alaska
- *004*. Pacific Standard Time (GMT-08:00) Pacific Time (U.S. and Canada); Tijuana
- *010*. Mountain Standard Time (GMT-07:00) Mountain Time (U.S. and Canada)
- *013*. Mexico Standard Time 2 (GMT-07:00) Chihuahua, La Paz, Mazatlan
- *015*. U.S. Mountain Standard Time (GMT-07:00) Arizona
- *020*. Central Standard Time (GMT-06:00) Central Time (U.S. and Canada)
- *025*. Canada Central Standard Time (GMT-06:00) Saskatchewan
- *030*. Mexico Standard Time (GMT-06:00) Guadalajara, Mexico City, Monterrey
- *033*. Central America Standard Time (GMT-06:00) Central America
- *035*. Eastern Standard Time (GMT-05:00) Eastern Time (U.S. and Canada)
- *040*. U.S. Eastern Standard Time (GMT-05:00) Indiana (East)
- *045*. S.A. Pacific Standard Time (GMT-05:00) Bogota, Lima, Quito
- *050*. Atlantic Standard Time (GMT-04:00) Atlantic Time (Canada)
- *055*. S.A. Western Standard Time (GMT-04:00) Caracas, La Paz
- *056*. Pacific S.A. Standard Time (GMT-04:00) Santiago
- *060*. Newfoundland and Labrador Standard Time (GMT-03:30) Newfoundland and Labrador
- *065*. E. South America Standard Time (GMT-03:00) Brasilia
- *070*. S.A. Eastern Standard Time (GMT-03:00) Buenos Aires, Georgetown
- *073*. Greenland Standard Time (GMT-03:00) Greenland
- *075*. Mid-Atlantic Standard Time (GMT-02:00) Mid-Atlantic
- *080*. Azores Standard Time (GMT-01:00) Azores
- *083*. Cape Verde Standard Time (GMT-01:00) Cape Verde Islands
- *085*. GMT Standard Time (GMT) Dublin, Edinburgh, Lisbon, London
- *090*. Greenwich Standard Time (GMT) Casablanca, Monrovia
- *095*. Central Europe Standard Time (GMT+01:00) Belgrade, Bratislava, Budapest, Ljubljana, Prague

Value

- *100*. Central European Standard Time (GMT+01:00) Sarajevo, Skopje, Warsaw, Zagreb
- *105*. Romance Standard Time (GMT+01:00) Brussels, Copenhagen, Madrid, Paris
- *110*. W. Europe Standard Time (GMT+01:00) Amsterdam, Berlin, Bern, Rome, Stockholm, Vienna
- *113*. W. Central Africa Standard Time (GMT+01:00) West Central Africa
- *115*. E. Europe Standard Time (GMT+02:00) Bucharest
- *120*. Egypt Standard Time (GMT+02:00) Cairo
- *125*. FLE Standard Time (GMT+02:00) Helsinki, Kyiv, Riga, Sofia, Tallinn, Vilnius
- *130*. GTB Standard Time (GMT+02:00) Athens, Istanbul, Minsk
- *135*. Israel Standard Time (GMT+02:00) Jerusalem
- *140*. South Africa Standard Time (GMT+02:00) Harare, Pretoria
- *145*. Russian Standard Time (GMT+03:00) Moscow, St. Petersburg, Volgograd
- *150*. Arab Standard Time (GMT+03:00) Kuwait, Riyadh
- *155*. E. Africa Standard Time (GMT+03:00) Nairobi
- *158*. Arabic Standard Time (GMT+03:00) Baghdad
- *160*. Iran Standard Time (GMT+03:30) Tehran
- *165*. Arabian Standard Time (GMT+04:00) Abu Dhabi, Muscat
- *170*. Caucasus Standard Time (GMT+04:00) Baku, Tbilisi, Yerevan
- *175*. Transitional Islamic State of Afghanistan Standard Time (GMT+04:30) Kabul
- *180*. Ekaterinburg Standard Time (GMT+05:00) Ekaterinburg
- *185*. West Asia Standard Time (GMT+05:00) Islamabad, Karachi, Tashkent
- *190*. India Standard Time (GMT+05:30) Chennai, Kolkata, Mumbai, New Delhi
- *193*. Nepal Standard Time (GMT+05:45) Kathmandu
- *195*. Central Asia Standard Time (GMT+06:00) Astana, Dhaka
- *200*. Sri Lanka Standard Time (GMT+06:00) Sri Jayawardenepura
- *201*. N. Central Asia Standard Time (GMT+06:00) Almaty, Novosibirsk
- *203*. Myanmar Standard Time (GMT+06:30) Yangon (Rangoon)
- *205*. S.E. Asia Standard Time (GMT+07:00) Bangkok, Hanoi, Jakarta
- *207*. North Asia Standard Time (GMT+07:00) Krasnoyarsk
- *210*. China Standard Time (GMT+08:00) Beijing, Chongqing, Hong Kong SAR, Urumqi
- *215*. Singapore Standard Time (GMT+08:00) Kuala Lumpur, Singapore

Value	■ *220.* Taipei Standard Time (GMT+08:00) Taipei
	■ *225.* W. Australia Standard Time (GMT+08:00) Perth
	■ *227.* North Asia East Standard Time (GMT+08:00) Irkutsk, Ulaan Bataar
	■ *230.* Korea Standard Time (GMT+09:00) Seoul
	■ *235.* Tokyo Standard Time (GMT+09:00) Osaka, Sapporo, Tokyo
	■ *240.* Yakutsk Standard Time (GMT+09:00) Yakutsk
	■ *245.* A.U.S. Central Standard Time (GMT+09:30) Darwin
	■ *250.* Cen. Australia Standard Time (GMT+09:30) Adelaide
	■ *255.* A.U.S. Eastern Standard Time (GMT+10:00) Canberra, Melbourne, Sydney
	■ *260.* E. Australia Standard Time (GMT+10:00) Brisbane
	■ *265.* Tasmania Standard Time (GMT+10:00) Hobart
	■ *270.* Vladivostok Standard Time (GMT+10:00) Vladivostok
	■ *275.* West Pacific Standard Time (GMT+10:00) Guam, Port Moresby
	■ *280.* Central Pacific Standard Time (GMT+11:00) Magadan, Solomon Islands, New Caledonia
	■ *285.* Fiji Islands Standard Time (GMT+12:00) Fiji Islands, Kamchatka, Marshall Islands
	■ *290.* New Zealand Standard Time (GMT+12:00) Auckland, Wellington
	■ *300.* Tonga Standard Time (GMT+13:00) Nuku'alofa
Example	*TimeZone = 030*
Registry Sub-key	HKLM\SYSTEM\CurrentControlSet\Control\TimeZoneInformation \DaylightName
Notes	■ If the entry is not present, the end user must select a time zone.
	■ If you do not configure a specific time zone setting, the default time zone depends on the language version of Windows XP Professional that is installed. For example, in the Japanese version, the default time zone is GMT+9 (Osaka, Sapporo, Tokyo).

[Identification]

The *[Identification]* section applies to unattended-setup answer files and Sysprep.inf.

The *[Identification]* section contains entries for specifying the network identification of a computer. If these entries are not present, Setup adds the computer to the default workgroup. If there is not enough information for this entry, Setup prompts the end user to provide this information. The following list describes each entry:

■ ***DomainAdmin***   Specifies the name of the user account in the domain that has permission to create a computer account in that domain.

■ ***DomainAdminPassword***   Specifies the password of the user account as defined by the DomainAdmin entry.

- ***JoinDomain***   Specifies the name of the domain in which the computer participates.

- ***JoinWorkgroup***   Specifies the name of the workgroup in which the computer participates.

- ***MachineObjectOU***   Specifies the full Lightweight Directory Access Protocol (LDAP) pathname of the organizational unit (OU) in which the computer belongs.

DomainAdmin

DomainAdmin specifies the name of the user account in the domain that has permission to create a computer account in that domain.

Syntax	*DomainAdmin* = account_name
Value	account_name
Dependencies	This entry is required if you set a value for *JoinDomain*, even though the computer account might already exist on the domain.
Example	*DomainAdmin = PatC*
Notes	For deployment, use an account with limited privileges that can only create computer accounts and join them to the domain. Alternatively, use the Visual Basic Script described in Chapter 13.

DomainAdminPassword

DomainAdminPassword specifies the password of the user account as defined by the *DomainAdmin* entry.

Syntax	*DomainAdminPassword* = "password_of_user_account"
Value	password_of_user_account
Dependencies	This entry is required if you set a value for *JoinDomain*, even if the computer account might already exist on the domain.
Example	*DomainAdminPassword = "abcdef123"*
Notes	■ The password is deleted from the $winnt$.inf file, which is a copy of the original unattended-setup answer file left on the computer after Setup completes. However, using *JoinDomain*, *DomainAdmin*, and *DomainAdminPassword* to join the computer to the domain is still a potential security issue because the password is in plain text. If anyone has access to the original answer file or Sysprep.inf file, they can use that password to access your network. ■ The recommended best practice is to use ADSI and Windows Script Host (WSH) to create a Visual Basic Script (VBScript) that automates the creation of computer accounts. A sample script is given in the Microsoft Knowledge Base, article Q315273 at *http://support.microsoft.com/default.aspx?scid=kb;en-us;q315273*. See Chapter 13 for more information.

JoinDomain

JoinDomain specifies the name of the domain in which the computer participates.

Syntax	*JoinDomain* = domain_name
Value	domain_name
Example	*JoinDomain* = *MYDOMAIN*
Notes	■ You can specify either this entry or the *JoinWorkgroup* entry, but you cannot specify both.
	■ Use an account with limited privileges that can create only computer accounts and join them to the domain.
	■ Instead of using *JoinDomain*, the recommended best practice is to use ADSI and WSH to create a Visual Basic Script (VBScript) that automates the creation of computer accounts. A sample script is given in the Microsoft Knowledge Base, article Q315273 at *http://support.microsoft.com/default.aspx?scid=kb;en-us;q315273*. See Chapter 13 for more information.

JoinWorkgroup

JoinWorkgroup specifies the name of the workgroup in which the computer participates.

Syntax	*JoinWorkgroup* = workgroup_name
Value	workgroup_name
Example	*JoinWorkgroup* = *MYUSERGROUP*
Notes	You can specify either this entry or the *JoinDomain* entry, but you cannot specify both.

MachineObjectOU

MachineObjectOU specifies the full LDAP pathname of the OU in which the computer belongs.

Syntax	*MachineObjectOU* = DNS_name, LDAP_path
Values	DNS_name, LDAP_path
Example	*MachineObjectOU* =" "OU = myou, OU = myparentou, DC = mydom, DC = mycompany, DC = com"

[RegionalSettings]

The *[RegionalSettings]* section applies to unattended-answer files and Sysprep.inf.

If you include *[RegionalSettings]* in the unattended-setup answer file, you must also use the **/copysource:**lang command-line option of Winnt32.exe so that Setup copies the appropriate language files to the hard disk. The command **winnt32 /copysource:**lang copies all the files in the i386\Lang folder from the source location to %SYSTEMROOT%\Lang folder on the target computer.

> **Note**   Any settings specified in the *[RegionalSettings]* section in your unattended-setup answer file do not persist if you run Sysprep on the computer. If the first-run experience is Windows Welcome, specify the corresponding settings in the *[Options]* section of Oobeinfo.ini. If the first-run experience is Mini-Setup, specify the corresponding settings in the *[RegionalSettings]* section of Sysprep.inf.

If you set *OEMPreinstall* to *Yes* in the *[Unattended]* section of your unattended-setup answer file and do not provide values for the *[RegionalSettings]* section, set *OEMSkipRegional* to *1* in the *[GuiUnattended]* section of the unattended-setup answer file or in the *[GuiUnattended]* section of Sysprep.inf to ensure that Setup completes without prompting for regional option information. However, do not distribute computers that do not have preconfigured regional, language, and keyboard settings; or enable the Regional and Language Options page during the end user's first-run experience.

To use *[RegionalSettings]* in Sysprep.inf, you must have all language files on the computer's hard disk. Specify the location of the files by using *InstallFilesPath* in the *[Unattended]* section of Sysprep.inf. The *InputLocale* and *InputLocale_DefaultUser* entries in Sysprep.inf do not work. To customize these settings, manually change the settings after first boot.

The following list describes the entries in the *[RegionalSettings]* section:

- *InputLocale*   Specifies the input locale and keyboard layout combinations to install

- *InputLocale_DefaultUser*   Specifies the input locale and keyboard layout combination for the default user

- *Language*   Specifies the language and locale to install

- *LanguageGroup*   Specifies the language group for this installation

- *SystemLocale*   Specifies the system locale to install

- *UserLocale*   Specifies the user locale to install

- *UserLocale_DefaultUser*   Specifies the user locale for the default user

InputLocale

InputLocale specifies the input locale and keyboard layout combinations to install.

Syntax	*InputLocale* = locale_ID:keyboard layout ID[, locale_ID:keyboard_layout_ID][, ...]
Values	locale_ID:keyboard layout ID[, locale_ID:keyboard_layout_ID][, ...]
Example	*InputLocale = 2058:40a, 1046:416*
Notes	<ul><li>The first keyboard layout specified is the default layout for the installation. One of the language groups defined in the *Language-Group* entry or the default language group for the language version of Windows XP Professional must support the specified combination. If an available language group does not support the combination specified, Setup uses the default combination. Setup also ignores this entry if you specify the *Language* entry.</li><li>Not supported by Sysprep.inf.</li><li>For a list of valid locale ID and keyboard layout combinations, visit the Microsoft Global Software Development Web site at *http://www.microsoft.com/globaldev*.</li></ul>

InputLocale_DefaultUser

InputLocale_DefaultUser specifies the input locale and keyboard layout combination for the default user.

Syntax	*InputLocale_DefaultUser* = locale_ID:keyboard_layout_ID
Values	locale_ID:keyboard_layout_ID
Example	*InputLocale_DefaultUser = 2058:40a*
Notes	<ul><li>One of the language groups defined in the *LanguageGroup* entry or the default language group for the language version of Windows XP Professional must support the specified combination. You must define the keyboard in the *KeyboardLayout* entry in the *[Unattended]* section of the unattended-setup answer file.</li><li>Not supported by Sysprep.inf.</li><li>For a list of valid locale ID and keyboard layout combinations, visit the Microsoft Global Software Development Web site at *http://www.microsoft.com/globaldev*.</li></ul>

Language

Language specifies the language/locale to install.

Syntax	*Language* = locale_ID
Value	locale_ID
Example	*Language* = 030
Notes	■ One of the language groups specified in the *LanguageGroup* entry must support this language. If an available language group does not support the locale, Setup uses the default language for this version of Windows XP Professional.
	■ If you specify this entry, Setup ignores the *SystemLocale*, *UserLocale*, and *InputLocale* entries.
	■ For a list of valid locales and their language groups, visit the Microsoft Global Software Development Web site at *http: //www.microsoft.com/globaldev*.

LanguageGroup

LanguageGroup specifies the language group for this installation.

Syntax	*LanguageGroup* = language_group_ID[, language_group_ID[, ...]]
Values	language_group_ID[, language_group_ID[, ...]]
Example	LanguageGroup = 2
Notes	■ You cannot specify a particular locale or language unless you install the appropriate language group.
	■ In Windows XP Professional, if you install one language group, you install all corresponding language groups. For example, if you install one language group from the set of East Asian language groups, you also install associated language groups. Likewise, if you install one language group from the set of complex script language groups, you install all complex script language groups.

Notes	■ The supported language group IDs are shown in the following list:

- *1.* Western Europe and United States (installed by default)
- *2.* Central Europe (installed by default)
- *3.* Baltic (installed by default)
- *4.* Greek (installed by default)
- *5.* Cyrillic (installed by default)
- *6.* Turkic (installed by default)
- *7.* Japanese East Asian Language
- *8.* Korean East Asian Language
- *9.* Traditional Chinese East Asian Language
- *10.* Simplified Chinese East Asian Language
- *11.* Thai Complex Script
- *12.* Hebrew Complex Script
- *13.* Arabic Complex Script
- *14.* Vietnamese Complex Script
- *15.* Indic Complex Script
- *16.* Georgian Complex Script
- *17.* Armenian Complex Script

■ For a list of specific languages that correspond to particular language groups, see the Microsoft Global Software Development Web site at *http://www.microsoft.com/globaldev*.

SystemLocale

SystemLocale specifies the system locale to install.

Syntax	*SystemLocale* = locale_ID
Value	locale_ID
Example	*SystemLocale* = *2058*
Notes	The system locale enables localized applications to run and display menus and dialog boxes in their native language. One of the language groups specified in the *LanguageGroup* entry or the default language group for the language version of Windows XP Professional must support the specified system locale. If an available language group does not support the locale specified, Setup installs the default system locale. Setup also ignores this entry if you specify the *Language* entry.

UserLocale

UserLocale specifies the user locale to install.

Syntax	*UserLocale* = locale_ID
Value	locale_ID
Example	*UserLocale = 2058*
Notes	The user locale controls the settings for numbers, time, currency, and dates. One of the language groups specified in the *LanguageGroup* entry or the default language group for the language version of Windows XP Professional must support the specified user locale. If an available language group does not support the locale specified, Setup installs the default user locale. Setup also ignores this entry if you specify the *Language* entry.

UserLocale_DefaultUser

UserLocale_DefaultUser specifies the user locale for the default user.

Syntax	*UserLocale_DefaultUser* = locale_ID
Value	locale_ID
Example	*UserLocale_DefaultUser = 2058*
Notes	The user locale controls the settings for numbers, time, currency, and dates. The specified user locale must be supported by one of the languages that is specified in the *LanguageGroup* setting or the default language for the Windows XP Professional version that is installed.

[SetupParams]

The *[SetupParams]* section applies to unattended-setup answer files.

This section is used to run an additional post-Setup command. It contains a single entry: *UserExecute*. The command specified with *UserExecute* runs immediately after Setup completes.

UserExecute

UserExecute specifies the command or application to run after Setup completes.

Syntax	*UserExecute* = path_and_file_name
Value	path_and_file_name
Default Value	none

Example	*UserExecute="C:\example.exe /s1 /s2"*
Notes	Enclose path_and_file_name in quotation marks if it is a long filename. You can omit the path only if the application is in the %SYSTEMROOT% or %SYSTEMROOT%\system32 folder or search path.

[TapiLocation]

The *[TapiLocation]* section applies to unattended-setup answer files and Sysprep.inf.

The *[TapiLocation]* section contains entries for specifying the Telephony Application Programming Interface (TAPI). It is valid only if a modem is present on the computer. If you use the Sysprep.inf file with Sysprep, the modem information (TAPI) and the Networking screens do not display during Mini-Setup. Setup uses the default networking components if you do not configure the networking components and if you do not specify them in Sysprep.inf.

To prevent the end user from being prompted for TAPI information during Windows Welcome, you can set TAPI location information in advance, and then set *TapiConfigured* to *Yes*.

The *[TapiLocation]* section supports the following entries:

- *AreaCode*   Specifies the area code for the computer's location.

- *CountryCode*   Specifies the country/region code to use for telephony.

- *Dialing*   Specifies the type of dialing to use for the telephony device in the computer.

- *LongDistanceAccess*   Specifies the number to dial to gain access to an outside line, such as 9.

AreaCode

AreaCode specifies the area code for the computer's location.

Syntax	*AreaCode* = area code string
Value	area code string
Registry Subkey	HKLM\Software\Microsoft\Windows\CurrentVersion\Telephony \Locations\Location1\AreaCode
Example	*AreaCode = 555*

CountryCode

CountryCode specifies the country/region code to use for telephony.

Syntax	*CountryCode* = country/region code number
Value	country/region code number
Registry Subkey	HKLM\Software\Microsoft\Windows\CurrentVersion \Telephony\Locations\Location1\Country
Example	*CountryCode* = 030
Notes	

- Use *1* for the United States. For more information, search the Internet for ISO 3166 for a list of valid country or region codes, or visit the International Telecommunication Union Survey Web site at *http://www.itu.int*.

- In some software modem drivers, particularly those used in portable computers, the default modem location is set to *USA*. To make sure that the correct location is chosen, use one of the following methods:

  - *Method 1*. Before running Setup Manager, add the following section to the unattended-setup answer file and set *CountryCode* equal to the appropriate number:

    ```
    [TapiLocation]
    CountryCode = number
    ```

  - *Method 2*. After using Setup Manager to create a configuration set, add the following section to the unattended-setup answer file in your configuration set and set *CountryCode* equal to the appropriate number:

    ```
    [TapiLocation]
    CountryCode = number
    ```

  - *Method 3*. In audit mode, use Device Manager to change the modem location from *USA* to the correct country or region before running **Sysprep -reseal**. Then, delete any TAPI locations using Phone And Modem Options in Control Panel (you can also delete the registry keys HKLM \Software\Microsoft\Windows\CurrentVersion \Telephony\Locations\LocationN).

Dialing

Dialing specifies the type of dialing to use for the telephony device in the computer.

Syntax	*Dialing = Tone	Pulse*
Values	■ *Tone* Specifies dialing with a multifrequency tone, such as a push-button phone.
	■ *Pulse* Specifies dialing with transmitting pulses of electricity, such as a rotary dial phone.
Example	*Dialing = Tone*

LongDistanceAccess

LongDistanceAccess specifies the number to dial to gain access to an outside line, such as 9.

Syntax	*LongDistanceAccess* = number to get outside line
Value	number to get outside line
Registry Subkey	HKLM\Software\Microsoft\Windows\CurrentVersion\Telephony\Locations\Location1\LongDistanceAccess
Example	*LongDistanceAccess* = 9

[Unattended]

The *[Unattended]* section applies to unattended-setup answer files and Sysprep.inf. Sysprep.inf supports a subset of this section's entries.

This section is required in unattended-setup answer files; otherwise, the setup program ignores the answer files. This section supports the following entries:

■ *ActivateProxy*   Specifies the proxy settings to use when connecting to the Internet to activate this installation of Windows XP Professional if you set *AutoActivate* to *Yes*.

■ *AutoActivate*   Specifies whether Setup attempts to activate this installation of Windows XP Professional automatically through an existing Internet connection.

■ *ComputerType*   Specifies the type of custom hardware abstraction layer (HAL) that Setup Loader loads and installs by text-mode Setup.

■ *CrashDumpSetting*   Specifies the creation and type of the dump file.

- ***DisableVirtualOemDevices*** Specifies whether to load virtual original equipment manufacturer (OEM) devices during Setup.

- ***DUDisable*** Specifies whether to connect to the Windows Update site to download updates during Setup.

- ***DUShare*** Specifies the location for downloaded Dynamic Update .cab files.

- ***DriverSigningPolicy*** Specifies how to process unsigned drivers during unattended Setup.

- ***ExtendOemPartition*** Specifies whether to extend the partition on which you install Windows XP Professional.

- ***FactoryMode*** Specifies whether %SYSTEMDRIVE%\Sysprep\Factory.exe runs on first boot.

- ***FileSystem*** Specifies whether to convert the primary partition to NTFS or to leave it alone.

- ***ForceHALDetection*** Specifies whether text-mode Setup examines the operating system and determines the most appropriate HAL to install during an upgrade.

- ***Hibernation*** Specifies whether to enable the hibernation option in the Power Options control panel.

- ***KeyboardLayout*** Specifies the type of keyboard layout to install during text-mode Setup.

- ***NtUpgrade*** Specifies whether Setup upgrades a previous version of Windows NT 3.51, Windows NT 4.0, Windows 2000 Professional, Windows XP Professional, or the Windows Server 2003 family.

- ***OemFilesPath*** Specifies the path to the \OEM folder (containing OEM files) if it does not exist under the i386 folder of the distribution share point.

- ***OemPnPDriversPath*** Specifies the path to one or more folders that contain Plug and Play drivers not distributed in Drivers.cab on the Windows XP Professional product CD.

- ***OemPreinstall*** Specifies whether Setup installs its files from distribution folders.

- ***OemSkipEula*** Specifies whether the end user must accept the End-User License Agreement (EULA) included with Windows XP Professional.

- ***OverwriteOemFilesOnUpgrade*** Specifies whether to overwrite OEM-supplied files that have the same name as Windows XP Professional or Windows Server 2003 operating system files during an unattended upgrade.

- ***Repartition*** Specifies whether to delete all partitions on the first drive of the client computer and to reformat the drive with the NTFS file system.

- ***TargetPath*** Determines the installation folder in which you install Windows XP Professional.

- ***UnattendMode*** Defines the unattended mode to use during GUI-mode Setup.

- ***UnattendSwitch*** Specifies whether Setup skips Windows Welcome or Mini-Setup when preinstalling Windows XP Home Edition or Windows XP Professional using the CD Boot method.

- ***WaitForReboot*** Specifies whether the computer waits 15 seconds after GUI-mode Setup finishes.

- ***Win9xUpgrade*** Specifies whether Setup upgrades previous installations of Windows 98, Windows 98 Second Edition, or Windows Millennium Edition (Windows Me) to either Windows XP Home Edition or Windows XP Professional, as specified in the *[Win9xUpg]* section.

ActivateProxy

ActivateProxy specifies the proxy settings to use when connecting to the Internet to activate this installation of Windows XP Professional if you set *AutoActivate* to *Yes*.

Syntax	*ActivateProxy* = section_name | *Proxy*
Values	■ section_name ■ *Proxy*
Example	*ActivateProxy* = *Proxy*
Notes	■ If section_name is *Proxy*, Windows Product Activation (WPA) uses the proxy settings specified in the *[Proxy]* section. If section_name is anything else, WPA uses the proxy settings specified in *[section_name]* in the unattended-setup answer file. The entries in *[section_name]* must match the syntax specified in the *[Proxy]* section. ■ If your network uses Web Proxy Auto-Discovery (WPAD), you may not need to set the proxy explicitly.

AutoActivate

AutoActivate specifies whether Setup attempts to activate this installation of Windows XP Professional automatically through an existing Internet connection.

Syntax	*AutoActivate* = Yes | *No*
Values	■ **Yes** Attempts to activate this installation of Windows XP Professional during unattended Setup through an existing Internet connection on the computer.
	■ **No** Requires the end user to activate Windows XP Professional either through an Internet connection or by phone.
Default Value	*No*
Example	*AutoActivate* = *Yes*
Notes	■ You must specify a valid Product Key in the *ProductKey* entry of the *[UserData]* section. If the Internet connection is through a firewall, you may need to specify the relevant proxy settings in the *ActivateProxy* entry.
	■ Always requires a Product Key.
	■ The Product Key you use to activate this installation using WPA must match the number on the Certificate of Authenticity (COA). The OEM packages the COA with the retail product or affixes it to the computer case.
	■ Standard licensing agreements specify that you can use a given Product Key to activate only one installation of Windows XP Professional on one computer. WPA enforces this requirement.
	■ If you use Winnt.exe to install Windows XP Professional, you must set *UnattendSwitch* to *Yes*.
	■ Setting *AutoActivate* to *Yes* does not guarantee successful activation of this installation of Windows XP Professional. For example, the activation attempt will fail if the computer cannot successfully connect to the Internet.

ComputerType

ComputerType specifies the type of custom HAL that Setup Loader loads and installs by text-mode Setup.

Syntax	*ComputerType* = HAL_description [, *Retail* | *OEM*]
Values	■ **Retail** Informs Setup that the HAL to install is part of Windows XP Professional or the Windows Server 2003 family.
	■ **OEM** Indicates that the HAL to load is OEM-supplied. If this is the case, you must also list the driver name in the *[OEMBootFiles]* section of the unattended-setup answer file.

Examples	*ComputerType* = *"OEM HAL"*, *OEM*
	ComputerType = *"Advanced Configuration and Power Interface (ACPI) PC"*, *Retail*
Notes	■ This entry is valid only when the value of *OemPreinstall* is *Yes*. If the *ComputerType* entry is not present, Setup attempts to detect the type of computer and install the appropriate retail HAL.
	■ The HAL_description string identifies the HAL to install. It must match one of the strings in the *[Computer]* section of TxtSetup.sif (for a retail HAL) or TxtSetup.oem (for an OEM HAL).

CrashDumpSetting

CrashDumpSetting specifies the creation and type of the dump file.

Syntax	*CrashDumpSetting* = *0	1	2	3*
Values	■ *0* Does not create a dump file.
	■ *1* Complete Memory Dump: Records the entire contents of system memory to %SYSTEMROOTt%\Memory.dmp when the system stops unexpectedly. If you choose this option, you must have a paging file on the boot volume large enough to hold all of the physical random access memory (RAM) plus 1 megabyte (MB).
	■ *2* Kernel Memory Dump: Records only kernel memory to %SYSTEMROOTt%\Memory.dmp when the system stops unexpectedly, which speeds up the process of recording information in a log. Depending on the amount of RAM in your computer, you must have 50 MB to 800 MB available for the paging file on the boot volume.
	■ *3* Small Memory Dump (64 K): Records the smallest set of useful information that can help identify the problem to %SYSTEMROOTt%\Mini.dmp. This option requires a paging file of at least 2 MB on the boot volume of your computer and specifies that Setup creates a new file each time the system stops unexpectedly.
Default Value	■ *3* for Windows XP Home Edition and Windows XP Professional
	■ *1* for the Windows Server 2003 family
Example	*CrashDumpSetting* = *0*
Notes	When the system fails, you can create a dump file that contains information useful for debugging. Dump file types vary by size. The system checks for available space on the boot volume and writes the largest possible dump file.

DisableVirtualOemDevices

DisableVirtualOemDevices specifies whether to load virtual OEM devices during Setup.

Syntax	*DisableVirtualOemDevices* = *Yes* | *No*
Values	■ **Yes** Disables loading virtual OEM devices during Setup.
	■ **No** Does not disable loading virtual OEM devices during Setup.
Default Value	■ *Yes* for preinstallation
	■ *No* otherwise
Example	*DisableVirtualOemDevices* = *Yes*
Notes	■ An example of a virtual OEM device is a RAM disk that has mass storage drivers, related .inf files, and so on.
	■ During attended Setup, you can disable loading of virtual OEM devices by pressing F4 at the prompt to press the F6 key.

DUDisable

DUDisable specifies whether to connect to the Windows Update site to download updates during Setup.

Syntax	*DUDisable* = *Yes* | *No*
Values	■ **Yes** Instructs Setup not to connect to the Windows Update site.
	■ **No** Instructs Setup to connect to the Windows Update site to download any available Windows XP Setup updates. Setup also downloads any necessary drivers that are not on the Windows XP Professional CD-ROM.
Default Value	*Yes*
Example	*DUDisable* = *No*
Notes	■ Specifies whether Setup connects to the Windows Update site to download any available Windows Setup updates or necessary drivers that are not on the Windows CD-ROM.
	■ DUDisable is equivalent to the command **winnt32 /unattend /dudisable.**
	■ Setup disables dynamic updates by default so corporate administrators can more easily standardize on a known set of Windows XP Professional system components.

DUShare

DUShare specifies the location for downloaded Dynamic Update .cab files.

Syntax	*DUShare* = path_to_downloaded_cabs
Values	path_to_downloaded_cabs
Example	*DUShare = "%SYSTEMDRIVE%\DU_Cabs"*
	Requires you to run **winnt32 /DUPrepare:**path_to_downloaded_cabs before using this entry.
Notes	When a path is specified, the Dynamic Update Wizard page is not shown and Setup does not try to connect to Windows Update. Instead, Setup uses the Dynamic Update .cab files from this share.

DriverSigningPolicy

DriverSigningPolicy specifies how to process unsigned drivers during unattended Setup.

Syntax	*DriverSigningPolicy = Block | Warn | Ignore*
Values	■ *Block* Setup does not install the unsigned device driver.
	■ *Warn* Setup stops the installation and prompts the end user for input before accepting the unsigned device driver.
	■ *Ignore* Setup continues despite the unsigned driver.
Default Value	*Warn*
Example	*DriverSigningPolicy = Block*

Notes

- Signed drivers have gone through the Microsoft driver testing and signing process to ensure that they are compatible with Windows XP Professional and the Windows Server 2003 family.

- Microsoft strongly advises against using *DriverSigningPolicy = Ignore* unless you have fully tested the device driver in your environment and are sure that it works properly. Using unsigned drivers increases the risk of device driver problems that can affect the performance or stability of the computer.

- If you are using *DriverSigningPolicy = Ignore* and you attempt to install a newer unsigned copy of a driver that distributed with Windows XP Professional or the Windows Server 2003 family, Setup installs the signed Windows XP Professional driver instead of the unsigned drivers, in accordance with the ranking process used by the operating system.

- A catalog certificate (.cat) file authenticates a driver signature. Microsoft can use the given certificate to sign drivers for only a finite length of time, generally six months. However, as long as you have a digitally signed driver, the subsequent expiration date of the certificate does not affect the status of the driver. A driver signature does not expire, even after the certificate used to sign the driver has expired.

- For more information, see the following Web sites:

    - Hardware Compatibility List (HCL) at the Microsoft Web site *http://www.microsoft.com/whdc/hcl/default.mspx*

    - Windows Driver and Hardware Development at *http://www.microsoft.com/whdc/hwdev/default.mspx*

    - Driver Signing for Windows Operating Systems at *http://www.microsoft.com/whdc/hwdev/driver/digitsign.mspx*

    - Windows Hardware Quality Labs Web site at *http://www.microsoft.com/whdc/hwtest/default.mspx*

    - Microsoft Device Development Kit at *http://www.microsoft.com /whdc/ddk/winddk.mspx*

ExtendOemPartition

ExtendOemPartition specifies whether to extend the partition on which you install Windows XP Professional.

Syntax   *ExtendOemPartition = 0 | 1 |* extra_size_in_MB

Values
- *0*   Setup does not extend the partition.
- *1*   Setup extends the partition to fill out the hard disk.
- **extra_size_in_MB**   Setup increases the current partition size by this amount. This is useful if you want to configure more than one partition on the hard disk.

Example	*ExtendOemPartition = 1000*
Notes	■ This entry causes Setup to extend this destination partition into any available unpartitioned space that physically follows it on the disk.
	■ *ExtendOemPartition* automatically leaves the last cylinder on the hard disk free to allow dynamic disk support.
	■ You can extend only NTFS file system partitions.
	■ When you use *ExtendOEMPartition* in Sysprep.inf for imaged computers, the destination computer's hard disk must be the same size or larger than the hard disk of the original master installation.
	■ The partition that you want to extend must have unpartitioned space available following the partition.
	■ If your manufacturing process requires FAT32, use the Oformat command-line tool included in the OEM Preinstallation Kit to format the hard disk so that you configure it for NTFS. Use the Convert command-line tool to convert the file system.
	■ You can also convert the partition during text-mode Setup by setting the *FileSystem* in the *[Unattended]* section of the unattended-setup answer file to *ConvertNTFS*. *FileSystem* is not a valid entry in Sysprep.inf. However, the hard drive performs better if you use the Convert command-line tool instead of the *FileSystem* entry.
	■ You can also use the *ExtendPartition* entry in the *[ComputerSettings]* section of Winbom.ini to extend the partition using the Factory tool.

FactoryMode

FactoryMode specifies whether %SYSTEMDRIVE%\Sysprep\Factory.exe runs on first boot.

Syntax	*FactoryMode = Yes	No*
Value	■ *Yes* %SYSTEMDRIVE%\Sysprep\Factory.exe runs on first boot.
	■ *No* %SYSTEMDRIVE%\Sysprep\Factory.exe does not run on first boot.
Default Value	*Yes*
Example	*FactoryMode = Yes*
Notes	Use this entry when performing a clean install of the operating system as the first step in building a master installation, which you then plan to duplicate onto multiple destination computers. *FactoryMode = Yes* will boot the computer into factory mode, where system configuration can be done before imaging. You must place the OPK tools in the %SYSTEMDRIVE%\Sysprep folder.

FileSystem

FileSystem specifies whether to convert the primary partition to NTFS or to leave it alone.

Syntax	*FileSystem = ConvertNTFS	LeaveAlone*
Values	■ ***ConvertNTFS*** Converts the primary partition to NTFS.
	■ ***LeaveAlone*** Does not change the primary partition file system.
Example	*FileSystem = ConvertNTFS*
Notes	■ This entry is provided for backward compatibility with the Windows 2000 Professional unattended Setup.
	■ For the Windows XP Professional and Windows Server 2003 family of operating systems, if your manufacturing processes require that you format the hard disk as FAT32, use the Oformat tool to create a FAT32 volume with clusters aligned in an optimal way for later conversion to the NTFS file system. Then use the Convert command-line tool to convert the file system to NTFS.
	■ You can also convert the partition during text-mode Setup by setting the *FileSystem* entry equal to *ConvertNTFS*. However, the hard drive performs better if you use the Convert command-line tool instead of the *FileSystem* entry.
	■ If you plan to use *ExtendOemPartition* during Setup, the file system must be NTFS.
	■ *FileSystem* is not a valid entry in Sysprep.inf.

ForceHALDetection

ForceHALDetection specifies whether text-mode Setup examines the operating system and determines the most appropriate HAL to install during an upgrade.

Syntax	*ForceHALDetection = Yes	No*
Values	■ ***Yes*** Installs the most appropriate HAL for the new operating system.
	■ ***No*** Keeps the HAL from the previous operating system.
Default Value	*No*

Example	*ForceHALDetection = Yes*
Notes	■ If *ForceHALDetection = Yes* during an upgrade, Setup may lose some user-specified hardware settings.
	■ If *ForceHALDetection = No* during an upgrade, Setup preserves user-specified hardware settings.

Hibernation

Hibernation specifies whether to enable the hibernation option in the Power Options control panel.

Syntax	*Hibernation = Yes	No*
Values	■ ***Yes*** Enables hibernation.
	■ ***No*** Disables hibernation.
Default Value	*Yes*
Example	*Hibernation = Yes*
Notes	■ Not supported on the 64-bit versions of the Windows Server 2003 family. This setting adds Hibernate to the Shutdown menu and creates the Hiberfil.sys file.
	■ To keep the size of your image file as small as possible, you may delete the hibernation file (Hiberfil.sys) (if it exists) from your master installation.
	■ The Hiberfil.sys file created during hibernation mode is as large as the available RAM on the computer. Before beginning hibernation mode, verify that the amount of free disk space on your computer hard drive is greater than or equal to the amount of RAM in the computer.
	■ Setup does not support hibernation if any driver or video card does not support Plug and Play.
	■ For Windows Server 2003, Enterprise Edition or Windows Server 2003, Datacenter Edition, you cannot use hibernation if the computer uses Terminal Server or if the Physical Address Extension (PAE) Kernel supports 3 GB or more of memory.
	■ For more information on the PAE Kernel, see the Microsoft Driver Development Kit (DDK), which you can order from the Microsoft DDK Web site at *http://www.microsoft.com/whdc/ddk/winddk.mspx*. You can also read the DDK documentation in the MSDN Library at *http://msdn.microsoft.com/library*.

KeyboardLayout

KeyboardLayout specifies the type of keyboard layout to install during text-mode Setup.

Syntax	*KeyboardLayout* = layout_description
Value	layout_description
Example	*KeyboardLayout = Us*
Notes	■ If this entry does not exist, Setup detects and installs a keyboard layout.
	■ This entry must match one of the right-hand strings (in quotation marks) in the *[Keyboard Layout]* section of TxtSetup.sif.

NtUpgrade

NtUpgrade specifies whether Setup upgrades a previous version of Windows NT 3.51, Windows NT 4.0, Windows 2000 Professional, Windows XP Professional, or the Windows Server 2003 family.

Syntax	*NtUpgrade = Yes	No*
Values	■ *Yes* Upgrades a previous version of Windows.
	■ *No* Does not upgrade a previous version of Windows.
Example	*NtUpgrade = Yes*
Notes	■ This entry is valid only for Winnt32.exe.
	■ To upgrade from Windows 98 or Windows Me, use the *Win9xUpgrade* entry.
	■ Set *NtUpgrade = Yes* to upgrade the previous Windows installation. If *OemPreinstall* is *Yes*, do not set *NtUpgrade* equal to *Yes*.
	■ This entry upgrades your previous version of Windows XP Professional, the Windows Server 2003 family, Windows 2000 Professional, Windows NT 4.0, or Windows NT 3.51. Setup takes all user settings from the previous installation and does not require end-user intervention.
	■ See Chapter 1, "Deployment Plan," for a list of valid upgrade scenarios.
	■ You can upgrade from Windows NT 4.0 Terminal Server Edition or Windows 2000 Application Server mode to Windows Server 2003 family, but Setup will warn you that it does not support Terminal Service Application mode.

OemFilesPath

OemFilesPath specifies the path to the OEM folder (containing OEM files) if it does not exist under the i386 folder of the distribution share point.

Syntax	*OemFilesPath* = path_to_OEM_folder
Value	path_to_OEM_folder
Example	*OemFilesPath* = "%SYSTEMDRIVE%\OEM_Files"
Notes	■ The path can be a UNC name. Enclose path_to_OEM_folder in quotation marks if it is a long filename. ■ For more information about the OEM folder, if you are a computer manufacturer, see the Microsoft Windows XP OEM Preinstallation Kit (OPK) User Guide. Otherwise, see the Microsoft Windows 2000 Server Deployment Guide. Chapter 7, "Distribution Points," describes how to create this folder.

OemPnPDriversPath

OemPnPDriversPath specifies the path to one or more folders that contain Plug and Play drivers not distributed in Drivers.cab on the Windows XP Professional product CD.

Syntax	*OemPnPDriversPath* = folder_1_on_system_drive[;folder_2_on_system_drive]...
Values	folder_1_on_system_drive[;folder_2_on_system_drive]...
Example	*OemPnPDriversPath* = MyFolder1; MyFolder2
Dependency	*OEMPreinstall* = Yes

Registry Subkey	HKLM\Software\Microsoft\Windows\CurrentVersion\DevicePath
Notes	

- The folders must contain all the files necessary to install the particular devices: catalog files, .inf files, and drivers.
- If you have a folder called Drivers with subfolders called Audio and Net, specify *OemPnPDriversPath = drivers \audio;drivers\net* in the unattended-setup answer file. Setup adds %SYSTEMDRIVE% to each of the folder names and the path for each subfolder to the Plug and Play device search path.
- The length of the *OemPnPDriversPath* entry in the unattended-setup answer file must not exceed 4096 characters.
- You cannot use environment variables to specify the location of a folder.
- Always use signed drivers. Signed drivers make the operating system more stable and significantly reduce requests for product support.
- When using *OemPnPDriversPath* in the unattended-setup answer file, be sure that the folders are available during GUI-mode Setup or the end user first-run experience. The easiest way to do this is to place the Plug and Play drivers in the OEM\$1 folder. To prevent end users from inadvertently deleting driver folders located at the root of the drive, you can place drivers under the OEM\$$ folder.
- If the drivers are not in the Drivers.cab file on the computer's hard disk or in the location specified by *OemPnPDriversPath*, Setup prompts the end user for the location of the drivers during the first boot of the machine, before Windows Welcome or Mini-Setup.
- You can also use the *[PnPDrivers]* section in Winbom.ini to update drivers on a previously-created image of the installed operating system.
- See Chapter 7 for a complete description of how to distribute third-party device drivers.

OemPreinstall

OemPreinstall specifies whether Setup installs its files from distribution folders.

Syntax	*OemPreinstall = Yes	No*
Values	

- **Yes**   Setup copies the subfolders and files contained in the \platform\oem folder.
- **No**   Setup does not copy these files.

Example	*OemPreinstall = Yes*
Notes	■ If *OemPreinstall = Yes*, do not set *NtUpgrade* to *Yes*.
	■ If *OemPreinstall = Yes*, unattended Setup automatically stops at the Welcome page. To avoid this pause in your factory environment, set *OEMSkipWelcome* to *1*. Do not distribute any computer with *OEM-SkipWelcome = 1*. Instead, set *OEMSkipWelcome* to *0* in the Sysprep.inf file you use before delivering the computer to the customer.

OemSkipEula

OemSkipEula specifies whether the end user must accept the EULA included with Windows XP Professional.

Syntax	*OemSkipEula = Yes	No*
Values	■ **Yes** Implies that the person performing the installation has read and agreed to the contents of the license agreement included with the product. It also implies that the end user on whose behalf you install Windows XP Professional has agreed to the license agreement.
	■ **No** Implies that the person performing the installation and the end user have not read and agreed to the license agreement.
Example	*OemSkipEula = No*
Notes	You must not use this entry to remove the Microsoft EULA screen because end users must see and accept it. Use Sysprep to ensure that end users see the EULA when the computer starts for the first time.

OverwriteOemFilesOnUpgrade

OverwriteOemFilesOnUpgrade specifies whether to overwrite OEM-supplied files that have the same name as Windows XP Professional or Windows Server 2003 family of operating system files during an unattended upgrade.

Syntax	*OverwriteOemFilesOnUpgrade = Yes	No*
Values	■ **Yes** Overwrites the files if found.
	■ **No** Does not overwrite the files if found.
Default Value	*Yes*
Example	*OverwriteOemFilesOnUpgrade = Yes*
Notes	This entry is provided for backward compatibility with Windows 2000 Professional unattended Setup.

Repartition

Repartition specifies whether to delete all partitions on the first drive of the client computer and to reformat the drive with the NTFS file system.

Syntax	*Repartition = Yes	No*
Values	■ **Yes** Deletes all partitions on the first drive and reformats the drive with NTFS.
	■ **No** Does not delete partitions or reformat the drive.
Example	*Repartition = Yes*
Notes	Repartition is valid only when performing an unattended Setup by booting the computer from the Windows XP Professional product CD.

TargetPath

TargetPath determines the installation folder in which you install Windows XP Professional.

Syntax	*TargetPath = * |* target_path
Values	■ * Setup generates a unique folder name for the installation.
	■ **target_path** Setup installs to the specified folder.
Example	*TargetPath = **
Notes	■ *TargetPath = ** indicates that Setup generates a unique folder name for the installation. The folder name given is usually Windows unless that folder already exists. In that case, Setup installs into Windows.x (where x is 0, 1, ... 999) if these folders do not already exist.
	■ The path must use 8.3 filenames. Do not include the drive letter in target_path. If you want to specify the target drive, you must use the **/tempdrive** command-line switch when you run **Winnt32.exe**.

UnattendMode

UnattendMode defines the unattended mode to use during GUI-mode Setup.

Syntax	*UnattendMode = DefaultHide	FullUnattended	GuiAttended	ProvideDefault	ReadOnly*

Values
- ■ *DefaultHide*   Specifies that answers in the answer file are defaults. Unlike *UnattendMode = ProvideDefault*, Setup does not display the user interface to end users if you specify in the answer file all the answers relating to a particular Setup page. If you specify only subsets of the answers on a page, the page appears with the provided answers. The end user can modify any of the answers on the displayed page. Use *UnattendMode = DefaultHide* in deployment scenarios in which an administrator might want only end users to provide the administrator password on the computer. This behavior is the default if you do not specify unattended mode.

- ■ *FullUnattended*   Specifies a fully unattended GUI-mode Setup. If you do not specify a required Setup answer in the answer file, Setup generates an error. During an attended Setup, improperly signed hardware drivers generate a warning dialog box. If *UnattendMode = FullUnattended*, Setup does not install hardware drivers unless they are properly signed. Use *UnattendMode = FullUnattended* in deployment scenarios in which you require a completely hands-off installation.

- ■ *GuiAttended*   Specifies an attended GUI-mode section of Setup. When specified, the end user must answer all questions in the GUI-mode portion of Setup before Setup finishes. Use *UnattendMode = GuiAttended* in preinstallation scenarios when you want to automate only text-mode Setup.

- ■ *ProvideDefault*   Specifies default answers in the answer file. In this case, Setup displays these default answers to the end user, who can change them if they are not appropriate. Use *UnattendMode = ProvideDefault* in preinstallation scenarios in which the OEM or administrator wants to give the person setting up the computer the option to change the predefined default answers (especially network options).

- ■ *ReadOnly*   Specifies read-only answers in the answer file if the Windows Setup pages containing these answers appear to the end user. Like *UnattendMode = ProvideDefault*, no user interface appears if the answer file contains all the answers on a page. Unlike *UnattendMode = DefaultHide*, however, the end user can specify only view answers on a displayed page. Use *UnattendMode = ReadOnly* in scenarios in which an administrator wants to force specific answers on one page but not on others.

Default Value   *DefaultHide*

Example   *UnattendMode = FullUnattended*

Notes   The default value is *DefaultHide* when you do not specify the entry. When you specify this entry, it fully automates text-mode Setup with or without the necessary answers.

UnattendSwitch

UnattendSwitch specifies whether Setup skips Windows Welcome or Mini-Setup when preinstalling Windows XP Home Edition or Windows XP Professional using the CD Boot method.

Syntax	*UnattendSwitch = Yes | No*
Values	■ **Yes** Instructs Setup to skip Windows Welcome. ■ **No** Instructs Setup not to skip Windows Welcome.
Default Value	*No*
Example	*UnattendSwitch = Yes*
Notes	■ Use *UnattendSwitch* only when you perform an unattended Setup with Winnt.exe, Winnt.sif, and the CD Boot method. This entry is not necessary if you use Winnt32.exe to run Setup. ■ *UnattendSwitch* is not the same as the *UnattendedInstall* entry in the *[Data]* section of the answer file. *UnattendSwitch* controls Windows Welcome; *UnattendedInstall* does not.

WaitForReboot

WaitForReboot specifies whether the computer waits 15 seconds after GUI-mode Setup finishes.

Syntax	*WaitForReboot = Yes | No*
Values	■ **Yes** Delays the reboot for 15 seconds after GUI-mode Setup finishes. ■ **No** Reboots immediately after GUI-mode Setup finishes.
Default Value	*Yes*
Example	*WaitForReboot = Yes*

Win9xUpgrade

Win9xUpgrade specifies whether Setup upgrades previous installations of Windows 98, Windows 98 Second Edition, or Windows Me to either Windows XP Home Edition or Windows XP Professional, as specified in the *[Win9xUpg]* section.

Syntax	*Win9xUpgrade = Yes | No*
Values	■ **Yes** Instructs Setup to upgrade the Windows installation, if found. ■ **No** Instructs Setup not to upgrade the Windows installation, if found.
Default Value	*No*

Example	*Win9xUpgrade = Yes*
Notes	This entry is necessary only when using an answer file to upgrade an existing Windows 98 or Windows Me computer to Windows XP Home Edition or Windows XP Professional. This entry is valid only for Winnt32.exe.

[UserData]

The *[UserData]* section applies to unattended-setup answer files and Sysprep.inf.

The *[UserData]* section contains entries for specifying user settings during Setup. It supports the following entries:

- **ComputerName**   Specifies the computer name

- **FullName**   Specifies the end user's full name

- **OrgName**   Specifies an organization's name

- **ProductKey**   Specifies the Product Key for each unique installation of Windows XP Professional

ComputerName

ComputerName specifies the computer name.

Syntax	*ComputerName = * |* computer_name
Value	■ *
	■ computer_name
Registry Subkey	HKLM\CurrentControlSet\Control\ComputerName\ComputerName
Example	*ComputerName = MYCOMPUTER*
Notes	■ If the *ComputerName* entry is empty or missing, the end user must enter a computer name.
	■ If the *ComputerName* entry is ***, Setup generates a random computer name based on the organization name specified.
	■ If computer_name is longer than 63 characters, the string truncates to 63 characters.

FullName

FullName specifies the end user's full name.

Syntax	*FullName = string*
Value	string
Registry Subkey	HKLM\SOFTWARE\Microsoft\Windows NT\CurrentVersion \RegisteredOwner

Example	*FullName = "Jerry Honeycutt"*
Notes	If the entry is empty or missing, the end user must enter a name, so that Setup can finish unattended.

OrgName

OrgName specifies an organization's name.

Syntax	*OrgName* = string
Value	string
Registry Subkey	HKLM\SOFTWARE\Microsoft\Windows NT\CurrentVersion \RegisteredOrganization
Example	*OrgName = "Microsoft Corporation"*

ProductKey

ProductKey specifies the Product Key for each unique installation of Windows XP Professional.

Syntax	*ProductKey = "xxxxx-xxxxx-xxxxx-xxxxx-xxxxx"*
Value	"xxxxx-xxxxx-xxxxx-xxxxx-xxxxx"
Example	*ProductKey = "12345-ABCDE-12345-ABCDE-12345"*
Notes	■ Each x is either an alphabetic character or a number. Requires the quotation marks and the hyphens.
	■ Always requires a Product Key.
	■ When using the unattended-setup answer file, this entry assigns the same Product Key to all computers on which you install Windows XP Professional or Windows Server 2003 family.
	■ Standard licensing agreements specify that you can use a given Product Key only to activate one installation of Windows XP Professional on one computer. WPA enforces this requirement.
	■ If you preinstall the Windows XP Professional or Windows Server 2003 family under a volume license agreement, consult your specific license agreement to determine the number of installations allowed per Product Key.

Appendix E

Batch Script Syntax

This book relies on batch scripts to automate many repetitive tasks. Batch scripts are not outdated. For example, simple two-line batch scripts can complete many tasks that require dozens of lines of Microsoft VBScript. Thus, I've included this appendix as a reference that you can use to better understand this book and write your own batch scripts to automate desktop deployment and management tasks. The description of each command comes directly from the command's help, which you can display by typing the name of the command followed by /?. I also used Microsoft Windows XP Professional Help and Support Center as a reference for documenting some of these commands.

A batch script is a plaintext file that contains one or more commands and has a *.bat* or *.cmd* filename extension. When you type the filename at the command prompt, Cmd.exe runs the commands sequentially as they appear in the file. You can include any command in a batch script. Certain commands—such as *For*, *Goto*, and *If*—enable you to do conditional processing of the commands in the batch script. For example, the *If* command runs a command based on the results of a condition. Other commands allow you to control input and output and call other batch scripts.

This appendix describes the commands that you can use to accept parameters on a batch script's command line and to control the command prompt. The remainder of this appendix describes the commands for controlling the execution of batch scripts.

> **Note** The majority of useful batch-scripting commands rely on command extensions. You can enable or disable command extensions through the registry by using Cmd.exe command-line options or by using the *setlocal* command in a batch script. See the section "Enabling Command Extensions" on page 840 for more information about enabling them using the registry or command-line options. See the section "*SetLocal*" on page 853 for more information about using the *setlocal* command. Command extensions are enabled by default, but be careful not to accidentally disable them. In general, I start each batch script using the *setlocal* command in order to ensure that command extensions are enabled. In this appendix, I indicate which commands require command extensions and which don't.

Batch Parameters

You can use batch parameters anywhere within a batch script to use options passed to it on the command line. Cmd.exe provides the batch parameter expansion variables *%0* through *%9*. When you use batch parameters in a batch script, *%0* is replaced by the batch script name, and *%1* through *%9* are replaced by the corresponding options that you type at the command line. To access options beyond *%9*, you need to use the *Shift* command. For more information about the *Shift* command, see "*Shift*," later in this appendix. The *%* batch* parameter expands to all the options that are passed to the batch script, not including *%0*.

You can also use modifiers with batch parameters. Modifiers use current drive and directory information to expand the batch parameter as a partial or complete file or directory name. To use a modifier, type the percent (**%**) character followed by a tilde (**~**) character, and then type the appropriate modifier (that is, *%~modifier*). Table E-1 lists the modifiers you can use in parameter expansion. This table uses *%1* as the example, but you can use any other batch parameters, *%1* through *%9*. The modifiers you see in Table E-1 do not work with batch parameters *%0* or *%**, though. You can combine modifiers to get compound results. The following list shows some examples of compound results:

- **%~dp1**   Expands *%1* to a drive letter and path.

- **%~nx1**   Expands *%1* to a filename and extension.

- **%~dp$PATH:1**   Searches the directories listed in the *PATH* environment variable for *%1* and expands to the drive letter and path of the first one found.

- **%~ftza1**   Expands *%1* to a dir-like output line.

Table E-1   Batch Parameter Modifiers

Modifier	Description
%~1	Expands *%1* and removes any surrounding quotation marks ("").
%~f1	Expands *%1* to a fully qualified pathname.
%~d1	Expands *%1* to a drive letter.
%~p1	Expands *%1* to a path.
%~n1	Expands *%1* to a filename.
%~x1	Expands *%1* to a file extension.
%~s1	Expands *%1* to short path- and filenames only.
%~a1	Expands *%1* to attributes of the file.
%~t1	Expands *%1* to date and time of the file.

Table E-1 Batch Parameter Modifiers

Modifier	Description
%~z1	Expands *%1* to size of the file.
%~$PATH:1	Searches the directories listed in the *PATH* environment variable and expands *%1* to the fully qualified name of the first one found. If the environment variable name is not defined or if the file is not found, this modifier expands to the empty string.

Note You cannot manipulate batch parameters in the same manner that you can manipulate environment variables. You cannot search and replace values or examine substrings, for example. However, you can assign the parameter to an environment variable and then manipulate the environment variable.

Batch Script Editor

My favorite text editor for batch scripts is TextPad from Helios Software Solutions. You can learn more about it and download it at *http://www.textpad.com*. It does everything from text sorting to syntax highlighting, and it has a powerful macro-recording feature. It's the perfect text editor for Windows Script Host scripts, *.reg* files, batch scripts, and answer files. UltraEdit is another popular text editor, which I've never used, but you can learn more about it at *http://www.ultraedit.com*.

The syntax-highlighting feature in TextPad makes editing batch scripts particularly easy. If you type a keyword correctly, TextPad highlights the keyword. If you mistype the keyword, the editor doesn't highlight it. That way, you're more likely to create error-free scripts. To use this feature for editing batch scripts, you'll need a syntax file, though, and I included one in the Samples\textpad folder on this book's companion CD, along with samples for .adm, .ini, .reg, .sif, and .vbs files. (The file is cmd.syn.) Using my syntax file, keywords are blue, comments are green, and everything else is black. Here's how to use it with TextPad:

1. Install TextPad.

2. Copy cmd.syn from the Samples\textpad folder on this book's companion CD to %USERPROFILE%\Application Data\TextPad.

3. Import cmd.reg from the Samples\textpad folder on this book's companion CD into the registry.

> This file configures the syntax file cmd.syn in TextPad. To configure the remaining syntax files, copy the appropriate .syn file as described in step 2, and then import the corresponding .reg file as described in step 3.

Cmd Options

Typing **Cmd** in the Run dialog box or at a command prompt starts a new instance of the Windows command interpreter, Cmd.exe. Typing this command in the Run dialog box opens a new window for the command interpreter.

Syntax

```
cmd [[{/c|/k}] [/s] [/q] [/d] [{/a|/u}] [/t:fg] [/e:{on|off}]
[/f:{on|off}] [/v:{on|off}] string]
```

Parameters

/c	Carries out the command specified by string and then stops. For compatibility, /r is the same as /c.
/k	Carries out the command specified by string and continues.
/s	Modifies the treatment of string after /c or /k.
/q	Turns the echo off.
/d	Disables execution of AutoRun commands.
/a	Creates American National Standards Institute (ANSI) output.
/u	Creates Unicode output.

/t:fg	Sets the foreground f and background g colors. The following table lists valid hexadecimal digits that you can use as the values for f and g.

- ■ **0**. Black
- ■ **1**. Blue
- ■ **2**. Green
- ■ **3**. Aqua
- ■ **4**. Red
- ■ **5**. Purple
- ■ **6**. Yellow
- ■ **7**. White
- ■ **8**. Gray
- ■ **9**. Light blue
- ■ **A**. Light green
- ■ **B**. Light aqua
- ■ **C**. Light red
- ■ **D**. Light purple
- ■ **E**. Light yellow
- ■ **F**. Bright white

/e:on	Enables command extensions. For compatibility, /x is the same as /e:on.
/e:off	Disables commands extensions. For compatibility, /y is the same as /e:off.
/f:on	Enables file- and directory-name completion.
/f:off	Disables file- and directory-name completion.
/v:on	Enables delayed environment-variable expansion.
/v:off	Disables delayed environment-variable expansion.
string	Specifies the command you want to carry out. Multiple commands separated by the command separator && are accepted for string if surrounded by quotes.
/?	Displays help at the command prompt.

Using AutoRun

If */d* wasn't specified on the command line, Cmd.exe looks for the following REG_SZ or REG_EXPAND_SZ registry values and executes them before executing any other commands, including strings:

- HKCU\Software\Microsoft\Command Processor\AutoRun

- HKLM\Software\Microsoft\Command Processor\AutoRun

Enabling Command Extensions

Command extensions are enabled by default. You may also disable extensions for a particular invocation of the command interpreter by using the */e:off* command-line option. You can enable or disable extensions for all invocations of Cmd.exe on a per-computer or per-user basis by setting either or both of the following REG_DWORD registry values to either 0x1 or 0x0:

- HKCU\Software\Microsoft\Command Processor\EnableExtensions

- HKLM\Software\Microsoft\Command Processor\EnableExtensions

The per-user setting in HKCU takes precedence over the per-computer setting in HKLM. The command-line options take precedence over the registry settings. The command extensions involve changes and/or additions to the following commands:

- *Del (Erase)*
- *Color*
- *Cd (Chdir)*
- *Md (Mkdir)*
- *Prompt*
- *Pushd*
- *Popd*
- *Set*
- *Setlocal*
- *Endlocal*
- *If*
- *For*
- *Call*
- *Shift*
- *Goto*

- *Start*

- *Assoc*

- *Ftype*

To get command-specific information about changes due to command extensions, type **cmd /?** at the command prompt.

Enabling Delayed Expansion

Delayed environment-variable expansion isn't enabled by default (see the section titled "*Set*" on page 850 for more information about delayed environment-variable expansion). You can enable or disable delayed environment-variable expansion for a particular invocation of the command interpreter with the */v:on* or */v:off* command-line options. You can enable or disable completion for all invocations of Cmd.exe on a per-computer or per-user basis by setting either or both of the following REG_DWORD values in the registry to either 0x1 or 0x0:

- HKCU\Software\Microsoft\Command Processor\DelayedExpansion

- HKLM\Software\Microsoft\Command Processor\DelayedExpansion

The per-user specific setting in HKCU takes precedence over the per-computer setting in HKLM. The command-line options take precedence over the registry settings. If delayed environment-variable expansion is enabled, the exclamation character can be used to substitute the value of an environment variable at execution time.

Enabling Name Completion

File- and directory-name completion isn't enabled by default. You can enable or disable filename completion for a particular invocation of the command interpreter with the */f:on* or */f:off* command-line options. You can enable or disable completion for all invocations of Cmd.exe on a per-computer or per-user basis by setting either or both of the following REG_DWORD values in the registry with the hex value of a control character to use for a particular function (for example, 0x4 is Ctrl-D and 0x6 is Ctrl-F):

- HKCU\Software\Microsoft\Command Processor\CompletionChar

- HKCU\Software\Microsoft\Command Processor\PathCompletionChar

- HKLM\Software\Microsoft\Command Processor\CompletionChar

- HKLM\Software\Microsoft\Command Processor\PathCompletionChar

The per-user settings in HKCU take precedence over the per-computer settings in HKLM. The command-line options take precedence over the registry settings. If completion is enabled with the */f:on* command-line option, the two control charac-

ters used are Ctrl-D for directory-name completion and Ctrl-F for filename completion. To disable a particular completion character in the registry, use the value for
space (0x20) because it is not a valid control character.

Completion is invoked when you type either of the two control characters. The
completion function takes the path string to the left of the cursor and appends a wildcard character to it if none is already present and builds a list of paths that match. It
then displays the first matching path. If no paths match, it just beeps and leaves the
display alone. Thereafter, repeated pressing of the same control character will cycle
through the list of matching paths. Pressing the Shift key with the control character will
move through the list backward. If you edit the line in any way and press the control
character again, the saved list of matching paths is discarded and a new one generated. The same occurs if you switch between file- and directory-name completion.
The only difference between the two control characters is that the file completion
character matches both file and directory names, whereas the directory completion
character matches only directory names.

If file completion is used on any of the built-in directory commands (*Cd*, *Md*,
or *Rd*), directory completion is assumed. The completion code deals correctly with
filenames that contain spaces or other special characters by placing quotes around
the matching path.

Also, if you back up and then invoke completion from within a line, the text to
the right of the cursor at the point completion was invoked is discarded. The special
characters that require quotes are

- <space>
- &()[]{}^=;!'+,`~

Preserving Quote Characters

If /c or /k is specified, the remainder of the command line after either option is processed as a command line, and the following rules are used to process quote (")
characters:

1. If all the following conditions are met, the command interpreter preserves
    quote characters on the command line:

    - No /s command-line option

    - Exactly two quote characters

    - No special characters between the two quote characters, where special is
      one of these: &<>()@^|

    - There are one or more whitespace characters between the two quote
      characters

    - The string between the two quote characters is the name of an executable
      file

2. Otherwise, the command interpreter checks to see whether the first character is a quote character. If so, it strips the leading quote character and removes the last quote character on the command line, preserving any text after it.

Batch Commands

The remainder of this appendix describes the commands you can use to control the execution of batch scripts. It describes the following commands:

- *Call*
- *Echo*
- *Endlocal*
- *Exit*
- *For*
- *Goto*
- *If*
- *Pause*
- *Rem*
- *Set*
- *Setlocal*
- *Shift*
- *Start*

Note   The Microsoft Windows Support Tools provide numerous command-line programs that are useful, particularly when you run them from batch scripts. The Windows Support Tools are on your Windows XP Professional product CD in the Support\Tools folder. Three of the most useful programs in the Windows Support Tools for deployment scenarios are Netdom.exe, Xcacls.exe, and Setx.exe. Netdom.exe is a program you use to manage computers on a domain. Xcacls.exe is a program you use to manage files' access control lists (ACLs). Setx.exe is a particularly useful program for batch scripts because you can use it to set environment variables with the contents of a registry setting or a file. You can read the user's name from the registry and store it in an environment variable by using Setx.exe, for example. Install the Windows Support Tools and explore the programs to become more familiar with what they can do.

Call

The *Call* command calls one batch script from another.

Syntax

```
call [drive:][path]filename [parameters]
```

The following syntax requires command extensions:

```
call label [parameters]
```

Parameters

Label	Specifies a label within the current batch script to call
[drive:][path]filename	Specifies the path and filename of the batch script to call
Parameters	Specifies any command-line options required by the batch script

Notes

With command extensions enabled, the *call label [parameters]* form of this command is available. When using this form, a new batch script context is created with the specified options, and control is passed to the statement after the label specified. You must *exit* twice by reaching the end of the batch script twice. The first time you reach the end, control will return to just after the *Call* command. The second time will exit the batch script. See the section "*Goto*" on page 848 for a description of the *goto :eof* extension that will allow you to *return* from a batch script.

Echo

The *Echo* command displays *message*s or turns command echoing on or off.

Syntax

```
echo [on | off]
echo [message]
```

Parameters

on	Enables command echoing
off	Disables command echoing
message	Specifies a message to display on the console

Notes

To output a blank line, use the command *echo.*, including the period at the end of the word *echo*.

Endlocal

The *Endlocal* command ends the localization of environment changes in a batch script.

Syntax

`endlocal`

Notes

Environment changes made after the *Endlocal* command are not local to the batch script; the previous settings are not restored after the batch script ends.

Exit

The *Exit* command quits the command interpreter or the current batch script.

Syntax

`exit [/b] [exitcode]`

Parameters

/b	Specifies to exit the current batch script instead of Cmd.exe. If executed from outside a batch script, it will quit Cmd.exe.
exitcode	Specifies a numeric number. If */b* is used, sets ERRORLEVEL to that number. If quitting Cmd.exe, sets the process exit code with that number.

For

The *For* command runs a specified command for each file in a set of files.

On the Resource Kit CD   This book's companion CD contains four examples of batch scripts that use the *For* command. They are forall.cmd, forcmd.cmd, fordirs.cmd, and forlist.cmd. The batch script forall.cmd runs a command for a specified set of files in a folder and all of its subfolders. The batch script forcmd.cmd runs a command for each line of output from a specified command. The batch script fordirs.cmd runs a command for each subfolder in a path. Last, the batch script forlist.cmd runs a command for each line of a text file. In all of these cases, you can pass the filename, line of output, or text file line to the command as a command-line option. These scripts are in the Scripts folder on the companion CD. Run them without any command-line options for help. Edit them in a text editor to see how they work.

Syntax

```
for %variable in (set) do command [parameters]
```

The following syntaxes require command extensions:

```
for /d %variable in (set) do command [parameters]
for /r [[drive:]path] %variable in (set) do command [parameters]
for /l %variable in (start,step,end) do command [parameters]
for /f ["options"] %variable in (file-set) do command [parameters]
for /f ["options"] %variable in ("string") do command [parameters]
for /f ["options"] %variable in ('command') do command [parameters]
```

Parameters

%variable	Specifies a single-letter replaceable parameter.
(set)	Specifies a set of one or more files. Wildcards may be used.
command	Specifies the command to carry out for each file.
parameters	Specifies parameters or command-line options for the specified command.
/d	If *set* contains wildcards, then specifies to match against directory names instead of filenames.
/r	Walks the directory tree rooted at *[drive:]path*, executing *command* in each directory of the tree. If no directory specification is given after */r*, the current directory is assumed. If *set* is just a single period (.) character, it will just enumerate the directory tree.
[[drive:]path]	Specifies the directory tree to walk when using */r*.
/l	The set is a sequence of numbers from *start* to *end* by *step* amount, so (1,1,5) would generate the sequence 1 2 3 4 5, and (5,-1,1) would generate the sequence (5 4 3 2 1).
start,step,end	Specifies the sequence of numbers from start to end by step amount when using */l*.
/f	Used with *file-set*. *File-set* is one or more filenames. Each file is opened, read, and processed before going on to the next file in *file-set*. Processing consists of reading in the file, breaking it up into individual lines of text, and then parsing each line into zero or more tokens. The body of the *for* loop is then called with the variable values set to the found token strings. By default, */f* passes the first blank separated token from each line of each file. Blank lines are skipped. You can override the default parsing behavior by specifying the *options* parameter. This is a quoted string that contains one or more keywords to specify different parsing options.

options	A string containing one or more of the following options, enclosed in quotes:

- *eol=c*. Specifies an end-of-line comment character.
- *skip=n*. Specifies the number of lines to skip at the beginning of the file.
- *delims=xxx*. Specifies a delimiter set. This replaces the default delimiter set of space and tab.
- *tokens=x,y,m-n*. Specifies which tokens from each line are to be passed to the *for* body for each iteration. This will cause additional variable names to be allocated. The *m-n* form is a range, specifying the *m* through the *n* tokens. If the last character in the *tokens=* string is an asterisk, an additional variable is allocated and receives the remaining text on the line after the last token parsed.
- *Usebackq*. Specifies that the new semantics are in force, where a back quoted string is executed as a command, and a single quoted string is a literal string command and allows the use of double quotes to quote filenames in *file-set*.

file-set	Specifies the set of files to parse when using */f*.
"string"	Specifies a string to parse when using */f*.
'command'	Specifies a command to run when using */f*. The *for* loop then parses the command's output.

Notes

- To use the *For* command in a batch script, specify *%%variable* instead of *%variable*. Variable names are case-sensitive, so *%i* is different from *%I*.

- The command for */f "eol=; tokens=2,3* delims=, " %i in (myfile.txt) do @echo %i %j %k* would parse each line in myfile.txt, ignoring lines that begin with a semicolon, passing the second and third token from each line to the *for* body, with tokens delimited by commas or spaces. Notice that the *for* body statements reference *%i* to get the second token, *%j* to get the third token, and *%k* to get all remaining tokens after the third. For filenames that contain spaces, you need to quote the filenames with double quotes. In order to use double quotes in this manner, you also need to use the *usebackq* option; otherwise, the double quotes will be interpreted as defining a literal string to parse.

- The variable *%i* is explicitly declared in the *for* statement, and the *%j* and *%k* are implicitly declared via the *tokens=* option. You can specify up to 26 tokens via the *tokens=* line, provided that it does not cause an attempt to declare a variable higher than the letter *z* or *Z*. Remember that *for* variables are single-letter, case-sensitive, and global; and you can't have more than 52 total active at any one time.

■ In addition, substitution of *for* variable references is enhanced. You can use the variable modifiers shown in Table E-1, earlier in this appendix.

Goto

The *Goto* command directs Cmd.exe to a labeled line in a batch script.

Syntax

```
goto label
```

The following syntax requires command extensions:

```
goto :eof
```

Parameters

Label	Specifies a text string used in the batch script as a label.
:eof	Transfers control to the end of the current batch script. This is an easy way to exit a batch script without defining a label. See the section "*Call*" on page 844 for more information about using *:eof*.

Notes

You type a label on a line by itself, beginning with a colon. In the following example, the *dir* command would not execute:

```
goto skip
dir
:skip
```

If

The *If* command performs conditional processing in batch scripts.

Syntax

```
if [not] errorlevel number command
if [not] string1==string2 command
if [not] exist filename command
if [not] errorlevel number (command) else (command)
if [not] string1==string2 (command) else (command)
if [not] exist filename (command) else (command)
```

The following syntaxes require command extensions:

```
if [/i] string1 compare-op string2 command
if [/i] string1 compare-op string2 (command) else (command)
if cmdextversion number command
if cmdextversion number (command) else (command)
if defined variable command
if defined variable (command) else (command)
```

Parameters

not	Specifies that the command interpreter should carry out the command only if the condition is false.
errorlevel number	Specifies a true condition if the last program run returned an exit code equal to or greater than *number*.
string1==string2	Specifies a true condition if *string1* and *string2* match.
exist filename	Specifies a true condition if the *filename* exists.
command	Specifies the command to carry out if the condition is met. *Command* can be followed by the *else* command, which will execute the command after the *else* command if the specified condition is false.
/i	Specifies to perform case-insensitive string compares. These comparisons are generic. If both string1 and string2 are composed of all numeric digits, the strings are converted to numbers and a numeric comparison is performed.
compare-op	*Compare-op* may be one of the following:

- *equ*. equal
- *neq*. not equal
- *lss*. less than
- *leq*. less than or equal
- *gtr*. greater than
- *geq*. greater than or equal

cmdextversion number	Works just like *errorlevel*, except it is comparing against an internal version number associated with the command extensions. The first version is 1. It will be incremented by one when significant enhancements are added to the command extensions. *cmdextversion* conditional is never true when command extensions are disabled.
defined variable	Works just like *exists* except it takes an environment variable name and returns *true* if the environment variable is defined.

Notes

The *else* command must occur on the same line as the command after the *If* command. For example:

```
if exist filename (
del filename
) else (
echo filename is missing.
)
```

Pause

The *Pause* command suspends processing of a batch script and displays the message Press any key to continue....

Syntax

```
pause
```

Rem

The *Rem* command records comments (remarks) in a batch script.

Syntax

```
rem [comment]
```

Parameters

Comment   Contains inline documentation for the script.

Set

The *Set* command displays, sets, or removes environment variables.

> **Note**   The *Set* command has one drawback: You can't load an environment variable with a registry setting or the contents of a file. If you want to load an environment variable with a registry setting or the contents of a file, try using Setx.exe instead. Setx.exe is in the Windows Support Tools, which you learned about earlier in this appendix. The Windows Support Tools are on the Windows XP Professional product CD in the Support\Tools folder. You can copy Setx.exe to a network share or add it to your disk image to make it accessible from your batch scripts.

Syntax

```
set
set [variable=[string]]
```

The following syntaxes require command extensions:

```
set /a expression
set /p variable=[prompt]
```

Parameters

variable   Specifies the environment-variable name.

string   Specifies a series of characters to assign to the variable.

/a   Specifies that the string to the right of the equal sign is a numerical expression that is evaluated.

expression   Contains the expression to evaluate when using /a. The expression evaluator is pretty simple and supports the following operations, in decreasing order of precedence:

- **()** grouping
- **! ~ -** unary operators
- *** / %** arithmetic operators
- **+ -** arithmetic operators
- **<< >>** logical shift
- **&** bitwise and
- **∧** bitwise exclusive or
- **|** bitwise or
- **= *= /= %= += -= &= ∧= |= <<= >>=** assignment
- **,** expression separator

If you use any of the logical or modulus operators, you will need to enclose the expression string in quotes. Any non-numeric strings in the expression are treated as environment variable names whose values are converted to numbers before using them. If an environment variable name is specified but is not defined in the current environment, a value of zero is used. If set /a is executed from the command line outside of a batch script, it displays the final value of the expression.

Numeric values are decimal numbers, unless prefixed by 0x for hexadecimal numbers and 0 for octal numbers. So 0x12 is the same as 18 and is the same as 022. Please note that the octal notation can be confusing: 08 and 09 are not valid numbers because 8 and 9 are not valid octal digits.

/p   Specifies to set the value of a variable to a line of input entered by the user. Displays the specified *prompt* before reading the line of input.

prompt   Specifies the prompt to display for the user. The option *prompt* can be empty.

Notes

- Type **set** without parameters to display the current environment variables.

- If command extensions are enabled, typing **set** variable, with no equal sign or value, displays the value of all variables whose prefix matches the variable. For example, typing **set p** displays all variables that begin with the letter *P*.

- The *Set* command will set *ERRORLEVEL* to 1 if the variable name is not found in the current environment.

- The *Set* command will not allow an equal sign to be part of the name of a variable.

- Environment-variable substitution has been enhanced. The command set variable = *%PATH:str1=str2%* would expand the PATH environment variable, substituting each occurrence of *str1* in the expanded result with *str2*. *str2* can be an empty string to effectively delete all occurrences of *str1* from the expanded output. *Str1* can begin with an asterisk, in which case it will match everything from the beginning of the expanded output to the first occurrence of the remaining portion of *str1*.

- You may also specify substrings for an expansion. set variable = %PATH:~10,5% would expand the PATH environment variable and then use only the five characters that begin at the 11th (offset 10) character of the expanded result. If the length is not specified, it defaults to the remainder of the variable value. If either number (offset or length) is negative, the number used is the length of the environment-variable value added to the offset or length specified. set variable = %PATH:~-10% would extract the last 10 characters of the PATH variable.

- set variable = %PATH:~0,-2% would extract all but the last 2 characters of the PATH variable.

- Support for delayed environment-variable expansion is available. This support is always disabled by default, but may be enabled as described in the section "Enabling Delayed Expansion," earlier in this appendix on page 841. Delayed environment-variable expansion is useful for getting around the limitations of the current expansion, which happens when a line of text is read, not when it is executed. The following example demonstrates the problem with immediate variable expansion:

```
set var=before
if "%var%" == "before" (
set var=after
if "%var%" == "after" @echo If you see this, it worked
)
```

  - This example will never display the message because the *%var%* in both *If* commands is substituted when the first *If* command is read because it logically includes the body of the *If*, which is a compound statement. So the *If* inside the compound statement is really comparing *before* with *after*, which will never be equal. Similarly, the following example will not work as expected:

    ```
    set LIST=
    for %i in (*) do set LIST=%LIST% %i
    echo %LIST%
    ```

  - It will not build a list of files in the current directory, but instead will just set the *LIST* variable to the last file found. Again, this is because *%LIST%* is expanded just once when the *For* command is read, and at that time the *LIST* variable is empty. So the actual *for* loop that's executing is the following:

    ```
    for %i in (*) do set LIST= %i
    ```

- Delayed environment-variable expansion allows you to use a different character (the exclamation mark) to expand environment variables at execution time. If delayed variable expansion is enabled, the previous examples could be written as follows to work as intended:

```
set VAR=before
if "%VAR%" == "before" (
set VAR=after
if "!VAR!" == "after" @echo If you see this, it worked
)
set LIST=
for %i in (*) do set LIST=!LIST! %i
echo %LIST%
```

- If command extensions are enabled, there are several dynamic environment variables that can be expanded but that don't show up in the list of variables displayed by typing **set**. These variable values are computed dynamically each time the value of the variable is expanded. If the user explicitly defines a variable with one of these names, that definition will override the dynamic one described as follows:

  - *%CD%*   Expands to the current directory string

  - *%DATE%*   Expands to current date using same format as *Date* command

  - *%TIME%*   Expands to current time using same format as *Time* command

  - *%RANDOM%*   Expands to a random decimal number between 0 and 32767

  - *%ERRORLEVEL%*   Expands to the current *ERRORLEVEL* value

  - *%CMDEXTVERSION%*   Expands to the current command extensions version number

  - *%CMDCMDLINE%*   Expands to the original command line that invoked the command interpreter

Setlocal

The *Setlocal* command begins localization of environment changes in a batch script.

Syntax

```
setlocal
```

The following syntaxes require command extensions:

```
setlocal enableextensions|disableextensions
setlocal enabledelayedexpansion|disabledelayedexpansion
```

Parameters

enableextensions	Enables command extensions
disableextensions	Disable command extensions
enabledelayedexpansion	Enables delayed variable expansion
disabledelayedexpansion	Disables delayed variable expansion

Notes

- Environment changes made after the *Setlocal* command are local to the batch script. The *Endlocal* command must be used to restore the previous settings. When the end of a batch script is reached, an implied *Endlocal* is executed for any outstanding *Setlocal* commands issued by that batch script.

- The *Setlocal* command will set the *ERRORLEVEL* value if given an option. It will be zero if one of the two valid options is given and one otherwise. You can use this in batch scripts to determine whether the extensions are available because the *Setlocal* command doesn't set the *ERRORLEVEL* value in older versions of the command interpreter, using the following technique. (The *verify* command with a bad option initializes the *ERRORLEVEL* value to a non-zero value.):

```
verify other 2>nul
setlocal enableextensions
if errorlevel 1 echo Unable to enable extensions
```

Shift

The *Shift* command changes the position of replaceable parameters in a batch script.
Syntax

```
shift
```

The following syntax requires command extensions

```
shift [/n]
```

Parameters

n	Specifies to start shifting at the *n*th command-line option.

Start

The *Start* command starts a separate window to run a specified program.
Syntax

```
start ["title"] [/dpath] [/i] [/min] [/max] [/separate | /shared]
[/low | /normal | /high | /realtime | /abovenormal | /belownormal]
[/wait] [/b] [command]
```

Parameters

"title"	Specifies the title to display in the window title bar.
path	Specifies the starting directory.
/b	Specifies to start application without creating a new window. The application has ^C handling ignored. Unless the application enables ^C processing, ^Break is the only way to interrupt the application.
/i	Specifies that the new environment will be the original environment passed to the Cmd.exe and not the current environment.
/min	Starts the window minimized.
/max	Starts the window maximized.
/separate	Starts 16-bit Windows program in separate memory space.
/shared	Starts 16-bit Windows program in shared memory space.
/low	Starts the application in the IDLE priority class.
/normal	Starts application in the NORMAL priority class.
/high	Starts application in the HIGH priority class.
/realtime	Starts application in the REALTIME priority class.
/abovenormal	Starts application in the ABOVENORMAL priority class.
/belownormal	Starts application in the BELOWNORMAL priority class.
/wait	Starts application and waits for it to terminate. If it is an internal command or a batch script, the command processor is run with the */k* command-line option. This means that the window will remain after the command finishes. If it is not an internal command or batch script, it is a program and will run as either a windowed application or a console application.
parameters	Specifies command-line options to pass to *command*.

Notes

- If command extensions are enabled, starting external commands through the command line or the *Start* command changes. Non-executable files may be invoked through their file association just by typing the name of the file as a command. (For example, typing **Word.doc** would launch the application associated with the *.doc* file extension.)

- When executing an application that is a 32-bit GUI application, Cmd.exe does not wait for the application to terminate before returning to the command prompt. This new behavior does not occur if executing within a command script. When executing a command line whose first token is the string *cmd* without an extension or path qualifier, *cmd* is replaced with the value of the *COMSPEC* variable. This prevents picking up Cmd.exe from the current directory.

- When executing a command line whose first token does not contain an extension, Cmd.exe uses the value of the *PATHEXT* environment variable to determine which extensions to look for and in what order. The default value for the *PATHEXT* variable is *.COM;.EXE;.BAT;.CMD*. Notice that the syntax is the same as the *PATH* variable, with semicolons separating the different elements. When searching for an executable, if there is no match on any extension, Cmd.exe then looks to see whether the name matches a directory name. If it does, the *Start* command launches Windows Explorer on that path. If done from the command line, it is the equivalent to typing **cd /d** path for that directory name.

Note If you've reached the end of this appendix and still don't see what you need, I recommend that you visit Dave Navarro's CMD Tools Web site: *http://www.cmdtools.com*. This handy Web site contains numerous command-line tools that you can use to write amazing batch scripts. Most of them are freeware, and many of them are flat-out cleverly useful. Another useful Web site is Rob van der Woude's Scripting Pages at *http://www.robvanderwoude.com*. This website covers the depth and breadth of most scripting languages. It's the single best resource I've found for writing batch scripts for Windows XP Professional, too. If you're writing batch scripts, you must spend some time at this website.

Index

Symbols and Numbers

Jerry Honeycutt

Jerry Honeycutt empowers people to work more productively by helping them deploy and use popular technologies such as the Microsoft Windows and Microsoft Office product families. As a best-selling author, Jerry has written more than 25 books, including, most recently, *Introducing Microsoft Windows Server 2003* (Microsoft Press, 2003) and *Microsoft Windows XP Registry Guide* (Microsoft Press, 2002). Most of his books are sold internationally and are available in a variety of languages.

Jerry is also a columnist for Microsoft's Windows XP Expert Zone, a Web site for Windows XP enthusiasts, and Microsoft TechNet. He makes frequent contributions to a variety of other content areas on Microsoft's Web site. Jerry has written more than 20 white papers on topics ranging from wireless networking to desktop deployment. He also contributes to various trade publications, such as *SearchWin2000* and *Storage Magazine*.

From 2000 through 2002, Jerry toured cities throughout the world to teach IT professionals how to deploy and manage the business desktop. These Microsoft seminars provided participants with best practices for deploying Windows 2000 and Office 2000 and offered hands-on workshops on deploying Windows XP Professional and Office XP Professional in a lab environment. Jerry is a frequent speaker at assorted public events, including COMDEX, Developer Days, the Microsoft Exchange Conference, and Microsoft Global Briefing. He also occasionally hosts chats on Microsoft's TechNet Web site.

In addition to his writing and speaking experience, Jerry has a long history of providing technical leadership to businesses. He specializes in desktop deployment, management, and networking—particularly using the Windows product family. Companies like Sunbeam Products, Capital One, Travelers, IBM, Nielsen North America, IRM, Howard Systems International, and NCR have all leveraged his expertise.

Jerry graduated from the University of Texas at Dallas in 1992 with a B.S. in Computer Science. He also studied at Texas Tech University in Lubbock, Texas. In his spare time, Jerry plays golf, is an avid amateur photographer, and travels. He lives in the Dallas suburb of Frisco.

For more information about Jerry and how he can help you deploy the business desktop, see his Web site at *http://www.honeycutt.com*, or send mail to jerry@honeycutt.com.

For *Windows Server 2003* **administrators**

Microsoft® Windows® Server 2003 Administrator's Companion
ISBN 0-7356-1367-2

The comprehensive, daily operations guide to planning, deployment, and maintenance.
Here's the ideal one-volume guide for anyone who administers Windows Server 2003. It offers up-to-date information on core system-administration topics for Windows, including Active Directory® services, security, disaster planning and recovery, interoperability with NetWare and UNIX, plus all-new sections about Microsoft Internet Security and Acceleration (ISA) Server and scripting. Featuring easy-to-use procedures and handy workarounds, it provides ready answers for on-the-job results.

Microsoft Windows Server 2003 Administrator's Pocket Consultant
ISBN 0-7356-1354-0

The practical, portable guide to Windows Server 2003. Here's the practical, pocket-sized reference for IT professionals who support Windows Server 2003. Designed for quick referencing, it covers all the essentials for performing everyday system-administration tasks. Topics covered include managing workstations and servers, using Active Directory services, creating and administering user and group accounts, managing files and directories, data security and auditing, data back-up and recovery, administration with TCP/IP, WINS, and DNS, and more.

Microsoft IIS 6.0 Administrator's Pocket Consultant
ISBN 0-7356-1560-8

The practical, portable guide to IIS 6.0. Here's the eminently practical, pocket-sized reference for IT and Web professionals who work with Internet Information Services (IIS) 6.0. Designed for quick referencing and compulsively readable, this portable guide covers all the basics needed for everyday tasks. Topics include Web administration fundamentals, Web server administration, essential services administration, and performance, optimization, and maintenance. It's the fast-answers guide that helps users consistently save time and energy as they administer IIS 6.0.

To learn more about the full line of Microsoft Press® products for IT professionals, please visit

microsoft.com/mspress/IT

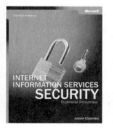

ᵒ k?

Do you have a few minutes to participate in a brief online survey? Microsoft is interested in hearing your feedback about this publication so that we can continually improve our books and learning resources for you.

To participate in our survey, please visit:

www.microsoft.com/learning/booksurvey

And enter this book's ISBN, 0-7356-1898-4. As a thank-you to survey participants in the United States and Canada, each month we'll randomly select five respondents to win one of five $100 gift certificates from a leading online merchant.* At the conclusion of the survey, you can enter the drawing by providing your e-mail address, which will be used for prize notification *only*.

Thanks in advance for your input. Your opinion counts!

Sincerely,

Microsoft® Learning

Microsoft | Learning

Learn More. Go Further.

To see special offers on Microsoft Learning products for developers, IT professionals, and home and office users, visit: *www.microsoft.com/learning/booksurvey*

* No purchase necessary. Void where prohibited. Open only to residents of the 50 United States (includes District of Columbia) and Canada (void in Quebec). Sweepstakes ends 6/30/2005. For official rules, see: *www.microsoft.com/learning/booksurvey*